GEORGE III,
NATIONAL REFORM, AND NORTH AMERICA

GEORGE III,
NATIONAL REFORM, AND NORTH AMERICA

"The True Essential Business of a King"

John L. Bullion

With a Preface by
Karl W. Schweizer

The Edwin Mellen Press
Lewiston•Queenston•Lampeter

Library of Congress Cataloging-in-Publication Data

Bullion, John L., 1944-
   George III, national reform, and North America : "the true essential business of a king"
/ John L. Bullion ; with a preface by Karl W. Schweizer.
      pages cm.
   Includes bibliographical references and index.
   ISBN-13: 978-0-7734-4079-1 (hardcover)
   ISBN-10: 0-7734-4079-8 (hardcover)
   1. Great Britain--History--George III, 1760-1820. 2. George III, King of Great Britain,
1738-1820. 3. Great Britain--Politics and government--1760-1789. 4. Monarchy--Great
Britain--History--18th century. 5. Great Britain--Colonies--America--Administration. 6.
United States--History--Revolution, 1775-1783--Causes. I. Title.
   DA505.B95 2013
   941.07'3092--dc23
                                2012044045

hors série.

A CIP catalog record for this book is available from the British Library.

Copyright © 2013 John L. Bullion

All rights reserved. For information contact

The Edwin Mellen Press	The Edwin Mellen Press
Box 450	Box 67
Lewiston, New York	Queenston, Ontario
USA 14092-0450	CANADA L0S 1L0

The Edwin Mellen Press, Ltd.
Lampeter, Ceredigion, Wales
UNITED KINGDOM SA48 8LT

Printed in the United States of America

FOR LAURA

For you have been my helper,
and under the shadow of your wings I will rejoice.
My soul clings to you;
your right hand holds me fast.
--Psalm 63: 7-8

Table of Contents

PART FOUR: ENDING WAR AND PREPARING FOR PEACE

PART FIVE: CONSEQUENCES

PART SIX: RETREATING FROM REFORM

i

Preface

Dr. John Bullion's long awaited collection of stimulating essays, based on fresh manuscript research, makes his work on 18th century Britain more readily accessible than before, and in more harmonized and coherent form. This it clearly deserves, partly because his writings have an inherent unity in theme and argument (especially prominent within a book format) and partly because this unity derives from a central intellectual intent: namely to illuminate the key personalities and issues operative in Britain's gradually changing socio-political profile during the Age of the American Revolution. These issues, which have engaged the author for many years—and variously still reverberate throughout the historiography of Georgian Britain—beg answers to such leading questions as: the king's role in the formulation of national policy after 1760; the complex dynamics between leading political figures, among them Pitt, Bute and Newcastle, and concomitant repercussions on the operation and rhetoric of formalized politics, the deeper intellectual context of political debates; the shaping of public opinion during an era of unprecedented press expansion; the wider determinants of military and foreign policy, and finally, the thought-world of George III—the framework of purposes and ideas instilled from early on and their implications for subsequent affairs of state. As such, *in toto*, Dr. Bullion helps clarify the complex synergy between the amorphous—but often competing—pressures, interests and opinions that collectively advanced the progressive liberalization of national political life. Essentially Dr. Bullion transmutes the rigors of archival exploration into a broader vision of Georgian politics, one that eschews the static, abstract paradigm of Namier (and post Namierites) for a more contextualized, time sensitive perspective (reminiscent of Namier's great opponent Sir Herbert Butterfield)[1] emphasizing narrative, depth, imagination, and evolving

---

[1] For a recent, exposition of the battle lines between Namier and Butterfield see: M. Bentley, *The Life and Thought of Herbert Butterfield* (Cambridge, 2011), pp. 253-256. See also the introduction in: K.W. Schweizer and P. Sharp, eds., *The International Thought of Sir Herbert Butterfield* (London/NY, 2007), pp. 1-6, 8-12.

historiography over theoretical acumen or stark scientific analysis—a major service to 18th century scholarship if not scholarship in general.

To close, the author's pioneering research, meticulous assessment of the sources, and understanding of the important current discussions among historians makes his book an admirable example of how we should approach our task of reclaiming the past.

Karl W. Schweizer, F.R.Hist.S., FRSA, FIBA

iii

Acknowledgements

I could not have written any of these essays without the advice and assistance of scores of dedicated archivists and librarians. It is thanks to them that so much of the past has been preserved and made accessible. In my experience, they are consummate professionals, maintaining the highest levels of performance despite budget cuts and understaffing—to say nothing of the challenges of working with historians! I want to recognize two by name: John Dann, the former director of the William L. Clements Library at the University of Michigan, and Alexander Hunter, archivist of the Bute MSS. at Mount Stuart on the Isle of Bute. John and Sandy stand out as extraordinary even among their splendid peers. I am also happy to acknowledge that the portrait of George III by Johan Zoffany on the cover was "supplied by the Royal Collection Trust/copyright HM Queen Elizabeth II 2012".

I have heard that relationships between editors and writers can be frequently strained and often even adversarial. If such is in fact the case, I count myself extremely fortunate never to have experienced this. Tim Parshall, the editor of my first book, proved to be the first of several who clarified my prose, straightened out organizational problems, and stimulated re-thinking of conclusions. Michael McGiffert, editor of the *William and Mary Quarterly*, and Michael Moore, editor of *Albion*, saw the angel in the marble of my early drafts and provided the chisel and the guidance for the creation of the final statues. One need only read the collections of essays edited and inspired by Karl Schweizer on Lord Bute and Clarissa Campbell Orr on queens and princesses in Britain from the seventeenth into the nineteenth century to appreciate their skills as editors. I benefited hugely from their attention and suggestions. What I admire most about Tim, the two Mikes, Karl, and Clarissa is an editorial gift they have in common. They not only tightened my focus by sharpening my prose and arguments, but they also encouraged me to widen my interpretive vision. Put another way, they insisted editorial fine tuning should not lead to narrowing the interpretive sweep of the work. For that, I am much in their debt.

Many of these essays were first tried out at scholarly conferences. Without exception, the commentators on my work improved my revisions of them for publication. Two in particular were extremely helpful: the late Milton Klein of the University of Tennessee, and Daniel Baugh of Cornell. Both were stringent and fair critics; each had the knack of being skeptical while being encouraging. They applied their own high standards to my papers. Trying to match their examples was challenging and rewarding.

For 25 years, Nancy Taube has prepared my manuscripts. In the process, she has applied her love for and mastery of the English language to my prose. She has always been particularly adept at finding contradictions in my essays and untangling my logic. Her keen sense of humor, often expressed in clever puns and sly word play, has kept life and work in perspective for me. I cannot imagine writing history without Nancy. And for the last year I have had the delightful pleasure of working with Pamela Schweizer on this book. From the first sentence she processed to the last entry in the index she prepared, every page in this book bears the mark of Pam's unfailing precision. I also deeply appreciate the enthusiastic encouragement she lavished on me. Having Nancy and Pam in my life are true blessings.

I've been a member of the Department of History at the University of Missouri-Columbia for thirty-four years and counting. It is impossible to calculate what I owe the department's faculty, staff, and students. They have made Read Hall an interesting (in all senses of that most suggestive word!) place to be. Three colleagues in particular have influenced my work: the late Gerard H. Clarfield, Robert M. Collins, and A. Mark Smith. But everyone has contributed to making the department an ideal place to learn, teach, and write history.

Roger J. Spiller, an old comrade from our days as apprentice instructors at Southwest Texas State University, was a perceptive critic of my work on Lord Bute and the British Army after 1763 and a thoughtful guide to the problems of writing political and military history. I continue to draw on those lessons after all these years. The late Philip Lawson made many trenchant suggestions that improved two of the essays considerably. Every eighteenth-century historian is the loser for his untimely death.

The scholar I owe the most to is Karl Schweizer. Thirty years ago, Karl asked me to contribute to a volume he was putting together on Lord Bute. That invitation was the most consequential of my scholarly career. It launched me on a series of investigations into the life and times of Bute and George III. Simultaneously, it gained me the advice and friendship of a great historian of Britain and Europe in the eighteenth century. Our collaboration has been as delightful as it has been productive. Through all these years, Karl has been a perceptive critic and a constant inspiration. His forays into twentieth century history helped determine me to write two books on Lyndon Johnson. Then, after my decade with LBJ, Karl encouraged me to return to the world of George III. Coming from him, that invitation was irresistible.

From start to finish on these essays, I have leaned on the love and support of my wife Laura and our children Jack and Chandler. Our son and daughter tolerated their father's journeys into an earlier century with good humor, and I appreciated them all the more after living with the adventures of raising and teaching George III. Our son-in-law Chris and our daughter-in-law Rachel have been equally good-humored and forgiving. All four rallied around me during Laura's recent serious illness, and I shall never forget their love and compassion. My heartfelt thanks go to my late friend Bud, faithful to us for seventeen years and never more so than during the toughest times.

Laura was present at the creation of all my work. From first thought to final draft, she has been my partner, keeping me focused on essentials and pretty much on schedule. Most important, she has always been my expert on life, and she has shared that expertise with love. Through teardrops and laughter, for richer or poorer, in sickness and in health, we have walked through the past and present worlds hand in hand. This book is dedicated to her with my love.

John L. Bullion

Introduction

All of the essays in this book examine "the true essential business" of King George III and other British politicians from the 1730s to the early nineteenth century. Although they deal with a variety of subjects, each one aims at answering four questions. What was their business? What did they think it was? What did they believe their business could and should be? How did they plan to convert thoughts about business into actions re-shaping it, and thereby transform proposals into policies?

Since business is essential to my essays, understanding what politicians meant at that time by it is essential. The easiest way to do that is to turn to the great pioneering work of English lexicography, *Samuel Johnson's Dictionary*, which was first published in 1755.

Dr. Johnson included several usages in his definition of business. Business referred to "employment and affair." It involved "serious engagement, in opposition to trivial transactions." It was "a point, a matter of question, something to be examined and considered." And that something was invariably significant and serious. Contemporaries knew that "to mean business is to be serious." Often very serious: as Johnson observed, the colloquial meaning of "to do one's business" was "to kill, destroy, or ruin [that person]."[1]

That George III and others defined some problems in domestic politics and international relations as business thus reveals they regarded the resolution of those issues as serious. And once they defined those issues as business, how they found answers was pre-determined. The king and his advisers used a knowledge of past and present business practices of dealing with affairs of politics, policies, and power to understand the dilemmas they faced and to devise solutions. So the crucial task for historians is asking and answering this question: how were things done then? This question is the foundation of the analysis and interpretation in my studies; each chapter in this book begins with accounts of how individuals understood existing political and administrative realities. That approach distinguishes my work from the histories of many other scholars of Britain during the Era of the American Revolution, if not other earlier periods.

Those studying the years 1750 to 1783 have long been aware of how pivotal those decades were. Such fundamental issues as the monarchy, parliamentary government, the nature of the British Empire, the conduct of war, the preservation, maintenance, and improvement of the fiscal machinery of the state, and the role of virtue and morality in politics and society were being constantly examined, tested, refined, reformed, and re-shaped. It was an unsettled and, in many ways, unsettling time for Britain's political elite. They were struggling to grasp what was going on and assess the significance of many changes, and those efforts competed for their attention with the ordinary, everyday concerns of patronage and politics first described and analyzed by Sir Lewis Namier. I do not deny the novelty of Sir Lewis's scholarship, but I do question how relevant its findings are to studying the business of formulating reactive policies to change and the direction of reform. Unfortunately, many studies of the politics of the time and their implications for policy continue to be shaped by Namierite preoccupations. The structure of British politics however remains a determining factor; the actual busy-ness of running the country and its colonies is—to the extent it is examined at all—a distinctly secondary concern.[2] Though this focus has produced many useful insights, it is significantly flawed. Demonstrating why is the purpose of this book.

Though the minutiae of patronage and political structures at Whitehall and Westminster often preoccupied George III and other leaders, they did not regard these details as their most significant business. They never questioned the pre-eminence of an insight memorably stated in Cicero's *Fifth Phillipic: nervi bellorum pecuniae*—money is the sinews of war. That phrase entered common usage in English by the mid-sixteenth century, and the cycle of wars with France during the eighteenth century confirmed its wisdom.[3] It is significant that British politicians took care to edit the original version. Cicero had observed that endless or infinite money was the sinew of war. Britain's leaders knew all too well that there was no endless supply of money, either from taxes or loans, and that the amount they could raise from both sources fell considerably short of infinite. Applying the great orator's adjectives to the nation's situation would only engender despair, for the wealth of all nations was finite and Britain's share of it was well below the actual and potential value of France's. [4] British leaders had to maneuver creatively and carefully. They had to know how to tax and what to tax and how much to tax. They had to know how to borrow and how to negotiate the best bargain possible with individuals and institutions willing to consider loaning money to the nation. That the youthful George III identified knowing this as the true essential business of a king is not surprising. Yet these subjects remain, with very few exceptions, unexamined by historians.[5] When they are touched on, the terse references are often uniformed by any knowledge of internal investigations and debates over alternatives at court and Whitehall. Sometimes the references are simply wrong. A historian who wrote a penetrating analysis of how paying taxes in the eighteenth century came to define patriotism and who was and was not a British subject marred his persuasive account of this development with errors of fact about British finance. He claimed that the annual £ 670,000 subsidy paid to Prussia during the Seven Years War equaled the yearly produce of British duties in peacetime. In reality, peacetime duties raised over £6,000,000 each year. The same book argues that the loans negotiated by Lord North during the American War were part of an oppressive fiscal plan that caused opposition to the war. There may have been opposition, but the role of North's plans in encouraging it was minimal. Until 1780 the loans he arranged were much smaller than the ones the nation struggled under during the Seven Years War. North's taxes fell chiefly on property rather than labor and avoided raising funds from the necessities of life by a creative and unprecedented use of lotteries.[6]

And the failure to understand the business of public finance can skew analysis of issues in less obvious but equally important ways. How this has been so is one of the purposes of my essays. Two examples follow as a preview of this thrust of the book.

Why did George Grenville decide that a stamp tax was the best way to raise a revenue in North America? He answered the question himself in the House of Commons on March 9, 1764. A stamp duty was "the least exceptionable" Parliament could impose on the colonies "because it requires few officers and even collects itself." The significance of this statement, obvious to his contemporaries, has been lost on many historians because they do not know what Grenville, a veteran financier, did. In Britain, many commercial, legal, judicial, and financial agreements were not legally binding unless they were on stamped paper. So if one wanted to buy or sell real or personal property, sue or defend oneself in court, loan or borrow money, enter into matrimony, play cards, shoot dice, advertise in a newspaper, or verify graduation from a university, one had to buy stamped paper and pay the stamp tax. Those duties covered the entire panorama of human activity in England by taxing enterprise, litigation, virtue (marriage licenses), vice (cards and dice), and minds (diplomas). One's self-interest thus required paying the stamp tax. It literally "collects itself." That it also was easy to administer and had a low overhead—"it requires few officers" to handle the distribution of stamped paper—were additional bonuses. Thus it was the ideal tax to impose on a people unfamiliar with paying parliamentary taxes and accustomed to defying or ignoring British legislation. And even if Grenville had been ignorant of these benefits, the self-appointed colonial expert Henry McCulloh, the subminister in the Stamp Office Thomas Cruwys, and the Secretary of the Treasury Charles Jenkinson called these characteristics of stamp taxes to his attention and urged their extension to the colonies. Excluding these considerations from accounts of the Stamp Act of 1765 leaves its formulation seriously incomplete. Yet most narratives of the genesis of the Stamp Act do not include these vital pieces of business.[7]

An example of the consequences of overlooking what recommended stamp duties to Grenville may be found in the standard accounts of the Rockingham Administration's initial reaction to widespread violent resistance to the tax in North America. Paul Langford's brief comment in his fine survey *A Polite and Commercial People: England, 1727-1783* is typical. "[The Duke of] Cumberland, who had a short way with rebels, thought of repressing American opposition by force. But neither the numbers nor disposition of troops in the colonies made this very practicable."[8] In fact, the evidence of Cumberland's intentions is ambiguous, and the Duke's sudden death prevented him from elaborating on them. Aside from that, Cumberland and his colleagues were perfectly aware the tax enforced itself in England. As time passed, tempers cooled, and a preoccupation with getting and spending replaced passion and uproar, the odds were the tax would begin to collect itself there as well, for the same reasons it was unavoidable in the Mother Country. Why go to the expense of ordering troop movements that would probably be unnecessary before orders from Whitehall reached army headquarters in New York? And this consideration was even more compelling in the case of moving regiments from Ireland or England to America. It would take time and money to write orders, prepare the regiments, gather their artillery, equipment, and supplies, find and pay for transports, and launch them into the North Atlantic on a journey made elongated and perilous by the winter season. Knowledge of what that business entailed, plus the nature of the tax, meant the administration never seriously considered the use of force during late 1765-early 1766.

Descriptions of how stamp taxes worked and how troops were moved are not to be found in the political files of British leaders. To gain enlightenment, historians must dig into the miscellaneous papers of First Lords of the Treasury and their advisers. Henry McCulloh's advice on stamp taxes was stuck away in the *omnium gatherum* files of the Duke of Newcastle, George Grenville, and the Marquis of Rockingham.[9]   Thomas Cruwys's analysis found its way into the files of the Earl of Hardwicke.[10]   Jenkinson's comments were probably parts of an *aide memoir* to help Grenville prepare for debates in the House of Commons; they are undated and placed in a volume with other drafts of speeches and statements of policy.[11]   The best guide to the Rockingham ministry's thinking during the fall of 1765 is an undated speech draft by Edmund Burke that is placed with other drafts in the Burke manuscripts at the Northamptonshire Record Office.[12] Learning how the self-enforcing tax worked depends upon searching outside the customary archival files for studies of the period. Doubtlessly clerks placed these undated comments with other drafts of speeches and reports.   Those miscellaneous files are precisely the places in my experience where historians can find out how things really worked. Mining them is the functional equivalent of discovering new archival sources.   That should be done more frequently and thoroughly.

The essays in his volume follow the pattern of these examples. They begin by asking how things work. "Why" questions are left for last. They start by asking and answering how, what, when, which, and where. How should parents prepare a young prince to rule his country? What is a mother's role in that preparation? When and where can secret tutoring be done? What is the role of gossip at court? Which taxes should be imposed to attract potential creditors to underwrite a huge debt? How much vote of credit should be sought in 1762? What terms of peace can be offered to the French and Spanish? Which conquests should be kept, and which returned? How large can the peacetime army and navy be? Where can new taxes be raised? Which taxes? How committed to reform were leading politicians? How committed were George III and George Grenville to reform? Where did their outlooks on reform come from? What policy could resolve the imperial crisis in 1775? Which changes would occur in Britain's situation after American independence was conceded? My essays establish the background to many decisions. They put those decisions in the context of true essential business. By so doing they deepen our understanding of why these decisions in the form and at the time they did. They supply new answers to the question why.

Those answers I found in archival sources that were either utterly neglected or under-used. The papers Prince George wrote under Bute's tutelage have been rarely studied. That is unfortunate, for they provide many clues to his later perspectives on individuals, issues, and events. The undated papers in his miscellaneous files include an interesting analysis of Britain's prospects after the American War. It had been overlooked by scholars for years. Despite the fact that many scholars have demonstrated the richness of the Earl of Bute's papers, and clearly provide the basis for a major biography of the king's "dearest friend," as yet none has been written. [13] It is also surprising that the documents in the earl's files that illuminate many plans for peacetime financial and military arrangements in Britain and the colonies remain comparatively neglected. The letters from George III are numerous and revealing, especially on plans for the army after the war and raising revenues in America. Romney Sedgwick did edit and publish some of this correspondence, but his book includes less than half of the entire corpus. [14] Bute's tenure as First Lord of the Treasury has only been treated in an unpublished dissertation. [15] When a monograph is written, it will have to draw upon the cache of official papers from his Treasury that were removed by Lord North, who served under Bute in 1762-1763. Ultimately these files found their way into MSS. North at the Bodleian Library, Oxford. These papers illuminate many fiscal decisions made during and in the aftermath of the Seven Years War. So do the papers of James Oswald, a Scots ally of Bute and a trusted advisor. Oswald's calculations of the cash on hand at the Treasury during the fall of 1762 decisively influenced peace negotiations. The correspondence of Samuel Martin, who undercut the Duke of Newcastle during the cabinet's dispute over continuing the Prussian subsidy and determining the vote of credit in May

1762, adds valuable details about the financial aspects of political struggles during that month. The papers of George Grenville, which have found homes in Los Angeles and London, contain relatively unexamined material. His actions as Secretary of State in 1762-1765 have informed studies of the diplomacy of the period. Interactions between Grenville and Thomas Whately, his "man of business," are critical to understanding his administration's colonial policies. And Grenville's collection of papers relating to his family's efforts to enclose common lands at Ashendon in Buckinghamshire have never been utilized. They not only lay out the process of parliamentary enclosures in the eighteenth century; they also shed light on Grenville's reforming spirit.[16] Finally, politicians frequently leaked materials on policy and cabinet disputes over it to friendly newspapers. They also commissioned pamphlets, some by Grub Street hacks, some by their intimate advisers. Politicians and the press have not been neglected: there have been some fine studies.[17] Nevertheless, I remain convinced that historians have not exhausted the possibilities of research on the politicians, the press, and public opinion. Finding explanations of decisions on policy, whether they are anonymous or signed with pseudonyms, has been and will be worth the search. The same can be said of all these sources.

These chapters are not the final word on their subjects. My intent in collecting them is to widen enquiry by calling attention to the individuals who ' made crucial decisions about what to do, then sought practical means for executing them. To be sure, historians influenced by the Annales School have taught us much about the *longue duree* and enriched our knowledge of impersonal forces in human affairs. But the men and women I have depicted in these essays did not see their lives and their duties in terms of a *longue duree*. They lived in the here and now, the real and practical. And they certainly did not see their decisions as mere ephemera, froth upon the waves of a boundless ocean. Such talk, they would have reasoned, equaled counsels of despair and rationales for inactivity. It was nonsense. They could not be inactive. They had to take care of business.

Endnotes

[1] Samuel Johnson, *A Dictionary of the English Language* (London, 1755). I have supplemented these entries with the definition of meaning business from *The Oxford English Dictionary*.

[2] The two classic works by Sir Lewis Namier are *The Structure of Politics at the Accession of George III* (London, 1928); and *England in the Age of the American Revolution* (London, 1929). The most influential and compelling Namierite studies of British politics and the American Revolution is the trilogy by Peter D. G. Thomas: *British Politics and the Stamp Act Crisis: The First Phase of the American Revolution, 1763-1767* (Oxford, 1975); *The Townshend Duties Crisis: The Second Phase of the American Revolution, 1767-1773* (Oxford, 1987); and *Tea Party to Independence: The Third Phase of the American Revolution, 1773-1776* (Oxford, 1991).

[3] For details on when Cicero's usage became widely used in English, see *The Oxford Dictionary of Phrase and Fable* (Oxford, 2006).

[4] For an influential estimate of France's superior resources, see Charles Jenkinson to Richard Neville, Nov. 14, 1762, Neville to Jenkinson, Dec. 2, 1762, and Jenkinson to Neville, Jul. 22, 1763, National Archives, PRO 30/50/48, fols. 45-46, 73; and PRO 30/50/52, fol. 59. Jenkinson assisted and advised the Earl of Bute and George Grenville at the Treasury; Neville was the Duke of Bedford's secretary in Paris during peace negotiations in 1762.

[5] One exception to this rule is the seminal work by John Brewer, *The Sinews of Power: War, Money, and the English State, 1688-1783* (Cambridge MA, 1990).

[6] See my review of Eliga H. Gould, *The Persistence of Empire: British Political Culture in the Age of the American Revolution* (Chapel Hill, NC, 2000) in *Albion* 33(2000), pp. 122-125.

[7] I have extracted this account from the treatment of the Stamp Act from my book *A Great and Necessary Measure: George Grenville and the Genesis of the Stamp Act, 1763-1765* (Columbia MO, 1982), pp. 104-107, 211-219, 224-229, 256. This includes a representative list of works that neglected to mention what made the tax attractive to Grenville. See for example Philip Lawson, *George Grenville: A*

Political Life (Oxford, 1984); and L. Stone, ed., *The Imperial State at War: Britain from 1689 to 1815* (London, 1994). For a recent omission, see Robert Middlekauff, *The Glorious Cause: The American Revolution, 1763-1789*, 2nd edition (New York, 2005), pp. 74-78.

[8] Paul Langford, *A Polite and Commercial People: England, 1727-1783* (Oxford, 1989), p. 366.

[9] Henry McCulloh's memoranda on the American stamp tax may be found in Newcastle Papers, British Library, Add. MSS. 33030, ff. 334-335; George Grenville Papers, Huntington Library, STG Box 12 (28); and Rockingham Papers, Sheffield Central Library, Wentworth Wodehouse Muniments, R. 65-6. There are also some McCulloh papers in the Henry Clinton Papers at the William L. Clements Library in Ann Arbor MI.

[10] Hardwicke Papers, British Library, Add. MSS. 35911, fol. 21.

[11] Liverpool Papers, British Library, Add. MSS. 38339, fol.131-135.

[12] The draft, which was titled "Speech on Stamp Act Disturbances," has been published in Paul Langford, ed., *The Writings and Speeches of Edmund Burke*, vol. II (oxford, 1981), pp. 43-44. See also "America," [Nov. 1765], Burke Papers, Northamptonshire Record Office, A. xxvii-81.

[13] Until this is done the collection of essays edited by Karl W. Schweizer, ed., *Lord Bute: Essays in Re-interpretation* (Leicester, 1988); and Schweizer's excellent 7,000 word entry on Bute in the *New Dictionary of National Biography* (Oxford, 2004) must suffice. I suspect that scholars have been discouraged by the necessity of understanding the intricacies of Scots politics and explaining and assessing Bute's work in botanical studies.

[14] Romney Sedgwick, *Letters from George III to Lord Bute* (London, 1939). There are over 500 letters in the Bute Archives that Sedgwick did not publish. He was unaware they were in the Cardiff Public Library. Namier was also unaware of this, and his failure to consult them adversely affected his treatment of George III and Bute. The Bute papers are now at Mount Stuart on the Isle of Bute, Scotland.

[15] J. D. Nicholas, "The Ministry of Lord Bute," Ph. D thesis, University of Wales, 1989.

[16] A fire at Grenville's country seat at Wotton in Buckinghamshire in 1820 not only destroyed many files but eventuated in the scattering of the rest. For work

on Grenville as Secretary of State, see Karl W. Schweizer, *Frederick the Great, William Pitt, and Lord Bute* (New York, 1991); and K.W. Schweizer, *England, Prussia, and the Seven Years War* (Lewiston NY, 1989). Also still useful is L. Wiggin, *The Faction of Cousins: A Political Account of the Grenvilles 1733-1763* (New Haven, 1958), and J.R. Tomlinson, ed., *Additional Grenville Papers 1763-1765* (Manchester, 1963).

[17] See Jeremy Black, *The English Press in the Eighteenth Century* (London, 1987); B. Harris, *Politics and the Rise of the Press* (London, 1996); and K.W. Schweizer, ed., *Parliament and the Press, 1689-1939* (Edinburgh, 2006).

PART ONE: MOLDING A PATRIOT KING
Chapter I
"To Play What Game She Pleased without Observation": Princess Augusta and the Political Drama of Succession, 1736-56*

Long after her death in 1771, the Earl of Shelburne assessed the part Augusta, Dowager Princess of Wales and mother of King George III, played in the politics of her time. He began by observing, "It seems to have been her fate through life to have been neglected and undervalued." This did not relegate her to obscurity and unimportance, however. Being overlooked and underestimated were, according to the Earl, the sources of her considerable influence. She was able "to play what game she pleased without observation." As a result, "under cover of that neglect," Augusta "compassed all her points and gained more power than would have fallen to the lot even of an ambitious person in her situation."[1]

Why the powerful and ambitious at court paid very little attention to Augusta until too late was not a subject that intrigued Shelburne. The answer was so obvious it did not interest him much. The Princess was skilled in the art of deception, and particularly adroit at convincing others that she was exactly as she appeared before them: a woman without a shrewd intelligence or a strong character, someone who had no grand designs for the future or ulterior motives to conceal. Put another way, she was very good at performing her chosen role. So good, in fact, that her audience at court did not realize she was acting. Shelburne included among the gullible not only those she fooled during the 1750s when she was a widow, but her husband Frederick while he was alive. How did Augusta gain influence over a man who insisted frequently and publicly that he would never be controlled by a woman, as his father George II was? Shelburne concluded that she accomplished this feat "by flattering [Frederick's] vanity, which was excessive, entering into all his little tricks to gain popularity, and offering herself [as] a ready instrument, in all his plans of falsehood and deception."[2]

Strip the malice from the Earl's judgments on Augusta, and what remains are statements both instructive and suggestive. They are instructive because they supply questions for closer examination. For example, what were Frederick's "little tricks to gain popularity"? How did his wife assist in them? They are suggestive because they point to the centrality of role-playing at eighteenth-century courts. What roles were Augusta expected to play as royal consort to the heir to the throne, as Dowager Princess of Wales, and as the mother of a future king? Equally important, how did she conceive of her various parts at court, and how did she execute them?[3] To investigate these matters, it is best to begin with Frederick.

Frederick's contemporaries at court knew he loved the theatre. He frequently attended performances at London's playhouses; he often acted in amateur theatricals at his residence; he was in the habit of staging and directing plays with his children and courtiers as actors; and he even co-authored with Lord Hervey a comedy put on by the Covent Garden company. What those in court did not notice, however, was the extent to which the Prince's character itself was theatrical in nature. His attachment to the theatre was encouraged by his affinity with the personalities and *personae* of actors and actresses.

The 1730s saw the beginning of what John Brewer has described as "the cult of the actor," when men like Colley Cibber and David Garrick, with their dramatic skills and their fascinating lives, "filled with drinking, impulsiveness, and a casual attitude to the marriage vows," elevated performers over dramatists in the public esteem. It was also a time when women on the stage were "universally regarded as beautiful, talented, vivacious and impulsive, rather than sober, chaste and discreet."[4] Impulsiveness was one of the characteristics Frederick shared with these objects of his and the public's affection, as were vivacity and personal charm. Perhaps most important, like the players of his day, the Prince had the ability to switch roles rapidly, depending on the audience and his own moods. The most vivid testimony to his versatility may be found in the diary of Lord Perceval, a man who liked Frederick despite not always approving of him. For instance, on October 13, 1731, Perceval commented, "The character of the P[rince] is this: he has no reigning passion," other than conversation with small groups of men. Though he was inclined toward generosity, he often spoiled it "by giving to unworthy objects." He had several mistresses, including an apothecary's daughter, "but is not nice in his choice, and talks more of feats this way than he acts." He was capable of talking "gravely according to his company, but is sometimes more childish than becomes his age." Insofar as the practicalities and maneuvers of politics and government were concerned, "he thinks he knows business, but attends to none." Frederick, Perceval judged, "likes to be flattered." He was also "good-natured, and if he the meets with a good Ministry [when he is King], may satisfy his people."[5]

Though Perceval did not note any parallels between the Prince and, as actors, it is obvious from this account that Frederick, like London's star players, enjoyed applause and admiration from his audiences. In effect, Perceval's words describe a series of performances, designed to create illusions and impressions, each intended to appeal to a specific audience. Moreover, these were disciplined performances. Perceval pointed out that Frederick enjoyed spending "the evening with six or seven others over a glass of wine and hear[ing] them talk of a variety of things, but he does not drink." This abstinence puzzled the diarist, even though what it reveals is not obscure. The Prince wanted to keep a clear head while he was observing and being observed in a social setting. He was fully aware he was on stage, and he meant to avoid every pitfall and enjoy all the triumphs of acting his part. Perceval noted that Frederick "loves play, and plays to win."[6] His observation described more than the Prince's enjoyment of gambling, and his determination to profit from his pastime. Without meaning to, Perceval also described his joyful pleasure at assuming a variety of roles, and his equal determination to achieve his goals by skillfully playing those parts.

Thus Frederick's personality impelled him to believe he was on stage constantly. The environment at court powerfully reinforced that perception. Just as the private lives of actors were public, so were the personal lives of royalty. Popular fascination with all aspects of the lives of those who performed in these two arenas guaranteed this would be the case. Brewer's assessment of actors— "Players made the stage seductive: their glamour and beauty, the virtuosity of their performances, their private lives, at once the focus of polite society and yet disreputable on its margins, all made the theatre a place of exciting dreams, fantasies, and illusions"— is equally apt when applied to princes and courts.[7] Compare, for instance, Brewer's colorful, trenchant description of the eighteenth-century theatre with Lord Hervey's memorable contemporary description of life at court. To do well at court, suggested Hervey acidly, one had to have sense enough to know the company was black and dirty; honour enough to despise them; goodness enough to hate them; and hypocrisy enough to tell them they were white and clean.[8] Despite these drawbacks, the lure of life at court was irresistible, and to no one more so than the cynical Hervey himself.

Aside from his affinity for actors, and from the similarities between the two milieus, the Prince was keenly aware of the political implications of his taste in drama and comedy. As relations with his parents worsened, Frederick's enthusiastic attendance at performances of Shakespeare became more frequent. George II and Caroline might prefer and patronize foreign music and Italian opera; their son's presence at stagings of the Bard stood as an obvious patriotic counterpoint. When he attended *The Beggar's Opera*, or plays satirizing the differences between him and the King and Queen, or productions that disguised George II thinly as the Golden Rump—a scandalous reference to the monarch's agonizing hemorrhoids and his notorious flatulence—Frederick drew visible battle lines between himself and those currently in authority. He may even have been inspired in his conception and enacting of the roles of patriot prince and the future people's king by what he saw and heard on stage. Addison's *Cato*, which featured a virtuous leader in a corrupt time, was one of his particular favorites. Of course, he was not blind to the possibility that others would identify him with the true citizen of Rome. During the autumn of 1737, "the Prince went from Kew to [a performance of *Cato*] in London, and was not only clapped at his coming into the house, which was the absurd compliment paid to any of the Royal Family on these occasions, but was also huzzaed." When the protagonist proclaimed, "'When vice prevails, and impious men bear sway, the post of honour is a private station,' there was another loud huzza, with a great clap, in the latter part of which applause the Prince himself joined in the face of the whole audience."[9]

Frederick's popularity with Londoners may have even depended to a large extent on his open enjoyment of the theatre and the *demi-monde* Brewer dubbed "theatreland:" the rowdy pit; the mob outside; the whores, pickpockets, cutthroats, and confidence men; the proud display of power, prestige, and position in the boxes.[10] Perhaps this explains why his theatrical disaster did not lower his standing in the eyes of audiences. The play he and Hervey wrote together under the *nom de plume* of Captain Bodin was at best a "dull comedy." At its first performance, two men who were specially vocal in their disapproval of Act I, were "hauled out of the gallery by soldiers for showing their disapprobation of the play" and thrown into the street. This example of the perils of criticism produced a relatively peaceful first performance, without affecting the inevitable. When the curtain next went up on the comedy, the audience "called out for another play," on the grounds "the highest power on earth should not force the free born subjects of England to approve of nonsense." Since staging another play "on the sudden" was impossible, the manager offered to refund the crowd's money. "The audience was contented, and all trooped home." Riots over "nonsense" were not, of course, unusual at London's theatres. Managers regularly had to repair the damage done by the customers to their buildings; players had to face at times real brick bats hurled by their critics. More noteworthy is what happened when the play was staged again. Frederick bravely showed up, he and "the audience out of respect to him made no disturbance."[11]

After her marriage to Frederick in June 1736, Augusta began attending the theatre with him. Clearly, this was at his command, because her grasp of English was limited at the beginning of her life in Britain. The colloquial language of the street, the contrasting pronunciations of the players, and the highly allusive nature of many of the dramas and comedies, must have made the experience a confusing blur of sound and sensation to her. This did not matter to her husband; what was important was that Londoners would see her at Covent Garden and Drury Lane, just as they would become aware that she accompanied him through the metropolis to enjoy conjurers and consult fortune tellers. As she presented herself publicly as a quick and enthusiastic convert to popular amusements in Britain, she would speedily overcome prejudices against her German origins. Compared to her, the King and Queen would seem more foreign, despite the fact that they had lived in the country much longer. The outcome of this strategy was much as Frederick desired. Audiences noticed her presence, and accounts about the royal couple at playhouses began to spread. That they occasionally had adventures together while attending the theatre helped. For instance, in January 1737, Londoners could enjoy this story:

> [It] appeared that one Francis Cooke, a gentleman's coachman, who had picked up a woman, did in a very impudent, saucy manner assault the sentry who had the case of His Royal Highness's chair in the playhouse passage and would force into the said chair the woman he had picked up to make, as he has the impudence to call it, a bawdy house of the Prince's chair . . . [This started] so great a disturbance and mob that the Captain of the Guard had much ado to quell the disturbance and prevent the mob from breaking into the playhouse where His Royal Highness, the Prince of Wales and the Princess of Wales were.

Thus Augusta was on public display, before the eyes of the crowd in and out of the theatre, enjoying the excitement and facing the risks of attending a play. Her virtue had its defenders, and they numbered more than the guards who kept the chair she shared with Frederick from becoming "a bawdy house."[12]

That Londoners could view the Princess going to the theatre and sitting in the royal box was important to Frederick. It was equally important to him that she not be seen as part of that world, similar to actresses or, for that matter, himself. If she were perceived as saucy, independent, skilled at assuming various roles and playing them believably, she would not be an appealing, popular consort. He wanted her to be recognized as a different type of woman. Here Augusta's nature assisted his plan. Imitating the *savoir faire* and practiced, worldly ways of women who performed on stage would have been extraordinarily difficult for her, if not absolutely impossible. Such a role would have compelled her to deny herself completely. Unlike the Prince, her personality was not outgoing and impulsive. Also in contrast to her husband, her character had been molded by a deep religious faith. For her to project his confident, worldly-wise swagger would have been impossible. Perceval, who witnessed her first meeting with the King and Queen, observed that she "had a great colour from the heat of the day and the hurry and surprise she was in." Her obvious nervousness and apprehension worried this veteran observer at court, though he did not comment on what it foretold about her future. Still, he noted "she has a peculiar affability of behaviour and a very great sweetness of countenance, mixed with innocence, cheerfulness and sense." To Frederick, all of these characteristics made her an ideal consort. He may have exaggerated a little when he told Queen Caroline that he "was exceedingly pleased with the Princess, and . . . that if he had been himself to look all Europe over, he should have pitched his choice on her," but not too much. Augusta suited his purposes perfectly, because she had qualities that would enable her to play the parts he had in mind for his wife.[13]

Frederick never described what impressed him about his bride-to-be at their first meeting. Undoubtedly he was moved by considerations similar to those detailed by Lord Hervey when he narrated her presentation to George II and

Caroline. Augusta's obvious and—to her unsympathetic observer—flamboyant deference to her royal in-laws, "joined to the propriety of her whole behaviour" on that occasion, "gave spectators great prejudices in favour of her understanding." Why? Hervey went on to explain that "she was but seventeen . . ., knew not a mortal here, and was suffered to bring nobody but one single man with her." Moreover, she came "from the solitude of her mother's country-house in Saxe-Gotha at once into the crowd, intrigues, and pomp of this court." In such a situation, "the bare negative good conduct of doing nothing absurd might reasonably prejudice sensible people in her favour." Sir Robert Walpole went further than that in his assessment of Augusta. He told Hervey that her impressing "the King last year in one interview enough to make him fond of the match and her behaving at Greenwich to the Prince in such manner as to put him in good humour with it, after all his Royal Highness had uttered against her before he had seen her, were circumstances that spoke strongly in favour of brains that had had but seventeen years to ripen."[14] By "brains," Walpole was referring to more than intelligence. Sir Robert discerned in her a precocious maturity and a fixed determination to be the Princess of Wales, and, ultimately, Queen of Great Britain.

Frederick saw these strengths as well, plus something else, something that made them peculiarly attractive to him. Augusta understood that the best way to realize her ambition was to please him and follow his directions. When she and the Prince first met, "she told him she had one request she should ever make him, which was that he would give leave for her governess to come over." She had asked the King for this favor so she could have the comforting presence in her new country of a woman who had been with her since childhood. George II had forbidden this, and the two had been separated in Holland when the Princess boarded the ship to Britain. Frederick responded that "there was nothing she desired but he would do, and accordingly sent an express to bring the governess over." At that moment, an important bargain was struck. From that point on,

Augusta promised to follow his lead. She had also demonstrated she was willing and able to oppose the King's commands in order to get what she and her husband wanted. Not yet man and wife, they had already bonded in a common enterprise.[15]

What roles Frederick wanted Augusta to play are illustrated by this story and its provenance. Perceval heard about her request immediately after the Prince made his decision. That was possible only if Frederick told the story, because the other person privy to the agreement knew no one and spoke so little English, that at her wedding, the Queen had to translate the vows for her. And, since Perceval did not say the Prince had directly told him this, unquestionably, Frederick had made certain it was widely known. It was not a tale intended to be kind to George II, who had, after all, denied to a young woman the presence of even one servant from Saxe-Gotha and thus consigned her to utter isolation at a strange court. Left unsaid, but clearly implied, was the conclusion that he was too cheap and mean-spirited to offer her any direct contact with the familiar, while he himself frequently traveled to Hanover to enjoy the favors of a new mistress there. In contrast, her future husband immediately agreed to a reasonable and understandable request and sent for the governess without delay. He was careful, though, to make sure others knew that Augusta had said this would be her first and last request of him. Once more, the morals were unstated but obvious. Unlike his father, whose lust for his mistresses and dependence on his wife, left him vulnerable to manipulation and domination by women, the Prince would be literally his own man. And, unlike Caroline, whom Frederick was fond of blaming for any difficulties he had in his relations with his father, Augusta would be properly subservient to her husband.[16]

Augusta's role in the drama Frederick was staging at court, in Parliament, at the theatre, and in London streets was performing as a vivid and more appealing contrast to Caroline. The Queen was sophisticated and cynical; therefore the Princess should be innocent and naive. It cannot have been a difficult role for her. She was, after all, a young woman, in a strange, complex place, surrounded by people she did not know, speaking a language she was still mastering. When servants spied her playing with a doll, and their amused recounting of the scene swiftly spread through the court, that contributed to her persona. Why she had not studied English during the year between the making of the match and her actual wedding—"her mother said it must be quite unnecessary, for the Hanover family having been above 20 years on the throne, to be sure most people in England spoke German (and especially at court) as often and as well as English"— increased sympathy for her.[17] Thus Augusta's claim in 1737 that she was surprised and dismayed to learn that her husband and her parents were bitter personal and political opponents was perfectly plausible to every one at court, even the King and Queen. If they had thought about this without seeing before them Augusta in her role as wide-eyed innocent, they would have realized how *implausible* such a claim was. Even before they married, Frederick and Augusta were defying the King's commands about her governess. There had been protracted disputes in the House of Commons during the parliamentary sessions of 1736-37 over doubling the Crown Prince's establishment from £50,000 to £100,000 a year, and the financing of their household was the sort of controversy she might be expected to follow. But the court did not make those connections.[18] Occasionally, the Queen would be sufficiently exasperated by her daughter-in-law's apparent ignorance of what was going on around her to lament her "flat stupidity." Invariably, she quickly regretted these criticisms, and reminded herself how sorry she felt for that "poor creature." "If she were to spit in my face," Caroline once remarked, "I should only pity her, for being under a fool's direction, and wipe it off."[19]

What the Queen did not realize was how Augusta, with the help of Frederick's direction, was creating an image the opposite of her own. Caroline was intensely political and deeply involved in advising the King and his ministers about public issues. The Princess was not political at all; she was a properly submissive and supportive consort. Ironically, the Queen burnished this image with her own words. Her considered judgment of Augusta was that "there was no sort of harm in her, that she never meant to offend, was very modest and very respectful."[20] The King and others at court agreed with this verdict. Horace Walpole expressed prevailing opinions about Augusta when he praised "the quiet inoffensive good sense of the Princess who had never said a foolish thing, or done a disobliging one since her arrival." This she accomplished, he noted, despite being "in very difficult situations, young, uninstructed, and besieged by the Queen, Princess Emily, . . . Lady Archibald [Hamilton]'s creatures, and very jarring interests."[21] Without question, Frederick's strategy succeeded. To their targeted audience, Augusta was obviously no Caroline: she was not sophisticated, independent, cunning, manipulative, cynical, disloyal to members of her family or contemptuous of the people of London and their pleasures. Indeed, her apparently awkward eagerness to maintain friendly relations with the King and Queen had the effect of harming their reputations while enhancing hers. And she did this without arousing any suspicions in George II or Caroline about the genuineness of the behavior she showed toward them or the existence of any ulterior motives on her part.

When the King and Queen dismissed Augusta as totally under Frederick's control, they were praising her guile without meaning to do so. This was precisely the impression she was trying to make. Moreover, they were mistaken. Frederick had to persuade Augusta to adopt his strategies; he could not command her to do his bidding. Hervey recorded an example of how the Prince had to rely on persuasion, without realizing what it revealed about the dynamics of his relationship with Augusta. When she decided she would only receive Holy Communion at a Lutheran chapel, rather than taking the sacrament according to the rites of the Anglican Church, he could not compel her to set aside her "scruples." As Frederick confessed to the Queen, "she only wept and talked of her conscience." Using arguments similar to those suggested by Sir Robert Walpole, he had explained to her that "when this thing came to take air, how ill it would be received not only by the bishops and clergy, but by the people of England in general; and what bad consequences it might have, by giving the whole nation prejudices against" her. This had no effect. Finally, the Prince added a point suggested by Hervey to Caroline and passed along from her to him. The Act of Succession required heirs to the throne "on no less a penalty than the forfeiture of the Crown, to receive the Sacrament according to the manner of the Church of England." This law might be applied to the Prince of Wales's wife. Continued refusal to participate in Anglican communions could lead to the annulment of her marriage and her return to Saxe-Gotha. Ultimately, as Hervey reported, "the Princess was convinced by her husband's reasonings, dried her tears, lulled her conscience, and went no more to the Lutheran Church."[22] In time, she became as devout an Anglican as she had been as a Lutheran.[23] She immediately agreed to send her governess, the very same governess whom Frederick had earlier helped her to retain, who according to Hervey "was thought to have put this conscientious nonsense into [her] head" and was "talking to her too freely also on conjugal points," back to Germany. Finally, at Frederick's behest, Augusta began regularly attending Anglican Services at the Royal Chapel in Kensington Palace. There she made her entrance as conspicuously as possible, providing undeniable proof of her commitment to the Church of England and the persuasive prowess of her husband.[24]

Alone among those watching her at court, Sir Robert Walpole appreciated Augusta's intelligence and perceived a tendency toward independence on matters important to her. These observations convinced him that the Princess would be capable of exercising considerable influence over Frederick's thoughts and acts. In fact, Walpole foresaw "no way of keeping the Prince within any tolerable bounds but by the Princess." He cautioned Caroline, however, not to begin cultivating Augusta too early. That would "only give the Prince a jealousy, and prevent his ever suffering his wife to have any interest with him or any influence at all over his conduct." The Queen must be patient. She had to give her daughter-in-law "time to form an interest in him before she went about to make any use of her Royal Highness to these purposes."[25] Frederick may have had similar thoughts, and decided to forestall the development of a friendship between the two women by keeping them as much apart as he could manage. Perhaps such a consideration explains the frequent trips he and the Princess took away from Kensington Palace. It may have even contributed to his dangerous decision to move Augusta from Hampton Court to St James's Palace when she went into labor with their first child.

Their dash to London, undertaken in haste, without informing anyone, over rough roads, and to a palace where no one had made preparations for the delivery of a baby or for the witnesses needed to confirm the live birth of an heir to the throne, infuriated the King and Queen. Because they doubted their son was capable of fathering a child, they suspected this might be a plan to palm off some "chairman's brat he had bought" as his offspring, thereby removing their second son, William, in Duke of Cumberland, from the line of succession. Once these fears were relieved—not only by the testimony of some who had hastened to St. James's and arrived just in time to see Augusta deliver her namesake, but by the fact the infant was a daughter rather than a son—they were outraged by the Prince's endangering the lives of mother and child.[26] But even this episode eventuated in the enhancement of Frederick's popularity. After the King angrily commanded that the Prince and his family leave St James's as soon as the Princess and her baby could safely move, and informed the court that no one who waited on Frederick would be welcome at royal drawing rooms and levees, Augusta suggested in an exchange of notes with the Queen that the blame should lie with the King and Queen. As Hervey aptly pointed out to Caroline, Frederick, by speaking through the Princess, "has by these means opportunities of saying things to [her] . . . , which he would not dare say to the King himself." In addition, however, she replied to Augusta she risked losing the battle for the public's opinion. If she softened the criticism she and George II had made of the Prince in a letter to his wife, she would give the impression she was retracting it out of fear. Alternatively, if she kept on painting him "in his true colours, people will certainly lay hold of that to blame you, and say you were not satisfied with turning him out of the house and blowing up his father against him, but that you endeavoured to set his wife against him too, and to make him uneasy there, by telling her she was married to a knave, a fool, and a liar." With Hervey's adroit editorial assistance, Caroline tried to slip through the jaws of this trap. She did not wholly succeed. Frederick's popularity in London rose, as did Augusta's, thanks in part to her reference in the published correspondence to the public's pleasure at the birth of their daughter.[27] As they left St James's, "there was a mob about [the Prince's] coach, who cried, 'God bless you!'" Not one to miss a fortuitously timed opportunity, Frederick responded, "'God bless the King and God bless the poor.'"[28] The Queen solaced herself as best she could, perhaps by recalling how she despised all popularity, and especially her son's, which "makes me vomit."[29] Had they known about this reaction, doubtless Frederick and Augusta would have been pleased.

The purpose of their actions is evident. Creating an unmistakable contrast to the Queen was vital to Frederick's strategy of succession. Let Augusta portray herself as a loyal, loving wife and consort and as a respectful, dutiful daughter-in-law, and she would become much more popular than Caroline. The Queen was already the target of criticism in London. Subjects in the metropolis tended to blame her for what went wrong in politics and government, while scorning the King as an absentee monarch who placed his beloved Hanover's interests over Britain's. As the reverse of Caroline, Augusta would enjoy public favor for that reason alone. Frederick staged performances of *Henry IV, Part I*; perhaps he realized that, similar to Prince Hal's, his wife's reputation "like bright metal on a sullen ground, /. . . Shall show more goodly, and attract more eyes / Than that which hath no foil to set it off."[31] Such a perception would help insure the popularity of the Prince and Princess before he took the throne, strengthen his political position during the years of waiting, and ease his succession when George II died. By that time, Augusta would no longer be the consort as contrast. She would be far along toward becoming the consort as exemplar.

In fact, Augusta assumed her new role as exemplar sooner than she or the Prince expected. After a brief but painful illness, the Queen died on November 20, 1737. Throughout her final days, she refused to see Frederick, despite his frequent, well-publicized efforts to speak with her. Whether he honestly wished to be reconciled with her is unknowable; mother and son certainly had detested each other for years, and Caroline's hatred for the heir apparent to the throne did not diminish at all as she faced death. Whatever his real feelings, the genuineness of his sentiments was beside the point as far as the public were concerned. The son was trying to do his filial and Christian duty; the mother was not doing hers. Perceval noted, "People speak hardly of her for not yielding to the Prince's repeated desire to see her." This, he thought, was too bad, for "she was otherwise a tender mother, beloved by all her children; who with watching and sitting up with her have quite worn down, and now are ill."[32] Frederick hardly needed this response from the public to convince him that his consort should try to be viewed as a good mother. That was already part of his plan. Surely, though, it confirmed for him the wisdom of that design. From this time until his death in 1751, he and Augusta conspicuously spent time with their children, often at the production of amateur theatricals. Even Horace Walpole, who despised the Prince, conceded after observing his behavior and gossiping with others about it, that Frederick was "a better natured man, and a much better father" than George II. The Princess was equally affectionate in public. To the Prince and Princess, it was important to establish themselves as clearly better parents than the older generation. This they succeeded in doing. The best portraits of Augusta painted during those years show her surrounded by her children, who eventually totaled nine in fourteen years of marriage. The artists duplicated with oil on canvas how she wanted to be perceived in real life by those at court and the public.

Augusta's role as mother underscored another distinction between her husband and his father. On her deathbed, Caroline urged the King to wed again. At this, George II's "sobs began to rise and his tears to fall with double vehemence" and, "sobbing between every word, with much ado he got out this answer: *"Non, j'aurai les maîtresses."*"[33] This meant Augusta would be the only royal consort in the realm after Caroline's death. Thus she was noticeably and unmistakably the embodiment of morality at court. Frederick himself was not immune to the charms of other ladies at court; indeed, Horace Walpole claimed "his chief passion was women," then made a joke of his lust by noting "like the rest of his race, for [the Prince] beauty was not a necessary ingredient. But," added Walpole, "though these mistresses were pretty much declared, he was a good husband," and the Princess "was likely to have always preserved a chief ascendant over him."[34] Proof of her ability to win and hold the affection and trust of her husband may be seen in the poem he wrote and then had published about her charms. In it, he celebrated

> . . . that gentleness of mind, that love
> So kindly answering my desire,
> That grace with which you look and speak and move,
> That thus has set my soul on fire.[35]

There is no reason to question his sincerity in "The Charms of Sylvia by The Prince of Wales to the Princess." There is equally no reason to doubt their determination to appear before the public in verse, on canvas, at court, in the royal box at the theatre, and among Londoners in the street as a loving couple: the picture of matrimonial and familial love, as opposed to an ageing keeper of a mistress at public expense.

George II was not merely infamous for his passionate attachment to mistresses. He was also well known—at least according to rumor—for being controlled by the women in his life. Frederick had always vowed that women would not dominate him; according to one of his sisters, this was the only belief he had ever held consistently.[36] When Sir George Lyttleton parodied the Prince's verses on his wife, he had Frederick proclaim he loved best

> "that all-consenting tongue,
>
> That never puts me in the wrong."[37]

Clearly the Prince tried to give the impression that Augusta did not influence his political thoughts and acts. Given his care about this, it is not surprising that there is no documentary record of any effects she possibly had on him.

What is recorded is her knowledge about what he was doing. Augusta was present during part of a confidential discussion Frederick had with his principal man of business in Parliament, the Earl of Egmont, in early 1751 about recruiting new MPs to their faction and establishing the Earl's position as its leader in the House of Commons. Egmont expressed no surprise at this in his notes on the conversation.[38] And, after the Prince's death in 1751, some Tories appealed to the Princess to confirm their version of negotiations with Frederick over parliamentary opposition to the ministry in 1747. So did Bubb Dodington, who wanted Augusta to inform the King that he and she wanted the Prince to follow "a plan of temper and moderation" in 1749.[39] Unlike the situation in 1737, when she successfully claimed to be ignorant of political issues affecting her, during the 1750s Augusta did not even attempt this role. Nor could she, and retain any reputation for truthfulness. When Dodington returned to the Prince's service in 1749, he took care to inform her about the terms of his agreement with Frederick and "to beg [her] protection." That she "answered me in the most obliging manner" obviously pleased him. As he later recalled, "knowing her right way of thinking, I ventur'd to communicate it to her, and beg'd her protection in the execution of it." He presumed that she, too, favored a muted opposition in Parliament and was willing to consider the possibility of a *rapprochement* with government. His other assumption, that her views would influence Frederick, reveals his conviction that she was an important player in the politics of the Prince of Wales's court.[40] Actually, she, like her husband, did not settle finally on either

Dodington's strategy or Egmont's plan for a vigorous parliamentary opposition. They kept their options open. Nor did they want to drive away any current supporters of the Prince or exclude any potential recruits to their cause. So Frederick constantly worked at boosting the morale and flattering the ambitions of both Dodington and Egmont. Augusta played the vital part of sympathetic listener and friendly intercessor for both men in their relations with their leader.

Thus in March 1751, it was Augusta's task to reassure Egmont about her husband's health. The Earl had been concerned about the Prince's illness and his "low spirits." After privately sending for him, Augusta talked with Egmont for nearly an hour, "telling me he was much better [and] only wanted to recover his strength." She observed Frederick was "always frightened for himself when he was the least bit out of order but that she laughed him out of it and never would humor him in these fancys." Then she passed along a message for Egmont from the Prince: "that he should not die this bout but for the future would take better care of himself, that he might live for the sake of me and the public."[41] The Earl went home more cheerful about Frederick's life and his own political future, just as she had intended.

Egmont's hopes were soon dashed. The Prince's condition was far more serious than Augusta believed; he died two days after her *tête-a-tête* with the Earl. This should not, however, obscure an important point: how practiced she was at manipulating Frederick's moods away from despair and toward optimism. She must have done the same when he fretted about the state of his political health. Certainly she knew about his detailed plans for opposition during the next parliamentary session and for the first days after his accession to the throne. And she knew where to find them: in three chests at Carlton House. When her husband died, she sent immediately for Egmont. The King might seize the chests, she pointed out to him, and "we might be ruined by these papers." Pulling "off the silk covers of the pillow of a couch in the Prince's dressing room to serve as a bag to put them in," she dispatched the Earl to retrieve them. When he returned with the chests, she extracted with no hesitation or search "a book in my own handwriting, containing the Prince's whole disposition" of places he would have to fill early in his reign, and gave it to its author. Because it was in the Earl's distinctive hand, the contents could not be proven to have been Frederick's work. Then "she opened one of the trunks which I found she knew contained the public papers of our projected settlement—his declaration speeches etc. and list of offices . . . [and] a state of the intended Civil List with reasoning and advice to the Prince upon it." These she ordered Dr George Lee to burn in the fireplace.[42] Not until the incriminating papers were ashes, did she begin thinking about what to do with her husband's body and when to tell her father-in-law. Her disciplined performance revealed more than her intimate knowledge of Frederick's schemes. It showed impressive political acumen and decisiveness. These were both traits she would have to call on again and again during Prince George's minority.

Augusta's first response to Frederick's death speaks volumes about her character. She obviously felt she could not waste time mourning the loss of her husband. Instead, she had to take stock of her political situation and act right away. She could not, she realized instantaneously, risk antagonizing George II. To help guard against this, the Prince's political papers had to be destroyed. If the King was angered by anything, it was entirely conceivable he might take George and Edward from her and put them in his household, just as George I had done to him and Caroline. He had disapproved of the Prince's choice of tutors for the boys, but could do nothing about it while Frederick was alive and George was not the next in line to the throne. That they were being taught lessons of factional opposition to the King's ministry had been beyond his control. Now it was not. This was a frightening prospect for the Princess, and not merely because she could no longer exercise any maternal authority over her sons. Once the new Prince of Wales was at St James's, the odds were she would not be the Regent if George II died before his grandson was eighteen. Instead, the Regent would be his uncle, the Duke of Cumberland. This, in Augusta's opinion, would not be just a political defeat for her. She firmly believed Cumberland might take advantage of his position and power as Regent to usurp the throne. In order to preserve her son's birthright and whatever influence she could have on him as his mother, she had to decide swiftly on how best to keep George in her household and to gain the King's support for her as Regent in the event of his death.[43]

Egmont's advice on how to accomplish this was so predictable, Augusta did not have to consult with him to know what he would say. The Earl believed it was essential to keep the parliamentary faction loyal to Frederick, intact and united. Those 40 to 60 votes in the House of Commons, he would argue, would deter George II and his ministers from taking the Prince away and naming his uncle Regent. To the newly widowed Princess such a strategy was a recipe for disaster. Adopting it would serve Egmont's self-interest, because it would demonstrate that his ambitions had not been wholly wrecked by his master's death. But it would guarantee that the Dowager Princess would lose her sons and any possibility of being Regent, because it would arouse George II's and his ministers' enmity while revealing to them they had nothing to fear from Egmont or Augusta. Before his death, Frederick and Egmont were having difficulty recruiting more MPs to their cause. Worse, they were having trouble maintaining the numbers of their supporters in Parliament. The message of this was clear to Augusta: "*if the Prince cannot hold them together how shall I?*"[44] She was, after all, a woman, and therefore, according to the conventions of the day, unsuited for political leadership. Even more important, she was not the heir to the throne, and thus had nothing to promise prospective allies. Under those circumstances, support for her at Westminster, risky at best, would rapidly melt away. Declaring opposition to the King and government while weakening by the moment in the House of Commons, was not the way to achieve her goals. She could not coerce the King or his ministers into giving her what she wanted. She would have to persuade them to do that.

Wounded by Augusta's decision, Egmont explained it by saying "she has been flattered" by his enemies in the moderate faction at Frederick's court "'into a total reliance on the King and has thought it necessary for her own purpose to abandon all the Prince's friends" in Parliament. In fact, she had reached these conclusions herself. It was no accident that Dr. George Lee, a leading moderate, was present with the Earl and the Princess at the destruction of Frederick's papers. Augusta summoned him there. This was not for advice about what to do; she could predict his position as easily as she could Egmont's. Lee was there to advise *how* this course of action was to be taken, and its possible consequences, not *whether* it should be. Nor was it accidental that Egmont, not Lee, was sent to Carlton House. If this errand became known (and it did), it could be plausibly explained as an effort by Egmont to protect his own interests (as it was).[45] Augusta was not manipulated by others into these decisions. She made them by herself, then *she* manipulated the late Prince's followers. The Earl's explanation of her strategy does not do her justice in another way as well. In her interviews with George II, Augusta did not simply throw herself on his mercy. In an effort to impress and sway the most important constituents of her life, she skillfully reprised a number of roles she had earlier played.

The Princess began the morning after her husband's death. Encouraged by two "very kind" messages of concern for her sent by the King, she played the dutiful daughter-in-law and loving wife and mother to his emissary, the Earl of Lincoln. "She received him alone; sitting with her eyes fixed; thanked the King much, and said she would write as soon as she was able; [and] in the meantime, recommended her miserable self and children to him."[46] Soon after Lincoln left, Augusta wrote a letter which reinforced her words and demeanor during that interview.

> The sorrow which overwhelms me does not make me the less sensible of the great goodness of Your Majesty. The only things, Sire, which can console me are the gracious assurances which Your Majesty has given

me. I throw myself together with my children at your feet. We commend ourselves, Sire, to your paternal love and royal protection.[47]

Horace Walpole guessed successfully at what was happening here. "The King and she, (Augusta)" he explained in his *Memoirs of George II*, "both took their parts at once; she, of flinging herself entirely into his hands, and studying nothing but his pleasure, but winding what interest she got with him to the advantage of her own and the Prince's friends." As for George II, he got the pleasure "of acting the tender grandfather, which he, who had never acted the tender father, grew so pleased with representing, that he soon became it in earnest."[48] The only flaws in Walpole's analysis sprang from the persistent tendency to underestimate the Princess that Shelburne called attention to years later. He, like Dodington, Egmont, and most of the men at court, had difficulty giving full credit to Augusta's intelligence, courage, and skill at political performances. In this case, Walpole failed to see that the Princess did not try to move the King to gain advantages for her political friends, but for herself and Prince George. Nor did he discern that she encouraged George II to take up the part of loving grandfather, a role she divined he was prepared to assume.

These were not the only ways in which Augusta improved her position with the King. She had long enjoyed a reputation for prudence and good sense. Her abrupt severing of contact with Egmont, whom she never again admitted into her presence after he brought back the Prince's papers, called attention to those traits. Moreover, she made sure others knew about the Earl's exclusion, by ordering her servants to broadcast it widely and to treat him rudely. For his part, Egmont understood that relying utterly on George II's goodwill and abandoning him and the Prince's other political allies was "not impolitic in her circumstances." Still, he faulted her for not "break[ing this news] decently to those who were so near her husband, and were so much concerned in it as I am, and so faithful to her and her children's interest."[49] What he did not comprehend was the fact that she could not be courteous to him and still appear to be a prudential, commonsensical woman. Seeing him would have become as widely and quickly known as refusing to meet with him at all was. And many at court, Whitehall, and Westminster would not regard a conversation between Augusta and her late husband's friend as an innocent exchange of kind condolences and courteous good-byes. To the contrary: the mere fact of their meeting would rouse suspicions about her motives and raise questions about the authenticity of her submission to the King and his ministers. It would also keep her from playing convincingly her final role in the crisis created by Frederick's death: that of a woman who was fundamentally uninterested in politics. Augusta was returning to the part she played first as the submissive, uninformed young Princess during 1736-37 and then occasionally thereafter when circumstances demanded it: the dutiful, apolitical consort. She played it as well in 1751 as she had earlier, though under changed circumstances.

By reprising this role, Augusta confirmed opinions the King already held about her. As Earl Waldegrave, who was one of George II's favorites, recalled, "The Princess of Wales, during the life of the Prince her Husband, had distinguished herself by a most decent & prudent Behavior." Noticing and approving of this, "the King, notwithstanding his aversion to his Son, behaved to her not only with great Politeness, but with the appearance of cordiality and Affection."[50] Augusta had taken a critical step toward winning his affection in February 1742. After that Sir Robert Walpole resigned as First Lord of the Treasury and Leader of the House of Commons, some in opposition called for an inquiry into his handling of secret service funds in the hope that grounds could be found for impeaching him for corruption. Determined to spare his longtime minister this indignity, the King took the extraordinary step of meeting privately with Augusta and asking her to persuade Frederick to tell his supporters to vote against any inquiry. Though the Princess respectfully requested to be excused from acting as her father-in-law's advocate, saying her practice was to take no part in politics, she did agree to pass the request along to the Prince.[51] That

Frederick ultimately did not do as George II wished, did not diminish his pleasure with Augusta's service as liaison between the two men. In 1751, she reaped the reward: "[H]is Majesty gave still stronger Proofs of his Favour and Confidence."[52] When he went to see the Princess on March 31, 1751, he would not sit in the chair of state prepared for his visit. Instead, he perched next to her on a couch. The two hugged each other, then wept together. When the children arrived, he "embraced Prince George, said he loved him, bid him to be honest and brave, and mind his mother who was the best of women." Next, he once more "embraced the Princess, desired nobody might come between him and her, and that he would do every thing for her." There was, Egmont gathered from the account almost instantaneously circulating in London, an "abundance of speeches and a kind behaviour to her and the children" that so "captivated Prince George" that he said "he should not be frightened any more with his grandpapa." In his memoirs, Waldegrave emphasized the political consequences of this meeting. The King "patronized the Act by which [the Princess] was appointed Regent, in case of a Minority: and, what was of greater Importance, he suffer'd the Heir Apparent to remain under her sole Direction."[54]

Augusta would have said Waldegrave exaggerated the extent of her victory. If George II died before his grandson's eighteenth birthday on June 4, 1756, she might be Regent, but she would have to share power with a council that would include Cumberland and many of the dead King's ministers. For her son's position to be as secure as she wished, Henry Pelham, currently First Lord of the Treasury, and his brother, the Duke of Newcastle, would have to remain opposed to Cumberland and his man of business, Henry Fox. Probably she was also aware that one reason her sons remained with her, was the Pelhams' fear that if they were moved to the King's court at St. James's, Cumberland and Fox might gain control of their education. Certainly Augusta knew that although the boys would stay at Leicester House, George II and his ministers would appoint their governors, preceptors and tutors. How and by whom George and Edward were educated would not be decided by her.[55] Against these limitations on her power, the Princess could balance the fact that she still had gained a great deal. To be sure, she could not exercise complete control over George's fate in the years immediately ahead. She did not even feel she could openly protest when she believed either the Pelhams or those they appointed in the Prince's household did not act properly or wisely. Clearly, she would not be able to cross swords with the King, however much it might seem justified to her. But she had positioned herself where she could maneuver behind the scenes and play time-tested roles to the best advantage of the future King.

The next years were hard ones for Augusta. She strained to achieve the appearance of what Waldegrave believed was reality before 1755: "the Princess's Behaviour to the King was wise and dutiful; she consider'd him as her Protector, Benefactor, and Friend; and took no Step, or any consequence without his Approbation."[56] In fact, she had nothing but contempt for him, scorning in particular to her *confidant* Dodington his inability to say "no" to his ministers. In her opinion, George II, despite his tantrums and grumblings, was a mere boy in their hands, whom they disciplined when necessary and tolerated at other times.[57] She, on the other hand, had to yield to him. "There were a hundred good reasons that tied her hands from interfering with the King; those about her children were obvious enough. If she was to stir," she reminded Dodington, "it would make things worse; she saw no way to extricate herself."[58] So she continued to play her role, and play it well. Although George II may have come to suspect her dislike for him, her prudential behavior prevented him from being certain and taking action against her.[59]

Augusta's hatred of Newcastle may have been even greater than her contempt for the King. "The weakness, meanness, cowardice and baseness of the Duke of Newcastle—all of which she echoed in the strongest terms"—were frequent subjects of her conversations with Dodington.[60] The Princess did not feel compelled to hide her feelings from Newcastle; during the 1750s, she criticized him to his face for yielding too much to Cumberland and Fox and for excluding Frederick's old supporters from office. Her inability to change his ways depressed Augusta. To her, it was an unmistakable sign of her own weakness that she could not bully the Duke as successfully as others who despised him did.[61] Finally, the performance of Prince George's governors and tutors dissatisfied her. George was not learning very much, and he remained disturbingly immature for someone who might be King in the near future. The lion's share of the blame for this she gave to the men appointed by George II and Newcastle.[62] But she knew she 'durst not recommend for fear of offense: while he had governors &c., [and] was under immediate inspection, all that they did not direct, would be imputed to her."[63] Once she began complaining, or appeared to be interfering, her enemies would remove "the Prince into those other hands, at last, by taking him from the people now about him and by degrees, consequently, from her."[64]

So Augusta accomplished what she could, sometimes by cautious stealth, more often by tightly controlling the contacts George and Edward had with the court and the outside world. Because "the young people of quality were so ill educated, and so very vicious, that they frighten'd her," she kept them as isolated as she could.[65] The Princess supplemented her close supervision of their social lives with determined efforts to instill her religious piety in them and with constant emphasis on proper and moral behavior. In particular, she was concerned about the potential that sexual temptations (because "the behaviour of the women was so indecent, so low, so much against their interest, by making them so cheap") and lust (because they were, after all, the sons and grandsons of men who kept mistresses) had to overturn their moral training and leave them under the domination of self-interested people who would not desire that they serve their nation well.[66] Edward, who evidently once had been her favorite, resisted these lessons and complained about his situation. George was his mother's son, to her relief and delight. Even so, Augusta realized she could not prepare him by herself to be a king. She could not provide the proper education for him, and he desperately needed a better teacher. Nor could she introduce him into the world of politics. The Princess did not believe "women could . . . inform him" about the realities of power. And, as he came closer to his eighteenth birthday, she "was highly sensible how necessary it was that the Prince should keep company with men."[67] Finding the right man to guide the Prince into an understanding of what the world he was entering was like and to teach what the duties of a king were in dealing with and overcoming that world, became her principal concern.

Augusta did not have many to choose from. Dodington knew the Prince, and had even discussed public finance with him, but the two had not established any close rapport. Besides, even though the Princess trusted Dodington enough to share her innermost personal thoughts with him, she did not believe he would reinforce her ideals of public and private morality, and she was so wary of his ambitions and motives, that she kept him utterly uninformed about her political activities. George would learn to accept things as they were, and to compromise with Newcastle and others on important points, if Dodington taught as he had acted.[68]

The other possible choice was the Earl of Bute, who had been a familiar at Leicester House since the mid-1740s. He had impressed her late husband and Egmont enough to be named a Lord of the Bedchamber at the Prince's court and to be slated for election as one of the 16 Scottish peers in the House of Lords when Frederick became King.[69] That the Prince also "used frequently to say Bute was a fine Showy Man, who would make an excellent Embassador in a court where there was no Business" did not disqualify him in her eyes.[70] To Augusta, this meant he was not enmeshed in the narrow practicalities of politics and government. Thus his vision of what a patriotic and moral monarch could accomplish was not bounded by narrow worldly criteria. Moreover, the fact that Bute did not have extensive contacts with politicians was an advantage. By itself, that proved his loyalty to Frederick's heir. Unlike many of the late Prince's supporters, he had not approached the ministry after his master's death in the hope of gaining a pension or an office. This was not due to a lack of connections at court. Bute's uncle, the Duke of Argyll, controlled Scottish patronage. Though his connection with Argyll had frayed over the years, certainly he could have appealed to his relative for aid had he so desired. His decision not to do this proved his commitment to Leicester House. Indeed, that attachment was so strong that he attempted to persuade Argyll to join the opposition to Newcastle's administration.[71] The absence of political connections also meant he would not be influenced in his future dealings with prominent politicians by past negotiations, arrangements, and alliances with them. Most important, the time they had spent together convinced the Princess that Bute shared her morality, her political ideals, and her ambition to make George a good monarch. If he could win her son's confidence, he would be ideal. Augusta did what she could to encourage this bonding. Waldegrave was convinced that "by the good offices of the Mother, [Bute] also became the avow'd favorite of the Young Prince."[72] No doubt he exaggerated her role, mostly because he was jealous of his successful rival for George's affections. The two establishment of a very close mentor—protégé relationship between the Earl and the Prince was chiefly Bute's doing. Augusta herself was more than happy to give him the credit and to delight in his success.[73]

Whether or not she helped create the foundation for an affectionate relationship between her son and the man who became his "dearest friend," the Princess did make a crucial contribution to its success. She arranged their meetings, and insured they would be secret even from her personal servants. This she achieved by giving the impression that Bute was visiting her and spending hours in *tête-à-têtes*. Dodington had no idea what was going on.[74] Inspired by the servants' talk about these meetings, Waldegrave leaped to the conclusion that Bute and Augusta were lovers. This impression was heightened by the behavior of the two toward each other in public. Bute, who inclined toward grand words and vivid gestures on every occasion, must have become even more theatrical out of gratitude to her. Augusta clearly did not conceal her feelings for her "best friend" in public.[75] As Horace Walpole later remarked, "the eagerness of the pages of the backstairs to let her know whenever Lord Bute arrived, a mellowness in her German accent as often as she spoke to him, and that was often and long, and a more than usual swimmingness in her eyes, contributed to dispel the ideas that had been conceived of the rigour of her widowhood."[76] Did she act and speak this way deliberately, in full awareness she was risking her reputation, in order to prevent anyone from guessing Bute's true role in her household, reporting it, and convincing George II to move his grandson to St James's? There is no way of determining this for sure. But if she did, playing this role was an extraordinary act of maternal love and courage.[77]

During the two decades between her marriage and her son's eighteenth birthday, courts were indeed stages for Augusta. In that time, she played many parts. Some were assigned to her, either by her husband or the realities of her situation. Some she chose. All she executed well. Throughout, her performances were inspired by a determination that her husband or her son would ascend to the throne under the most favorable circumstances possible, popular with his people, independent of the politicians of the old order, and prepared to take up the role of patriot king immediately. What she said about the future George III she had felt about Frederick as well: she "could have nothing so much at heart as to see him do well, and make the nation happy."[78] To fulfill that goal, and her other wish, that he be "great and happy for [his] own sake," Augusta was ready to adopt whatever roles might be required of her, whether they were the dutiful daughter-in-law, the submissive, supportive, and loving wife, the affectionate mother, the prudent, decent, and apolitical woman, perhaps even the lover of Bute.[79] She understood that all of these in turn were necessary for playing well the most crucial parts of her life, as Princess of Wales and as the mother of a king who would make himself and his nation "great and happy."

*This chapter first appeared in: Clarissa Campbell Orr, ed., *Queenship in Britain, 1660-1837: Royal Patronage, Court Culture, and Dynastic Politics* (Manchester University Press, 2002), pp. 207-235.

Endnotes

[1] The Earl of Shelburne, "Autobiography," in: Lord Fitzmaurice, *Life of William Earl of Shelburne Afterwards First Marquess of Lansdowne With Extracts from His Papers and Correspondence*, 2 vols, 2nd ed. (London, Macmillan, 1912), I, pp. 46, 49.

[2] *Ibid.*, I, p. 49

[3] Shelburne commented on role-playing at court and Augusta's aptitude for it: "Naturally given to dissimulation and intrigue she had both time and opportunity to improve these important qualifications; she was surrounded by nothing else, and the perpetual mortifications she submitted to pressed and obliged her to exert both." He also pointed out that she was very observant, "had resolution equal to any enterprise, and had a perfect command of temper." *Ibid.*, I, p. 49.

[4] J. Brewer, *The Pleasures of the Imagination: English Culture in the Eighteenth Century,* (New York, Farrar, Straus, & Giroux, 1997), pp. 334-48.

[5] Viscount Perceval, "Diary," Nov. 13, 1731, ed. R. A. Roberts, Historical Manuscripts Commission, *Manuscripts of the Earl of Egmont. Diary of Viscount Percival Afterwards First Earl of Egmont*, 3 vols., (London, His Majesty's Stationery Office, 1920-23), I, pp. 207-8. In the text, I have spelled "Perceval" the way most members of the family wrote it, and not "Percival" as this viscount did.

[6] *Ibid.*, Nov. 13, 1731, I, pp. 207-8.

[7] Brewer, *Pleasures*, p. 334.

[8] Lord Hervey, *Memoirs of the Reign of George the Second From his Accession to the Death of Queen Caroline*, ed. J. W. Croker, 2 vols., (London, John Murray, 1848), I, p. 90.

[9] *Ibid.*, II, p. 406. For a discussion of the political implications of operas and plays, see: Brewer, *Pleasures*, pp. 369-83.

[10] Brewer, *Pleasures*, pp. 325-56.

[11] Perceval, "Diary," Oct. 11, 1731 and Jan. 16, 1731-2, I, pp. 205, 216. For another example of Frederick's personal courage in public, see: *ibid.*, Oct. 1, 1735, II, pp. 197-8.

[12] Quoted in Brewer, *Pleasures*, p. 350. For Augusta's unfamiliarity with English, see: Hervey, *Memoirs*, II, p. 115 and Perceval, "Diary, Apr. 27, 1736, II, p. 264.

For another example of how the Prince displayed and proclaimed Augusta's virtues on London's streets, see Perceval: "Diary," May 1, 1736, II, p. 267.

[13] Perceval, "Diary," Apr. 27, 1736, p. 264. Perceval had become the 1st Earl of Egmont in 1734. I continue to refer to him by his family name to distinguish him from his son, the 2nd Earl of Egmont, who became one of Frederick's principal advisers during the 1740s and who also kept a journal of events that I quote from in this chapter.

[14] Hervey, *Memoirs*, II, pp. 114-15.

[15] Perceval, "Diary," Apr. 27, 1736, II, p. 264.

[16] *Ibid.*, II, p. 264. For an example of Frederick's penchant for blaming his mother for his difficulties with the King, see Perceval, "Diary," Sept. 21, 1737, II, p. 435.

[17] Hervey, *Memoirs*, II, p. 115. As Hervey sarcastically observed, this was "a conjecture so well founded that I believe there were not three natives in England that understood one word of it better than in the reign of Queen Anne."

[18] For a contemporary account of this episode, see: *ibid.*, II, pp. 407-8. The source for this was Monsieur Dunoyer, a dancing master at court, who, according to Hervey, "was a sort of licensed spy on both sides," sometimes reporting to the King and Queen about events at the Wales's court, sometimes to the Prince about their Majesties and the courtiers around them. In his account, Augusta accosted him privately, after the Prince had retired, and asked if there was trouble within the family, "adding with great vehemence, that she would know." When Dunoyer "pretended ignorance, she burst into tears, flew into a greater passion than he thought her capable of, and by these means had forced him, half out of fear and half out of pity, to tell her all he knew." This has all the marks of a staged scene, one designed to limn further a perception of the Princess's concern about relations with her in-laws while extracting information out of the dancing master.

[19] *Ibid.*, II, pp. 132-3.

[20] *Ibid.*, II, p. 133.

[21] Horace Walpole, *Memoirs of King George II*, ed. J. Brooke, 3 vols., (New Haven, Yale University Press, 1985), I, p. 53. Lady Archibald Hamilton was reputed to be the Prince's mistress. He had prevailed upon Augusta to make her one of his Ladies of the Bedchamber, despite the opposition of the Queen. See Hervey, *Memoirs*, II, pp. 119-20, 131-2.

[22] Hervey, *Memoirs*, II, pp. 129-30. During the eighteenth century, it was a common practice in the Church of England to take the sacrament of Holy Communion only two or three times a year. Augusta was attending other Anglican services, but she did not feel she could in good conscience take communion according to those rites.

44

[23] For a discussion of her piety as an Anglican, see J. L. Bullion, " 'George, Be a King!': The Relationship between Princess Augusta and George III," in: S. Taylor, R. Connors and C. Jones (eds.), *Hanoverian Britain and Empire: Essays in Memory of Philip Lawson* (London, Boydell Press, 1998), pp.180-1, 189. Reprinted as ch. III in this book.

[24] Hervey, *Memoirs*, II, pp. 129-31. "Whether by grandeur or by chance," according to Hervey, Frederick and Augusta "used generally to come to chapel at Kensington after the service had been some time begun." This meant the Princess had "to crowd by the Queen," which irritated Caroline considerably. Hervey believed this was designed by the Prince to provoke a quarrel so he could then describe his mother as unreasonable and difficult to live with. It seems equally probable that a late arrival called attention to Augusta's presence and underscored her commitment to the Church of England. Once this point was established, and it was clear the Queen was not going to rise to the bait, Augusta did not attend this service when she could not be there when it started.

[25] *Ibid.*, II, p. 121.

[26] *Ibid.*, II, pp. 362-78; the quotation is on p. 372.

[27] *Ibid.*, II, pp. 426-41, 457-8.

[28] Perceval, "Diary," Sept. 21, 1737, II, p. 435.

[29] Hervey, *Memoirs*, II, p. 210.

[30] For examples, see *ibid.*, II pp. 190-5, 210-11, 223-4.

[31] For an example of Frederick's productions of *Henry IV, Part I*, George Bubb Dodington, "Political Journal," Jan. 11, 1751, in: J. Carswell and L. A. Dralle (eds.), *The Political Journal of George Bubb Dodington* (Oxford, Clarendon Press, 1965), p. 95. Interestingly George II saw parallels between Shakespeare's creation and his own situation. One morning in late 1735 "he indulged himself in another sally . . . against his son by saying whilst he was talking of the actors he had seen in the play of Harry the Fourth the night before, that there were really some good ones, but for the Prince of Wales he must own he never saw so awkward a fellow and so mean a scoundrel in his life." Everyone present, noted Hervey, grasped George II's meaning "but all very properly pretended to understand his Majesty literally joined in the censure and abused the theatrical Prince of Wales." Hervey, *Memoirs*, II, pp. 53-4.

[32] Perceval, "Diary," Nov. 20, 1737, II, p. 445. A full account of Caroline's final illness may be found in: Hervey, *Memoirs*, II, pp. 490-539.

[33] Hervey, *Memoirs*, II, pp. 513-14.

[34] Walpole, *Memoirs of George II*, I, p. 53.

[35] *Ibid.*, III, p. 145.

[36]Hervey, *Memoirs*, II, p. 211.

[37]Walpole, *Memoirs of George II*, III, p. 145n.

[38]Earl of Egmont, "Memorandum Book," [Mar. 12, 1751], in: A. N. Newman (ed.), "Leicester House Politics, 1750-60, From the Papers of John, Second Earl of Egmont," in: *Camden Miscellany Vol. XXIII* (London, Royal Historical Society, Camden Fourth Series Volume 7, 1967), p. 196.

[39]Dodington, "Political Journal," Oct. 2, 1751, Jul. 16, 1752, pp. 135, 165.

[40]*Ibid.*, Jul. 18, 1749, p. 7. When Dodington reminded Augusta about their conversation later, she confirmed his understanding of it. "It was," she said, "very true, she was a good witness of it, and would always say it, &c." *Ibid.*, Jul. 16, 1752, p. 165.

[41]Egmont, "Memorandum Book," [Mar. 18, 1751], p. 197.

[42]*Ibid.*, [Mar. 20, 1751], pp. 198-9. Egmont noted that Augusta opened one of the trunks briefly even though "I knew there was nothing [there] and she too." This indicates he was well aware she was very familiar with her late husband's most secret records.

[43]Augusta's acts can be followed and her motives inferred from *ibid.*, [Mar. 20-Apr. 13, 1751], pp. 198-213.

[44]*Ibid.*, [Mar. 26, 1751], p. 205, italics in original. For the Prince and Egmont's problems in the House of Commons, see the Earl's entry for [Mar. 12, 1751], p. 196.

[45]*Ibid.*, [Mar. 28, 1751], p. 206. Augusta even accused Egmont of spreading the story himself, either personally or by encouraging his servants to do it, in order to inflate his own reputation. He protested his innocence, observing as he did so that by the time he got home after the destruction of the papers his servants already knew he had retrieved them from Carlton House. He also asked her to try to remember if she had told anyone. Augusta did not respond to this thinly veiled accusation.

[46]Walpole, *Memoirs of George II*, I, pp. 54-5.

[47]Quoted in J. Brooke, *King George III* (New York, McGraw Hill, 1972), p. 26.

[48]Walpole, *Memoirs of George II*, I, p. 55.

[49]Egmont, "Memorandum Book," [Mar. 27, 1751], p. 205.

[50]Earl Waldegrave, "Memoirs of the Leicester House Years, 1752-1756," in: J. C. D. Clark (ed.), *The Memoirs and Speeches of James, 2nd Earl Waldegrave, 1742-1763* (Cambridge, Cambridge University Press, 1988), p. 162.

[51]See: Morris Marples, *Poor Fred and The Butcher: Sons of George II* (London, Michael Joseph, 1970), p. 97. Soon after George II and Augusta had their

conversation in February 1742, the King and Frederick met for the first time in four and a half years. It was a formal occasion at court, intended to signal to the political world that the two were interested in a reconciliation. After the Prince kissed his father's hand, George II broke their long silence by asking, "How does the princess do?" Then he added, "I hope she is well." These sentiments not only artfully called attention to the two men's common affection for Augusta, surely one of the few beliefs or feelings they shared. It also hinted at the King's hope she might become the means for drawing him and the Prince closer together politically and personally. For this exchange, see: J. Walters, *The Royal Griffin: Frederick, Prince of Wales, 1707-51*(New York, Stein & Day, 1972), p. 183.

[52] Waldegrave, "Memoirs," p. 162.

[53] Walpole, *Memoirs of George II*, I, p. 58; and Egmont, "Memorandum Book," Mar. 31, 1751, p. 207.

[54] Waldegrave, "Memoirs," p. 162.

[55] See: Walpole, *Memoirs of George II*, I, pp. 60-105.

[56] Waldegrave, "Memoirs," p. 163.

[57] Dodington, "Political Journal," Feb. 8, 1753, p. 203.

[58] *Ibid.*, May 27, 1755, p. 299.

[59] According to Walpole, after the passage of the Act of Parliament making Augusta the Regent, George II claimed he had "assumed to himself the chief direction of the bill." Then he added in remarks he made to Henry Fox, "I have a good opinion of the Princess, but I don't quite know her." Walpole, *Memoirs of George II*, I, p. 103. Walpole also heard that the King told Henry Pelham soon after Frederick's death "You none of you know this woman, and you none of you will know her till I am dead." Quoted in: Clark, "Introduction," Waldegrave, p. 54.

[60] Dodington, "Political Journal," May 27, 1755, p. 298.

[61] *Ibid.*, Feb. 8, 1753, pp. 204-5.

[62] Bullion, "George, Be a King!", pp. 186-8.

[63] Dodington, "Political Journal," May 29, 1754, p. 271.

[64] *Ibid.*, Dec. 28, 1752, pp. 192-3.

[65] *Ibid.*, Oct. 15, 1752, p. 178; see also the entry for Dec.18, 1753, p. 244.

[66] *Ibid.*, May 27, 1755, p. 300. See also Bullion, "'George, Be a King!'" pp. 190-5.

[67] Dodington, "Political Journal," May 27, 1755, p. 300.

[68] On Aug. 6, 1755, Dodington talked "with the Prince, about funding, &c., and other serious things" and he "seem'd to hear with attention and satisfaction." "Political Journal," p. 318. But the Princess's friend emphasized teaching the wisdom of the world, and he often urged Augusta to end George's isolation at court. Although she found it politic to agree with him in principle on these occasions this was not the sort of advice she welcomed or had any intention of taking. For examples of Dodington's educational philosophy and the Princess's temporizing responses see: "Political Journal," Oct. 15, 1752, Dec. 18, 1753 and May 27, 1755, pp. 178, 244, 300.

[69] Egmont, "A Plan for the New Parliament," [Apr. 1749], in: Newman (ed.), "Leicester House," p. 171. Frederick made Bute a Lord of the Bedchamber on October 16, 1750. This was not a minor appointment. The Prince reserved these positions for politicians whom he expected could help him in increasing the numbers of his supporters. No doubt he anticipated Bute would assist in the recruitment of Scottish MPs. Such appointments served another purpose as well. Accepting them publicly bound men like Bute to Frederick's cause, and thus improved his reputation and position as leader of the opposition to government. Since the Prince insisted that those accepting posts from him resign places and give up pensions they held from the King, their commitment to him became all the more noticeable. Bute relinquished a pension from the crown. See: A.N. Newman, "Communication: The Political Patronage of Frederick Lewis, Prince of Wales," *Historical Journal*, 1 : 1 (1958), pp. 73-5.

[70] Waldegrave, "Memoirs," pp. 163-4. Given this description of him as a "fine Showy Man,," it is interesting that Walpole believed what first commended Bute to the Prince was the Earl's skill at acting "in private companies with a set of his own relations." Walpole, *Memoirs of George II*, I, pp. 32-3. Shelburne remembered the same story. Shelburne, "Autobiography," I, p. 51.

[71] See A. Murdoch, "Lord Bute, James Stuart Mackenzie and the Government of Scotland," in: K. W. Schweizer (ed.), *Lord Bute: Essays in Re-interpretation* (Leicester, Leicester University Press, 1988), pp. 119-22.

[72] Waldegrave, "Memoirs," p. 176.

[73] See J. L. Bullion, "The Prince's Mentor: A New Perspective on the Friendship between George III and Lord Bute during the 1750s," *Albion*, 21: 1 (1989), pp.34-55.

[74] There is no hint in Dodington's "Political Journal" that he was aware Bute was tutoring Prince George secretly. Augusta's efforts at deception were successful. "She may deceive me," mused Dodington, "but I am persuaded that she has no flx'd digested political plan at all; or regular communication in politics, with anybody, but Mr. [James] Cresset," her private secretary. These exchanges illustrate how carefully and skillfully the Princess kept the reality of Bute's significant influence at Leicester House not only from the prying eyes of enemies,

but from friends like Dodington as well. Dodington, "Political Journal," July 21, 1755, Aug. 6, 1755, pp. 310-11, 317.

[75] Augusta called Bute her "best friend" in an undated letter to him reprinted in R. Sedgwick (ed.), *Letters from George III to Lord Bute, 1756-1766* (London, Macmillan, 1939), p. 4. For an account of how they behaved toward each other in public during 1755-56, see: J. L. Bullion, "The Origins and Significance of Gossip about Princess Augusta and Lord Bute, 1755-1756," *Studies in Eighteenth-Century Culture*, 21: 1 (1991), pp. 357-8 (chapter II in this volume).

[76] Walpole, *Memoirs of George II*, II, 151. Clark persuasively argues that Waldegrave was Walpole's source for these observations. "Introduction," *Waldegrave*, p. 78. See also Brooke's notes on this passage in Walpole's *Memoirs of George II*, pp. 251-2n.

[77] An account of their relationship during the two years before George's eighteenth birthday, including a discussion of whether Augusta deliberately risked her reputation, may be found in: Bullion, "The Origins and Significance of Gossip," pp. 245-65.

[78] Dodington, "Political Journal," Oct. 15, 1752, p. 180.

[79] The quotation describing this wish of Augusta is from Earl of Bute to Prince George, [June 1755], in: Sedgwick (ed.), *Letters from George III to Lord Bute, 1756-1766*, p. liii.

Chapter II

The Origins and Significance of Gossip about Princess Augusta and Lord Bute, 1755-1756*

Where two or three gather in faith, St. Paul informed us, there is the church. When men in business meet, warned Adam Smith, a conspiracy in restraint of trade is a distinct possibility. And when politicians conversed or corresponded in eighteenth-century Britain, they frequently gossiped.[1] Their observations on a speech in Parliament, of a smile or a frown from royalty at a drawing room or from a minister at a levee, of business and pleasure at court, of meetings between people who should (or should not) have been together, were the grist of a gossip that was endlessly fascinating—to them. Moreover, their interpretations of what these observations meant for the present and future seemed enormously significant at the time. Thus, termed conventionally, gossip fills their papers.

The phenomenon of gossip has proved to be equally fascinating to scholars in a number of diverse disciplines.[2] In eighteenth-century studies, Patricia Meyer Spacks, in particular, has drawn upon these findings and her own wide-ranging and sensitive knowledge of the literature of the period to produce a remarkable and suggestive study.[3] Historians of eighteenth-century British politics, however, are exceptions to this rule. By and large, they have neither explored the role of gossip nor investigated particular episodes in which it played a critical role.[4] Political gossip is a potentially promising area of inquiry for a number of reasons. The gossip of politicians can yield interesting insights into the behavior of their fellows at court and in Parliament. It can reveal the personalities and characters of the gossips themselves. Finally, the mere fact that some people were gossiped about in certain ways at specific moments could, in different ways, influence the historical events of their time.

In this chapter, I will discuss one of the most important of those moments. I will examine the origins of rumors about the relationship between the Earl of Bute and Augusta, Dowager Princess of Wales. Then I will call attention to the effect that the rapidly spreading conviction that they were lovers had on British politics during the 1750s and 1760s.

Both of these subjects have been hitherto overlooked by historians. I think there are two explanations for this. First, scholars have assumed that the rumors about Augusta and Bute had no real historical significance during the 1750s. According to the prevailing wisdom, if this talk about an affair had any importance at all, it did so because it contributed to Bute's unpopularity during the early years of George III's reign. Studying the gossip during the 1750s in much detail thus would divert one's attention from more central issues. Second, historians have without exception dismissed the rumors as almost certainly false. To the extent that they have examined them at all, they have busied themselves in amassing circumstantial evidence that—to their minds at least—substantiates that assumption.[5] This preconception about the significance of the gossip before George II's death, and the focus on "proving" that Augusta and Bute were not lovers, have caused historians to neglect other areas of inquiry. Even a matter as basic to historical research as determining the chronology of an event has remained unexplored. *When* did the rumors about the princess and her friend begin? No one has as yet pinpointed that time. It is no wonder that, having failed to inquire about such an obvious point, historians have not understood one of the most important consequences of those rumors. As we shall see, establishing that they began during the late summer and early fall of 1755 raises interesting questions about their origins. Even more important, it yields a crucial clue to their significance for the intense and momentous friendship between Bute and the future George III.

Historians have also failed to recognize the strengths and weaknesses of the sources of the gossip about Augusta and Bute, and to use that knowledge to inform an analysis of both the rumors and their relationship. Spacks's shrewd comments about what made the eighteenth century "a great age of gossip"—the minute attention to detail and the penchant for interpreting character on the basis of those observed details of behavior—have not informed their analyses. As a result, scholars have not fully credited how keenly and carefully observant eighteenth-century politicians were of the words and actions of those around them. Two examples will illustrate this trait and its significance.

The editors of the political journal of George Bubb Dodington note that his words are the records of "the day-to-day work of a man whose object and political training it was to be accurate about the affairs that interested him."[6] What was true of Dodington was true of others as well. Men who hoped to establish their careers at Westminster, Whitehall, and particularly the king's court at St. James or the princess's at Leicester House, soon learned that it was crucial to observe the behavior of their superiors carefully and to describe it accurately. The accounts left by many politicians are often striking in the density and specificity of physical and conversational detail their descriptions provide.

An example is Princess Augusta's account, as recorded by her friend Dodington, of the flirtation of her sister-in-law, Princess Amelia, with the earl of Chesterfield. Augusta began by criticizing Amelia's gambling for high stakes in public at Bath. When Dodington asked with whom, she seized the chance to tell him "It was prodigious the work she made with Lord Chesterfield. When he was in Court," she recalled, "[Amelia] would hardly speak to him; at least as little as was possible to a man of his rank." But now, "she sent to enquire of his coming before he arriv'd; when he came sent her compliments and that she expected he should be of all her parties at play; that he should sit by her always in the public rooms, that he might be sure of a warm place, etc."[7] Notice how closely Augusta and her informants had observed Amelia at St. James and in Bath, how carefully they listened to her, and how quickly they noticed differences in her behavior *vis-a-vis* the earl. Whether or not one believes, as Augusta did, that this flirtation was improper and might well indicate the potential, if not the actuality, of an affair, the description of Amelia at play with games of chance and Chesterfield is vivid and convincing.

Another example is Horace Walpole's account of a wit telling a joke about Bute and the princess. "George Selwyn," wrote Walpole, "hearing some people at Arthur's t'other night lamenting the distracted state of this country joined in the discourse with the whites of his eyes and his prim mouth, and fetching a sigh, said, 'Yes, to be sure it is terrible! There is the Duke of Newcastle's faction, and there is [Henry] Fox's faction, and there is Leicester House! Between two factions and one fuction, we are torn to pieces!'"[8] The joke itself is feeble, what sticks in the mind is Walpole's sketch from life of Selwyn's mannerisms, timing, and delivery. As was the case with Dodington's account of Augusta's censure of Amelia, the description of the event in question is persuasive, whatever one thinks about the principal message of the passage. An eye for the telling detail, and the capacity to communicate it effectively—these abilities were shared by the Princess, Dodington, Walpole, and other contemporaries.

An understanding of why they watched so closely and wrote so carefully reveals why historians should respect their descriptions of behavior. Eighteenth-century men and women constantly observed and communicated others' acts because they believed that outward behavior provided the only reliable clues to inner human motives. In so doing, they adopted a remarkably legalistic way of assessing intent, and it is not surprising that the most precise statements of their criterion of assessment may be found in opinions from the bench. "We must judge of a man's motives," declared Lord Kenyon, "from his overt acts." Mr. Justice Willis elaborated on this point: "What passes in the mind of man is not scrutable by any human tribunal; it is only to be collected from his acts."[9] Those who traded in political and social gossip used the same standard of judgment. This may be clearly seen in the following discussion by Lord Hervey of the relationship between Frederick, the Prince of Wales, and Lady Archibald Hamilton during the

1730s. "There are always some people," Hervey noted, "who doubt of the most notorious intrigues." So some thought, or pretended to think, that the "commerce between Lady Archibald Hamilton and the Prince was merely platonic." But "stronger symptoms of an *affaire faite* never appeared on any pair than were to be seen between this couple," Harvey claims in rebuttal of such views. And here is the evidence: Frederick often saw her at her house; he often met her at her sister's; he walked with her "day after day for hours together *tête-a-tête* in a morning in St. James Park; and whenever she was at the drawing-room (which was pretty frequently), his behavior was so remarkable that his nose and her ear were inseparable, whilst, without discontinuing, he would talk to her as if he had rather been relating than conversing from the time he came into the room to the moment he left it, and then seemed to be rather interrupted than to have finished."[10] To Hervey, this was proof positive they were lovers.

Is it, though? The evidence of his senses was enough for Hervey, but historians need not accept his conclusions. In fact, some have doubted that there was any sexual liaison between the prince and Lady Hamilton.[11] We cannot be certain, for the affair, if there was one, was never openly acknowledged by the participants, as understandably was the liaison between George II and the countess of Yarmouth. The best rule of thumb for assessing eighteenth-century gossip is to keep the distinction between witnesses' observation and the same observers' interpretation firmly in mind. One should regard descriptions of observed acts by politicians who were practiced at watching the people around them as basically accurate, unless, of course, there is factual information that contradicts their narratives of events, or convincing reasons to believe that biases about the people involved or preconceptions about the audience hearing the story distorted their accounts. One may also, I think, rely on people at court to notice and to describe carefully behavior that was out of the ordinary in political or social interaction. As the preceding examples demonstrate, contemporaries were keenly alert to unusual displays of interest between men and women. Their explanations of what these acts revealed are more problematical, however. They were, then as now, obviously quicker to see lust in operation and an affair in progress than to view an emotional reaction between a man and a woman as friendship, affection, or some socially acceptable form of love. Historians should not rush to the same judgment in the absence of compelling supporting evidence. In my analysis of the gossip about the princess and Bute, I have tried to keep observation and interpretation separate, and to give the former the credit it deserves while recognizing the limitations of the latter.

I

During the summer of 1755, reports began to circulate about Augusta's reactions to the crisis in relations with France and her political intentions. Dodington, who paid close attention to the political gossip of London's coffee houses, soon heard them, and shared what he had discovered with the princess in early August. She expressed surprise, protesting that she was not involved in any schemes to oppose the government, and pointing out that certainly "nobody could stand clearer than she; that everyone must know everybody that she saw, and when." Dodington laughed at this, and joked that he "had some thoughts of writing her life and transactions, as I pick them up, and presenting it to her, of which, I was persuaded, that she knew nothing at all." Augusta "seem'd mightily pleas'd with the idea, and after laughing, took serious pains to convince me that she had no fix'd settlement, or connexions, at all."[12] It is unlikely that Dodington would have attempted such a joke if he had heard any rumor about an "intrigue" between the princess and Bute at that time, the possibility for embarrassment and loss of her favor would have been too great. Yet no more than six weeks after his conversation with her, that talk had begun. Within a week after his return from Hanover on September 16, George II had received from Earl Waldegrave, the governor of the Prince of Wales, "thorough information" about the political plans of Leicester House. And, though Waldegrave discreetly avoided any direct comment on this subject in his *Memoirs*, it seems likely he also informed the king of his conviction that Augusta and Bute were lovers.[13] Certainly by early October, the countess of Yarmouth, Newcastle, and Newcastle's closest friend, the earl of Hardwicke, had heard the story. All of them apparently believed it.[14] They did not remain alone in that belief. The news passed quickly through court, and then on to the wider world of London. Soon the story about an "intrigue" at Leicester House was widely known and commonly believed.

Why did these rumors spread so rapidly? In part, they did simply because of human nature, then and now, but also because a liaison with the princess helped to explain Bute's role in arranging an alliance between Leicester House and William Pitt in opposition to the government.[15] For example, the countess of Yarmouth discounted hopes that Augusta would remain aloof from opposition politics by reminding Newcastle that the princess "'is in the hands of those who will not permit that' and then [added] with a smile, 'we both know what we mean, though neither of us will speak.'" Moreover, as Spacks has observed, sex was the most popular subject of gossip at the time, with the possible exception of money. Reports of sexual misconduct by Augusta appealed to what Sir Horace Mann singled out as characteristic of "the greatest gossips, [they] are always fond of the marvelous."[16] That the dowager princess of Wales would take a lover fit Samuel Johnson's definition in his *Dictionary* of "the marvelous" as "wonderful," meaning a "surprise caused by something unusual or unexpected." Her friends and enemies unanimously regarded her as a prudent woman, one who was discreet and cautious, who weighed alternatives carefully and had the ability to discern and follow the most politic and profitable course of action. By 1752, according to Dodington, she "had establish'd a character for prudence;" in 1755, Waldegrave recalled that she "was reputed by those who knew her imperfectly a Woman of excellent Sense and extraordinary Prudence."[17] Thus the possibility that she would discard caution, reject morality, and risk reputation by yielding to an illicit passion fascinated people in the political and social worlds that orbited around the court. Their fascination with the difference between public reputation and private reality, plus the political import of the "intrigue," sped the rumors on their way.

What were the origins of these rumors? What first aroused the suspicions of observers at Leicester House? The answer must be that during the summer of 1755, Augusta's behavior toward Bute dramatically changed. She had known the earl since the late 1740s, and no scandal had been attached to their relationship, even though gossips later speculated that an affair between them might have begun then.[18] The changes that happened in 1755 have been detailed by Walpole in his *Memoirs of the Reign of King George II*. Drawing upon conversations with his friend Waldegrave, he recalled that "the eagerness of the pages of the backstairs to let her know whenever Lord Bute arrived, a mellowness in her German accent as often as she spoke to him, and that was often and long, and a more than usual swimmingness in her eyes, contributed to dispel the ideas that had been conceived of the rigour of her widowhood."[19] This was clearly conduct well out of the ordinary for the usually discreet, prudent Augusta. Any observant person—and Waldegrave certainly was one—could not have missed it. Bute's responses attracted his notice as well. "The favoured personage," continued Walpole, "naturally ostentatious of his person and of haughty carriage, seemed by no means desirous of concealing his conquest. His bows grew more theatric, his graces contracted some meaning, and the beauty of his leg was constantly displayed in the eyes of the poor captivated Princess."[20]

As these passages indicate, Waldegrave believed that the Princess's obvious enchantment with Bute was the outward manifestation of a powerful sexual attraction to him. He could think of nothing else. The earl had no respect for Bute's intelligence, learning, or political acumen. To the contrary: his contacts with "the favoured personage" at court caused him to dismiss Bute as a pompous lightweight, a man deserving to be called *Bombastus Vigorosus* by more discerning persons. Waldegrave conceded, however, that Bute was a physically striking man. "He was above the middle size, had broad shoulders, great muscular strength, and remarkable fine legs. Those bodily perfections . . . ," Waldegrave later observed with bitter sarcasm, "sometimes may have attracted vulgar widows." In 1755, he felt no animus toward Augusta, and certainly did not regard her as a "vulgar widow." Even so, he was certain during that summer that she was susceptible to Bute's physical grace and beauty. Perhaps he recalled, as did Walpole, that "the nice observers of the court thermometer, who often foresee a change of weather before it actually happens, had long thought her Royal Highness was likely to choose younger ministers than [her two advisers], that formal piece of empty mystery, [James] Cresset; or the matron-like decorum of Sir George Lee." After all, "her eyes had often twinkled intelligibly enough at her countryman Prince Lobkowitz." Whether or not Waldegrave heard and credited the same gossip, he clearly believed that her friend's appearance and mannerisms had transfixed the Princess. To him, it was obvious that she was either helpless, or did not try, to conceal her passionate fascination.

Waldegrave was equally sure that the two were actually having an affair. The basis for his confidence was his knowledge that they had created ample opportunities for themselves to consummate and continue a sexual relationship. The earl evidently heard on the authority of "three old Ladys, one Gentleman Usher, and two Pages of the Back Stairs" that Augusta and Bute were together alone for lengthy periods walking in the gardens at Kew and Carlton House, or meeting in her private apartments at Leicester House.[21] Walpole translated walking into a metaphor for sexual relations, his own contribution to the gossip about the princess and her friend. "As soon as [Prince Frederick] was dead," he archly noted, the Princess and Bute "walked more and more in honour of his memory." His conviction that these private meetings were more devoted to lovemaking than to more innocent activities was shared by Waldegrave and many others. Even when they learned—perhaps from the same servants who informed them about the meetings between the princess and Bute—that he at least occasionally saw the prince, they did not change their minds. These encounters, they were sure, "were less addressed to the Prince of Wales than to his mother." Indeed, to Waldegrave, what he saw and heard admitted of only one explanation: the two were lovers who through foolishness and arrogance had thrown caution to the winds. He carefully noted the details that convinced him in his interviews with the king and the ministers, and later in conversations with friends such as Walpole. Those details, plus Waldegrave's reputation for being both sagacious about politics and worldly-wise about society, persuaded them as well about the reality of an intrigue between Augusta and Bute.[22]

II

Historians have been far less impressed by Waldegrave's testimony. They have not been persuaded by his certainty that the Princess and Bute were lovers, and they have been unconcerned about his description of their behavior. Yet Waldegrave's observations are worthy of attention and explanation. They were the products of an experienced observer and judge of both political and social behavior, whose description and interpretation of the events at Leicester House during the summer of 1755 were uncolored by malice. To be sure, he never liked Bute, and a year later, after he learned in June 1756 that he would not be Groom of the Stole for the Prince of Wales, that dislike widened to include Augusta and deepened into hatred for them both. But until that disappointment, Waldegrave recalled later, "the Princess and her Son seem'd fully satisfied with my Zeal, diligence, and faithful Services, and I was treated with so much Civility, that sometimes I thought myself almost a Favorite." As Clark points out in his introduction to Waldegrave's memoirs, the earl had reason to believe that he and young George were on good terms even as late as June 1756. Waldegrave, enjoying as he did a pleasant relationship with Augusta, and heartened by the prospect of preferment and power in the next reign, had no reason to exaggerate or distort the evidence of his eyes and ears. He did, however, have a duty to the sovereign he respected, George II, to report fully and precisely on events at Leicester House. An intimate connection—be it political or personal—forged between Augusta and anyone could have a significant impact on relations between her court and the king's, and on the balance of power between the forces of government and opposition in Parliament. Waldegrave was therefore obliged to bring his observations of the conduct of the princess and Bute, and the conclusions he drew from them, to the king's attention. That duty he fulfilled as loyally and conscientiously as he did other responsibilities during his tenure as governor to the Prince of Wales.[23]

But one need not merely rely on Waldegrave's reputed powers of observation and his fidelity to George II to substantiate the accuracy of his description of changes in Augusta's behavior toward Bute and the intensity of her attachment to him. A comparison of reactions at court to her relationship with Dodington with her responses to Bute in 1755 reveals that Waldegrave had indeed seen an unmistakable change in her usual conduct and attitudes toward her friends. The princess frequently spent time alone with Dodington. His discussions of his meetings with her during 1752—1755 are peppered with notations that they walked together for two or three hours in the garden, that they met in private, and that he was shown immediately by her pages to her chambers when he saw only her, and, on occasion, her children. When together, they shared "much talk upon all matter of private subjects, serious and ludicrous."[24] In particular, Augusta was remarkably candid in discussing her concerns about her son's development and education with Dodington. The two also had a number of guarded but reasonably frank exchanges about political events and prospects. She liked and trusted Dodington. This was no secret at court. So, why were there no rumors about a possible sexual involvement, given their private meetings, their obvious rapport, and Dodington's reputation as a veteran of affairs of the heart?[25]

Part of the answer must be his appearance. Unlike Bute, Dodington was "short, dumpy . . . comically fat and ugly, with an absurd uptilted nose, large mouth, protruding eyes, and pudgy hands." He affected the manners and dress of his youth, a style which had been out of fashion for thirty years.[26] If Augusta had a fondness, as observers claimed, for younger, graceful, handsome men, she would have found nothing in this friend to tickle her fancy. But more to the point, Augusta never displayed in public any trace of an intense emotional attachment or commitment to Dodington. (Nor did she show any such commitment in private. There is not the least hint of any sexual attraction or deeply affectionate connection between the two in his notes on their meetings.) Observers of them in public concluded—correctly—that theirs was a friendship that both found frequently useful, occasionally amusing, and nothing more. The speculation sprang up that her attachment to Bute was of a very different nature, gives us ample reason to believe that Waldegrave in fact did see something unprecedented in Augusta's behavior during the summer of 1755. Private meetings that no one thought worthy of remark when she saw Dodington, were regarded as occasions for adultery in the case of Bute. The princess's obvious excitement and eagerness when she greeted the earl unquestionably revealed feelings for him that were far stronger than for her other friend, feelings too powerful to conceal from alert, knowing eyes.

Conceding that Waldegrave first recognized, then accurately described Augusta's powerful attachment to Bute does not mean, however, that we are compelled to agree with his interpretations of what he saw. Were the two lovers? Conclusive evidence of a sexual affair was lacking at the time, and none has been unearthed since. Indeed, to the extent that Waldegrave's confidence was based on his conviction that they had ample opportunities for lovemaking during the long periods of time they spent together alone, it rested on an uncertain foundation. What seemed to him to be suggestive and suspicious behavior with Bute may with equal plausibility be explained as another example of the way Augusta usually behaved with trusted political and personal friends. Besides, asking whether they were lovers is, in important ways, following the scent of a red herring. It was so for contemporaries; as we shall see, it has been for historians for too long. That question has distracted us from asking what caused the princess's conduct toward

Bute to change so suddenly and dramatically during the summer of 1755. Waldegrave and Walpole believed that sexual desire was the principal, if not the sole, explanation. We need not accept this, even though the earl was practiced at assessing attractions between men and women. He overlooked a persuasive alternative explanation for the princess's obvious affection for Bute. And the fact that he failed to consider this possibility had a significant impact on the history of his time.

III

Augusta herself once said that "nobody but God could judge of the heart," and, insofar as her relationship with Bute was concerned, only she and the Almighty ever completely knew for sure about its nature. Still, there was one passion in Augusta's life that we can be sure of, for she freely confessed to it. "She could," the princess told Dodington, "have nothing so much at heart as to see [George] do well [as king], and make the nation happy." She knew, however, that he was not doing well preparing himself for the monarchy. She was pleased that he was "a very honest boy," but she also wished when he was fourteen that "he were a little more forward, and less childish, at his age." Augusta hoped that as George learned more from his tutors, he would mature. Unfortunately, in May 1755, when he was nearly seventeen, she lamented to Dodington that "his education had given her much pain. His book-learning," she continued, "she was no judge of, [but] suppos'd it small, or useless." She had "hop'd he might have been instructed in the general course of things," and Waldegrave had disappointed her even in this modest expectation.

Still, the passage of time had convinced the princess that the fault was not wholly the pupil's. In 1752, she had despairingly said to Dodington that he knew George "as well as she did." By 1755, she felt she knew her son's qualities. "He was not," according to her, "a wild, dissipated boy, but good natur'd, and cheerful, but with a serious cast, in the whole." Waldegrave and his tutors, she scornfully observed to Dodington, "knew him no more than if they had never seen him: . . . he was not quick, but with those he was acquainted with, applicable and intelligent." Her friend soon had proof of this. Perhaps inspired by Augusta's remarks, Dodington "afterwards [had] much talk with the Prince about funding, etc., and other serious things, [which he] seem'd to hear with attention and satisfaction."

Dodington's experience with George indicated, in a small way, how sensible was a desire the princess had expressed to him almost a year earlier. Then she had "wish'd he had an acquaintance older than himself" to instruct him. At that time, she could not intervene by placing appropriate men around the prince to guide him. She "durst not recommend," she recognized, "for fear of offence: while he had governors etc., [and] was under immediate inspection, all that they did not direct, would be imputed to her." Such charges, she also knew, could be dangerous. In 1752, Augusta had discerned that some political opponents were trying to intervene in the prince's education and "by taking him from the people now about him . . . by degrees, consequently, from her." Part of their plot, she believed, was "to get the Prince to their side, and then, by their behaviour, to throw her off from her temper and so make their complaint to the King stronger and make her disoblige him, in defending the accus'd." They were certain, she was further convinced, that "if they could force her into any indiscreet warmth" when she supported George's present instructors, they would make "so plausible a story to the King as might have compass'd their ends" by convincing him that he should move his grandson to Kensington Palace. She had evaded this effort to trick her into appearing to interfere with the prince's education, and she had every intention of resisting the temptation to intervene in reality. At present, she could do nothing. She consoled herself, however, with the belief that "in a year or two, [the prince] must be thought to have a will of his own, and then he would, she hop'd, act accordingly."

After one of those two years passed, Augusta decided to act. During the summer of 1755, she asked Bute to begin tutoring her son in secret.[27] Two reasons probably determined her choice. She regarded the earl as the only one of Prince Frederick's former associates who had always been loyal to her.[28] Such loyalty was essential in this situation; if Waldegrave, the ministers, or George II got wind of the princess's intervention, they certainly would try to remove Bute. That removal would take the form of separating George from his mother and placing him within the king's household. As she told Dodington in May 1755, "there were a hundred good reasons that tied her hands from interfering with the king," emphasizing "those about her children, [which] were obvious enough. If she was to stir," she continued, "it would make things worse." The events of 1752 had stayed fresh in her memory. Who educated the next king, and what they taught him, could quickly become politically controversial issues. The raising of such questions that year had eventuated in the removal of Lord Harcourt and the bishop of Norwich from their posts as Governor and Preceptor of the prince, and threatened the careers of even such eminent men as William Murray, a famous attorney and important politician, and Andrew Stone, the duke of Newcastle's secretary. At that time, the princess had grown "quite weary" of hearing "such an outcry at [Harcourt and the bishop's] leaving them, as if they were the most considerable men in the nation."[29] That outcry, she could anticipate, would be even louder and the consequences more dire for her, should news leak out that she was decisively intervening on her own initiative in her son's education. She had to proceed with the utmost secrecy. Therefore she could call upon only the most reliable friend. Moreover, Bute's views on personal and political morality corresponded to hers. Unlike Dodington, who was convinced the prince needed to be more frequently with people his own age and doubted the usefulness of much book learning, Augusta held strong opinions about "the universal profligacy . . . of the young people of distinction" and had a high regard for formal education.[30] Bute shared these convictions. On the grounds of prudence, morality, and pedagogy, he was the obvious, if not the only, choice.

Delighted by Augusta's proposal, Bute eagerly accepted. For obvious reasons: not only did this role appeal to his sense of himself and his duty, but also, if he were successful, he would become the most powerful politician in the realm when George succeeded his grandfather. His private letter of thanks to her after he began instructing the prince is the effusive written equivalent of the noticeably and unusually dramatic—even for the normally theatrical Bute—bows he made to her in public during that summer. "How great the confidence she is pleased to place in him," he wrote, in the third person. "How immense the obligation laid upon him . . . . He feels her favor as he ought, he has a heart that can feel it, it will palliate a thousand other ills, nor shall he easily repine at anything but at those bounded faculties so little suited to the great trust reposed in him. What is however wanting in talents shall be sup plied with industry and the great business of his life shall while the Princess pleases point to that one center." This flow of language ultimately roused even Bute's concern that it might seem too grateful. "Let not Her Royal Highness," he hastily added, "think that these are words of course or affected phrases, 'tis the language of his heart."[31] Judging from the vigor with which Bute conducted the education of the prince, the flowery language expressed honest sentiments and truly arose from powerful emotions.

Nor is there any reason to question how pleased Augusta was by the earl's taking up the challenge, and how moved she was when it became clear he was succeeding. Bute evidently preserved only one of the princess's letters to him; it is not surprising that he kept this one. "I cannot express the joy I feel to see he has gained the confidence and friendship of my son. Pursu (sic) my worthy friend those instructions you have begun, and imprint your great sentiments in him, thos (sic) will make my son and his mother happy. Ld. Bute forbids his best friend to speak what she feels, but he must allow her to be grateful."[32] The gratitude and affection she felt for a friend who was bringing toward reality her ambitions for her son are obvious in this letter. Even though Bute forbade "his best friend to speak what she feels," her feelings compelled her to disobey. They were equally compelling on public occasion. She did not conceal them in the drawing rooms and in front of servants. Always alert for changes in relationships at court, Waldegrave and others heard and saw her indiscreet words and acts. Moreover, these observers were not wrong. Augusta's behavior did betray a passionate attachment to Bute. But they did not intuit what the princess identified as the most important component in that friendship. Waldegrave never perceived that he was seeing the visible expressions of a mutual joy and gratefulness that a very difficult and supremely important task—the preparation of George for the throne—was going very well. That failure had important consequences.

IV

By now, the significance of the talk about an intrigue involving the princess and Bute that began during the late summer of 1755 should be clear. That confident interpretation of their behavior in public prevented some usually acute observers from realizing the truth about Bute and the Prince of Wales.

So "fond of the marvelous," and thus so certain that the earl and the princess were involved in an affair were observers, that no one divined that (at least some of) Bute's trips up the back stairs ended in tutoring sessions with George, and that many long hours when the earl was in the royal gardens and chambers were spent with the heir to the throne, not Augusta. The court knew that Bute was sometimes with the prince, but this was seen as incidental to, and perhaps an excuse for, his being with the princess. During 1755—1756, according to Walpole, it was "whispered that the assiduity of Lord Bute at Leicester House, and his still more frequent attendance in the gardens at Kew and Carlton House, were less addressed to the Prince of Wales than to his mother."[33] In fact, the reverse was true. Had Waldegrave realized this, he would have informed the king, and thereby set in motion a chain of events very different from what did occur. George II had no respect for Bute, and in any case wished to remove his grandson from the princess's court.[34] News about the earl's secret usurpation, with Augusta's approval and assistance, of the role of the prince's governor would have inspired the monarch and his ministers to make serious efforts to take George away from his mother and her friend. But neither Waldegrave nor anyone else discerned what was going on behind closed doors and garden walls. They were stunned to discover when George came of age in June 1756 that he wanted his "dearest friend" to be his Groom of the Stole and ultimately to become "the minister" when he took the throne. Compelling a minor to change palaces and friends would have been politically difficult enough, but it might have been managed. Forcing a young man who would reign when his grandfather died, who would not be dependent on a council of regency, to drop his firmest commitments, soon proved impossible. George II and his ministers had to yield, and Bute became a powerful man, one who would have to be reckoned with in the present and future.

Why did no one suspect that Bute was forging an intimate relationship with the prince? It was partly the result of the contempt Waldegrave and others had for the princess's friend. They simply could not believe that his pompous, stilted words and mannerisms would attract the notoriously withdrawn George. That he would succeed where better men had failed, obviously never occurred to them. In their eyes, Bute was a sententious yet insignificant player in the politics of the court. But their misreading of the earl seems minor indeed compared to their underestimation of the princess. Neither Waldegrave, nor George II, nor anyone else at court except Bute, who was necessarily privy to her secret, knew how attached Augusta was to the future king, and how determined she was to fulfill her wish that he be "great and happy for [his] own sake."[35] Thus they did not anticipate the lengths she would go, and the risks she would run, for her son. That she would look for a different tutor for him, find one she judged loyal, intellectually capable, and morally sound, arrange secret meetings between them, and conceal many of the sessions by providing the misleading appearance that the prince's new mentor was meeting her—these suspicions never crossed their minds. Yet that was the plan her concern for her son caused her to conceive and to execute.

Of course, we know now that Augusta was risking not only discovery of her plot, which did not happen, but scandalous whispers about her morality, which did. Did that possibility ever occur to her? Did she decide to put her reputation at jeopardy as well? If she did, it was an extraordinary act of maternal love and courage. As Spacks has emphasized in *Gossip*, eighteenth-century women depended completely on their reputations for sexual virtue, and had no means of effectively refuting any scandals that put their good names in doubt or of retaliating against their persecutors.[36] There is no sure way of ascertaining whether Augusta was aware of this danger, but the possibility cannot be dismissed entirely. The princess certainly was aware, as she told Dodington, "that everyone must know everybody she saw and when." She also knew that those at court watched the behavior of men and women together closely for signs of impropriety. Augusta herself avidly played the game of assessing the potential for lust and adultery on occasion, and seems to have been as quick as anyone else to conclude sexual misconduct was occurring and to gossip about it. From this, she might have guessed that her good name could be jeopardized. Still, her knowledge of and her participation in the realities and rituals of life at court, do not prove that she consciously risked her own reputation. Barring the discovery of other evidence, that must remain unknown.

When the prince first heard the rumors, his determination not to be separated from his mother and his mentor was strengthened. "I will ever remember," he vowed, "the insults done to my mother, and never will forgive anyone who shall offer to speak disrespectfully of her." And "in the same solemn manner" he resolved, "I will defend my Friend . . . and will more and more show to the world the great friendship I have for him, and all the malice that can be invented against him shall only bind me the stronger to him."[37] Ironically, George never realized how crucial the blackening of their reputations had been for him

68

and Bute. It provided a necessary protective coloration, and thus permitted the germination and flowering of that intense friendship that so strongly influenced events in Britain, Europe, and the empire during the 1760s.[38]

*This chapter first appeared in: *Studies in Eighteenth-Century Culture* 21 (1991), pp. 245-265.

Endnotes

[1] I have borrowed this introduction from J. H. Hexter, *Doing History* (Bloomington: Indiana University Press, 1971), p. 85. In his version, the gossips are historians, not eighteenth-century politicians.

[2] For an excellent bibliography of studies of gossip as a social phenomenon, see Edith B. Gelles, "Gossip: An Eighteenth-Century Case," *Journal of Social History* 22 (1989), p. 679, n. 4.

[3] Patricia Meyer Spacks, *Gossip* (New York: Knopf, 1985). For Spacks's comments about studies of gossip by social scientists, see p. 34.

[4] As Gelles's bibliographical notes make clear, those eighteenth-century historians who have most frequently studied gossip are social historians. Gelles's own article, for example, deals with the role of gossip in determining an appropriate husband for Abigail Adams Junior, the daughter of John and Abigail Adams. The role of gossip in polities has remained unexamined.

[5] For examples of the tendencies described above—all of them in solid studies of the period — see John Brewer, "The Misfortunes of Lord Bute: A Case-Study in Eighteenth-Century Political Argument and Public Opinion," *The Historical Journal* 16 (1973), pp. 3-4, and Brewer's book, *Party Ideology and Popular Politics at the Accession of George III* (Cambridge: Harvard University Press, 1973), pp. 152-53, 294n; Frank O'Gorman, "The Myth of Lord Bute's Secret Influence," in: *Lord Bute: Essays in Re-interpretation*, ed. Karl W. Schweizer (Leicester: Leicester University Press, 1988), pp. 59-60; and John Brooke, *King George III* (London: Constable, 1972), pp. 48-49.

[6] The quotation is from the introduction by John Carswell and Lewis Arnold Dralle, eds., *The Political Journal of George Bubb Dodington* (Oxford: Oxford University Press, 1965), xxiv. For examples of the special care Dodington took in recording conversations and describing facial expressions, see pp.180, 198, 244, 399.

[7] Dodington, p. 174. As this conversation reveals, Augusta did not mind telling Dodington about her personal reactions to people. She was much more cautious in discussing political events with him. Dodington had been a follower of her late husband Prince Frederick, and kept in close contact with her after his death in 1751. Because of her frankness with him, especially about her sons, and because

of his skill as an observer, his *Journal* is the most reliable source for her opinion on personal matters during the early 1750s.

[8] *The Yale Edition of Horace Walpole's Correspondence*, 48 vols. (New Haven: Yale, 1937-1983), 9, p. 202. Leicester House was Augusta's official residence in London. Its name was used as a shorthand reference to the faction which supported her interests in policies. As John Cannon observed, Selwyn's humor, "so greatly admired in his lifetime, seems to have depended for its effect upon a mock-serious delivery: in print, it appears laboured." See Cannon's entry on Selwyn in: Sir Lewis Namier and John Brooke, eds., *The History of Parliament: The House of Commons, 1754-1790*, 3 vols. (London: Oxford University Press, 1964), 3, p. 421.

[9] I owe this point, and the quotations illustrating it, to J. C. D. Clark, *The Dynamics of Change: The Crisis of the 1750s and English Party Systems* (Cambridge: Cambridge University Press, 1982), p. 19. For a similar comment by Dodington, see p. 301.

[10] Lord Hervey, *Memoirs*, ed. Romney Sedgwick (London: W. Kimber, 1952), pp. 138-39. An "intrigue" in eighteenth-century usage was a clandestine illicit intimacy between a man and a woman.

[11] For example, Sir George Young, *Poor Fred: The People's Prince* (Oxford: Oxford University Press, 1937), pp.79-80, 169.

[12] Dodington, pp. 316-17. In fact, Augusta had commissioned Bute to negotiate with William Pitt, a political alliance that she took pains to conceal from Dodington. Dodington believed her on this occasion, but at other times he suspected, rightly, that the princess withheld political intelligence from him. For example see: p. 227. It must be emphasized that while Dodington's *Journal* is an invaluable source for Augusta's personal opinions, historians should use it very carefully on matters political.

[13] "Memoirs of 1754-1757," in: *The Memoirs and Speeches of James, 2nd Earl Waldegrave*, ed. J. C. D. Clark (Cambridge: Cambridge University Press, 1988), pp.169-71. See also Clark's introduction to this splendid edition, pp. 76-79, for a judicious discussion of Waldegrave's possible role in the spread of rumors about the princess and Bute. Clark argues that the evidence for Waldegrave's role is not conclusive, yet he himself notes that "the clear implication" of passages in the *Memoirs* "is that Waldegrave himself told George II everything that happened at Leicester House." As the earl later told the prince of Wales, "I was accountable to his Majesty, and it was my Duty to give Informations as to some particulars, when he required it: or supposing it had been my Intention to deceive the King, even in that case it would have been absurd to have denied those things, which might be seen at every Drawing room, and were the subject of conversation at every Coffee House." Waldegrave's reference to "every Drawing room" is crucial to an understanding of this passage. In contemporary usage, a "drawing room" referred

to the formal levee, a reception held in the morning, by a member of the royal family or a person of rank. The earl was pointing out that he and others had observed unmistakably suggestive behavior between Augusta and Bute at her levees, and that he had discussed those observations with George II.

[14]The duke of Newcastle to the earl of Hardwicke, Oct. 4, 1755, and Hardwicke to Newcastle, Oct. 13, 1755, in: Philip C. Yorke, *The Life and Correspondence of Philip Yorke, Earl of Hardwicke, Lord High Chancellor of Great Britain*, 3 vols. (Cambridge: Cambridge University Press, 1913), 2, pp. 250-52.

[15] Sir John Pringle, the queen's physician after 1761, and Horace Walpole believed that there was another political consideration that helped explain the speed with which the rumor circulated. Both asserted that powerful men at the king's court broadcast the story in an effort to discredit Augusta and to prevent Bute from becoming the preeminent politician in the kingdom during the next reign. The two differed on one significant detail. Sir John was convinced "a party of the great people" had concocted the rumor themselves with those ends in mind. Walpole knew the real source of the story (i.e., Waldegrave), believed in the purity of his motives and the accuracy of his observations, and therefore was absolutely certain that the princess and Bute were lovers. To him, the role of the great men—specifically Hardwicke—was confined to spreading the news in the expectation it would serve them politically No evidence has been found in the extant papers of prominent politicians during the 1750s that supports either version of events. For Pringle's and Walpole's accounts, see Clark's introduction to Waldegrave, pp. 77-78, with n. 251; see also *The Yale Edition of Horace Walpole's Memoirs of King George II*, ed John Brooke, 3 vols (New Haven Yale University Press, 1985), 2, pp. 160-61.

[16] Sir Horace Mann to Walpole, Oct. 25, 1755, Walpole Correspondence 20, p. 505.

[17] Dodington, p.180, Waldegrave, p. 159. Even Horace Walpole, who held no brief for Augusta, praised "the quiet inoffensive good sense of the Princess (who had never said a foolish thing, or done a disobliging one since her arrival [in England], though in very difficult situations . . .)" in his account of 1751 *Memoirs*, p. 153.

[18] For speculation that the affair started sooner than 1755, see Walpole, *Memoirs* 2, p.151, and Waldegrave, "An Allegory of Leicester House," p. 229.

[19] *Memoirs*, 2, p. 151. Brooke (2 251-52n) and Clark (introduction, Waldegrave, p. 78) are certain that Waldegrave was the source of Walpole's information about Leicester House. Their assumptions are justified, with this passage compare Waldegrave's memoirs, particularly his revealing and bitter "An Allegory of Leicester House," pp. 163-64, 229-231, 233. Thanks to Brooke, we know that Walpole wrote this section between Aug. 6 and Oct. 6, 1758. Since this was

before he had access to Waldegrave's papers, he must have relied on conversations with the earl.

[20] *Memoirs*, 2:151. John Brooke helpfully supplies in his notes different versions of this passage. In an earlier draft, Walpole described Bute's actions thus: "the veins in the calf of his leg were constantly displayed in the eyes of the poor captivated Princess, and of a court who maliciously affected to wonder that they preserved so much roundness." Though Walpole's dislike of Bute is obvious in these passages, one should not conclude that the description in them of the earl's figure and mannerisms was inaccurate. Alan Ramsay's portrait of Bute, which was done in 1758 at the order of the Prince of Wales, is visual confirmation of the words of Walpole and Waldegrave. As he posed, Bute carefully gathered his robe in his right hand in order to display his legs. He also crossed them in such a way that the observer's eye is drawn to them. The general effect is of a man proudly conscious of his physical attributes, and practiced at presenting himself in such a way as to call attention to them and to heighten their attractiveness. Owned by the present Marquess of Bute, this portrait is on loan to the National Galleries of Scotland. Scholars may see an unfortunately dim reproduction of it, with comments, in John Brewer, "The Faces of Lord Bute: A Visual Contribution to Anglo-American Political Ideology," *Perspectives in American History* 6 (1972), pp. 96-97.

[21] "An Allegory of Leicester House," Waldegrave, *Memoirs*, p. 231; Walpole, *Memoirs*, 2:151. Servants at Leicester House continued to supply tidbits of information about the behavior of Bute and members of the royal family to interested politicians during the early years of George III's reign. See, for example, the duke of Devonshire's diary, Nov. 2, 1761, in: *The Devonshire Diary: William Cavendish, Fourth Duke of Devonshire, Memoranda on State of Affairs, 1759-1 762*, ed. Peter D. Brown and Karl W. Schweizer, Camden, 4th ser. 27 (London: Royal Historical Society, 1982), p. 147.

[22] For Waldegrave's knowledge about politics and society, see Clark's excellent account of his life in his introduction to Waldegrave's memoirs, especially pp. 41-64. The earl's description so completely persuaded Walpole that during the 1780s he told John Pinkerton, the antiquary and historian, "I am as much convinced of an amorous connection between B[ute] and the P[rincess] D[owager] as if I had seen them together." *Correspondence*, 12:262n.

[23] On Waldegrave's punctilious performance of his duties as governor, see Clark and the earl's own comments, pp.57-64, 71-76, 169-71, 176-83.

[24] Dodington, pp. 164, 173 (for the quotation), 189, 202, 197, 227, 240, 243, 245, 249, 263, 271-72.

[25] For Dodington's reputation as a lover see: Walpole's "Brief Account of George Bubb Dodington, Lord Melcombe," an appendix to *Memoirs*, 3: pp.160-61.

[26] The description of Dodington is from Carswell and Dralle's introduction, xii-xiii. Their description is borne out by Lord Townshend's caricature of Dodington, which is reproduced in their frontispiece.

[27] The beginning of Bute's efforts to educate the prince of Wales may be dated by a letter from the prince to Bute (Jul. 1, 1756), in which he observed, "I have had the pleasure of your friendship during the space of a year." *Letters from George III to Lord Bute, 1756-66*, ed. Romney Sedgwick (London: Macmillan, 1939), p. 2.

[28] James Lee McKelvey, *George III and Lord Bute: The Leicester House Years* (Durham: Duke University Press, 1973), p. 21.

[29] For an account of the controversy over the prince's education in 1752, see: Brooke, *George III*, pp. 35-39. The princess's views may be found in Dodington, pp.189-195 (quotation 190).

[30] Dodington, p. 300. For Dodington's views on education, see p. 178. Augusta had never hesitated to talk to Dodington about her dissatisfaction with George's progress. Nor did she hide the fact that she blamed it on his governor Waldegrave and his tutors. She had even hinted on May 29, 1754, that she might in the future look for someone to assume control of her son's education. But her habitual caution when discussing political issues with Dodington asserted itself once she settled on Bute. She never told him about her decision.

[31] Bute to Augusta [summer 1755], in: *Letters from George III to Bute*, pp. li-lii.

[32] Augusta to Bute, [1755?], *Letters from George III to Bute*, p.4n.

[33] Walpole, *Memoirs*, p. 2:151.

[34] Waldegrave told Augusta in 1756 that whenever he mentioned the possibility of Bute's being appointed the prince's Groom of the Stole to George II, he "never obtain'd a serious Answer; and . . . as often as I touched on the Subject, [the king] immediately laugh'd in my Face." He also recalled that before 1756 George II had "already declared his opinion, by speaking of the Princess's Favorite, and of her Partiality towards him, with the greatest Contempt." For the king's intention to move the prince away from his mother to Kensington Palace, see Brooke, *George III*, pp. 50-51.

[35] Bute to the prince [1755], *Letters from George III to Bute*, pp. liii-liv.

[36] For other penetrating comments about the importance of women's sexual reputations in the eighteenth century, see: Lawrence Stone, *The Family, Sex and Marriage in England, 1500-1800* (London: Harper and Row, 1977), pp. 501-507.

[37] Jul. 1, 1756, *Letters from George III to Bute*, p. 3. George apparently never forgave Waldegrave for what he believed was the earl's role in creating and spreading these rumors. In 1804, he described Waldegrave as "a depraved worthless man." See Clark, introduction to Waldegrave, *Memoirs*, p. 53. Gossip

about his mother and his "dearest friend" may have also taught George to be more aware of how servants could initiate stories and cause mischief. When he heard the first news about his grandfather's death, he "order'd all the servants that were out to be silent about what had passed as they value their employments." Later, he insisted that his bride-to-be limit the number of servants she would bring with her from Mecklenburg-Strelitz. "The utmost she can bring is one or two *Femes de Chambres*, which I own I hope will be quiet people, for by my own experience I have seen these women meddle much more than they ought to do,." *Letters from George III to Bute*, pp. 48, 58.

[38] The impact of George's and Bute's friendship has been analyzed many times. In particular, see John Brewer, "The Misfortunes of Lord Bute: A Case-Study in Eighteenth-Century Political Argument and Public Opinion," *The Historical Journal* 16 (1973), pp. 3-43; and K.W. Schweizer, ed., Lord *Bute: Essays in Re-interpretation*, the collection cited above, ch.. 5; K.W. Schweizer, *Frederick the Great, William Pitt and Lord Bute* (NY, 1991), esp. chs. V, VI, VII.

Chapter III

"George, Be a King!": The Relationship between Princess Augusta and George III*

When textbooks in history focused on kings, queens and presidents more than they do today, writers sought the origins of the American Revolution in the characters of the most prominent participants. The role of principal villain was George III's, and authors seeking to explain why he took that part often referred to what he learned as a youth from his mother, Augusta, the dowager princess of Wales. "George," Augusta commanded the boy, "be a King!" Her son took this injunction to heart, and resolved to assert his personal authority over his subjects. Ultimately this resolution fated him to be the last king of most of Britain's North American possessions.[1]

However familiar the story of the princess's command was to generations of schoolchildren in Britain and America, scholars of eighteenth-century Britain have long regarded it as apocryphal. To support this judgment, they have pointed to its provenance. None of the great memoirists *cum* gossips of the 1750s and 1760s mentioned such a vignette. Nor is there any reference to it in contemporary letters, diaries, pamphlets or caricatures. The story first appeared in 1820, in the autobiography of John Nicholls who had been a student at Exeter and Oxford during the 1750s, and had no contact whatsoever with the court at Leicester House, the princess's residence. Thus historians have seen fit to dismiss it as a piece of unsubstantiated gossip, passed off as fact, and of no great historical import. So skeptical of the truth of Nicholls's tale was the great historian Sir Lewis Namier that he was wont to joke that Augusta was probably criticizing her son's table manners. The Namier version went this way: "George! sit up straight! take your elbows off the table! don't gobble your food! do you want to look like your uncle Cumberland? George, be a King!"[2] Whether or not other scholars agreed with Sir Lewis's explanation, they clearly shared his doubts about the significance of Nicholls's account. Augusta's impact on her son has been left largely unexplored, except for some perfunctory condemnations of her for isolating the prince of Wales from society and politics. Far more attention has been paid to the critical part George's "dearest friend," the earl of Bute, played in shaping his character during the 1750s and determining his political fate in the 1760s.[3]

This oversight needs correcting. Certainly Bute did have a significant effect on his young protégé, but it is equally certain he had the opportunity to accomplish what he did solely because Augusta chose him to tutor the prince in secret. Precisely how she explained her decision to George is unknown. A surviving letter from the earl to his royal pupil does reveal, however, that she stressed to her son that Bute was her trusted friend.[4] That recommendation may have had an important effect at the beginning of the intimate friendship the prince and his mentor formed. The man who served as George's governor during that period, Earl Waldegrave, was positive that it was "by the good offices of the Mother" that Bute "became the avow'd favorite of the Young Prince."[5] Embittered by her friend's usurpation of his responsibility, Waldegrave later claimed that "long before [George's] coming of age, none who approached him preserved the least influence, except the mother and those who she confided in."[6] To test the truth of these charges, looking at the relationship between mother and son is necessary.

Waldegrave's recollections point to another reason to assess Augusta's role in the life of George III. The earl was positive that the dowager princess had a definitive impact on the young prince as his character developed. When Waldegrave began his service as governor, he "found his Royal Highness uncommonly full of Princely Prejudices, contracted in the Nursery, and improved by the society of Bed Chamber Women and Pages of the Back Stairs:" this situation he blamed on Augusta.[7] Other contemporaries were equally convinced. Indeed, they believed that the princess's sinister control over her son continued after the advent of Bute, and was even heightened by the earl's winning of George's heart and mind. Vivid proof of the popular convictions about Augusta's role may be found in the satirical caricatures that appeared in London windows after George III's accession to the throne.

Constantly, she and her reputed lover were portrayed as duping, or blindfolding, or lulling into a politically and personally damaging slumber, or even poisoning—*à la* Claudius and Gertrude in *Hamlet*—the young king. These images not only effectively undercut the royal authority, they served as well to communicate and confirm widespread fears about the power George's mother had to narrow his vision of reality and to lead him astray. Given the widespread broadcasting of such "verses and indecent prints," it is not surprising that on November 16, 1760, immediately after his accession, George III heard "in the avenues to the Play house the mob crying out No Scotch Government, No Petticoat Government."[8]

Historians should not, of course, accept Waldegrave's opinion and popular caricatures as incontestable proof of Augusta's power over her son. Nevertheless, that so many were so certain that she enjoyed great influence over him and used it to control his thoughts and acts makes an investigation of the accuracy of their perceptions worthwhile. That requires a careful analysis of the relationship itself; and of the extent and significance of his mother's role m George III's life. The proper place to begin that analysis is with Augusta herself.

I

Before her husband Frederick died in 1751, few people at court paid much attention to Augusta. When they did, it generally was due to some *gaffe* of his. Two examples must suffice.

Although the sexual liaisons of George II were openly conducted and widely known, the king did not treat his wife publicly as the prince did his. During their marriage, the court was sure Frederick had two mistresses, Lady

Archibald Hamilton and Lady Middlesex. Each was a frequent source of embarrassment to Augusta. Immediately after their marriage in 1736, the prince persuaded his wife to name Lady Archibald Hamilton, one of the ladies of the bedchamber, after Queen Caroline had refused to do so, saying, "it was impossible for her to put Lady Archibald about the princess without incurring the contempt of the whole world."[9] The court's reaction to Augusta's yielding to her husband's wishes was not contempt, however. Rather, it was one of sympathy for her, and appreciation for her willingness to obey and endure. The queen was "always remarkably and industriously civil" to Augusta, and thought "there was no sort of harm in her, that she never meant to offend, was very modest and very respectful." To be sure, Caroline considered Augusta to be neither witty nor intelligent. Still, she invariably reproached herself whenever exasperation led her to lament "the silent stupidity" of her daughter-in-law and forget her virtues.[10]

In a like manner, Frederick's behavior with his other mistress elicited from observers pity for her situation and respect for her behavior. While Lady Middlesex was enduring a difficult pregnancy in 1750, Horace Walpole reported that the prince attended her as constantly as did the midwife. One morning "the Princess came [to Lady Middlesex's house] to call him to go to Kew; he made her wait in her coach above half an hour at the door."[11] Episodes such as these led even Walpole, who came to detest Augusta and pilloried her in his memoirs as a passionate and domineering woman, to praise "the quiet inoffensive good sense of the Princess (who had never said a foolish thing, or done a disobliging one since her arrival [in England] though in very difficult situations)."[12]

Caroline's comments, and those of Walpole, reveal the perspective they and others at court had on Augusta. To them, her virtues were apparent. She obeyed her husband and followed his directions, just as the social mores of the eighteenth-century court demanded. She accepted the twin realities that men could commit adultery with virtual impunity from society's censure, and that men with royal blood could conduct their affairs in public, without any protest. The fact that she did not respond to Frederick's actions, which went beyond the acceptable boundaries of even royal behavior by exposing her to public humiliation, improved others' opinion of her.[13] It is important to note, though, that this did not mean these observers had great respect for the princess's abilities. Implicit in their remarks is the judgment that Augusta's preservation of dignity and adherence to society's standards was more passive than active, the reaction of a person of limited wits, spirit and experience rather than the calculated determination of an intelligent, politically and socially aware woman. In this reading of her character, they were mistaken. When the earl of Shelburne summed up his impressions of Augusta, he observed, "it seems to have been her fate through life to have been neglected and undervalued."[14] Whatever the truth of these remarks for her later years, they certainly described her fate while she was Frederick's wife.

Shelburne himself did not feel the princess's virtues had been underestimated. Instead, he believed the court had not accurately gauged her natural aptitudes for "dissimulation and intrigue," which "the perpetual mortifications she submitted to pressed and obliged her to exert."[15] These cutting words were deliberately chosen by a man who intensely disliked the princess. What they amount to is this: Augusta successfully concealed from interested observers at court her real strengths as a person and as a princess. A central part of her character, her devoutness, went largely unspoken of. Yet when she first came to Britain, she insisted that her beliefs would not allow her to take communion in the Church of England, and went instead to a Lutheran chapel. The argument of the prince, that when this became known it would be very unpopular, had no impact on her. According to Frederick, "she only wept and talked of her conscience." Ultimately a political point overrode her scruples. The Act of Succession required heirs to the crown to take communion only from the Church of England on pain of losing the throne if they did not comply. When Augusta learned that this could possibly be applied to her, and if so would result in her being sent back to Germany, she "dried her tears, lulled her conscience, and went no more to the Lutheran Church." She began regularly attending Anglican services at the chapel at Kensington, and "received the sacrament like the rest of the royal family."[16] Undoubtedly, this decision was inspired in the first instance by political expediency. Still, there is reason to believe that once made, the change in communions was not continued cynically. Augusta's critical attitude during the 1750s toward the immorality of young aristocrats, and the freedom with which an intimate adviser of hers could criticize latitudinarian clergy, indicate that she had genuinely transferred her religious commitment to a strict Anglicanism.[17]

Augusta's ability to adapt her commitment to ideals to the reality of the particular circumstances of her life in Britain is evident in other areas as well. Most notably, she succeeded in winning the affection and trust of a difficult and capricious husband. Despite Frederick's apparent infatuation at different times with other women, she learned how to attract and hold his attention The proof of this is not merely the birth of nine children in 14 years of marriage. It may be found as well in "The Charms of Sylvia," a poem written by Frederick in praise of his wife. In it, he celebrated the princess's "lovely range of teeth so white," her "gentle smile . . . with which no smile could e'er compare, that chin so round, that neck so fine, those breasts that swell to meet my love," and "that easy sloping waist, that form divine." The verses themselves are awkward and hackneyed, and afforded much amusement to London's *cognoscenti*, but Frederick was sufficiently pleased with them and his wife to publish them. Significantly, he emphasized in the poem that Augusta's physical attractions "below" and "above"—as he gracelessly referred to them—were not what bound him most closely to her.

No—tis that gentleness of mind, that love
So kindly answering my desire,

That grace with which you look and speak and move,

That thus has set my soul on fire.[18]

One example of how the princess's "gentleness of mind" comforted and strengthened Frederick has survived. During his fatal illness in 1751, Augusta, who believed he was getting "much better [and] only wanted to recover his strength," confided to the earl of Egmont, his closest political adviser, that the prince "was always frightened for himself when he was the least out of order but that she laughed him out of it and never would humor him in these fancys." After these wifely ministrations he had as always—in this case, incorrectly—concluded "he should not die this bout but for the future would take more care of himself."[19] Long familiarity with her husband's fears and foibles enabled her to manipulate his moods away from despair and toward optimism.

Frederick's affection for his wife was matched by his trust in her discretion. Those politicians who plotted with the prince to oppose the king's government sooner or later realized that the princess was privy to his political secrets. It is doubtful that she played an active role in formulating his plans, for her husband's proudest boast was that he, unlike his father, would never fall under the domination of his wife.[20] But Augusta was present on one occasion when Frederick and Egmont sifted through the political loyalties of some M.P.s, and the fact that the earl expressed no surprise in his diary that she remained in the room indicates that he did not find this unusual. Once the two men were ready to begin discussing their strategies for establishing themselves firmly in power immediately after George II's death, however, "the Princess at [Frederick's] intimation then withdrew." Probably the prince wanted to underline his freedom from feminine control. It is also conceivable he did not want Augusta to know that he was taking the dangerous step of loaning Egmont a copy of his scheme for a few days.[21] Certainly she was familiar with the plan's existence and its details. When Frederick died unexpectedly on March 20, 1751, he was not even cold before she sent for Egmont. Mastering her shock and horror at her husband's death, she warned the earl that "she did not know but the King might seize the Prince's papers—that they were at Carlton House—and that we might be ruined by these papers." She gave Egmont the keys to three trunks there, commanded him to hurry to Carlton House, remove incriminating evidence, and bring it back to her. She even supplied him with a pillow case to hide the papers in. After the earl accomplished his mission, she supervised the destruction of the plans. Only then did Augusta turn to considering what to do about Frederick's body and when to inform his father.[22] It was an impressive and disciplined performance, one that revealed not only her knowledge of her husband's schemes, but a political acumen and decisiveness that would have surprised many.

When Augusta remarked "we might be ruined by these papers," she was not including Egmont in her thoughts. The earl served a useful purpose by smuggling the dangerous material out of Carlton House, but the princess was already determined to sever her ties with him. What concerned her was the possibility that George II would seize upon any plausible excuse to take her children away from her control. In particular, she feared that the new heir to the throne, her son George, would be removed to the king's household. In the time immediately after Frederick's death, the purpose behind Augusta's maneuvers was to avoid giving George II any justification for that measure. Thus she destroyed Frederick's plans, stopped seeing Egmont, and sought a reconciliation with the king.[23]

The princess succeeded in her design, and convinced George II to agree to her becoming regent should he die before his grandson came of age. On March 30, the two met for 15 minutes, then sent for the children. According to Egmont's informant, "the King embraced Prince George, said he loved him, bid him be honest and brave, and mind his mother who was the best of women." Then he "embraced the Princess, desired nobody might come between him and her, and that he would do everything for her." This "abundance of speeches and a kind behaviour to her and the children" ended by "captivate[ing] Prince George who said he should not be frightened any more with his grandpapa."[24] Augusta's performance at what was the supreme political and personal crisis of her life to that point, plus the reaction of her son, meant that George and the other children would continue to be with her. She would have the opportunity to mold the character of the next king of Britain. Perhaps because she was so keenly aware that she might have lost it had she not disarmed the suspicions of George II, she intended to make the most of this opportunity.

II

The historical record is nearly silent about what sort of parent Augusta had been for George and her other children before Frederick's death. Almost all contemporary comment centered on the prince, and focused in particular on his obvious preference for his second son, Edward.[25] His "great Passion" for this boy was openly avowed. It also inspired Frederick to use Edward to execute his favorite political plan of separating Great Britain from Hanover. When he became king, he informed Egmont in 1750, he would make his second son the elector of Hanover. George would not dare object, he went on. Frederick intended to force him to acquiesce by first offering him an annual allowance of £100,000, and then withholding it until he agreed to this settlement.[26]

The prince planned to manipulate his heir in other ways as well. Aware that George might want to command the army, he intended to make him lord high admiral instead. The reasoning behind this decision was no compliment to George. Frederick believed "if he was to be bred among Troops [it] might turn his head dangerously to a love of regular Troops with all the fopperies of the Trade which naturally captivate young men." Being lord high admiral would "turn his attention and vanity to the fleet." One should not be deceived by the prince's reference to the natural tendency of young men. That was not what worried Frederick. He believed Edward could avoid the temptations army service provided, for he meant to give his second son command of a regiment of guards. What concerned the prince was a weakness he perceived in George's character, a weakness that would make him unable to avoid the showy follies and idle affectations of importance that Frederick identified with officers in the regular army. Only if George was placed in a better environment would his attention and pride be turned toward proper objects; left to himself; he could not do it.[27]

Why the prince reached this conclusion is not clear. As Horace Walpole archly observed, "it ran a little in the blood of the family to hate the eldest son," but this does not seem to have been the case with Frederick. Even Walpole conceded he was a much better parent than George II.[28] His preference rested on a different foundation, one made up at least in part of Edward's physical and psychological resemblance to him. In appearance, Edward looked much more like Frederick than George did. The second son's mercurial moods and his often indiscreet glibness also perfectly matched his father's temperament.[29] George was much the quieter child, with a less facile mind and tongue. His social mannerisms were marked by, as the sympathetic Lady Louisa Stuart observed, an "awkward hesitation." While Edward was praised, when George "ever faltered out an opinion, it was passed by unnoticed [and] sometimes knocked down at once with: "Do hold your tongue, George, don't talk like a fool."[30] In his father's mind, he was the son who would require careful guidance and supervision, or he would learn the wrong lessons.[31] This did not mean that Frederick was unremittingly harsh or cruel to George. The few surviving letters from him to his eldest son reveal a father capable of mixing judicious encouragement and mild criticism.[32] Nevertheless, the prince was determined to monitor and control George's life closely, and could not help comparing this necessity with what he presumed to be Edward's intelligence, spirit and independence.

At least outwardly, Augusta concurred with her husband's assessment of their two oldest sons. Lady Louisa Stuart recalled that she openly preferred Edward, often ignored George, and at times corrected him sharply.[33] Other observers' memories were much the same.[34] Of course, after Frederick's death the situation changed dramatically. George would obviously become king far sooner than anyone could have anticipated. Paying less attention to him than to the favorite son was no longer possible; his preparation for the throne could not be delayed. The princess accordingly began to focus her attention and efforts on George.

During the first months after Frederick's death, Augusta learned very little about "the real disposition" of George. At the end of that time, she complained to one of her husband's old political allies that he knew her son almost as well as she did. He was, she thought, "very honest." Still, "she wish'd he were a little more forward, and less childish, at his age." He also was not learning his schoolwork as rapidly as she had hoped. This slowness as a student concerned her rather less, though, than his immaturity. Augusta believed his instructors bore the lion's share of the responsibility for his lack of progress in education. But his childishness meant the boy remained dangerously impressionable. His character was still malleable, and therefore the possibility of his being impressed by the wrong people was still very real. For the present, Augusta was "very glad" that George did not take "very particularly to anybody about him but his brother Edward. The young people of quality," she believed, "were so ill educated, and so very vicious, that they frighten'd her." She hoped that his instructors would soon succeed in improving the boy's studies and his maturity. For now, she could summarize what was good in George's character more briefly: "he was a very honest boy, and . . . his chief passion seem'd to be Edward."[35]

George's learning did not improve during the next three years. Even after Bute became his "dearest friend" and tutor, he continued to be afflicted by a debilitating indolence in intellectual pursuits. (One of Bute's greatest accomplishments was convincing his pupil that he could resist this weakness).[36] Nor did George's childishness wane. His mother complained about it and feared its possible consequences for years. When an effort was made to remove some of the prince's instructors on the grounds of Jacobitism, Augusta's sensitivity to George's vulnerability to manipulation caused her to see it as a plot to remove him from her. The aim of her enemies, she believed, was "to get the Prince to their side, and then, by their behaviour, to throw her off from her temper, and so make their complaint to the King stronger and make her disoblige him [by] defending the accus'd." They were confident "if they could have forc'd her into any indiscreet warmth," that they would carry "the Prince into those other hands, at last, by taking him from the people now about him and by degrees, consequently, from her." Augusta was sure she defeated this only by keeping George II "in very good humour with her and the children."[37] Later she justified her suspicions and actions by recalling that Lord Harcourt, the prince's governor, "always spoke to the children of their father, and his actions, in so disrespectful a manner, as to send them to her almost ready to cry, and did all he could, to alienate them from her." After Harcourt's removal, the boys themselves became aware of his attempts. "George . . . mentioned to her once, that he was afraid he had not behav'd to her so well as he ought sometimes, and wonder'd he could be so misled." Augusta soothed her son by assuring him that he had never acted improperly toward her, but only "now and then" treated her "not with quite so much complaisance, as a young gentleman should use to a lady."[38] But she did not wonder at his being misled so easily. This narrow escape strengthened her conviction that she must maintain her pre-eminent influence on the life of her immature son. It would be up to her to imprint certain virtues on his heart and mind, virtues that would enable him to live up to her ideas of what a king should be.

III

As had been Frederick's habit, Augusta often defined what a king should be by what she believed George II was not. A monarch should not be dominated by his ministers, unlike George II, whom "she reckon'd . . . no more than one of the trees we walk'd by (or something more inconsiderable, which she named)."[39] A king should maintain his dignity and authority, and not childishly claim to be able to accomplish deeds he could not. The man presently on the throne "would sputter and make a bustle, but when [ministers] told him that it must be done from the necessity of his service, he must do it, just as little Harry [her son Henry, who was eight] must when she came down" to discipline him.[40] A king should observe his obligations to his family, without caviling or being tightfisted. George II was notoriously miserly, and ever ready to divert funds that should have gone to his grandchildren to his own purse.[41] A ruler of Great Britain should not favor the interests of Hanover when they conflicted with those of Britain. Augusta "wish'd Hanover in the sea, as the cause of all our misfortunes; in the manner it had been treated [by George II], it had been the foundation of all just complaints, and bad measures."[42] Finally, a king should not be governed by the women his love and lust attracted him to. "Princes when once in women's hands," she believed, "make miserable figures."[43] She was determined that her son would be the reverse of his grandfather, and not simply because she "could have nothing so much at heart as to see him do well, and make the nation happy."[44] Her determination was also fuelled by a dislike for the king so intense that a friend could only remember her speaking favorably of him once, and by the bitter awareness that she had to behave prudently, stay in his good graces, and never reveal her dislike and contempt as long as he lived.[45]

Augusta had three basic strategies for molding her son into the right sort of man and monarch. One was the time-honored parental stratagem of seizing on appropriate chances to reinforce good and criticize bad behavior. We have seen how she reminded George that a gentleman should always be complaisant toward ladies, when he was remorseful about his behavior toward her. Similarly, whenever George and Edward "behav'd wrong or idly (as children will do) to any that belong'd to the Prince, and are now about her, she always ask'd them how they think their father would have lik'd to see them behave so to anybody that belong'd to him, and that he valued." "They ought," she reminded the boys, "to have more kindness for them, because they had lost their friend and protector, which was [the children's] also." This effort to induce feelings of loyalty and obligation to one's friends, she found, "made a great impression upon them."[46] Augusta also made certain that her sons showed the proper respect to the rank, of those who were trying to serve them. Although she regarded the bishop of Norwich as an enemy, she assured him that she had constantly supported him as the prince's preceptor, and "always inculcated to the children to show him great respect." "Not for love of you, my Lord," she bluntly told the bishop, "but because it is fitting and necessary; for if they are suffer'd to want respect that is due to one degree, they will go on to want it to another, till at last it would come up He to me, and I should have taught them to disregard me."[47] This took a considerable act of will on her part. Both Augusta and the boys thought the bishop was an incompetent instructor, and the princess probably shared her secretary's opinion that his latitudinarianism made him virtually an atheist.[48] Nevertheless, paying the respect owed a man of his station was an important enough principle that it could not be overlooked, even in this case. Not that Augusta blinked at criticism at the right times when it was called for. She regularly assessed the moral fitness of those about her, and those in politics and at court. It must be assumed that she passed both these judgments and her readiness to judge along to George. As Waldegrave later remarked, even as a young man he paid "rather too much attention to the sins of his neighbour."[49]

Augusta's second stratagem was also traditional; one customarily resorted to by devout parents. Although direct evidence on this is lacking, it seems likely that the woman who had insisted on taking communion in the Lutheran chapel until she was convinced this was politically unwise, encouraged her children to observe the rites of the Anglican church faithfully and wholeheartedly. Her efforts were most successful with her eldest son. Well before he ascended the throne, George had concluded that the God's will applied to kings as well as to lesser mortals, and had to be accepted and obeyed.[50] He had a sense of the active role of providence in the lives of men and nations that was far keener than most of his contemporaries in Britain, and resembled more closely the providentialism of his subjects in New England.[51] These convictions were genuinely held. As Waldegrave remarked, George's "Religion is free from all Hypocrisy." The earl did qualify this observation by noting it "is not of the most the charitable sort."[52] One should recall, though, that this was the critique of a worldly man not particularly concerned about the presence of sin in himself or others.[53] What Waldegrave's comment unintentionally points out about George is his knowledge of Christianity's moral rules and his conviction that he and others should live by these precepts.

But could her son manage to live by these rules? This question haunted Augusta. He was childish and impressionable, and the weak will and heedlessness of children did not bode well for resisting the temptations and snares of the world. The princess had no reason to be confident in his capacity for resistance, even with her aid and the church's counsel. Indeed, she had reasons other than her son's temperament to be apprehensive. Augusta had managed to get her way on important points with both her husband and her father-in-law, but she had no illusions about the limits of her powers. The diary of her confidante George Bubb Dodington offers ample evidence of her frustrations over her inability to change George II and the necessity of prudently avoiding antagonizing the king.[54] If the world ever gained a foothold within her son, and offered him a rationale for gratifying impulses, the influence she had might not be sufficient to overcome it. When Dodington claimed that "all good men plac'd their chief hopes in the Prince's continuing chiefly in her hands and direction, and in her preserving this influence over him which was justly due to her from her prudence as well as from nature," he articulated her heartfelt convictions.[55]

To accomplish this, Augusta adopted her third stratagem. She was certain it was essential to isolate her son as much as possible from worldly contaminations. "The young people of quality," as we have seen, "were so ill educated, and so very vicious, that they frighten'd her." Thus she was glad in 1752 that George clung to the company of his family, and encouraged this tendency in her eldest son.[56] When Edward complained in 1753 about this "subjection . . . and of his brother's want of spirit," she was alarmed. At this time, Dodington argued that the prince should have more company, but the princess "seem'd averse to the young people, from the excessive bad education they had, and the bad examples they gave."[57] This close supervision of their social life continued to chafe Edward, while George bore it docilely. In 1755, Augusta conceded that he needed the company of men, because "women could not inform him" about his duties in government and opportunities in politics. "But if it was in her power absolutely," she rhetorically asked Dodington, "where could she address him? What company could she wish him to? What friendships desire he should contract? Such was the universal profligacy, and the character and conduct of the young people of distinction" that she did not know where to turn. Then Augusta revealed her deepest concern. "She would be in more pain for her daughters," she told her friend, "than for her son, if they were private persons, [because] the behaviour of the women was so indecent, so low, so much against their interest, by making them so cheap."[58] The princess had realized that the wedge which could split George apart from her, and destroy what potential he had for being a good monarch, was unbridled sexual appetite. All her careful instruction in morals and manners, she believed, would be swept aside if he ever yielded to lust.

Augusta did not spell out to Dodington why she believed this, but her reasoning may be easily inferred. In part, she assumed that her son, like other men, had powerful sexual hungers to satisfy. She was certain, as she told her friend, that he would have "many" children.[59] In part, too, she had the example of what lust had done to George II. To the princess, the king's unrestrained pursuit of sexual pleasure had helped make him a cipher. Finally, it is possible that Augusta blamed Frederick's erratic behavior on his penchant for adultery, and resented the way his amours had exposed her to public humiliation. She was determined to prevent the still immature George from repeating the mistakes of his grandfather and father. To do this, she tried to isolate him from feminine temptation for as long as she could, until, she hoped, he accepted the necessity of avoiding the dangers of lust. Her efforts were successful. Augusta did not manage to keep George completely separated from women she regarded as immoral Indeed, George Lewis Scott, the prince's subpreceptor from 1750 to 1756, noticed that his pupil "has the greatest temptation to gallant with the ladies, who lay themselves out in the most shameful manner to draw him." But she did persuade him that "Princes when once in their hands make miserable figures, the annals of France and the present situation of government in the Kingdom I most love are convincing proof of" that. She taught him to believe that such women were attracted not to him but to his power, and sought an ascendancy over him to turn that power to their own purposes. He learned that lesson well enough to remark to Scott that "if he were not what he is, they would not mind him." Finally, she convinced him that he had to resist the passions of "boiling youth," in the expectation that in time a proper "marriage will put a stop to this combat in my breast." Fortified by these precepts, the prince had, as Scott noted, "no tendency to vice, and . . . as yet very virtuous principles;" the ladies' efforts were "to no purpose."[60] Another, and more important, proof of the princess's success came in August 1755. Rumors were circulating that George II was thinking of arranging a match between his grandson and a princess of Brunswick. To Augusta, such a marriage was premature and, because of the personality of the proposed bride, unwise. She was delighted when she found that George understood her objections, and, far from yielding to lust, "was much averse to [the marriage] himself."[61]

Underlining what the princess had achieved is important. She had taught her son, by frequent precept and with the assistance of isolating him as much as she could from contact with "indecent" and "cheap" women, that chastity before marriage and fidelity afterwards were virtues. This was an unusual lesson, to say the least. Augusta lived in an age when male fornication and adultery were at worst venial sins, and often expected behavior. Chastity and fidelity were strictly feminine virtues. Under this double standard, royal males differed from their aristocratic and commoner counterparts only in the fact that they conducted their sexual adventures more publicly.[62] Augusta succeeded in training her eldest son so well that even when he was most afflicted with "boiling youth," he shrank from any lustful, immoral designs on women.[63]

Edward did not absorb these lessons. To his mother's disgust, he celebrated coming of age by courting a married woman, sleeping with whores and professing latitudinarian religious doctrines that permitted him to do both without feeling guilty.[64] The difference between the two brothers was aptly summarized by another son, Prince Frederick. In 1759, the nine year old Frederick and George saw a famous courtesan pass by. "The child named her—the Prince, to try him, asked, who that was?—"Why, a Miss"—"A Miss," said the P[rince] of W[ales], why, are not all girls Misses?" Frederick replied that she was a certain kind of miss, one who sold oranges. George teasingly asked, "Is there any harm in selling oranges?" The boy rose to this bait by answering, "Oh! but they are not such oranges as you buy—I believe they are of a sort that my brother Edward buys."[65]

As time passed, it became clear Frederick was a consumer of the fruit Edward bought. Among Augusta's sons, George alone adopted the virtues that she taught them all.[66] He became an anomaly not only at court and in politics, but within his family as well: a man who believed being virtuous meant being chaste and faithful, and practiced those womanly virtues. This pleased his mother greatly. In August 1755, she proudly informed Dodington that the prince of Wales "was not a wild, dissipated boy, but good natur'd, and cheerful, but with a serious cast in the whole." She also told her friend that "those about [the prince] knew him no more than if they had never seen him; that he was not quick, but with those he was acquainted with, applicable and intelligent."[67] These were the words of a mother satisfied with her son's moral progress and confident he would realize his potential as a king. Although Dodington neither knew nor guessed this, these were also the sentiments of a woman who knew that the final step in the molding and maturation of George's character was taking place. Unknown to the politicians at court, the princess's friend Lord Bute had begun to tutor the prince. Moreover, Bute was proving to be a remarkably successful instructor.[68]

This success was crucial to Augusta's plans for her son. As early as May 1754, she had "wish'd [the prince] saw more company." By this, she meant that "he had acquaintance older than himself." More specifically, she wanted him to know men who could guide him in the ways of politics without compromising her efforts to make him virtuous. Even that early she may have had Bute in mind. But she "durst not recommend," she told Dodington, "for fear of offense: while he had governors &c., was under immediate inspection, all that they did not direct, would be imputed to her." Unwilling to give George II any excuse for taking his grandson from her, she refrained. "In a year or two," she hoped, the prince "must be thought to have a will of his own, and then he would, she hop'd, act accordingly."[69]

The reason for her concern is clear. Augusta had learned from Frederick's detailed plans for his first days on the throne that "it was of infinite consequence how a young reign set out." The fact that George was leading an isolated life had thus far yielded very good results, but, if it continued much longer, it might have very bad ones. The princess did not believe that "women could . . . inform him" about the realities of power, and she "was highly sensible how necessary it was that the Prince should keep company with men."[70] This was the case in part because she thought men had political skills and knowledge not available to women. Moreover, Augusta worried that unscrupulous men might convince George that his reliance on his mother was unmanly, and thus sever their relationship. Bute expressed her fear vividly in a letter to the prince, when he warned him against those who "sooner or later" would whisper in his ear that "Lord Bute . . . only means to bring you under your mother's government, sure you are too much of a man to bear that."[71] Driven by her sense she had to do something soon, not merely to forestall such tactics, but because of George II's advancing age and the deepening crisis with France, she decided during the early summer of 1755 to ask Bute to take over the education of the prince. To prevent discovery, the two adopted the subterfuge that the earl was visiting her.[72] Bute and George established with surprising quickness a rapport that went well beyond the usual teacher-pupil relationship. Delighted that a male friend who shared her ideas about morality and her commitment to making George a patriot king was now her son's "dearest friend," Augusta urged Bute to continue to pursue his "worthy efforts" and "imprint his grate sentiments" on the prince.[73] Her choice of "imprint" to describe this process is significant. She expected Bute would duplicate in his political education of George her own successful effort to fix within his heart and mind her religious and moral beliefs and practices. This duplication would not merely complete the fashioning of his character as a virtuous man and monarch. It would also guarantee that the ways of the world would not overturn the lessons of his mother.

IV

Augusta's success with her son was soon obvious, at first to those who saw him most frequently at court, and then to the wider world that gossiped and speculated about events at Leicester House. His devotion to religion and his insistence on maintaining morality were apparent to Waldegrave, who viewed them coolly, and to Bute, who was overjoyed by his protégé's willingness to submit to the laws and the will of God.[74] His commitment to chastity excited even more comment. No doubt this was because it had no precedent among his male ancestors in the house of Hanover and was so different from the reactions of Edward, who could not wait to embrace both latitudinanan religion and all available women.[75]

The fact that George's "chastity had . . . remained to all appearance inviolate, notwithstanding his age and sanguine complexion," did not surprise the cynical Horace Walpole. He explained the princess's success by confidently asserting that she had "fettered" George's mind. Indeed, Walpole believed that "could she have chained up his body" as well, "it is probable she would have preferred his remaining single" in order to maintain her control over him.[76] Such an interpretation is unjust to Augusta. She expected her son would marry, and wanted him to as a means of preserving the line of descent. She also knew that his most intimate male advisers would come to have, and rightly so, more influence on his political behavior than she ever would. As for fettering his mind, she clearly had less impact on Edward and her other sons than she did on George. Other explanations for her decisive role in shaping his character must be sought.

Foremost among these must be George's receptiveness to her moral training. Augusta was right when she realized that the young prince was pliable, was susceptible to having patterns of thought and behavior imprinted on him. She was also correct to observe that he was "good natur'd," not merely in the sense that he was complaisant, but in the fact that he wanted to be virtuous. What his mother accomplished was convincing him that he could be good, that virtue was within his power if he committed himself to Christianity and to following its rules of morality. Bute then built upon this foundation, by persuading his pupil that a monarch could be moral politically as well as personally, and could be a patriot king if he learned and observed certain procedures and policies.[77] Both his mother and his "dearest friend" appealed to the deep-seated desire within George to be a good man and monarch. Far more than his other brothers, he was in this crucial respect his mother's son.

V

Gauging the historical significance of Augusta's influence on George requires asking two separate questions. The first is the more difficult to answer. How did George's perceptions of himself as an honest and moral man, a faithful husband and a conscientious father, affect his political judgments? Such a question must be answered in the immediate context of his decisions, and the answers will on occasion not be obvious. To return to Augusta's putative role in the coming of the American Revolution: if as some scholars have argued, that revolution may be understood in important ways as a revolt against patriarchalism, how would a king determined to be a good father to his family and his people react to an assault on his paternal as well as his political authority? George III's correspondence after the beginning of armed conflict in 1775 reveals his absolute commitment to reducing the mother country's rebellious children to obedience. P. D. G. Thomas has suggested that this deeply felt determination was the result of his personal character, "a resolution not to give way, that is very marked throughout his political life, combined with an inability to see an opponent's point of view; perhaps also a sense of lese-majesty towards himself as sovereign."[78] Asking whether the king's sense of himself as a virtuous man with moral imperatives he had to follow helped form these character traits and contributed to his determination, might illumine his own character and his role in the American Revolution further. Certainly such subjects deserve careful and sensitive examination.

The other question involves assessing the significance of his people's perceptions of George III as a moral, religious monarch who was particularly and conspicuously virtuous in the domestic sphere of his family. Here Linda Colley has provided us with some intriguing food for thought. As Colley has pointed out, George's public reputation improved dramatically after the end of the American War of Independence. Central to that improvement, according to her, was the king's "undoubted domestic probity and obstinate patriotism." In a time of national flux and humiliation, these qualities "seemed to many to represent a reassuring stability . . . [and] honest uncomplicated worth in contrast with those meretricious, complex and/or immoral politicians who had failed." As years passed, George III's morality and stability seemed even brighter and more meritorious in contrast to his heir's sexual and political escapades. In this case, the king may have been the beneficiary of "a general rise in female politicization" in the early nineteenth century.[79] That should not be surprising. Many of the virtues George's people had come to prize—his unfeigned commitment to

Christianity, his fidelity to his wife, his morality in general and his dedication to domestic responsibility in particular—were, then considered, as we have seen, feminine.

That George III had these virtues was the result of his mother's efforts and example. She served him well. George reigned during a time when European monarchs were toppled from their thrones by popular revolutionary fervor and war. In contrast to them, he enjoyed the support and affection of his people, and became the national symbol of resistance to French ideas and armies. That affection was deeply rooted in the morality the princess imprinted within him. John Brooke closed his comments on Augusta by asserting that "during the reign of her son she was of no consequence in politics."[80] This is true only in the most literal sense, in terms of direct intervention in political events. Insofar as broad influences on George III were concerned, it was she, after all, who instilled in him what it meant to be a king. Indeed, she did more than that. Years after her death, her lessons of domestic virtue and genuine piety helped him remain one.

*This chapter first appeared in: Stephen Taylor, Richard Connors and Clyve Jones, eds., *Hanoverian Britain and Empire*, (Boydell and Brewer, 1998) pp. 177-197.

Endnotes

[1] For a description of this story, see John Brooke, *King George III* (1972), pp. 86, 390. I can remember reading this story in an elementary school textbook during the 1950s.

[2] *Ibid*, p. 390. For biographical details about John Nicholls, see Sir Lewis Namier and John Brooke, *The House of Commons 1754-1790* (3 vols., 1964), III, 202. J. C. D. Clark has also cautioned historians about the possibility that Nicholls may have nursed a grudge against Augusta and her son. His father, Dr. Frank Nicholls, had been one of George II's physicians. When George III succeeded his grandfather, Dr. Nicholls lost his position to a Scotsman who, according to Samuel Johnson, was "very low in his profession." *The Memoirs and Speeches of James, 2nd Earl Waldegrave, 1742-1763*, ed. J. C. D. Clark (Cambridge, 1988), p. 129 n.

[3] See the treatment of Augusta and Bute in: Brooke, *George III*, pp. 29-72; Stanley Ayling, *George the Third* (New York, 1972), pp. 33-60; Sir Lewis

Namier, *England in the Age of the American Revolution* (2nd ed. 1961), pp. 83-93; idem, "King George III," in: *Crossroads of Power. Essays on Eighteenth-Century England*(1962), pp. 124-40; and John L. Bullion, "The Prince's Mentor: A New Perspective on the Friendship between George III and Lord Bute during the 1750s," *Albion*, xxi (1989), pp. 34-55. cf ch. II in this volume.

[4] *Letters from George III to Lord Bute, 1756-1766*, ed. Romney Sedgwick (1939), pp. liii-liv: earl of Bute to the prince of Wales [summer 1755].

[5] Earl Waldegrave, "Memoirs of 1754-1757," in: *Memoirs and Speeches of Waldegrave*, ed. Clark, p. 176.

[6] *Ibid.*, p.229.

[7] *Ibid.*, p. 176. See also Waldegrave, "An Allegory of Leicester House," in: *ibid.*, p. 229.

[8] Examples of these prints and a stimulating analysis of their content and significance may be found in: Vincent Carretta, *George III and the Satirists from Hogarth to Byron* (Athens, GA 1990) pp. 68-71. The quotations are from "Leicester House Politics 1750-1760, From the Papers of John Second Earl of Egmont," ed. Aubrey N. Newman, *Camden Miscellany XXIII* (Camden 4th ser vii 1967) p. 227: diary of the earl of Egmont, Nov. 16, 1760. See also K.W. Schweizer, "English Xenophobia in the 18th Century," *Scottish Tradition*, vol. 22, (1997), pp. 6-26.

[9] *Lord Hervey's Memoirs, Edited From a Copy of the Original Manuscript in the Royal Archives at Windsor Castle*, ed. Romney Sedgwick (1952), p. 176.

[10] *Ibid.*, pp. 186-7.

[11] *The Yale Edition of Horace Walpole 's Correspondence*, ed. W. S. Lewis *et al.* (48 vols., New Haven, 1937-83), xx, 122: Horace Walpole to Sir Horace Mann, Feb. 25, 1750.

[12] Horace Walpole, *Memoirs of King George II*, ed. John Brooke (3 vols. New Haven, 1985), I, 53.

[13] For comments about contemporary attitudes toward adultery see: Lawrence Stone, *The Family, Sex, and Marriage in England 1500-1800* (1977) pp. 501-7.

[14] Lord Fitzmaurice, *Life of William, Earl of Shelburne Afterwards, First Marquess of Lansdowne, with Extracts from his Papers and Correspondence* (2 vols. 1912), I, 46.

[15] *Ibid.*, p. 49.

[16] *Hervey's Memoirs*, ed. Sedgiwck, pp. 182-3. Augusta's presence at the chapel at Kensington was conspicuous because, according to Hervey, Frederick insisted

that she arrive late. Perhaps he did so to draw attention to her observance of Anglican rites.

[17] Augusta frequently complained about the immorality of young people at court, both to people she was personally close to such as George Bubb Dodington, and those she was less well acquainted with such as Earl Waldegrave. For example, see Dodington's diary entry for May 27, 1755 in: *The Political Journal of George Bubb Dodington*, eds. John Carswell and Lewis Arnold Dralle (Oxford, 1965), p. 300; and Waldegrave, "An Allegory of Leicester House," in: *Memoirs and Speeches of Waldegrave*, ed. Clark, p 229. For the scathing comment by James Cresset that the latitudinarian bishop of Norwich was a "bastard and atheist" see: *Walpole's Correspondence*, ed. Lewis, xx, 344: Walpole to Mann, December 11, 1752.

[18] Frederick, "The Charms of Sylvia," in: Walpole, *Memoirs*, ed. Brooke, III, 145. A parody of the poem circulated in London that included these lines: "No—tis that all-consenting tongue/That never puts me in the wrong." See also Walpole's comment on Frederick as poet in: *ibid.*, I, 54.

[19] "Leicester House Politics," ed. Newman, p. 197.

[20] Princess Caroline, who detested her brother, once scornfully rejected Lord Hervey's hypothesis that, if Frederick became king; within a month Queen Caroline "would have more weight with him than anybody in England" with these words: "Jesus! . . . My good Lord, you must know him very little if you believe that; for in the first place he hates Mama; in the next, he has so good an opinion of himself that he thinks he wants no advice, and of all advice no woman's; for the saying, no woman ought to be let to meddle with business or ever did any good where they did meddle, is perhaps the only thing in which I have not heard him ever contradict himself." *Hervey's Memoirs*, ed. Sedgwick, pp. 218-19. See also: Brooke, *George III*, pp 29-30.

[21] "Leicester House Politics," ed. Newman, pp 196-7. Others also assumed Augusta was conversant with Frederick's political negotiations. After his death in 1751, some Tories appealed to the princess to confirm to George II that they had rejected his overtures in 1747 to join him and his friends in an open opposition to the ministry. During the next year, Dodington asked the same favor of her, reminding Augusta as he did so that they had both hoped Frederick would follow "a plan of temper and moderation" in 1749. *Dodington Journal*, eds., Carswell and Dralle, pp. 135, 165, Oct. 2, 1751 and Jul.16, 1752.

[22] "Leicester House Politics," ed. Newman, pp. 198-9.

[23] Augusta's maneuvers may be followed in detail in: *ibid.*, pp. 199-213.

[24] *Ibid.*, p.207.

[25] For example, see: Walpole, *Memoirs*, ed. Brooke, I, 51; and Brooke, *George III*, p. 41.

[26] "Leicester House Politics," ed. Newman, pp. 175, 193.

[27] *Ibid.*, p. 175. For a contemporary understanding of what "foppery" meant, see Samuel Johnson's *Dictionary of the English Language*.

[28] Walpole, *Memoirs*, ed. Brooke, I, 51.

[29] Henry Fox remarked on the physical and psychological resemblance between Frederick and Edward by noting the son was the "express image of his worthless father." Henry Fox, "Memoirs on the Events Attending the Death of George II, and the Accession of George III," in: *The Life and Letters of Lady Sarah Lennox 1745-1826*, eds., the countess of Ilchester and Lord Stavordale (1902), p. 12. Walpole also called attention to the similarities between the two in a letter to Mann, May 24, 1767. *Walpole's Correspondence*, ed. Lewis, xxii, 521. For some remarks on Edward's notorious indiscreetness, see Horace Walpole, *Memoirs of the Reign of King George III*, ed. G. F. Russell Barker (4 vols., 1894), I, 110; and *Walpole's Correspondence*, ed. Lewis, vii, pp. 365-6: "Account of the duke of York's Journey to Paris and Comprègne, and his death at Monaco," [1767].

[30] Quoted in Brooke, *George III*, p. 41.

[31] For examples of Frederick's political advice to his children, see his remarks on Sir Robert Walpole, in: *Walpole's Correspondence*, ed. Lewis, xviii, 219: Walpole to Mann, April 25,1743; on George II, in "Leicester House Politics," ed. Newman, p. 207; and on his brother, the Duke of Cumberland, in: Fox, "Memoirs," in: *Lady Sarah Lennox*, ed. Ilchester and Stavordale, pp. 33

[32] These letters are described in: Brooke, *George III*, p. 23.

[33] *Ibid.*,p. 41.

[34] For example, see Shelburne's comment that the treatment of George by his mother and father "went the length of the most decided contempt of him, if not aversion, [by] setting up his brother [Edward's] understanding and parts in opposition to his, and undervaluing everything he said or did." Fitzmaurice, *Life of Shelburne*, I, pp. 53-4. The surviving letters from Frederick to George strongly suggest that this account is too harsh.

[35] *Dodington Journal*, ed. Carswell and Dralle, pp. 178-9: October 15, 1752.

[36] See Bullion, "The Prince's Mentor," pp. 43-6.

[37] *Dodington Journal*, ed. Carswell and Dralle, pp. 192-3: Dec. 28, 1752. Lucid accounts of this struggle maybe found in: Brooke, *George III*, pp. 35-9; and in Clark's introduction to *The Memoirs and Speeches of Waldegrave*, pp. 54-63.

[38] *Dodington Journal*, ed. Carswell and Dralle p. 207, Mar. 3, 1753

[39] *Ibid.*, p. 199: Jan. 25, 1753.

[40] *Ibid.*, p 203: Feb. 8, 1753.

[41] *Ibid.*, pp 176-7: Oct. 15, 1752. See also entry for May 29, 1754; *ibid.*, pp 271-2.

[42] *Ibid.*, p 316: Aug. 6, 1755.

[43] One can see what Augusta taught George about the consequences of the king's attraction to women in a letter from the prince to Bute in 1759 in: *Letters from George III to Bute*, ed Sedgwick, p 37. The princess was hardly the only person who believed a succession of women had essentially ruled George II. See Hervey *Memoirs*, ed. Sedgwick, p 194.

[44] *Dodington Journal*, ed. Carswell and Dralle, p. 180: Oct. 15, 1752

[45] *Ibid.*, p. 215: Mar. 29, 1753. There are indications that George II sensed Augusta's real feelings, yet felt himself thwarted by her prudence from taking action. Horace Walpole heard that the king told Henry Pelham soon after Frederick's death that "You none of you know this woman, and you none of you will know her until I am dead." Quoted in: *The Memoirs and Speeches of Waldegrave*, ed. Clark, p. 54.

[46] *Dodington Journal*, ed. Carswell and Dralle, p. 179: Oct. 15, 1752. See also entry for Nov. 17, 1753: *ibid.*, p. 241.

[47] *Ibid.*, p. 191: Dec. 28, 1752.

[48] For their reaction to the bishop of Norwich as an instructor, see: *ibid.*, p. 203, Feb. 8, 1753. George and Edward had been complaining about the bishop for some months prior to this. See Clark's introduction to *The Memoirs and Speeches of Waldegrave*, p. 54. For Cresset's remarks about the bishop's religious views see n. 17 above.

[49] Waldegrave, "Memoirs," in: *The Memoirs and Speeches of Waldegrave*, ed. Clark, p. 148.

[50] See: *Correspondence of George III with Bute*, ed. Sedgwick, p. 31: the prince to Bute, [September 7, 1759]. In his reply, Bute recalled that the prince's religious feelings were not new, for he was "accustomed from [his] childhood to look up to Heaven" so he could "in the day of affliction put full confidence in Him who gives and resumes at pleasure." The cause of George's unhappiness was the death

of his sister Elizabeth. A few years later, when he drafted a "sketch of the Education I mean to give my Sons," George III noted, "Religion should be instilled from the most tender Youth as that teaches that the All Wise Creator is not a respecter of persons and that in his Eyes all Men are judged by their conduct not their birth." For this reason he believed the end of their education should be "the making them Christians, & Usefull (*sic*) Members of Society." Royal Archives, Windsor Castle, Add. Georgian MS 32/1732-3: "The Plan of Education for a Prince." I would like to thank Her Majesty The Queen for her gracious permission to quote from papers in the Royal Archives.

[51] It is striking to compare the prince's providentialism with that of the Massachusetts soldiers so well described by Fred Anderson in: *A People's Army. Massachusetts Soldiers and Society in the Seven Years' War* (Chapel Hill, NC, 1984), pp. 196-7, 209-10, 216-18. For examples of George's providentialism during the Seven Years War, see: Bute Papers (the marquess of Bute, Mountstuart, Isle of Bute), Correspondence with George III, nos. 73, 25: the prince to Bute [early Aug. 1759], [Oct. 19, 1759]; and in: *Letters from George III to Bute*, ed. Sedgwick, p. 32: the prince to Bute [Oct. 19, 1759].

[52] Waldegrave, "Memoirs," in: *The Memoirs and Speeches of Waldegrave*, ed. Clark, p. 148.

[53] For an excellent description of Waldegrave's social milieu and his worldliness, see Clark's introduction in: *ibid.*, pp. 41-8.

[54] *Dodington Journal*, ed. Carswell and Dralle, pp. 177-8, 193-4, 197-200: Oct. 15, Dec. 28, 1752, Jan. 25, 1753.

[55] *Ibid.*, p. 194: Dec. 28, 1752.

[56] *Ibid.*, p. 178: Oct. 15, 1752.

[57] *Ibid.*, p. 244: De. 18, 1753.

[58] *Ibid.*, p. 300: May 27, 1755.

[59] *Ibid.*, p. 317: Aug. 6, 1755.

[60] Augusta's precepts are revealed in *Letters from George III to Bute*, ed. Sedgwick, p. 37: the prince to Bute [1759]. In it, George told Bute that he had "long resisted the charms of those divine creatures," which indicates that the moral he stated in the letter dated from before his friendship with Bute. His mother's observation about people flattering him because of his position rather than his personal qualities clearly impressed the young prince. He remembered it for years. Indeed, when he planned the education of his sons, he commented that "the most severe trials a Prince has to combat are those occasioned by his rank; the most efficacious means of destroying this dangerous charm would be the

making him acquainted nth his own weakness, his own ignorance, and the keeping him perhaps distant from Courts." The king even mused that it might be wise "to hide his rank from him till he shall possess virtue enough to be frightened at the being acquainted with it." He conceded, however, that "custom, that most powerful of Tyrants, will never permit this to be adopted." Royal Archives, Add. Georgian MS 32/1732: George III, "The Plan of Education for a Prince." The comments in this paragraph by George Lewis Scott are quoted in: Ayling, *George the Third*, p. 36. Waldegrave, a much less sympathetic judge of the prince than Scott, confirmed his resistance to temptation. The earl pointed out that George had "great command of his Passions," and noticeably avoided the pursuit of pleasure. Waldegrave, "Memoirs," in: *The Memoirs and Speeches of Waldegrave*, ed. Clark, pp. 148-9.

[61] *Dodington Journal*, ed. Carswell and Dralle, p. 317: Aug. 6, 1755.

[62] See Stone, *Family, Sex, and Marriage*, pp. 503-7.

[63] See *Letters from George III to Bute*, ed. Sedgwick, pp. 36-39: two letters from the prince to Bute [1759]. In describing his infatuation with Lady Sarah Lennox, George protested "before God I never have had any improper thought with regard to her, . . . having often flatter'd myself with hopes that one day or other you would consent to my raising her to a Throne."

[64] For Edward's pursuit of Lady Essex, and the princess's presumed reaction to it, see: *Walpole's Correspondence*, ed. Lewis, xxi, 53-4: Walpole to Mann, January 29, 1757. Two weeks later, on Feb. 13, 1757, Walpole wrote to Mann: "Prince Edward's pleasures continue to furnish conversation: he has been rather forbid by the Signora Madre to make himself so common; and has been rather encouraged by his grandfather to disregard the prohibition." *Ibid.*, p. 57. For Edward's relationship with the earl of Eglintoun, who encouraged his protégé in both pleasurable activities and latitudinarianism, see: Fox, "Memoir," in: *Lady Sarah Lennox*, ed. Ilchester and Stavordale, pp. 16-17; and *James Boswell: The Earlier Years 1740-1769*, ed. Frederick A Pottle (New York, 1966), pp 47-52. Boswell, in his "Sketch of the Early Life of James Boswell Written by Himself for Jean Jacques Rousseau, 5 December 1764," explicitly linked latitudinarianism and sexual license in this way: "My Lord [Eglintoun] made me a deist. I gave myself up to pleasure without limit. I was in a delirium of joy." *Ibid.*, p. 4. Eglintoun was Edward's mentor as well.

[65] *Walpole's Correspondence*, ed. Lewis, ix, 237: Walpole to George Montagu, May 16, 1759.

[66]Indeed, Frederick may have been precocious. When nine, he unbuttoned his trousers and offered to show Lady Charlotte Edwin how eunuchs were made. *Ibid.*, For his later escapades, and those of his other brothers, see: Brooke, *George III*, pp. 270-82.

[67] *Dodington Journal*, ed. Carswell and Dralle, p. 318: Aug. 6, 1755.

[68] Bute began his work with George in Jun.– Jul. 1755. See *Letters from George III to Bute*, ed. Sedgwick, p. 2: the prince to Bute [Jul. 1, 1756].

[69] *Dodington Journal*, ed. Carswell and Dralle, p. 271: May 29, 1754.

[70] *Ibid.*, p. 300: May 27, 1755. For Frederick's detailed plans for the first days of his reign, and Augusta's knowledge of them, see: "Leicester House Politics," ed. Newman, pp. 104-20, 198.

[71] The quotation is from *Correspondence of George III with Bute*, ed. Sedgwick, p. liii: Bute to the prince [1755]. Bute went on to note that if the prince were "well acquainted with this nation, with the people you are to govern, with the individuals you are one day to employ, with the business of the Kingdom, you would have no occasion for the Princesses advice nor would she offer it." Until that time, however, he warned George to "look on him as your most determined enemy who attempts to breed suspicions in your breast against her."

[72] This deception led observers at court to conclude that Augusta and Bute were having an affair. The gossip about them played a crucial role in preventing politicians from guessing that the earl was in fact tutoring the prince. This episode and its importance are discussed by John L. Bullion, "The Origins and Significance of Gossip about Princess Augusta and Lord Bute, 1755-1756," *Studies in Eighteenth-Century Culture*, xxi (1991), pp. 245-65; ch. II in this volume.

[73] *Letters from George III to Bute*, ed. Sedgwick, p. 4: Augusta to Bute [1755].

[74] Waldegrave, "Memoirs," in: *Memoirs and Speeches of Waldegrave*, ed. Clark, p. 148; *Letters from George III to Bute*, ed. Sedgwick, p. 31: Bute to the prince [Sept. 7, 1759], also: Bute to the Prince, Oct. 21, 1759, Bute MSS (Mt. Stuart).

[75] Even before Edward came of age, Scott observed that he was "of a more amorous complexion" than his older brother. Quoted in: Ayling, *George the Third*, p. 36.

[76] Quotations from an excerpt from Walpole's original draft of his "Memoirs of George III," published in: *Walpole's Correspondence*, ed. Lewis, xxi, 517 n. 15: Walpole to Mann, Jul. 23, 1761.

[77] Bullion, "The Prince's Mentor," pp. 44-7.

[78] For the interpretation of the American Revolution as a revolt against paternalism, see Jay Fliegelman, *Prodigals and Pilgrims: The American Revolution against Patriarchal Authority 1750-1800* (Cambridge, 1980); for Thomas's remarks see: P. D. G. Thomas, "George III and the American Revolution," *History*, LXX (1985) pp. 30-1.

[79] Linda Colley, "The Apotheosis of George III: Loyalty, Royalty and the British Nation, 1760-1820," *Past and Present*, 102 (1984) pp.104-5, 124-5.

[80] Brooke, *George III*, p. 266.

Chapter IV

The Prince's Mentor: A New Perspective on the Friendship between George III and Lord Bute during the 1750s*

The effects of the intense personal and political relationship between the young George III and his "dearest friend," the earl of Bute, are well known to scholars of eighteenth-century Britain. The prince's affection and respect raised Bute, an obscure though well-connected Scottish nobleman, to the highest offices of state and to the absolute pinnacle of power. The earl's instruction and advice governed George's reactions to men and measures from 1755 until 1763. Even after Bute's influence waned following his resignation as First Lord of the Treasury, the lingering suspicions at Whitehall and Westminster that the king still listened to him in preference to others complicated relations between George III, his ministers, and Parliament.[1]

This chapter examines the origins of the friendship between the king and the earl, and the features of it that strengthened and preserved their attachment during the 1750s. These are questions that have not engaged the attention of many students of the period. The long shadow the relationship cast over politics during the 1760s has intrigued far more historians than its beginnings. They have been content to leave efforts to understand that subject to Sir Lewis Namier, who was inclined toward making psychological judgments of eighteenth-century politicians, and John Brooke, who was compelled to do so by the demands of writing a biography of George III.[2] Both of these men asserted that the personal and affectionate aspects of the connection between the prince and Bute far outweighed the political and ideological during its early years. Their arguments have evidently convinced historians of politics to pass over what made Bute "my dearest friend" and press on to matters they assumed to be more relevant to their interests. The concern of this chapter is to demonstrate that this assumption is incorrect. It will show that political and ideological considerations were in fact utterly critical to this friendship at its inception and throughout its development during the 1750s, with consequences which profoundly affected the political history of the first decade of George III's reign. A mistaken reliance on works by Namier and Brooke has prevented scholars from perceiving these realities. Thus it is necessary to begin by indicating the serious flaws in their interpretations.[3]

Namier's analysis of the young prince and Bute is strikingly shallow. To Sir Lewis, George was "the neurotic boy, bitter in soul and mentally underdeveloped, [who] concentrated on [King George II] the hostility of the heir and rival, while his love went out to Lord Bute, to him the incarnation of a tutelary paternal spirit." After this opening blast, one might reasonably expect Namier to define what he meant by neurosis and to demonstrate how the prince fit the definition. No such definition was forthcoming. In its place, Sir Lewis substituted his own prejudices and gave full rein to his obvious dislike of the prince. He asserted that George was more dependent than "a normal youth" of the 18th century should be. But he provided no basis for comparison, either by referring to modern concepts of normal behavior for young men or by discussing the norm for contemporary 18-year-olds. He diagnosed the prince's conscience as "diseased," because George harshly criticized the political morality and perceptiveness of all statesmen except Bute.[4] Yet the prince's judgments differ more in degree than in kind from the reactions of, say, the duke of Newcastle to William Pitt, and *vice versa*. Indeed, they are almost identical to George II's opinions of the leading politicians of his day before he ascended to the throne. That prince, according to Lord Hervey, "used always to speak of [Sir] Robert Walpole as a great rogue, of [Horace Walpole] as a dirty buffoon, of [Newcastle] as an impertinent fool, and of [Lord Townshend] as a choleric blockhead."[5] George II's temperament and morals were vastly different from his grandson's, so the congruency of their views toward men who served the monarch rather than the prince suggests that these opinions would be better explained as the results of the difficult circumstance of being a relatively powerless heir apparent to the Crown than as symptoms of a diseased conscience or neurotic personality. Finally, Namier even went so far as to wonder "whether it would not have been better for England had the Prince of Wales had a gay mistress instead of a sententious preceptor, wrongly described as a 'favourite.'" Why wonder? The career of George IV would seem to offer an obvious chance to investigate the point. Sir Lewis chose not to compare father and son as Princes of Wales, however. Here, as elsewhere, there is no theoretical or scholarly rigor to his treatment of the two men's friendship. Instead, Namier indulged himself with a series of sweeping, unexamined judgments, culminating in this: "The biggest blunders in the world are committed by men with serious faces who feel uncomfortable in their own minds, talk a great deal, and never enjoy themselves."[6] Perhaps so, but these and other *obiter dicta* tell us more about Namier than about George III and Bute.

Where Namier saw a neurotic personality, and interpreted the two men's friendship as a result and expression of it, Brooke viewed the prince as a victim of circumstances, not of neuroses. George's father, Prince Frederick, had died when he was twelve. By all accounts, his mother, Princess Augusta, was not an openly affectionate parent. Moreover, she was determined to keep her son isolated from "the young people of quality," who "were so ill educated, and so very vicious, that they frighten'd her."[7] She distrusted and disliked the boy's grandfather, and feared the influence and intentions of his uncle, William, Duke of Cumberland. The prince absorbed her prejudices against these men, and neither of them had the ability or the inclination to overcome her opinions. In this environment, the boy grew up both alone and lonely, isolated and starved for affection, aware that he would be king yet impotent to prepare himself for the throne. Thus Bute's influence can be explained, according to Brooke, "simply." The earl "was the first person to treat [the prince] with kindness and affection." Given the life the boy had led, "it was certain that the first person who did this would win his confidence." Then, "just as the prince was approaching manhood, came Bute, a man of culture and learning, a former follower of his father, imbued with his ideas, sympathetic and encouraging. Here was a man in whom the prince could confide, who would show him the way his father would have him tread. No wonder he put his trust in Bute!"[8]

Brooke's portrayal of the young prince's life at Leicester House is touching, and clearly is colored by a humane sympathy for George. Still, his explanation for the beginning of the friendship with Bute is not convincing. Bute was not the first to treat the prince in a kindly fashion and try to win his confidence. Earl Waldegrave, his governor from 1752 until 1756, was, according to his mother, "very well bred, very complaisant, and attentive, etc." In 1753, Augusta noted that George and his brother Edward "liked him extremely." She added that if "this man, by his manner, should hit upon the means" of improving their education, "I shall be mightily pleased."[9] Far from being insensitive to the boy's isolation from the world, Waldegrave blamed it for his educational and social backwardness. As we shall see, he devised a method of instruction that he hoped would enable the prince to shake off the bad effects of his isolation.[10] He failed where Bute succeeded, but that failure cannot be said to be due to a cold, insensitive approach.

The reason for his failure was no mystery to Waldegrave. He believed Augusta must have persistently criticized him in private, and destroyed any chance of success. Brooke agreed with this judgment. But Waldegrave himself had no proof supporting his accusation. Indeed, his papers and memoirs reveal that he felt no concern about the princess's attitudes toward him until after Bute had clearly become the prince's friend.[11] Moreover, the evidence that has survived shows that she was eager for him, or anyone, to succeed in educating George. When one of Waldegrave's predecessors complained that people in the prince's household were challenging his authority, she protested her innocence eloquently and convincingly. "[I] always," she said, "inculcated to the children to show him great respect, and was very far from endeavouring, or even wishing, it should be lessen'd: . . . 'not from love of you, my Lord, but because it is fitting and necessary; for if they are suffer'd to want respect that is due to one degree, they will go on to want it to another, till at last it would come up to me, and I should have taught them to disregard me.'"[12] In the absence of direct evidence to the contrary, to assume that she reversed her practice in Waldegrave's case is unjustified. Those who taught the prince, before she felt compelled by their lack of results to ask Bute to make an effort, had her full support. The earl's friendship inspired her to ask him to become the prince's *de facto* tutor, but his success in forming a friendship with her son was not the result of her supporting him where she had undercut others.

In his account of the origin of the friendship, Brooke emphasizes one other factor: Bute had been a friend of Frederick, and shared his political ideals and goals. This, he suggested, contributed significantly to George's enthusiastic reaction to the earl. Brooke does not spell out why he believed this was so important. Apparently he, like Namier, assumes the boy hungered for "a paternal tutelary spirit" and saw Bute, who had supported his father and still held to his opinions, as "the incarnation" of it. There are ways of testing this assumption. Did memories of Frederick mean much to George before he met Bute? Did the political ideals his father espoused attract the prince before 1755? Was Bute the first to appeal to his affections for Frederick? Did Bute deliberately try to call the prince's attention to similarities between himself and Frederick? Curiously, Brooke does not try to answer these questions. Had he done so, he would have found evidence that seriously qualifies his argument.

Before he died, Frederick prepared a political testament for his son, which he left in the princess's hands, with instructions to "read it to You from time to time and . . . give it to You when you come of Age or when You get the Crown." Augusta complied with his wish, so the prince at least heard his father's ideas during the early 1750s. He received the testament itself when he turned eighteen in 1756.[13] Augusta also carefully tried to preserve "[George's] affections towards his father's memory." She happily reported to one of Frederick's followers that "he seem'd to have a very tender affection for the memory of his father," adding that "she encourag'd it as much as she could."[14] She evidently succeeded. Lord Harcourt, the prince's governor in 1752, "always spoke to [George and his brother] of their father, and his actions, in so disrespectful a manner;" the boys' response was to come to their mother nearly in tears.[15] This reaction implies that the prince retained feelings of affection for Frederick, and disliked criticism of his political career and ideas.

But were these feelings of crucial importance to Bute's success with him? There is reason to doubt they were. Bute was not the first of the prince's tutors to refer respectfully to Frederick. According to Augusta, Andrew Stone, George's sub-preceptor during 1752, "always spoke of the [late] Prince with great respect, and with great civility of all those that he knew the Prince had a real value for."[16] Despite this, Stone was unable to cajole or compel the boy to concentrate on his studies. Bute was also, in all probability, not the first of the prince's tutors to agree with some of the ideas expressed in Frederick's testament. Frederick had called for economy in government, reduction of taxes, and payment of the national debt. Waldegrave was just as convinced of the wisdom of these policies, and stated in the House of Lords that he would teach the reasoning behind them to the prince.[17] No tutor before Bute believed as Frederick did, that the connection between Britain and Hanover should be severed. The teaching of that doctrine was novel to George. But before endowing this with much significance, it should be asked if Bute himself believed that the opinions he shared with Frederick and his friendship with the dead prince would assist him in establishing and maintaining a relationship with George.

When he began tutoring the prince, Bute regarded his friendship with Frederick as a mixed blessing. He was apprehensive that others might use his old connection with the father as a wedge to split him apart from the son. So he assured George, "I glory in my attachment to the Princess, in being called your fathers friend, but I glory in being yours too; I have not a wish, a thought but what points to your happiness alone."[18] Perhaps that same concern governed his handling of the similarity between his political ideas and Frederick's. Bute did not use that to lend authority to his views. He may not have even called his royal pupil's attention to it. George never mentioned his father in his surviving correspondence with Bute, and he repeatedly identified his political vision as the one held by his "dearest friend." If Bute himself rejected the role of purveyor of paternal values, his former connection with Frederick and the fact that his political opinions closely resembled the late prince's cannot have been as central to the origins of his intense relationship with George as Brooke argues.

In sum, the explanations by Namier and Brooke of the friendship's beginnings are both seriously flawed. Namier's judgment of the prince as a neurotic desperately seeking someone to depend upon is not sustained either by reference to any psychological theory or by research in contemporary sources. Brooke assumes that because Bute played a unique role in George III's life, he must have been unique in the prince's experience from the beginning of the relationship. This is a plausible hypothesis for investigation, but in his biography it remains only that. Analysis of the evidence reveals Brooke did not succeed in isolating the quality or qualities that made Bute unique. The sources of their friendship, and the causes of its intensity and duration, remain obscure.

An examination of the relationship between George III and Bute from the perspective provided by Daniel J. Levinson's theories about the role mentors play in the development of adult personality clarifies much of the obscurity presently surrounding the origins and dynamics of the friendship.[19] It provides a new angle of vision on the two men, one which focuses attention on certain aspects of their time together during the 1750s. That focus, in turn, permits the isolation of characteristics which truly did make Bute unique in the prince's experience, and which explain the sense of purpose that animated both men and had such a striking impact on politicians and policy during the early 1760s.

Levinson's description of the relationship between a young man and his mentor can be briefly summarized. Typically, the young man is between the ages of 17 and 33, and experiences himself "as a novice or apprentice to a more advanced, expert, and authoritative adult." The mentor is almost always an older man. He is a mixture of parent and peer, and in some ways is seen as a responsible, admirable older brother. But the process of mentoring, as opposed to the perceptions of it, is "defined not in terms of formal roles but in terms of the character of the relationship and the functions it serves." According to Levinson, a mentor

> may act as a *teacher* to enhance the young man's skills and intellectual development. Serving as *sponsor*, he may use his influence to facilitate the young man's entry and advancement [in the adult world]. He may be a *host* and *guide*, welcoming the initiate into a new occupational and social world and acquainting him with its values, customs, resources, and cast of characters. Through his own virtues, achievements, and way of living, the mentor may be an *exemplar* that the protégé can admire and seek to emulate. He may provide *counsel* and moral support in time of stress.

For all these reasons—and for another, particularly crucial one I shall describe later—the mentoring relationship is "one of the most complex and mentally important a man can have in early adulthood."[20]

Does Bute's relationship with the prince fit Levinson's model of mentoring? Obviously, a precise match cannot be expected. Levinson developed his theory after a decade of intensive study of the lives of 40 contemporary American men, divided equally among hourly workers in industry, business executives, university biologists, and novelists.[21] George and Bute fall into none of those categories, to say nothing of their living in the cloistered atmosphere of the prince's court at Leicester House and in a vastly different society and era. After excising the purely contemporary, professional, and occupational aspects of Levinson's model, nonetheless his definition of mentoring describes Bute's role in the prince's life. Numerous examples from the notes George sent Bute before he became king support this conclusion. One of the most striking is a letter he wrote on July 1, 1756, after he had had "the pleasure of your friendship during the space of a year." At that time, George II was trying to remove Bute from the prince's household. The prince and his friend were resisting the combination of threats and blandishments being offered them.[22] Written in the middle of this confrontation within the royal family, the letter documents some of the chief sources of George's attachment to Bute. Those sources correspond closely to the different aspects of mentoring Levinson called attention to in his definition.

One year's experience had made the prince appreciative of his friend's pedagogical skills. As *teacher*, Bute was already a spectacular success, not least because he had made his pupil aware of his deficiencies and inspired him to change. From the earl's friendship, "I have reap'd great advantage, but not the improvement I should [have] if I had follow'd your advice; but you shall find me mak[ing] such a progress in the summer, that shall give you hopes, that with the continuation of your advice, I may turn out as you wish."[23] George also anticipated that Bute would serve as his *sponsor* as he took "upon me the man in every thing" and prepared for his destiny as monarch. "I hope my dear Lord you will conduct me through this difficult road and will bring me to the gole." Bute would be his *host* and *guide* on this road. It was his friend who warned him "the Ministers have done everything they can to provoke me, . . . [and] have call'd me a harmless boy." George II's ministers attacked his mother as well, "because she is so good to come forward and preserve her son from the many snares that surround him," and Bute, "not for anything he has done against them, but because he is my friend, and wants to see me come to the throne with honor and not with disgrace and because he is a friend to the bless'd liberties of his country and not to arbitrary notions." To deal with these men, the prince recognized he must defend Bute, show "the world the great friendship I have for him," inform him of all malicious attacks on him, and resist "all the allurements my enemies can think of, [and] the threats that they may pour out upon me." Absolutely crucial to his success in doing this, George believed, was his friend's *counsel* and support. "I will exactly follow your advice, without which I shall inevitably sink," he promised, and then elaborated, "I am young and unexperienc'd and want advice. I trust in your friendship which will assist me in all difficulties." It is not surprising, given this trust, that George regarded Bute as an *exemplar*, a true friend both to him and to "the bless'd liberties of his country. I know few things I ought to be more thankfull (*sic*) for to the Great Power above," he observed, "than for its having pleas'd Him to send you to help and advise me in these difficult times."[24]

To be sure, the prince's perceptions of Bute do not correspond to Levinson's description of present-day protégés' attitudes toward their mentors. As we have seen, George did not identify the earl as a person or a politician with his deceased father. Nor did he see Bute as a responsible, admirable older brother. He was too keenly aware that this should be his role in the royal family to make that sort of projection.[25] Rather, he viewed Bute from a perspective that was appropriate to his position and his time: friendship. Bute was—to borrow from Harold Perkin's skillful dissection of the various meanings of that "integral part of the texture of life" in eighteenth-century England—a man "in whom [George] recognized special merit or services to [him]self."[26] Indeed, because the prince believed he had extraordinary merit and was performing supremely valuable services, the earl was not merely a friend, but "my dearest friend." Social psychologists of our own day would call a person such as Bute a mentor. George never used that word. It was not in common usage during the 1750s,[27] and, in any case, to him "my dearest Friend" perfectly expressed the part Bute was playing in his life and the deep admiration and affection he felt for the earl. To historians, however, there are important advantages to seeing the prince and his friend as an eighteenth-century example of Levinson's model of the mentoring relationship. Principal among these is the insight his explanation of the most essential help a mentor provides in the transition from young man to adult gives us into the origins and dynamics of the friendship.

As they interviewed their subjects, Levinson and his colleagues gradually uncovered a profound influence on these men's development which they called "the Dream." "The Dream," argued Levinson, "plays a powerful and pervasive role in early adulthood." More detailed than pure fantasy, less articulated than a plan, it begins as a vague sense of one's potential roles and powers in the adult world. At this stage, it has "the quality of a vision, an imagined possibility that generates excitement and vitality." It is "only tenuously connected with reality, although it may contain concrete images such as winning the Nobel Prize," or being economically successful, or a great artist, or a good provider and parent. Whatever the Dream's nature, "a young man has the developmental task of giving it greater definition"—in other words, converting vision into a rational plan of action—"and finding ways to live it out"—that is, devising practical procedures for attempting its execution in the adult world. Crucial to his success at these tasks is forming a mentoring relationship. The mentor, in turn, has the role of "support[ing] and facilitate[ing] the *realization of the Dream.*" This is "developmentally the most crucial" function of the mentor. "He fosters the young adult's development by believing in him, sharing the youthful Dream and giving it his blessing, helping to define the newly emerging self in its newly discovered world, and creating a space in which the young man can work out a reasonably satisfactory life structure that contains the Dream."[28]

This aspect of Levinson's model of mentoring raises interesting questions about the prince and Bute. Did George have an equivalent of "the Dream"? Did Bute help him define it, and assist him in planning for its realization? Did this role explain the beginning of their friendship? Did it account for the intensity of their relationship during 1755—1763?

If the youthful prince began to envision a dream between 1751, when his father died, and 1755, when Bute assumed *de facto* responsibility for his education, he did not try to articulate it to his mother. Nor did he discuss any vision of his future with those officially charged with preparing him for the throne. Had either Augusta or his tutors been asked if he had one, they would have answered no, on the basis of their experience with George as student. Unquestionably, he was an uninspired pupil, and an uncommonly indolent one. Waldegrave was struck by a "want of application and aversion to business" in the prince that amounted to "a state of total inaction."[29] Augusta supposed in 1755 that the sum total of his "book-learning" was "small or useless." She even doubted that he had been successfully taught "the general course of things."[30] There is no reason to doubt the accuracy of their description; George himself frequently testified to the power "that indolence which if I don't soon get the better of will be my ruin" had over him after Bute began to rouse him from it.[31] So crippling an affliction must have prevented him from working out any well-defined hopes for his reign. It certainly kept him from thinking of ways to accomplish them, and then preparing himself intellectually and emotionally for the effort.

George also did not attempt to form with anyone a mentoring relationship similar to the one he later had with Bute. All of the officials around him at Leicester House would have been eager to encourage him had he tried. Waldegrave, who had no political ambition for high office, would have done so out of a sense of duty to the nation and personal loyalty to George II, who had pleaded with him to oversee the prince's education. Others would have added to patriotism their own self-interested motives. George was going to be king, and given his grandfather's age and health, sooner rather than later. Anyone who established close ties with the next monarch would become an extremely important figure at court in the years ahead. When the bishop of Norwich became the prince's preceptor in 1751, he was told "that Lord Harcourt [the governor] was only a cipher; that as [Norwich] had parts and abilities, he might easily get the whole in his own hands." His friend therefore "advis'd him not to omit so fair an opportunity."[32] The prince was outwardly civil to Waldegrave, the bishop, and the others in his establishment.[33] Inwardly, how ever, he responded no more to their willingness to forge intimate links with him than he did to their efforts to better educate him for his future responsibilities.

Why was George's reaction to Bute so different? In July 1756 the prince noted that he and the earl had been friends for a year, but none of their letters from 1755 have been found.[34] There is one clue, however, to their friendship's beginning that historians have overlooked: the differences between the pedagogical methods and goals of George's official instructors, and those of Bute. Despairing of teaching the prince by "a right system of education," Waldegrave settled for trying "to give him true notions of common things." The method chosen to accomplish this was instruction by conversation, rather than by books, and "sometimes, under the disguise of amusement, to entice him to the pursuit of more serious studies."[35] What "true notions of common things were" is easy to infer. Waldegrave was exposing the prince to the worldly-wise counsel of a Whig courtier who accepted the *status quo* in politics. It was a world view that explicitly and implicitly stressed the checks on kings' powers and the limits on what any man or monarch could accomplish. It offered no prospect either of significant improvement in political morality, or of fundamental changes in national policies. Its vision, insofar as it could be said to have one, was of a reign similar in all important respects to that of George II, whom Waldegrave fully respected and faithfully served. He wanted to prepare the prince to be a king like his grandfather, with the same ideas about the monarch's role in government, and the same realistic (in Waldegrave's eyes, at least) approach to politics and policies. This Whiggish wisdom struck no responsive chords in George. Indeed, after three years of studying with Bute, he condemned "the negligence, if not wickedness of those around me in my earlier days," and blamed them for helping keep him from "that degree of knowledge and experience in business one of my age might reasonably have acquir'd."[37]

Bute's educational methods and purposes were quite different, and met with a quite different reception. From the beginning of their relationship as tutor and pupil, he insisted that George had to be a serious student of books. Worldly wisdom was no substitute for learning first principles of government, politics, and finance; history revealed that the education of princes often determined, for good or ill, the fate of their people. A prince's honor, honesty, and virtue were also more valuable than being worldly-wise, for virtuous princes could change nations for the better. And Britain needed reformation; of that Bute was sure. His was not the perspective of the courtier, accepting things as they were and skeptical of the possibility and efficacy of change. Bute looked at the future from the view of the country, not the court; he believed that George III should reduce the national debt and retrench the nation's finances, avoid the entanglements with European conflicts from George II's attachments to Hanover, and—most important of all— work to free the monarchy from ministerial control and the political world in general from corruption. The earl was also certain George could accomplish these reforms. He assured his pupil that although "you are not accustomed to serious things, . . . yet your temper is extremely formed for it, formed for manly ideas and even refinements in virtue." Acquiring the habits of serious study and political virtue would, he told George, "make everything easy."[38]

Without question, the prince was captivated by this confidence in him and this vision of what a virtuous king could achieve. Augusta, who was elated that Bute had "gained the confidence and friendship of my son," recognized the transforming impact his ideals were having on the prince. "Pursue my worthy friend," she urged him, "those instructions you have begun, and imprint your great sentiments in him, those will make my son and his mother happy."[39] George later testified to the accuracy of her observation and the prescience of her prediction. He fondly recalled his and Bute's anticipation of "the hour . . . which has been so long been wished for by my D. Friend, I mean the entering on a reformation in Government."[40] Purging corruption would have meant, he remembered, "when we were both dead our memories would have been respected and esteemed to the end of time."[41] He vowed only to accept the throne "with the hopes of restoring my much loved country to her antient state of liberty; [and] of seeing her in time free from her present load of debts and again famous for being the residence of true piety and virtue."[42] Bute had supplied the prince with a dream which kindled his ambitions and energies. George recognized that Bute was his inspiriting agent. That recognition impelled him to feel a keen sense of affection and gratitude to the earl. He expressed his gratitude in terms of a deeply felt obligation to live up to the standards and example of Bute, both as prince and, ultimately, as king. "I will constantly reflect," he promised, "whether what I am doing is worthy of one who is to mount the Throne, and who owes everything to his friend."[43]

Namier and Brooke dismissed Bute's vision as politically naive. Both of them were certain that teaching the prince "common things," either by Waldegrave's methods or perhaps via a gay mistress's ministrations, would have served him better. In and of itself, this proposition seems dubious as a guide to educating the young. Even if a hard-and-fast distinction could be made in practice between "realism" and "idealism" as a philosophy of instruction, powerful arguments could be made in favor of the idealistic approach. Should not students, whether kings or commoners, take their orientation toward their lives by attempting to conceive what their possible perfection would be? Whatever the answer, it is clear that Bute was the first to give George a coherent vision of what his future could be that was attractive to him. It is equally clear that he responded to this vision enthusiastically. Thus inspired, he began to exchange his former indolence and inattention for energy and concentration on his preparation for the crown. Their bunkered outlook kept Namier and Brooke from recognizing the crucial significance of Bute's passionate advocacy of his political vision to his relationship with the prince, and from seeing that it was this that made him unique in George's experience.

That same commitment to "realism" prevented Namier and Brooke from appreciating an equally significant contribution Bute made to George's development. The earl fulfilled the other crucial role of the mentor in Levinson's model: he devised a practical plan for realizing the dream. It was a plan they dismissed as naive, and they explained the prince's attraction to it as a result of either a neurotic dependence on Bute or "his limited acquaintance with men."[44] Yet, scorning the ideas Bute had about executing the vision he shared with the prince as impractical, does not take into account the fact that important elements of his plan became reality. Bute did become the First Lord of the Treasury and the most powerful politician in the kingdom. He and George accomplished this by following his plan. To be sure, they did not achieve their lofty goals. This failure, however, was not due to any flaws in their design for grasping political power.

To Bute, it was obvious his pupil could not accomplish a reformation of British politics by himself. Because the prince was inexperienced in politics and administration, he would be unprepared to answer the arguments and resist the proposals of those who would inevitably oppose his goals out of self- interest. George needed no convincing on this point. He agreed that he lacked knowledge and experience in political business, and that it would take years for him to acquire them. "Therefore if I should mount the Throne without the assistance of a friend, I should undoubtedly be in the most dreadful of situations."[45] That friend, of course, was to be—indeed, had to be—Bute. His experience and knowledge would make up for the prince's deficiencies. His use of those superior qualities to further the cause of reform would enable George to employ the full range of royal prerogatives to achieve their common vision of the future.

The design of their plan was simple. Bute would be First Lord of the Treasury in the new reign. By serving in a responsible ministerial office, he would not be vulnerable to politically and personally wounding charges that he was a royal favorite, exercising illegitimate and unchecked power behind the curtain.[46] As First Lord of the Treasury, he would control the fountainhead of places and pensions. Hopes of power, wealth, and honors would always be the principal motives of men; these considerations Bute and the prince did not expect to change. Rather, they planned to use ambition and greed to help transform the present system of government. Under George's monarchy and Bute's Treasury, "noble actions and generous sentiments shall lead to the royal favour, and prostitution of principle, venality, and corruption meet with their just reward." "The honest citizen, the zealous patriot," would be uplifted as they deserved; "the degenerate mercenary sons of slavery," compelled to conform to virtue.[47] Finally, the Treasury was as central to government as it was to politics. It was responsible for establishing and executing the nation's fiscal policies. Bute and the prince believed it was essential to reduce the national debt through economy in expenditures and enhancement of revenues by a judicious extension of excise taxes. These measures, so necessary to the financial strength and political security of the state, were so controversial and far- reaching "that no man but he that has the Prince's real affection can go through" with them.[48] Bute as First Lord would command that affection and support, and could accomplish these fiscal reforms.

The king's role would be straightforward. He had to remember that "every step of a Prince is of consequence," and do nothing that might inadvertently diminish his friend's power.[49] In practice, this meant he should always "speak firmly" with his other ministers, and never "be stagger'd if they say anything unexpected." George assured Bute that neither "they, nor no one else, shall see a want of steadiness either in my manner of acting or speaking." If surprised, he would "give fifty sorts of puts off, till I have with you thoroughly consider'd what part will be proper to be taken."[50] This last comment reveals what the two men intended to be the extent of Bute's power. Not only would he control the Treasury, but also his approval would also be necessary for any measures other departments of state contemplated taking. Though neither he nor the prince used the term, they planned that he would be the prime minister. The king would elevate him to that commanding position, and then maintain him there with watchful and unswerving support.

Insofar as politics outside the palace and Whitehall were concerned, the prince and Bute planned to convince the people that George III would be the long-awaited "Patriot King." In particular, they wanted to make the prince's coolness toward Hanover and toward Britain's deepening involvement in the war in Germany apparent from the first days of his reign.[51] They also intended to demonstrate his commitments in favor of economy and against corruption immediately, by asking Parliament for the fixed sum of £800,000 per annum for the civil list.[52] Finally, the new king would not exclude Tories and political independents from offices and places at court. This would dramatically signal that George III was no respecter of old political arrangements and factions.[53] Bute and the prince anticipated that all this would make George very popular with Parliament and the public, and assist in enlisting his subjects in the cause of moral and political reformation.

This plan for realizing his dream seemed without weakness to the prince. "A proper steadiness of conduct," he predicted, "added to your friendship, will carry me hereafter with honor through the difficultys (*sic*) I shall meet with from the ingratitude of some, the pusillanimity and enmity of others. The game," he concluded, "will ever be in my favor" if he could avoid yielding to personal weaknesses.[54] Certainly he was not disheartened by the political vicissitudes of 1759-1760. The thought that circumstances might prevent Bute from immediately taking the Treasury merely caused him to promise "you will for all that be Minister; for all men will find the only method of succeeding in their desires, will be by first acquainting you with what they mean to request before they address themselves to me."[55] With his dream in focus, and his plan set, George was eager to become king. "Whilst my Dearest is near me," he confidently told Bute in May 1760, "I care not who are the tools he may think necessary to be in [the] Ministry."[56] Apparently he was as sure then as he had been when he wrote his essay on British politics that after his accession, "a generous reformation will ensue."[57] That Bute had furnished the prince with a dream of political reformation and regeneration and a plan for achieving that vision is clear. In the fullest and most significant meaning of that role in Levinson's model, he was the prince's mentor.

To view George as protégé and Bute as mentor makes understandable the origin, intensity, and endurance of their friendship. Bute's political ideals and plans struck sparks in the prince, igniting a compelling interest and affection, and creating an attachment that was given great emotional force by an inspiring common vision of Britain's future. When George wholeheartedly adopted Bute's dream as his own, and Bute's plans as the means of implementing that vision, he made a deeply felt commitment that sustained the friendship through thick and thin from 1755 into the mid-1760s. The prospect of a regenerate politics in the kingdom and a determination to combine the power of the monarchy and the Treasury to achieve that goal—these thoughts, and the emotions they excited, were at the core of the relationship, defining its essence, and making it valuable beyond compare to both men.

To be sure, they felt affection for each other. But the personal qualities that aroused and preserved their affection were political virtues as well, and esteemed as such. George admired Bute's honesty and his disinterested support in large part because he presumed other politicians lacked these qualities. "As to honesty," he wrote in 1760, "I have already lived long enough to know that you are the only man I shall ever meet with who possesses that quality, and who at all times prefer my interest to your own."[58] "I look on the majority of politicians as intent on their own private interests instead of that of the public;" Bute, because he was in the minority, deserved his respect and affection.[59] Bute's forthright criticism of the prince's indolence and his short comings as a student won his pupil's respect and love too, and not just because it was to better George personally. The "unwearied pains" his mentor took, and "the many truths" he revealed about the prince's "unhappy nature" were not only "for my future quiet and honour," but also for "the happiness of this my dear Country."[60] In contrast, his earlier tutors, through "negligence, if not wickedness," endangered both the prince and the nation.[61] Finally, George recognized that Bute's friendship in and of itself had momentous political implications for his and the country's future. He therefore valued it accordingly.[62]

Bute did not separate personal and political virtues when he examined his friendship with George. For example, when he expressed pride over the prince's improvement as a student during 1755—1756, he described the change in terms of politics.

> "My young friend, My hopes, the only Hopes the *Spes ultima* of this poor countrey, grows every day more firm, More steady. May his future Subjects," he wished, "be as fond of Liberty as he is; May they have as Strong an aversion to Vice, Corruption & Arbitrary Power, & they will be a happy people; He a happy [prince]."[63]

The specific qualities Bute urged on George, and was delighted to find developing—"steadiness, warmth on proper occasions, and resolution"—were intended to prepare him to be a patriot king.[64] Furthermore, Bute warned the prince that their friendship could not survive anything that would weaken the earl politically. "Anything that has the least colour of coolness or reserve" on the part of the prince toward Bute would sap the power of Bute's political situation and make his situation as George's friend unbearable to him.[65] To see personal affection as something divisible from the compelling political commitment to the two men made, and then give it an equal or greater emphasis in explaining the beginning, intensity, and endurance of their friendship, is to misread their relationship completely.

To look at Bute as mentor and George as protégé also makes clear the answer to an interesting and important question. Why, despite some serious misgivings, did Bute continue to plan on becoming, and then in May 1762 actually take on the burdens of being, First Lord of the Treasury? As early as December 1758, he began to express doubts to the prince about being First Lord when George became king. The reasons he cited were those of political expedience; he could not safely defy the opposition of "these great Greenvilles," Pitt and his three brothers-in-law, Earl Temple, George Grenville, and James Grenville.[66] This did not ring true to the prince. "When I compare the many things I have heard you say on the subject"—that is, about the necessity of taking the Treasury and the practicality of doing so despite the expected opposition from self-interested men—he could only conclude "tis owing to some diffidence of me." The prince therefore reiterated his commitment to their strategy and the tactics they devised to execute it in an effort to reassure his friend.[67] In fact, Bute did not need reassuring about George's determination. As many historians have pointed out, he doubted his own ability and will to function effectively as "the Minister" in government. Those doubts were apparently serious enough for him to hint to the prince that he would not be able to accept any ministerial employment.[68]

Had the prince responded to this either by accepting that his friend would be more comfortable as a courtier, or by conceding that Bute would have to share power with other ministers, the political history of the early years of his reign might have been significantly different. Although neither Pitt nor Newcastle was happy about Bute's influence with George III and the necessity of his sitting in the Cabinet, they accepted the situation. Each saw the wisdom in the duke of Devonshire's observation: "There ought to be an inclination to indulge a young King in regard to one he was so fond of," provided that "those whose abilities and situation rendered them the most considerable" continued to have power as well.[69] The politicians also did not object to Bute's becoming a Secretary of State, reasoning that he "would be more tractable and more dependent when he was in a responsible office."[70] The extraordinarily violent and persistent opposition to the earl that John Brewer has so well analyzed did not begin until after Pitt's resignation in October 1761, when it began appearing to politicians and the public that Bute had his eye on becoming the dominant figure in government. After

Newcastle left the Treasury in May 1762, that opposition, fueled by the conviction that Bute had flouted the constitutional principle of ministerial responsibility and aimed at absolute rule, intensified. It did not abate when the earl left office. It retained its fervor long after he was out of politics. Most important, it poisoned relations between George III and the politicians for at least a decade and, as Bute himself observed, prevented a young and personally virtuous monarch from enjoying the popularity he might have had with his subjects.[71] This progression of events and consequences was set in motion by George's unyielding commitment to his dream, his plan, and his dearest friend. Also crucial to the process was the earl's unwillingness to insist upon changing their design. Why did he decide against pressing his arguments? The answer may be found in the prince's response to his misgivings when he first raised them. "I don't deny," George admitted, "that the scene looks very black; and that his situation is far from being desirable. But, if his is such, what is mine?" Without sufficient knowledge or experience, "if I should mount the Throne without the assistance of a friend, I should undoubtedly be in the most dreadful of situations." He hastened to explain why he said without a friend. If Bute did not take office, "the voice of envy will call him the Favourite which would I am sure make him leave me, to do the best way I can with these men, who are either biass'd by ambitious or avaricious views." Then he concluded, "I would not have my friend imagine that altho' I look on this thought of his, if ever effected, as my ruin, that I can ever blame him for taking that part."

Without exception, historians have viewed this letter as proof of Bute's manipulation of the prince's dependence on him. Brooke goes so far as to see it as evidence of the earl's practicing "a subtle form of moral blackmail" on George. Only an unquestioning and incorrect certainty that Bute pulled all the strings in their relationship could have prompted such a reading. Who is trying to manipulate whom here? Do as you desire, and I will not blame you, the prince was saying, even though it will ruin me personally and politically. In other words, you will bear the whole responsibility, if not the outright guilt, for this catastrophe. "Do as you wish," he told Bute, "even though you will be compelled to stop advising me. Put another way, do not expect you can play any political role during the next reign, or do anything to reform the present corruption, or preserve our dear friendship." All this told to Bute more or less between the lines, George claimed he would not press his friend to change his mind. Then he closed by doing exactly that: "I can only set before him how dreadful the day that gives me the Crown will appear to me, if I have not him in my Ministry and I leave to him to see if he can no way palliate to himself the accepting the said offer."[72]

Bute was a more sensitive person than his later interpreters. To him, the thrust of the letter was unmistakable. Refusing to take office would be a dreadful day for him as well as the prince. If he would not execute his role in the plan, his relationship with George would be irrevocably ended. Mentors who abruptly doubt the practicality of the plan for realizing a dream, who seem to question their protégés' abilities and commitment, and who suggest that their own prowess to advise and assist may be insufficient, do not remain dearest friends. Bute did not want to stop being the prince's mentor, and thus the trap for him and his protégé was set.[73]

George gained confidence from this harrowing episode. When his friend expressed doubts about the Treasury in May 1760 and May 1762, he brushed them aside with brisk, optimistic comments.[74] Only when it was obvious to him that Bute had been exhausted by the difficulties of making peace with France and Spain and shaken by the vituperation heaped upon him did George III again adopt the tone of his letters of December 1758.[75] By then those arguments did not work. Bute no longer believed in the dream, and he was certain he did not want to go on in office.[76] If the price of leaving politics was the end of his special relationship with the king, he was ready to pay it.

Pay it: Bute did. The two men tried to remain close during 1763-1766, going to considerable pains to maintain clandestine contact with each other.

During that time, though, the earl's influence perceptibly waned, and he became "my dear friend." A sharp exchange between the two in July-August 1766 ended their personal friendship; the mentor-protégé relationship already belonged to the past.[77]

More than two decades later, the two men did manage a partial reconciliation. The passage of time restored Bute's personal affection for George. During the constitutional crisis of February-March 1783, he told his son, "My heart bleeds for my Dearest." Time evidently also healed some wounds for the king. In early 1788, for an unknown reason he decided to sum up for "my d. Friend" the lessons of 50 years of life and 28 years on the throne. "Every day makes me more a philosopher," he observed. "[I] attempt to keep my desires within a narrow compass, that my disappointments may be fewer. When one is within a few months of 50," he went on, "one has acquired little advantage from the experience of a toilsome life if one has not learned to be moderate in expectations and thankful to divine Providence for the good one possesses, and full of diffidence of one's attempts and therefore not surprised when they prove abortive." Almost certainly these words were not meant to hurt, and did not. In the following year, the king invited the earl and his family to a ball at Windsor. They accepted, despite Bute's frail health.[78]

Still, George III's "philosophical" statement was a final repudiation of the political vision and commitment that had created and strengthened their intense friendship years before. They did not try at this late date to recover what they once had been: mentor and protégé, the dearest of friends.

* This chapter first appeared in: *Albion*, 21 (1989), pp. 34-55.

Endnotes

[1]There is no good biography of Bute, but many aspects of his career have been discussed in: Karl W. Schweizer, ed., *Lord Bute: Essays in Re-interpretation*, (Leicester, 1988). The best studies of his impact on politics are John Brewer, "The Misfortunes of Lord Bute: A Case-Study in Eighteenth-Century Political Argument and Public Opinion," *The Historical Journal* 16 (1973):3-43; and Frank

O'Gorman, "The Myth of Lord Bute's Secret Influence," in Schweizer, *Lord Bute*, pp. 57-81. For his role as statesman and diplomat see: K.W. Schweizer, *Frederick the Great, William Pitt and Lord Bute* (New York, 1991); *idem.*, *England, Prussia and the Seven Years War* (Lewiston, 1989); *idem*, "Lord Bute: 1713-1792," *Oxford Dictionary of National Biography*, (Oxford, 2004), vol. 53, pp. 173-180.

[2] Lewis Namier, *England in the Age of the American Revolution*, 2nd ed. (London, 1961), pp. 83-93; and "King George III" in: *Crossroads of Power: Essays on Eighteenth-Century England* (London, 1962), pp. 124-140. Sedgwick advanced a similar explanation of the relationship in: *Letters from George III to Bute*, pp. lvii-lx. J. H. Plumb attempted a different psychological approach in his 1977 George Rogers Clark Lecture, subsequently printed as the pamphlet *New Light on the Tyrant George III* (Washington, D.C., 1978). In it, he argued that the key to understanding the king's behavior during his reign was an awareness of his obsessive temperament. Because Plumb concentrated on George's interests and avocations after he became king, and did not analyze the origins and significance of his friendship with Bute, I will not discuss his interpretation in this chapter. For the results of a biographical approach, see: John Brooke, *King George III* (London, 1972), pp. 44-72; and Stanley Ayling, *George the Third* (London, 1972), pp. 39-54.

[3] For example, Brewer and O'Gorman in the articles cited in endnote 1 do not discuss the origins of the friendship. Brewer refers to it only briefly in his essay on Bute in Herbert van Thal, ed., *The Prime Ministers: From Sir Robert Walpole to Edward Heath* (New York, 1975), pp. 105-113. James Lee McKelvey, *George III and Bute: The Leicester House Years* (Durham, N.C., 1973) focuses almost exclusively on the two men's political relations with the various ministries of the 1750s.

[4] Namier, *England*, pp. 84-85, 87, 92. I am not the first to note Namier's dislike of George III. See Stephen B. Baxter, "The Conduct of the Seven Years War," in *England's Rise to Greatness* (Berkeley, 1983), pp. 324-325.

[5] Hervey, *Memoirs*, Romney Sedgwick, ed. (London, 1952), pp. 34-35.

[6] Namier, *England*, pp. 87, 92.

[7] For the quotation, see George Bubb Dodington, entry in his political journal for October 15, 1752, in John Carswell and Lewis Arnold Dralle, eds., *The Political Journal of George Bubb Dodingion* (Oxford, 1965), p. 178 [hereafter cited as *Political Journal*]. A supporter of the late Prince Frederick, Dodington maintained a close relationship with the Princess Dowager of Wales during the 1750s. His comments about George's education are the only reliable extant sources of Princess Augusta's views on her son's instruction before Bute.

[8] The quotations are from Brooke, *King George III*, p. 53; for his account of the prince's environment at Leicester House, see pp. 26-44.

[9] Dodington, Feb. 8, 1753, *Political Journal*, pp. 202-203.

[10] Earl Waldegrave, *Memoirs from 1754 to 1758 by James, Earl Waldegrave, Knight of the Garter, One of His Majesty's Privy Council in the Reign of George II and Governor of the Prince of Wales, Afterwards George III* (London, 1821), pp. 9, 63-64.

[11] See *ibid.*, pp. 63-69; and Brooke, *King George III*, pp. 5 1-52.

[12] Dodington, Dec. 28, 1752, *Political Journal*, p. 191; see also the entry for Jan. 25, 1753, p. 200.

[13] Frederick, "Instructions for my Son George, drawn by my-Self, for His good, that of my Family and for that of His People, according to the ideas of my Grandfather, and best Friend, George I," [Jan. 13, 1748/9], in: Sir George Young, *Poor Fred: The People's Prince* (Oxford, 1937), pp. 172-175. Since Augusta destroyed all the rest of Frederick's political papers, it seems reasonable to assume that she complied with the requests in this one surviving document.

[14] Dodington, Oct. 15, 1752, *Political Journal*, p. 179.

[15] Dodington, Mar. 3, 1753, in: *ibid.*, p. 207.

[16] *Ibid.* Augusta appreciated Stone's civility deeply, because he served one of Frederick's most vigorous opponents, the duke of Newcastle.

[17] See: John L. Bullion, "To know this is the true essential business of a king': The Prince of Wales and the Study of Public Finance, 1755-1760," *Albion* 18 (1986): 429-431. (See ch. VI in this volume).

[18] The most convenient source for this quotation from the earl of Bute to the prince of Wales, [1755] is Sedgwick, *Letters from George III to Bute*, p. liii, but scholars should be aware that Sedgwick's summary of the parts of the letter he deleted is misleading. The original is in the Bute Letterbooks in the British Library, Add. MSS 36769, fos. 69-70.

[19] J. Levinson, with Charlotte N. Darrow, Edward B. Klein, Maria H. Levinson, and Braxton McKee, *The Seasons of a Man's Life* (New York, 1978), pp. 97-101. Other historians have used the word "mentor" to describe Bute; see Ayling, *George the Third*, pp. 41, 52; Plumb, *New Light on the Tyrant*, p. 6; and Brewer, "Bute," in van Thal, *Prime Ministers*, p. 107. Brewer also uses "protégé" to describe George in "Misfortunes of Lord Bute," p. 8. But Ayling, Plumb, and Brewer did not explore the implications of these terms.

[20] Levinson, *Seasons of a Man's Life*, pp. 97-101. For efforts to sharpen his definition of mentoring, see Nancy W. Collins, *Professional Women and Their*

Mentors: A Practical Guide to Mentoring for the Woman Who Wants to Get Ahead (Englewood Cliffs, N.J., 1983), pp. 24-25; and Sandra Riley and David Wrench, "Mentoring among Women Lawyers," *Journal of Applied Social Psychology* 15 (1985), pp. 376-79, 384-85.

[21] For Levinson's assumptions and methodology, see *Seasons of a Man's Life*, pp. ix-xii, 4-63.

[22] The prince to Bute [Jul. 1, 1756], in Sedgwick, *Letters from George III to Bute*, p. 3. A concise account of their difficulties with George II may be found in *ibid.*, pp. xlix-li, 2-3n.

[23] *Ibid.*, p. 3. I shall discuss Bute's pedagogical philosophy and methodology in greater detail below.

[24] *Ibid.*, pp. 3-4. The prince's comments about political attacks on his mother refer to the rumors that she and Bute were having an affair.

[25] See the prince to Bute [Jul. 30, 1759] and [Mar.1760], in *ibid.*, pp. 27, 41.

[26] Harold Perkin, *The Origins of Modern English Society, 1780-1800* (London, 1969), pp. 45-50; the quotations are on pp. 48, 49.

[27] "Mentor" does not appear in Samuel Johnson's *A Dictionary of the English Language* (London, 1755).

[28] *Seasons of a Man's Life*, pp. 91-93, 98.

[29] Waldegrave, *Memoirs*, pp. 9, 30.

[30] Dodington, August 6, 1755, *Political Journal*, p. 318.

[31] The prince to Bute [Jul. 1, 1756], in Sedgwick, *Letters from George III to Bute*, p. 4.

[32] Dodington, Feb. 8, 1753, *Political Journal*, p. 203; see also Waldegrave, *Memoirs*, p. 69.

[33] Dodington, Oct. 15, 1752, *Political Journal*, p. 178; and Waldegrave, *Memoirs*, p. 64.

[34] The Prince to Bute [Jul. 1, 1756], in Sedgwick, *Letters from George III to Bute*, p. 2. Since the publication of these letters, over 500 additional ones from George to Bute have been discovered at the Bute family seat at Mount Stuart, Isle of Bute, Scotland. With very few exceptions (and those trivial in content), these letters are political rather than personal. Internal evidence indicates none of them was written in 1755. They are now located at Mt. Stuart, Isle of Bute.

[35] Waldegrave, *Memoirs*, pp. 63-64.

[36] An idea of Waldegrave's views can be gathered from *ibid.*, pp. 4-7; and from Waldegrave, drafts of speeches on the education of the Prince of Wales [early 1753, 1754, and 1755], Holland House Papers, BL, Add. M55 51380, fos. 119-122, 126-128, 239. For an illuminating discussion of the world view of the quintessential Whig courtier Lord Hervey, see Reed Browning, *Political and Constitutional Ideas of the Court Whigs* (Baton Rouge, 1982), pp. 35-66.

[37] The prince to Bute [Dec. 19, 1757], in Sedgwick, *Letters from George III to Bute*, p. 21.

[38] The quotations are from Bute to the prince, [1755] in *ibid.*, pp. lii-liv. For discussions of Bute's ideas, see Brooke, *George III*, pp. 55-66; and Bullion, "The Prince of Wales and the Study of Public Finance," pp. 431-49.

[39] Augusta to Bute [1755] in Sedgwick, *Letters from George III to Bute*, p. 4n.

[40] George III to Bute [Nov. 1762], in *ibid.*, p. 167.

[41] George III to Bute [Nov. 1762], in *ibid.*, p. 166.

[42] The prince to Bute [Jun. 1757], in *ibid.*, p. 6.

[43] The prince to Bute [Mar. 25, 1757], in *ibid.*, p. 5 (for similar sentiments see two letters written in Sept. 1758 on pp. 13-15).

[44] The quotation is from Brooke, *King George III*, p. 66.

[45] The prince to Bute, [Dec.19, 1758], in Sedgwick, *Letters from George III to Bute*, p. 21. For Bute's diagnosis of George's shortcomings in 1755, see *ibid.*, p. liv.

[46] The prince to Bute [Dec. 19, 1758], in *ibid.*, p. 21. This tactic did not, of course, keep the politicians and the public from identifying Bute as "the Favourite," even while he held office.

[47] The prince's essay on the British political system, quoted in Brooke, *George III*, pp. 65.

[48] The quotation is from George III to Bute [Nov. 1762], in Sedgwick, *Letters from George III to Bute*, p. 166. For an account of the two men's views on specific fiscal policies, see Bullion, "The Prince of Wales and the Study of Public Finance," pp. 444-46.

[49] The prince to Bute [Winter 1759-1760], in Sedgwick, ed., *Letters from George III to Bute,* p. 36.

[50] The prince to Bute [Dec.1758], *ibid.*, p. 20.

[51] See Brooke, *George III*, p. 75. For other indications of thoughts by Bute and George on how to make the new king popular, see John L. Bullion, "From 'the French and Dutch are more sober, frugal, and industrious' to the 'nobler' position: Attitudes of the Prince of Wales toward a General Naturalization and a Popular Monarchy, 1757-1760," *Studies in Eighteenth-Century Culture* 17 (1987): 159-172, chapter V in this work.

[52] See Bullion, "The Prince of Wales and the Study of Public Finance," pp. 444, 451-52.

[53] See Linda Colley, *In Defiance of Oligarchy: The Tory Party, 1714-1760* (Cambridge, 1982), pp. 267, 285-91.

[54] The prince to Bute [Winter 1759-1760], in Sedgwick, *Letters from George III to Bute*, pp.36-37.

[55] The prince to Bute [May 4, 1760], in *ibid.*, p. 45.

[56] *Ibid.*, The prince did, however, except Pitt, "the blackest of hearts," from this rule.

[57] See Brooke, *King George III*, p. 65.

[58] The prince to Bute [Apr. 23, 1760], in Sedgwick, *Letters from George III to Bute*, p. 43.

[59] The prince to Bute [May 4, 1760], in *ibid.*, pp. 45-46.

[60] The prince to Bute [ca. Sept. 1758], in *ibid.*, pp. 14-15.

[61] The prince to Bute [Dec. 19, 1758], in *ibid.*, pp. 21.

[62] The prince to Bute [Winter 1759-1760], in *ibid.*, p. 35-36.

[63] Bute to Gilbert Elliot, Aug. 16, 1756, in: McKelvey, *George III and Lord Bute*, p. 42. See also Bute to Earl Talbot, Apr. 23, 1760, in *ibid.*, p. 89.

[64] The prince to Bute [Dec. 1758], in Sedgwick, *Letters from George III to Bute*, p. 22.

[65] The prince to Bute [Winter 1759-1760], in *ibid.*, p. 36.

[66] The prince to Bute [Dec. 1758], in *ibid.*, p. 19.

[67] *Ibid.*, p. 20.

[68] The prince to Bute [Dec. 19, 1758], in *ibid.*, p. 21.

[69] The duke of Devonshire, diary entry for Nov.12, 1760, in Peter D. Brown and Karl W. Schweizer, eds., *The Devonshire Diary: William Cavendish, Fourth Duke of Devonshire, Memoranda on State of Affairs, 1759-1762*, Camden, 4th ser., vol. 27 (London, 1982), p. 57.

[70] Jan. 16, 1761, in *ibid.*, p. 72.

[71] In "The Misfortunes of Lord Bute," Brewer failed to call attention to the fact that violent opposition to Bute did not begin until after Pitt's resignation. Nor did he note the politicians' earlier acquiescence and—in some cases—eagerness for Bute to hold responsible office. Richard Pares's stimulating discussion of Bute in office in *King George III and the Politicians* (Oxford, 1953), pp.100-108, also suffers from these oversights. For a more accurate account of the politicians' opinions, see O'Gorman, "The Myth of Lord Bute's Secret Influence," pp. 58-59, and K.W. Schweizer, "Lord Bute and William Pitt's Resignation," *Canadian Journal of History*, VII, 2, (1973), pp. 111-125.See also: *Devonshire Diary*, pp. 76-92. For Bute's awareness of his impact on the king's popularity, see Bute to Henry Fox, Mar. 2, 1763, Holland House Papers, BL, Add. M55 51379, fos. 140-41.

[72] The prince to Bute [Dec. 19, 1758], in: Sedgwick, *Letters from George III to Lord Bute*, p. 21. For Brooke's comment, see: *King George III*, p. 62.

[73] In *ibid.*, p. 53, Brooke remarks that it was a pity Bute did not merely wish to be the prince's teacher and friend without wanting to be his prime minister. Such a relationship could not have been possible. Certainly by Dec. 1758 it was impossible for Bute to change their relationship by becoming simply teacher and friend.

[74] George III to Bute [May 4, 1760], [May 13, 1762], and [May 19, 1762], in Sedgwick, *Letters from George III to Bute*, pp. 45, 103, 109

[75] George II to Bute [November 1762], [early Mar. 1763], [Mar. 5, 1763], in *ibid.*, pp. 166-67, 196-98.

[76] Bute to Thomas Worsley, Nov. 28, 1762, Bute Letterbooks, BL, Add MSS 36797, fol. 24; and Bute to Fox, Mar. 2, 1763, Holland House Papers, BL, Add. MSS 51379, fos. 140-41.

[77] This exchange is in Sedgwick, *Letters from George III to Bute*, pp. 250-58. Accounts of the two men's relationship from 1763-1766 may be found in O'Gorman, "The Myth of Lord Bute's Secret Influence," and Peter D. Brown, "Bute in Retirement," in Schweizer, *Lord Bute*, pp. 62-69, 241-252.

[78] For Bute to Charles Stuart, Feb. 25, 1783, and the invitation to Windsor in 1789, see *ibid.*, pp. 268-69. Brown speculated that the reconciliation was perhaps fostered by Charles Stuart's support for William Pitt the Younger during the

Regency crisis of 1788, but George's letter quoted above antedates those events. For it, see George III to Bute [1788] Bute Papers, Mount Stuart, Box VIII.

PART TWO: LEARNING REFORM

Chapter V

From "the French and Dutch are More Sober, Frugal and Industrious" to the "Nobler" Position: Attitudes of the Prince of Wales toward a General Naturalization and a Popular Monarchy, 1757-1760*

During the years 1757-1760, as the Earl of Bute contemplated how to prepare the future George III for his destiny as king, he decided that his royal pupil must understand the causes of, and the best solution for, a situation that many contemporaries believed to be the principal danger to the future expansion of British commerce: the high cost of labor in Britain. Accordingly, he assigned the relevant literature, indicated his own preferences among the competing theories, and required the prince to write essays on this and related subjects.[1] In all but one of these essays, George argued that the expense of labor was directly related to the weight of taxation on the "necessaries" of the poor, such as candles, soap, malt liquor for brewing beer, and the leather and skins necessary for making shoes and clothes. Such taxes raised the price of these necessities of life, and were "in their own nature severe and offensive, because they fall heavy on the poorest of the people who cannot indemnify themselves but by raising the price of their labor." They were also "contrary to sound politics, as the price of manufactures rise[s] with the price of labor." The end result of this process was obvious. "The sale of our manufactures . . . must diminish by every such aggravation of the price of them, as the cheapest [goods] at foreign markets are generally preferred to the best." Any decline in trade was harmful to Britain, for "our national profits sympathize with our foreign sales." And "what is of more importance than all the rest," the prince concluded, "these [taxes] give a rigid and oppressive air to government, which becomes odious from the minute it appears to be so."[2] Thus they "ought to be removed entirely, or reduced to very moderate [duties]."[3]

In one essay, however, which he wrote in 1757, and titled "On Industry in Great Britain," George questioned the significance of these opinions. Without denying that taxes on necessities raised wages, he claimed that they were a minor cause of the high price British manufacturers paid for work. And without discarding his conviction that the burden of taxation on the poor should be lightened, he proposed other, more radical cures for the heavy expense of labor. Thus, a description of "On Industry in Great Britain" permits scholars to know the full range of ideas and policy alternatives that Bute and the prince seriously considered.[4] Moreover, an understanding of the reasons why they finally rejected the policies espoused in that essay gives an insight into the political strategy Bute and George developed during the 1750s for governing Britain.

I

The prince began "On Industry in Great Britain" by referring to general principles. "The number of inhabitants, and particularly of laboring people, provided they are employed," he asserted, "is the real wealth and strength of a state." On the other hand, "an idle and debauched populace [is] one of the greatest grievances a commercial state can labor under." Such an unproductive populace diminished a state's commerce, and "without commerce, no country can grow rich. What is worse," a country without commerce "can never be secure against the encroachments of ambitious neighbors." And, as George recognized, the fact that Britain was an island would not preserve her security should she lose her trade. "An island without foreign commerce," he pointed out, "can have but an indifferent navy, [and] consequently cannot protect itself."

Having established to his satisfaction the premier importance of productive laborers to commerce, and of commerce to the state, the prince briefly sketched the development of manufacturing in Europe and in England. In his account, he emphasized two factors. One was the decisions governments made about trade and manufacturing, for the prince was certain that intelligent political leadership could overcome many obstacles. The other was the national characters of the various peoples of Europe. "Queen Elizabeth," for example, "with the assistance of able ministers and the wisdom of Parliament, carried the superiority of both [commerce and manufacturing] to an amazing height." Among other decisions, the encouragement they gave to highly skilled, "naturally industrious" Flemish workers to immigrate to England helped make English manufacturers "the best and most perfect in Europe." As the trade in these goods flourished, the navy "soon became the terror of the world." But when the quality of English leadership declined, the Dutch and the French began to enjoy the advantage in trade. In part, this was due to wise decisions in those countries, but it owed even more to the fact that "the French and Dutch are more sober, frugal, and industrious than the English." In the prince's opinion, an understanding of this difference in national character was crucial to any grasp of the success and failure in a nation's commerce, and central to any plans for meaningful change.

George's commitment to this concept may be clearly seen in his explanation of why France, "by underselling the English, have got the greatest part of [the] Turkish, Italian, and Spanish trades." As he noted, "Malachy Postlethwayt gives the national debt, and the continuation of taxes, as the cause of this."[5] "Perhaps he may be right in part," the prince conceded, "but undoubtedly the national debt is not the principal source of the high price of labor." Rather, that was "the general disposition of the manufacturers to idleness and debauchery." What caused the general disposition to idleness? Because the number of laborers in Britain was relatively small compared to other countries, and because they could be confident of finding employment whenever they wanted it, they could choose when, how much, and how efficiently they worked. What they decided depended on the price of basic necessities. "When provisions are cheap," according to the prince, "they work less. When they are dear, they work better and more constantly, [and] therefore their work is cheaper." But the poor were not merely idle, they were also debauched by a taste for things beyond their station in life, the result of "the manner of living" they enjoyed in Britain. "If the poor will give up superfluities, and pay taxes only on their necessaries," the prince calculated that their taxes "will not amount to a thirty-sixth part of what they earn." In contrast, the Dutch paid six times more in taxes on necessities. Thus it did not surprise George to learn that "the necessaries the poor ought to consume are not dearer in England than in France and Holland." The crucial difference was not taxes, but habits of consumption. "When wheat is very dear, the French poor eat but little bread and content themselves with roots, while our manufacturers cry out they are starving unless they can eat the finest bread in as great quantities as when wheat is very cheap." This "indulgence in unnecessary things" was not confined to the finest bread, either. The prince believed the taste for luxuries "is carried to a very extraordinary height in this kingdom, for the manufacturing populace consume brandy, gin, tea, sugar, foreign fruit, strong beer, printed linens, snuff, tobacco, etc." While they had "these superfluities," George concluded, "no one can think the price of labor too low." He pointed to the example of "one little manufacturing town in the west of England, of about 3,000 inhabitants, [where] excise [duties are] paid for 2,000 hogshead on strong beer, beside what is spent in spirituous liquors." To the prince, this was "a strong proof of exorbitant wages." Moreover, there was other proof that "our manufacturing poor instead of being the strength and riches of the state, have become a burden to it." Presumably because many were unwilling to work, "the poor rate [has] increased within the last century from £700,000 to £2,500,000 *per annum*." But even more to the point, the relative scarcity of productive labor enabled those who did work to command higher wages and thus both to feed and to stimulate further their extraordinary appetite for luxuries. Thus the high cost of labor in Britain, though affected to a certain extent by taxes, was in fact largely due to the scarcity of labor and to the way of life of the poor there. Lowering the cost of labor would therefore require more than lowering taxes.

According to the prince, one course of action in particular would both increase the numbers of the laboring poor and improve their moral and economic behavior. Borrowing from Elizabeth's example, he argued that "the most expeditious means of increasing the number of people, of keeping down the price of labor, of enforcing industry, and of improving our manufacturers, is by a general naturalization" of foreign Protestants. By "general naturalization" George meant permitting foreigners to become subjects merely by swearing the appropriate oaths to the government and taking communion in any Protestant church, rather than restricting naturalization to each individual immigrant who had the time, money, and connections to obtain a private Act of Parliament Removing this restriction would, he was sure, encourage many foreign Protestants to immigrant to Britain.[6] These people, who were accustomed to hard work, low wages, and a less luxurious manner of living, would by their numbers and industriousness compel native Britons to work harder and cheaper. Thus "the gentry, the clergy, and the farmers would be benefited by the improvement of their lands." English manufactured goods "would be improved and rendered cheaper, which would increase foreign trade," which in turn would increase "the number of ships and sailors thus employed [which are] the means of a large navy." A general naturalization would also, the prince predicted, induce "many rich men," already attracted by "the excellence or our constitution," to settle in Britain, and by their wealth improve the resources of the nation.

But as obvious as the benefits of a general naturalization law were to the prince, he was well aware that others "violently opposed" it. So he proposed, "if this remedy cannot be adopted, the example of the Dutch ought to be followed," and laborers compelled "to work moderately six days in the week. This would," George believed, "be equal to an increase of one-third of [the] manufacturing people, [and] some think it would amount to above twenty millions' more *per annum* in commodities than are now produced." He advised supplementing this policy by using "every means . . . to oblige the poor [were not working] to work six days in the week," which would produce "an addition of ten millions' worth of commodities *per annum*." He concluded by insisting that without a general naturalization, "the only method of preventing the French and Dutch from underselling us is to establish a good policy by which the poor would be kept to work, and less given to luxury, idleness, and debauchery." George was not sanguine about the ease with which establishing that good policy could be achieved. As he commented, "Making laws to answer this object [is] difficult." Still, he obviously felt that the benefits of success would justify the effort.

After making these bold proposals for lowering the price of labor, the prince ended "On Industry in Great Britain" in a less controversial fashion, by listing nine "general commercial maxims [which] are invariable unless from a great change of circumstances." Most of these stressed the interdependence of the commercial and landed interest, and the crucial importance of maintaining a favorable balance of trade, both with foreign nations and with colonies. Unsurprisingly, he noted that "the prosperity of our trade depends very much on the encouragement given to our manufactures, or laws made relative thereto." It also, he observed, "depends upon the judicious manner of laying and collecting our taxes, and upon the ease, readiness, freedom and cheapness of exportation." This observation did not contradict his basic position in the essay. He had not insisted that taxation played no role in establishing wages; rather he argued it was a comparatively less important factor. George concluded his list with this maxim: "the prosperity, strength, riches, and even the well-being of this kingdom depends on our being able to sell our native produce and manufactures as cheap, and as good in quality, in foreign markets as any other commercial state." No doubt the prince's acknowledgement of this truth strengthened his conviction that the cost of labor had to be lowered, either by a general naturalization or by a stricter regulation of laboring people.

II

The source for the prince's ideas and reforms in "On Industry in Great Britain" is obvious. All of the ideas expressed in this essay—the stinging critique of the "manner of living" of Britain's manufacturers, the effect of their habits on the price of labor, the insistence that that cost must be lowered or trade would suffer, the unfavorable comparison of English with European laborers, the citation of examples from the Tudor era, the various advantages of encouraging immigration, and the plans for compelling the poor to work more regularly and constantly—had been used by those who favored a general naturalization in Parliament and in pamphlets for many years.[7] In particular, "On Industry in Great Britain" bears the marks of its author's familiarity with the arguments and proposals of one of the ablest and most outspoken proponents of that policy, Josiah Tucker.[8] These ideas were not, of course, original with either Tucker or other supporters of relaxing the laws governing naturalization. During the seventeenth and the first half of the eighteenth centuries, most who theorized about the economic roles of the poor posited a direct relationship between the cost of labor and the volume of trade, stressed the necessity of providing regular, constant employment for the poor and requiring them to work, and enlivened their arguments with "frequent blasts against 'idleness.'"[9] Those who favored a general naturalization adopted these doctrines enthusiastically. They justified encouraging immigration by referring to them as undeniable descriptions of present reality and irrefutable prescriptions for future policy. As they did so, they ignored or discounted the ideas of men such as Daniel Defoe, who had questioned the prevailing views by arguing instead that high wages did not necessarily hinder productivity or stagnate trade, and that idleness was often the result of an absence of incentives for laborers.[10] Even Tucker, whose subtle and powerful mind was attracted by the objections Defoe and, later, David Hume raised against the assumption that a growing trade required low wages, submerged his interest in their arguments whenever he advocated a general naturalization.[11] Thus the prince and Bute were left unexposed to any views which challenged the orthodoxies of the seventeenth and early eighteenth centuries' economic thought when they read tracts espousing that policy.

Unquestionably, when George wrote "On Industry in Great Britain," he and his tutor were convinced by Tucker's arguments, and persuaded of the wisdom of his solutions. Bute did not design his assignments merely to acquaint his pupil with the various positions on public issues. Rather, the aim of his pedagogy was to teach the prince whatever Bute believed was the correct position. What cannot be known with certainty is which argument, or consideration, moved first the tutor, then the student, to champion the cause of a general naturalization. Probably its supporters' emphasis on the moral shortcomings of the poor played an important part in that decision. Bute referred to the people of Britain as "prostituted" in 1756, and added that they did not have "as strong an aversion to vice, corruption, and arbitrary power" as the young prince. The future king, he averred, would have to bring liberty and virtue to them.[12] George accepted his mission willingly, vowing to Bute that he would not accept the throne unless he could reasonably hope to make Britain "again famous for being the residence of true piety and virtue."[13] To men convinced that Britons were not virtuous enough, and committed to replacing vice with virtue, an argument that stressed the economic significance of "the general disposition of the manufacturers to idleness and debauchery" must have seemed persuasive, and remedies that promised to change that disposition equally so.

Whatever the reasons why arguments in favor of a general naturalization and policing the activities of the poor at and away from work impressed Bute and the prince, certainly they were not blind to the unpopularity of these policies and the political difficulties of implementing them. Removing restrictions on naturalization had been "violently opposed," as George noted, and successfully as well. Despite the full support of the Whig oligarchy and the ministries of the day, naturalization bills failed in the House of Commons in 1746, 1747, 1748, and 1751. Opponents of those measures argued that the true cause of high wages was high taxes on the necessities of the poor, predicted that a general naturalization would tempt only "some inconsiderate foreigners, especially Germans . . . not celebrated either for their sobriety or abstemiousness," and concluded that the policy would enrage the people without producing the desired effect.[14] These points were as popular in the country as in the House. In 1751, a Bristol crowd celebrated the defeat of a naturalization bill by burning an effigy of Josiah Tucker.[15] Three years later, after the repeal of the Jewish Naturalization Act of 1753, another crowd in the same city chanted during the parliamentary elections, "No general naturalization! No Jews! No French bottle-makers! No lowering wages of laboring men to 4d. a day and garlic!"[16]

Comparing the reactions of Tucker and Bute to these events is instructive. Popular and parliamentary opposition to his theories and proposals did not keep Tucker from continuing to espouse both a general naturalization and a stricter regulation of the poor. It did, however, cause him to reconsider his role as an instructor to the prince. The bishop of Norwich, who served as preceptor to the prince from 1751 to 1753, had asked Tucker "to put into the hands of his royal pupil such a treatise as would convey both clear and comprehensive ideas on the subject of natural commerce," and be free from "the narrow conceptions of ignorant or the sinister views of crafty and designing men." Tucker began to work "with all imaginable alacrity," but never completed the treatise. The furious opposition to his ideas by "the herd of mock patriots" in Parliament and by the people, inflamed "by misrepresentations and false alarms," convinced him that publishing such a work under the royal patronage "might disserve [the prince] in the eyes of others," because "of the many jealousies to which it was liable and the cavils which might be raised against it."[17] To be sure, neither Bute nor George anticipated publishing "On Industry in Great Britain." Still, nothing in that essay reveals any apprehensions about the effect of the identification of the prince with Tucker's analysis of and remedies for the high price of labor on his subjects' attitudes toward him. Nor is there any hint that the widespread opposition to these ideas should deter the prince from encouraging another attempt to relax restrictions on naturalization and, if that again failed, from trying to compel the people to lead more industrious and less luxurious lives. The point of "On Industry in Great Britain" is clear: the new king should advocate these reforms, despite their unpopularity. Such was the position of Bute and the prince in 1757.

III

It was not their position for long. In every other essay he wrote before succeeding to the throne that touched on the cost of labor in Britain, beginning with "On methods to be used in writing a history of revenues and taxes after the Revolution" in 1758, George stressed that the remedy for high wages was lowering taxes on the necessities of the poor. He never again argued in favor of a general naturalization of Protestants or a stricter regulation of the poor. The explanations he used to justify the wisdom of reducing taxes disclose why he and Bute came to endorse a policy they had regarded as essentially ineffectual in 1757.

Just as they had done when the prince wrote "On Industry in Great Britain," the two men appropriated basic arguments and conclusions from other sources, in this case from prevailing contemporary views on taxes and their effects. Since the excise crisis of the early 1730s, the opposition viewpoint of that era that taxes on necessities were harmful to the poor and to trade, had become an axiom of taxation policy. Proponents of that orthodoxy emphasized in their arguments that these duties inevitably and quickly raised wages and thus increased prices of manufactured goods.[19] Bute and George, who had earlier been impressed by the questions Tucker raised about this portrayal of the relationship between taxes and wages, now referred to that relationship as an undeniable fact of economic life. Significantly, however, the two men went beyond this justification for lowering taxes. They added to it an argument that was uniquely their own, one which they believed to be more compelling than compassionate, fiscal, or commercial considerations. "Of more importance than all the rest, these [taxes on necessities] gave a rigid and oppressive air to government, which becomes odious from the minute it appears to be so."[20] Since the composition of "Industry in Great Britain," Bute and the prince had become concerned with popular appearances, perceptions, and opinions. They had concluded that if the new king's subjects perceived him and his government to be oppressive, they would detest the monarch and his ministers. This concern was one reason why the two men worried during the summer of 1758 about the ability of their ally, William Pitt, to resist pressure to send British troops to Germany. "If this unhappy measure should be taken," the prince predicted, "we shall be drawn deeper in a continent war than ever." Because he believed continental involvement was as unpopular with his subjects as it was at Leicester House, he feared that Pitt's implication in such a policy would mean "when I mount the throne, I shall not be able to form a ministry who can have the opinion of the people."[21] That same concern with popular opinion explained his *volte-face* on the primary cause of and best remedy for the high cost of labor in Britain. Had Bute and the prince been persuaded by purely intellectual arguments that "On Industry in Great Britain" was incorrect, the prince would have written an essay similar to it in form and subject, exposing how those doctrines misrepresented and misinterpreted reality. No such essay has been found. Political reality, as they saw it, not intellectual reconsideration, convinced them to elevate the reduction of taxes to a much more important role than George assigned it in 1757, and to discard his earlier recommendations.[22] The two men had realized that the prince could not espouse a general naturalization or a regulation of the lives of the poor without forfeiting the good opinion of his people. That was a price they were unwilling to pay.

Why not? Bute and George wanted to win and retain the affections of the people because they had come to believe that "the nation's confidence [and] the people's love" would be necessary both to preserve Britain's place in the world and to accomplish the political, fiscal, and moral reforms they thought should be made.[23] This belief can only have been strengthened by George's growing disenchantment during 1758 with politicians in general—all of whom he felt were greatly deficient to Bute in integrity and ability—and with "the great orator" Pitt in particular, who by late 1758 was acting an "infamous and ungrateful part."[24] In contrast, the prince's opinions of his subjects improved as time passed. Not only did he never repeat the unfavorable comparison he made between them and European laborers in "On Industry in Great Britain," but he even criticized "the odious doctrine that the poor were mere beasts of burdens and should be treated accordingly, as in France and Holland; that the harder they labored and the less they received, the less time and money they would have to idle away, and the more governable they would be found." The "nobler" position, according to him, recognized the differences between Britons and "continental slaves." Moreover, he concluded that "in subduing the ill qualities of the poor, we might subdue their good ones too; and that if once tamed to the degree desired at home, they might become in the same degree spiritless and unserviceable abroad."[25] With these words, the prince implicitly rejected one of the reforms he proposed in "On Industry in Great Britain." He still wanted to restore virtue in his kingdom, but he now believed that the prerequisite for this was not the regulation of the poor, but winning the people's confidence and support. To accomplish that goal, Bute and he started to consider how to make him a popular monarch, beginning with his first official remarks as George III.[26]

IV

What, then, is the historical significance of "On Industry in Great Britain?" If it resulted in nothing, not even another essay on the subject, should it be regarded only as interesting juvenilia, an exception that proves the rule? I think not. That Bute and the prince would even temporarily endorse policies that had been violently opposed and would be difficult to implement reveals their genuine concern about the future of British trade and manufacturing, and their firm conviction that measures had to be taken to lower the high cost of labor. Moreover, the reason why this essay was unique is significant in itself. The ending of harsh criticism of the poor, and the discarding of thoughts about supporting legislation providing for a general naturalization of foreign Protestants and compelling the poor to work harder and lead more virtuous and frugal lives, are important indications of how committed George and Bute became to making sure he would be perceived as the "much-vaunted and long-awaited 'patriot king.'" Scholars have only recently begun to appreciate how carefully George III and Bute worked to make the new king popular during the days immediately after his accession.[27] The abandonment during 1758 of the controversial policies the prince endorsed in "On Industry in Great Britain" in favor of a commitment to the more popular doctrine that reducing or repealing taxes on the necessities of the poor would lower the cost of labor indicates that the two men were preparing to pursue that goal well before October 1760.

*This chapter first appeared in: *Studies in Eighteenth Century Culture* 17 (1987), pp. 159-172.

Endnotes

[1] Bute's pedagogical methods are best described in John Brooke, *King George III* (London: Constable, 1972), pp.107-108. The prince himself commented that he prepared for his essays by reading "the history of the time, journals, debates, political pamphlets, and manuscript collections." On methods to be used in writing a history of revenues and taxes after the Revolution," [1758] Royal Archives, Additional Georgian Manuscripts, 32/1225. (Hereafter manuscripts from this source will be cited as RA, Add.) This essay may be dated by the reference to the current national debt, which corresponds to the debt for 1758. Many of George's essays may be dated by using this method; others can be assigned approximate dates because he wrote his essays on historical periods in chronological order. The 12 essays by him that discuss the cost of labor may be found in RA, Add. 32/259-261, 1087-449, and 1531-696.

[2] "Account of sessions of Parliament and taxes raised during the reign of William and Mary up to 1694," [1759-1760], RA, Add. 32/1403. The prince's convictions that English laborers were paid more than their counterparts in Europe, and that French manufactured goods cost less than British products, were shared by virtually all of his contemporaries. How accurate were these beliefs? Calculating wages and prices for the eighteenth century is extremely difficult, owing to the paucity of data covering extended periods of time and all regions and countries, and to the questionable accuracy of most contemporary statistics. Still, careful analysts of eighteenth-century economies believe that British labor commanded a

higher price, and enjoyed a better standard of living than European workers did. Scholars also have discovered that after 1750 the proportion of British domestic goods sold in Europe declined, and Britons were compelled to make up the differences by seeking and developing markets elsewhere. These historians tend to explain this by referring to European tariffs, rather than to the cheaper labor there. Whatever the explanation, however, it seems clear British manufacturers were being undersold in European markets. Finally, Ralph Davis has convincingly argued that the establishment of linen and silk industries in Britain during the 1700s was the result of the passage of protective tariffs. Without that legislation, British manufacturers would have been unable to compete with French producers of those goods in British markets. In conclusion, contemporary perceptions about wages in Britain and about the prices of manufactured goods there and abroad were most likely correct. See Phyllis Deane, *The First Industrial Revolution* (Cambridge: Cambridge University Press, 1965), pp. 55, 56, 142, 43; Phyllis Deane and W. A. Cole, *British Economic Growth, 1688-1959: Trends and Structures* (Cambridge: Cambridge University Press, 1969), pp.18-22, 82-88; and Ralph Davis, "The Rise of Protection in England, 1689-1786," *Economic History Review*, 2nd. ser., (1966), p. 316.

[3] "On methods to be used in writing a history of revenues and taxes after the Revolution," [1758], RA, Add. 32/1228. For a full discussion of George's ideas about taxation, see chapter VI in this volume.

[4] "On Industry in Great Britain," [1757] RA, Add. 32/259-261. For the date, see note 5. Quotations in section I are from this source.

[5] A comparison of passages in the prince's essay with Malachy Postlethway *Britain's Commercial Interest Explained and Improved*, 2 vols. (London: D. Browne, 1757), , pp. 11-14, 43-51, reveals that he borrowed from it when he wrote "On Industry in Great Britain."

[6] The prince did not define "general naturalization" in: "On Industry in Great Britain," but he clearly used the term in the same way the supporters of a bill for naturalizing foreign Protestants in 1748 did. See "Arguments in support of the bill for naturalizing foreign Protestants," February 4, 1748, in: T. C. Hansard, ed., *The Parliamentary History of England, from the Earliest Period of the Year 1803*, Ser. 1, 41 vols. (London: Longman, 1806-1820), 14, pp. 137-40.

[7] A convenient contemporary source for these arguments is *ibid*. For good surveys of opinion for and against a general naturalization, see: Thomas W. Perry, *Public Opinion, Propaganda, and Politics in Eighteenth-Century England: A Study of the Jew Bill of 1753*, Harvard Historical Monographs 51 (Cambridge, MA., Harvard University Press, 1962), pp. 31-44 and 72-89; and W. George Shelton, *Dean Tucker and Eighteenth-Century Economic and Political Thought* (New York, St. Martin's, 1981), pp.70-87.

[8] Compare "On Industry in Great Britain" with Josiah Tucker, *A Brief Essay on the Advantages and Disadvantages which respectively attend France and Great Britain, with Regard to Trade*, 3rd edition (London, T. Trye, 1753), iv, pp.14, 36-38, 53, 54n, and 65-84.

[9] D. C. Coleman, "Labour in the English Economy of the Seventeenth Century," *Economic History Review*, 2nd. Ser., 8 (1955-56), pp. 280-281. Coleman's essay is usefully elaborated upon in Joyce Oldham Appleby, *Economic Thought and Ideology in Seventeenth-Century England* (Princeton, NJ, Princeton University Press, 1978), pp. 73-98, 129-157. For the period 1700-1750, see: A. W. Coats, "Changing Attitudes to Labour in the Mid-Eighteenth Century," *Economic History Review*, 2nd. Ser., 11(1958-59), pp. 35, 36.

[10] For the views of those who dissented from orthodoxy, see *ibid.*, pp. 35-37; and Richard C. Wiles, "The Theory of Wages in Later English Mercantilism," *Economic History Review*, 2nd. Ser., 21(1968), pp. 113-26.

[11] At times during the 1750s, Tucker argued publicly that "there was no necessary reason why high wages should act as an obstacle to continuous economic expansion." In other pamphlets, however, he urged the reduction of wages, and bitterly criticized English labor's idleness and immorality. Coats, "Changing Attitudes," *Economic History Review*, 2nd. Ser., 11(1958-59), p. 51; see also Wiles, "Theory of Wages," *ibid.*, 21(1968), pp. 124-26. Tucker espoused the latter positions whenever he argued for a general naturalization. When analyzing why he did so, scholars would be best advised to eschew attempts to reconcile Tucker's various positions on wages during the 1750s, and rather remember Coats' wise warning: "In considering the activities of propagandists it is easy to underrate the extent to which established doctrines are adapted or distorted to suit the needs of a particular interest group." A. W. Coats, "Economic Thought and Poor Law Policy in the Eighteenth Century," *ibid.*, 13(1960-61), p. 40.

[12] The earl of Bute to Gilbert Elliot, Aug. 16, 1756, quoted in: James Lee McKelvey, *George III and Lord Bute: The Leicester House Years* (Durham, NC, Duke University Press, 1973), pp. 42-43.

[13] The prince to Bute, [early Jun. 1757?], in: Romney Sedgwick, ed., *Letters from George III to Lord Bute, 1756-1766* (London, Macmillan, 1939), p. 6.

[14] See "Arguments against the bill for naturalizing foreign Protestants," February 4, 1748, Hansard, ed., *Parliamentary History* 14 pp.141-47. The quotation is from page 145.

[15] Shelton, *Dean Tucker*, p. 70

[16] Quoted in: Linda Colley, *In Defiance of Oligarchy The Tory Party, 1714-1760* (Cambridge, Cambridge University Press, 1982), p.155

[17] Josiah Tucker, *Four tracts together with two sermons on political and commercial subjects* (Gloucester R Raikes, 1774), ix-xi

[18] "On methods to be used in writing a history of revenues and taxes after the Revolution," [1758], RA, Add 32/1220-1232.

[19] See William Kennedy, *English Taxation 1640-1799: An Essay on Policy and Opinion* (London G Bell, 1913), pp.104-23. It is difficult to measure to what extent these arguments were correct. Most contemporaries simply assumed the arguments correctly depicted reality, without ever testing their accuracy by looking for an increase in wages and prices after the imposition of a duty on a specific necessity. Among modern scholars, how much taxes on necessities affected trade and industry in eighteenth-century England is a matter of controversy. All would agree, however, that the impact was less immediate and dramatic than eighteenth-century observers believed. For a discussion of the difficulties of determining these effects, see William J. Hausman and John L. Neufeld, "Excise Anatomized the Political Economy of Walpole's 1733 Tax Scheme," *The Journal of European Economic History* 10 (1981) pp. 131-32, 141-43.

[20] "Account of sessions of Parliament and taxes raised during the reign of William and Mary up to 1694," [1759-1760] RA, Add 32/1403.

[21] The prince to Bute, [ca. Jul. 2, 1758], in Sedgwick, ed., *Letters from George III to Bute*, 11.

[22] This decision was more a change in emphasis than a change of opinion. In "On Industry in Great Britain," the prince had acknowledged that heavy taxes and the tastes and vices of manufacturers both contributed to high wages in Britain. So did Postlethwayt and Tucker. The former supported a more liberal naturalization policy; the latter was certain "our trade is greatly burdened by the *nature* of *most of our taxes, and the manner of collecting them.*"(Postlethwayt, *Britain's Commercial interest*, 2. pp. 532-33; Tucker, *Brief Essay*, p. 38). What divided opinion in the pages of pamphlets and essays was which was the more important. In the political world, one of the options had been foreclosed.

[23] The prince's essay on the British political system, quoted in Brooke, *George III*, pp. 121-22

[24] The prince to Bute, [ca. Jul. 2, 1758], [December ?, 1758], and [Dec. ?, 1758], in Sedgwick, ed., *Letters From George III to Bute*, pp.11 and 17-19.

[25] "Account of sessions of Parliament and taxes raised during the reign of William and Mary up to 1694," [1759-1760] RA, Add. 32/1409. As Coats noted in "Changing Attitudes," *Economic History Review*, 2nd Ser., 11(1958-59): pp. 35-51, from the 1750s to the publication of *The Wealth of Nations*, more sympathetic attitudes toward laborers came to predominate in economic thought. Particularly toward the end of that period, theorists began to argue that depressing wages

would encourage idleness, because the laborer would have no incentive to work. Higher wages, conversely, would stimulate him to greater productivity. Moreover, they asserted that the English worker's taste for luxuries (redefined in their writings as "comforts" and "conveniences") would operate as a powerful and beneficial incentive as well. The prince certainly became more sympathetic to laborers in his later essays, but there are no indications in them that he did so because of these, or any, economic considerations. On the crucial question of the level of wages, George continued to advocate keeping it as low as possible. Political motives, not new theories about economic activity, explained his change of heart.

[26] See Earl Fitzmaurice, *Life of William, Earl of Shelburne, Afterwards First Marquess of Landsdowne*, 2 vols. (London: Macmillan, 1912), 1, p. 33.

[27] See John Brewer, *Party Ideology and Popular Politics at the Accession of George III* (Cambridge: Cambridge University Press, 1976), pp. 47-48 and 101-102; the quotation is from 101.

Chapter VI

"To know this is the True Essential Business of a King": The Prince of Wales and the Study of Public Finance, 1755-1760*

By the middle of the eighteenth century, the growth of the national debt, the burden of the taxes necessary to support it, and the effect of this system of public finance on the politics, economy, and society of Britain, deeply concerned politicians in opposition.[1] Their frequent expressions of concern were sufficiently persuasive to induce similar apprehensions on occasion in politicians at court. In 1753, when the national debt was a little over £74,000,000, earl Waldegrave, a personal favorite of George II, felt compelled to tell the House of Lords about a "consideration of very great importance, . . . the state of our national debt [the heavy taxes which are the consequences of this debt." The situation required, he went on, "prudent measures of government, with that strict national economy which must be our only remedy." Waldegrave did not go so far as to believe the nation was on the verge of collapse. As he pointed out, "a country and a government like ours has so many and so great resources that we may bear a great deal and still be in a flourishing condition. Yet as long as this evil does subsist," he warned the House, "we can never expect fully to exert our proper strength." He concluded, "Till this burden is removed it will remain a check to our trade, will be still heavier on the landed interest, must lessen our credit and influence abroad, and will be a cause of discontent if not of disaffection at home."[2]

The context of Waldegrave's remarks is interesting: the earl was telling the House of Lords how he planned to supervise the education of the Prince of Wales, the future George III, and what he believed the young prince should learn. Although Waldegrave soon despaired of teaching the prince anything "by books," and gave up trying to do more than "to give him true notions of common things, [and] to instruct him by conversation," it seems unlikely he would have neglected to mention a subject he thought was so important for George to know.[3] That the prince absorbed much from any conversation with the earl about the national debt and the burdens of taxation is doubtful, but clearly he did learn and adopt a conclusion very similar to Waldegrave's from the man who succeeded the earl as tutor, and became his confidant and "dearest friend," the earl of Bute. In June 1757, George vowed to Bute that he would only accept the throne if he could reasonably hope to realize two goals. The first was "restoring my much loved country to her ancient state of liberty. Seeing her in time free from her present load of debts and again famous for being the residence of true piety and virtue" was the other.[4]

The fact that the future monarch had expressed a hope that Britain would one day be free from the burden of debt would probably have satisfied Waldegrave. Bute, to his credit, insisted that the prince go further, and study carefully the historical background of the fiscal situation he would have to confront as king. Under his direction, George read histories of England and English finances, studied journals of the House of Commons and accounts revealing the extent of debt and the yields of various taxes, and wrote between 1755 and 1760 a series of essays on subjects relating to public finance.[5] He began the last of these early in 1760, only months before his grandfather's death in October elevated him to the throne. There can be no doubt that the two men took these exercises very seriously indeed. As the prince observed apropos of the study of the history of the nation's financial system and the effects it had on Britain's power and prosperity, "to know this is the true essential business of a king."[6] Moreover, both he and his instructor assumed that Bute should and would become First Lord of the Treasury in the new reign. Whenever the earl thought about "not accepting the Treasury in a future day," the prince stiffened his friend's resolve by reminding him how he saw "with horror . . . the inevitable mischiefs that would arise from your taking such a step to this poor country, and consequently to myself; for I fear I should not only find how differently that board would be managed, but also that you would give me less of that wholesome advice, that alone can enable me to make this great nation happy."[7] As the earl of Shelburne later recalled, Bute "panted for the Treasury, having a notion that the king and he understood it from what they had read about revenue and funds while they were at Kew. He had likewise," Shelburne also remembered, "an idea of great reformations, which all men who read the theory of things, and especially men who look up at being ministers, and want to remove and lower those that are, make a great part of their conversation."[8] The essays the prince wrote while under Bute's tutelage give historians a unique opportunity to study the ideas the two men had about public finance, and what thoughts they had about the possibilities of reform, before they came to power.

I

The prince's study of the origins and progress of the national debt confirmed the belief he expressed in June 1757, that one day freeing the nation from this burden would be highly desirable. To George, the beginnings of the debt during the reign of William and Mary owed more to the weaknesses and corruption of politicians and their calculated and pernicious aims than to any necessity of financing a just war by this means. The government at that time, he asserted, could have raised the money needed to pay for the war against Louis XIV by increasing taxation, but instead chose a method that would "tempt. . . individuals to live and die without the least regard to posterity, a way of thinking," he added, "now become fatally prevalent."[9] The surrender of Parliament to this temptation was analogous to the thoughtlessness of "a young spendthrift who eagerly compounds for a present convenience at the expense of any future encumbrance, however burdensome or reproachful."[10] The motives of William III and his ministers, however, were less thoughtless than calculated. According to the future king, his predecessor was compelled by his difficulties with France to come each year to Parliament "with much to ask, and much to conceal."[11] William had involved England in the war on the European continent, and this involvement, according to the prince, offered the first proof supporting an axiom he accepted as true: "Ruin and distress approach in proportion as opposition slackens to foreign expense and continental measures."[12] The king and his ministers anticipated that opposition would most likely be inspired by the expense of that involvement, for "it demanded great sums annually." Thus "the fear of alarming the people by raising all the money necessary for the current service within the year produced a plan the most opposite to the true interest of this country that ever entered into the heart of man." This plan was "that of anticipating the revenue by borrowing immense sums to supply the yearly services of the state, and to lay no more taxes upon the subject than what would suffice to pay the annual interest of the money borrowed." George concluded, "Here then, is the melancholy foundation of what is called the national debt."[13]

Founded to support a policy harmful to the national interest by tempting the politicians and the people to postpone paying for it, the debt continued to grow as British governments continued to pursue continental measures. Moreover, those governments first discovered, then continually used a method to help pay for it by supplementing tax receipts in a way that further corrupted the people. The first lottery was instituted by Parliament in 1694, and the experiment proved successful enough to be continued ever since.[14] According to the prince, the lottery of 1694 was "a most pernicious precedent, too often made use of since, as it serves not only to excite, but even to authorize, a spirit of gaming in every man who is able to raise a few pounds, though perhaps at the expense of his morals, credit, and character." Lotteries also had the harmful effects of "rendering the poor impatient of labor and the tradesman dissatisfied with moderate profits, [and of] possessing the rich with the rage of accumulating." Finally, George sourly observed, they encouraged the people, as well as the state, to live beyond their income.[15]

The prince was aware that Parliament had, in 1717, made a serious attempt to arrange for paying off the debt. In that year, "the surpluses . . . of the aggregate, general, and South Sea funds that remains after paying their respective interests and annuities [were] by the 3d Geo. I, c.7, brought together and called the Sinking Fund, because [it was] originally destined to sink the national debt." This fund generally produced about £2,000,000 per year which could be applied to the principal of the debt and, as George pointed out, "upon this depends all our hopes of being ever free from debt. Moreover," he observed, "this can alone furnish us with future supplies on any sudden emergency, which makes the application of the money arising from this fund a point of the utmost importance." As time passed, however, the money generated by the fund was "applied often . . . to very different purposes" than its original one. Indeed, at the present time, "the sinking fund is in the first place applied to the making up [of] deficiencies arising in other funds; secondly, it is usual to make up from thence [deficiencies in] the supplies of the current year; lastly it is applied to its original purpose of discharging by degrees the public debt."[16] Under the present system, the fund intended to retire the national debt was no longer used exclusively, or even chiefly, to achieve that goal.

The prince knew that some defended the expansion of public credit by pointing to "the large fortunes possessed by individuals, and the quantity of money in the funds." To him, though, all this is far from being real. "This money," he noted, "exists in name, in paper, in parliamentary security; amply sufficient indeed for the creditors of the public, but what is the pledge given for that security?" The answer was "the land, trade, and personal industry of the subject, from whence the produce of the product of the several taxes arise. In these, then, and these only subsist the property of the public creditor," concluded the prince, "and," he then observed, "these diminish in their value in proportion to the mortgages upon them." The "great accession of wealth and fortune in this kingdom, and the immense riches of the public funds . . .," therefore, "are in truth nothing more than the riches of one or more individuals transferred to another, without the least accession to the public." Even the man "thus grown immensely opulent at the expense of some of his fellow citizens" did not benefit as much as he thought. "Heavy taxes must be imposed by the public to pay the interest of the debt owing him; he not only must bear his proportion of these taxes, but must also suffer a great diminution of income by the enhanced price of every commodity." Upon the whole," the prince summed up his findings, "the property of a public credit consists in a certain proportion of national taxes, and whatever increase of riches he has by them, by so much are those of the public lessened. No advantage therefore accrues to a nation by public debts, on the contrary many disadvantages."[17]

Under Bute's direction George's studies of the history and development of "the enormous debt the nation labors under" and of "this intricate system" of public finance resulted in the prince's concluding that both were immensely harmful to Britain.[18] Posterity's prosperity was mortgaged to maintain an ill-advised and pernicious continental involvement; the system for retiring the debt had been diverted from its original purpose; the management of the debt encouraged bad habits of personal industry and finance (*vide* the lottery), and far from generating new wealth for the nation, diminished its present resources. The prince was not ignorant of other versions of the history of public finance that reached different conclusions. For instance, he read White Kennet's defense of the court Whigs and Bishop Burnet's *History of My Own Time* before he prepared his essays on finance during the reign of William and Mary.[19] He could hardly have been unaware of how speculation in the public funds operated to assist in raising money in the short term for government: that sort of information was readily available in not only certain histories, but, among other places, the pocket appointment books sold for gentlemen's and ladies' convenience.[20] Instead, George and his tutor consciously rejected favorable interpretations of the national debt and methods of financing it. As a result, the doctrines expressed in the prince's essays seem to be strongly influenced by the arguments parliamentary oppositions had made against the various Whig governments since the 1690s. Indeed, many of his opinions about fiscal decisions made during the 1690s were in general agreement with those of prominent members of the proscribed Tory party. Sir Roger Newdigate, for example, believed that the Whigs, "the boasted friends of civil liberty" had oppressed "the people with taxes unknown under the Stuarts," and by creating a moneyed interest that was inimical to the landed interest, were "zealous to support tyranny in King William which they abhorred under Charles and James."[21] John Brewer has pointed out that insofar as George III's readiness to deny the reality of party distinctions and to trumpet the necessity of royal independence was concerned, he differed from George II by being "a 'country' Whig."[22] The essays the prince wrote on public finance before 1760 also reveal his and Bute's predilection for country ideas.

Some of George's most critical words about the system of public credit were written before or during 1758, when the national debt was £77,780,386, and Britain's prospects in the war seemed, if no longer dark, at least still dim. In 1759 and 1760, the nation's army and navy went from victory to victory, while the national debt rose steadily, from £82,776,589 on January 5, 1759, to £90,365,586 on January 11, 1760. It was also clear that by January 1761, the debt would increase by another £8,240,000.[23] One might expect that the growth of the debt would, if anything, sharpen the prince's criticism of Britain's financial system. But in 1760, despite the dramatic growth of the debt, with no end in sight, and as the time of the prince's accession to the throne was obviously closer, his and Bute's attitudes toward the immediate usefulness of public credit began to resemble the court's view more than the country's. In the essay he wrote in 1760 on the last years of William III's reign, the prince noted "what great things could be done by public credit," and then closed a reference to England's victories under the duke of Marlborough by observing, "We have seen the effects of this mighty engine, [even though it was] at no time supposed to exceed fourteen millions." Then he commented that one could see the same effects "even in our present melancholy circumstances, when we can scarce expect a peace before we have increased our debt to £130 or £140,000,000." Even now, "we may still derive some consolation from this great national strength, even against Sir Robert Walpole's suggestion, who affirmed national bankruptcy to be the consequences of our debt arising to £100,000,000."[24] George did not explain the reason why he now focused on the debt's benefits, but it is obvious. As in William's time, a triumphant war was being fueled by public credit. Moreover, Bute and the prince had weighed the advantages of stopping the debt's increase against the disadvantages of giving up conquests by making a precipitate peace. They sensibly decided in favor of continuing the borrowing to preserve and, if possible, increase the fruits of victory. Since the other choice would have been political disaster for a new king, no doubt their decision was easy to make.[25] Still, they remained determined to lighten the burdens on posterity as much as they could, and as soon as they dared.

II

"Every thing except the water and the air," an anonymous adviser complained to Bute in 1759, "is . . . in consequence [of the national debt] severely taxed." He exhorted Bute to teach the Prince of Wales about the dangers of this, particularly to "our mercantile interest, clogged as it is by taxes" which raised the price of materials and cost of labor, and thus made British goods less competitive in foreign markets. The prince had to be aware that when he came to the throne, he would have to take measures both to improve the mercantile interest and to govern with "extreme frugality," because "he will find the kingdom poorer, and more exposed, than he will find any example in history that it has been before his time."[26] This advice must have pleased Bute, for he had already begun teaching these lessons to the future George III. Those lessons, however, were of comparatively recent origin.

The prince had reached a strikingly different conclusion about the threat posed to British trade and manufacturing in "On Industry in Great Britain."[27] In this essay, the prince observed that "France is our most dangerous rival in trade... [and] by underselling the English have got the greatest part of Turkish, Italian, and Spanish trades." What explained this? In his volumes on British commerce, Malachy Postlethwayt gave "the national debt, and the continuation of taxes as the cause."[28] George conceded that "perhaps he may be right in part," but then argued, "undoubtedly the national debt is not the principal source of the high price of labor." That was caused by "the general disposition of the manufacturers to idleness and debauchery." Because labor was scarce in Britain, manufacturers could indulge their taste for these vices. "When provisions are cheap," the prince explained, "they work less; when dear, they work better and more constantly, therefore their work is cheaper." Furthermore, English manufacturers did not merely indulge their fondness for idleness at every opportunity. They also had a taste for luxuries that their French and Dutch counterparts did not share. According to George, the necessities that the poor should have consumed were not more expensive in Britain than in France or Holland. But on the continent, the poor reacted to increases in the price of wheat by eating "but little bread" and contenting themselves "with roots." The British poor, in contrast, claimed they were starving unless they could eat the finest bread in as great quantities as when wheat is very cheap. "The difference therefore," he concluded, "lies in the manner of living." More proof of the "very extraordinary height" luxury was carried to in Britain could be found in the taste of the manufacturing population for brandy, gin, tea, sugar, foreign fruit, strong beer, printed linens, snuff, tobacco, etc. "While they can have these superfluities," the prince argued, "no one can think, the price of labor too low." He then pointed to a small manufacturing town of about 3,000 population in the West Country that annually paid excise taxes on 2,000 hogsheads of strong beer, "besides what is spent [on] spirituous liquors, a strong proof of exorbitant wages." To the future king, "our manufacturing poor, instead of being the strength and the riches of the state, are become a burden to it," a burden best described by the growth of the poor rates over the last century from £700,000 to £2,500,000 a year.

Lowering taxes would obviously not solve the popular fondness for idleness and indulgence. Moreover, taxes on the necessaries of life seemed already low to the prince. He believed the Dutch paid "six times as much [in those taxes] as our poor are obliged to do. If the poor will give up superfluities," he continued, "and pay taxes only on their necessaries, they will not amount to a thirty-sixth part of what they earn." George evidently did not dismiss the idea of lowering taxes as completely pointless. Indeed, he noted in "On Industry in Great Britain" that "the prosperity of our trade depends upon the judicious manner of laying and collecting our taxes." But he emphasized in that essay the wisdom of taking other courses of action. He argued that relaxing the naturalization laws would be "the most expeditious means of increasing the number of people, of keeping down the price of labor, of enforcing industry, and of improving our manufactures." He also recognized, however, that "this idea [had] been violently opposed" in the past, and might not be easily adopted in the future. If naturalization proved to be too politically unpopular, he suggested that "the example of the Dutch ought to be followed;" that is, "oblige the laborers to work moderately six days in the week. This," the prince calculated, "would be equal to an increase of one-third of manufacturing people, [and] some think it would amount to above 20 millions more per annum in commodities, than now are produced." He also recommended that "every means should be employed to oblige the [non-working] poor to work six days in the week." This, he guessed, would increase Britain's production by another 10 million pounds' worth of goods a year. As production increased, the price of British goods would decrease. But if these reforms were not made, foreign manufactured goods would continue to enjoy a competitive advantage. "The only method," George argued, "of preventing the French and Dutch from underselling us is to establish a good police by which the poor would be kept to work, and less given up to luxury, idleness, and debauchery." He did admit, however, "the making laws to answer this objective are difficult."

The prince did not reveal the sources for the doctrines he expounded in "On Industry in Great Britain." Still, there are obvious clues to the provenance of his opinions. The supporters of general naturalization bills frequently argued that they were necessary because they would "not only teach our lower sort of people to be more frugal and parsimonious, but [also] render it necessary for them to be so." Because foreigners "have been bred up to a harder way of living than is usual among such sort of people in this country, their spare way of living would enable them to work for less wages, and this would necessarily in a short time reduce the . . . wages even of our own people, in all those branches of manufacture, where the wages . . . are higher here than among our rivals the French."[29] Thus the prince surely learned his lessons about "the general disposition of the manufacturers to idleness and debauchery" and the wisdom of general naturalization from the proponents of that policy. One of those advocates may have been Dr. Thomas Hayter, the bishop of Norwich and the preceptor of the prince from 1751-1753, who must have been an enthusiastic supporter of naturalization. Had he not been so, he would not have commissioned one of its ablest and most outspoken defenders, Josiah Tucker, to write "a treatise as would convey [to the prince] both clear and comprehensive ideas on the subject of national commerce, freed from the narrow conceptions of ignorant [men] or the sinister views of crafty and designing men."[30] Perhaps Hayter anticipated the completion of this work by discussing Tucker's ideas with the prince, and the stinging critique Tucker made of the morals and work habits of British manufacturers and the poor struck a responsive chord in a young man who paid, as Waldegrave later observed, "rather too much attention to the sins of his neighbors."[31] Certainly the prince never read Tucker's projected *magnum opus*, for the good reason that he stopped writing it soon after he began. As Tucker later explained, his analysis and proposals were so unpopular that publishing them under the royal patronage would do a disservice to the prince himself.[32]

Though there is no direct evidence on this point, Bute and the prince must have dropped any idea of advocating a general naturalization of foreign Protestants for the same reason. Certainly the two men knew that it had been "violently" and successfully opposed when the parliamentary opposition had defeated the government's bills liberalizing naturalization in 1746-1747, 1748, and 1751, and succeeded in compelling the repeal of the Jewish Naturalization Act of 1753.[33] Thus the prince would be committing his prestige against a successful opposition, one that opposed naturalization on principle and enjoyed popular support. Moreover, the men who opposed naturalization also opposed men in government whom the prince despised, and thus he hoped to make them his allies. It is not surprising that George and Bute bowed to these political realities. The prince's advocacy of naturalization was fleeting. Instead, he committed himself in his own essays to an argument that was popular with the opponents of naturalization, that taxes caused the high cost of labor in Britain.

What about George's alternative to a policy of general naturalization, regulating the lives of the poor to compel them to be more industrious and less debauched? To call making such regulations "difficult," as the prince did, was to understate reality. Had he publicly espoused compelling the people to work six days a week, and preventing them from enjoying their usual food, drink, clothes, and pastimes, he would have been widely detested by the people he hoped to govern. Since he vowed in September 1758 that he had "too much love for any countrymen to mount this throne and be their detestation," he and Bute soon realized clearly that attempting to compel the poor to change their lives would end any hope of winning their love.[34] In essays he wrote after "On Industry in Great Britain," he never mentioned again the controversial remedies he favored in that work. He also dropped the sharp criticism of his countryman's "manner of living" that he made in that essay. Instead, he criticized "the odious doctrine" he found in some people during the 1690s "that the poor were mere beasts of burden, and should be treated accordingly, as in France and Holland; that the harder they labored and the less they received, the less time and money they would have to idle away, and the more governable they would be found." The "nobler" position, according to George, recognized that there were differences between Britons and "continental slaves." These nobler attitudes also had the advantage of preserving two of the most useful attributes of the poor: their aggressiveness and patriotism which could be harnessed to the purposes of the state in the army and navy. "In subduing the ill qualities of the poor," warned the prince, "we might subdue their good ones too, and that if once tamed to the degree desired at home, they might become in the same degree spiritless and unserviceable abroad."[35] Just as George began to find the national debt more useful as the time of his accession approached, he also came to appreciate more the martial virtues of his subjects.

As time passed, too, the prince and Bute began to emphasize more the significant effects that taxes had on Britain's trade. In the list of commercial maxims he prepared for "On Industry," George had noted that the prosperity of Britain's trade depended upon laying and collecting the nation's taxes judiciously.[36] He expanded upon this maxim in essays he wrote later, by using historical examples and observations as illustrations of its truth. Unlike some critics of the system of public finance, George was not principally disturbed by the burdens it put directly on the landed interest.[37] Indeed, he argued that even during the session of 1692, when Parliament passed the first modern tax on land, it laid proportionately heavier burdens on trade and manufacturing.[38] Parliament continued to follow this pernicious precedent throughout William's reign, and thus "laid the foundation for the innumerable oppressive taxes under which industry and trade at present groan."[39] The damage these taxes did to industry and trade was not minor; indeed, it was there that the taxes necessary to fund the national debt did their most serious harm to the nation.

Moreover, the prince now believed that the taxes on the necessities of the poor were the most harmful. "Taxes on necessities," the prince wrote in his essay "Account of Sessions of Parliament and Taxes Raised During the Reign of

William and Mary up to 1694," "are in their own nature severe and offensive, for they fall heavy on the poorest of the people, who cannot indemnify themselves but by raising the price of their labor." They were also, he continued, "contrary to sound politics, as the price of manufactures rise with the price of labor." The effect of rising prices on trade was obvious to the prince. Since "the cheapest [goods] at foreign markets are generally preferred to the best," fewer British goods would be sold abroad. Since "our national profits sympathize with our foreign sales," as taxes on the poor's necessities caused a decrease in commerce, they naturally harmed the economy and, ultimately, the power of Great Britain. Serious though the economic consequences could possibly be, they were not the worst result of taxes on necessities. There was a political consequence "of more importance than all the rest." Taxes on necessities, George explained, "give a rigid and oppressive air to government," and government "becomes odious from the minute it appears to be so."[40]

It was the political consequence of taxing necessities that explains why he stopped regarding them as unburdensome and essentially irrelevant to increases in wages and started thinking they either "ought to be removed . . . or reduced to very moderate duty."[41] Other men who reached this conclusion emphasized other considerations to explain their decision. Either they stressed the need to be compassionate toward the poor or they argued that taxes on necessities inevitably and quickly raised the price of manufactured goods, or they combined these two inconsistent points.[42] The prince adopted these arguments, but unlike other thinkers on taxation during this period, he gave primacy of place to the political necessity of opposing taxes on the poor. Bute and he had realized that a new king could not afford to appear "rigid and oppressive." If he did, he would immediately become "odious" to the people. The prince and his tutor intended that George III would be a popular monarch. Part of the price they would have to pay was revising their opinions about the national debt and the reduction of taxes to fit the circumstances of the times. It was a price they were willing to pay, because they believed that only a popular king could effect real changes in Britain.

III

What reforms did Bute and the prince have in mind? Insofar as the present system of public finance was concerned, they did not plan to make any changes that would have immediate and drastic effects. The huge national debt was, as they recognized, a fact of life that could neither be wished away nor speedily retired. They also knew that it would continue to grow rapidly until the war was over. The best that the next king could hope to accomplish immediately was the careful, economical management of the civil list. In the first year of George II's reign, Parliament had granted the king £800,000 for the civil list, the money to be raised from the produce of certain excise and customs duties.[43] Bute and the prince had noticed that these taxes in fact produced enough to yield to George II more than £800,000 a year. Indeed, they discovered in 1760 that the average produce for his reign had been £811,834 *per annum*, and probably also knew that the yearly average for the last decade had been £823,956.[44] Returning the produce of those taxes to the public in return for Parliament's agreeing to grant the king the flat sum of £800,000 a year during his life for the civil list, they decided, would provide both more money for fighting the war and an unmistakable and popular example of the new king's commitment to economy. They also intended to spend the £800,000 in ways that were more obviously efficient than the old king was doing.[45]

Constraints similar to those that restricted their speculation on possibilities for reducing the national debt limited the prince's and Bute's thoughts about reducing taxation. So long as the war went on, preserving the nation's credit by not merely maintaining the present taxes, but finding new sources of revenue, would be imperative. The prince and his tutor might recognize the future desirability of lowering taxes on the necessities of the poor, but they could do nothing in the present to lighten these burdens. Moreover, the two men were aware that even under the most promising of circumstances, reduction of taxes would be very difficult. George noted that the study of public finance might "show where injudicious burdens have been laid upon the necessary materials for manufactures, and thus lead to the necessary alterations that might be made for the salvation of [the] kingdom." But he also observed that reducing these taxes, "from their delicacy of consequence, may perhaps from the natural propensity of the people to discontent, never be put into execution."[46] The prince also believed that it "has been the known interest of ministers to prefer a multiplicity of taxes" in order to provide a multiplicity of jobs to use for their own corrupt purposes, and he might have anticipated that these practitioners of corruption would not readily accept the diminution of the source of their power.[47] Still, this appreciation of the difficulties ahead did not prevent him from considering how best to raise the revenue the state needed without hindering commerce or raising prices to the point that they might increase the cost of British manufactured goods.

Concern about the cost of manufactures led the prince to favor increasing the number of excise taxes. To him, the advantages of this form of taxation could be most clearly seen by comparing it to customs duties. He conceded that "prudently managed" customs duties were "the least felt by the people." The merchant, who paid them at the ports and then added them to his price, and who knew "they do not come out of his pocket, cannot complain; and the consumer is apt to forget the burden by confounding it with the price of the commodity." But customs duties had, in his opinion, two serious weaknesses that undercut that virtue. First, if they were so heavy "that the value of the commodity shall bear too small a proportion to the duty imposed," the results were "many checks upon trade." Moreover, heavy duties encouraged "that pernicious custom of smuggling, to which there had not been any proper remedy adopted." Logically, the remedy to this seems to be to keep duties low, and rely on the increase of trade to supply additional revenue, but the prince apparently was not attracted to this argument, probably because of the other weakness of customs duties. "The earlier any commodity is taxed," he pointed out, "the dearer it comes to any consumer in the end," because, "every trader takes his profit not only upon his own labor, time, and materials, but also upon the tax itself, which the first importer advanced to the government." For example, a merchant who imported paper from Holland, paid the duty and laid "several months out of his money, is entitled to a profit upon the duty so paid," and passed it on to the stationer. Ultimately, "the person in whose library the book is finally deposited, not only pays the original duty, but the profits taken by . . . intermediate traders." As the prince knew, "in a more complicated branch of trade, [this process] might be carried to an amazing increase."[48]

In contrast, an excise tax "is an inland imposition paid either on the retail or consumption of the commodity." Without doubt, the prince concluded, this was "the most economical way of taxing the subject, for the whole charge of levying and managing the excise duties amounts to but 20*d*. in a pound." Moreover, "the commodity comes . . . cheaper to the consumer than it would if charged with the same duty of custom, because it is generally paid [at] a later stage of its progression." Such duties did, however, have their drawback. Because retailers and consumers so frequently tried to defraud the collector of excises, it was necessary to give the government's servants broad powers of search and seizure, and to make trials summary and without benefit of juries. "It must be owned," admitted the prince, "that the extreme harshness and arbitrary proceedings of the excise laws are not the most suited to the spirit of a free people." Indeed, "from its first origin till now the name of an excise man has been odious to the people." The prince recalled that even Sir Robert Walpole, at the height of his power in 1733, had to drop his "favorite scheme," excises on wines and tobacco, because of intense popular opposition. Bute and the prince regarded this development as unfortunate. Walpole's excise on wines was probably impractical, "but as to the tobacco, it is certainly feasible, and would produce a large increase of public revenue." Furthermore, "the method of warehousing [tobacco] now established is a very good preparation towards it."[49] When an excise tax would not fall on a necessity of life, when opinion might be reconciled toward an additional tax by changes in the methods of storing and retailing it, and when the revenue would benefit considerably, the prince and his friend were willing to risk proposing and then imposing such a tax. They also seemed aware that the king would have to take that risk. As the prince observed, there were some necessary changes in taxation "that no minister dare make of himself in points of such immense consequence, and of so delicate a nature."[50] The monarch therefore would have to use the full weight of his authority to encourage his ministers and to support them in making these changes. Then, having accomplished that, he would have to use his authority again to persuade his subjects to accept them.

The analysis Bute and the prince made of the history of the system of public finance in Britain reveals why the two men felt that the proper use of the king's authority was so necessary for the success of fiscal reform. They believed that Britain's fiscal problems were not merely fiscal in nature. Had they been so, they would have been relatively easy to solve, for the fiscal solutions to the problems were obvious and uncomplicated. But in fact the real crisis facing the nation was more moral than it was fiscal. According to the prince's version of events, the national debt had begun as the devious way William III and his advisors avoided serious questions about the cost and the worth of involvement on the European continent. They deliberately designed this disingenuous policy to appeal to "the general bias of the times, [which leaned] strongly to relieving the present the expense of the future," and they chose well, for, as George philosophized, "the world ever produces wrong headed individuals who would rather pay £10 in perpetuity than £4 out of their pockets at once."[51] Moreover, in addition to taking advantage of the politicians' shortsighted and conscienceless disregard of posterity, William and his ministers appealed to their selfishness and cupidity as well. The many taxes they proposed and Parliament passed to pay the interest on the debt burdened trade more than the landed interest, which directly benefited most M.P.s, and created numerous places with salaries, which tempted the politicians with the prospect of personal gain and patronage. As this system of public finance took root and grew, it also tempted and corrupted the people. The lottery legitimized "a spirit of gaming," and openly enticed men of all ranks to play even "at the expense of [their] morals, credit, and character." It likewise undermined virtuous habits of economic life, "rendering the poor impatient of labor and the tradesmen dissatisfied with moderate profits, possessing the rich with the rage of accumulating."[52] The prince did not repeat in later essays his critique in "On Industry in Great Britain" of "the general disposition to idleness and debauchery," but he did point to an equally dangerous development. Heavy customs duties involved people as participants in or supporters of "that pernicious custom of smuggling," and excise taxes elicited so many frauds that extreme powers of search, seizure, and trial were necessary.[53] In both cases, that respect for law and government which was a necessary bulwark of the state was diminished. The weight of taxes on necessaries also engendered disaffection from the government. Finally, in the opinion of Bute and the prince, this system played a crucial role in the corruption of the monarchy itself. By providing the funds needed to support involvement on the continent, the fiscal system catered to the "partiality [George II] has for that horrid Electorate [of Hanover], which has always lived upon the very vitals of this poor country."[54] Thus the duke of Newcastle was always "possessed of a powerful remedy to allay [the king's] passions" and was "sure of carrying every point by satiating his avarice."[55] With this hold over George II, plus the power his control of Treasury patronage gave him in the House of Commons, the duke of Newcastle could, according to the prince, bend the king himself and the power of the crown to his own purposes. In sum, the system of public finance begun in the 1690s pandered successfully to the most selfish, shortsighted, corrupt, and immoral instincts of the monarch, the politicians, and the people. Given this analysis of the history of public finance, it is not surprising that the prince linked together in his vision of the future "seeing

[Britain] in time free from her present load of debts and again famous for being the residence of true piety and virtue."[56]

Because the prince and Bute believed that the national debt and the system of public finance that serviced it were rooted in moral shortcomings and could only flourish in such soil, they concluded that the first, and most essential, step toward fiscal reform had to be moral reformation. That reformation would have to begin with a new king, for only a monarch who had not been ensnared by the past system and renounced it from the beginning of his reign would have the power and prestige necessary to bring about change. So Bute prepared his royal pupil by constantly reminding him that he had to master his own weaknesses, particularly "that incomprehensible indolence, inattention and heedlessness that reigns within [the prince],"[57] He also emphasized that "a prince ought to endeavor in all his thoughts and actions to excel his people in virtue, piety, generosity, and nobility of sentiment," so "when they have occasion to approach him, they may do it with love and veneration, and feel he merits, by his own virtue and not the fickle die of fortune, the vast superiority he enjoys above them."[58] For his part, George vowed "the interest of my country ever shall be my first care; my own inclinations shall ever submit to it. I am born for the happiness or misery of a great nation," he realized, "and consequently must often act contrary to my passions."[59] The example of his mastery of himself, and his commitment to rewarding virtue in others, Bute and the prince expected, would inspire a similar discipline and commitment in others. They also planned that the attraction of this example of virtue would be enhanced by the new king's popularity. They were aware that the prince had "some advantages, which none of his family have had before him," advantages which could make him a far more popular monarch than George I or George II. In particular, he "[was] not a foreigner, but a prince born and bred in the country: which is of some advantage everywhere, and perhaps no place more than here." He was not connected with any faction, so he had not "rendered himself odious to any part of the nation from the [Orkneys] down to the south of

Britain." He also "will have no predilection of any other country, nor any prejudices of foreign policy." These advantages, plus the affection felt for his mother, would "prepare mankind . . . to expect their political salvation from his government."[60] Bute and the prince planned to seize the opportunity offered by these advantages and to effect that salvation. "Let the day once come," George wrote in his essay on the British constitution, "in which the banner of virtue, honor, and liberty shall be displayed, that noble actions and generous sentiments shall lead to the royal favor, and prostitution of principle, venality, and corruption meet their just reward," and the prince would gain "the nation's confidence [and] the people's love." Supported by that, the king "will silence every clamor, be able to apply proper remedies to the heavy taxes that oppress the people, and lay a sure foundation for diminishing the enormous debt that weights this country down and preys upon its vitals."[61]

IV

What effect did these ideas about the national debt and taxation and about the necessity for moral reform have after the prince's accession to the throne on October 25, 1760? It is clear to historians now that Bute and the new king were being reasonably straightforward when they insisted that the duke of Newcastle remain First Lord of the Treasury, though Newcastle at the time had doubts about their real intentions.[62] They realized that huge sums of money would have to be raised quickly to continue the war, and Newcastle had the experience and the contacts in the City of London to do so. Bute also intended that William Pitt would continue to direct the war effort with his usual vigor and determination, even though it would be expensive. Intervening precipitately in the financing and prosecution of the war would mean running a considerable risk of damaging both the nation's interests and the king's popularity, and Bute had no intention of taking that chance. The king was far less committed to keeping Pitt on, and once even burst out that he "ought to risk everything rather than submit" to bondage to the Great Commoner. Finally, however, he deferred to Bute's judgment on this point, and took the safer course.[63]

Even as they moved cautiously, though, the two men still tried whenever possible to distinguish their views from those of George II's last administration. This practice disturbed the old ministers, whose collective opinion was best expressed by the duke of Devonshire when he complained, "Lord Bute . . . seems not only ignorant of business but visionary."[64] The first indication of a new vision of the future came only hours after George II's death, when his successor pledged that "as I mount the throne in the midst of a bloody war, I shall endeavor to prosecute it in the manner most likely to bring an honorable and lasting peace." Pitt, who immediately recognized the barely concealed criticism of the human and fiscal cost of the war and the implications of the omission of any reference to Britain's ally Prussia, successfully bullied Bute and the king into calling the war "expensive but just and necessary" and saying peace would be made "in concert with our allies" before the speech was published. Even so, the news about the original draft clearly signaled George III's views to the political world.[65]

On October 31 the king gave another signal of his intentions, this time to all his subjects, by issuing a proclamation "for the encouragement of piety and virtue, and for [the] preventing and punishing of vice, profaneness, and immorality." In it, he observed that vice by its "frequent ill examples" had had "so fatal a tendency to the corruption of many of our loving subjects, otherwise religiously and virtuously disposed," and promised that in the future only the virtuous would receive the royal favor and that "all persons of honor, or in place of authority, will give good examples by their own virtue and piety."[66] Such sentiments from a new monarch were not novel, of course. Both George I and George II had issued similar proclamations upon their accessions, and neither was a morally scrupulous man. George III, however, had every intention of acting on these principles and thus setting himself apart from his royal ancestors. The king's speech opening Parliament in November gave him his next chance to call his subjects' attention to what he felt was another crucial difference between him and his predecessor. To this end, he commanded Newcastle to insert in the speech the words "born and educated in this country, I glory in the name of Britain; and the peculiar happiness of my life will ever consist in promoting the welfare of a people, whose loyalty and warm affection to me, I consider the greatest and most permanent security of my throne."[67] These words vividly conveyed the promise that the new king would not be prejudiced in favor of continental alliances that had been so expensive in British blood and treasure.

At the same time, George III also tried to convince Newcastle "to mention care and attention to the preserving inviolably the sinking fund, as one of the chief supports of the public credit in the speech." He must not have pressed the matter, though, as the speech did not include any reference to the sinking fund.[68] Instead, the king demonstrated his commitment to economy and fiscal responsibility by asking Parliament to vote to him for life £800,000 a year for the civil list, and, in return, being "ever desirous of giving the most substantial proofs of his tender regard to the welfare of his people," consented that "such disposition may be made of [his] interest in the hereditary revenues of the crown, as may best conduce to the utility and satisfaction of the public."[69] To the satisfaction of the king, this message was "much applauded in the House [of Commons]."[70]

Finally, after George Grenville openly opposed on December 16th the administration's proposal to add three shillings per barrel to the duty on strong beer, the king's reaction was, in the opinion of Newcastle and Devonshire, "very suspicious."[71] Clearly this tax would raise the price of a drink the London poor regarded as a necessity. It was the very type of tax the king and Bute believed should be if possible reduced, and certainly not raised. Neither, however, had expressed any objection to the proposal to Newcastle, evidently because the duke firmly believed that this tax was necessary to pay the interest on a new loan of £12,000,000 for 1761, and the two men were willing to let him bear the responsibility for raising the money for the largest single loan in British history.

Grenville argued in the House that it would be better to avoid taxing this necessity. He suggested instead raising the money by increasing the duties laid on wines and spirits during the last parliamentary session, and appropriating the money for the loan of 1761.[72] His view did not prevail in the House, but it won him favor in the royal closet. "I have some notion," Newcastle wrote Devonshire, "that what George Grenville did (so disapproved by *all* his brothers) was approved by my lord Bute: for when I told his majesty how *well* things had gone in the House of Commons that day, he was *graciously* pleased to say *nothing*." Newcastle believed Bute wanted to make Grenville Chancellor of the Exchequer, "and some friend of [Bute's] at the head of the Treasury."[73] Soon afterwards, when George III and the duke discussed the possibility of Grenville's becoming Speaker of the House, the king "commended . . . Grenville extremely, approved him very much. . . , but would himself have rather kept him for some employment of greater consequence." This employment, Newcastle was sure, was Chancellor of the Exchequer. He was also certain that the king's opinion would probably help persuade Grenville not to become Speaker. This prospect did not please Newcastle, who was determined not to allow the king to force Grenville on him.[74] For their part, George III and Bute were delighted. They wasted no time perfecting their relationship with a man who was well-versed in the technicalities of finance and thought as they did on broad fiscal issues.[75]

In less than three months after becoming king, George III had acted on his principles and taken the first steps toward the regeneration of the nation's morals and the reform of its finances. Although certainly not all had gone as he wished during that time, he remained convinced that he could and would realize his goals. Indeed, so certain was the king that he and Bute could accomplish great changes that the earl's counsels of caution and patience in dealing with Pitt at times chafed him. "Foreboding thoughts," he assured Bute, were foreign to him, for "I am happy enough to think I have [at] present the real love of my subjects."[76] He did not realize that his real education in "the true essential business of a king" had only just begun. And yet, already there was "strange talk of [Bute] and [the king's mother], verses and indecent prints published, [and] even in the avenues to the playhouse the mob crying out, 'no Scotch government, no petticoat government,' in the very hearing of the king as he passe[d] along."[77]

*This chapter first appeared in: *Albion* 18 (1986), pp. 429-454.

Endnotes

[1]For brief descriptions of the opposition's arguments against the national debt and the financial system servicing it, see: Isaac Krammick, *Bolingbroke and his Circle: The Politics of Nostalgia in the Age of Walpole* (Cambridge, MA, 1968), pp. 43-55; Reed Browning, *Political and Constitutional Ideas of the Court Whigs* (Baton Rouge, 1982), pp. 187-188; and Linda Colley, *In Defiance of Oligarchy: The Tory Party, 1714-1760* (Cambridge, 1982), pp. 157-161. For convenient sources for opposition statements in Parliament on the debt and taxation see Sir John Barnard's motion to reduce the interest on the national debt, Mar. 14, 1737, and his motion for "taking off the taxes that oppress the poor and the manufacturers," [Apr. 1737], in: T. C. Hansard, ed., *The Parliamentary History of England, from the Earliest Period to the Year 1803*, Ser. 1, 41 vols., (London, 1806-1820), 10, pp. 71-187; and the summary of the opposition's arguments against the bill for naturalizing foreign Protestants, Feb. 4, 1748, in *ibid.*, 14, pp. 141-148. Frederick, Prince of Wales, was virtually the head of the opposition from 1746 until his death in 1751, and his "Instructions for my son George, drawn by myself, for his good, that of my family, and for that of his people, according to the ideas of my grandfather, and best friend, George I," Jan. 13, 1748-9, include typical opposition prescriptions for dealing with problems of public finance. "Instructions for my son George" has been published in Sir George Young, *Poor Fred: The People's Prince* (Oxford, 1937), pp. 172-175.

[2] Earl Waldegrave, draft of a speech on the education of the Prince of Wales, [early 1753], B.L., Add. MSS. 51380, f. 121. I have changed spelling and punctuation in all the quotations in this essay to conform to modern English usages, except in the case of italicized words, which appeared in the original. The principal of the national debt on Jan. 20, 1752 was £74,309,562. *Journals of the House of Commons*, 26, pp. 387-388.

[3]Earl Waldegrave, *Memoirs from 1754 to 1758 by James, Earl Waldegrave, Knight of the Garter, One of His Majesty's Privy Council in the Reign of George II and Governor of the Prince of Wales, Afterwards George III* (London, 1821) pp. 63-64. Even if Waldegrave neglected to discuss the national debt, the prince doubtless was aware of it. If the prince's mother read to him the instructions left by her late husband as she was supposed to, the prince learned that his father advised him to "employ all your hands, all your power to live with economy, and

try never to spend more in the year than [the money raised by] the malt [tax] and [a] two shillings in the [pound] land tax." If he could do so, "you will be able to reduce the national debt, which if not done, will surely one time or the other, create such a disaffection and despair, that I dread the consequences for you." George was also told "the sooner you have an opportunity to lower the interest [on the national debt], for God's sake, do it." Frederick further advised George to ask the moneyed interest firmly for "their assistance and support, to ease the land[ed interest] of the vast burden it is loaded with, which can only be done, by reducing the national interest." Finally, he advised his son that "a good deal of the national debt must be paid off, before England enters into a war." Prince Frederick, "Instructions for my son George," Jan. 13, 1728-9, in Young, *Poor Fred*, p. 173. Moreover, the Bishop of Norwich, the prince's preceptor before Waldegrave took control of his education, was interested in introducing the prince to fiscal and commercial issues, and probably saw to it that he began studying them during 1751-1753. For Norwich's interest in teaching the prince about these subjects, see Josiah Tucker, *Four Tracts Together with Two Sermons on Political and Commercial Subjects* (London, 1774), pp. ix-xi, quoted in Walter Ernest Clark, *Josiah Tucker, Economist: A Study in the History of Economics* (New York, 1903), pp. 63-64.

[4] The prince of Wales to the earl of Bute, [early Jun. 1757?], in Romney Sedgwick, ed., *Letters from George III to Lord Bute, 1756-1766* (London, 1939) p. 6.

[5] Bute's method of instruction is described in John Brooke, *King George III* (London, 1972), pp.107-108. Very little is known about the reading he assigned to the prince (*ibid.*, p. 608). A few of the book orders for the prince have survived in the Bodleian Library, MSS. North, A. 4, ff. 82, 86, 95, 98, 126, 222, 224, 267, and 297. The prince's essays on public finance and related subjects have been preserved in the Royal Archives at Windsor, Additional Georgian Manuscripts, in RA, Add. 32/259-261, 1087-1449, 1531-1696, 1700-1728. In addition, the prince occasionally touched on matters relating to public finance in other essays (see Brooke, *George III*, pp. 118-119, 121- 122). This article will focus on the prince's essays on finance from the Glorious Revolution to his day to the exclusion of his studies of taxation in earlier periods, because he believed the origins of Britain's present difficulties began in the 1690s.

[6] "On methods to be used in writing a history of revenues and taxes after the Revolution," RA, Add. 32/1226 [hereafter cited as "On methods to be used"]. In this essay, the prince referred to "78 millions national debt." *Ibid.*, p. 1232. Thus the essay was written after Mar. 6, 1758, when the total of the principal of the debt was £77,780,386, and before Mar. 15, 1759, when the total was announced as £82,776.586. See "A state of the national debt," Mar. 6, 1758, Bodleian Library, MSS. North, A. 4, ff. 163-166; and Mar. 15, 1759, *Common Journals*, 27, p. 485.

[7] The prince of Wales to Bute, [Dec. 1758], Sedgwick, ed., *Letters from George III to Bute*, p.19; see also the prince's letter to Bute, Mar. 4, 1760, in *ibid.*, p. 45.

[8] Lord Fitzmaurice, *Life of William, Earl of Shelburne, afterwards First Marquess of Landsdowne, with Extracts for his Papers and Correspondence*, 2 vols. (London, 1912), 1, p. 111.

[9] "Account of sessions of Parliament and taxes raised during the reign of William and Mary up to 1694," RA, Add. 32/1272, 1371 [hereafter cited as "Account of sessions . . . up to 1694"]. I think the prince wrote this essay sometime during 1759-1760 for two reasons. First, its subject suggests that it was written immediately prior to the essay that covers William's reign from 1694 to his death. Second, on Mar. 5, 1759, the prince received several unspecified volumes on modern English history. See "Book order for the prince of Wales," Mar. 5, 1759, Bodleian Library, MSS. North, A. 4, f. 222. The prince's reading for this essay included history from the Whigs' point of view in Bishop Burnet's *History of My Own Times*, and from the Tory perspective in the works of Viscount Bolingbroke and Jonathan Swift. *Ibid.*, RA, Add. 32/1233-1270. In an earlier essay, "History of taxes and impositions from the Norman invasion to the Revolution," RA, Add. 32/1102-1109 he had practiced analyzing "the passions and prejudices of the several historians" of English antiquity. In the case of the reign of William and Mary, the prince clearly found the passions and prejudices of Bolingbroke and Swift to be more persuasive.

[10] Account of sessions . . . up to 1694," RA, Add. 32/1367-1368.

[11] *Ibid.*, RA, Add. 32/1381.

[12] *Ibid*, RA, Add. 32/1384.

[13] "On methods to be used," RA, Add. 32/1230. The consensus of modern scholarship is that the prince's views are incorrect, because during the 1690s "it proved impossible to pay for the war from current income, and a vast machinery of public credit was hastily erected to serve the requirements of the state." See: J. V. Beckett, "Land Tax or Excise: the levying of taxation in seventeenth- and eighteenth-century England," *English Historical Review* 100 (1985): 307; and P. G. M. Dickson, *The Financial Revolution in England: A Study in the Development of Public Credit, 1688-1756* (London, 1967), pp. 9-12, 46-75.

[14] "Abstract of debts and taxes from the Revolution," RA, Add. 32/1164.

[15] "Account of sessions . . . up to 1694," RA, Add. 32/1402. For the expression of similar views by members of the parliamentary opposition, see: "Debate in the Commons on the Lottery," [Mar.-Apr. 1755], in Hansard, ed., *Parliamentary History*, 15, pp. 513-517.

[16] "On methods to be used," RA, Add. 32/1231-1232. See also "Extract from an essay on the sinking fund, asserting the right of the public to the fund," RA, Add. 32/1692-1696. The prince's descriptions of the sinking fund, its original purpose,

and the uses to which it was ultimately put are, though brief and tinctured with his conviction that it was being misused, historically accurate. For a modern discussion, see: Dickson, *The Financial Revolution in England*, pp. 82-89, 204-212.

[17] "On methods to be used," RA, Add. 32/1230-1231.

[18] The quotations are from "A history of the revenue from the Revolution to the present time," RA, Add. 32/1198-1199. The titles indicate that the prince wrote this essay after he wrote "On methods to be used." It would seem logical to study methodology and sources first, and then write the history. There are also many similarities in the texts of the two essays. Compare, for example, RA, Add. 32/1198-1199 with RA, Add. 32/1220. Thus "A history of the revenue from the Revolution to the present time" was probably composed sometime between Mar. 6, 1758 and Mar. 15, 1759.

[19] For the prince's knowledge of Burnet, see: "Account of sessions . . . up to 1694," RA, Add. 32/ 1233-1270. The prince also had in his library another Whig history of the times, White Kennet's *History of Britain*. "Book order for the prince of Wales," Dec. 10, 1757, Bodleian Library, MSS. North, A. 4, f. 126.

[20] See, for example, *The Daily Journal; or, The Gentleman's and Tradesman's complete annual account book for the pocket, or desk for the year of our Lord 1761* (London, 1760), pp. 1-5.

[21] See Sir Roger Newdigate, undated note on political parties, Warwickshire County Record Office, Newdegate MSS., B. 2539/1.

[22] John Brewer, *Party Ideology and Popular Politics at the Accession of George III* (Cambridge, 1976), p. 135.

[23] For the debt in 1758, see "a state of the national debt," Mar. 6, 1758, Bodleian Library, MSS. North, A. 4, ff. 163-166; in 1759, Mar. 15, 1759, *Commons Journals*, 27, p. 485; in 1760, *Annual Register* 3 (1760), pp. 196-197; and in 1761, February 2, 1761, *Commons Journals*, 28, p. 1052.

[24] "Account of sessions of Parliament and taxes granted from 1694 to the death of William III," [1760], RA, Add. 32/1448 [hereafter cited as "Account of sessions . . . to the death of William III]. This essay was probably written in 1760 before George became king. The prince's optimism that Britain could safely raise the national debt to £130 or £140,000,000 contrasted starkly not only with the opinion of Walpole, but also with the apprehensions of the present First Lord of the Treasury, the duke of Newcastle. In October 1760, Newcastle fretted that it would be scarcely practical to raise the debt to £110,000,000. Newcastle, "State of expenses for 1760, with requirements for new taxes," October 4, 1760, B.L., Add. MSS. 33040, ff. 63-69. In *King George III*, pp. 118-119, John Brooke argued that the prince's expressions of concern in his essays about the national debt and the weight of taxes in fact reflected "Bute's jealousy of Pitt's success in waging war."

"With monotonous regularity," he continued, "the prince dwelt on the increase of the national debt, with the implication that this more than offset all the victories which had been gained." Evidently Brooke was unaware of the appreciation of "this mighty engine" of public credit that the prince wrote in 1760. Brooke's argument is questionable for other reasons as well. The prince expressed his concern about public finance in a letter he wrote in Jun. 1757 and in essays he wrote between Mar. 1758 and Mar. 1759. Thus he had held these views for some time before the great victories of the *annus mirabilis*, 1759. See the prince to Bute, [early Jun. 1757?] in Sedgwick, ed., *Letters from George III to Bute*, p. 6; "On methods to be used," and "A history of the revenue from the Revolution to the present time," RA, Add. 32/1194-1232.

[25] Frederick, who advised his son that "a good deal of the national debt must be paid off, before England enters into a war" in his next words qualified that advice by adding, "at the same time never give up your honor nor that of the nation." His son also recognized that there were times when it was unwise to follow too slavishly the best fiscal advice. Prince Frederick, "Instructions to my son George," Jan. 13, 1748-9, in Young, *Poor Fred*, p. 173.

[26] Anon., "the education of the prince," [after Jan. 5, 1759], Mount Stuart, Isle of Bute, Scotland, Bute Papers in the possession of the Marquess of Bute, Box VII, pp. 10-16. James Lee McKelvey erred when he argued in *George III and Lord Bute: the Leicester House Years* (Durham, NC, 1973), p. 85n, that this essay was written in either 1755 or early 1756. The anonymous author referred to a national debt of "more than four-score millions!" In Jan. 1759, the debt was £82,776,589. Moreover, since the essay was written in 1759, it could not have been "in effect a prospectus for the instruction of the prince," as McKelvey asserted.

[27] "On Industry in Great Britain," RA, Add. 32/259-261. An exact date cannot be determined for this essay, but some clues are provided by the prince's reference to Malachy Postlethwayt's argument that the high taxes necessitated by the national debt was the principal reason why labor was more expensive in Britain than in Europe. Postlethwayt first made the argument explicitly in his article on "Labor" in Postlethwayt, *The Universal Dictionary of Trade and Commerce*, 2 vols. (London, 1751, 1755), 2, pp. 1-6. Since volume two of the *Dictionary* was published in 1755, the prince might have written the essay as early as that year. But Postlethwayt made the same argument in his works *Britain's Commercial Interest explained and improved . . .* , 2 vols. (London, 1757), 1, pp. 43-51; and *Great Britain's True System . . .* (London, 1757), pp. 143-185. I believe that George had read *Britain's Commercial Interest* before he wrote his essay, because there are similarities in argument and phrasing between his essay and that work (compare *Britain's Commercial Interest* 1, pp. 11, 14 with RA, Add. 32/261). I also think it was written before 1759-1760, because the prince's growing concern to be a popular king makes it doubtful he would have espoused even privately in 1759 or 1760 the unpopular opinions and plans that he enthusiastically embraced in "On Industry in Great Britain."

[28] "On Industry in Great Britain," RA, Add. 32/259. All quotations in this and the next two paragraphs are from this essay.

[29] Arguments in support of the bill for naturalizing foreign Protestants, February 4, 1748, Hansard, ed., *Parliamentary History*, 14, p. 139. A Tory opponent of this bill characterized this argument in favor of naturalization thusly: "Our laborers and mechanics, 'tis said . . . live too high and extravagantly . . . [while foreigners live] upon herbs and roots and drink water." Quoted in Colley, *In Defiance of Oligarchy*, p. 156.

[30] Tucker, *Four Tracts*, pp. ix-xi, quoted in: Clark, *Josiah Tucker*, p. 63. For summaries of Tucker's ideas, see: Clark's monograph; Robert Livingston Schuyler's introduction to *Josiah Tucker: A Selection from His Economic and Political Writings* (New York, 1931), pp. 3-49; and W. George Shenton, *Dean Tucker and Eighteenth-Century Economic and Political Thought* (New York, 1981). For some of Tucker's writings concerning naturalization, see: *A Brief Essay on the Advantages and Disadvantages which Respectively Attend France and Great Britain With Regard to Trade* (London, first edition, 1749; second edition, 1750; third edition, with a new appendix, 1753; fourth edition, printed in Glasgow, 1754); *Reflections on the Expediency of a Law For the Naturalization of Foreign Protestants in Two Parts; Part I* . . . (London, 1751); *Reflections on the Expediency of a Law For the Naturalization of Foreign Protestants in Two Parts: Part II* . . . (London, 1751); *A Letter to a Friend Concerning Naturalizations* . . . (London, first and second editions, 1753); and *A Second Letter to a Friend Concerning Naturalizations* . . . (London, 1753).

[31] Waldegrave, *Memoirs*, p. 8.

[32] Tucker, *Four Tracts*, pp. ix-xi, in Clark, *Josiah Tucker*, pp. 63-64. Tucker had first-hand experience of the unpopularity of his ideas. He wrote his pamphlets on naturalization while serving as rector of All Saints' Church in Bristol, and in 1751 a mob, displeased with the tenor and thrust of his arguments, dressed an effigy in full canonicals and burned it. *Ibid.*, P. 29.

[33] The quotation is from "On Industry in Great Britain," [1757-1758?], RA, Add. 32/259. For information on the successful opposition to naturalization, and arguments against it, see: Colley, *In Defiance of Oligarchy*, pp. 155-156; Thomas W. Perry, *Public Opinion, Propaganda, and Politics in Eighteenth-Century England: A Study of the Jew Bill of 1753* (Cambridge, MA, 1962), p. 178; and "arguments made use of against naturalization," February 4, 1748, Hansard, ed., *Parliamentary History*, 14, pp. 142-143.

[34] The prince to Bute, September 25, 1758, in Sedgwick, ed., *Letters from George III to Bute*, p. 13.

[35] "Account of sessions . . . up to 1694," RA, Add. 32/1409.

[36] On Industry in Great Britain," RA, Add. 32/260.

[37] For examples of other men's emphasis on the damage done to the landed interest, see the opinions of Waldegrave and Newdigate, which are cited in notes 2 and 21 above.

[38] "Account of sessions . . . up to 1694," RA, Add. 32/1272.

[39] "Account of sessions . . . to the death of William III," RA, Add. 32/1449. How "oppressive" these new taxes were on trade and industry is a matter of controversy among modern scholars. For a discussion of the difficulties of determining the economic effects of taxation in eighteenth-century Britain, see: William J. Hausman and John L. Neufeld, "Excise Anatomized: the Political Economy of Walpole's 1733 Tax Scheme," *The Journal of European Economic History* 10 (1981), pp. 131-132, 141-143.

[40] "Account of sessions . . . up to 1694," RA, Add. 32/1403.

[41] "On methods to be used," RA, Add. 32/1228. The prince defined taxes on necessaries as taxes on "candles, soap, malt liquor (at the brewery), leather and skins at the tanner." In "On Industry in Great Britain," RA, Add. 32/259, he defined strong beer as a luxury, not a necessity.

[42] See: William Kennedy, *English Taxation, 1640-1799: An Essay on Policy and Opinion* (London, 1913), pp. 104-123. As Kennedy pointed out, the notion that the government should avoid taxing the necessities of the poor became "a first principle of tax policy" during this period (p. 123).

[43] On methods to be used," RA, Add. 32/1232.

[44] "Production of civil list revenues, down to Oct. 10, 1760," Bodleian Library, MSS. North, A. 4, f. 307. For the yearly average for the last decade, see: E. A. Reitan, "The Civil List, 1761-77: Problems of Finance and Administration," *Bulletin of the Institute of Historical Research* 47 (1974), p. 187.

[45] The prince's father committed himself publicly in 1747 to a civil list fixed at £800,000 a year in an effort to make himself more popular. Presumably this precedent, and a similar desire for popularity, inspired the prince's and Bute's decision about the civil list. See: E. A. Reitan, "The Civil List in Eighteenth-Century British Politics: Parliamentary Supremacy verses the Independence of the Crown," *The Historical Journal* 10 (1966), p. 322. Reitan has also discussed the commitment of George III and his Lord Steward, earl Talbot, to economy in the affairs of his household ("The Civil List, 1761-77," pp. 190-191). For George III's personal involvement in settling the wages and privileges of the royal laundresses and thus preserving his "plan of economy' see: George III to Bute, [January 1761], Mount Stuart, Bute Papers, Correspondence with George III, nos. 122/2-3 and 123/1-3.

[46] "A history of the revenue from the Revolution to the present time," RA, Add. 32/1201.

[47] "Account of sessions . . . up to 1694," RA, Add. 32/1398.

[48] "On methods to be used' RA, Add. 32/1227-1228.

[49] *Ibid.*, RA, Add. 32/1228. The prince's emphasis on raising money by extending excise duties tends to confirm Beckett's point that politicians during the eighteenth century regarded excise taxes as the principal means of increasing the government's revenues ("Land Tax or Excise," p. 286).

[50] "On methods to be used," RA, Add. 32/1225.

[51] "Account of sessions . . . up to 1694," RA, Add. 32/1398.

[52] *Ibid.*, RA, Add. 32/1402.

[53] "On Industry in Great Britain," RA, Add. 32/259; and "On Methods to be used," RA, Add. 32/1227-1228.

[54] The prince to Bute, Aug. 5, 1759, in Sedgwick, ed., *Letters from George III to Bute*, p. 28.

[55] Bute to George Grenville, Oct. 13, 1761, in: K. W. Schweizer, "A lost letter of John Stuart, 3rd Earl of Bute, to George Grenville, 13 Oct. 1761," *The Historical Journal* 17 (1974): 439. Bute went on to tell Grenville that now "the scene [is] changed; a determined young prince holds the scepter . . . [and his] virtues and his way of thinking excludes the possibility of getting at him by these methods formerly practiced."

[56] The prince to Bute, [early Jun. 1757?], in: Sedgwick, ed., *Letters from George III to Bute*, p. 6.

[57] The prince to Bute, two letters [Sept. 25, 1758] and [Sept. 1758?], *ibid.*, pp. 14-15.

[58] Bute to the prince, Sept. 7, 1759, *ibid.*, p. 31n.

[59] The prince to Bute, [winter 1759-1760], *ibid.*, p. 39. The "passion" uppermost in the prince's mind at that moment was his infatuation with Lady Sarah Lennox. Bute had just advised him not to marry an English woman, and the prince resolved to follow that advice.

[60] Anon.,"the education of the prince," [after Jan. 5, 1759], p. 17, Mount Stuart, Bute papers, box VII. The prince's father had offered him similar advice: "Convince this nation that you are not only an Englishman born and bred, but that you are also this by inclination." Prince Frederick, "Instructions for my son George," Jan. 13, 1748/9, in: Young, *Poor Fred*, p. 174.

[61] Quoted in: Brooke, *King George III*, pp. 121-122. For a more general statement by the prince on what a virtuous king could accomplish even "in the worst corrupted times, in storms of inward faction and the most threatening circumstances without," see "Essay on King Alfred," quoted in: Sir Lewis Namier, *England in the Age of the American Revolution*, 2nd ed., (London, 1961), p. 93. Bute noted to a friend in 1756 how unprecedented in history it was for a

prince to be so committed to liberty and so averse "to vice, corruption, and arbitrary power" to bring liberty to "a prostituted people," and then promised when George came to the throne, "the experiment will for the first [time] be tried." Bute to Gilbert Elliot, Aug. 16, 1756, quoted in: McKelvey, *George III and Lord Bute*, pp. 42-43.

[62] For Newcastle's doubts, see: the duke of Devonshire, "Memoranda on state of affairs, 1759-1762," Oct. 27, 1760, in: Peter D. Brown and Karl W. Schweizer, eds., *The Devonshire Diary: William Cavendish, Fourth Duke of Devonshire: Memoranda on State of Affairs, 1759-1762*, Camden Miscellany, vol. XXVII, Camden, 4th Ser. (London, 1982), pp. 42-43.

[63] George III to Bute, [mid-Nov. 1760], in: Sedgwick, ed., *Letters from George III to Bute*, pp. 49-50.

[64] Devonshire, "Memoranda on state of affairs, 1759-1762," Oct. 27, 1760, in: Brown and Schweizer, eds., *Devonshire Diary*, p. 43.

[65] For a description of the controversy on Oct. 25, 1760 over the king's speech to the Privy Council, see: Brooke, *King George III*, pp. 135-138. As he later reminded Bute, George III was "very averse to the altering [of] my declaration," and did so only because Bute insisted on it. George III to Bute, [mid-November 1760], in: Sedgwick, ed., *Letters from George III to Bute*, p. 49. For the effect of this and other episodes of friction between Bute and the king on one hand, and Pitt and Newcastle on the other, see: Philip Lawson, *George Grenville: A Political Life* (Oxford, 1984), pp. 115-116; and the earl of Egmont's diary entries for Oct. 27 and Nov. 6 and 16, 1760, in: Aubrey N. Newman, ed., "Leicester House Politics, 1750-60, from the papers of John, second earl of Egmont," *Camden Miscellany Vol. XXII*, Camden 4th Ser., 7 (London, n.d.), pp. 214- 217, 224, and 226-227.

[66] "By the King, a Proclamation, for the encouragement of Piety and Virtue, and for preventing and punishing of Vice, Profaneness, and Immorality," Oct. 31, 1760, in: *Annual Register* 3 (1761), pp. 241-243. This proclamation commanded royal officials to enforce existing laws regulating the morals of the people, which probably was as far as the king and Bute felt they could go in realizing the goal of establishing "a good police by which the poor would be kept to work."

[67] For the king's command to Newcastle, see: Bute to Newcastle, Nov. 15, 1760, B.L., Add. MSS. 32914, f. 355. In contemporary accounts of the speech, "Britain" was often misprinted as "Briton." See Nov. 20, 1760, *Commons Journals* 28, p. 935.

[68] "Memorandum on the speech from the king," [Nov. 1760], B. L., Add. MSS. 32914, f. 393.

[69] Nov. 25, 1760, *Commons Journals* 28, p. 947.

[70] Charles Townshend to Bute, [Nov. 25, 1760], Mount Stuart, Bute Papers, box II, no. 259.

[71] Devonshire to Newcastle, Dec. 21, 1760, B.L., Add. MSS. 32916, ff. 232-233.

[72] For an account of Grenville's remarks in the House of Commons against the tax, see: Sir Roger Newdigate's notes on the Committee of [Ways and Means], Dec. 17, 1760, Warwickshire County Record Office, Newdegate MSS., B. 2540/5. Grenville explained his opposition later by recalling he had "undertaken the defense of the laborer and manufacturer, by [my] opposition to the tax on strong beer." [George Grenville], *A reply to a letter addressed to the Right Honorable George Grenville* . . . (London, 1763), p. 7. Richard Rigby emphasized in his account a different aspect of Grenville's remarks, his anger at not being consulted by Newcastle during deliberations on the tax. According to Rigby, Grenville "made a speech in which he animadverted upon the new tax, or rather upon those who framed it not having previously acquainted him with it." Rigby to the duke of Bedford, Dec.18, 1760, Bedford Estates Office, London, Bedford Papers, XLII, no. 270.

[73] Newcastle to Devonshire, Dec. 19, 1760, B.L., Add. MSS. 32916, f. 209. Grenville's brothers included his brother-in-law, Pitt, who felt compelled to answer Grenville with a strong defense of the tax and the Treasury. See Newcastle to the earl of Hardwicke, Dec. 17, 1760, B.L., Add. MSS. 35420, ff. 144-145. Philip Lawson has argued that "there is no doubt that [Grenville] consulted Bute before this move, using [Charles] Jenkinson as the intermediary." Lawson, *George Grenville*, p. 116. In fact, there is no direct evidence bearing on any consultation between Bute and Grenville on the tax before Dec. 17. Lawson cited as partial proof for his assertion a letter from Jenkinson to Grenville that was published in: W. L. Smith, ed., *The Grenville Papers: Being the correspondence of Richard Grenville, Earl Temple, KG., and the Right Hon. George Grenville, their friends and contemporaries*, 4 vols. (London, 1852-1853), 1, pp. 356-357. But Jenkinson mentioned nothing about taxation in his letter. Moreover, even if he had discussed the Treasury's plans for new taxes, he could not have passed on information or opinions about a tax on strong beer. Since Jenkinson referred to Lord George Sackville's presence at the king's levee as fresh news, he must have written the letter soon after Oct. 30. Until around Nov. 19 or 20, Newcastle planned to lay additional duties on malt, not strong beer. See: John Roberts to Newcastle, Oct. 26, 1760, B.L., Add. MSS. 32913, ff. 349-350; William Mellish to Newcastle, Nov. 19, 1760, B.L., Add. MSS. 32914, f. 425; Bartholomew Burton to Newcastle, Nov. 20, 1760, *ibid.*, ff. 432-434; Newcastle, "Considerations on laying an additional duty on beer," [Nov. 20, 1760], *ibid.*, ff. 432-434; and the earl of Mansfield to Newcastle, Dec. 10, 1760, B.L., Add. MSS. 32915, f. 378. Lawson also relied on Newcastle's suspicions that the king and Bute approved of Grenville's behavior in the House on Dec. 17, and hoped to make him Chancellor of the Exchequer. But Newcastle made these speculations on Dec. 19, and, since he was not explicit on this point in his letter to Devonshire,

he may have been referring to an approval that was given after the event, not before. When the duke heard of Grenville's intentions before the debate he merely noted "Mr. G. Grenville will oppose the tax on the brewery, and propose that of the spirituous liquors." Newcastle, "Memorandum," Dec. 16, 1760, B.L., Add. MSS. 32999, f. 125. If this intensely suspicious and insecure man had heard one breath about prior consultation between Grenville and Bute, surely he would have recorded it. In sum, as yet no direct evidence dated before Dec. 17 has been found to support Lawson's assertion.

[74] Newcastle to Hardwicke, Jan. 9, 1761, B.L., Add. MSS. 35420, ff. 158-160.

[75] See: Lawson, *George Grenville*, pp. 117-119.

[76] George III to Bute, [mid-Nov. 1760], in: Sedgwick, ed., *Letters from George III to Bute*, p. 50.

[77] Nov. 16, 1760, Egmont diary, in: Newman, ed., "Leicester House Politics, 1750-60," Camden 4th Ser., 7, p. 227.

Chapter VII

A New Vision of Empire? Attitudes of George III and Lord Bute toward North America, 1757-1760

The commitment British politicians made to taxing colonists and strengthening imperial authority was the immediate cause of the American Revolution. On this point, there is no disagreement among historians. There is, however, an interesting and significant controversy over when and why imperial leaders made this commitment. Most scholars of the period believe it was the result of problems created by the Seven Years War, especially the enormous increase of Britain's national debt between 1754 and 1763 and the inescapable necessity of defending new and old possessions after the Peace of Paris. In contrast, Jack P. Greene has argued that Britain's government had decided before the war to embark on the fateful course of taxation and reform. According to him, a fixed determination to institute these policies existed well before any British politician could have anticipated the eventual size of the debt or the extent of the nation's conquests.

This disagreement should not be dismissed as a quibble over the timing of decisions in London. It has important implications for our understanding of the political origins of the Revolution. Ever since Bernard Bailyn published his magisterial *The Ideological Origins of the American Revolution*, historians have interpreted colonists' fears of a deep-seated conspiracy against their liberties as the overwrought and essentially unjustified results of their ideological biases.[1] But if British politicians were already committed to imperial reform before the Seven Years War, then the claims made by George Grenville and others in 1763-65 that the cost of the struggle compelled them to tax the colonies deliberately concealed this fact. If that was the case, Americans' profound distrust of the Mother Country's motives and intentions should be viewed as a clear-sighted understanding of realities in London rather than a near-paranoiac fantasy.

Examining Greene's thesis thus serves a useful purpose. Although his arguments have not escaped challenge, they have not been effectively refuted. This chapter will evaluate their validity by applying a test that both he and his principal critics overlooked. Before doing so, describing his interpretation and the critique of it is necessary.

I

Among Greene's many strengths as a historian of the first British Empire is his grasp of the roles political and bureaucratic institutions played in shaping events. In their routine procedures, Greene has often found significant clues to the ideas directing decisions on great issues. He centered his research on imperial policy before the Seven Years War, characteristically by studying the records of the ministry responsible for colonial affairs. There he found activities and interests that went well beyond the mundane duties of corresponding with royal officials and vetting provincial laws. As early as 1748, the able and energetic first Lord of Trade, the earl of Halifax, was impressed by the rapid expansion of population and wealth in Britain's North American colonies. These developments, Halifax believed, had profound significance for the Mother Country's future. Assisted by his well-informed under secretary, John Pownall, the earl calculated that trade with North America comprised an important and growing percentage of Britain's overseas commerce. Moreover, the multiplying numbers of British Americans, and their geographical spread, made them crucial factors in devising the nation's military strategies against its inveterate enemies, France and Spain. This realization of the economic and military importance of the American colonies did not brighten the vision Halifax and his colleagues had of the years ahead. As men at Whitehall figured the value of the mainland colonies, they fretted that this growth heightened the possibility of American independence. The keenness of their concern was honed by knowledge that London had been unable to exercise effective control over America in the past. After consulting their information and their apprehensions, Halifax and the other lords of Trade reached what seemed an undeniable conclusion: the Mother Country had to exert herself quickly and effectively to stave off a national disaster. That conclusion impelled them first to conceive, and then work to achieve specific changes in colonial policy. Those reforms addressed problems of executing the Acts of Trade and Navigation, forcing assemblies to obey instructions from London, and—most ominously when seen from the vantage point of later events—finding and raising permanent sources of revenue to support royal authority in America.[2]

During the 1750s, these plans bore no fruit. Halifax did not succeed in persuading any ministry to adopt them. Greene argued, however, that focusing on the earl's failure obscures the long- range importance of the Board of Trade's work. His wide-ranging research convinced him that Halifax and his colleagues spread their perceptions and programs beyond the narrow boundaries of ministerial offices into the wider world of politicians, pamphleteers, and self-appointed "experts" on Britain's empire. Dissemination of the Board's opinions about the value of North America and the danger of independence, he asserted, resulted in "a major reversal in the tone and quality of imperial behavior toward the colonies."[3] That reversal was virtually complete by the time Britain declared war on France in May 1756. Only the exigencies of war prevented the implementation of efforts to improve metropolitan authority over the American colonies. Thus the war, in Greene's view, was but an intermission. The only effect the experience and expense of fighting the French in the Western Hemisphere had was to sharpen the sense of urgency in London. At the war's end, British politicians simply returned to the earlier laid plans with the firm intention of executing them. The meaning of this for understanding the origins of the American Revolution was clear to Greene. "The decision by colonial authorities in Britain to abandon [Sir Robert] Walpole's policy of accommodation and to attempt to bring the colonies under much more rigid controls"—a decision that he called "the salient precondition" of the Revolution—was made "not abruptly in

1763, as has been traditionally supposed, and not even in 1759, as Bernhard Knollenberg has recently argued, but gradually in the decade beginning in 1748."[4]

Historians have accepted Greene's deft summary of the Board of Trade's plans and policies during 1748-1756 as accurate. The same may not be said of his conclusion about the timing of Whitehall's commitment to strengthening the Mother Country's control over her North American colonies. To Robert W. Tucker and David C. Hendrickson, Greene did not satisfactorily answer a crucial question. They pointed out that Halifax and his colleagues never gained any ministerial statements of support for their proposals. Nor did the Board of Trade persuade others in government to press for parliamentary intervention in colonial affairs. "If imperial officialdom was determined to impose a much tighter regime on the colonies," asked Tucker and Hendrickson, "why did a variety of ministers uniformly fail to respond to the Board of Trade's initiatives throughout this period?" In their opinion, Greene had found no evidence that both explained official inertia on America and buttressed his interpretation. His argument that the necessity of concentrating on fighting the French deterred any attempts at colonial reform did not convince them. To Tucker and Hendrickson, the complete absence of any sign of interest from important politicians in the Board of Trade's proposals justified rejecting Greene's effort to place the origins of the American Revolution between 1748 and 1756. They denied any meaningful transformation in attitudes toward North America or imperial reform occurred among Britain's rulers during that time. If there was no new vision of empire then, the beginnings of the fall of the First British Empire were to be found elsewhere.[5]

Tucker and Hendrickson's refutation of Greene's arguments would be persuasive, *if* the men in power in the 1750s had also been the progenitors of the colonial policies of the early 1760s. But they were not. No one who served in the cabinet during peace and war from 1748 to 1760 was responsible for those fateful decisions. Indeed, the dominant figures in politics during those years, the duke of Newcastle and William Pitt, had no part whatsoever in determining the official posture toward America immediately after the war. Conversely, the men who did play the major political roles during 1762-1763 had no power to shape events in the earlier decade. The most significant of these were the Prince of Wales, the future George III, and his "dearest friend" and mentor, the earl of Bute, who served as first lord of the Treasury from May 1762 to April 1763. They decided to balance the competing demands of security and economy by committing the British government in 1763 to raising a revenue in North America by parliamentary taxation.[6] Moreover, it was Bute who reportedly observed in early 1763 that "it appeared to him to be of much greater importance to bring our old Colonies into order, than to plant new ones," and who told the earl of Shelburne in June of that year that the Board of Trade "at the critical moment of this peace, appears to me one of the greatest situations this country can afford, and the very noblest field you can possibly exercise your talents in."[7] What were Bute's ideas, and those of his royal protégé, about the empire during the 1750s? Tucker and Hendrickson did not investigate this, so there is an important gap in the evidence supporting their contentions against Greene. The same gap exists in Greene's research. He, too, did not include the prince and Bute in his discussion of the 1750s. Correcting this omission will complete the description of attitudes toward North America and imperial reform during that decade. In fact, it does more than that. For a number of reasons, an analysis of their beliefs during the 1750s is an ideal measurement of the validity of Greene's argument.

Obviously, one of those reasons is the importance of the king's and Bute's commitment to making Americans pay for their own defense. Simply put, between the signing of the preliminary treaty of peace in November 1762 and the earl's resignation from the Treasury in March 1763, they approved and designed policies that eventuated in resistance and revolution. Did prior conceptions about the colonies inspire these decisions? Investigating that question provides a significant test of Greene's thesis.

In addition, the thoughts and acts of George and Bute during the late 1750s offer telling clues about the pervasiveness of Halifax's ideas. This is so because the prince and his mentor were determined that George would be a patriot king, bringing about fundamental changes in politics and policies. Unlike most men who had any pretensions or expectations in the 1750s of exercising power, the two ardently believed that reform was essential to Britain's future strength and prosperity. George eagerly anticipated "the hour . . . which has been so long wished for by my D. Friend, I mean the entering on a reformation in Government."[8] They planned to free the monarchy from ministerial control and the political world from corruption. Equally necessary, they were sure, were dramatic changes in the present system of public finance. They intended to reduce the national debt by frugally administering government, and finding more equitable and productive taxes that would enhance the public revenue without harming the nation's commerce. In foreign affairs, Bute and the royal heir apparent opposed Britain's current involvement in European alliances. To them, such connections meant that the nation was entangled in every European dispute, and consequently embroiled in every war on the continent. They argued that George II had favored the interests of his native country, the Electorate of Hanover, over those of Britain, with these harmful results: Hanover was guaranteed protection; European nations friendly to the Electorate received financial subsidies and the support of British troops; and Britain got stuck with high bills in money and blood. "Ruin and distress," the two men were convinced, "approach in proportion as opposition slackens to foreign expense and continental measures."[9] In the future, British diplomacy should aim at reducing the country's obligations to European nations. Such a goal would, as George and Bute knew, reverse the central thrust of London's foreign policy since the Glorious Revolution, just as rooting out corruption and reducing the debt would alter the current direction of Britain's politics and public finances.

This enchantment with political, fiscal, and diplomatic change reveals that the prince and his dearest friend were no respecters of the old ways past and present ministers had done things. Instead, they were committed to looking at problems of government from different perspectives, with an eye toward finding new approaches to dealing with them. Where they found these approaches is telling. Neither Bute nor George was an original thinker. They gathered their rationales and plans for reform from others, especially men in opposition to the ministries of the day. To a considerable extent, they gauged the worth of these schemes by how critical they were of present policy. And vice versa: the errors in other ideas they often measured by how closely they corresponded to the positions of the venal and shortsighted politicians in power.[10] The implications of their predilection for reform, and their preference for ideas associated with the country ideology and the parliamentary opposition, for an assessment of Greene's assertions about Halifax's influence should be clear. If the Board of Trade's activities had in fact widely transformed opinions about the significance of America and the wisdom of imperial reform, the prince and Bute would have known about it. Moreover, they would have embraced the Board's proposals for improving imperial control. If America was important to the Mother Country's trade now, and would become even more so in the future, the colonies there could help solve many of Britain's pressing fiscal and commercial difficulties. For this reason, imperial reform would be a necessity. Also, as the significance of America increased, the importance of Europe would proportionally decline: an excellent justification for turning away from systems of European alliances. Finally, that these ideas had not persuaded the Pitt-Newcastle ministry to act would positively recommend them to the prince and Bute. It would be one more proof that men presently in power were either ignorant of the country's true interests, or too corrupt to do what was best for Britain. Their deep commitment to reform, plus their belief that the ministers were fools or knaves, makes George and Bute's attitudes toward North America a perfect litmus to test for the transformation of thought and planning Greene claimed occurred before the end of the 1750s.

Fortunately, the sources have survived to enable historians to make this test. Bute saved hundreds of letters George wrote to him. In them, the earl's protégé discussed a wide variety of personal and political matters with unguarded candor. His ideas, and by inference those of Bute as well, may be confidently extracted from this correspondence. Furthermore, as part of the prince's education during 1755-1760, Bute assigned his pupil essays on issues he felt would confront him during his reign. During the process of reading and analysis, Bute let his student know what the correct approach to these issues was. The essays therefore completely expose the attitudes the two men had toward difficulties facing the present and future reigns. Since neither anticipated these youthful exercises would ever be published, they were as frank as the private letters between them.[11] If North America loomed larger in their minds toward the end of the 1750s, that would be reflected in their correspondence and in the prince's essays on public finance and commerce. Their advocacy of reform would establish the validity of Greene's interpretation. On the other hand, if George and Bute did not espouse the ideas and policies of Halifax's Board of Trade, there is ample reason to dismiss the conclusions Greene reached as incorrect.

II

When Bute chose assignments for the prince, he focused on what he believed would be the three issues of transcendent importance during the next reign. What personal characteristics should a monarch have? George learned from the history of earlier kings and queens that virtue was essential to the conduct of politics and governance. What should Britain's system of public finance be? Bute stressed the adverse impact of a burgeoning national debt on politics, trade, the economy in general, and the morality of the public. He also emphasized the different strengths and weaknesses of various taxes. Finally, what was the impact of war on nations? In this part of his studies, George paid particular attention to

Britain's experiences in European conflicts. Knowing the right answers to these questions, as the prince remarked in one essay, "is the true essential business of a king."[12]

Britain's North American colonies were not of sufficient significance to be added to this group. Nor did Bute regard them as important enough to make assignments devoted to them alone. The future king never analyzed at length the role the colonies had played in the past or would take in the future. To be sure, scattered references to them may be found in his essays. It is even possible to pluck these statements out of the essays and arrange them into a coherent statement on the colonies. I must emphasize, however, that this order has been imposed on them by me, not by George or Bute. Moreover, it is an order that is not informed by considerations of chronology. Not only did the prince fail to date his work, but also he usually did not leave clues in the text that permit precise dating by the reader. As a result, I cannot infer any development of their views over time.[13] One inference does seem persuasive to me, though: the absence of a rigorous analysis of Britain's colonies in the prince's papers demonstrates that Bute and he did not believe they were as important as royal virtue, the system of public finance, and relationships with European nations.

I have organized George's remarks into three sections. The first contains all of his references to the value of the American colonies and trade with them to the Mother Country. It also includes why he thought they were valuable, and what he believed the role of the Acts of Trade and Navigation were. In the second section, I deal with their position on the possibility of raising a revenue in America from parliamentary taxation. The third section discusses the views of the prince and Bute on how best to fight France in the present war and how they treated America in their discussion of that issue.

The Value of the North American Colonies

One of the first subjects Bute assigned to George was an analysis of industry in Great Britain. This essay concluded with a list of nine "commercial maxims" which were "invariable unless from a great change of circumstances." That list began with the most fundamental propositions about any nation's economy. The first axiom posited "That the prosperity of the landed interest of any state depends upon foreign commerce"; the second, "That the increase of the Riches of a State, depends upon exporting more in value of its native produce and manufactures, than is imported of manufactured commodities from other states." Then, having established how crucial a favorable balance of trade with foreign nations was to the most powerful political interest in the country, George proceeded to outline in the remaining six maxims how that desirable situation could be achieved and sustained. It was necessary that all commerces be open to anyone: "monopolies and exclusive Charters are very prejudicial to the Trade of a state, and therefore should be discouraged." An "increase of trade and navigation greatly depends upon the increase of the husbandry and agriculture." Furthermore, "the prosperity of our Trade depends very much on the encouragement given to our manufactures, on laws made relative thereto." His point made, the prince moved on to describe how to insure that those laws would be well-founded. "The Success of our Trade greatly depends on the knowledge our nobility and gentry have of all its various movements, connections, and dependencies, in a national light, as ambassadors and Senators, and more particularly, on the wise regulation of our board of trade and Plantations." "The prosperity of our Trade" rested on a broader foundation than just a wise regulation of commerce and an encouragement of manufacturing, though. It also depended "upon the judicious manner of laying and collecting our Taxes, and upon the ease, readiness, freedom and cheapness of exportation." The eighth maxim dealt with the colonies. "The prosperity of this Nation as well as that of her Colonies, depends very much on the harmony, mutual confidence, and extension of their commerce with each other." George ended his list by rephrasing the second maxim, and underlining its significance. "The prosperity, strength, riches, and even the well being of this kingdom, depends upon our being able to sell our native produce and manufactures as cheap, and as good in quality in foreign markets, as any other commercial state."[14]

What does this litany reveal about the prince and Bute's attitudes toward the North American colonies and imperial reform? It is impossible to give a precise answer. In his eighth maxim, George did note that the prosperity of Britain and her colonies "depends very much on . . . the extension of their commerce with each other." But this comment grouped together the mainland and Caribbean possessions of the nation, without giving any indication of their comparative importance to the Mother Country. Moreover, the eighth maxim must be read in the context of the others. These make it clear that George and Bute did not regard trade with the colonies as the most lucrative and vital part of Britain's commerce. Successful competition in foreign markets was far more crucial. Indeed, a favorable balance of trade in those markets, according to the two men, determined whether the country would be economically prosperous and militarily secure in the future. What constituted success in foreign trade was not the re-exportation of goods grown in the New World to Europe. Rather, it was the sale of produce and manufactures grown and made in Britain.

The laws of Parliament and the regulations of the Board of Trade applied to foreign as well as colonial trade, so one cannot presume that the prince's remarks about the necessity of wise laws and regulations clearly refer to Halifax's ideas of imperial reform. In fact, his stress on encouraging domestic manufacturing and on providing for "the ease, readiness, freedom, and cheapness of exportation" from Britain hints that he may have been more concerned with the Board's regulations affecting European trade. Based on this list, the most one can say about the two men's opinion of the British commerce with the colonies was that it was important, but not essential—definitely a contributor to prosperity, but by no means a determinant of national wealth and security at present or in the years ahead.

The prince gave greater weight to Britain's trade with her colonies when he briefly described the reign of Elizabeth I. As he discussed her, he pointed out that the Caribbean colonies had been the base the nation's economic power rested on. George praised the queen for "encourage[ing] trade and open[ing] a passage to the Indies, which has since been the foundation of the wealth of the nation." In the same essay, he also called attention to an unusual characteristic of Britain's American colonies. "Contrary to the . . . effects of the plantations of other nations, our number of people is not lessened, but increased since our settlements abroad." This development, he opined, "has enabled [us] to carry on the long and bloody wars we have." Why did Britain's overseas possessions sustain an increase in the Mother Country's population, rather than draining people from her? At first glance, "this may seem odd, but [when?] considered, [the reason] will be plainly seen." British subjects "who are settled in the colonies take more of our manufactures than if they had stay'd at home, so they employ large numbers of hands here." George did not elaborate on this last point, probably because he had often explained to Bute how regular work kept people from emigrating, and steady wages encouraged them to marry and have children. Instead, he concluded by wryly pointing out what made monarchs popular before and during Elizabeth's era. Those who made military conquests were the more popular; those who did not soon had political difficulties.[15]

Were the British West Indies the foundation of the nation's wealth? Did America's colonists, by purchasing manufactured goods, sustain her military power? Or was the colonial trade an important contributor to national prosperity and security, but no more so—and perhaps less—than Britain's commerce with Europe? Resolving these differences by referring to the prince's essays is impossible. In nearly 2,500 folio pages of youthful exercises, these are the only times George assessed the value of the American trade. And these two assessments were not extended discussions of the topic. A much more accurate description of them is brief, unsupported assertions. Exactly the same may be said of all of his references to the colonies. In his essays, George only occasionally mentioned them. He never discussed them at great length. I have included every reference to the American colonies I have found in the discussion that follows.

In one of these, the colonies are mentioned only in passing. As he discussed the history of taxation, the prince claimed that James I increased the lottery "upon [the] pretense of planting the English colony in Virginia." Whether James "got anything by this, or whether it was laid out according to its definition is a secret to this day."[16] George did not approve of lotteries, arguing that they debauched the people without assisting the state. This clearly was another example of its shortcomings.[17] His reference to Virginia was meant to support this position, rather than to demonstrate the value of the Chesapeake.

Similarly, the prince cited the colonial experience to illustrate a point he was trying to make about historical trends in the price of labor in England. He explained why wages were comparatively higher in medieval England by noting "the reason is plain: when a nation is barbarous & thinly populated, the poor can live without work, & will therefore insist on high wages, as we see in our plantations. But in a populous trading country," he went on, "the poor must either starve, or be contented with a little."[18] Obviously, one should not base sweeping conclusions about the state of the prince's knowledge about North America on a brief comment in an essay written about another subject. Still, it is fair to say that though he grasped that high wages in the colonies were partially the result of a scarcity of labor and an abundance of land, he either was ignorant of or chose not to point out the rapid growth of the population and commerce of America in recent decades. As was the case with his discussion of James's lottery, George was much more interested in describing what happened in England than in writing about the New World.

Given this apparent lack of interest in America, that Bute and the prince never studied how well the imperial system worked is not surprising. The two did think that the Acts of Trade and Navigation were very important. When George discussed the actions of Charles II and his brother, the Duke of York, immediately after the Restoration, he praised York for doing all he could to advance trade. "Parliament," he added, "pressed by the king, and their [duty, [made] it flourish by [passing] the Act of Navigation for encouraging trade and building ships."[19] In another essay, George observed that these laws distinguished modern colonies from ancient ones. With the exception of Spain, European nations now "planted colonies with a view to commerce," not as "place of conquest." Thus Britain's "colonies are very different to anything known by the ancients, [for they are] kept in an almost entire dependence on the Mother Country, with whom alone they are permitted to trade."[20]

Despite these expressions of respect for the importance of the Acts of Trade and Navigation in regulating colonial commerce, Bute and George did not believe coercive legislation, strictly enforced, explained the prosperity of Britain's possessions and their trade. "With regard to colonys (sic) this Island sends out," explained the prince, "they will be rather tended to extend its commerce than Dominion." This did not mean "they will . . . fail of being peopled," however, because "they enjoy the same common liberty" as subjects in Britain.[21] The royal public and his teacher believed American growth and prosperity was due to the liberties guaranteed by the British constitution, not to laws that controlled their development. In this, they were in much closer agreement with Americans than with Halifax. The role of liberty was so important to them, in fact, that they diagnosed the failure of Spain's West Indian colonies as the absence of mild government and the presence of restrictive laws. Spain's "government in the West Indies," the prince argued, "ought to be made so easy to the people that they could not be so happy under any other nation." It was also in her best interests to open her colonies in the East and West Indies to foreign trade. This would greatly increase the revenue of that nation. Moreover, Spain would "be sure of a true and sincere friend in Great Britain."[22] The prince did not elaborate further on the reasons why Spain should open her West Indian possessions to foreign ships and merchants. As a result, it is impossible to tell if he and his mentor were inspired by knowledge of the brisk commerce at the Dutch free port on St. Eustacia or the lucrative illicit Caribbean trade by Americans for Spanish bullion and French molasses. Clearly, though, he regarded liberty as one of the essential principles of colonial government. Acts of Trade and Navigation were essential as well, probably because, as he said apropos of the Spanish West Indies, "it is but right Spain should make reasonable gain by their plantations though they allow a moderate advantage in trade" to others.[23] The aim of restrictive legislation was to enable the Mother Country to make a reasonable profit. But that profit depended on colonists' having political liberty and the opportunity to seek commercial advantages. George evidently had this in mind when he included this among his 'general commercial maxims': "that the prosperity of this Nation, as well as that of her Colonies, depends very much on the harmony, mutual confidence, and extension of their commerce with each other."[24]

In summary, Bute and the prince did not devote much time to the study of the American colonies. They accepted that Britain's trade with them was important enough to justify once calling it the foundation of national wealth and elsewhere saying that prosperity depended very much on extending it. And it did not preoccupy them, as it did Halifax and his colleagues at the Board of Trade. Other problems and possibilities, Bute and George were certain, demanded their attention much more. Surely one reason for their certainty was this: they did not believe that imperial control over the colonies had to be tightened or Britain might lose her possessions in North America. To the contrary: their brief comments indicate they thought that the present situation was working well and that a critical component of that success was the liberty common to British subjects everywhere. These positions may or may not have been an explicit rejection of

Halifax's arguments. He was never mentioned in the essays, so this cannot be resolved. But whether they knew about his arguments or were utterly ignorant of them, the thoughts of Bute and the prince on the American trade and future relations between the Mother Country and her colonies were far from Halifax's convictions.

Parliamentary Taxation of the Colonies

In contrast to the sporadic attention and mild interest Bute and George expended on trade between Britain and her North American colonies, the two men regarded public finances as a vitally important subject and frequently assessed the advantages and disadvantages of various taxes. Typical of the prince's approach to these matters was his lament in one essay that

> for many Years just raising the Supply within the Year has been impossible in cases of immergeancy, & the present exercion of our money 'd force seems to be so great, & every commodity so thoroughly tax'd, that should Calamitys happen, & bring with them the necessity of greater Supplys, it is hardly possible to conceive where the new Impositions can be made.[25]

After the war, the North American colonies would be an obvious place to raise money to George and Bute. When the prince wrote this essay, that thought had evidently not yet crossed their minds. Instead, they advocated increasing the number of excise taxes in Britain. Especially attractive to them was an excise on tobacco sold within the realm. "It is certainly feasible," the prince observed, "and would produce a large increase of public revenue." Moreover, "the method of warehousing [tobacco] now established is a very good preparation towards it.[26] Of course, tobacco was grown in North America. Its production there in huge amounts revealed to those who thought about it the prosperity of the Chesapeake colonies. Yet George and Bute looked to raise money from its consumers in England, not from those who grew it across the water.

The reason for this is clear. When the prince and his "dearest friend" singled out excise duties on goods consumed in England as the most promising source of additional revenue for the state, they were following the precepts of most politicians who thought about taxes. There was nothing original about their attraction to that type of tax or to an excise on tobacco.[27] In contrast, had the two men suggested levying taxes on colonists, they would have been breaking new ground. Failure to speculate that the colonies might contribute to relieving the nation's fiscal difficulties was not unique to the prince and his tutor during the late 1750s. In William Pitt's papers may be found lengthy lists of possible taxes the Treasury sent him for comment. These include not only the predictable—increases in existing customs, excise, and stamp duties—but also some ingenious extensions of the revenue officer's grasp: taxes on dogs, bachelors, pistols and arms, horses and geldings, lace and jewels, signs, glue, servants, and coarse salt for manure.[28] Writers in the newspapers were equally inventive. Without neglecting the usual sources of revenue, they ranged as far afield as proposing that groups as diverse as Roman Catholics, Methodists, and ladies of pleasure be heavily taxed to help support the war.[29] But neither Treasury officials nor Grub Street hacks ever suggested taxing the king's subjects in the New World.[30] That no one in or out of power made that suggestion at a time when everyone was searching for ways of increasing the nation's revenues does not speak well for Greene's assertion that before the war information about North America's expanding wealth had been broadly disseminated and the wisdom of taxing Americans widely accepted. The prince and Bute shared the general obliviousness to the possibility of tapping the prosperity of the colonies by parliamentary taxation. Indeed, they were not simply unmindful of the prospects for a colonial revenue. They were unaware of an important previous effort to tax Americans. When George listed and described taxes passed by Parliament between 1701 and 1756, he omitted the law that imposed a *6d* per gallon duty on foreign molasses imported into North America, the Molasses Act of 1733.[31] They were also either ignorant of, or they were unimpressed by, Halifax's arguments in favor of taxing the colonies.

War Against France

How could war against France best be fought? How important were the enemy's colonies and her trade with them to sustaining her power? What role should Britain's North American colonies play in the conflict? These, and similar questions, were frequently asked and answered in Parliament and in pamphlets, at Westminster and in Whitehall, during the 1750s. They were also discussed at Leicester House, where Bute and George worked to prepare themselves for power. What is unusual about their answers is Bute's decision against requiring his pupil to advocate the usual alternative to the present strategy for fighting France.

George and Bute were not alone in arguing that making alliances with European nations and sending money and troops to support them had caused monarchs and ministers to overlook the true interests of the country while increasing the burdens of debt and taxation to a nearly unbearable weight. But other opponents of the continental policy spelled out what the nation's true interests were: the development of her colonies and the improvement of her foreign commerce. Then they argued forcefully for attacking France where she was very vulnerable and could be hurt the most: her merchant fleet and her navy on the high seas, and her colonies around the world. For years, these positions had been staple arguments of the opposition to the government, and integral parts of the Tory and Country agendas for the regeneration of Britain. But though Bute and George enthusiastically argued for other positions associated with the opposition and the country—chief among these the reduction of the debt and the ending of political corruption—they never explicitly called for a maritime, colonial strategy to replace the concentration on the continent of the past 60 years.[32] This omission suggests that their opposition to a continental strategy was not inspired by any appreciation of the colonies' economic and military significance. Rather, the prince's vehement critique of European alliances was fueled by his hatred for George II. According to the king's grandson, the reigning monarch's "partiality . . . for that horrid Electorate which has always liv'd upon the very vitals of this poor Country" was to blame for the adoption of the wrong policy.[33] The accession of a king who was a native Briton and had no ties to Hanover would solve the problem. Led by him, the government could proceed to adopt new strategies for dealing with European affairs in war and peace. Describing in the essays what those strategies would be, or what role Britain's overseas interests would have in formulating them, did not interest George or Bute. They narrowed their focus to the present situation in Europe and the man they believed should be blamed for it.

In conclusion, reading the prince's essays leaves a clear impression of his and Bute's attitudes during the 1750s toward the American colonies. They believed America was important to Britain. This was so principally because colonists purchased British manufactured goods. The American market provided a foundation for economic prosperity and encouragement for population growth, both of which contributed vitally to the Mother Country's power. Insofar as George and Bute thought about how the empire should be run, they were convinced that the Acts of Trade and Navigation guaranteed Britain would receive a reasonable profit from colonies she established essentially for commercial gain. Yet the spirit of commercial and political liberty had to animate that empire. Liberty, they asserted, was crucial to its prosperity. No thought was given by Bute and the prince to attempting to tax colonists, even though they had strongly held ideas about the best ways to tax Britons. Nor did the two men articulate any concept of how British and French colonies and commerce should influence military strategy, despite their vigorous opposition to the nature and extent of the nation's involvement in Europe during the eighteenth century.

None of these attitudes reveals either a knowledge of or an affinity for Halifax's analysis of the situation in North America and his proposals for imperial reform and taxation. But one must go beyond my explanation of the scattered references to America in the essays to measure the full dimensions of Halifax's lack of influence on them. Taken as a whole, these essays are evidence that during 1755 to 1760, as the prince and Bute were preparing for the new reign, their principal focus was elsewhere, on problems and prospects in Britain and Europe.

Interestingly, one of the most persistent and self-interested advocates for tightening trade restrictions on Americans and taxing them understood this. Henry McCulloh pressed these schemes on Halifax, Newcastle, and the duke of Bedford during the 1750s. Yet when he approached Bute in the course of his ceaseless efforts to gain the favor of influential politicians, he did not supply the earl with a rationale and a plan for improving the Mother Country's control over her American provinces. Instead, he sent Bute a discourse on "the system of our public boards from the reign of Henry VII until the Revolution."[34] To his mind, helping the prince learn the lessons of the past from his instructor was a surer route to favor than trying to convert Bute and George to changing the governance of America. McCulloh's instinct—or, perhaps, his information—was correct. There is no reason to conclude from George's essays that he and Bute believed imperial reform and taxation were vital for Britain's future.

III

The correspondence between the two men gives a different perspective on their thoughts between 1755 and George's accession to the throne. When he designed his essay assignments, Bute looked to the future. These exercises were meant to prepare his young charge for becoming a reforming, regenerating patriot king. The letters were concerned with the present; by and large, they are reactions to immediate situations. Often those situations involved North America. The war began there, and it remained one of the principal theaters of combat throughout the fighting. A major goal of the British government from the war's beginning to its end was defending North America from French attacks. The locus and purpose of the conflict would, one would think, compel George and Bute to turn their thoughts toward those colonies.

This did occur, though far less than might be expected. Taken as a whole, George's correspondence with Bute centers on the same subjects as his essays for his teacher. Even in the midst of a war fought in large part to secure the North American colonies, the prince and the earl focused on Europe. Their correspondence does not contain any discussion about the war during its first two years. This is curious in itself, considering the unrelieved record of military disaster and disappointment in America.[35] George ended this silence by commenting in early November 1757 on the rumor that Frederick the Great had signed a treaty with France and was moving his troops into Silesia. What inspired his remarks is clear: the prince feared that Frederick's actions might end in catastrophic defeat for Britain. "This will certainly bring the French back to their native air, and enable them by putting soldiers into their ships to man a great fleet; I begin now to think that you and I, my Friend, shall see the end of this once great and glorious country." George resolved not to "give way to black thoughts," and news from Europe soon revealed the rumor to be false and his apprehensions of an invasion of Britain unfounded.[36] Far from reaching a rapprochement with the French, Frederick was in the process of defeating them at Rossbach and the Austrians at Leuthen. The moral was clear to the prince: "the conduct of the Great King through the whole war is a convincing proof that resolution & steadiness will beat the world."[37]

After November 1757, George followed developments in the European war closely. Usually he and Bute were not as pleased—not even temperately—as they had been earlier by Frederick's victory and example. In particular, they strenuously objected to sending large numbers of British troops to the continent. "If this unhappy measure should be taken," opined the prince in July 1758, "we shall be drawn deeper in a Continent War than ever; and when I mount the Thr[one] I shall not be able to form a M[inistr]y who can have the opinion of the people."[38] When the ministers decided that month to commit a substantial British force to western Germany, the two men were furious with Pitt, who had reversed a lifelong opposition to continental measures, and George II.[39] This anger inspired George to describe in his letters what he had left out of his essays: the military strategy he and Bute preferred for dealing with France in Europe. They advocated taking advantage of Britain's naval supremacy to land troops on the French coast. Once there, British forces could seize ports and fortifications long enough to destroy them. Such attacks, and the threat of more to follow, they expected, would keep France from exerting her full force in Germany. This would achieve victory for Britain's allies there much more cheaply and effectively than the presence of a British army in central Europe. Thus the expedition against St. Malo and Cherbourg in the summer of 1758 had their full support.[40] After some initial success, this attack failed. Efforts to distract and weaken France by a series of "descents" on the coast ended. Even so, the prince and Bute were not persuaded by this disappointment to adopt a maritime, colonial strategy. Instead, they paid even closer attention to campaigns on the continent. George constantly noted and commented on activity in the European theater of war during 1758-1760.[41]

The prince first mentioned America in his correspondence with Bute on August 11, 1758. After saying that "nothing can give me truer joy than the appearance of our affairs in France"—British forces had just captured Cherbourg—he added, "I don't think it unlikely but in a few days news of consequence may arrive from America which will crown all, and enable us when we please to make a lasting and honourable peace."[42] The news he awaited was the outcome of the attack on Louisburg. Why he expected that fortress's fall would insure a lasting and honorable peace is unknown. Perhaps he anticipated that Britain would keep Cape Breton after the war ended. Controlling French access to the St. Lawrence River would enable British forces to prevent the reinforcement of Canada in future conflicts. Conversely, he might have been thinking of the precedent of the treaty of Aix-la Chapelle in 1748. At that time, British diplomats returned Louisburg to France. This secured a French withdrawal of forces from the Low Countries, where they would have posed a constant threat to the sea lanes used by British shipping and to the safety of England itself from invasion.[43] Whichever he had in mind—and he may have been thinking of both— it is worth underlining that George thought Louisburg alone would guarantee a good peace. He would have been satisfied with less than the conquest of Canada. Moreover, the prince did not specify what a lasting peace would mean for Britain. He only observed that after the war ended, "if vice and faction can be got the better of, this nation will again appear in her antient (*sic*) lustre."[44] The forecast of good news from North America was thus bracketed in his letter between expectations of military triumph in France and hopes for political regeneration at home. Furthermore, if the prince thought at all about benefits a secure American empire might confer on the Mother Country, he did not discuss them.

British forces did conquer Louisburg, but the troops under General James Abercromby suffered a bloody defeat at Ticonderoga. George reacted to the news by predicting "this check will prevent . . . pushing towards Crown Point," and hoping that the divine assistance given British arms at Louisburg would result in "further marks of His goodness." Then he proceeded to refer again to his plans to try "with vigor to restore religion and virtue with I mount the throne." He fortified his determination by telling Bute, "I have no fears with regard to a future day provided you keep your health."[45] As for the earl himself, he consoled Pitt by telling him, "valour was despised, America neglected, and you left single— handed to plead the cause of both" until recently.[46] He did not divulge that he and his protégé had been among those neglecting the American colonies. Nor did he take these words to heart. During 1759, the famous year of victory, the two men continued to mention affairs in America only sporadically, concentrating instead on the European side of the Atlantic.

In August 1759, intelligence of the allied victory at Minden encouraged George to "think Providence seems now to be more in our favour than last year, which makes me flatter myself that the affairs in America will also succeed better; & that with proper care this kingdom may in a number of years again humble her foes."[47] Six weeks later, the prince celebrated the news of a victory at Crown Point. "What a providential stroke this is, it will make us certain of a good piece; if the King will but with vigor push on the war."[48] Once more, George was regarding victory in America, in this case British control of Crown Point, just as he had the anticipated conquest of Louisburg—as the guarantee of an honorable and beneficial peace. Removing the French from the Hudson River Valley was evidently sufficient security for the American colonies in the future. The key to preserving this advantage was a continued effort in the war so the French could not, because of conquests elsewhere, compel cessions in northern New York.

In October, dispatches arrived in London from Quebec. "Heaven be prais'd for this great news," the prince wrote Bute. "It puts an end to the French dominion in America." But George did not reflect on the meaning of this for British North America in the years ahead. Instead, he was pleased that this "will enable us to have some troops from that quarter."[49] These reinforcements could help defend Britain against any invasion from France, a possibility that had seemed real enough during the spring and summer.[50] Understandably, the defense of England was more important to him than contemplating whether Britain could keep all of Canada after the war. How remote that thought was from his present concerns may also be seen in his philosophical reaction in June 1760 to "a melancholy account" that a French force was on the verge of re-taking Quebec. "We must meet with some disappointments," he told Bute. "I hope this will be the only one this campaign though I fear it will not end here."[51] When a reassuring report reached him that the British occupying force had been reinforced, the prince reacted calmly. He was "glad" Quebec had been held, adding "[I] hope this will encourage the French to sue for peace."[52] In this instance, the importance of Canada to him was not that Britain could legitimately claim it in future negotiations. Rather, he hoped that its seizure would so discourage the French as to persuade them to begin serious peace talks.[53]

It did not. The war dragged on, with no end in sight to the loss of men and money in Germany. This disappointment contributed to the prince's petulant response to the conquest of Montreal and the end of French resistance in North America. "I wish my Dearest Friend joy of this success," he wrote Bute, "but at the same time I can't help feeling that every such thing raises those I have no reason to love." News of "an extended expedition to France," the very sort of attack he and Bute favored, did not lighten his mood. Sourly George remarked, "I myself imagine 'tis intended sooner or later for Germany if that should be the case I hope this nation will open her eyes and see who are her true friends, and that her popular man is a true snake in the grass."[54] The conquest of Canada inspired only frustrated, bitter words about Pitt and the British involvement in Germany from the prince. The possible implications of that conquest for Britain and North America in the years ahead did not interest him in October 1760.

To sum up the evidence of the correspondence between Bute and George from 1757 until he became king on October 25, 1760: by far, the two men paid the closest attention to events in Britain and Europe. When they referred to any development in America, they customarily gauged its significance in terms of effects on their two areas of principal concentration. What they meant by a "good," "honorable," and "lasting" peace was not defined in their letters. They gave no indication that they believed the retention of all Canada was essential to the future security of British North America. There is also no hint that they felt those colonies would be supremely important to Britain after the war ended. As for imperial reform and taxation, the prince and Bute did not in these letters place them on their agenda for change. Their absence cannot, moreover, be explained by lack of familiarity with Halifax. In December 1758, George claimed that "[Henry Bilson] Legge, Lord George [Sackville], Lord Halifax, [Henry Seymour]Conway, and more that could [be] named were equal in abilities" to Pitt and his three brothers-in-law, Earl Temple, George Grenville, and James Grenville. He qualified his assessment, however, by telling Bute he thought none of these men was honest. In addition, "as to opinion, I can never have much of any of these people, for I find they all of them waver like the wind" on the issue of committing greater numbers of troops and larger amounts of money to Europe.[55] Not on his ideas about the importance of North America, nor on his conviction of the necessity of establishing imperial authority, nor on his plans for colonial taxation, but on his presumed complicity in political corruption and on his anticipated position on continental involvement: thus did the prince judge and condemn Halifax! As a measure of what the two men felt was truly important, these reactions were perfectly consistent with the rest of the prince's correspondence with Bute during 1757-1760.

IV

Soon after George became king, he and Bute embarked upon their self-appointed mission of reforming Britain. The new monarch immediately informed his ministers and his subjects that he expected greater morality in their personal lives and planned to extinguish party in politics, by issuing a proclamation encouraging piety and virtue and by appointing Tories to positions of honor at court.[56] Insofar as the nation's finances were concerned, George III made it clear to Newcastle that he wanted "care and attention [paid] to the chief supports of the public credit."[57] He also demonstrated his commitment to economy and fiscal responsibility. George asked Parliament to vote £800,000 per year to him during his life for the civil list, and, in return, he would agree that "such disposition may be made of [his] interest in the hereditary revenues of the crown, as may best conduce to the utility and satisfaction of the public."[58] Finally, on the first day of his reign, the new king let the Privy Council know that he was no friend of European alliances or the British role in the war in Germany. He omitted any reference to Britain's allies in his speech that day, and only after vigorous objections from Pitt did he and Bute consent to promise that peace would be made "in concert with our allies" in the published version of his remarks.[59] George bitterly resented having to yield on this point, and he must have relished delivering this promise on November 20, 1760 in his first speech to Parliament: "born and educated in this country, I glory in the name of Britain; and the particular happiness of my life will ever consist in promoting the welfare of [that] people."[60] What this public repudiation of his ancestors' attachment to Hanover foretold was unmistakable. George III would favor a new approach to European affairs. In diplomacy, as in politics and finance, he and Bute had revealed they had a new vision of Britain's future.[61]

That vision did not include new plans for the empire. The king and Bute made no statements about any contribution North America might make to the Mother Country in the years ahead. Nor did they indicate any interest in changing the present imperial system or taxing colonists. They began their tenure together in power with the same preoccupations with Britain and Europe and the same agendas for domestic reform that they had while they prepared for power and waited for George II death. In time, of course, the North American colonies became critically important to them, the means of reconciling the requirements of military security and fiscal economy. But that did not happen in the way described by Greene. During the 1750s, the prince and Bute only occasionally turned their attention to America. They never considered taxing colonists, even though they looked for new sources of revenue. They never entertained thoughts of imperial reform, either. Far from thinking regulation of the colonies' trade had to be tightened, they believed the present system, channeled by the Navigation Acts and energized by the spirit of political and economic liberty, was working very well. Finally, although they worried about national bankruptcy, political corruption, moral decay, continental involvement, and foreign invasion, they never expressed any fear of American independence. Greene argued there was a significant continuity of attitudes about and plans for North America from the early 1750s to the early 1760s. This does not describe the experience of George III and the earl of Bute. Their ideas about America did not remain the same; they changed fundamentally after George became king. What caused that change were the currents and eddies of negotiations with France, and the twists and turns of domestic politics, during the years 1761-1763.[62]

Endnotes

[1] Bernard Bailyn, *The Ideological Origins of the American Revolution*, (Cambridge, MA., 1967). Bailyn did not examine whether American beliefs in conspiracy were well founded. At one place in his analysis, however, he came close to stating that the patriots' distinctive way of assessing the significance of political acts led them to mistake the intentions of the British government. *Ibid.*, p. 95.

[2] Jack P. Green, "An Uneasy Connection: An Analysis of the Preconditions of the American Revolution," in Stephen G. Kurtz and James H. Hutson, eds., *Essays on the American Revolution*, (Chapel Hill, 1973), pp. 65-80; and "'A Posture of Hostility': A Reconsideration of Some Aspects of the Origins of the American Revolution," *Proceedings of the American Antiquarian Society* LXXXVII (1977), pp.27-68. Greene made the same points in summary form in "The Seven Years War and the American Revolution: The Casual Relationship Reconsidered," *The Journal of Imperial and Commonwealth History* VIII (1980), pp. 85-92. For examples of how Greene has brilliantly used institutional history to illuminate broader issues, see: *The Quest for Power: The Lower House of Assembly in the Southern Royal Colonies. 1689-1776* (Chapel Hill, NC, 1963); and "Political Mimesis: A Consideration of the Historical and Cultural Roots of Legislative Behavior in the Eighteenth Century," *American Historical Review* LXXXV (1969-1970), pp. 337-360, with "A Comment" by Bernard Bailyn and Greene's "Reply," *ibid.*, pp. 361-367.

[3] The quotation is from Greene, "An Uneasy Connection," in Kurtz and Hutson, eds., *Essays on the American Revolution*, p. 71. He made a similar statement in "'A Posture of Hostility,'" *Proceedings of the American Antiquarian Society* LXXXVII (1977), pp.65-66.

[4] Greene, "An Uneasy Connection," Kurtz and Hutson, eds., *Essays on the American Revolution* 65; see also "'A Posture of Hostility," *Proceedings of the American Antiquarian Society* LXXXVII (1977), p. 29. How the experiences of the war intensified opinions about North America formulated during 1748-1756 is discussed by Greene in "The Seven Years War and the American Revolution," *The Journal of Imperial and Commonwealth History* VIII (1980), pp. 92-95.

[5] See Robert W. Tucker and David C. Hendrickson, *The Fall of the First British Empire: Origins of the War of American Independence* (Baltimore, MD, 1982), 160n, for their discussion of Greene. In contrast, they argued that the imperial policies of the 1760s had their roots in the Seven Years War and the problems it generated, not in the thoughts and acts of the Board of Trade before that conflict. See *ibid.*, 9-105.

[6] See John L. Bullion, "Security and Economy: The Bute Administration's Plans for the American Army and Revenue, 1762-1763," *William and Mary Quarterly* 3d Ser., XLV (1988), pp. 499-509, chapter XII in this work.

[7] William Knox, *Extra-Official State Papers addressed to the Right Hon. Lord Rawdon* 2 vols. (London, 1789), II, 29; and the earl of Bute to the earl of Shelburne, Jun. 12, 1763, Bute Letterbook, Add. MSS. 36797, fol. 54, British Library, London.

[8] George III to Bute, [Nov. 1762], in Romney Sedgwick, ed., *Letters from George III to Lord Bute, 1756-1766* (London, 1939), 167.

[9] The quotation is from an essay written by Prince George for Bute during the late 1750s, "Account of sessions of Parliament and taxes raised during the reign of William and Mary up to 1694," Additional Georgian Manuscripts, BA, Add. 32/1381, Royal Archives, Windsor, England. For descriptions of the prince and Bute's commitment to reform in general and their thoughts about specific changes, see chapters III, IV, and VI.

[10] For examples of how Bute and the prince borrowed ideas from men in opposition to government, and denigrated the efforts of ministers, see chapter VI and John Brooke, *King George III* (London, 1972), pp. 58-63.

[11] For discussions of how Bute used the essays to instruct the prince, and the lessons he tried to teach, see Brooke, *King George III*, pp. 55-58; and chapter VI.

[12] The essays George III wrote during the 1750s may be found in RA, Add. 32/1-2483. The quotation is from "On methods to be used in writing a history of revenues and taxes after the Revolution," [between Mar. 6, 1758 and Mar. 15, 1759], *ibid.*, 1232. For the dating of this essay, see chapter VI.

[13] For examples of the difficulties in precisely dating the prince's essays, see *ibid.*, 431n, 432n, 435n, and 438n.

[14] "On Industry in Great Britain," [before 1757-1758?], RA, Add. 32/260. A discussion of the complete content of the essay and its probable date of composition may be found in chapter VI.

[15] "On Great Britain's relations with foreign powers," [n.d.], RA, Add. 32/257-258.

[16] "A short history of England from the earliest times to the succession of the Hanoverians," [n.d.] BA, Add. 32/168.

[17] For George's critique of lotteries, see chapter VI.

[18] "History of taxes and impositions from the Norman invasion to the Revolution," [n.d.] RA, Add. 32/1101.

[19] "A short history of England from the earliest times to the succession of the Hanoverians," {n.d.] RA, Add. 32/208.

[20] "Laws relative to government in general," [n. d.], RA, Add. 32/903.

[21] *Ibid.*, RA, Add. 32/825.

[22] "On Spain," [Sept.-Oct., 1760], RA, Add. 32/479. The prince abstracted in this essay several memorials presented by the Spanish ambassador to George II and his ministers. The last one he summarized was dated Sept. 9, 1760, so he wrote "On Spain" after then. He finished it before Oct. 25, because his grandfather died that day and the many demands on a new monarch's time, attention, and energy were too great for him to continue his studies.

[23] *Ibid.*

[24] "On Industry in Great Britain," [1757-1758] RA, Add. 32/260.

[25] Prince George, "Essays on methods to be used in writing a history of revenues and taxes after the Revolution," RA, Add. 32/1231, Royal Archives.

[26] *Ibid.*, RA, Add. 32/1228, Royal Archives.

[27] See J. V. Beckett, "Land Tax or Excise: the levying of taxation in seventeenth- and eighteenth-century England," *English Historical Review* C (1985), p. 286.

[28] See "Taxes proposed, 1758," and "Taxes proposed, 1758 and 1759," in Chatham Papers, N.A. 30/8/81, part I, fos. 140-141, 148-151, National Archives, London.

[29] For these suggestions, and a lengthy compendium of taxes proposed in letters to London newspapers, complete with witty commentaries on them, see Jeremiah Henriques to the printer, *St. James Chronicle*, Feb. 16-18, 1762.

[30] Lawrence Henry Gipson in volume X of *The British Empire Before the American Revolution* claimed that Samuel Martin, a Secretary to the Treasury, suggested to the duke of Newcastle in 1759 that stamp duties be imposed on colonists. *The Triumphant Empire: Thunder-Clouds Gather in the West 1763-1766* (New York, 1961), pp. 258-259. That claim is repeated in John L. Bullion, *A Great and Necessary Measure: George Grenville and the Genesis of the Stamp Act 1763-1765* (Columbia, MO, 1982), 12. In fact, Martin was discussing English, not American taxes in his letter to Newcastle. See Samuel Martin to the duke of Newcastle, Feb. 26, 1759, Newcastle Papers, Add. MSS. 32888, fol. 252, British Library.

[31] "Account of sessions of Parliament and taxes granted from 1701 to Dec. 1756," RA Add. 32/1611-1614.

[32] For George and Bute's views on the pernicious effects of British involvement in fighting in Europe, see Prince George, "Account of sessions of Parliament and taxes raised during the reign of William and Mary up to 1694," RA Add. 32/1381-

1384; K. W. Schweizer, "The Draft of a pamphlet by John Stuart, 3rd Earl of Bute," *Notes and Queries*, ccxxxii (1987), pp. 343-5; *idem.*, "Lord Bute and British Strategy in the Seven Years War: Further Evidence," *Notes and Queries*, ccxxxvi (1991), pp. 189-91; *idem.*, "Some Additions to the Dodington Diary," *Notes and Queries*, (Mar. 1992), pp. 56-61. For excellent analyses of the arguments of the proponents of a maritime strategy, see Richard Pares, "American versus Continental Warfare, 1739-1763," *English Historical Review* LI (1939), pp. 429-465; and Daniel A. Baugh, "Great Britain's 'Blue Water' Policy, 1689-1815," *The International History Review* X (1988), pp. 33-58.

[33] The prince to Bute, [Aug. 5, 1759], in Sedgwick, ed. *Letters from George III to Bute*, 28.

[34] Henry McCulloh to Bute, Dec. 13, 1756, Bute Papers, Box 1, no. 101, Mount Stuart, Isle of Bute, Scotland. For McCulloh's background, see Charles G. Sellers, Jr., "Private Profits and British Colonial Policy: The Speculations of Henry McCulloh," *William and Mary Quarterly* 3rd Ser., VIII (1951), pp.535-551.

[35] The two sources for the correspondence between George III and Bute, Sedgwick's *Letters from George III to Lord Bute* and the over 500 letters in the Bute Papers, Correspondence with George III, at Mount Stuart, include no letters from 1755 and only a few that can be dated in 1756. It is possible that there were letters from these years that were lost, but I doubt the number is large. Bute clearly went to pains to preserve his correspondence with his protégé, even when it was politically dangerous to do so.

[36] The prince to Bute, [Nov. 5, 1757), Sedgwick, ed., Letters from George III to Lord Bute 7. George's remarks reveal that he understood how Britain benefited from continental alliances, a fact that lends credence to the suspicion that his and Bute's most deeply felt objection to them was their identification of this policy with George II and the defense of Hanover. The end of this letter underscores how the prince personalized diplomatic issues. He would not despair, but rather "consider that having you is worth more to me and my dear country than these foreign and home friends that are daily changing. If you are but well and Providence assist us, England may yet be free and happy."

[37] The prince to Bute, [Dec. 1757], Bute Papers, Correspondence with George III, no 75.

[38] The prince to Bute, [Jul. 2, 1758], Sedgwick, ed., *Letters from George III to Bute*, 11.

[39] See *ibid.*, and the prince to Bute, [Aug. 5, 1759], Sedgwick, ed., *Letters from George III to Bute*, 28. For Bute's anti-continental views see also: K.W. Schweizer, "Lord Bute and British Strategy during the Seven Years War: Further Evidence," *Notes and Queries*, (Oxford), Jun. 1991, vol. 236, pp. 189-191.

[40]The prince to Bute, [Jul. 2, 1758], *ibid.*, pp.10-11; and the prince to Bute, [Sept. 1758], Bute Papers, Correspondence with George III, no 48.

[41]For the prince's comments during this period, see his letters to Bute in Sedgwick, *Letters from George III to Bute* 7-47; and Bute Papers, Correspondence with George III, nos. 49, 59, 60, 73, 74, 75. See also: K. W. Schweizer, "British Foreign Policy 1689-1763," *Journal of the History of European Ideas*, (Fall 1992), vol. 14, pp. 275-282.

[42]The prince to Bute, [Aug. 11, 1758], Sedgwick, ed. *Letters from George III to Bute*, 11.

[43]See Baugh, "'Blue-Water' Policy," *The International History Review* X (1988), pp. 46-47.

[44]The prince to Bute, [Aug. 11, 1758], Sedgwick, ed., *Letters from George III to Bute*, 11.

[45] The prince to Bute, [Aug. 20, 1758], *ibid.*, pp.12-13.

[46] Bute to William Pitt, [Aug. 20, 1758], William Stanhope Taylor and John Henry Pringle, eds., *Correspondence of William Pitt, Earl of Chatham*, 4 vols. (London, 1838), I, 336.

[47]The prince to Bute, [early Aug. 1759], Bute Papers, Correspondence with George III, no. 73.

[48]The prince to Bute, [after Sept. 18, 1759], *ibid.*, no. 25.

[49]The prince to Bute, [Oct.19, 1759], Sedgwick, ed., *Letters from George III to Bute*, 32.

[50]The impact of fears of an invasion from France on ministerial policies during 1759 is discussed in Richard Middleton, *Bells of Victory: The Pitt-Newcastle Ministry and the Conduct of the Seven Years War, 1757-1762* (Cambridge, 1985), pp.107-129. For their effect on the prince of Wales, see his letters to Bute during Jun.-Jul. 1759 in Sedgwick, ed. *Letters from George III to Bute*, pp. 24-27.

[51]The prince to Bute, [between Jun. 17-27, 1760], Bute Papers, Correspondence with George III, no. 77.

[52] The prince to Bute, [soon after Jun. 27, 1760], *ibid.*, no. 66.

[53]The prince and Bute were not alone in this opinion. Pitt later reacted to the fall of Quebec by observing that it, Montreal, and Louisburg should " 'not be given up for nothing' but were certainly 'proper matters of negotiation.'" Newcastle to the earl of Hardwicke, Oct. 31, 1759, quoted in Middleton, *The Bells of Victory*, p.183. Indeed, as late as Mar. 1761 Pitt conceded that under certain circumstances it might be wise and necessary to Britain to give up all or part of Canada. *Ibid.*, 184. These observations raise some questions about how valuable Pitt thought the

North American colonies were. At least from late 1759 until early 1761, he was willing to contemplate leaving them with less than total security from the French in Canada in order to gain concessions elsewhere. Such willingness on the part of a man identified by contemporaries and historians as committed to the North American colonies calls the validity of Greene's thesis into further question.

[54]The prince to Bute, [Oct. 5, 1760], Sedgwick, ed., *Letters from George III to Bute*, p. 47.

[55]The prince to Bute, [Dec. 1758], *ibid.*, 19.

[56]For the king's proclamation "for the encouragement of Piety and Virtue, and for preventing and punishing of Vice, Profaneness, and Immorality," Oct. 31, 1760, see *Annual Register* III (1760), pp. 241-243. For reactions of Newcastle to the appointment of Tories and the rumor that the king intended to spend no Treasury money on candidates in the general election of 1761, see Sir Lewis Namier, *England in the Age of the American Revolution* 2d edition (London, 1961), pp. 134-142.

[57] Newcastle, "Memorandum on the speech from the king," [Nov. 1760], Newcastle Papers, Add. MSS. 32914, fol. 355, British Library.

[58] The king's message, Nov. 25, 1760, *Journals of the House of Commons* XXVIII, 947.

[59] For a description of this controversy, see Brooke, *King George III*, pp.135-138.

[60]The king's speech, Nov. 20, 1760, *Commons Journals*, XXVIII, 935. George later remembered that he was "very averse to the altering [of] my declaration." The king to Bute, [Nov. 1760], in Sedgwick, ed., *Letters from George III to Bute*, p. 49.

[61]The king's ministers certainly recognized this. The duke of Devonshire reflected their collective judgment by describing Bute as a "visionary." He also spoke for them when he complained that the earl was "ignorant of business." To Devonshire and his colleagues, this was an alarming combination. The duke of Devonshire, "Memoranda on state of affairs, 1759-1762," Oct. 27, 1760, in Peter D. Brown and Karl W. Schweizer, eds., *The Devonshire Diary: William Cavendish Fourth Duke of Devonshire: Memoranda on State of Affairs. 1759-1762 Camden Miscellany Vol. XXVII* Camden, 4th Ser. (London, 1982), 43. For the concrete impact of this change in priorities see: K.W. Schweizer and M. Schumann, *The Seven Years War: A Transatlantic History* (London, 2010), esp. pp. 181-197.

[62] For a description of the king and Bute's attitudes toward North America during 1761-1763, and the factors determining those attitudes, see John L. Bullion, "Securing the peace: Lord Bute, the plan for the army, and the origins of the American Revolution," in Karl W. Schweizer, ed., *Lord Bute: Essays in Reinterpretation* (Leicester, Engl., 1988), pp. 25-35; Bullion, "Security and

Economy," *William and Mary Quarterly* XLV, 499-509; and John L. Bullion and Karl W. Schweizer, "The Use of Politicians' Private Papers in the Study of Policy Formulation in the Eighteenth Century: The Bute Papers as a Case Study," *Archives* XXII (1995), pp. 34-44, chapters XI, XIII, and X in this work.

PART THREE: FINANCING WAR

Chapter VIII

The *Monitor* and the Beer Tax Controversy: A Study of Constraints on London Newspapers, 1760-1761*

During the Seven Years War, William Pitt usually enjoyed the support of most London newspapers. First in loyalty to him through the thick and thin of politics, however, was the weekly essay paper, the *Monitor*. Founded in August 1755 by Richard Beckford, its original aims were to serve the interests of that family and to encourage the growth of Toryism, both in the City and in the nation. Beckford died in January 1756, and by the following November his brother William had given the paper an additional purpose: furthering the cause of the Great Commoner. After that date, the *Monitor* was almost always unstinting in its praise of Pitt and his policies, and unsparing in its attacks on his opponents.[1]

In January 1761, the *Monitor* temporarily departed from its usual enthusiastic support of Pitt. On December 17, 1760, he had vehemently defended the Treasury's proposal to impose an additional three shillings per barrel tax on strong beer in the House of Commons. The paper, in contrast, sharply attacked the tax on January 3. What explains this anomalous behavior? Marie Peters, a sensitive student of Pitt's wartime popularity, concluded that the *Monitor* was simply reflecting the City's immediate hostile reaction to the proposal. By early February, she argued, the paper had returned to Pitt's fold, and "dutifully moderated its views."[2]

This brief interpretation is not entirely satisfying, because Peters left two questions unasked. One is suggested by her interpretation itself. Why was the popular reaction in London so intense that the *Monitor* did not defend Pitt's position? The other arises naturally from a reading of the texts of the two editions.

The *Monitor* did more on February 7 than merely moderate its January 3 opinions. As the following examples reveal, it reversed them.

On January 3, the paper predicted that a new tax on beer would justly "give the inferiour Stations of Life a very mean Opinion of the Understanding and Honesty of the Guardians of their Liberty and Property." Furthermore, it stressed that "equality in the bearing of publick Burthens is a Plea every Freeman has a right unto, and every Subject, who apprehends himself in Danger of being thereby injured, ought not to be denied the Liberty to remonstrate against, and to endeavour to avoid the Evil."[3] In the later essay, the *Monitor* did not dispute that "this new tax may be accounted not to be so equitable as some others and as all impositions for raising money in a free nation ought to be." But then it harshly criticized the fact that "not only the [beer tax], but those suspected of advising, or in any wise contributing to its formulation and effect, are set up by somebody to be the object of public hatred." The paper also avowed: "Far be it from a Free people, who boast of their loyalty and justice, to usurp upon the prerogative of their guardians and rulers, by an unreasonable and unwarrantable opposition to an act of the legislative power; and to give credit to the many ill grounded reports spread to defame and injure individuals under the specious appearance of Liberty and Publick Good."[4] These accusations of excess on February 7 could with some justice be leveled against the essay of January 3.

The two *Monitor* essays also contradicted each other over the fiscal consequences of an additional levy on beer. The edition of January 3 speculated that it would reduce consumption, and thus collections as well. The paper estimated that the new tax might be "insufficient to raise one Third of the Sum" necessary to fund the loan for 1761. Such a shortfall in revenue would be disastrous for future loans. "Who will venture their Fortunes on a precarious Fund? Who will subscribe again, when they have lost by a former Loan?" And a failure of public credit, the *Monitor* reminded its readers, "will blunt our Swords, muzzle our Guns, . . . sink our Interest," and compel the nation to accept disadvantageous terms of peace.[5] Thirty-five days later, readers learned a different lesson from the same journal. "That [the tax] may fall very short of its calculation in the produce expected may be feared." Still, Englishmen need not be overly alarmed about the consequences. "If a money bill should happen to fall short of the expectation of those who bring it into the House, it is no novelty; it has been frequently the case."[6] From disaster to the ordinary: the *Monitor*'s fiscal analysis of the beer tax had traveled a long way in five weeks.

Does a desire to return to supporting Pitt completely explain the *Monitor*'s *volte-face*? This chapter will argue that it does not. Rather, the opinions printed in the two issues about the beer tax vividly illustrate the constraints on newspapers during the early 1760s. They show how careful the press had to be to keep from overstepping those boundaries in reporting and commenting on political events. They also reveal that some considerations were more important to the *Monitor* than reporting a true account of events to its readers. Indeed, these were so important that the paper's editors thought it better to mislead, than to inform, the public. To appreciate the conditions under which the *Monitor* and other papers wrote about the new duty without an awareness of the particulars of the government's proposal of it is impossible. It is therefore necessary to begin by determining as precisely as possible what was said in the House of Commons on December 17, 1760.

I

When the House went into the Committee of Supply on that day, Henry Bilson Legge, the Chancellor of the Exchequer, rose to present the Treasury's estimate of the nation's fiscal needs for 1761. He told the M.P.s that it would be necessary to borrow twelve million pounds. An agreement had been reached between the Duke of Newcastle, the First Lord of the Treasury, and bankers in the City on the terms. To pay the annual interest on this loan, the government would have to collect at least an additional £480,000 in revenue a year. The Treasury proposed that this be done by imposing an additional three shillings tax on each barrel of strong beer, to be paid by the brewer within two weeks of its production. This duty, according to Legge, would comfortably generate enough revenue to fund the debt. He estimated that it would raise £509 ,084 *per annum.*[7]

Before Legge began, he already knew that the Treasury's recommendation would be opposed. George Grenville, the Treasurer of the Navy, had told Newcastle on December 16 that he objected to taxing beer, and would propose an alternative. He went on to inform the duke that he favored appropriating the surplus revenues from the duties imposed on foreign brandies and domestic spirits in 1760 to the service of the loan for 1761. The difference between that amount and the £480,000 the government needed, he planned to say, could be made up by imposing additional duties on spirituous liquors.[8] Legge did not try to anticipate his fellow minister's arguments. He said nothing about why the Treasury preferred taxing strong beer rather than other commodities.[9] Grenville would have to make his case himself; the Treasury bench would not help him by introducing the question of possible alternatives. There was one subject, though, that Legge had to bring up: the effect of this tax on the cost of strong beer to the consumer. The House would want to know what the government's reaction would be to any attempt by the brewers to raise their prices. Memories of the near confrontation between them and the Treasury over prices in February 1760 were still fresh in men's minds, and rumors of an imminent price hike had excited much comment in the City and in the press generally as recently as October.[10]

Since the possibility of conflict between the industry and the government is important to an understanding of events between December 1760 and February 1761, a few words about it are in order. A series of medieval and Tudor statutes forbade combinations and conspiracies to raise the price of beers and ales. Since the late seventeenth century, the Treasury had successfully insisted that brewers observe the spirit and letter of these laws. When strong beer was introduced in London in 1722, it cost beer drinkers 3 d. per quart pot. The price was the same in December 1760, even though taxes had been levied on both the brewing and selling of beer during the intervening years. In 1753, the government had required victuallers to obtain an annual license for retailing beer. In February 1760, the voracious appetite of the war for money compelled Parliament to impose an additional duty of 3 d. per bushel on malt. Brewers had already been talking among themselves since 1758 about the desirability of raising prices. This new expense made charging more for strong beer seem even more advisable. According to their calculations, this new tax on malt would make the cost of brewing strong beer go up by one shilling a barrel. London breweries were large-scale operations, some producing as many as a thousand barrels a week. To the men who ran these enterprises, one shilling was "a sum too large to be borne patiently, if at all."[11]

When the brewers met privately in February 1760 to discuss the situation, some insisted that now was the time to claim that neither they nor the publicans could stay in business unless they raised the price of strong beer from 22-23s. per barrel to 27s., and from 3d. to 3 1/2d. per pot. Others held back. Not because they disagreed with the recommended prices: there was a general consensus on that. The timing, however, troubled them. They pointed out that the breweries currently had about a year's supply of strong beer at various stages of aging. None of that had been brewed with the more expensive malt. Raising prices on it might well result in the government's intervention. They suggested doing nothing at present beyond agreeing "to review their Plan" after one year passed, "when their Old Stocks of Beer were exhausted." This proposal was adopted, and a possible confrontation averted for the time being.[12]

Newcastle, Legge, and others at Whitehall regarded this as only a temporary reprieve. They interpreted the brewers' discussions and their agreement to review the plan as meaning that they "would certainly carry their proposal into Practice" in early 1761.[13] Members of Parliament might not be as knowledgeable about the details as men at the Treasury were, but certainly they could read newspapers and thereby discover that plans to raise beer prices were in the wind.

Thus the Chancellor of the Exchequer could not avoid disclosing on December 17 what the administration's policy on the price of strong beer would be.

Legge announced that the government would not oppose an increase in price from 3 to 3 1/2 d. per pot.[14] As he justified this decision, he revealed the extent to which Whitehall had come to sympathize with the brewers' point of view. He noted that the present price of a barrel to victuallers was 24 shillings.[15] The Treasury would not object to the brewers adding five shillings to this charge. Three of those five shillings would cover the new tax on strong beer. Another shilling would recompense them for the expense of the malt tax of 1760. The fifth shilling, Legge explained, would be their "profit" for paying the other four shillings before they sold the barrel, and would protect them against the possibility that some of their customers might not pay for the beer they ordered and received.[16] This would make the price of a barrel to victuallers 29 shillings. The government also would take no action against victuallers retailing that beer at seven farthings a pint and 3 1/2 d. a quart. Such increases, Legge summed up, would give "Brewer and Victualler . . , an allowance to reimburse them for their former Grievances of Licenses etc."[17] After this explanation of the government's position on the price of strong beer, Legge moved that the committee report out an additional three shilling tax on strong beer.

Grenville then made "a strong but not very lively speech against [the Treasury]."[18] In it, he "delivered his opinion fully against the propriety of this tax, representing the particular severity it would be attended with . . . for the labouring and manufacturing part of his Majesty's subjects." They would pay more for a necessity because of this proposal and the government's willingness to allow the brewers to raise their price. And what if they refused to spend more for strong beer? In that case, Grenville pointed out, the tax, "by diminishing the consumption of that commodity, . . . must certainly lessen the public revenue." He urged the House to raise the money from new and old duties on foreign brandies and domestic spirits. This would cause the burden to fall on a more appropriate source of revenue: well-to-do people who were consuming luxuries, not the working poor who were drinking a staple of their lives.[19] Familiar with the details of taxes on spirits—he had devised the most recent duties, then shepherded the bill through the House in early 1760—Grenville drew upon his expertise to make a lengthy presentation designed to convince M.P.s that his proposals would produce enough money to fund the loan.[20]

Pitt responded to his brother-in-law's speech. His remarks were probably extemporaneous, for when Newcastle had warned him the day before about Grenville's intentions, he "seemed not to believe" the duke.[21]

Certainly he was angry at this apostasy, and that anger fueled a speech that was everything Newcastle could have wished. His defense of the beer tax was so enthusiastic that the Earl of Hardwicke briefly wondered if he had been responsible for choosing it.[22] "Mr. Pitt . . . answered Mr. Grenville's objections, strongly supported the propriety and expediency of the tax upon beer, declaring that he did it from the fullest conviction, and that he rejoiced that [the surplus gained from the duties imposed on spirits in 1760] was ready for the service of another year [1762]."[23] He praised the Treasury's performance extravagantly. "He had," he claimed, "a great dependence upon those who had considered [taxing beer], and prepared it"; indeed, no Treasury Board could have done better in arranging for financing the war effort.[24] He even went so far as to compliment Legge, whom he detested, and to "treat his honourable kinsman (as he called Grenville) with contempt."[25]

Grenville did reply, "adhering to his former opinion," but the outcome, which had never been in doubt, was now obviously a foregone conclusion.[26] Legge's motion was reported out of committee without a dissenting vote. The rest of the stages of legislation clearly would be a formality. Details might be changed, but there would be an additional three shillings tax on strong beer. Elated, Newcastle wrote Joseph Yorke that the House had "passed . . . the tax on the brewery which we suppose will produce upwards of £500,000 p. a."[27] The duke did not pass along any news about the probable effect of the new tax on the price of beer. Apparently he felt this was less worthy of note, and would not particularly interest the British minister at The Hague.

II

The same could not be said of Londoners and the newspapers published in the metropolis. One observer in the *Public Ledger* computed "the beer-drinkers in and about [London] to be about 4 fifths of the people," and then pointedly commented that "4 fifths of the people may justly be called the public."[28] To the labouring poor, strong beer was a necessity of life, as essential to productive work as to the enjoyment of leisure. (Indeed, its popular name, porter, testifies to its identification with men doing manual labor.) Moreover, strong beer was considered a socially beneficial beverage, because it contributed much more than other drinks to the longevity and vigor of men and women's lives. One need only glance at Hogarth's "Beer Street" and "Gin Lane" to have visual confirmation of this belief. Even small beer was held to be deficient in its healthful properties to porter. For example, in 1764 soldiers in the Hampshire militia blamed the sudden death after maneuvers of a popular comrade on his "drinking cold small beer." They inscribed an appropriate moral on his gravestone:

Soldiers be wise from his untimely fall
And when ye're hot drink Strong or none at all.[29]

Understandably, therefore, any hint of an increase in the price of strong beer was of intense interest to Londoners. Newspapers trying to swell circulation were eager to pass those hints along to them, garnished with appropriate attacks on the brewers, and did so during the fall of 1760.

In October, rumors that the brewers were ready to raise the cost of a pot immediately, had been common currency at Whitehall and in the City. The Treasury responded by ordering its solicitor "to cause immediate prosecutions against any persons concerned in a combination for raising the price of beer and ale."[30] The same reports of "a Scheme amongst the Brewers to raise the price of Beer and Ale" reached the press, and the discussion of them in print resulted m "the Clamour now arising amongst the common people against it."[31] To "An Anti-Monopolist" writing in the October 25 *Public Advertiser*, the "timely complaints of the public caused [the brewers] to drop for the present their wicked designs."[32] With an eye to equal success in the future, the same newspaper ran an unsigned paragraph on November 10 on why some necessities cost more than they did a few years earlier. "Those who endeavour to *throw* this upon our taxes," the author warned, "willfully *mistake* the matter." In fact, "the legislature have been remarkably careful in avoiding, as far as possible, to tax *those things* that are most needful." Rather, "monopolists and confederations of suppliers are to blame" for higher prices.[33] Applied to brewers, this meant their complaints about the burden of the new malt duty were deliberately misleading.

So, for a variety of reasons, the debate in the House on December 17 was vitally interesting to both press and public. Although it is impossible to tell when news about these proceedings began to seep out, it cannot have been long afterwards. There were hundreds of witnesses present, some of them sitting from London seats, some of them brewers, some not even M.P.s.[34] From several standpoints, the debate was a striking one: the announcement of the largest loan in history; the proposal of a new tax on beer; the ministry's promise not to prosecute men who raised the price of strong beer to 3 1/2 d. per pot; and the political and personal drama of the public disagreement of ministers over fiscal policy and the clash between the two brothers-in-law, with all that portended for politics within the administration. All these elements encouraged discussion of the day's events outside of doors. That men at the *Monitor* knew the details before the edition of January 3 is not surprising.

Knowing, however, was one thing; publishing, another. In 1738, at the instigation of the Speaker, Arthur Onslow, the House of Commons had decided that "it is an high Indignity to, and a notorious Breach of, the Privilege of this House" for any writer or printer "to give [in newspapers] any Account of the Debates, or other Proceedings of this House, or any Committee thereof, as well during the Recess, as the Sitting of Parliament." If this privilege was violated, "this House will proceed with the utmost Severity against such Offenders."[35] This threat was sufficient to intimidate London newspapers during the 1750s.[36] When four newspapers tested it on January 31, 1760 by publishing Speaker Onslow's communication of the House's vote of thanks to Admiral Hawke, and Hawke's reply, punishment swiftly followed. The publishers were summoned to the bar of the House, examined, and found in contempt. Because they expressed sorrow for publishing these proceedings, they were dismissed after receiving on their knees a reprimand from Onslow and paying the usual fees of attendance. One of the printers had claimed he was unaware of this privilege. Ignorance did not exempt him from being held in contempt and, in any case, no one could plead it after this episode.[37] Moreover, publishing a formal vote of thanks to a naval hero—hardly a controversial measure—was innocuous compared to informing the public about the debate on December 17 in the Committee of Supply. No daily or tri-weekly newspaper in London was willing to be the first to break the news about the beer tax and risk the wrath of Arthur Onslow and the House of Commons. After some consideration of the best way to avoid winding up on their knees in St. Stephen's Chapel, the editors of the *Monitor* were prepared to run that risk.

Why? Certainly the answer is the *Monitor*'s firm ideological commitment to the rights of the people that Marie Peters has so well described. " 'Every true Briton,' 'every private subject,' " to the *Monitor*, "has the right to watch over those who rule him, to express opinions on what they do, to take measures to prevent harm to the constitution and expose public inequities." That right included Parliament as well as kings and ministers.[38] In this case, the people's interests would obviously be adversely affected by the ministry's proposals and the House's reaction to them on December 17. That their governors planned to impose a direct tax on strong beer was bad enough. Among other harmful consequences, this would give brewers another excuse to try to raise prices. But the administration had gone even further than that, by promising not to oppose anyone charging 3 1/2 d. per pot of porter. That would guarantee an increase in the cost of a necessity of life. Those who had not heard this news had to be informed. Those who already knew—and the *Monitor* was ready to claim the prospect of this tax "already alarms the disinterested and industrious part of the nation"—needed to be encouraged in their opposition.[39] On this occasion, the commitment of the paper's editors to the people's rights overrode their admiration for that prominent defender of the beer tax, William Pitt.

III

The tactic the *Monitor* adopted to tell its readers about the government's tax was straightforward. Without referring to any debate, the paper noted in the first sentence: "Amongst the Taxes for the Current Year, we are informed there is proposed a new Duty upon Beer and Ale." The *Monitor* then wasted no time in attacking:

> a Tax, which already alarms the disinterested and industrious Part of the Nation: And which will, it is apprehended, prove greatly Detrimental to the Revenue arising from the Brewery, insufficient for the Payment of the Loan intended, and injurious to that Part of the People, on whom the Consumption of the Common Brewery chiefly depends; while such as Brew their own drink are totally exempt from the Payment of three Shillings on each Barrel of Strong Beer and Ale; besides what may be further added to the Price of a Pot of Beer by the Publican.

Note the last two parts of this opening blast. In them the *Monitor* flatly stated that the consumers of strong beer would bear the burden of the tax, plus whatever profit the publican would seek, by paying a higher price for beer. Without mentioning Legge's concession to the brewers, or the specific price he said government would not oppose, the paper had managed to tell its readers that a price hike would be the inevitable result of the passage of this tax. Keeping the Treasury's offer from the public protected the *Monitor* from being in contempt of the House. Referring to an increase as inevitable, and criticizing sharply the government proposal that caused it, fulfilled its obligation to the people.

The *Monitor* spoke eloquently of the consequences of a higher price for porter. "The Increase of the Price of Strong Beer and Ale," it asserted, "will necessarily revive the almost abolished Practice of guzzling Small Beer [mixed with] Gin, amongst those who love Strong liquor, and the Hard Labourers, who [will be unable to] purchase Strong Beer." This would "encourage Drunkenness, entail upon the Nation those Evils and Vices which once disgraced this Island, enervated our Soldiers, Sailors and Labourers [and] disabled our Manufacturers." Aside from these social evils that would have serious effects on Britain's domestic economy and international trade, the *Monitor* predicted that the nation's finances would seriously suffer as well. As consumption of beer decreased, revenue from that source would decline. When collections could not adequately service the nation's debts, it "would injure publick Credit in a most Essential Manner, and might become the secret Engine to force Britain to accept of disadvantageous Terms of Peace."

By themselves, these were harsh criticisms of the tax. But the *Monitor* reserved its most stinging indictment for another flaw it could see in the proposal. This tax was improper, because it was flagrantly unequal. "Where is the Equality of a Tax," it pointedly asked, "which leaves the Noble, the Rich, and the Opulent Part of the Subjects in a State of Exemption, and must be gathered out of the Industry of the middling and inferiour Classes?" The well-to-do brewed their own strong beer, and all who brewed solely for domestic consumption were not required to pay the three shilling tax. Their cellars could be full of porter, their tables covered with pints and quarts, and they would pay nothing to the excise man. In contrast: "the poor Man, who warms himself at the Publican's Fire, is obliged, if he calls for Beer, to contribute in its Price to the Support of publick

Liberty, and the Defence of the rich Man's property." The *Monitor* did not favor any new imposition on beer, either on the finished product or any of the raw materials. Malt, according to the paper, was already taxed too much. But of the choice between two evils, taxing malt again was far more preferable than adding another duty to beer. Everyone would have to pay that tax, rich and poor, and distillers as well as brewers.

The *Monitor*'s final judgment on the ministry's proposal was blunt and uncompromising: "This three Shilling Tax, in every Prospect, is productive of disagreeable and dangerous Effects." On that note, the paper rested its case. No doubt its editors were happy to have once again defended the rights of the people and the economic interests of "the middling and inferior Classes," without exposing the *Monitor* to parliamentary reprisals.[40]

IV

The *London Evening Post* printed lengthy excerpts from the *Monitor*'s essay on the first page of its January 6 edition.[41] That same day, the *London Chronicle* published much briefer excerpts dealing with the inequality of the tax, without identifying the source.[42] No other paper followed their lead. For ten days, no further news about the imminent beer tax and the resultant price hike appeared in the press.

During that time, two of the protagonists in the drama moved ahead with their plans. Legge smoothly steered the bill through the various stages of legislation. The House of Commons approved it on January 14 *nemiente contradiente*; the House of Lords, by the same vote on January 20. The king assented to the legislation on the same day.[43] Meanwhile, the brewers tried to take full advantage of the interval between December 17 and the enactment of the tax. The government's bill did not impose the three shilling duty on beer brewed before that tax became law. So, after the vote on December 17, they began brewing as much porter as they could. They also initiated measures to-raise the price of their strong beer immediately to the levels Legge had indicated the government would not oppose. The brewers informed their publican customers that the new price of a barrel would be twenty-nine shillings, and urged them to retail the beer at 3 1/2 d. per pot. From the brewers' perspective, the rush was understandable. For some time to come, they would be selling beer made before the passage of the new tax. Profits earned during this period would be higher than they would be after the old stocks were depleted, and would provide a useful cushion against the day when the government began collecting the extra three shillings. The publicans were more reluctant. They knew full well who would be dealing directly with an irate public across the bar, and were justly apprehensive.[44] Even before that occurred, however, all of the parties concerned had to deal with some angry essays in the press.

On January 17, the *Evening Post* published some bitter paragraphs against the inequality of the impending tax. "In the Business of Taxation, all Christian Governments should ever be careful not to *grind the Faces of the Poor*." Therefore, the paper continued, no tax on necessities should be adopted: "if it bears harder on the Indigent than the Wealthy, because this would gradually impoverish the middle Class to such a Degree, that at last there would be but two Distinctions left in a Nation, *Princes and Beggars*." Then the anonymous author pointedly asked: "While *Financiers* seem to be at a loss to raise a Fund for paying the Interest of necessary Loans, is it not surprising that a *certain Tax* remains *unrectified?*" In contrast to poorer Britons, many well-off landowners could use loopholes in the land tax to avoid paying their full share. He estimated that one-half of them were thus able to save money and then lend it to the exchequer, when they should be paying revenue into it.[45] In the same edition, "Philo-Patriae" also stigmatized the tax "now about to be laid upon Beer" as unequal and profoundly harmful to the interests of the laboring poor, who would pay the entire tax. As if this were not sufficient to excite resentment, he predicted that between the brewers and the publicans the price of a pot would rise to 4d.[46] "Paul Porter," writing in the next issue of the *Evening Post*, made the same prediction about price, the usual observations about who would bear the whole burden of the tax, and recommended that the government not make the tax perpetual. Limit its duration to a few years, he suggested. If the people knew that it and the price increase it caused were temporary, they would pay even 4d. a pot gladly to help support the war effort.[47]

Few other papers in London followed the *Evening Post*'s lead. Most did not discuss the beer tax at all. It is somewhat ironic, therefore, that despite the *Evening Post*'s uncompromising hostility to the measure, the attack that aroused the most interest and comment appeared in another newspaper. On January 20, the *Public Ledger* published the following unsigned paragraph:

> When *over-grown* dealers in any of the necessaries of life meanly project and apply for a new tax upon themselves, that they might plead an excuse for raising from the public twice the sum they advance to the government, and this too chiefly from the poor and labouring part of the nation, who, under such pressures, have neither leisure nor money enough to help themselves, and elude the duty, would it not be doing them justice if they were, by a subsequent act, restrained from raising the price of their commodity? Upon a fair enquiry into their profits, it might be found they would still gain more than most of them deserve.[48]

That the brewers were greedy was not a novel story to readers: the accusation that they had advised the government to impose this tax, however, was new indeed. Moreover, though the *Public Ledger* maintained a discreet silence on the ministers' role, the implication of this paragraph was unmistakable. In return for the brewers' support of the three shilling duty, the government had agreed to permit a price increase. The paper could not explicitly charge the ministers with being a party to such a harmful bargain without prompting parliamentary action against it. The clearest indication that such a deal might have been struck was Legge's speech on December 17, and directly referring to it would violate the House's privilege. So the *Public Ledger* proceeded to expose what it believed was collusion between the Treasury and the brewers to the detriment of the laboring poor by innuendo, in the expectation that the public would make the connection.

That expectation was justified. Before a week was out, some brewers who were "being very much censured as promoters of the present additional tax upon strong beer" assured Londoners via the *Public Advertiser* that "all the reports are false and absurd, maliciously and enviously given out to disturb the peace, for private; wicked, and very base purposes."[49] In fact, they had cause for complaint. They truthfully protested in the *Public Advertiser* that they had not advised imposing this tax, that they had been surprised by the government's proposal of it, and that they had privately remonstrated against it to officials at the Treasury.[50] To the beer drinking public, though, the brewers protested too much. These Londoners noted the efforts by some publicans to raise the price of a quart to 3 1/2d., and concluded that the brewers were trying to realize their part of the bargain. "The lower Class of People in this Metropolis," noted the *London Evening Post* on January 29, "are far from being reconciled to the Act lately passed for laying an additional Duty on Strong Beer, as it chiefly affects them most." The paper followed this observation with reports of assaults on brewers, threats to level pubs that charged their prices, and boycotts of publicans who intended to charge 3 1/2d. per pot. Understandably, "some publicans, who raised the Price of their Beer Yesterday Morning, thought proper to lower it again before Night." The editors did concede that "the Exigencies of Government may have made [this tax] necessary." Even so, they predicted, the public would never permit brewers and publicans to raise the price of porter.[51]

The crowd found another target for their resentment as well: George III himself. When the young king attended the theatre in late January, parts of the audience raised "the clamour about the beer." This demonstration, which "dissatisfied" him and his mentor, the Earl of Bute, revealed that beer drinkers in London blamed the king's government as much as the brewers for the recent attempt to raise prices.[52] To their minds, George's ministers had accepted the brewers' advice and assistance, and given them permission to increase their profits in return. The paragraph in the *Public Ledger* had struck a responsive chord, and had been seemingly confirmed by two later developments. The government had done nothing when the brewers had tried to raise prices. Moreover, when *Lloyd's Evening Post* examined the act itself, the editors made, and then published, a significant discovery. Contrary to earlier reports, the paper noted, there was no clause in it restraining brewers and publicans from raising prices.[53] Because of his association with Bute, George was far less popular than a young prince who had just ascended to the throne and gloried in the name of Britain would have otherwise been.[54] His assent had made the beer tax the law of the land. His presence at the play was, therefore, a perfect opportunity for Londoners to express their discontent with their rulers.

No newspaper carried any account of this episode at the time it occurred. The reason for their silence is clear: they believed government officials would interpret publication as encouraging more insults to the king, and charge the offending paper with sedition. This assessment was well- founded. On February 6, the Solicitor-General, the Solicitor to the Treasury, and the famous Westminster justice of the peace Sir John Fielding met to discuss "the mob, the [*Gazetteer* and *London Daily*] *Advertiser*, [and]the tax on beer."[55] Six days later, the law officers of the crown determined that there was no libel in the *Gazetteer* of February 3. The paragraph marked for their consideration described the king's daily schedule, nothing more.[56] Some ministers apparently believed that this might be intended to assist "the mob" in planning and executing future confrontations over the tax and the cost of beer with George III. The influence of the press on popular disturbances seemed obvious to them. In this case, the cooler heads of the attorneys prevailed. Moreover, politicians and the king's law officers did not have to consider prosecuting any newspapers over the beer tax again. The events of late January caused the papers involved in the campaign against the tax to examine the effect of their arguments, and then change them.

V

Once more, the *Monitor* took the lead. In its February 7 edition, the paper explained the reasons why anger at the beer tax spread through London. Then it noted: "the contagion spreads so wide, that it is become the most ready means of designing men to spirit up the populace, to assist them in working the ruin of the innocent; and of the Disaffected to quench the ardour of our Governors, and to insult Majesty itself." The *Monitor* could understand why the tax would disturb people. No tax pleased everyone, and this one appeared to be less equitable than some others might be. But this objection, plus the charge that it would not raise enough money, should not be given too much weight by the people. Other taxes failed to produce the estimated sum without ill effects. And however understandable the dissatisfaction of the community in general was with an apparently inequitable tax, that did not justify "those heats and excesses, with which they publickly insult their Governors; are drawn to forget their duty to the King, and licentiously endeavour to degrade some of the most respectable manufacturers in the brewery, by imputing unto them an intention to injure their own trade." By signing the act, the king had merely followed the advice of Parliament. The ministers had conceived and formulated the act "upon most rational and just observances." In particular, they proceeded "not with an inclination to enhance the price in the retail way, but to squeeze some part of those vast profits out of the wholesale manufacturer, for the relief of the national burden." As for the brewers, common sense should have persuaded people against believing they would try to injure their own trade by advising the imposition of another tax on it. If officials did happen to consult with them about details of the bill, such a step was not sinister. Rather, it indicated that the government was properly trying to learn as much as possible about the trade before proceeding.

The only danger to consumers that the *Monitor* could foresee was the brewers' effort to raise prices. At the present time, "while they were amusing the people with objections and misrepresentations of persons and things," they were also filling their cellars with beer brewed before the tax went into effect. They also "seem resolved not to increase their stocks, till they can find an opportunity to bring that very stock, not charged by the late act, into the market at [an] advanced price of *five shillings* per barrel." Such an increase, the *Monitor* insisted: "must not in any sort be placed to the account of the promoters of the said act, but is entirely to be attributed to the insatisfiable thirst of the brewers, who snatch at every incident to improve their lucrative trade." Only "artful, designing, and seditious men" would make such "bad use" of the tax as to suggest that government bore any blame for the brewers' actions. Such men were trying to inspire porter drinkers—who were "of all his Majesty's subjects the most exposed to temptations for interpreting and destroying the peace and harmony of the society"—to a factious and destructive opposition to authority. To disarm these enemies, the government should "suffer not the price of *Porter* to be raised at the will and pleasure of the brewer" by using the authority of the Privy Council to prevent any increase.[57]

Certain aspects of this essay deserve emphasis. Its overt purpose is clear. The *Monitor* wanted to deflect popular anger over the threatened price hike away from the tax and the government and toward the brewers and their "insatisfiable thirst" for greater profits. Central to realizing this goal was an insistence that the planners of the duty designed it to fall solely on the profits of the brewery. The authorities, the *Monitor* claimed, did not expect that higher prices to the consumer would be the result of taxing strong beer. Those who said otherwise were "artful, designing, seditious" men. Of course, making that claim meant that the paper had to cover up what Legge had said on December 17. Rather than informing the public that the government had indicated it would not oppose an increase in the price of a barrel of porter by five shillings, the *Monitor* had to imply that the recent effort of the brewers to charge that price had received no official encouragement of any sort. A paper committed to informing the people on matters affecting their interests was now misleading them about the government's true positions.

What caused the editors not only to reverse their prior arguments against the beer tax, but also their ideological commitment to the public's right to know? Probably their decision was based on a conviction that a strict regard for consistency and truth in this case was undesirable, from the standpoint of both self-interested and patriotic motives. It was obviously unwise for the *Monitor* and other papers to print opinions that officials might reasonably construe as seditious libel. If they continued to criticize the government directly and indirectly, and if crowds continued to insult the king, and perhaps some ministers as well, they were in danger of having that happen. Expediency dictated that the *Monitor* do more than simply disavow the mob's activities. The paper had to leave no doubt in its readers' minds that it was not encouraging further outrages by continuing to hold the government partly responsible for any rise in porter prices. Such expediential reasoning surely played a role in the paper's decision.

But not the only role: there are reasons to assume that the editors had come to believe that attacking the ministry on this issue really was close to being seditious. As Peters points out, the paper never supported mob violence. To the *Monitor*, the "middling sort" was the most valuable part of the people. It regarded the lower classes, "the most exposed to temptations for interrupting and destroying the peace and harmony of the society," with suspicion.[58] In this case, the mob were challenging the sovereign's authority and dignity, and calling into question the wisdom and honesty of Parliament. That amounted to an attack on the constitution, which the *Monitor* believed was "the most perfect form of government, that ever was instituted, better . . . than that of any other nation now existing."[59] Finally, by attacking a tax that was intended to help the government fight France vigorously, the mob could conceivably hamper the war effort. The *Monitor* was fully committed to the war. It was equally committed to gaining at the peace terms commensurate with the blood and treasure Britain had spent and the victories she had won. Part of the price of good terms was supporting a vigorous conduct of the war by paying taxes. "If [this tax] answers the ends of government," the paper argued on February 7, "the subject has no reason to complain. Let us, therefore, whatever may be the event of this act," it advised, "study to be quiet."[60] For its own and the nation's sake, the *Monitor* planned to follow this strategy henceforward.

VI

Other newspapers were not willing to remain entirely quiet on the subject of beer, but they did adopt many of the *Monitor*'s tactics. The *Public Ledger*, for example, published a piece by "Publico" on February 12 which asserted that the king and Parliament "never imagined brewers and publicans would boldly attempt to make the poor pay one farthing a quart to themselves, as an increase of profit, besides the farthing paid to the government."[61] On February 18, *Lloyd's Evening Post* printed a lament by "Norvicensis" about the false accusations against the government that was quickly extracted and published again by the *London Chronicle* and the *Public Advertiser*. "Norvicensis" was shocked "that an act, never intended to oppress the poor, should excite a murmur against the best of sovereigns."[62] And, even as the papers defended the king and the administration, they were also focusing the debate on the brewers and their attempt to raise prices. In the even-handed tradition that typified the way newspapers dealt with domestic controversies of this period, publishers opened their columns to the brewers' defenders as well as to their opponents. Neither side in the debate referred to the government's proposals of December 17.[63]

Certainly London's beer drinkers did not remain quiet. Disagreements between brewers and publicans, and the threat of violence and boycotts had prevented any increase in the price of beer in February. When brewers and publicans tried again in late June to raise the price to 3 1/2d. per pot, the same types of crowd actions occurred. Such were reported in the *St. James Chronicle* and the *Whitehall Evening Post*, without reference to any official role.[64] These attacks on the brewers did not trouble the *Monitor* in the least. It published a biting essay accusing them of trying to injure labor, industry, and the interest of the nation by a selfish attempt to raise prices. Again, the paper insisted that the tax was meant to fall on the profits of manufacturers and purveyors of porter. The *Monitor* did not specifically condone violent acts against them, but clearly it was less troubled by the mob when it attacked brewers rather than the king and his government.[65]

Indeed, only twice was the silence about the government broken. A paragraph in the *Public Ledger* noted that it had been informed that: "had a certain great financier then in place [Legge] rightly represented its consequences, the bill might have received a negative."[66] This notice relieved the present ministers and the House from any blame, and placed responsibility squarely on a man currently in the political wilderness. It also, of course, reversed what actually happened during the debate of December 17. "Simplicitor," a defender of the brewers, hinted on June 23 that the reality of December 17 was different than what the public was being told. He argued in the *London Chronicle* that it should not be vainly imagined that Parliament intended that only brewers and publicans would pay the tax.[67] But this was the only attempt by the brewers and their allies to suggest that Legge had said something about price increases six months earlier.

Instead, they asked the Treasury to acknowledge Legge's pledge. On July 22, a committee of brewers presented a memorial to the Treasury Board. It described the necessity of a price increase, and the opposition they had met with. Then they prayed for some relief from the Treasury "either by intimating it was the sense of Parliament [that] the price of strong beer should be advanced from 3 d. to 3 1/2 d. a quart, or by any other method that may be thought proper." Not surprisingly in light of the public's reaction to the prospect of paying 3 1/2 d., the lords of the Treasury decided they could not give any relief to the petitioners.[68] Ultimately, however, the government had to respond as the brewers wished. Faced with the possibility that porter brewing might entirely stop in December

1761, the Treasury entered into negotiations with them. The result was a clause in an act amending the beer tax of 1761 which ordered that no brewer or victualler should be "sued, impleaded, or molested . . . by indictment, information, popular action or otherwise" for charging more for beer.[69] The papers did not report this news.[70] Occasional essays on the brewers pro and con appeared during the next few months, but the controversy did not excite much interest in the pages of newspapers or in the streets of London. Beer drinkers in the metropolis accepted the inevitable. The brewers and publicans got their price increase; the government, £571,042 in revenue during 1762 as consumption stayed at pre-tax levels.[71] *Lloyd's Evening Post* commended the common people for submitting to the tax and the increase "not only quietly, but many even cheerfully." The author could not help adding, though, that now porter, "so far from being inviting, is flat, mawkish, and disgust[ing]."[72]

VII

In retrospect, however, when one considers the *Monitor* and some other papers on the beer tax controversy, the impression that lingers is not flat, watered beer or greedy brewers and publicans. Rather, the limits within which the press had to work are the most striking aspects of the whole episode. Some were imposed and enforced by institutions of government.

The *Monitor* had to avoid infringing upon parliamentary privilege when it alluded to the debate of December 17. The paper had to be equally careful not to appear to encourage riots and other popular demonstrations, and to keep its criticism of ministers away from the boundaries marked by seditious libel. To be sure, the *Monitor* was committed to and celebrated openly the people's right to know about the activities of their rulers and to prevent harm being done to the constitution or to their interests. But in 1760-61, this commitment did not inspire its editors to challenge either the House's definition of privilege or the legal concept of seditious libel.

It also seems apparent from its various reactions to the beer tax that internal, as well as external, constraints played a major role in shaping the *Monitor*'s editorial policy The editors did venerate the constitution, and were determined to maintain it. They also believed that threats to the government and the society could come from the lowest as well as the highest ranks. When the laboring poor of London attacked the king, the head of government and the visible symbol of authority, the *Monitor* discountenanced them, and ceased its sharp criticism of the ministry and the duty on beer. The paper's unswerving support for a vigorous military effort against the French also tilted it away from questioning the wisdom of the ministers and the tax, and toward accepting the expediency of their proposal That doing so required misleading the public about Legge's comments regarding an increase in the price of porter did not deter the editors of the paper. During 1760-61, the *Monitor*'s conception of what was in its own and the nation's interest outweighed its commitment to the people's right to know.

*This chapter first appeared in a book version of *Studies in History and Politics/Études d'Histoire et de Politique*, eds., K.W. Schweizer and J. Black, (Edwin Mellen Press, 1989).

Endnotes

[1] Marie Peters, *Pitt and Popularity: The Patriot Minister and London Opinion during the Seven Years' War* (Oxford, 1980), pp. 13-16.

[2] *Ibid.*, p. 179.

[3] *Monitor*, Jan. 3, 1761.

[4] *Ibid.*, Feb. 7, 1761.

[5] *Ibid.*, Jan. 3, 1761.

[6] *Ibid.*, Feb. 7, 1761.

[7] Henry Bilson Legge's speech, Dec. 17, 1760, in: Sir Roger Newdigate, Parliamentary Diary, Newdegate MSS., B. 2540/ 5, Warwickshire County Record Office, Warwick, England.

[8] The Duke of Newcastle, "Memorandum," Dec. 16, 1760, Newcastle Papers, Add. MSS. 32999, f. 125, British Library.

[9] The reasons why the Treasury decided on a direct tax on beer rather than levying another duty on malt may be found in a letter and enclosure from an influential Commissioner of the Excise, William Burton, to Newcastle, Nov. 20, 1760, Newcastle Papers, Add. MSS. 32914, fos. 432-36. Burton's basic points—that there was a higher rate of fraud in malting, that the brewers had to pay in a shorter period, and that a direct tax on beer would probably increase the price to the consumer less than an additional tax on malt—are briefly summarized in Peter Mathias, *The Brewing Industry in England, 1700-1830* (Cambridge, 1959), p. 360.

[10] For the February confrontation, see *ibid.*, pp. 359-60; for the October rumors, see the Earl of Hardwicke to Newcastle, Oct. 19,1760, Newcastle Papers, Add. MSS. 32913, f. 205, and *Public Advertiser*, Oct. 25, 1760.

[11] For legislation concerning the price of beer and ales, see Mathias, *Brewing Industry*, p.110, and *London Evening Post*, Jan. 31, 1761; for the price of strong beer and taxes on the industry, see Mathias, *Brewing Industry*, pp. 110-11, 359-60; and for a lucid account of the taxes and the brewers' meetings in February 1760, see John Bindley, "Considerations on Beer and Malt," sent to Charles Jenkinson, [Dec. 1763], Liverpool Papers, Add. MSS. 38335, fos. 310-11, British Library. The quotations in this paragraph are from this paper. Very knowledgeable about both the brewing industry and distilleries, Bindley served first as Secretary to the Commissioners of the Excise, and then as a Commissioner, during this period.

[12] See Bindley, "Considerations on Beer and Malt," [Dec. 1763], Liverpool Papers, Add. MSS. 38335, f.310. Mathias evidently did not consult this paper, with the result that he mistakenly assumed that the brewers held back because some feared the higher price would reduce demand, *Brewing Industry*, p 359.

[13] Bindley, "Considerations on Beer and Malt," [Dec. 1763], Liverpool Papers, Add MSS 38335, f 310.

[14] For Legge's announcement, see *ibid.*, and Legge's speech, Dec. 17, 1760, Newdigate Diary, Newdegate MSS., B. 2540/5. Other references to the Chancellor of the Exchequer's remarks about raising the price of beer may be found in a memorial from London brewers to the Treasury Jul. 22, 1761, Treasury Minutes; T. 29/34, f. 78, N.A., London; and London brewers, "Proposals for consideration," [December 12, 1761], Treasury Papers, T. 1/408, f. 279, N.A.. To the best of my knowledge, no historian has hitherto noticed that Legge promised that the government would not intervene against a price increase to 3 1/2 d. per pot.

[15] In *Brewing Industry*, p 359-360, Mathias observed that the usual price per barrel to the victuallers in Feb. 1760 was 22-23s. Legge and others at the Treasury apparently believed that brewers had raised this to 24s. in order to share the burden of the additional malt duty with the victuallers.

[16] As a supporter of the brewery later noted "When a Tax is laid upon any sort of Consumption, the Dealers always add to it, if not double it, and they must do so, in order to compensate their bad Debts, because when a Customer becomes Insolvent [dealer] lose not only the prime Cost [the goods they sold to him], but also the Tax they have paid" *Public Advertiser*, Oct. 13, 1762. The government recognized the wisdom of this practice, and thus was ready to allow the brewers the fifth shilling.

[17] Bindley, "Considerations on Beer and Malt," [Dec. 1763], Liverpool Papers, Add MSS 38335, f. 310.

[18] This judgment is from Newcastle to Joseph Yorke, Dec. 19, 1760, Newcastle Papers, Add MSS 32916, fos. 193-94.

[19] This account of Grenville's speech draws heavily upon a report about the debate of Dec.17, 1760 in the *St. James Chronicle*, Dec. 23-25, 1762. At that time, the Earl of Bute and his followers were trying to refute the current rumors that he had devised the beer tax and supported it in Parliament. This paragraph was part of that effort, for another, see *London Chronicle*, Dec. 9-11, 1762. A comparison of Grenville's views as attributed to him in the *St. James Chronicle* with statements he later made indicates that his remarks were accurately summarized. See: George Grenville, *A reply to a letter addressed to the Right Honourable George Grenville. . .* (London, 1763), p. 7; and Grenville's speech in the House of Commons, Feb. 3, 1766, in R. C. Simmons and P. D. G. Thomas, eds., *Proceedings and Debates of the British Parliaments Respecting North America, 1754-1783* (London, 1982-), vol. 2, p. 145.

[20] Grenville's figures may be consulted in Dec. 17, 1760, Newdigate Diary, Newdegate MSS., B. 2540/5. No doubt it was this part of the speech that made it "not very lively."

[21] Hardwicke to Lord Royston, Dec. 17, 1760, Hardwicke Papers, Add. MSS. 35352, f. 157, British Library.

[22] *Ibid.*

[23] *St. James Chronicle*, Dec. 23-25, 1762.

[24] Newcastle to Hardwicke, Dec. 17 ,1760, Hardwicke Papers, Add. MSS. 35420, fos. 144-45.

[25] Henry Fox to the Earl of Ilcester, Dec. 20, 1760, Holland House Papers, Add. MSS. 51420, fos. 125-26, British Library.

[26] *St. James Chronicle*, Dec. 23-25, 1762. Even the exceptionally insecure Newcastle expressed no fears about the debate when he first learned of Grenville's intention, a sure sign of the ministry's confidence. "Memorandum," Dec. 16, 1760, Newcastle Papers, Add. MSS. 32999, f. 125.

[27] Newcastle to Yorke, Dec. 19, 1760, Newcastle Papers, Add. MSS. 32916, fos. 193-94.

[28] "An Honest Drayman," *Public Ledger*, Jun. 26, 1761.

[29] For an account of the untimely end of Thomas Thetcher (1738-1764), see his gravestone at Winchester Cathedral. The original stone was restored in 1781, then twice replaced, in 1802 and 1966, thus proving the truth of another moral on his monument: "An honest Soldier never is forgot/Whether he die by musket or by Pot."

[30] James West to Philip Carteret Webb, Oct. 10, 1760, Treasury Papers, T. 27/28, p. 101.

[31] Hardwicke to Newcastle, Oct. 19, 1760, Newcastle Papers, Add. MSS. 32913, f. 205.

[32] *Public Advertiser*, Oct. 25, 1760.

[33] *Ibid.*, Nov. 10, 1760.

[34] For a list of brewers sitting in the House, see Mathias, *Brewing Industry*, p. 333; for an assessment that "strangers" were usually in the galleries during debates, see P. D. G. Thomas, *The House of Commons in the Eighteenth Century* (Oxford, 1971), pp.. 139-40. Whether brewers were present as Members, or strangers, or not at all, they quickly heard about Legge's statement on prices. See the two memorials to the Treasury cited in n. 14.

[35] April 13, 1738, *Journals of the House of Commons*, vol. 23, p. 148. See also the account of Onslow's role in Thomas, *House of Commons*, p. 336.

[36] P. D. G. Thomas, "The Beginning of Parliamentary Reporting in Newspapers, 1768-1774," *English Historical Review*, vol. 74 (1959), pp. 623-24.

[37] *Ibid.*, p. 624; and *Commons Journals*, vol. 28, pp. 741, 745. The newspapers were the *London Chronicle*, *Public Advertiser*, *Daily Advertiser*, and *The Gazetteer and London Daily Advertiser*.

[38] Marie Peters, "The *Monitor* on the constitution, 1755-1765: new light on the ideological origins of English radicalism," *English Historical Review*, vol. 86 (1971), p. 714. Curiously, when Peters discussed the *Monitor* and the beer tax in *Pitt and Popularity*, p. 179, she did not recognize that the paper's Jan. 3, 1761 edition was a perfect example of the point she had made about its ideology in her earlier article.

[39] The quotation is from *Monitor*, Jan. 3, 1761.

[40] All quotations are from *ibid.* The arguments in the *Monitor* parallel Grenville's arguments in the House, but one should not assume that the paper was merely

paraphrasing his speech. These objections to a tax on beer were commonplace in contemporary discussions of finances. For example, see Burton's knowledge of them in his comments to Newcastle, Nov. 20, 1760, Newcastle Papers, Add. MSS. 32914, fos. 432-36. It is certainly unlikely that Grenville "leaked" his remarks to the *Monitor*, given the distaste for assisting popular agitations against taxes he expressed on Feb. 3, 1766, in: Simmons and Thomas, eds., *Proceedings and Debates*, vol.2, p. 145.

[41] *London Evening Post*, Jan. 3-6, 1761.

[42] *London Chronicle*, Jan. 3-6, 1761.

[43] *Commons Journals*, vol. 28, pp. 1007, 1010, 1016, 1018, 1021, and 1030.

[44] For these developments, see *London Evening Post*, Jan. 27-29 and Feb. 7-10, 1761.

[45] *Ibid.* Jan. 15-17, 1761.

[46] *Ibid.*

[47] *Ibid.*, Jan. 17-20, 1761.

[48] *Public Ledger*, Jan. 20, 1761. See also "Some QUERIES relating to the BREWERY" in *Lloyd's Evening Post*, Feb. 6-9, 1761, which includes this question: "Whether some intelligent Brewers were not consulted and advised with on the Strong Beer Bill, by persons in the Government's service?"

[49] *Public Advertiser*, Jan. 26, 1761.

[50] An advertisement signed by Samuel Whitbread, in *ibid.* Feb. 2, 1761. I have found no evidence to support the charge that the brewers proposed the tax; that honor belonged to some Commissioners of the Excise. Moreover, there is no evidence that they learned about it before Legge spoke on Dec. 17, 1760. Finally, no record survives of any protest they made against it. Such a protest would have had to be verbal, however. The rules of the House of Commons prevented subjects from petitioning against a tax before it was imposed. So it is possible that the brewers made their objections known orally and informally.

[51] *London Evening Post*, Jan. 27-29, 1761. See also *Public Ledger*, January 29, 1761, and *Whitehall Evening Post*, Jan. 29- 31, 1761, for other examples of the activities of the crowd.

[52] The diary of George Bubb Dodington, Feb. 2, 1761, in John Carswell and Lewis Arnold Dralle, eds., *The Political Journal of George Bubb Dodington* (Oxford, 1965), p. 417. This entry does not describe the particulars of the incident. It may have been similar to an episode that occurred in late 1761 which

is described in Mathias, *Brewing Industry,* p. 113. No scholar has yet noted that this identification of George III with the beer tax may have contributed to his unpopularity during the early years of his reign.

[53] *Lloyd's Evening Post,* Jan. 23-26, 1761.

[54] For an indication of George's lack of popularity soon after he became king, see the Earl of Egmont's diary entry for November 16, 1760, in Aubrey N. Newman, ed., "Leicester House Politics, 1750-60, from the papers of John, second earl of Egmont," *Camden Miscellany Vol. XXII,* Camden 4th Ser., vol. 7 (London, n.d.), p. 227.

[55] Newcastle, "Memorandums," Feb. 6, 1761, Newcastle Papers, Add. MSS. 32918, f. 312.

[56] Report of the law officers, Feb. 12, 1761, in *ibid.,* f. 519. In f. 521 may be found the only extant copy of the Feb. 3, 1761 *Gazetteer.*

[57] *Monitor,* Feb. 7, 1761.

[58] Peters, "The *Monitor,*" *English Historical Review,* vol. 86 (1971), p. 716; and *Monitor,* Feb. 7, 1761.

[59] Peters, 'The *Monitor,*" *English Historical Review,* vol. 86 (1971), p. 709.

[60] *Monitor,* Feb. 7, 1761. For one of many examples of the paper's fervent commitment to vigorous campaigns against the French, particularly in the West Indies, see the Feb. 14, 1761 issue.

[61] *Public Ledger,* Feb. 12, 1761.

[62] *Lloyd's Evening Post,* Feb. 16-18, 1761, *London Chronicle,* Feb. 17-19, 1761, and *Public Advertiser,* Feb. 20, 1761

[63] For essays in favor of the brewers, see *London Evening Post* Feb. 12-14 and 19-21, 1761; *Public Advertiser,* Feb. 17, 20 and Mar. 7, 1761; and *Lloyd's Evening Post,* Mar. 2-4, 1761.

[64] *St. James Chronicle,* Jun. 23-25 and 25-27, 1761, and *Whitehall Evening Post,* Jun. 23-25 and 25-27, 1761.

[65] *Monitor,* Jul. 11, 1761.

[66] *Public Ledger,* Jun. 22, 1761. George III hated Legge, and succeeded in having him dismissed as Chancellor of the Exchequer in Mar. 1761.

[67] *London Chronicle,* June 20-23, 1761.

[68] Action on a memorial from London brewers to the Treasury, Jul. 22, 1761, Treasury Minutes, T 29/34, f. 78.

[69] Mathias, *Brewing Industry*, p 113

[70] Much later, the *Gazetteer* noted the existence of the clause, but interpreted it as forbidding an increase to 3 1/2 d. per pot under usual circumstances. "The late act, allowing brewers etc to raise their price reasonably, does by no means authorize the present extravagant rise, as the apprehensions upon which the allowance was granted, have not yet been realized, malt and hops continuing to be sold at a moderate price" Once again, a paper was willing to suggest that the ministry had more benign motives than might first meet the eye. *Gazetteer*, Jul. 27, 1762.

[71] For the collections from the additional three shillings on strong beer, see "Gross Produce of the Excise, 1760-1762," [Mar. 1763], in the Charles Townshend Papers, 8/3B/2, William L. Clements Library, Ann Arbor, Michigan.

[72] *Lloyd's Evening Post*, June 11-14, 1762. The author was voicing the widely held suspicion that the brewers were not only charging more, but also were reducing the expenses of production by adulterating or watering their porter.

Chapter IX

The Vote of Credit Controversy, 1762*

The political consequences of the controversy within the British Cabinet over the vote of credit for 1762 are well known to historians of the eighteenth century. George III's decision to reject the advice of the first Lord of the Treasury, the Duke of Newcastle, occasioned Newcastle's resignation and marked the end of his 40 year career in important office. This driving from the Treasury of a man who had served George I and George II faithfully and at considerable cost to his own fortune signaled the closing of an era in British politics. From that time onward, the Duke's friends and enemies from the next generation took the lead at court, Whitehall, and Westminster. First among these to assume power was George III's 'dearest friend', the Earl of Bute,[1] who succeeded Newcastle at the Treasury. Bute's rise—he had been made Secretary of State the previous year—had already inspired a bitter press debate over the propriety and wisdom of permitting a royal favorite to play an important role in government.[2] That controversy intensified after 1762, and ensured that the young king became unpopular with the public and was distrusted by the politicians. Even after Bute resigned in April 1763, the prevailing suspicion that he continued to manipulate George III from behind the curtain, poisoned relations between the king and his ministries during the 1760s.[3] The circumstances of Newcastle's fall lent considerable credence to widespread doubt about the King's real attitudes towards his governments.

Despite these results of the vote of credit controversy, its causes have never been discussed in detail. This failure has left a gap in the historiography of eighteenth-century politics. Moreover, and equally important, it leaves our understanding of the Seven Years War and the long-standing controversy between proponents of a continental strategy and those who argued for colonial/maritime warfare incomplete as well. Few other episodes in the political and diplomatic history of the eighteenth century highlight so vividly the deep disagreements over England's continental policy that perplexed and divided ministers of state. Newcastle had steadfastly defended the idea of European alliances as a barrier to French aggression for many years.[4] He did so again in 1762. The Duke's arguments about the necessity of a continuing involvement on the continent were strengthened by his experiences in 1748 and 1749, when Britain had been compelled to return colonial conquests to regain losses in Europe. Bute, *per contra*, had long subscribed to the theory that George II's continental focus—his attachment to Hanover especially—had needlessly entangled Britain in European affairs and caused the government to neglect national interests elsewhere.[5] In so far as the immediate situation was concerned, the Earl was convinced that the administration had to negotiate an advantageous peace, one that satisfied national interests and thereby enhanced the prestige of both the government and the new king.[6] Keenly aware of the animus directed at him, sorrowful that his royal protégé was being wounded by it as well, he regarded the peace negotiations as crucial. He believed they had the potential, if to successful; to establish George III's popularity beyond partisan attack, and preserve his independence from the men who had dominated his grandfather.[7] Unsuccessful negotiations would weaken the King severely, perhaps even beyond the hope of recovery. The clash between Newcastle and Bute in 1762 over finances revealed their significant divisions over means and ends in policy, their differing assessments of the dangers in Britain's situation, and their bitter distrust of each other's judgment and motives. This essay seeks to describe and explain these divisions and the attitudes that engendered them. It will also, by reassessing the controversy from the standpoint of Bute, illustrate the connection between domestic political pressures and foreign policy formulation.

Throughout December 1761, the king and his Cabinet had come to accept the imminence of war with Spain—a prospect which raised the greatest concern.[8] An additional enemy meant that new burdens would be imposed on an already seriously overstrained Exchequer, with predictable and potentially disastrous results. Spain, it was expected, planned to invade Portugal to whose defense Britain was pledged both by treaty and economic interests,[9] while expanded operations overseas created new financial, naval, and troop demands. Even before Britain's decision to declare war, Newcastle had already calculated the government's need at £14 million to cover the anticipated fiscal requirements for 1762, though his City advisers recommended that he ask for £2 million less.[10] A larger sum, they feared, would risk a collapse of confidence in public credit. Newcastle agreed but then discovered that he could only raise that money by consenting to pay an effective rate of five percent interest on the loan, the highest interest the government had yet been compelled to offer during the war. He also had to tempt subscribers with additional capital by charging them only £80 for every £100 of stock.[11] To his relief, this agreement was finalized and the loan approved by Parliament before the king broke relations with Madrid. Had this not been the case, Newcastle was certain that he would have had difficulties borrowing money on any terms, however favorable.[12]

Still, the 1762 supply—laboriously negotiated—did not relieve concerns at the Treasury about Britain's future capacity to finance an extended war. The Chancellor of the Exchequer, the Earl of Barrington, was very pessimistic about the impact of a Spanish war. Fighting with Spain would endanger British commerce in the Iberian peninsula, in the Mediterranean, and in the Caribbean.[13] As that trade shrank, so would the receipts of the sinking fund, because many of the taxes supplying that fund were imposed on the Spanish trade.[14] Barrington had earlier suggested taking £2 million from that fund for the budget of 1762—a strategy he now dismissed as too precarious. One possible solution was to ask the House to approve an increase in supplies, then try to borrow more money for future needs.[15] Newcastle, however, was apprehensive that such a request would adversely affect public credit, perhaps even jeopardize the quarterly payments on the loan he had just negotiated.[16] Moreover, aside from his concern about the effect of imposing another loan by public finance, the duke was afraid that such an attempt would lead to renewed demands for cost saving measures: specifically, the withdrawal of British troops from Western Germany and the termination of subsidies paid to Prussian and other British allies since the outset of war.[17] Such a step, Newcastle believed, might be popular politically but would prove disastrous for British diplomacy and for the war effort—tantamount to giving France control in central Europe and thus permitting the unhampered concentration of French resources on the struggle overseas. Accordingly, the duke was determined to maintain Britain's commitments abroad at all costs.[18]

Bute anticipated that Newcastle and his allies in the Cabinet would fight hard to preserve the existing continental system. He also foresaw that they would be cool towards any provision of funds for the protection of Portugal against invasion from Spain. To forestall any objections that this might cost too much in men and money, Bute arranged, on his own initiative, to send 7,000 British regulars under Lord Loudon to Portugal and then sprang the news on Newcastle at a meeting on December 26, 1762. Understandably the duke was upset at not being consulted beforehand. Unmollified by Bute's lame promise to consult him whenever money was involved, the Duke angrily exclaimed: "My Lord, troops are *money*."[19] And yet Newcastle did not, then or later, share his (and Barrington's) concerns about the nation's fiscal capability. He realized that a full discussion of Barrington's reservations would not convince his colleagues to modify their stand on Portuguese aid but merely add weight to their arguments in favor of abandoning the German war.[20]

Newcastle's circumspection did not prevent the issue of the German war from being raised in the Cabinet on January 6, 1762. After the ministers had approved attacks on Havana and Manila and a new deployment of the navy in the Mediterranean, Bute brought up "the great question, *for consideration only*, of withdrawing all our troops from Germany and giving up the German war."[21] In justification of this discussion, he recalled that Newcastle had often doubted

Britain's ability to "carry on the whole war."[22] Bute cannot have expected that reminding the Duke of arguments he had made against declaring war on Spain would suddenly convince him to end German involvement. He was aiming to extract a firm statement from Newcastle that Britain's finances would be strong enough for the nation to fight on in Europe and against Spain without the need for troop withdrawal or request for additional funds. The Earl was not disappointed in either expectation. Newcastle and the Duke of Devonshire rehearsed once more the familiar arguments against withdrawal from Germany, and defended them against George Grenville, who stressed the necessity of concentrating on maritime-colonial objectives.[23] And Newcastle at this meeting, and again in a letter to Bute on January 13, 1762, expressed his hope that by anticipating revenues for 1763 by a vote of credit, and leaving a "pretty great" arrears for another year, Britain could make it through 1762.[24]

George III's reaction to his first Lord of the Treasury's comments is instructive. "The reasons that actuate the Duke of Newcastle are very easily explained," he fumed to Bute. "He looks on the lessening of our expense in any quarter as the means of supporting the war: while if the burden is too great for us, that we shall then be forced to make peace."[25] "If Newcastle refused to listen to reason on the German war, the King went on; he should be allowed to resign from office. It would be better to do that, rather than "have myself and those who differ from him made unpopular, and perhaps forced to put our hands to [terms of peace that] we now would start at having only mentioned."[26] There is no reason to believe that George was exaggerating. He genuinely believed that Newcastle and his allies in the Cabinet were quite capable of deliberately creating a situation where Britain would have to make peace in 1762 because she could not afford to fight on. Such an accusation could only spring from a profound dislike and distrust of the Whigs in general and Newcastle in particular.

What caused this lack of trust? It cannot, we think, be explained merely by referring to the king's youth, inexperience, and long-standing hatred of

Newcastle.[27] What George was remembering was the scenario of August 1761, when Newcastle, Devonshire, the Earl of Hardwicke, and the Duke of Bedford threatened to resign if the Cabinet did not moderate its demands on France. Bute and the king had yielded to them at the time, despite their feelings that Britain was unwisely giving up its claim to valuable conquests in the West Indies and the lion's share of the fishing waters off Newfoundland.[28] George could see a repetition of this tactic on the horizon, and warned Bute against it.

Bute was less ready to force Newcastle and friends out of government. Still, he shared his royal master's apprehensions concerning the management of Treasury affairs. It therefore seemed essential to him to obtain an independent assessment of the finances of the kingdom from a knowledgeable and informed source—namely Samuel Martin, secretary to the Treasury.[29] Martin had been Treasurer to the Dowager Princess of Wales since 1757 and had no great affection for Newcastle. He took up with zeal the role of adviser and conductor of Treasury accounts to Bute. Before the end of January, he sent Bute some detailed "Observations on the money faculties of the state, 1762."[30]

"Observations" was sobering reading for Bute. Martin began by asserting "that the faculties of this country are very considerably impaired since the beginning, and in consequence of, the present war." To prove his point, he noted that the sinking fund produced £650,000 a year less than it did in 1757. Taxes now produced £1,400,000 more per year, but these increased taxes diminished the capacity of the government to raise more revenue in this fashion. Loans relieved some of that burden, but loans required new taxes to pay the annual interest. That interest had increased from 2.7 percent in 1757 to the present 5 percent, which, on a loan of £12 million, meant the nation had to raise £600,000 more per year. New taxes could easily have the effect of interfering with the collection of present ones, and could even reduce the money generated by the taxes that contributed to the sinking fund. Martin's central point seemed clear. Britain was approaching the point where she could raise no more revenue and would begin consuming the sinking fund. When this occurred, faith in her public credit would vanish. Unable to tax or borrow, resources drained, Britain would have to beg for peace on any terms.[31]

That time could come soon. Martin carefully called Bute's attention to another fiscal problem, "a new debt by anticipation, whereby the effective revenue of a future year is rendered entirely inapplicable to the public service of that year." This was accomplished by issuing exchequer bills, by contracting for short-term loans through parliamentary votes of credit, and by charging some expenses to the sinking fund. These expedients permitted the Treasury to pay bills drawn on it with cash borrowed from the Bank of England, on the security of Parliament's promise to repay those loans out of the first supplies voted for the following year. For 1762, Martin predicted, the Treasury would get a vote of credit for £1,000,000, would issue exchequer bills for £1,500,000, and would charge £2,000,000 on the sinking fund. Thus before any money could be appropriated for 1763, Parliament would have to vote £4,500,000 immediately to the public's creditors. Nor was this all. In 1761, services incurred and not provided for in the supplies for that year equaled £2,312,046. Assume the same amount in 1762, and the government would be obliged to pay £6,812,046—a staggering sum—before it could begin to provide for the needs of 1763. Continuing the war in 1763 under these circumstances would be difficult indeed.[32]

Bute clearly respected Martin's advice, for—as will be seen—he continued to consult him during the rest of the year.[33] "Observations" armed the earl with accurate, informed knowledge about Britain's fiscal situation. Still, Bute did not act upon it in January 1762. Evidently he believed—or hoped—that Britain could fight on vigorously on all fronts in 1762 and make a good peace during the year. Certainly he resisted Bedford's attempt in early February to put the House of Lords on record as favoring an immediate withdrawal of British forces serving abroad.[34] But peaceful relations within the Cabinet were short-lived. Frederick the Great's behavior later that month greatly displeased and

264

disturbed the king and Bute.[35] This, in turn, raised the question of whether Britain should continue to pay the annual subsidy of £670,000 per year to the Prussian court.[36] At the same time, the Dutch states pressed the government for a guarantee that Britain would come to their defense if France attacked.[37] Bute responded to this news from Europe by again pressing Newcastle for assurance on the nation's finances. Bute asked, on February 22, if the Duke thought he could pay and support an army of 70,000 men in Western Germany.[38] Newcastle replied: "If the expense of Portugal does not go beyond what appears at present, and there are no other new expenses, I am of opinion I can support them for this present year." The Duke did, however, reserve his judgment on 1763, saying he "could only answer for this year." According to Devonshire, Bute was "well pleased" by this reply and inclined toward giving assurances to Holland and keeping British troops in action on the lower Rhine.[39]

Newcastle gave his assurance to Bute in good faith. Even granting that he placed more stress on his cautious escape clause (if Portuguese expenses remained within the anticipated limits, the war could be successfully financed) than Bute did, the Duke was reasonably confident that Britain would be able to wage war in all theatres without fiscal collapse. On February 1 he had briefly considered asking for a vote of credit of £2 million, rather than the £1 million granted in 1759, 1760, and 1761. He quickly decided that would not be necessary.[40] In keeping with his general policy of speaking only in cautious generalities when talking about finances with Bute, he supplied the Earl with no details about his thoughts. His distrust about what Bute would do with the figures and the information that he was thinking of asking for an unprecedentedly large vote of credit was to serve him ill during the next two months. But for the present, he and his friends remained hopeful that they could. continue to reassure Bute and to move him by a series of decisions to support their policies on the German war, the Prussian subsidy, and the terms of peace with France and Spain. Devonshire suspected that Bute's misgivings on a number of issues were politically inspired, rather than matters of conviction. "Lord Bute would rather be adverse, that in case the peace should be unpopular, the odium might be thrown upon us, and if it proved otherwise, he would then assume the merit of it." Newcastle's friend was quietly confident that "if the terms were reasonable we would force them to be accepted."[41]

Neither Newcastle nor Devonshire anticipated, however, that Barrington would decide in April 1762 that the supplies voted for 1762 would not come close to satisfying the demands liable to be made on the Treasury during that year. The Chancellor of the Exchequer's calculations dramatically changed the political situation within the Cabinet. For Barrington proved, to his own and to Newcastle's satisfaction, that a vote of credit for £1 million would fall far short of paying the army in 1762. The most conservative calculation (too conservative, according to Barrington) put the shortfall at a little over £455,000. A more realistic estimate amounted to nearly, if not over, £1 million. Thus Barrington urged Newcastle to seek a vote of credit for £2 million.[42] He understood that interest on a short-term loan of this size would be high, but could see no alternative. In the present condition of the public finances, postponing payment on immediate obligations might be interpreted as the first sign of impending national bankruptcy. Popular apprehensions of bankruptcy could, according to the wisdom of the day, bring on the event itself, by making it impossible for the government to borrow money in the future. Newcastle's initial reaction to Barrington's report indicates that he was not as concerned about that prospect as the less experienced Chancellor of the Exchequer. The Duke was initially confident that around £500,000 of the bills could be successfully treated as services incurred and not provided for, and put off until 1763. He was, however, sufficiently worried about expenses in Portugal (which could not be predicted on the basis of past experience) to agree to ask Parliament's approval for a vote of credit of £2 million.[43] Half of that sum would be allocated to Portugal; the other, to German expenses. Such a vote would have the additional benefit, Newcastle thought, of ensuring that the government could cover the Prussian subsidy of £670,000. Newcastle made this decision quickly. On April 5 he received Barrington's calculations and recommendations, and on April 8 the Cabinet met at the Duke's request, so that he could "lay before them the state of the expense that would attend war in Portugal and to consider the method of laying it before Parliament." He did not let anyone know in advance that he planned to ask for a vote of credit for £2 million.[44]

Newcastle's reluctance was the result of his knowledge that his opponents were continuing to muster arguments in favor of withdrawal from Europe and against renewal of the Prussian subsidy—a key symbol of Britain's continental commitment. Though in the previous year Parliament had voted the subsidy (albeit with noticeable reluctance),[45] by 1762 the expense appeared less justifiable than ever. Now that British maritime predominance was assured, co-operation with Prussia—always justified as a diversion of French resources—seemed no longer essential or worth the funds required. Moreover, Prussia's military fortunes had recently revived, owing to the death of the Czarina Elizabeth, the accession of her nephew, the Prussophile Peter III, and the subsequent withdrawal of Russia's powerful army from the war. Convinced that these developments would greatly enhance Frederick's prospects of peace now that his bargaining position had improved, the British government repeatedly urged the king to initiate negotiations with Austria, but without success.[46] Prussia, as shown by subsequent events, saw in Russian changes an opportunity to fight the Austrians with renewed activity and win fresh victories which might compensate for past losses.[47] Another complication was Britain's growing concern at this time over Prussia's ambiguous involvement in Russo-Danish hostilities over the Schleswig-Holstein issue—a concern intensified by Frederick's persistent refusal to divulge the instructions given to Colonel Goltz, his newly appointed envoy at St. Petersburg. This secrecy inevitably caused Britain to suspect the worst: that Prussia had indeed promised to assist the Czar militarily and hence was requesting the subsidy merely to defray the expenses of Russo-Prussian mobilization against the Danes.[48] These circumstances, naturally, were to have direct implications both for the subsidy and for the German war. Already in February, complaining that Prussia had offered no indication of her plans, for peace or war, Bute had suggested that the new situation in Russia might make the subsidy unnecessary.[49] Influencing his thinking was the argument advanced by Lord Mansfield: if Prussia was freed of her deadliest enemy, Russia, Britain conversely had acquired two additional burdens—war with Spain and the defense of Portugal. On the basis of disproportionate need, therefore, the subsidy ought not to be paid.[50] Ultimately, faced with strong counter-arguments from Newcastle and Hardwicke, Bute compromised, informing the Prussian envoys on February 26 that the money would be remitted but made conditional on the clarification of Frederick's military and diplomatic plans.[51] In the event, the king indignantly rejected the conditions Bute sought to impose. On March 17, on hearing of the difficulties still being made about the grant, Frederick ordered his ministers to discontinue all further deliberations—a decision clearly indicating how far the entente with Russia had diminished his dependence on British financial support.[52]

It was to be some weeks, however, before Frederick's revised position became known in London. Meanwhile, the subsidy question remained a divisive issue on the cabinet agenda. When, in early March, Newcastle briefly switched positions, arguing against paying the subsidy until Frederick offered explicit plans for peace, he was promptly challenged by Hardwicke—the most statesmanlike of the Whig lords, with a broad vision of national integrity and interest. The money, Hardwicke reminded Newcastle, had already been promised, at least in principle; only the time and method of payment were still undecided. Once England and Prussia had settled this matter, the subsidy could not properly be withheld despite Frederick's admittedly provocative conduct. Still more, were Britain to suspend payment, it might be interpreted as a prelude to ending the German war and would probably alienate the pro-Russian Czar whose friendship was so vitally important. Indeed, concluded Hardwicke, "for the sake of securing the Emperor of Russia, it is be worthwhile to give the subsidy to Frederick, although it should have no other effect."[53] This, the traditional Whig view, Newcastle found persuasive, as did the Duke of Devonshire, another notable Cabinet member, and in the following weeks both, thus converted, likewise attempted to convince Bute and the King. The perception creating consensus among Newcastle and friends was the need for a long-term policy—that is, the avoidance of diplomatic isolation and the maintenance of a European system to counteract the combination of Bourbon courts lately reinforced by the connection with Austria: that military/diplomatic cooperative which, despite recurrent strains, was to last until at least the 1770s. Against this preponderance, Britain could not easily stand alone; hence the need to avoid an economy measure which short-sightedly sacrificed future security. Precisely because, they agreed, diplomatic configurations were currently uncertain, Britain's national interests, if not international stature, now depended more than ever on her continued cooperation with Russia and Prussia respectively. From this wider perspective, even £670,000 seemed a negligible sum compared with the prospect of being left "without one single friend or ally in Europe."[54] However, prompted more by personal and economic considerations than by tradition or design, Bute declined to give way, maintaining that Frederick's persistent reserve verging on enmity could not be excused. He protested in this sense to the Prussian ministers and, writing officially to A. Mitchell on April 7, strongly disapproved Prussia's unilateral proceedings, warning that only upon proof of Frederick's non-involvement in Peter III's anti-Danish schemes could the subsidy possibly be paid.[55] No doubt Bute anticipated the Prussian monarch's refusal to accept the money on the conditions attached, which perhaps explains why he made the demand; certainly Hardwicke thought such was the case.[56] Indeed, by now, it was becoming increasingly apparent that Bute, having combined the German war and the subsidy into two aspects of one interrelated issue, was effectively seeking an opportunity to end both. Hence, during the Cabinet meeting on April 8, mentioned earlier, Bute strongly supported Grenville when the latter urged immediate withdrawal from the continent and seriously advised against any further financial aid to Prussia on economic, political, and military grounds.[57] He also took Grenville's side in the vote of credit dispute, challenging Newcastle's request for a further £1 million by emphasizing that savings in the war zones such as America and Belleisle would more than cover the cost of war with Spain: to vote increased supplies could only encourage extravagance and waste in Germany.[58] Though the Cabinet adjourned, the major issues still unsettled, Newcastle's strategy had appreciably lessened the scope for compromise; rather it heightened the sense of financial urgency and suggested a compelling necessity of choosing between Germany and Portugal. As Gilbert Elliot told Newcastle's closest adviser at the Treasury: "we shall fight our Portugal war against [your] German war."[59]

That fight came to pass because Bute, Grenville, and their supporters distrusted Newcastle's intentions and therefore his figures as well. Grenville himself relied on two compelling arguments when discussing the vote of credit with Bute. First, he pointed out that a vote of £2 million meant the anticipation on 1763's supplies would equal at least £8 million. To have to pay that sum, then find enough money from taxes and loans to cover the cost of full-scale war, would be impossible. Second, Grenville asserted that if Britain could hold down expenses now, and reduce them where it was practical, the nation could fight on longer. Indeed, he was confident that if the ministry withdrew troops from Europe and concentrated on the maritime conflict, Britain could easily remain at war for two or three more years. In that space of time, she could compel France to yield satisfactory terms of peace. In private, Grenville buttressed these points with two others. One need not presume, he told Bute's secretary that the war would necessarily continue into 1763. If the government showed France that it would keep expenses under control while still fighting, the enemy would lose its last hope that Britain's finances might collapse. Thus asking for the usual vote of credit of £1 million, plus, Grenville urged, ending British involvement in Germany, could terminate hostilities before the end of 1762.[60]

These arguments were persuasive to George III, who was ready to respond to the request of £2 million by reducing commitments abroad and thus obviating the need for that sum.[61] Bute was more cautious than the king, even though he believed Martin was right about the desperate state of Britain's finances and feared that doubling the vote of credit might bring on bankruptcy. Impressed also by the practical, military, and diplomatic difficulties attending withdrawal from Germany, he decided to determine whether the soldiers there and in Portugal could be supported with a lesser vote of credit. Asking Martin for his opinion on these figures, Bute was eventually informed that the real demands on the Treasury would amount to no more than £200,000 above the £1 million—a gap which could be bridged either through slightly higher allocations or with the money saved by not renewing the Prussian subsidy.[62] Since in subsequent discussions both Newcastle and Barrington remained adamant about the need for a second million,[63] Grenville, prompted by Bute, advanced the following solution. Parliament was scheduled to meet in November; what if it were summoned in early October? Would this, Grenville wondered, enable the Treasury to meet expenditures through the summer with only the cash available from a vote of credit for £1 million? Bute passed on Grenville's observations to Martin who, after further calculations, agreed that if Parliament met in October, £1 million would indeed suffice—without the interim necessity of recalling Britain's forces on the continent but, hopefully, with some economies elsewhere, the Prussian subsidy being an obvious item of contraction. Grenville's arguments and figures plus Martin's confirmation of them settled the matter for Bute and the king: operations in Germany would be continued, the Prussian subsidy dropped, and the savings thus effected applied towards defraying the formidable cost of the Spanish war.[64]

A final decision on the subsidy was taken on April 30, shortly after the arrival of disturbing additional evidence concerning Frederick's apparent complicity in Peter III's Danish campaign. Put to the vote, the question was defeated 5 to 3. Only Newcastle, Devonshire, and Hardwicke spoke in favor of the payment; the remaining ministers, including Bute, Grenville, and the Lord Chancellor, all argued for rejection and they carried the day.[65]

On the whole, this resolution of the Prussian subsidy and the vote of credit had little direct diplomatic impact, save that now the existing alienation between England and Prussia was publicly advertised. As for the conflict of opinion within the Cabinet, at one level certainly it was personal—a direct confrontation between Newcastle and Grenville; on another, it signified a final and complete rejection of Newcastle (and Newcastle's war policy) by the Court. The aversion to continental intervention characteristic of those opposed to Newcastle and friends stemmed, at least in part, from their conviction that the fiscal and domestic situations precluded limitless reliance on national credit and confidence—that funding capacity upon which government and an active foreign policy depended.[66] Unlike politicians solidly committed to a system in Europe, with attachments to particular powers (usually either Austria or Prussia), George III and Bute took a more prudential line on the issue of alliance necessity, the desirability of particular allies, the expenditures and concessions involved in securing or retaining an alliance. As such, they represent what has been called the "Tory" view of international relations—a view characterized by opposition to involvement in Europe, dislike of Hanover, and aversion towards alliance commitments.[67] This position, whatever its ideological roots, was certainly shaped in part by ministerial distrust of colleagues committed to European involvement and sensitivity to domestic pressures, thus illustrating clearly the impact of internal prejudices, processes, and constraints on diplomatic maneuvers. Not only was foreign policy a central topic of debate in Parliament; it was also one of the areas in which a ministry was vulnerable to attack. A policy not assured of political support and funding, as Jeremy Black has stressed,[68] could prove dangerous, if not futile; hence, of necessity, Bute's stand on the subsidy and vote of credit issues was shaped by the need to reconcile diplomatic imperatives with fiscal exigencies and parliamentary requirements. All this, obviously, made it unlikely that he would be willing to adopt the potentially damaging (in a domestic context) compromises and concessions necessary for the implementation of a viable alliance strategy. His suspicion—and, of course, George III's conviction—that the supporters of continental intervention might possibly court bankruptcy and a less than satisfactory peace to preserve their system made compromise even more unlikely. The same considerations were also to play a role in the post-war world, the generation of ministers who sought to tax cider or redefine the financial nature of Anglo- American relations being similarly reluctant to underwrite ventures having little apparent relevance to British diplomatic traditions or current priorities. To an equal degree—in a less conscious sense perhaps—the Cabinet's decision was symbolic of a more abstract, more deeply rooted issue: namely dissociation from "Hanoverian" tradition which, in the minds of George III and Bute, was inextricably fused with Germany, the continental war, and hence the Prussian alliance. Seen from this perspective, the fundamental motive for ending the subsidy and limiting the vote of credit was not merely fiscal and political, but psychological as well: the need to banish the specter of George II, his ministerial supporters, and the tradition they represented from British foreign policy. The same consideration (among others) also essentially explains why the Court would gladly have withdrawn from Germany had circumstances been more favorable and the attendant risks less daunting.

The chief political consequence of the decisions of late April and early May was the resignation of Newcastle. As the Duke himself commented to friends, he could hardly have done otherwise: Grenville's opinions on Treasury affairs counted more than his and two lords of the Treasury, James Oswald and Gilbert Elliot, and secretary Martin had defected over the vote of credit. Indeed,

Martin was now collecting information relating to possible savings from withdrawing troops from Germany.[69] Newcastle's honor and credit in the political world obviously depended on his leaving office. Nevertheless, his attachment to office was so great that George III felt "great astonishment" when told that he planned to resign.[70] However surprised he may have been, neither he nor Bute asked Newcastle to reconsider. As Grenville observed, letting Newcastle have his way on the vote of credit after so much controversy would be tantamount to making him the dominant political figure in the Cabinet and perpetuating his European policy.[71] Moreover, after the work of Grenville and Martin, whatever trust they had had in Newcastle's handling of the nation's finances and his analysis of Britain's fiscal situation was gone. Before the crisis had erupted, Grenville had observed on December 9, 1761 that "it would be wise amidst the luster of great events to think of the unerring evidence of figures."[72] Bute and George III believed they had learned during the next five months that figures could err, could even mislead, if they were being manipulated by men seeking the furtherance of their own pet policies. George III reported to Bute on 27 May 1762 that Bedford believed Newcastle had resigned over the German war and "said [he] had been by the late King turned from an Englishman into a German."[73] The young king left unspoken the obvious moral: for that reason, Newcastle had to go.

*This chapter first appeared (with Karl W. Schweizer) in: *British Journal for Eighteenth-Century Studies* 15, (1992), pp. 175-188.

Endnotes

[1] Among the most elusive and misunderstood figures of Hanoverian politics, Bute still lacks a full-length scholarly biography. Vital aspects of his career have been reassessed on the basis of then new research in: *Lord Bute: Essays in Reinterpretation*, ed. by K. W. Schweizer (Leicester, 1988). See also more recently, incorporating new work, *idem*, "John Stuart, third Earl of Bute (1713-1792) in: *Dictionary of National Biography* (Oxford, 2004), pp. 173-179 and the various chapters touching on Bute in: Schweizer, *Statesmen, Diplomats and the Press: Essays on 18th Century Britain* (Lewiston, 2002). For Bute as minister and statesman see: K.W. Schweizer, *Frederick the Great, William Pitt and Lord Bute: The Anglo Prussian Alliance 1756-1763* (Garland, NY, 1991) and the relevant

chapters in: K.W. Schweizer and M. Schumann, *The Seven Years War: A Transatlantic History* (London, 2010).

[2] For detailed accounts see J. Brewer, "The misfortunes of Lord Bute: a case study in 18th- century political arguments and public opinion," *Historical Journal,* 16 (1973), pp.113-43; D. George, *English Political Caricature to 1792: A Study of Opinion and Propaganda* (London, 1959), pp.119-32, 133-38; K.W. Schweizer, "The Origins of the Press War of 1762 Reconsidered," in: *Lord Bute,* ch. IV; idem, "English Xenophobia in the 18th Century: The Case of Lord Bute," *Scottish Tradition* 22 (1997), p. 6-25.

[3] F. O'Gorman, "The Myth of Lord Bute's secret influence," ch. 3 in: *Lord Bute,* pp.57-81; J. Brewer, "The faces of Lord Bute: a visual contribution to Anglo-American political ideology," *Perspectives in American History,* 6 (1972), pp. 95-116.

[4] On Newcastle's diplomacy and its underlying assumptions see H. M. Scott, "The Duke of Newcastle and the Idea of the Old System," in: *Knights Errant and True Englishmen: British Foreign Policy, 1660-1800,* ed. by J. Black (Edinburgh, 1989), pp.55-91; K. W. Schweizer, "Lord Bute, Newcastle, Prussia and The Hague overtures: a re-examination," *Albion,* 9 (1977), 72-97; D. B. Horn, "The Duke of Newcastle and the origins of the diplomatic revolution," in: *The Diversity of History: Essays in Honour of Sir Herbert Butterfield,* ed. by J. H. Elliott and H. G. Koenigsberger (London, 1970), pp.247-68; B. Sims and T. Riotle, eds., *The Hanoverian Dimension in British History, 1714-1837* (Cambridge, 2007), pp. 22-55, pp. 271-276; J. Black, "The British Attempt to Preserve Peace in Europe, 1748-1755" in: H. Durchhardt, ed., *Zwischenstaatliche Friedenswahrung im Mittelalter und Früher Neuzeit* (Cologne, 1991); R. Middleton, *The Bells of Victory, The Pitt-Newcastle Ministry and the Conduct of the Seven Years War* (Cambridge, 1985), *passim.*

[5] "Account of sessions of Parliament and taxes raised during the reign of William and Mary up to 1794:" RA Add. 32/1381, Royal Archives, Windsor; Bute to Pitt, Summer 1757 and Jun. 8, 1758: PRO 30/8/24, fol. 327 and fol. 308; Newcastle to Hardwicke, Oct. 14, 1761: BL Add. MSS 32929, fols 262-63; Newcastle to J. Yorke, May 14, 1762: BL Add. MSS 32938, fols 239-49.

[6] K. W. Schweizer, "Lord Bute, William Pitt and the peace negotiations with France, April-Sept. 1761," ch. 2 in: *Lord Bute,* pp.41-55; K. W. Schweizer, *England, Prussia and the Seven Years War* (Lewiston/Lampter, Wales, 1989), pp. 106-110.

[7] Bute to Gen. Townshend, Nov. 2, 1762: BL Add. MSS 36797, fols 16-17; Bute to Sir James Lowther, 17 Nov. 1762: BL Add. MSS 36797, fols 22-33.

[8] For a detailed account of Anglo-Spanish differences leading to war see A. Christelow, "The Economic Background of the Anglo-Spanish War," *Journal of Modern History,* 28 (1946), 22-36; C. Petrie, *King Charles III of Spain* (London,

197!); BL Add. MSS 38334, CXLV, fols 80-89, "Heads on the declaration of war with Spain."

[9] By the Methuen Treaty of 1703, England was pledged to assist Portugal against invasion with 20 cruisers, 10,000 infantry and 25,000 cavalry: BL Add. MSS 36807, fols 243-44; *The Consolidated Treaty Series*, ed. by C. Parry (New York, 1969), XXIV, 401-407.

[10] Newcastle to Barrington, Oct. 22, Nov. 22, 176!: Barrington Collection, East Suffolk Record Office, Ipswich; Newcastle to Devonshire, Oct. 31, 1761: BL Add. MSS 32930, fols 220-31.

[11] Minutes—1762 Loan, Dec. 3, 1761: BL Add. MSS 32931, fols 383-84; An Act for Raising by Annuities [...] the Sum of Twelve Million Pounds, Statutes at Large, ch. 10, 2, Geo. III.

[12] Newcastle to Yorke, Dec. 11, 1761: BL Add. MSS 342932, fols 123-25; Newcastle to Barrington, Dec. 27, 1761: *ibid.*, fol. 377; "Considerations relating to the present situation of affairs," Jan. 1762: BL Add. MSS 32999, fols 362-65.

[13] Barrington to Newcastle, Jan. 3, 1762: BL Add. MSS 32933, fols 50-54.

[14] *Ibid.*

[15] *Ibid.*, fols 53-54; Memd., "Proposal to raise 2 million": BL Add. MSS 32999, fols 98-99.

[16] "Considerations," Dec. 31, 1761: BL Add. MSS 32932, fols 419-20; Memorandum for Lord Barrington, Jan. 8, 1762: BL Add. MSS 32933, fol. 128.

[17] Newcastle to Hardwicke, Oct. 18, 1761: BL Add. MSS 35421, fol. 124; Newcastle to Rockingham, Nov. 19, 1761: BL Add. MSS 32931, fols 147-48; Newcastle to Devonshire, Dec. 26, 1761: BL Add. MSS 32932, fols 362-64; Newcastle to Hardwicke, Dec. 25, 1761: BL Add. MSS 35421, fols 141-45.

[18] Newcastle to Hardwicke, Oct.18, 1761: BL Add. MSS 32929, fols 356-60; same to same, Nov. 15, 1761: BL Add. MSS 342931, fols 45-49; Newcastle to J. Yorke, Jan. 8, 1762: BL Add. MSS 32933, fols 112-18.

[19] Newcastle to Devonshire, Dec. 26, 1761!: BL Add. MSS 32932, fols 362-64; Newcastle to Hardwicke, Dec. 31, 1761: *ibid.*, fols 419-20.

[20] Newcastle to Hardwicke, Dec. 25, 1761: BL Add. MSS 32931, fols 345-51: "I never saw this nation so near its ruin, as at present. What remedy will be proposed, I know not. I see by Mr. Grenville, his *inclination* is to withdraw our army in Germany immediately and send them to Portugal, or employ them against Spain. To me, that is the weakest and would expose us more to the contempt of France and Spain than any other measure [...]."

[21] *The Devonshire Diary, 1759-1762*, ed. by P. D. Brown and K. W. Schweizer, Camden 4th Series, vol. 27 (London, 1982), p.154.

[22] *Ibid.*

[23] *Ibid.*, pp.154-55; Newcastle to Hardwicke, Jan. 10, 1762: BL Add. MSS 32933, fols 179-82; Cabinet Minutes, Jan. 6,1762: PRO 30/47/21 Egremont MSS.

[24] Newcastle to Bute, Jan. 13, 1762: Bute MSS; cf. BL Add. MSS 32933, fols 267-68; *Devonshire Diary*, p.154.

[25] *Letters from George III to Lord Bute*, ed. by R. Sedgwick (London, 1939), p.78.

[26] *Ibid.*, p.79.

[27] The argument advanced by Namier and generally endorsed by his disciples, e.g. L. B. Namier, *England in the Age of the American Revolution* (London, 1961), pp.310-25; J. Brooke, *King George III* (London, 1972), pp.93-98; R. Browning, *The Duke of Newcastle* (New Haven, 1975), p.288.

[28] For full details see K. W. Schweizer, "William Pitt, Lord Bute and the Peace Negotiations with France, 1761," *Albion*, 13, no. 3 (198!), 262-75; *idem*, "The Cabinet Crisis of August 1761: Unpublished Letters from the Bute and Bedford Manuscripts," *Bulletin of the Institute of Historical Research*, 59, no. 140 (1986), pp.225-29.

[29] On Martin see: A. Valentine, *The British Establishment 1760-1874* (Norman, OK, 1970), II, p. 585; *The House of Commons, 1754-1790*, ed. by L. B. Namier and J. Brooke, 3 vols (London, 1964), III, pp.114-17. For the Martin papers see: BL Add MSS 41348-57. These cover the period 1755-1763.

[30] BL Add. MSS 38334, fols 246-47. See also BL Add. MSS 51435, fols 238-39 (Martin Papers).

[31] BL Add. MSS 38334, fol. 246 r/v.

[32] *Ibid.*, fols 246-47.

[33] Samuel Martin to Bute, Mar. 18, 1762, May 1762, June 4,1762: Bute MSS, Mt Stuart; *Devonshire Diary*, p.162.

[34] See K. W. Schweizer, "The Bedford Motion and the House of Lords Debate, Feb. 1762," *Parliamentary History*, 5 (1986), pp.107-23.

[35] Especially his persistent refusal to provide precise details of his military plans and determination to continue the war with Austria, despite Britain's repeated urgings that he think of peace.

[36] On the declining state of Anglo-Prussian relations at this time see K. W. Schweizer, *England, Prussia and the Seven Years War* (Edwin Mellen Press,

1989), pp.97-245; R. Lodge, *Great Britain and Prussia in the 18th Century* (New York, 1972, reprint), ch. 4; K. W. Schweizer, *Frederick the Great, William Pitt and Lord Bute*, chs. VII-XI.

[37] Joseph Yorke to Bute, Jan. 19, 1762, Feb. 5, 1762: PRO/SPF 84/495.

[38] Newcastle to Hardwicke, Feb. 22, 1762: BL Add. MSS 32935, fols 9-13, giving an account of his meeting with Bute.

[39] *Devonshire Diary*, pp.159-60.

[40] "Memd.," Feb. 1762: BL Add. MSS 32999, fol. 390.

[41] *Devonshire Diary*, p.160; Newcastle to Devonshire, Feb. 23, 1762: Chatsworth MSS 182/224.

[42] "Lord Barrington's Paper on the Supply for 1762," Mar. 31, 1762: BL Add. MSS 33040, fols 317-19; cf. "Paper written in March 1762 to show that more than a million vote of credit would be wanting," Barrington MSS, HA 174.1026. 4a.

[43] "Memd.," Lord Bute, Apr. 7,1762: BL Add. MSS 32936, fol. 412. "Portugal," Mar. 27, 1762: BL Add. MSS 32999, fols 441-43.

[44] *Devonshire Diary*, p.166; Newcastle to Barrington, Apr. 8, 1762: BL Add. MSS 32936, fols 440-41; Egremont's minutes of Apr. 8. 1762: PRO 30/47/21.

[45] C. W. Eldon, *England's Subsidy Policy Towards the Continent during the Seven Years War* (Philadelphia, 1938), pp.142-43; Jenkinson to Bute, Dec. 9 and 17, 1761: Bute MSS; Symmer to A. Mitchell, Nov. 20, 1761 and Dec. 11, 1761: BL Add. MSS 6839, fols 238-39 and 242-43.

[46] Bute to A. Mitchell, Jan. 8, 1762: PRO/SPF 90/79.

[47] *Devonshire Diary*, pp.158-59, 167-70; Schweizer, *England, Prussia and the Seven Years War*, pp.167-75; 187-210; Newcastle to Hardwicke, Feb. 22, 1762: BL Add. MSS 35421, fols 194-95.

[48] K. W. Schweizer, *England, Prussia and the Seven Years War*, p.174; K. W. Schweizer, "Lord Bute and the Prussian Subsidy 1762: An Unnoticed Document," *Notes and Queries* (Mar. 1989), pp.58-6 Bute to A. Mitchell, Apr. 9, 1762: PRO/SPF 90/79; Newcastle to Bedford, Apr. 12, 1762: Bedford MSS, vol. 45 (1762), fol. 70; Newcastle to Devonshire, Apr. 13, 1762: BL Add. MSS 32937, fols 86-87.

[49] Bute to Newcastle, Feb. 23, 1762: BL Add. MSS 32935, fol. 37; *Devonshire Diary*, p.159.

[50] Newcastle to Hardwicke, Feb. 25, 1762: BL Add. MSS 35421, fol. 21; "The Prussian Subsidy, 25 Feb. 1762: Arguments Against It:" BL Add. MSS 32999, fols 414-16.

[51] Bute to A. Mitchell, Feb. 26, 1762: PRO/SPF 90/79.

[52] K. W. Schweizer, *England, Prussia and the Seven Years War*, pp.22; K. W. Schweizer and M. Schumann, *The Seven Years War: An International History* (London, Routledge, 2010), p. 216.

[53] Hardwicke to Newcastle, Apr. 14, 1762: BL Add. MSS 32937, fols 103-104. cf. Hardwicke to Newcastle, Feb. 25, 1762: BL Add. MSS 32935, fols 76-77.

[54] Newcastle to Devonshire, Apr. 13, 1762: BL Add. MSS 32937, fol. 87.

[55] Bute to A. Mitchell, Apr. 9, 1762 (secret): PRO/SPF 90/79.

[56] Hardwicke to Newcastle, Apr. 7, 1762: BL Add. MSS 32936, fols 414-15; same to same, Apr. 10, 1762: BL Add. MSS 32937, fols 17-19.

[57] "Minutes," Apr. 8, 1762: *Devonshire Diary*, p.166; "Memd.," Apr. 8, 1762: BL Add. MSS 33000, fols 41-42.

[58] Newcastle to Barrington, Apr. 8, 1762: BL Add. MSS 32936, fol. 440.

[59] Gilbert Elliot to James West, joint secretary to the Treasury since 1757: *Devonshire Diary*, p.167.

[60] Grenville to Bute, May 3 and 21, 1762: Bute MSS, Mt Stuart; Newcastle to Devonshire, Apr. 17, 1762: BL Add. MSS 32937, fols 188-92; Newcastle to Hardwicke, Apr. 17, 1762, *ibid.*, fols 183-86; cf. "Account of Mr. Grenville as to a sufficiency of £1 million vote of credit for 1762 with his Majesty's answer," May 2, 1762: Bute MSS, Mt Stuart (Library Papers).

[61] George III to Bute (mid-Apr. 1762): Sedgwick, p.91.

[62] Martin to Bute, Mar. 18, 1762, May 1762: Bute MSS, Mt Stuart; "Mr. Martin's observations on the quantum of the vote of credit wanted for 1762," Apr. 25, 1762: Barrington MSS, HA/ 1026/4(a).

[63] Lord Barrington's Paper (Apr. 1762): Barrington MSS, HA/ 1026/1; Barrington to Newcastle, Apr. 17, 1762: BL Add. MSS 32937, fols 194-96.

[64] *Devonshire Diary*, pp.166-67; Grenville to Bute, Apr. 29, 1762: Grenville Papers, I, 440-42; same to same, May 3, 1762: Bute MSS, Mt Stuart; Newcastle to Hardwicke, Apr. 30, 1762: BL Add. MSS 32937, fols 450-51; Bute to Prince Ferdinand, April 13 and 30, 1762: PRO/SPF 87/46; Knyphausen to Frederick III, Mar. 30, 1762, DZA Rep. 96.33, fols 106-107, reporting a conversation with Bute.

[65] Mitchell to Bute, Apr. 2, 1762: PRO/SPF 90/80; George III to Bute, Apr. 29, 1762: Sedgwick, Devonshire Diary, p. Bute to Bedford, May 1, 1762: Bedford MSS, Vol. 45, no. 8, fols 106-107; Newcastle to Hardwicke, May 2, 1761: BL Add. MSS 32928, fols 20-21.

[66] Schweizer, *England, Prussia and the Seven Years War*, pp. 235-36.

[67] For further details see J. Black, "The Tory View of 18th century British Foreign Policy," *Historical Journal*, 31 (1988); K. W. Schweizer, "The Draft of a Pamphlet by John Stuart, 3rd Earl of Bute," *Notes and Queries*, 34 (1987), pp. 343-45.

[68] J. Black, "Britain's Foreign Alliances in the 18th Century," *Albion*, 20, no. 4 (1988), 573-602.

[69] Cf. Newcastle to Hardwicke, Apr. 17 1762: BL Add. MSS 32937, fols 183-86: "Mr. Grenville and I cannot *jointly* have the conduct of the Treasury."

[70] George III to Bute, May 7, 1762: Sedgwick, p.100.

[71] *Ibid.*, pp.99-100.

[72] Grenville to Bute, Dec. 9, 1761: Bute MSS, Mt Stuart.

[73] Sedgwick, p.109.

Chapter X

Peace or War, 1762*

One of the central concerns of historians of any era and any subject is to determine how and why decisions are made. In the case of the political and diplomatic history of the eighteenth century British state, scholars have sought answers to this question in the public records of the period. Documents in the files of the great offices of government, and the records of parliamentary debates, have been scoured again and again for clues to understand the process and motivation of policy formulation. Far less examined are the papers of the politicians involved in the decisions. In part, this failure results from the fact that these papers are often not centrally located, in the great archives in London and at Oxford and Cambridge. In part, too, there is an understandable tendency among modern historians to presume that civil servants had as strong an influence on policy in the eighteenth century as they have in the twentieth. Finally, scholars have tended to assume that everything dealing with official policy in the eighteenth century must be within official records. But whatever the reason, or combination of reasons, they do not reflect the reality of either eighteenth-century life or record keeping. Politicians often took public papers with them when they left office. Moreover, decisions were frequently not made at Whitehall, but in the drawing rooms in London during parliamentary sessions and in the deceptive calm of rural estates in the summer months. In both cases, correspondence between political and personal friends inevitably discussed decisions of policy as well as politics and patronage, mixing these concerns together in significant and revealing ways. Thus the study of politicians' private papers is essential to an understanding of the official world of eighteenth-century Britain.

This chapter will illustrate this general point by describing a particular case. John Stuart, the 3rd earl of Bute, was a central figure in politics during the

1750s and 1760s. His political role as the "dearest friend" of the young George III has been often described. Yet Bute also was an important player in the formulation of diplomatic and fiscal policy during the first years of George's reign. How important he was can only be determined by studying his own private papers and those of his most intimate advisers. Bute, therefore, is an interesting case study of how private political papers can enhance our knowledge of events that he and his contemporaries regarded as among the most crucial in their lives.

The golden age of diplomatic history, as Jeremy Black has observed[1], was the late nineteenth and early twentieth century—an age in which foreign policy issues were prolifically explored in many still important monographs, articles, and documentary collections. In both Britain and continental Europe—the leading areas in this research—the historical literature developed distinctive methodologies and approaches: a near total concentration on diplomatic records— for British historians, sources mainly in the Public Record Office and British Library; an emphasis on description over explanatory analysis; less concern with processes than specific conjunctures; and, above all, the perception of foreign policy as a rational, self-contained activity, the product of distinct bureaucratic structures, unaffected by external forces or pressures. This in turn matched the assumption that "foreign policy was substantially divorced from domestic politics, the clear pursuit of national interest of the former contrasting with the vagaries— to diplomatic historians usually trivial or disastrous—of the latter."[2]

Such studies have suffered a relative decline since, due partly to shifts towards newer fields of historical specialization, but also—in the case of British foreign policy—due to the influence of Sir Lewis Namier and his followers, whose preoccupation with factional intrigue led to the neglect of larger questions of policy, foreign as well as domestic. Indeed, when Sir Herbert Butterfield 30 years ago reviewed British diplomacy after the Seven Years War, the only substantial work available to him was Frank Spencer's edition of the Sandwich correspondence, the sole study of foreign policy sponsored by Namier.[3]

For a long time, British historians remained confined within the Namierite mold. Diplomacy became a marginal subject—dismissed as overspecialized, its concerns considered trivial, its methods regarded as outmoded in comparison with newer fields of scholarly concentration. This situation has altered over the last few decades. British scholarship has experienced a notable revival of interest in foreign policy, and recent studies reflect increasing growth in both scope and sophistication.[4] Since the 1970s, diplomatic historians have not only broadened their perspectives, addressing wider questions like the intellectual assumptions of national policy, the military/naval dimensions of diplomatic action and the links between diplomacy and domestic developments. They have also gradually expanded the range of sources consulted. Indeed, these new facets are interrelated. The shift from microscopic studies of particular diplomatic episodes to the more complex processes behind decision making has required a corresponding supplementation of the traditional diplomatic records by other relevant material, especially the personal papers of ministers, officials, and diplomats. These constitute a mine of information that remains to be fully investigated. Such documentation is especially valuable because in the eighteenth century, ministers and officials routinely retained possession of whatever papers they chose and normally made no distinction in the case of sensitive or secret material.

Formerly housed in two locations—at Mt Stuart, Isle of Bute, and the Cardiff Public Library—the Bute papers were consolidated in 1980. They are now kept at the Bute ancestral home where they can be consulted by serious scholars with prior approval from the archivist and the present Earl's secretary. Other Bute material relating to public affairs is located at the British Library (Add. MSS 36796-814). His Treasury papers are among the North manuscripts at the Bodleian Library. Finally, Bute correspondence is scattered throughout the major documentary collections of the period. Traditionally, use of the Bute papers has tended to be minimal. Sir Lewis Namier and R. Sedgwick are the only notable scholars prior to World War II to consult the papers—but only those from Mt

Stuart and then only a portion, in transcript, made by the History of Parliament Trust, the Cardiff manuscripts remaining undiscovered until the early 1950s. Although these scholars and their followers—the so-called Namier school—touched on various important aspects of Bute's career, their focus was never on Bute directly nor were they interested in issues of statesmanship, foreign policy, and political/ideological controversy—all areas in which Bute was active or influential.[5] This, together with the limited use of Bute material, led the Namierites to underestimate Bute's role in national affairs and to endorse uncritically the earl's negative reputation as shaped and transmitted by Whig historical tradition. Some advances were made in the 1970s and early 80s with the publications of Mc Kelvey, Brewer, and Marie Peters[6], but it is only relatively recently that Bute has undergone extensive scholarly re-appraisal. Key aspects of his career have been reinterpreted on the basis of new documentation, central to which are the Bute manuscripts themselves. In light of this research, it now appears that contrary to accepted belief, Bute was a competent, hard working and dedicated Secretary of State, with a good knowledge of European affairs, and quite capable of pursuing coherent policies with intelligence and resolution.[7] This has been substantiated by work on the 1761 Anglo-French negotiations for peace, demonstrating that Bute not Pitt, as traditionally believed, was the dominant figure throughout the discussions with a decisive role in devising the proposals submitted to France.[8] Bute's record as diplomat has also been reassessed in connection with Russia and, more controversially, Prussia—Britain's ally during the Seven Years War. Expanding upon the earlier writings of von Ruville, Dorn and Spencer, a series of recent studies—again enhanced by previously neglected Bute material—have vindicated Bute from the charges of treachery which a generation of German historians had leveled against him. They also have re-examined Bute's diplomacy within a wider interpretative framework: with reference to inherited problems, the interplay of domestic and foreign pressures, the exigencies of wartime politics, and in relation to the transformations throughout the European system as a whole towards the close of the Seven Years War and beyond. Combining evidence from European and British archives, this research has led scholars to conclude that the negative aura surrounding Bute's foreign policy owed less to deficient statesmanship than to domestic/political and financial constraints, new international tensions, and above all, a fundamental shift in the pattern of European alliances which seriously diminished Britain's continental stature and influence after 1763.[9] From this perspective, Bute's diplomacy has been judged basically effective in difficult circumstances: adapted to political requirements, fiscal capability and international dynamics, its overall objectives were achieved. There is, furthermore, increasing recognition that on many diplomatic issues, Bute merely brought to successful completion policies initiated earlier, between 1757 and 1761, by the Pitt-Newcastle administration. This suggests that the contrasts between Bute's ministry and that of his immediate predecessors, certainly in foreign affairs, were less dramatic than usually assumed—an important conclusion with wide implications for Bute's historical stature. In this sense, the new material from the Bute archives can be used both for specific information and for general interpretations of British diplomacy and its practitioners.

Another topic requiring investigation—and where the Bute papers at Mt Stuart would prove rewarding— is the influence of George III in the foreign policy realm. A recent obvious trend in work on the Hanoverian period (associated with such historians as J. C. D. Clark, J. Black, R. Hatton, and S. Baxter) has been to emphasize the importance of monarchical authority in national affairs and to identify foreign policy as a crucial field of royal concern in which the king's wishes usually accorded with but sometimes took precedence over ministerial views. At least in constitutional theory, the king concluded treaties and formalized alliances, made peace and declared war. Despite Parliament's growing influence in foreign affairs after 1714, there was general recognition that Britain's diplomacy remained the prerogative of the Crown.[10]

This general impression, however, still needs to be refined by closer studies of particular monarchs. Invariably, they had differing views and pursued distinctive strategies to secure their goals—suggesting that, in practice, royal influence was generally more dependent on circumstances and personal factors than simply constitutional principle. Although the official diplomatic records contain little evidence of royal activity—these essentially registering Cabinet decisions—there is material on the theme among the Bute archives, some of which has already been put to good use. Thus we now have a clearer picture of George III's upbringing under the tutelage of Lord Bute during the 1750s and the significance of their association for his ideas on government, finance, and diplomacy.[11] Raised within the opposition environment of Leicester House, George from an early age developed firmly held ideas about public finance—specifically concern over the national debt and its impact on government credit—that fostered a striking aversion to expensive British military and diplomatic commitments abroad.[12] Both the king's and Bute's opposition to European involvement were convincingly demonstrated by the events of 1762, especially their cancellation of the subsidy convention with Prussia which hastened the dissolution of the Anglo-Prussian wartime alliance and foreshadowed Britain's post-war diplomatic isolation.[13] Here recent work has shown that the aversion of George III, Bute and their supporters to continental intervention stemmed, in large measure, from their conviction that Britain's fiscal and political situation precluded limitless reliance on national credit and confidence—that funding capacity upon which government and an active foreign policy depended.[14] Unlike politicians solidly committed to a system in Europe, with strong attachments to particular powers, George III and Bute took a more prudential line on the issue of alliance necessity, the desirability of particular allies, the expenditures and concessions involved in securing or retaining an alliance. This also explains their opposition to anything that might favor Hanover, long a contentious issue politically, with the result that after 1760, British diplomacy was far less affected by electoral concerns than before the

Seven Years War. As such, they represent what has been called the Tory/Country view of international relations—a view traditionally hostile to continental connections but strongly favoring concentration on maritime/colonial objectives.[15] Whatever its ideological roots, this policy was shaped in part by ministerial and royal sensitivity to domestic pressures, thus illustrating the impact of internal processes and constraints on diplomatic maneuvers. What remains to be explored is the precise extent to which George III's views influenced ministerial actions and thereby the course of British diplomacy after 1763. The fact that British policy retained its anti-French orientation into the 1770s suggests that interventionism by way of a continental strategy remained dominant among the political elite and that here official diplomacy aligned with royal wishes. But since no alliance was actually concluded, one must wonder about inhibiting forces and competing priorities, even while acknowledging the diminishing opportunities for British diplomacy amidst the changing conditions of post war Europe. Foreign affairs may not have been consistently at the centre of political debate after 1760, but it certainly remained a subject of abiding interest for both George III and Bute judging by the many diplomatic memoranda preserved at Mt Stuart and in the Royal Archives at Windsor. From these documents it is clear that foreign affairs were viewed by both men from the sole perspective of confrontation with the Bourbons, a tendency they shared with successive ministries and, according to Hamish Scott, a major reason for the inflexibility characterizing British diplomacy in the 1760s and 1770s.[16] One important dimension of Britain's post-war continental policy was the intermittent quest for alliances, ideally with Russia, alternatively with her traditional ally, Austria—but on what terms? There was an obvious need for concessions in order to secure foreign allies but this option frequently conflicted with a more circumspect approach advocating restraint in terms of commitments and expenditures—an approach with which George III (and Bute) were closely identified. It is quite possible to see this as a conscious disengagement from the interventionist tradition epitomized by the earlier Hanoverians and to argue that, consequently, there is an important sense in which non-intervention—as part of a continuing Tory/country ideology bridging the 1750s and the early reign of George III—retained an influence on foreign policy whose precise nature and extent scholars should explore further.[17] Such work may well invalidate H. Scott's recent dismissal of the "Tory" approach to foreign policy as a minority persuasion,[18] with little impact on policy decisions. Additional research among the Bute collection should prove most valuable in this connection.

Just as the Bute papers at Mt Stuart permit historians to reassess his role in the diplomacy of his era, so do the papers of James Oswald at Hockworthy House, Wellington, Somerset, and volumes in MSS North at the Bodleian Library permit students to gauge more accurately his performance as First Lord of the Treasury from May 1762 to April 1763.[19] It is not surprising that Oswald's papers would provide insights into Bute's performance at Downing Street. Though the two Scotsmen were political foes during the 1750s, by March 1761 they had become close enough for Bute to insist that Oswald be reappointed as a junior lord of the Treasury. Fifteen months later, Oswald had established himself, according to the duke of Newcastle, as one of the "real council whom [Bute] consults upon everything." Among the earl's most trusted confidential advisers, he was the one whose opinion carried the most weight on fiscal matters.[20] His papers therefore enable us to see which issues most engaged Bute's attention during his tenure at the Treasury. It is much more surprising to find an even more important cache of Treasury documents in the papers of Frederick, Lord North. Volumes a. 4 and a. 6, b. 4-6, and c. 1-3 in MSS North contain a remarkable number of the earl's papers and even include accounts and book orders of the Prince of Wale's household during the late 1750s.[21] How these records of Bute's service as Groom of the Stole to the future George III found their way in North's files is unknown. The presence of Treasury papers from May 1762—April 1763 is more understandable: North served on the board that Bute presided over.[22] Whatever their provenance, these volumes substantially flesh out our knowledge of the earl as a wartime finance minister.

What do these sources reveal about Bute? To begin with, they call into question the earl of Shelburne's oft-quoted assessment. Bute, Shelburne cunningly wrote, "panted for the Treasury, having a notion that the king and he understood it from what they had read about revenue and funds while they were at Kew." His ambitious arrogance, Shelburne went on, was also fuelled by "an idea of great reformations, which all men who read the theory of things and especially men who look up at being ministers, and want to remove and lower those that are, make a great part of their conversation."[23] This judgment, which helped inspire John Brooke to dismiss Bute as the quintessential don lost in the real world of politics, has some merit as a description of the studies the earl and his royal protégé made of public finance during the 1750s.[24] The two did see themselves as committed reformers. They were eager to reduce the national debt and the corrupt politics it engendered. They did want to economize wherever possible in administration. And they did wish to lighten tax burdens, particularly on the necessities of the industrious poor, by a judicious increase in the number of excise taxes. But before they came to power, there is ample evidence in George's essays that they appreciated how difficult fiscal reform would be, especially in wartime. Most striking of all, the two had noticed "what great things could be done by public credit." Marlborough's victories, according to the prince, showed "the effects of this mighty engine," even when the debt went beyond what leaders of the time felt were safe limits. The same effects could be seen "even in our present melancholy circumstances, where we can scarce expect a peace before we have increased our debt to £130 or £140,000,000." George derived "some consolation from this great national strength, even against Sir Robert Walpole's suggestion, who affirmed national bankruptcy to be the consequences of our debt arising to £100,000,000." When he ascended the throne, and his mentor became one of the most powerful men in Britain, they were already determined to make full practical use of the existing system. Reform would have to wait until the war against France was over.[25]

The experience of exercising power during a war confirmed, of course, Bute's opinion about the necessity of postponing reform. But it also gave him a special perspective on fiscal issues. During most of the time between 1760-63, his years at the center of the nation's politics, the earl never grappled with the problems of peacetime finance. Instead, as a member of the cabinet, he became familiar with the balancing of two demands, the need for taking vigorous military actions, and the need for preserving Britain's fiscal strength. The two ideally could be complementary. Money raised by taxes and loans would pay for successful campaigns. Unfortunately, they could as easily compete with each other in damaging and dangerous ways. Too tight-fisted a control over finances could weaken an offensive thrust or a defensive stand fatally. Too free a hand with money could make it impossible to raise enough in succeeding years to prosecute the war successfully. The necessity of balancing the two demands weighed on the minds of Bute and the young king and influenced all their reactions to financial questions.

Their focus on these intertwined necessities was heightened by the fact that each of them had a powerful champion against the other in the cabinet from October 1760 to May 1762. William Pitt endlessly insisted that military requirements take precedence over fiscal concerns, which he confidently asserted were largely illusory. Newcastle at the Treasury had no such confidence; indeed, he saw bankruptcy and disaster lurking around every corner. Bute had to deal with both men, each in his own right an experienced, successful politician. Further complicating his relationship with them was their agreement on one policy: Britain had to support the war in Germany vigorously. As we have seen, George III and Bute wanted to reduce the influence of Hanover on British policy. Continental involvement was, in theory at least, anathema to them. This prejudice had as its most pronounced effect the growing distrust of both men towards

Newcastle. Once Pitt resigned as Secretary of State in October 1761—the result of an alliance between Bute and Newcastle against his demand for a pre-emptive strike against Spain—the king and his "dearest friend" became convinced that Newcastle was perfectly capable of creating a situation where Britain would have to make peace in 1762 because she could not afford to fight another year. Thus it behooved Bute to learn as much as he could about the true state of the nation's finances. He could not trust Newcastle to do this, so he had to look elsewhere.[26]

Bute began his process in November 1761, by asking George Grenville, the Leader of the House of Commons, to report to him about the Treasury's budget for 1762. After outlining it, Grenville noted that it did not as yet reflect the real expenses of 1761. "The Navy," he wrote, "is contracting a debt during the course of the year." Moreover, the army had incurred expenses not yet provided for. So far expenses for the navy and army equaling £1,353,662 had been reported. There would be more after the holidays. These Parliament would have to pay before providing for 1762, so the cost of the war was really greater than it appeared.[27]

The news evidently decided Bute to delve deeper into the Treasury's accounts. In January 1762, he secretly approached Samuel Martin, secretary to the Treasury, and asked him for a thorough analysis of Britain's ability to make war. No friend of Newcastle's, and the Treasurer to the Dowager Princess of Wales since 1757, Martin readily agreed. Before the end of the month, his "Observations on the money faculties of the state, 1762" was in Bute's hands. From it, the earl learned that the situation was indeed precarious. His informant was especially helpful in reinforcing Grenville's point about "a new debt of anticipation, whereby the effective revenue of a future year is rendered entirely inapplicable to the public service of that year." By issuing short-term exchequer notes, charging some expenses to the sinking fund, and by contracting for short-term loans through parliamentary votes of credit, the government increased the funds available to it in 1762 by an estimated £4,500,000. These would have to be repaid out of the supplies for 1763, before Parliament appropriated any money for that year. Add to this the amount of services incurred and not paid for in 1762 which in 1761 was £2,312,046—and the government would have to pay a staggering sum before it even began to support the war in 1763. This report did more than alert Bute to the dangers of a prolonged war. It made him pay close attention to any effort to increase the vote of credit. In April 1762, this is precisely what Newcastle recommended to the cabinet. Bute immediately opposed it as unnecessary, wasteful, and dangerous.[28]

We have examined the vote of credit controversy in some detail elsewhere. For present purposes, it is sufficient to say that after Martin and Grenville examined the figures provided by the Chancellor of the Exchequer, the earl of Barrington, they convinced the king, Bute, and Oswald that no increase in the vote of credit was necessary. As soon as Parliament rose, Newcastle resigned as First Lord. Bute reluctantly stepped into his place. He must have realized that this was the only way he could be certain of fully knowing the real condition of the nation's finances. The king's encouragement was also crucial in his decision. George took care both to disparage his friend's "talk . . . of his own ignorance in business" and to remind him he could "put his chief confidence in Oswald as to Treasury matters."[29] The documents in the Oswald and North Papers reveal that he followed the king's advice: Oswald did become his principal *confidante*, adviser, and administrator at the Treasury. They also show that it was Bute who directed Owald's efforts toward the issues the earl identified as most important.

The earl began by demanding an account of the cash in the exchequer, both to reassure himself that the government could pay its bills until Parliament met again and to plan disbursements. Although he was pleased with a highly favorable report that predicted the Treasury would not need to borrow a farthing before October 31, he still charged his principal adviser with the management of the cash. This duty Oswald executed with such skill as to keep the government solvent until the end of November.[30] Bute's foresight and the delegation of a supremely important job to a talented subordinate enabled the Treasury to avoid the bankruptcy Newcastle had warned against.

In his role as the king's chief minister, Bute's preoccupation during the summer of 1762 was to try to achieve a satisfactory peace. At the Treasury, though, he had to assume the war would continue into 1763. This meant he had two tasks: finding ways to reduce present and future military expenses as much as he could, and determining what the cost of another year of war would be as accurately as possible. These were by no means straightforward tasks, because the cabinet was divided on the best strategy for prosecuting the war in the future. One option was to continue in 1763 the present level of involvement of British troops and money in Germany. Withdrawing men and gold from central Europe, disbanding some of the land forces, and concentrating on a maritime war aimed at French commerce and Spanish colonies was the second. The proponents of the second alternative insisted that this strategy would be so much cheaper the nation could indefinitely fight on against the Bourbon powers. They also argued that this sort of war was by far the most effective way of maintaining Britain's current advantage over the enemy. Bute unquestionably was tempted by this alternative. Indeed, he was even willing to consider removing British troops from Germany in 1762 if the amount thereby saved would significantly improve the country's fiscal condition. The earl therefore ordered an inquiry into how much withdrawal would reduce expenses in the short run, as well as an investigation into the relative costs of the two strategies if fighting went on into 1763. Martin and his assistants did the initial work, then Oswald commented on their figures and recommendations.[31] By the end of summer, they had answers for Bute.

The Treasury noted in August that Grenville and others had estimated that Britain would save £1,755,378 if troops were withdrawn from Germany before the end of that month. But that amount of savings, Oswald reminded Bute, would not remain constant. The Treasury calculated it would decrease at the rate of at least £300,000 per month.[32] The implications for Bute were clear. Obviously no withdrawal could be executed by August 31. Troops could not be removed from an active theatre of war in the blink of an eye. It would take months to plan, organize, and execute, and every day that passed would reduce savings. For strategic, logistical, and diplomatic reasons, withdrawal could not be expected until winter. The savings to be gained would be minimal, if not non-existent. No doubt Oswald's findings helped Bute resist pressure to remove the army from western Germany during 1762.

What about the costs of continuing to fight in 1763? Martin and Oswald scouted various ways of saving money, including disbanding regiments and changing the victualling system in North America. Once they took these into account, and hypothesized that British involvement in Germany would be ended and "the restricted plan of war" pursued, they estimated that the government would still have to borrow £9,000,000. With admirable precision, Oswald set the figure at £9,070,342 9s.o¾d.[33] The political significance of his finding was great. Grenville had calculated that the maritime/colonial war could be financed safely with a loan of £6,500,000. That Bute's most trusted adviser thought this estimate was far too low and raised serious questions about the wisdom of trusting Grenville's counsel on the great issue of peace or war. Bute's removal of him as Secretary of State in October 1762 may have been inspired in part by Oswald's report. In any event, the departure of Grenville from the cabinet removed the last stumbling block within the ministry in the way of a final, concerted effort to reach agreement with France and Spain.[34]

Not even Oswald could determine precisely the cost of continuing the present scope of the war into 1763. The best he could provide was a projection that the government would need to borrow somewhere between £13,000,000 and £15,000,000.[35] Whatever the final amount, it would be the largest loan in British history, coming at the end of a long, bloody, and expensive struggle that had already strained the public credit severely. If Bute needed another reason to pursue a settlement vigorously during the fall of 1762, Oswald and Martin had just supplied him with one. Arranging a loan of £9,000,000 would be difficult enough. Getting £13-15 millions might prove impossible. By themselves, these two estimates were powerful arguments for making peace in 1762.[36] At one point, Martin tried to be helpful by suggesting Bute should ask some "moneyed men [to] subscribe . . . to a declaration that they will be ready to assist government with certain sums of money, if they should be wanted to carry on the war."[37] Bute wisely decided he could not risk this. Any such discussion might require him to divulge these estimates, with unpredictable results in diplomacy and on the Exchange.

The Treasury never considered what new taxes would be necessary to secure the loans for military campaigns in 1763. Nothing could be decided about taxation until the cabinet determined whether the German war would continue. That point was never debated; the signing of the preliminaries of peace in Paris in early November foreclosed any consideration of the issue. Nor could Bute and his colleagues begin immediately discussing what the peacetime budget would be. As Oswald pointed out, that depended on how large the government felt the army and navy should be, and on how many soldiers and sailors could be discharged before the first of January. Moreover, no budget could be formulated until the Treasury could figure out how much money was owed for services in 1762 that were incurred but not provided for in that year's supply. One estimate from outside the Treasury incredibly predicted that the administration would have to borrow £10,000,000 to balance the budget for the first year of peace. Oswald scornfully rejected this as much too high, and underscored his point by noting that it was more than any estimate of the loan necessary to fight a maritime war.[38] But this sensible response highlighting the different magnitudes of budgets in war and peace could not prevent Bute from approaching the problems of peace from the perspective of war. Apprehensive of a vengeful attack by France on the nation's new possessions, fearful that the enemy's finances would recover before Britain's, Bute was certain that imperial security depended on keeping the largest peacetime force in arms in the country's history. Yet he was equally certain Britain could not afford to pay for these forces, and that the utmost economy was required to restore its fiscal strength. Thus the earl's analysis kept him confronted with the familiar wartime dilemma: balancing considerations of military security and fiscal economy. Other politicians, most notably Pitt and Newcastle, did not believe seeking such a balance was desirable or necessary. They were not in power; Bute, who knew only the lessons of wartime, was. The search for security and economy led him and his colleagues to make fateful decisions about the size of the army in North America and the necessity of obtaining a revenue from the colonies. To be sure, the Treasury moved cautiously, postponing any duties for a year in order to learn more about conditions in America. Still, the commitment given in Parliament to make colonists pay for their own defense was the first step toward resistance and revolution.[39] In that sense, the American Revolution was a heritage of Bute's Treasury.

Furthermore, their caution on colonial duties may have been less a sign of carefulness by Bute than a result of his growing disenchantment with office. To look for any indications of interest in new sources of revenue in Oswald's or North's papers is to look in vain. Decisions on specific taxes were left in the hands of the Chancellor of the Exchequer, Sir Francis Dashwood, who could not understand a tax on linen prepared by Oswald and substituted a politically embarrassing excise on cider. When pressed on his role in this, Bute could honestly say he had none. "He had thought little of taxes," he told Charles Yorke after his retirement; "his object was the Peace."[40] This admission reveals his limitations as a First Lord of Treasury. When finances directly affected the great issues of war and peace, and the nation's military and fiscal safety, he conscientiously performed the duties of his office and informed himself thoroughly about the options available. When they did not, he could not sustain any interest in the public finances or any commitment to the office. Physically ill, sick of politics and politicians, unnerved by savage attacks on him, Bute was ready to leave politics months before he resigned as First Lord of the Treasury. At the end, he could force himself to make broad policy decisions affecting the security and economy of Britain. The details, even the important ones of revenue legislation, he left to others. That they did not consult him did not trouble Bute.[41]

What, then, do the papers at Hockworthy House and in MSS North reveal about Bute as finance minister? Clearly, they correct Shelburne's harsh judgment. Bute did not "pant" for the Treasury. He took on that duty at the insistence of the king and because he believed he could trust no one else to give him accurate information about the fiscal situation. In office, he relied on the expert advice of a skilled and loyal colleague, just as other eighteenth century First Lords invariably did. Bute directed Oswald's attention to the most crucial issues facing the Treasury during his tenure, the management of its cash reserves, and the estimation of the costs of fighting on into 1763. Then the earl used that information to fight off the proponents of a naval war in 1763 and to add urgency to the quest for a settlement. Contrary to Shelburne, schemes of reform, whether visionary or not, had no place on his agenda while at the Treasury. He was a responsible, cautious minister, who maintained his concentration on the most important issues. This accomplishment commands all the more respect because he had no aptitude for or interest in mastering the details of public finance, and he did not intend to remain at the Treasury any longer than he had to.

Reaching this assessment of Bute at the Treasury would be impossible without the records in these collections. The official files at the Public Record Office do not contain Oswald's painstaking work and do not demonstrate how the earl used it to guide his diplomatic and political strategies. As was the case with his diplomacy, only the personal collections of politicians show the full range of alternatives available to him and how and why he decided between them. The eighteenth was a century in which no hard and fast distinction between the public, political, and private concerns of politicians existed. Papers relating to policy decisions are promiscuously mixed with documents on patronage and even personal business—a situation which accurately reflects the impact of individuals' personalities on the resolution of the great issues of their time. It also reflects the sometimes casual, sometimes deliberate way politicians stripped the records of their offices when they moved on to other duties or, in Bute's case, retirement. For these reasons, those who overlook collections of personal papers do. so at their scholarly peril. Put more positively, those who mine these sources will, just as we have in the earl of Bute's papers, find a rich reward. What is true for Bute is doubtless the case with other eighteenth-century politicians as well.

* The chapter was originally presented as a paper, co authored with Karl W. Schweizer, at the Nineteenth Annual meeting of the Western Conference on British Studies, Boulder, Colorado, October 10, 1992 and subsequently published in: *Archives*, vol. XXII, (April 1995), pp. 34-44.

Endnotes

[1] J. Black, "Archives and the problem of diplomatic research," *Journal of the Society of Archivists* 8 (1986), pp. 104-05.

[2] *Ibid.*, p. 104.

[3] H. Scott, *British Foreign Policy in the Age of the American Revolution* (Oxford, 1990), pp. 1-2; H. Butterfield, "British Foreign Policy 1762-1765," *Cambridge Historical Journal*, 6 (1963), pp. 131-40.

[4] For a full bibliography, see Black, "British Foreign Policy in the 18th Century: A Survey," *Journal of British Studies*, vol. 26, no. I (5987), pp. 26-53.

[5] K. W. Schweizer (ed.), *Lord Bute: Essays in Reinterpretation* (Leicester, 1988), p. 6.

[6] James McKelvey, *George III and Lord Bute, The Leicester House Years* (Durham, NC, 1973); John Brewer, "The Misfortunes of Lord Bute: A Case Study in 18th Century Political Argument and Public Opinion," *Historical Journal*, XVI (1973) pp. 113-43; Marie Peters, *Pitt and Popularity* (London, 1980); cf. Schweizer, "Lord Bute and William Pitt's Resignation," *Canadian Journal of History*, VII no. 2 (1973), pp. 111-125; Schweizer, "John Stuart, 3rd Earl of Bute (1713-1792), *Oxford Dictionary of National Biography*, (Oxford, 2004), vol. 53, pp. 173-180; K. Schweizer, *Statesmen, Diplomats and the Press: Essays on 18th Century Britain*, (Lewiston, 2002), ch. I.

[7] Bute certainly made a good impression on the foreign envoys in London— invariably shrewd and well informed—as industrious, perceptive and

competent—qualities considerably higher than his historical reputation suggests. Galitzin to Kauderbach, Mar. 31, 1761; Hop to Greffier, Nov. 4, 1760. Bute MSS "Odd Papers." Recent work on the parliamentary session of 1762 further indicates that, again contrary to the hitherto accepted view, Bute was a proficient public speaker. See Schweizer, "The Bedford Motion and House of Lords Debate, Feb. 5, 1762," *Parliamentary History*, V (1986), pp. 107-23.

[8] K. W. Schweizer, *Lord Bute*, ch. II.

[9] K. W. Schweizer, *Frederick the Great, William Pitt and Lord Bute: Anglo-Prussian Relations 1756-1763* (New York, 1991); Scott, *passim*; Black (ed.), *Knights Errant: and True Englishmen: British Foreign Policy 1660-1800* (Edinburgh, 1989).

[10] Scott, p. 15.

[11] J. Bullion, "'To know this is the true essential business for a king,' The Prince of Wales and the Study of public finance, 1755-1766," *Albion*, XVIII (1986), pp. 431-39. *idem*, "The Prince's mentor: A new perspective on the friendship between George III and Bute," *Albion*, XXI (1989), pp. 44-51. Reprinted as chs. IV and VI in this volume.

[12] K. W. Schweizer, "Some additions to the Dodington Diary," *Notes and Queries*, 237 (March 1992), pp. 56-61.

[13] Schweizer and Bullion, "The Vote of Credit Controversy: 1762." *British Journal of 18th Century Studies*, xv (1992), pp. 175-88, ch. IX of this work.

[14] *Ibid.*, pp. 1-9; Schweizer, *England, Prussia and the Seven Years War* (Lewiston, 1989), pp. 235-36. See also chs. VI and VII in this volume.

[15] Schweizer, "The Draft of a Pamphlet by John Stuart, 3rd. Earl of Bute," *Notes and Queries*, September 1981, pp. 343-44; H. Scott, *op. cit.*, p. 42. More recently some of this research has resurfaced, not always with due acknowledgement in: B. Simms and T. Riotte, *The Hanoverian Dimension in British History, 1714-1837*, (Cambridge, 2007), esp. chs. III and IV. See also: introduction.

[16] *Ibid.*, p. 8.

[17] As recently advocated by J. Black and the present author. See: Black, "The Tory view of 18th century British Foreign Policy," *The Historical Journal*, XXXI (1988), pp. 469-77; Schweizer, "Some additions to the Dodington Diary," *passim*.

[18] Scott, "The Second Hundred Years War, 1689-1815," *The Historical Journal*, 35, 2 (1992), p. 450.

[19] Oswald Family Papers, Chest IV, in the possession of Mrs. Daphne Bruton, Hockworthy House, Wellington, Somerset; and MSS North, a. 4 and a-6, b. 4-6, c. 1-3, Bodleian Library, Oxford. We acknowledge the kind permission of Mrs. Bruton and the Bodleian Library to quote from these documents.

[20] The most convenient source of information about James Oswald is in Sir Lewis Namier and John Brooke (eds), *The History of Parliament: The House of Commons, 1754-1790*, 3 vols, (Oxford, 1964), III, pp. 237-240. The quotation from the Duke of Newcastle is in *ibid.*, p. 238.

[21] MSS North, a. 6 includes plans for the Prince of Wales's establishment in 1756, book orders for the prince during 1757 and 1759, suggestions for taxation, accounts from the commissariat in Germany in 1758, the national debt in 1758, the navy's debt for 1757, the produce of various taxes in Scotland, and the produce of civil list revenues from 1727 to Oct. 10, 1760. All of these supplement our knowledge about Bute and the future George III during the late 1750s. Because none of them pertain to Bute's tenure at the Treasury, they are not discussed in this chapter.

[22] The most convenient source of information about Lord North is Namier and Brooke (eds), House of Commons, III, pp. 204-12.

[23] Lord Fitzmaurice, *Life of William, Earl of Shelburne, afterwards First Marquess of Lansdowne, with Extracts from his Papers and Correspondence*, 2 vols. (London, 1912), I, III.

[24] Brooke, *King George III* (London, 1972), p. 47.

[25] Bute's views on public finance during the 1750s may be discovered in the essays the Prince of Wales wrote on that subject for him during that decade. These essays are in the Royal Archives at Windsor, Additional Georgian Manuscripts, RA, Add. 32/259-261, 1087-1449, 1531-1696, and 1700-1728. They are discussed fully in chapter VI of this volume.

[26] For Bute's relationship with Newcastle and William Pitt, see Bullion, "Securing the peace: Lord Bute, the plan for the army, and the origins of the American Revolution," and Schweizer, "Lord Bute, William Pitt, and the peace negotiations with France, April-September 1761," in Schweizer (ed.) *Lord Bute* pp. 25-30, 41-55. For the earl's mistrust of Newcastle's performance at the Treasury, see chapter IX.

[27] [George Grenville] to Bute, [Nov.-Dec. 1761], Bodleian Library, MSS North, c. i, f. 251.

[28] Samuel Martin, "Observations on the money faculties of the state, 1762," [Jan. 1762], BL. Add. 38334, ff. 246-47. For the author's identity, and the date, see BL. Add. 51435, ff. 238-39. For a full account of the conflict between Bute and Newcastle, see ch. IX.

[29] George III to Bute [May 19, 1762], in Romney Sedgwick (ed.) *Letters from George III to Lord Bute, 1756-1766* (London, 1939), p. 109.

[30] "A particular state of the public cash for the service of the year 1762," [after Jun. 3, 1762], Bodleian Library, MSS North, c. 2, 1. 140; and George III to Bute [Oct. 30, 1762], Sedgwick (ed.), *Letters from George III to Bute*, p. 153.

[31] See the paper endorsed "Oswald's Observations" by Bute [Aug. 1762], Bodleian Library, MSS North, b. 6, ff. 287-89; and a paper on the supplies for 1763, [Nov. 1762], Hockworthy House, Oswald Papers, Chest IV.

[32] [Oswald], "Observations on a paper containing an estimate of the supply for 1763, and dated Aug. 26, 1762," [after Aug. 26, 1762], Bodleian Library, MSS North, C. 2, f. 178.

[33] Paper endorsed "Oswald's Observations" by Bute [Aug. 1762], Bodleian Library, MSS North, b. 6, f. 289.

[34] [Grenville], "Abstract of the supply of 1761 and 1762 and a state of the ways and means for those years; and an estimate of that of 1763" [Aug. 1762], Bodleian Library, MSS North, b. 5, ff. 47-48. Oswald later recalled with some asperity that Grenville and his allies "deemed [his estimate of a loan of nine millions] a mere exaggeration." Oswald, paper on the supplies for 1763 [Nov. 1762], Hockworthy House, Oswald Papers, Chest IV. For Bute's reaction to Grenville during the fall of 1762, see chapter XI.

[35] Paper endorsed "Oswald's Observations" by Bute, [Aug. 1762], Bodleian Library, MSS North, b. 6, 1. 289.

[36] The arguments in favor of peace in the famous letter from a gentleman in Wandsworth to a gentleman in the City, reprinted in *St. James Chronicle*, Sept. 7-9, 1762, stress the necessity of borrowing "immense sums, the burden of which we will feel hereafter [for years to come]" as a powerful reason for peace. Though those immense sums were not specified, it is probable the author was referring to Martin and Oswald's estimates. Historians have generally attributed this influential article to Edward Richardson, a hack in Bute's pay. It is worth noting, however, that Richardson did not live in Wandsworth. Oswald did. See the return address on Oswald to Bute, [Feb. 1763], Hockworthy House, Oswald Papers, Autograph Letters.

[37] Martin to Bute, [early fall 1762], Mount Stuart, Bute Papers, box VI (undated), U85.

[38] Oswald, paper on supplies for 1763 [Nov. 1762], Hockworthy House, Oswald Papers, Chest IV. Oswald thought the estimate of a £10,000,000 loan even if peace was made was concocted "to disappoint the . . . plan of showing the necessity of peace" by "assuming" that the expense would be so great in any case that Britain might as well fight a maritime war.

[39] For Bute's unique effort to balance the two considerations, Chapter XIII. For the Treasury's caution, see George III to Bute [Mar. 18, 1763], Sedgwick (ed.), *Letters from George III to Bute*, pp. 201-02.

[40] See Bullion, *A Great and Necessary Measure: George Grenville and the Genesis of the Stamp Act, 1763-1765* (Columbia, MO., 1982), pp. 27-33, 36-42; the quotation is on p. 28.

[41] Charles Jenkinson to Bute [early Mar. 1763], Bodleian Library, MSS North, b. 5, ff. 85-86.

PART FOUR: ENDING WAR AND PREPARING FOR PEACE

Chapter XI

Securing the Peace: Lord Bute, the Plan for the Army, and the Origins of the American Revolution*

When the Earl of Shelburne praised the preliminary treaty of peace in the House of Lords on December 9, 1762, he emphasized that "the security of the British colonies in North America was the first cause of the war." That security, he boasted, "has been wisely attended to in the negotiations for peace." Removing the French from Canada and the Spanish from Florida would improve commerce, increase navigation and naval power, and "of millions more consequence than all our other conquests, . . . insures to Great Britain the pleasing hopes of a solid and lasting peace."[1] Were these hopes realistic? Shelburne and other spokesmen for the Bute administration tried to convince their audiences that they were. But Lord Bute and his colleagues were keenly aware that success in this war did not guarantee security in the present or in the future. That security would depend upon planning wisely for the army after the war. As Bute later remarked, "I hope this peace will be [as] permanent as it is great, but certainly a respectable force kept up will not lessen its duration."[2]

The King took the responsibility for drafting the plan for that respectable force upon himself. He began in early September 1762, two months before the signing of the preliminaries.[3] Throughout the process he and Bute had "two things principally in view: security and economy," which they felt "ought certainly to go together."[4] Economy they defined without difficulty: it meant keeping the expenses of the army in 1763 from exceeding the cost of the army in 1749, the first year of peace after the War of the Austrian Succession.[5] Though no papers describing why they settled on this definition have yet been found, their reasoning may be safely inferred from a number of sources. As an official at the War Office observed, in planning for the post-war army, it was necessary to begin by "follow[ing] some Rule," and "'it seemed the most natural" to start with a knowledge of the numbers and cost of the military in 1749.[6] The fiscal and political advantages of reducing the army's expenses to that level were obvious. Doing so would enable the ministry to devote more of the government's resources to restoring its financial strength, which the King, Bute, and the consensus of political opinion agreed had been seriously weakened by a long and expensive war.[7] Moreover, the ministers would not have to justify spending more on the army in 1763 than in 1749 to a skeptical House of Commons that would certainly be economy-minded.[8] Security, however, could not be defined so quickly and precisely. That definition involved both analysis of military problems Britain faced in the past, and predictions of the sorts of problem she would confront in the future. In particular, it included assessments of where Britain would be vulnerable in the years ahead, and of the capacity and will of the nation's enemies to take advantage of any opportunities. Once these decisions were made, it involved planning the practical details of the size, establishment, and disposition of the post-war army. While working on these details, the King and Bute had to be careful not to go over the cost of the army in 1749, so security and economy would indeed "go together."[9] George III and his "dearest friend" planned for Britain's security conscientiously and boldly, departing from precedent as they did so. They knew that the consequences of their efforts could be momentous, either for good or bad.

As events transpired, the consequences of their plan for the American army were unexpected. Efforts to keep the cost of the army below the 1749 level by taxing colonists for the support of the regulars stationed there precipitated the imperial crisis of 1765-6, and ultimately helped bring about the American Revolution. It is fair to say that that revolution began with the plan formulated by the King and Bute, and approved by the ministry and Parliament. What that plan was, and the considerations that inspired it, are the subjects of this chapter.

To the King and Bute, it was obvious that Britain had to station a large force of regulars in America. As early as September, *The Briton* warned that "considerable supplies of men" would be necessary "to maintain all the countries and islands which we have wrested from the enemy."[10] The only question was, how large should that force be? The Duke of Newcastle was confident on December 23, that the ministry meant to station 12,000 regulars in America.[11] Whether his information was accurate or not is unknown, since no evidence confirming it has yet been discovered. The King's plan, which was ready on December 27, called for 10,542 officers and men in the New World. These troops were to be organized into 21 battalions.[12] This number of battalions discloses that King George intended that these units would have many fewer enlisted men than was usual in a peacetime establishment, but would retain an unusually large number of officers. "Small corps with a great many officers" was the way Welbore Ellis, the Secretary at War, later depicted the American establishment, and his statement accurately described this aspect of the King's plan.[13]

George did not indicate in this plan how he wanted to finance the 21 battalions. Indeed, he did not even estimate their cost. Before the Cabinet met on December 28 to consider the plan, someone (probably Ellis) estimated the expense of the American army at £225,159 per year. When Bute and his colleagues in principle approved stationing 21 battalions in the colonies, they decided that this expense would be borne by Great Britain in 1763.[14] If they went on to discuss the future financing of this force on December 28, no record of their considerations has so far surfaced. Still, one needed only to glance at the total expense of the army in 1749 and in 1763 to realize that a larger American army, if paid for by Britain, meant that the cost of the entire army in 1763 would be higher than in 1749.[15] This violated the King and Bute's principle of economy. Thus it is not surprising that whenever the King and his ministers began discussing the future financing of the force in America, they determined that colonists should pay for the troops defending them in 1764 and thereafter. That revenue, they further decided, would be raised by parliamentary taxation. For a time, they evidently were optimistic that they could levy a tax on colonists that would support the army in 1763. In early February, George sent Bute a note, enclosing a comparison he had devised between the army's size and cost in 1749 and its projected size and cost in 1763. That comparison did not include troops in the colonies. "I have not put down the 10,000 in America," he explained, "as [it is] proposed that being no expense to Great Britain." The postponement of that scheme did not weaken their determination to tax the colonists in 1764, and lower the cost of the army that year to below the level of 1749.[16]

Why did the King and his ministers believe a large army organized in "small corps with a great many officers" was necessary in the colonies? "As to the 10,000 in America," George observed to Bute, "that is become necessary from our successes."[17] Though he did not elaborate on this flat statement, his meaning is clear. In part, the King was alluding to problems identified by one of Bute's hired hacks months earlier. *The Briton* had noted "the extent of our conquests in North America, peopled by new subjects, indisposed to our dominion from national as well as religious aversion, and surrounded by innumerable nations of fierce Indians, whom it will be absolutely necessary to over-awe and restrain by a chain of strong forts and garrisons," then predicted that these circumstances called for "considerable supplies of men."[18] When Ellis justified the number of troops for America to the House of Commons on March 4, 1763, he referred to the same considerations. He pointed out that Britain had acquired "90,000 Canadians . . . besides Indians" as new subjects. Then he observed that "French missionar [ies had] interwove politics with religion" in Canada, and "combined their prejudices," with the result that the new subjects were "not familiaris'd (*sic*) to civil government unsupported by arms."[19] In order to preserve British authority against the possibility or the reality of internal disturbance, the government of Canada would need the support of a considerable force of regulars. Moreover, these problems of internal government had grave implications for the external security of all British colonies in America. Disaffection in Canada, and troubled Indian relations, would be serious enough in times of the profoundest peace. During periods of international tension or actual war, the connections the *habitants* and Indians had with European enemies could be disastrous for Britain. Apparently the ministers thought that the best solution to these related problems of internal and external security was peopling the conquered territories with Britons and Anglo-Americans, for the King asked Parliament to "consider of such methods in the settlement of our new acquisitions as shall effectually tend to the security of those countries."[20] Until this could be effected, a large army would be necessary in the New World.

The size of that army was only one of its strengths. From the viewpoint of the King and his ministers, its establishment was equally important. The extent of territory in Canada, and the isolation of the conquered islands from other British possessions required creating and garrisoning many small posts. "No post can be without a commissioned officer," Ellis pointed out, "nor with one only. From this, a greater number of officers are clearly necessary," and this necessity justified an establishment of "small corps with a great many officers."[21] Even more significant, however, was the advantage such an establishment promised to hold when war broke out again. The King and Bute were convinced that keeping a large number of battalions, with "a great many officers," on active duty meant that the army in the colonies could expand rapidly and quickly. Rather than trying to activate regiments and staff them with officers from the half-pay list during a national emergency, the government could simply recruit more enlisted men. As Ellis put it, "you will have the bottom of an army easily . . . augmented" in the colonies. The difference between this army and the force in America in 1749 was dramatic. "Then you had only four battalions in America. Now you will have the foundations of a great army there."[22] That army would be prepared for the next war. It would need to be, according to the King. "The reason for keeping so many nominal corps," he reminded Bute, "is that an army may be formed on any new war."

"If we don't take the precaution," George predicted, "I will venture to affirm whenever a new war breaks out we shall run great risk of losing the great advantages we are at this hour to be blessed with by this great, noble, and perfect definitive treaty."[23]

The King's words aptly summarize the reason why he and the ministers decided to station a large force in America. They believed new possessions were vulnerable to French and Spanish aggression, especially at the beginning of war. Britain therefore had to prepare to defend them. Although later colonists—and much later, historians as well—argued that the regulars were also in America to help enforce imperial regulations in the older colonies, there are no indications that George III, or Bute, or the other ministers contemplated using them for this purpose during 1762-3.[24] Instead, considerations of military security dictated their presence in those numbers with that establishment. Furthermore, the government made that decision before late February 1763, when London learned about "the royal edict of France in a gazette. They are to have 23,000 men, half in their [West Indian] islands, and half on board their fleet, to serve alternatively." Such "a great force" obviously threatened British possessions in the Caribbean, and heightened concern about relations with Canadians and Indians. As Ellis told the House, this French military presence was "a sufficient reason for our keeping a great force in America."[25] It also confirmed the Bute administration's suspicions about French intentions for the future and concern about the enemy's power. Clearly, now, the ministry had not erred by preparing to meet France's challenge to British security in the New World with an army than was larger, better able to expand rapidly and efficiently, and, after 1763, less expensive than the force in America in 1749.

The plan for the American army was not the only effort the government made to be ready to defend the new possessions at the beginning of the next war.

The King's plan for the establishment of regiments to be stationed in Britain followed the same principles as that for those in America.[26] The purpose of that establishment was the same as well. "You could not increase your army when war came suddenly so conveniently by [creating] new corps—more speedy, more effectual this way," Ellis explained to the House. And, just as he observed about the American army, the Secretary at War emphasized, "Without exceeding the cost of 1749 [for troops in Britain], you will have an army more ready, more convenient, etc."[27] The major reason why the King and Bute were eager to take advantage of what they supposed to be the willingness of the Irish parliament to pay for 6,000 more troops in Ireland, organized into 15 battalions of infantry, was their conviction that these units, once expanded, could be of crucial importance in helping defend the new possessions in time of war.[28] Like the regulars in the colonies, these battalions would be no expense to Britain. Indeed, by employing officers who otherwise would be on half pay, they would reduce the cost of the British establishment.[29] Thus in this case; too, the nation would have the benefit of an army that was larger and readier to expand for less money than in 1749.

During their planning for the peacetime army, the government did not neglect "that part of our force in which our safety is most immediately concerned." The First Lord of the Admiralty, George Grenville, had been interested in improving the recruitment of experienced sea men into the navy since the 1750s.[30] As the end of war approached, he recalled the "constant complaint that as soon as the peace is concluded the government of Great Britain has no longer given any attention necessary for maintaining that peace by keeping the kingdom in as respectable a situation as is consistent with that economy which is always desirable and which is now indispensable." To remedy this complaint, he began thinking about employing some of the seamen the navy would discharge during peace in ships to be rented by the customs service, for use in patrols against smuggling. Such a measure would improve Britain's revenues and commerce. When the next war began, these seamen would be readily available for service in the fleet. By neglecting to take measures such as this in the past, "we have labored under very great disadvantages whenever we have been obliged to enter into a new war, and we have been at an immense expense before we get together and put into action that national strength which is necessary for our own defense and the annoyance of our enemies." In previous wars, Britain had been fortunate that enemies gave her the time to augment her forces. In the future, the First Lord implied, she might not be so lucky.[31]

Grenville's reasoning on the necessity for preparing to expand the navy's manpower swiftly and efficiently obviously duplicated the thoughts of the King and Bute on the army. That it was attractive to them is not surprising. On December 1, after informing the House that the administration planned to keep more seamen on active duty than after the previous war, Grenville disclosed that it was also contemplating making "provisions for the disbanded [seamen]" and for officers who would otherwise be on half pay 'by employing. . . [them] against smuggling etc." The plan he settled on called for 2,060 officers and men in 60 vessels, to be stationed off the coasts of Great Britain and Ireland. For reasons that remain unknown, the administration did not act on the plan. Still, Grenville's work may have been the initial inspiration for its decision to improve the enforcement of customs laws by increased use of the navy's ships as water patrols.[32]

From this record of thought and action on the army and navy, it is clear that the King and Bute firmly rejected the course of following the example of earlier monarchs and ministers at the beginning of peace. Obviously, their determination was grounded in part on their conviction that the new circumstances of defending an enlarged empire, one which now included recent enemies, demanded new policies. Yet what is illuminated even more vividly by a consideration of their plans during 1762-3 is their awareness of the transitory nature of peace, and of the formidable power and inveterate hostility of France. That awareness inspired them to commit themselves and the administration to preparing militarily for the beginning of the next war at the end of the present one. What caused them to be so sensible of a French threat to peace? And which considerations persuaded them to try to meet that threat with their plan for the army? In answering these questions, knowledge of the reactions of other politicians to the post-war situation and to the plan is useful. Comparing their ideas with those of the King and Bute reveals not only the differences between them, but also some illuminating similarities.

The Tories had been staunch supporters of George III since the early days of his reign, and of the ministry during the parliamentary debates over the preliminaries. Still, they balked at supporting the plan for the army. Part of their reaction was due to their traditional opposition to large standing armies and to anything that promised to in crease the crown's influence, such as keeping large numbers of officers on active duty. "To keep up . . . so large a number of corps in time of peace . . . which may soon be raised to their old complement," Sir John Phillips told Bute, "was unconstitutional." Sir John also noted that he and many other Tories thought there was no military justification for so large a force now, when so large a body of well-trained militia are in the kingdom, ready and able to defend it against the attacks of any power whatever, and at the beginning of such a peace that is likely to continue. "Let not the first measure taken after obtaining a safe and honorable peace be to demand a large standing army, unnecessary for his majesty's and the kingdom's safety," he pleaded, before proceeding to threaten that the Tories would oppose the plan in the House.[33]

Tory reasoning impressed neither George III nor Bute. The King thought their analysis of the military situation was entirely founded on their political and military prejudices, not on any assessment of present realities. The militia did not lessen the need for a large regular army, he protested to Bute, no doubt recalling that militia units had not faced regular soldiers during the last war and could not be sent out of England. Their presence and numbers did, however, make any Tory fears of an absolute monarchy patently ridiculous. "If the government yielded to

Tory passion," he angrily wrote Bute, "tis not worthwhile to consider two minutes what is to be done."[34] Tory political power, however, could not be shrugged off. Ultimately the ministers gave up their hope of adding 6,000 troops to the Irish establishment, gaining in return Tory support for the rest of the plan. Since this apparent concession to the Tories was due at least as much to opposition in Dublin, it may well have been an artful maneuver that got Tory support for the British and American establishments in return for a change the administration had to make anyway.[35] The loss of these troops displeased the King and Bute, for they did not share the Tories' optimism that a smaller regular army would be sufficient to maintain the security of Britain and the empire.[36]

The Duke of Newcastle and his allies and supporters had opposed the ministry since the opening of the parliamentary session. Unsurprisingly, they opposed the plan for the army. To them, it obviously increased the influence of the King and his favorite.[37] Equally important, they believed it was the wrong way to secure the nation in the future. They did not deny that the French would pose a threat to peace in the future. As H.B. Legge, former Chancellor of the Exchequer, noted in the House, the continuation of the Bourbon alliance between France and Spain, the retention by France of a share in the Newfoundland fisheries, and the restoration of French sugar islands would "in a short time furnish them with the means of maintaining another war." Britain was not so fortunate. Her acquisitions would require improving for many years before they added to the nation's power and wealth. Before that time was up, "we shall have this dance to go over again with [a debt of] 140 millions upon our backs."[38] But the way to prepare for that day was not by enlarging the military. Instead, the government should follow France's example, reduce the army to below the strength of 1749, and concentrate on improving revenues. Preparation for the next war should be devoted to fiscal retrenchment and reform, not military enlargement.[39]

In contrast, William Pitt, who opposed the government during the debate on the preliminaries, felt that the ministry's plan was the right idea but not carried far enough. He favored keeping more officers and men on active duty, and increasing the number of troops in Britain and America. Pitt professed he "was for economy, but in great matters, not a starving, penurious economy in little offices that amounted to nothing material and only rendered the promoters ridiculous." In so far as military preparedness was concerned, "in so early a peace, the nation ought to show itself on a respectable footing. The peace was inadequate, precarious, and hollow; . . . it would soon be broke; . . . [and] whenever France broke with you, she would do it without giving notice."[40] The major reasons why Pitt regarded the peace as "an armed truce only" were the same as those Legge mentioned when he predicted France would soon be able to fight again: the Bourbon alliance, the fisheries, and the French sugar islands.[41]

Comparing the King and Bute's views with those of Pitt and Newcastle is more difficult than with the Tories' opinions. Pitt and Newcastle's followers in the House announced they would not vote against the army estimates, so there was no cause for a ministerial rebuttal on March 4. Moreover, because the ministers were determined to defend the peace treaty against the criticism of Pitt and Newcastle, they portrayed it in public in glowing terms. When he sought to persuade, Bute did not hesitate to "be bold enough to affirm that this country has not made so great, so safe, and so permanent a peace (for so it promises) as this, for some hundred years past."[42] In private, he and his colleagues were satisfied that by their conviction "we had obtained the highest conditions that could be got."[43] The difference is a telling one. The King and Bute were genuinely proud of the treaty, they honestly regarded it as "great, noble, and perfect," but pride did not blind them to the reality that it did not attain everything they had wished for.[44] How it fell short of their desires, and their assessment of the significance of those shortcomings, are revealed by their opinions during the peace negotiations of 1761-2.

The King and Bute had agreed with Pitt in June 1761 that excluding the French from the Newfoundland fisheries would be "a vast thing for us."[45] Such a stroke would bring considerable commercial advantages to Britain, while denying any profits from the trade to France. Of even greater significance, it would "incapacitate them from being any longer a naval power," and thus secure Britain and her possessions from attack.[46] Unlike Pitt, the King and Bute did not want to make exclusion a *sine qua non* for peace. They did not think the fisheries were worth prolonging the war over. It was, however, worth a try, particularly as an opening gambit. "As the Fishery, which was proposed to be left to France, would be a ruined Fishery," Bute told the Cabinet on June 25, 1761, "it was possible that they might give it up now." The moderates in the Cabinet, Newcastle and his allies, were less sanguine. They did not quarrel about the benefits Britain would gain from excluding the French from Newfoundland; they opposed making the proposal because they were sure France would never agree to it, and a good chance for peace might be lost.[47] Events immediately bore out their prediction, and ultimately their fear. The French not only refused to give up all of the Newfoundland fisheries, but they insisted on the right to continue fishing in the Gulf of St Lawrence, and the cession of a suitable *abri* there for their fishing fleet to shelter and to dry the catch, as well as demanding a place on the coast of Newfoundland to dry cod caught in those waters. The Cabinet countered by proposing that the French get a share of the fishing off Newfoundland, plus a drying station on that island, on condition the fortifications at Dunkirk be destroyed. Bute agreed reluctantly. He did so "because the Council thought it was right," but he bluntly told Newcastle "that he regretted that concession [of the right to dry fish] more than anything else."[48] His hopes of Britain's dominating the cod commerce and seriously weakening, if not destroying, France's naval power were clearly fading. What followed utterly extinguished them.

In early August, the enemy's counter-proposals arrived in London, and the Cabinet discovered that France still insisted on part of the St Lawrence fishery and an *abri* in the Gulf, preferable Cape Breton or St John's. Bute's immediate response was to consider this "as a declaration of war." Significantly, Newcastle "thought it was very bad but hoped Lord Bute would not however lose sight of Peace:" the first sign of a crisis within the Cabinet fully as grave as the one in the negotiations.[49] Initially, Bute sided with Pitt, and argued for a flat rejection of the French ultimatum. Newcastle, the Earl of Hardwicke, and the Duke of Bedford urged acceptance of the demands in principle in the interest of making peace, then limiting the damage by refusing to grant Cape Breton or St John's as the *abri*. By a majority of one, Pitt and Bute prevailed in the first vote. At this point, as the Duke of Devonshire observed to Bute, "our situation at home appeared to me as serious as that abroad. I feared," he continued, "we should break to pieces,"[50] and the moderates leave the ministry. The King and Bute fully appreciated the implications of such a withdrawal. Aware this would leave them dependent on Pitt, and thus shackled to his policy of continuing the war until French power was crushed; fearful that Britain's finances might collapse before this occurred; believing that diplomacy rather than *force majeure* was the best way to end the war, and cognizant that they must have the moderates' support to pursue negotiations, the two men yielded on the St Lawrence fishery and on an *abri*. The realism of their decision did not blind them to what had been lost, however. Even as he conceded, Bute could not help reminding the Cabinet that he had favored excluding the French from the entire fisheries, and that now "he could not . . . but consider the favorite object the Fisheries as in a great measure by their means given up."[51] He clearly believed that, during the next peace, France would again enjoy the commercial and military advantages she had reaped before from the fisheries.

Bute also believed that Britain had not demanded adequate compensation for her concessions on the fisheries. On June 26, he had declared that "the King would not consent to leaving to France the Right of fishing given them by the Treaty of Utrecht without receiving some great Compensation in return," and hinted that the prize should be Guadeloupe.[52] This met with no positive response from the Cabinet, either at that time or later. When the Cabinet decided to agree to let France dry fish on Newfoundland in exchange for the demilitarization of Dunkirk, Bute asked Bedford how they could "advise the king to sit down satisfied with a barren country [Canada] not equal in value to the duchies of Lorraine and Barr, and yet an acquisition invidious from its vast extent, while the French have restored to them the very essence of the whole?" Instead, he went on, why not keep "something that will bring in a clear, certain, additional revenue, to enable [posterity] to pay the interest of the enormous debt we have, by this most expensive war, laid upon them?"[53] During the first debates on France's ultimatum in August, Bute was against granting France an *abri* "unless we insisted on Guadeloupe instead of [the fishery]."[54] Since no one agreed to that, he argued against further concessions on the fishery on these grounds: "that we ought after our successes to reap some advantage from the war, that we have given up *Sugar Islands* . . . which brought a revenue of £4 or £500,000 to France, and had only a long barren tract of country that did not produce £40,000 p.a.; that therefore if we had not the Fishery we really got nothing."[55] This argument was as unsuccessful as his use of the King's name in June. After he and the King accepted the moderates' position, their only solace was Bute's *cri de coeur* on August 19.

> He was by no means convinced that we had not gone much too far in our concessions, that his conscience told him, that we had; and that he was averse to every step that had been taken towards conceding to the French any share in the Fisheries; or if this was to be conceded that we . . . demand some great compensation in return and particularly the Island of Guadeloupe etc.; and that in giving up his opinions on this head he had only submitted to the Majority.[56]

This outburst, and Bute's other comments during the negotiations of 1761, are interesting. His criticism of the concessions on the fisheries, his estimate of the value of Canada without a virtual monopoly of that commerce, and his appreciation of the comparatively much greater worth of Guadeloupe, are indistinguishable from the charges his opponents leveled at the peace during 1762-3. His assessment in 1761 of the significance of these terms for France's economic and military power in the future was identical as well. It is clear that Bute had hoped and tried to achieve in 1761 what they claimed the treaty failed to accomplish. His principal goal had been to gain complete military security for Britain's American possessions, plus a virtual monopoly of a lucrative commerce, by ending entirely or restricting sharply French participation in the fisheries. If the French would not agree to that, he wanted Guadeloupe in return for the fisheries, which would amount to British domination of the even more lucrative sugar trade, and provide the means for a faster restoration of the nation's finances. He got neither of his wishes. Moreover, his analysis of the reasons why he got neither convinced him that he had to change his priorities to conform to the reality of Britain's and his own situation.

During the negotiations of 1761, Bute learned that the French would not "hold . . . out their throats to be cut."[57] The enemy would fight on rather than make a concession that would ruin France's navy and ensure the military security of British possessions in the New World. The question had become whether Britain should continue the war in the hope that more victories would compel France to give in on this point. Bute had never shared Pitt's facile confidence in Britain's fiscal strength, and thus had never regarded another year of war with the same equanimity. Moreover, important members of the Cabinet did not believe British arms were capable of accomplishing that end, and regarded attempting it as very likely ruinous. No matter how reluctantly he had done it, Bute had cast his lot with these men. When he did so, he effectively gave up the hopes he had had when the negotiations began. None of the moderates believed Britain should demand Guadeloupe as compensation for the fisheries. All of them explained the "reason why France has not made peace" by noting "if these concessions [the Cabinet made on the fisheries] had been sooner made it would have [been] better." The first British proposals caused the French to look for assistance from

Spain, and, having been granted it, to raise their demands. To make peace, Britain would have to be more reasonable in her demands. The French would respond favorably if convinced their antagonists wished for peace, without having to have it, and offered moderate terms.[58] France's obduracy over the fisheries, his own convictions about the advisability of concluding peace soon, and his political allies' opinions on what a reasonable peace was and how it could be obtained, made Bute change his goals. Never again after August 19, 1761 did he express any regret about Britain's failure either to keep most of the fisheries, or to get Guadeloupe instead of them. He accepted the reality that he could not ask for either of these and hope to end the war. Thus when Bute made his secret attempts during the period from November 1761 to January 1762 to renew negotiations with France, he encouraged his Sardinian go-betweens to intimate "that as there was no great seeming difference between us when the negotiation broke off, it might be easily accommodated if France was disposed to peace." Pleased by the Duc de Choiseul's reply to this, and convinced Choiseul genuinely desired peace in 1762, he responded by indicating "we should be ready to treat on the same terms" as the last two ultimatums exchanged in 1761.[59]

This meant that from the beginning of the negotiations of 1762, Bute recognized that although Britain would retain Canada, the future security of her North American colonies would not be completely assured, because she could not exclude the French from "the nursery of seamen," the fisheries. He also was aware that since he had no support within his own government for keeping Guadeloupe, France would enjoy again the considerable benefits of the sugar trade, with the consequence that both her navy and her revenues would be restored more quickly than would otherwise have been the case. He quickly had to acknowledge another reality as well. With the entrance of Spain into the war in January 1762, adjusting what had seemed in 1761 to be minor differences between Britain and France became much more difficult. France now had an ally, one which had not been weakened by six years of fighting. Britain now had an additional drain on her human and fiscal resources, which the war had already seriously depleted. Bute could expect that the French would be more optimistic at the very time that mounting expenses would make a speedy peace all the more necessary for Britain.

To deal with this situation, Bute and his colleagues decided to strike a telling blow against Spain in the Caribbean by conquering Havana, while sending troops to assist against any attack on Portugal. The loss of Havana, the ministers reasoned, would make Spain amenable to ending the war quickly.[60] In order to relieve the fiscal strain of another year of fighting and a new foe, the Cabinet also looked for ways of reducing expenses in Germany. Ultimately, Bute did not act on the advice many pressed on him, to withdraw British troops from western Germany. Still, the fact that he seriously contemplated a measure that was fraught with logistical difficulties, and might conceivably expose Britain itself to invasion, reveals the depth of his concern about the nation's finances.[61] That concern heightened his determination to make an honorable peace in 1762.

What was an honorable peace as far as the New World was concerned? Bute defined it first to the Cabinet in late April, then in a letter to Bedford on May 1. Britain would restore Martinique and Guadeloupe, with Marie Galante, to France. The neutral islands and the Grenadines would be British. On the North American continent, "to prevent future disputes," the Mississippi River would be the boundary between the two nations' possessions. Thus the French would part with nothing in America they had a legal claim to, "and we secure in perpetuity our Northern conquests, from all future chicane." This last point deserves elaboration; because it discloses what Bute aimed at after recognizing that the concessions on the fisheries and in the Caribbean would prevent both the establishment of complete military security for North America and the monopoly of a lucrative commerce. The French had, in his opinion, a well-deserved reputation for chicanery, the use of legalistic artifices to claim what was not rightly theirs, thereby prolonging or initiating conflicts. The Mississippi would be a precise and unmistakable boundary, offering no opportunity for this favorite tactic of the enemy's.[63] Remove this potential *casus belli*, and one could expect that the chances for a longer peace would be increased. Put another way, the possibility of any renewal of a military struggle with a renascent France in the near future would be lessened.

How could the French be induced to accept an honorable peace? To Bute, the success of diplomatic efforts would depend on recognizing France's determination to maintain her pre-war position in the West Indies, and being reasonable about demands in that area. Thus he warned the Cabinet in late April that the French would never agree to the cession of Guadeloupe or Louisiana in return for the restoration of Martinique. To prevent the breakdown of negotiations and the continuation of the war, it would be necessary to restore the two islands in exchange for the four neutral islands and the Grenadines.[64] Privately, Bute was willing to go further than that. In June, he secretly offered to give up Santa Lucia, the most important of the neutral islands. He was ignorant neither of the "worth of St Lucia compared with the three others," nor of the consequences of that cession.[65] The French wanted Santa Lucia because it was vital to them commercially and militarily. When their demand became known to members of the Cabinet, George Grenville strenuously objected to it. Yielding that island, he argued, meant the French would be in a better military and economic position in the West Indies than before the war. They would dominate the sugar trade, and engross most of its wealth. That trade would improve their merchant navy, and train and employ seamen who would man their fleet in wartime. The fine harbor and windward position of Santa Lucia would give their navy the strategic advantage during war, and pose a continual and grave threat to the security of the British islands. Grenville formally notified the King of his dissent, and the reasons for it.[66] Bute did not dispute Santa Lucia's value. In his mind, however, that value was outweighed by two considerations. The first was the risk Britain would run by continuing the war to try to retain it. As the King noted, if the fighting went on, "in a year or two from being brought to a state of beggary we shall be forced to sue for peace," and the ministers would be responsible for "having drawn this nation into the shameful situation of setting down with what it may be permitted to keep by the French."[67] The second was the risk of a quickly renewed conflict even if Britain did succeed in keeping Santa Lucia. In terms reminiscent of his explanation of the rationale for making the Mississippi River the boundary in America, Bute explained to Bedford and the French the cession of the island by observing it was done "not only with a view to cut off all other present matters in dispute between us . . . but chiefly to render the peace stable and permanent: to remove everything likely to produce animosities thereafter."[68] He assumed, as Devonshire did, that if France did not get Santa Lucia, she would not rest until she regained it.[69] Restoring it would certainly speed the end of the war, and probably lengthen the peace. Ultimately, he persuaded his colleagues to agree to its return.

Bute stuck with this strategy for the remainder of the negotiations. He was ready to make concessions to Spain's vital interests in the Caribbean, even going so far as to argue in the Cabinet in favor of returning Havana without seeking an equivalent. When his colleagues insisted that the nation must have some compensation for that important conquest, he persuaded them to leave the Spanish with the choice of ceding Florida or Puerto Rico. This enabled Spain to preserve her West Indian possessions intact. In exchange for this moderation, he insisted on keeping the boundary between Canada and Louisiana as precise as possible, on an unequivocal statement of the right to cut logwood in Spanish possessions in Central America, and on as clear a demarcation and as wide a separation as possible between British and French fishing areas.[70] As had been his intent in returning Santa Lucia, his motive was removing what would otherwise obviously be causes of dispute in the future. To critics such as George Grenville, the economic and military effects of Bute's concessions "undermine[d] the strategic advantage gained over France during the war."[71] But to the King and Bute, and ultimately to other members of the Cabinet as well, trying to achieve the degree of strategic advantage and security that Grenville wished for would be an unmitigated disaster. As one of Bute's defenders pointedly asked: "Is there any reason to believe that France is reduced so low as to surrender at Discretion; to give up everything but France itself; to give up its existence as a Trading State and a Maritime Power?" The answers were clear: there was no justification for such "a precarious, nay, an improbable, Supposition." Even assuming the government could raise "the immense Sums required for another Year . . . there is no certainty, no Likelihood of compelling France to submit to Terms better for us than now offered, by another Campaign, and another after that." What was certain was "if the War continues, our Distress is near at hand." That distress would be felt for years, too, for "France supports the Expense of this War with an immediate and cruel Taxation; we borrow immense sums, the Burden of which we shall feel hereafter."[72] This reasoning led to an inescapable conclusion. The administration had to make an honorable peace, one which gained Canada, parts of the fisheries, and some West Indian islands while removing as soon as possible potential causes for a quick renewal of conflict. The preliminary articles of peace, signed by Bedford and approved by the King in November 1762, fulfilled these criteria to the satisfaction of Bute and his colleagues. They "had obtained," Bute told Henry Fox, Paymaster of the Forces, "the highest conditions that could be got."[73]

Those conditions were not, of course, what Bute and the King had hoped for in 1761. In the future, Britain would still have to deal with a powerful France, and her old antagonist would be restoring her full naval and commercial strength through the fishery and the sugar trade. France would also have important military advantages in the Caribbean, particularly the strategically important island of Santa Lucia. The course of the negotiations of 1761-2 had impressed the value of these concessions on George and his "dearest friend." Indeed, they had conceded them only because of the dynamics of the Cabinet's internal politics in 1761 and their sense of Britain's overriding need for an honorable (but not wholly triumphant) peace in 1762. Their awareness that France had the means at hand to restore her strength quickly strongly influenced their planning for the peace.

So did their assessment of France's intentions for the peace. If the French did not intend to renew the struggle as soon as they were able, the ministry could rest easier about her return to full power. The King and Bute did not, however, feel that Britain could safely rely on France's goodwill in the years ahead. The concessions the government had made in the interests of a "stable and permanent" peace had not been founded upon the expectation that they would mitigate or remove entirely French hostility in the future. Bute only voiced that hope publicly, to the French or to politicians whose support he hoped to gain for the preliminaries. In private, it is clear that he made those concessions to facilitate the conclusion of the present war, and to guard against French "chicane." The fact that he believed it was necessary to prevent chicanery from the very beginning of the peace reveals that he had no confidence whatsoever in any remission of France's hostility toward Britain. Had he ever had any such faith, it would have been removed by the twists and turns of negotiations during September and October 1762. In the same letter in which he held out the hope of a stable and permanent peace to the French, Bute complained to Bedford about "all the French evasions" that were "obstacles to the peace," and told him to warn them that any departure from articles already agreed upon would mean the continuation of the war.[74] Bute was proceeding according to the same rule he had formulated in 1761: the French invariably reacted to signs of weakness by raising their demands.[75] There are no indications that he stopped following that rule after the preliminary articles were signed, even though they guarded against the aggressive use of chicanery by the enemy. "A respectable force," he told Phillips, "will not lessen [the peace's] duration."[76] Indeed, he expected such a force would lengthen it, by serving as visible proof of Britain's strength and determination.

One other consideration probably strengthened Bute's resolve to maintain a respectable force from the very beginning of peace. Soon after the conclusion of the preliminaries, he discovered that he could not assume that, in the immediate future at least, France's fiscal problems would be as serious as Britain's. During the war, he had never been as sure as Pitt that France's finances were in a perilous condition. To help in planning for the peace, in November 1762 he had Charles Jenkinson write to Richard Neville in Paris, asking him to procure as soon as possible 'as exact accounts as possible of the present state of the French finances." Neville replied on December 1 that the public credit of France was in good condition. The government did not contemplate laying any new taxes, and would not have even if the war had continued, and did not intend borrowing any more money. He also noted that the Comptroller-General had told him that France "had one advantage of us in respect to finance which must at least bring on our ruin first." That was, "their expenses in war never exceeded their revenue above one-fourth, whereas we were constantly obliged to borrow three-fourths, or very near." Neville hoped this information 'may facilitate the loans we must want in England.' His letter arrived in London as the King, Bute, and other ministers were concentrating on planning for the future. It was received there as "some very useful intelligence."[77] There was, therefore, good reason for Bute, who tended toward a dark view of fiscal affairs anyway, to be apprehensive that France was in better fiscal condition than Britain. Together with the reasons he had for believing that France, though defeated and weakened, had the means at hand to restore her power in a relatively short time, and the will to keep testing Britain's strength and resolve, this was an additional cause for concern for Britain's security in the future. Moreover, this news not only indicated that Britain should maintain a large peacetime force, but also revealed that she should look for external sources of revenue to help pay for it, in order to lighten her fiscal burdens, and improve her fiscal situation *vis-à-vis* France. There are no hints that Bute had revised in 1762 the pessimistic estimate of the immediate value of Canada to Britain's commerce and revenue he made in 1761. Nor did he anticipate that the nation's acquisitions in the West Indies would provide much help soon.[78] This meant that the revenue would have to come from the older colonies.

It is not surprising, therefore, that Bute and the King believed that the security of Britain's new possessions depended upon stationing a large force which could be easily expanded in America. In the future, Britain would still confront a powerful enemy, one which was rapidly renewing its strength through the fisheries and the West Indies trade. That enemy would also enjoy important military advantages in the Caribbean, particularly the strategically important island of Santa Lucia. Finally, France would continue to look for opportunities to defeat Britain, and would try to take advantage of any weaknesses. Given these circumstances, if Bute and his colleagues had ever considered reducing the army to 1749 levels, as both the Tories and the Newcastle Whigs thought advisable, they would have instantly rejected it. Such a plan would leave Britain's new possessions far too vulnerable to a powerful, vengeful France.

It is also not surprising that Bute and George III would conclude that the safety of Britain depended as well upon keeping military expenses at the level of 1749, or below. Britain's fiscal condition, especially considered in comparison with France's, demanded the strictest economy. Pitt might scorn certain measures of economy; Bute and the King did not believe the nation could afford to follow his advice. They also believed that economy could not be achieved without finding new sources of revenue from outside Britain, and that this revenue would not be found immediately from the new possessions. Raising revenue in the older colonies was as necessary to security as a large army. Thus the origins of the American Revolution may be found in the imperatives of imperial security, as perceived by George III and Lord Bute.

*This chapter first appeared in: K.W. Schweizer,(ed.), *Lord Bute: Essays in Reinterpretation* (Leicester University Press, 1988).

Endnotes

[1] Quoted in R.B. Morris (ed.), *The American Revolution, 1763-1783: A Bicentennial Collection* (Columbia, SC, 1970), pp. 13-14.

[2] Bute to Sir John Phillips, Feb. 23, 1763, BL Add. MSS 36797, f. 34.

[3] George III to Bute, Sept. 13, 1762(?), in R. Sedgwick (ed.), *Letters from George III to Lord Bute, 1756-1766* (1939), p. 135.

[4] Bute to Phillips, Feb. 23, 1763, BL Add. MSS 32797, f. 34.

[5] George III to Bute, Sept. 13, 1762(?), in Sedgwick, *op. cit.*, p. 135. For further examples of this definition of economy, see chapter XII.

[6] "A representation designed to shew what were the Forces kept up in the year 1749, and upon what Establishment: The Reduction necessary to be made in the present Forces to bring them to the same Numbers and Establishment, and what will then be the Charge of the Half Pay at the Conclusion of the War," Oct. 1762, Charles Townshend MSS, 299/3/16.

[7] For the King and Bute's concern about Britain's financial strength, see George III to Bute, Jul. 26, 1762, in Sedgwick, *op. cit.*, p.126.

[8] The ministry's estimate of the mood of the House is in the King's speech, Nov. 25, 1762, *Journals of the Home of Commons*, XXIX, p. 354.

[9] It is instructive to compare the King and Bute's understanding of the relationship between security and economy with the one expressed in 1767 by Charles Jenkinson, who had been Bute's private secretary in 1762 and privy to the plans made then for the post-war army. Jenkinson observed in 1767: "The two great ends of security and economy may seem at first view to combat each other, but it is our duty to reconcile them. Security must have the first place. Without this the whole may be lost, the whole at least is in danger. Economy can save a part only. The first therefore must be obtained, but in obtaining we should apply every principle of economy to render the burden as light as possible, and when once obtained there we should stop" (Jenkinson, "naval argument," Jan.-Feb. 1767, BL Add. MSS 38336, f. 361): In contrast to this view—which was informed by Jenkinson's knowledge in 1767 that military costs could not safely be reduced below those of 1749—the King and Bute were determined to make security and economy equal priorities, and planned accordingly.

[10] *The Briton*, Sept. 25, 1762.

[11] The Duke of Newcastle to the Duke of Devonshire, Dec. 23, 1762, BL Add. MSS 32945, f. 335.

[12] Enclosure in Richard Rigby to the Duke of Bedford, Dec. 27, 1762, Bedford MSS, XLVI, nos. 218, 224. Henry Fox identified this as "his majesty's plan" in his letter to Bute, Dec. 30, 1762, Bute MSS, Fox Correspondence.

[13] Charles Jenkinson, notes, Mar. 4, 1763, R.C. Simmons and P.D.G. Thomas (eds), *Proceedings and Debates of the British Parliaments Respecting North America* (1982), I, p. 440.

[14] "State showing the number of land forces proposed to be kept for the service of the year 1763" [early Jan. 1763], Charles Townshend MSS, 299/3/15. Fox told Bute he had sent Townshend these estimates; see: Fox to Bute, Jan. 5, 1763, Bute MSS, Fox Correspondence.

[15] Compare "State showing the number of land forces proposed to be kept for the service of the year 1763" with Dec. 16, 1748, *Journals of the House of Commons*, XXV, pp. 671-2.

[16] George III to Bute, [early Feb. 1763], Bute MSS, Correspondence with George III, no. 414. This letter may be approximately dated by its reference to 10,000 troops in America. In early February, the ministry decided to reduce the number of battalions to be stationed there from 21 to 20. See Bullion, *op. cit.*

[17] George III to Bute, [c. Feb. 17, 1763], Bute MSS, Correspondence with George III, no. 274. For a discussion of the significance of this letter, see Bullion, *op. cit.*

[18] *The Briton*, Sept. 25, 1762.

[19] Gilbert Elliot, notes, Mar. 4, 1763, in Bullion, *op. cit.*

[20] The King's speech, Nov. 25, 1762, *Journals of the House of Commons*, XXIX, p. 354.

[21] Sir Roger Newdigate, notes, Mar. 4, 1763, and Jenkinson, notes, Mar. 4, 1763, in: Simmons and Thomas, *op. cit.*, I, 440.

[22] Newdigate, notes, Mar. 4, 1763, in *ibid*. To my knowledge, no historian has previously called attention to this aspect of the plan for America. Yet Ellis publicly and the King privately stressed the importance of the speed and efficiency with which "nominal corps" could expand. George III to Bute, [c. Feb. 17, 1763], Bute MSS, Correspondence with George III, no. 274.

[23] *Ibid.*

[24] See: Bullion, *op. cit.*

[25] Newdigate, notes and Jenkinson, notes, Mar. 4, 1763, in: Simmons and Thomas, *op.cit.*, I, p. 440.

[26] George III to Bute, Sept. 13, 1762(?), in: Sedgwick, *op. cit.*, p. 135; enclosure in Rigby to Bedford, Dec. 27, 1762, Bedford MSS, XLVI, no. 224; and "State showing the number of land forces proposed to be kept for the service of the year 1763," [early Jan. 1763], Charles Townshend MSS, 299/3/15.

[27] Newdigate, notes, Mar. 4, 1763, Newdigate MSS B. 2543/11.

[28] George III to Bute, [c. Feb. 17, 1763], Bute MSS, Correspondence with George III, no. 274. For a discussion of the background of the attempt to station more troops in Ireland, see J. Shy, *Toward Lexington: The Role of the British Army in the Coming of the American Revolution* (Princeton, NJ, 1965), pp. 73-8.

[29] Bute to Phillips, Feb. 23, 1763, BL Add. MSS 36797, f. 34.

[30] S.F. Gradish, "Wages and Manning: the Navy Act of 1758," *EHR*, XCIII (1978), pp. 63-5.

[31] [George Grenville], "Some thoughts upon a plan for the useful employment of a body of seamen in the king's pay in time of peace and for the suppression of the dangerous and infamous practice of smuggling," [Oct. 1762], BL Add. MSS 57834, fos 109-10.

[32] See Sir James West to Newcastle, Dec. 1, 1762, BL Add. MSS 32945, f. 233, for Grenville's speech, in which the First Lord announced the government would keep 16,000 officers and men, including 4,000 marines, on the peace establishment. For the navy establishment in 1750s, see Feb. 18, 1750/l, *Journals of the House of Commons*, XXVI, 45. For the plan, see "Proposals . . .", Dec. 1762, George Grenville MSS, STGI8-(30); for the government's ultimate action, see Mar. 24, 1763, *Journals of the House of Commons*, XXIX, 609.

[33] Phillips to Bute, Feb. 17, 1763, Bute MSS, 11/34/1-4.

[34] George III to Bute, [c. Feb. 17, 1763], Bute MSS, Correspondence with George III, no. 274.

[35] When the King learned that Bute "seems to doubt whether the Irish will agree to pay the additional 6000," he immediately suggested an alternative plan for reduction that did not include the 15 battalions. George III to Bute, Feb. 5, 1763, Bute MSS, Correspondence with George III, no. 195. This letter bears out the suspicion voiced in Shy, *op. cit.*, 76.

[36] Bute to Phillips, Feb. 23, 1763, BL Add. MSS 36797, f. 34.

[37] H.B. Legge to Newcastle, Feb. 26, 1763, and Newcastle to the Earl of Hardwicke, Mar. 3, 1763, BL Add. MSS 32947, fos 98, 163-4.

[38] Legge's speech, Dec. 10 1762, in Simmons and Thomas, *op. cit.*, I, 426.

[39] Legge's speech, Mar. 4, 1763, in Newdigate, notes, Newdegate MSS B. 2543/11; and Elliot, notes, NLS MS 11036, f. 47.

[40] West to Newcastle, Mar. 4, 1763, BL Add. MSS 32947, fos. 265-6.

[41] Pitt's speeches, Mar. 4, 1763 and Dec. 9, 1762, in Simmons and Thomas, *op. cit.*, I, 441, 419-22.

[42] Bute to the Marquis of Granby, Nov. 5, 1762, BL Add. MSS 38200, f. 93.

[43] Bute to Fox, Nov. 30, 1762, BL Add. MSS51379, f. 118.

[44] George III to Bute, [c. Feb. 17, 1763], Bute MSS, Correspondence with George III, no. 274.

[45] Newcastle to Devonshire, Jun. 28, 1761, BL Add. MSS 32924, f. 314. The best analysis of the negotiations during the summer of 1761 is Karl W. Schweizer, "William Pitt, Lord Bute, and the peace negotiations with France, May-September 1761," *Albion*, XIII (1981), pp. 262-75. For a lengthy description, see Z.E. Rashed, *The Peace of Paris 1763* (1951), pp. 56-114.

[46] Bedford to the Earl of Gower, Jun. 27, 1761, PRO 30/29/1/14. fos. 527-8.

[47] Jun. 25, 1761, Jenkinson, notes on cabinet meetings, Jun.-Sept. 1761, BL Add. MSS 38336, fos. 237-8. These notes are based on conversations Jenkinson had with Bute, and thus constitute the Earl's record of the meetings, and the most complete account of his statements at them. Jenkinson used these notes while he was working on an answer to the French memoir on the negotiations of 1761. That answer was never published, because Bute feared it might hinder his secret contacts with the French during Nov. 1761- Jan. 1762, see Rashed; *op. cit.*, pp. 112-14. For notes on cabinet meetings by an influential colleague of Bute's, see the Duke of Devonshire's diary, in P.D. Brown and Karl W. Schweizer (eds), *The Devonshire Diary: William Cavendish, 4th Duke of Devonshire; Memoranda on State of Affairs, 1759-1762* (1982), pp. 99-120.

[48] Jul. 15, 1761,Jenkinson notes, BL Add. MSS 38336, f. 249.

[49] Aug. 6, 1761,Jenkinson notes, BL Add. MSS 38336, f. 253.

[50] See Schweizer, *op. cit.*, pp. 272-3; and Karl W. Schweizer, "The cabinet crisis of August 1761: unpublished letters from the Bute and Bedford manuscripts," *Bull. Institute for Historical Research*, LIX (1986), pp. 225-9. The quotation is from Aug. 14, 1761, Brown and Schweizer, *op. cit.*, p. 110.

[51] Aug. 19, 1761, Jenkinson notes, BL Add. MSS 38336, f. 264.

[52] Jun. 26, 1761, Jenkinson notes, BL Add. MSS 38336, fos. 241-2.

[53] Bute to Bedford, Jul. 12, 1761, in Lord John Russell (ed.), *Correspondence of John, Fourth Duke of Bedford, Selected from the Originals at Woburn Abbey* (1846), III, 32.

[54] Aug. 13, 1761,Jenkinson notes, BL Add. MSS 38336, f. 254.

[55] Aug. 14, 1761, Brown and Schweizer, *op. cit.*, 109.

[56] Aug. 19, 1761, Jenkinson notes, BL Add. MSS 38336, fos. 265-6.

[57] The phrase in quotations is the Earl of Gower's, in a letter to Bedford, Jul. 3, 1761, Bedford MSS, XLIV, no. 90.

[58] Sept. 15, 1761, Brown and Schweizer, *op. cit.*, pp.123-5.

[59] Jan. 8, 1762, *ibid.*, p.155. For an account of these negotiations through the Sardinian envoys in London and Paris, see Rashed, *op. cit.*, pp.113-22.

[60] Jan. 6, 1762, Brown and Schweizer, *op. cit.*, p. 154. For a full discussion of the benefits to be gained by taking Havana, see Henry Ellis to the Earl of Egremont, Jan. 16, 1762, PRO 30/47/14/1, fos. 240-5. An account of the planning may be found in R. Middleton, *The Bells of Victory: the Pitt- Newcastle ministry and the Conduct of the 72 Seven Years' War, 1757-1 762* (1985), p. 205.

[61] This struggle over the war in Germany may be followed in Brown and Schweizer, *op. cit.*, pp. 154-70; and in the King's letters to Bute from Jan. to May 1762 in Sedgwick, *op. cit.*, pp. 78-101. George's willingness to remove British troops from Germany is a sure sign that Bute seriously considered a withdrawal. For another indication, see Jenkinson to George Grenville, Apr. 13, 1762, in W.J. Smith (ed.), *The Grenville Papers: being the correspondence of Richard Grenville Earl Temple, K.G., and the Right Hon. George Grenville, their friends and contemporaries* (1852-3), I, 440.

[62] Bute to Bedford, May 1, 1762, in Russell, *op. cit.*, III, p. 76.

[63] For the contemporary definition of "chicane," see the *Oxford English Dictionary*. France's reputation as a "chicaning power" was proverbial at the time. See Bedford to Bute, May 4, 1762, in Russell, *op. cit.*, III, 77.

[64] Bute to Bedford, May 1, 1762, in Russell, *op. cit.*, p. 76.

[65] For the secret concession of Santa Lucia, see Rashed, *op. cit.*, pp. 149-50; for the awareness of the value of that island, see Grenville's notes on cabinet meetings, Mar. 18, 1762, George Grenville MSS, STG 17-(43). There is a modern transcription of these notes in BL Add. MSS 57834, fos. 59-62.

[66] See Grenville, notes on the French statement, Jul. 1762, George Grenville MSS, STG17-(35); Edward Weston to Grenville, Jul. 1762, *ibid.*, STG 17- (37); and George III to Bute, Jul. 1762, Bute MSS, Correspondence with George III, no. 188.

[67] George III to Bute, Jul. 26, 1762, Sedgwick, *op. cit.*, p. 126.

[68] Bute to Bedford, Sept. 28, 1762, BL Add. MSS 36797, f. 12. See also Bute to Fox, Oct. 26, 1762, *ibid.*, fos 14-15.

[69] Devonshire to Newcastle, Aug. 25, 1762, BL Add. MSS 32942, fos. 9-10.

[70] Rashed, *op. cit.*, pp. 179-80.

[71] Phillip Lawson, *George Grenville: A Political Life* (1984), p.136.

[72] [James Oswald], *A letter to a gentleman in the City, St James Chronicle,* Sept.7-9, 1762. For a brief account of the success of this essay, more generally known as "the Wandsworth letter," see John Brewer, *Party Ideology and Popular Politics at the Accession of George III* (1976), p. 223; for responses to it by

Bute's enemies, see *St James Chronicle*, Sept. 11-14, 1762, and *North Briton*, XV.

[73] Bute to Fox, Nov. 30, 1762, BL Add. MSS51379, f. 118.

[74] Bute to Bedford, Sept. 28, 1762, BL Add. MSS 36797, f. 12. For a contrary argument, that Bute hoped to end French hostility toward Britain, see R. Hyam, "Imperial interests and the Peace of Paris (1763)," in R. Hyam and G. Martin, *Reappraisals in British Imperial History* (1975), pp. 34-5; for a convincing rebuttal of Hyam's interpretation, see R.W. Tucker and D.C. Hendrickson, *The Fall of the First British Empire: Origins of the War of American Independence* (Baltimore, MD, 1982), pp. 40-1.

[75] Bute to Bedford, Jul. 12, 1761, in Russell, *op. cit.*, III, pp. 32-3.

[76] Bute to Phillips, Feb. 23, 1763, BL Add. MSS 36797, f. 34.

[77] Jenkinson to Richard Neville, Nov. 14, 1762, and Neville to Jenkinson, Dec. 2, 1762, and Neville to Jenkinson, Dec. 2, 1762, PRO 30/50/48, fos 45-6, 73. The judgement on the usefulness of Neville's intelligence is in Jenkinson to Neville, Jul. 22, 1763, PRO 30/50/52, f. 59. Neville was Bedford's secretary when the latter was negotiating peace in Paris.

[78] In his speech to Parliament on Nov. 25, 1762, *Journals of the House of Commons*, XXIX, 354, the King emphasized the necessity of improving the new acquisitions. Though the speech understandably emphasized their potential for future improvement, such an argument implicitly recognized that these additions to the empire would not be much present help to the nation.

Chapter XII

"The Ten Thousand in America:" More Light on the Decision on the American Army, 1762-1763*

Although historians have long recognized the significance of the British administration's decision in 1762-1763 to station 10,000 regular soldiers in the colonies—it had the momentous consequence of bringing on a confrontation with colonists over parliamentary taxation—they have not found very much contemporary evidence bearing on it. *When* was the decision made? The records that John Shy examined as he prepared his magisterial study, *Toward Lexington: The Role of the British Army in the Coming of the American Revolution*, do not reveal precisely when the earl of Bute's ministry committed itself to maintaining an army in America. As a result, Shy concluded that "the decision . . . was not really *made*" but "was simply assumed by the time the preliminaries of a peace settlement had been worked out in late 1762."[1] *Why* was the decision taken? After a thorough search, Shy noted that "there is no authoritative expression of the reasons for keeping an army in peacetime America."[2] Finally, *how* did the ministry explain the decision to the House of Commons on March 4, 1763? In particular, did its spokesman, Secretary at War Welbore Ellis, explicitly promise that Americans would pay for the soldiers? Until Peter D. G. Thomas recently added to knowledge about Ellis's speech by publishing excerpts from two newly discovered accounts of the debate on the army—one by Charles Jenkinson, an M.P. and Bute's private secretary, the other by Sir Roger Newdigate, a prominent Tory M.P.—information on these important points was scanty as well.[3]

In the course of research on the Bute administration and the origins of the American Revolution, I have found fresh, significant documentation on all these questions. This evidence reveals the date at which the ministry committed itself in principle and yields an authoritative explanation of its motives. Another set of notes on the debate of March 4, in the handwriting of Gilbert Elliot, a Scottish

M.P., provides a means of checking the accuracy of statements attributed to Ellis by Jenkinson and Newdigate.[4] Because of this evidence, historians can now be confident that they know when and why the administration decided to put a large army in America, and what Ellis said about that army and the ministry's plans for subsidizing it.

Although the records Shy studied did not permit him to establish when the ministers began thinking about the American army, he could discern when they made their "final," official decision on that subject. He pointed out that on February 12, 1763, Ellis officially notified Sir Jeffrey Amherst, the commander in chief in America, that the king intended to keep 20 battalions there, comprising 10,000 officers and men. He assumed that the ministers must have made the final decision shortly before that date.[5] This assumption, I think, is most likely correct. Since the ministers wanted Amherst to send them his plan for distributing the troops as quickly as he could for the king's inspection and approval, they had every reason to transmit news about the colonial establishment to America soon after they officially decided on its numbers.[6] But Shy was unaware of other contemporary records that show that the decision of February 1763 concerned numbers only. He also was unaware that the necessity for an American garrison was not "simply assumed . . . in late 1762" without planning or discussion by George III and his ministers. To the contrary: the king had concluded, for good and sufficient reasons, that a large army in the colonies was necessary and had devised a specific plan for one, before the end of 1762. His ministers considered the plan, and committed themselves to the principle that inspired it, fully six weeks before Ellis wrote to Amherst.

On December 27, 1762, Richard Rigby informed the duke of Bedford that their mutual friend Ellis "finds work enough upon his hands with settling the reduction of the army." Rigby added that the general plan for the peacetime army "is the business which chiefly engrosses the attention at Court at present" and promised that he would send the duke a copy as soon as he could get one.[7] He obtained one that same day, which he enclosed in his letter with the remark, "This is not absolutely fixed, the ministers have a meeting on it tomorrow." He predicted, though, that "it will be this plan, or [one] very near it." The plan Rigby sent to Bedford called for 10,542 men, distributed into 21 battalions, for North America.[8]

The cabinet met on December 28 and discussed what Henry Fox, Paymaster-General of the Forces and Leader of the House of Commons, identified as "his majesty's plan." Bute and his colleagues reached no firm decision on the American army that day, for Fox urged the earl two days later that the plan should be "fixed as soon as may be."[9] But though they made no final decision, they certainly came close to doing so. Early in the new year, Charles Townshend, who had served as Secretary at War until December 8 and was mulling over whether to accept the presidency of the Board of Trade, received a paper from Fox titled "State showing the number of land forces proposed to be kept for the service of the year 1763." According to this paper, the administration intended to station 21 battalions in the colonies, at an estimated expense of £225,159 per year.[10] Also in January, Ellis provided the earl of Egremont, the Secretary of State responsible for the colonies, with an estimate of the numbers and expense of the American army for 1763. The War Office's "Estimate . . . for the service in North America" calculated that the 21 battalions to be kept there would cost £224,904.[11] The ministry decided in February to reduce the number of battalions in America to 20 and the number of men to 10,000; but the estimates Townshend and Egremont received show that the ministers had been committed in principle to stationing a large army in the colonies since the meeting of December 28. The decision to reduce the number of battalions by one was a last-minute adjustment of an existing commitment, not the commitment itself.

The timing of the commitment raises the question of when the king and the cabinet decided to finance the enlarged army in America by making Americans pay for it. Was this subject discussed, and a commitment in principle made, at the December 28 meeting? I have uncovered no new evidence on this point. It is possible, however, that a letter from the king to Bute in March 1763 may provide an answer. On March 18, Charles Townshend unexpectedly moved in the House of Commons to lower the duty on foreign molasses imported into America from 6d. to 2d. per gallon, with the revenue going to support the army. Angered that none of the ministers spoke against "this insidious proposal," George III reminded Bute that lack of preparation could not excuse their silence, because "this subject was new to none, having been thought of this whole winter."

"All ought to have declar'd," he went on, "that next session some tax will be laid before the House but that it requires much information before a proper one can be stated."[12] The king may have been remembering discussions on December 28. Even if he was not, his comments reveal that whenever the financing of the American army began to be considered, the ministers focused their thoughts not on whether the colonists should pay, but how, and not on whether they should be taxed, but when. The letter also discloses that this focus did not change: the ministers remained committed throughout their deliberations to the principle that colonists should support the American army.

Two other pieces of evidence substantiate the king's recollection of discussions about financing the army. One is a letter from Jenkinson to Bute on March 18, which confirms that the Treasury had been considering reducing the molasses tax during the winter.[13] The second is a note George III sent to Bute in early February, enclosing a comparison he had devised between the size and cost of the army in 1749, the first year of peace after the War of the Austrian Succession, with the government's plans for the army in 1763. That comparison did not include the colonial garrison. "I have not put down the 10,000 in America," explained the king, "as [it is] proposed that being no expense to Great Britain."[14] Subsequent to the writing of this letter, the government decided to postpone taxing Americans until 1764. That was the only change in this proposal, which became official policy before the end of the third week in February. By

February 19, news had begun to circulate among opponents and supporters of the ministry that Ellis would recommend to the House putting 20 battalions overseas, to "be paid another year by the colonies themselves."[15]

What motives persuaded first the king, then his ministers, to commit themselves to stationing a large army in North America? Shy argued in *Toward Lexington* that they believed such a force was necessary to defend the new conquests and to back up the management of Indian affairs. He also asserted that the ministers seriously thought of using the army to control the older colonies and that, to them, the plan "had the added attraction of putting some teeth in the imperial system."[16] This analysis of the government's motives has been adopted by nearly all scholars of the period, with only R. C. Simmons dissenting. The absence of any positive statements on the subject by men in authority apparently led Simmons to doubt that "any important British politician subscribed to the view that military forces should remain in America to guarantee colonial subordination or cooperation."[17] Some comments by the most important politician of all, George III, reveal that such doubts are well founded.

On February 17, 1763, the king wrote to Bute in response to disturbing news of Tory opposition to the plan. Sir John Phillips, a leader of the Tory M.P.s, had written to the earl that day warning him that "the proposed regulation of the army . . . gives very great uneasiness" to many Tories, because "they judge it unconstitutional to keep up an army consisting of so large a number of corps in time of peace." Tories objected to the ministers' plan to maintain "a large standing army" that numbered, by their calculations, nearly twice as many troops as any previous peacetime establishment, with more regiments and more officers, though fewer enlisted men, on active duty. Phillips found no military justification for so large a force, especially one in which regiments "may soon be raised to their old complement" simply by enlisting more soldiers, at the beginning "of such a peace that is likely to continue." He diplomatically stated that he believed that this proposal was attractive to the king because it rewarded "the merit of

those brave officers who have ventured their lives in the service of their country"
by keeping them on active duty, but he cautioned Bute that it could "be construed
by his enemies to be a design (which both his royal heart and your loyal breast
abhors) to make himself an absolute monarch and your lordship an absolute
minister." Then he pointedly added, "There is nothing I dread so much as the
forcing those who are extremely desirous of supporting his majesty's
administration to join in any measures with those who are watching all
opportunities to defeat it."[18]

When the king read this letter, he felt the prick of that point keenly, and
Phillips's diplomatic phrases did not moderate his immediate reaction. He was
outraged by the Tories' objections, which to his mind were based on nothing but
their traditional prejudice against standing armies, no matter what the
circumstances, and by their lese majesty. "If government is to yield everything to
men who only rebel because they have never been accustomed to act by any rule
but passion," he angrily told Bute, "tis not worthwhile to consider two minutes
what is to be done. I deny every reason Sir John gives," he declared, and
reminded Bute why he and the ministry had settled on this plan. "As to the 10,000
in America, that is become necessary from our successes." One does not need
clairvoyance to read the king's mind. Britain's new territories and subjects had to
be governed and defended. France might at any time renew the struggle; the treaty
of 1763 had secured a cessation of hostilities, not a permanent peace.
Accordingly, a large army, with means to expand its numbers rapidly in an
emergency, was necessary in America. "If we don't take precaution," the king
predicted, "I will venture to affirm whenever a new war breaks out we shall run
great risk of losing the great advantages we are at this hour to be blessed with by
this great, noble, and perfect definitive treaty."[19] This was the royal rationale—
this, and no more. Nowhere in his letter to Bute did George III refer to the
possibility of using the American regiments to control the older colonies by
enforcing imperial law there.

The absence of any such reference is significant, for reasons best illuminated by a brief description of the king's involvement in the planning for the postwar army during 1762-1763. As early as September 1762, George had taken upon himself the primary responsibility of drafting a plan for the peacetime establishment.[20] He devised the plan the cabinet discussed and approved in principle on December 28. In early February, when his ministers began to fear that the Irish Parliament might balk at paying for the six thousand soldiers that plan added to the usual peacetime establishment in Ireland, he worked out an alternative scheme for the government to fall back on if the threatened Irish opposition materialized.[21] When the ministers looked for ways after February 17 to persuade the Tories to support the original plan, they borrowed his idea of comparing the size and cost of the army in Britain in 1749 and 1763 to demonstrate the government's concern for economy as well as security.[22] Finally, the king participated in, and agreed with, the decision to compel colonists to pay for the soldiers defending them. Given this record of royal interest and activity, it is evident that Bute was not exaggerating when he remarked to Fox that his majesty "looked upon the army to be his own department."[23] The king knew the reasons why the government believed that Britain needed 20 battalions in America. Furthermore, there are no grounds for believing he would leave out any justification for that decision in a personal letter to his "dearest friend." His letter of February 17 has, in fact, all the characteristics that distinguish his private correspondence with Bute: passionate and unguarded language; frank and informed analyses of issues and alternatives; vigorous and unrestrained expression of opinions.[24] George III's rationale for "the 10,000" reveals that he and his ministers were not thinking of using those troops as imperial police in the older British colonies when they made their decision about the American army.

How did Ellis justify the policy to the House of Commons? Did his public explanation differ in any significant way from the king's private justification? And what did the Secretary at War say about meeting the costs of the American army? In answering these questions, Gilbert Elliot's notes are of considerable value, in large part because of his experience as a parliamentarian and his connections with the ministry. He and Bute had had an "affectionate attachment" since 1755, and the earl appreciated his friend's skill as a politician and parliamentary debater, respected his judgment on issues and men in politics, and trusted his advice. In October 1761, Elliot had served Bute as go-between in delicate, confidential negotiations with George Grenville. After Grenville succeeded William Pitt as Leader of the House of Commons, Elliot gave him effective support during the debates in December 1761 over the conduct of the war in Germany and negotiations with Spain. In May 1762, he helped convince the king and Bute that a vote of credit for one million pounds would enable the Treasury to pay the most pressing current accounts until Parliament met in the fall. When Bute became first lord of the Treasury after the decision on the vote of credit drove the duke of Newcastle from office, he named Elliot Treasurer of the Chamber. This lucrative sinecure freed him from the routine duties of a junior lord of the Treasury and permitted him to concentrate on business in the House of Commons and "attendance on the king." The most crucial business he dealt with was the crisis in the cabinet during September and October 1762 over the terms of peace. Elliot was one of four members of Bute's "real council" who persuaded the earl to remove Grenville from the post of Secretary of State and to replace him as Leader of the House with Fox.[25] Without question, therefore, Elliot's notes of March 4, 1763, were taken by an experienced, skilled politician who was accustomed to focusing on the most salient issues for the administration in political situations and who was practiced at assessing, from the standpoint of the ministry, the significance of arguments made during parliamentary debates. It is not likely that he missed or mistook any point he regarded as important.

What did Elliot think was important in Ellis's remarks? He believed that the ministry's justifications for stationing a large army in America and its assurances about the present and future expense of that force were the most significant parts of the speech, as the following notes make clear.

> . . . American Army
>
> Ten thousand divided into 20 Battalions
>
> Model in America . . .
>
> 2 Batt[alions] to Jamaica.
>
> 1 Antigo
>
> 1 Grenadoes
>
> 1 for small Islands
>
> 1 Domin[ica] Tobago, St. Vin[cent], Provid[ence],
>
> Bermudas by [undecipherable word] of [undecipherable word]
>
> 2 St. Augus[tine] Florida etc. etc.
>
> 4 Mobile Lusiana Senegal East Indys
>
> 90 thousand Canadians acquired. besides Indians. French missionary, interwove Politicks with Religion—combined their prejudices—not familiaris'd to civil goverment, unsupported by arms. Royal edict of France 23 thousand men, half to serve in their Islands half in their fleet alternately. Comparison 1749 with present model increase of this
>
> 2,554   932,20
>
> Exceeding this year in expense
>
> 111217
>
> £70,000
>
> suppose this plan for 1764.
>
> a saving to this country
>
>   105,000
>
> America paying its own troops . . . [26]

Much of what Elliot extracted from Ellis's speech requires little or no comment, especially when compared with Jenkinson's and Newdigate's notes. The organization of the speech is clear. Ellis began by describing the disposition of battalions in the West Indies, Louisiana, Senegal, and the East Indies, and then explained why Britain needed to station a large number of regulars in Canada. In one respect, Elliot took more detailed notes than the other two on the official justification for the ministry's decision. He was impressed by Ellis's point that French missionaries "interwove Politicks with Religion [and] combined their prejudices" when they ministered to Indians. As a result, the Indians of Canada were "not familiaris'd to civil government, unsupported by arms." To maintain British authority over those Indians, as well as over the "90,000 Canadians," required a substantial force. Elliot also noted, as Jenkinson and Newdigate did, Ellis's argument for defense against an unusually large French force in the Caribbean that could quickly invade British possessions in event of war.

After justifying the largest peacetime army in British history, Ellis went on to demonstrate that maintaining it would not be ruinously expensive, either in 1763 or later. To accomplish this, he adopted the tactic the king had used in February to emphasize the attention paid to keeping expenses as low as possible. Ellis compared the numbers and expense of the army in 1749 with the estimated numbers and expense of the army for 1763 and 1764. To make the comparison easier to understand, and to establish the cost of the army in 1764, he calculated what the cost for 1763 would have been if the ministers had had to ask Parliament to support the army for a year, rather than merely for the eight months from April 24 to December 24.[27] When Ellis presented the results to the House on March 4, Jenkinson thought he "was too minute," though he "did it in general well."[28] Elliot must have agreed that Ellis was too detailed, for he jotted down only those figures that seemed significant to him.[29]

He noted that Britain would have 2,554 more officers and men on active duty in 1763 than in 1749. The cost would be approximately £932,200 over a twelve-month period, £111,217 more than in 1749. Of course, since the army would need support only for the last eight months of 1763, the real increase over 1749 was around £70,000. And, if Britain kept the same number of troops in 1764, there would be no excess in expenditure over 1749 at all. Indeed, the larger army of 1764 would cost the nation £105,000 less then the army of 1749. This "saving to this country" would come about because in 1764 "America [would be] paying its own troops."

These last words are somewhat cryptic, owing to the brevity of Elliot's notes on this point and to Ellis's desire to avoid specifics of future policy. The accounts by Jenkinson and Newdigate leave no doubt that the troops Americans were going to pay were British regulars, not a colonial force, and that all the colonies would contribute to supporting them. Ellis deliberately gave no indication of how the colonists would contribute, because the ministry wanted to delay discussion of that topic until it presented a "proper" tax the next year.

After the promise that Americans would pay for the army in 1764, Elliot took no further notes on Ellis's comparison, though Newdigate recorded the Secretary at War as continuing, "then you had only four battalions in America. Now you will have the foundations of a great army there."[30] Perhaps he felt that Ellis had already made his point. The figures he recited, plus his unambiguous assurance that in 1764 the colonies would support the battalions stationed there, had conveyed to the House the ministry's commitment to making Britain more secure than she had been after the last war, and at less cost.

Elliot's notes do not offer new insights into Ellis's speech. Rather, their value to historians rests on their congruence with the accounts of Newdigate and Jenkinson. These notes by an experienced, perceptive politician leave little room to doubt the accuracy of those two accounts and give scholars convincing reasons to be confident that they know essentially what Ellis said about the decision to station an army in America on March 4, 1763. Thus we can be sure that Ellis justified the action as essential for securing the new possessions from disturbances within and the whole empire from a military threat from without. Moreover, the agreement between Ellis's remarks on that decision and the king's recollection of the reasons for it shows that the secretary gave a straightforward, complete account of the government's motives. Historians can also be sure that Ellis assured the House of Commons that the army would be not only the largest peacetime British army in history but also less expensive than a comparable army had been. Finally, we can be certain that that assurance depended upon a commitment that the Secretary at War explicitly made: in 1764, Americans would pay for the troops that defended them.

In sum, the new evidence on the decision on the American army makes clear that George III and his ministers decided after due deliberation in December 1762 that stationing a large force in North America was necessary. Contrary to Shy, this decision was really made, and not simply assumed. Moreover, the king's comments to Bute in private, and Ellis's remarks to the House in public, show that it was based upon the belief that Britain could not otherwise achieve imperial security. Neither the king nor the cabinet was influenced by thoughts that the regulars could also serve to police the older colonies. And neither the monarch, who happily told Bute on March 4 that "the army debate has succeeded to the utmost of my wishes," nor the ministers, who doubtless shared his satisfaction, shrank from promising the House that "next year America [would] pay itself" for its security.[31] They did not foresee the revolutionary impact of this promise, when implemented by acts of Parliament, on American public opinion. In fact, at no time during their deliberations do they appear to have considered American opinion at all.

* This chapter first appeared in *William and Mary Quarterly* 43, 1986 pp. 646-657.

Endnotes

[1] Shy, *Toward Lexington: The Role of the British Army in the Coming of the American Revolution* (Princeton, NJ., 1965), pp. 45-46. This conclusion has had a considerable influence.

[2] *Ibid.*, p. 67.

[3] Peter D. G. Thomas, "New Light on the Commons Debate of 1763 on the American Army," *William and Mary Quarterly*, 3d Ser., XXXVIII (1981), pp.110-112. These excerpts may also be found in R. C. Simmons and P.D.G. Thomas, eds., *Proceedings and Debates of the British Parliaments Respecting North America, 1754-1783* (London, 1982-), I, pp. 440-441.

[4] [Gilbert Elliot], notes [Mar. 4, 1763], Minto Papers, MS 11036, fols. 46-47, National Library of Scotland, Edinburgh.

[5] Shy, *Toward Lexington*, pp. 64, 79.

[6] Welbore Ellis to Sir Jeffrey Amherst, Feb. 12, 1763, War Office Papers, W.O. 4/987, fols. 3-6, Public Record Office.

[7] Richard Rigby to the duke of Bedford, Dec. 27, 1762, Bedford Papers, XLVI, no. 218, Bedford Estates Office, London.

[8] Enclosure *ibid.*, no. 224.

[9] Henry Fox to the earl of Bute, Dec. 30, 1762, Bute Papers in the possession of the marquess of Bute, Fox Correspondence, Mount Stuart, Isle of Bute, Scotland. Shy was aware that the ministers met on Dec. 28 but mistakenly believed that they confined their discussion to the peacetime establishment in Ireland (*Toward Lexington*, p. 74).

[10] "State showing the number of land forces proposed to be kept for the service of the year 1763" [Jan. 1763], Charles Townshend Papers, 299/3/15, William L. Clements Library, Ann Arbor, MI.; Fox to Bute, Jan. 5, 1763, Bute Papers, Fox Correspondence.

[11] "Estimate . . . for the services in North America" [Jan. 1763], Egremont Papers, P.R.O. 30/47/24, bundle 3, fol. P.R.O. There is no apparent reason for the difference in the cost of 21 battalions between this estimate and the estimate in the Townshend Papers.

[12] The king to Bute [Mar. 19, 1763], Romney Sedgwick, ed., *Letters from George III to Lord Bute, 1756-1766* (London, 1939), p. 202.

[13] Charles Jenkinson to Bute [Mar. 8, 1763], Simmons and Thomas, eds., *Proceedings and Debates*, II, pp. 562-563.

[14] The king to Bute [early Feb. 1763], Bute Papers, Correspondence with George III, no. 414. References to the plan for stationing 10,000 soldiers in America and to "some impertinent letters" from the duke of Brunswick that arrived in London in early Feb. date this letter. The comparison itself has not been found.

[15] The duke of Newcastle, "Mems. Definitive Treaty, Plan of the Army," Feb. 19, 1763, Newcastle Papers, Additional Manuscripts, 32947, fol. 48, British Library. Contemporaries used "another year" to refer to the following year. See also Rigby to Bedford, Feb. 23, 1763, Bedford Papers, XLVIII, no. 70.

[16] Shy, *Toward Lexington*, p. 67. Shy essentially based his conclusion "that the ministry, before making their decision, considered how the army might be used against rebellious Americans" on two anonymous papers read by more than one minister between Feb. and May 1763. One of these was "Hints respecting the settlement of our American provinces"; the other, "Plan of forts and garrisons."

"Hints" is dated Feb. 3, 1763; internal evidence indicates that "Plan" was finished sometime between Feb. and May 1763. Obviously, neither paper could have influenced the commitment the ministers made on Dec. 28, 1762, to station troops in the colonies. Thus even without other new evidence discussed in this essay, Shy's conclusion has to be regarded as questionable.

[17] R. C. Simmons, *The American Colonies: From Settlement to Independence* (New York, 1976), p. 291.

[18] Sir John Phillips to Bute, Feb. 17, 1763, Bute Papers, 11/34/1-4.

[19] The king to Bute [Feb. 17, 1763], Bute Papers, Correspondence with George III, no. 274.

[20] The king to Bute [Sept. 13, 1762], in Sedgwick, ed., *Letters from George III to Bute*, p. 135.

[21] The king to Bute [Feb. 5, 1763], Bute Papers, Correspondence with George III, no. 195.

[22] "Account of the meeting at Sir Francis Dashwood's on the army plan," Feb. 25, 1763, Newcastle Papers, Add. MSS 32947, fol. 93.

[23] Bute to Henry Fox, Mar. 2, 1763, Holland House Papers, Add. MSS 51379, fol. 141, British Library. Shy described the king's interest in the army during 1762-1763 in *Toward Lexington*, pp.68-69, but because he was unaware that George III drafted the plan discussed on Dec. 28, devised a contingency plan for Ireland on Feb. 5, and compiled the first comparison of the army estimates for 1749 and 1763, his account underestimates the extent and significance of the king's involvement.

[24] Scholars may conveniently study this remarkable correspondence in Sedgwick, ed., *Letters from George III to Bute*. Over 500 letters were subsequently discovered (after Sedgwick's edition) at the Central Library, Cardiff, Wales, (depositor unknown) and these were transferred in the early 1980s to the central Bute collection at Mt. Stuart, Isle of Bute.

[25] This sketch is based on Sir Lewis Namier and John Brooke, eds., *The History of Parliament: The House of Commons, 1754-1790*, 3 vols. (Oxford, 1964), II, pp. 390- 394, and on G.F.S. Elliot, *The Border Elliots and the Family of Minto* (Edinburgh, 1897), pp. 333-376.

[26] [Elliot], notes [Mar. 4, 1763], Minto Papers, MS 11036, fols. 46-47. Elliot took notes on other parts of Ellis's speech and on remarks made by other speakers during the debate, but he did not record any other comments on the American army.

[27] For the official request for funds from Apr. 24 to Dec. 24, 1763, see Feb. 25, 1763, *Journals of the House of Commons*, XXIX, pp. 501-507. For examples of comparisons between the estimates for 1749 and the estimates for 1763, figured

for 12 months rather than 8, see two documents prepared at the War Office: "Estimate of the charge of his majesty's forces in Great Britain . . . for 1749 and 1763" [mid-Feb.1763], and "Forces voted for the plantations, Minorca, and Gibraltar in 1749 and 1763" [mid-Feb.1763], Chatham Papers, P.R.O. 30/8/76, fols. 72, 219. That Ellis did not use these comparisons when he prepared his speech to the House is suggested by Newdigate's notes of Mar. 4 showing that he mistakenly stated the number of troops in 1749 as 29,214, or 815 more than the correct 28,399. Newdigate, notes, Mar. 4, 1763, Newdigate MSS, B. 2543/11, Warwickshire County Record Office, Warwick, England.

[28] [Jenkinson], notes [Mar. 4, 1763], MSS North, B.5, fol. 94, Bodleian Library, Oxford. Jenkinson did not take any notes on the comparison.

[29] For a complete record of the entire comparison see Newdigate, notes, Mar. 4, 1763, Newdigate MSS, B. 2543/11. Since the figures in Elliot's account correspond closely with Newdigate's, historians can tell what the numbers Elliot jotted down refer to, and can be certain that the two sets of notes are basically accurate. (The figures in both sets also correspond closely to the two War Office estimates, when the numbers and expense of the 815 men Ellis inadvertently included in his calculations for 1749 are added to those estimates.) Because Thomas deleted all references to the comparison of 1749 and 1763 when he published excerpts from Newdigate's notes, readers of them cannot possibly know that the "saving" of £105,133 in Sir Roger's notes referred to the difference between the projected cost of the military establishment in 1764 and the cost of the establishment in 1749. Thus they would have missed an important point Ellis was trying to make, that in 1764 Britain's army would be not only larger than in 1749 but less expensive. The value to scholars of the passage Thomas reproduced is further diminished by his failure to notice and call attention to an error in Newdigate's notes. Sir Roger wrote down that the estimated cost of the army in America for 12 months was £114,340. In fact, the estimate was £214,340. See "Forces voted for the plantations, Minorca, and Gibraltar in 1749 and 1763," Chatham Papers, P.R.O. 30/8/76, fol. 219.

[30] "New Light," *William and Mary Quarterly*, 3d Ser., XXXVIII (1981), p.112.

[31] The quotations are from the king to Bute [Mar. 4, 1763], Bute Papers, Correspondence with George III, no. 222, and Thomas, "New Light," *William and Mary Quarterly*, 3d Ser., XXXVIII (1981), p. 112.

Chapter XIII

Security and Economy: The Bute Administration's Plans for the
American Army and Revenue, 1762-1763*

On March 4, 1763, Welbore Ellis, secretary at war in the Bute administration, informed the House of Commons about the ministry's proposal to station twenty battalions of regulars in America. After describing the establishment of that force, he announced that he was "authorized to say it is the intention of government that another year, this country shall not be loaded with this corps[,] but that the country who have immediate benefit shall pay them." Then, after justifying the presence of so large an army in the colonies, Ellis again explicitly promised "next year America to pay itself" for the troops there.[1]

The significance of this commitment is obvious: the attempt to support the army by taxing colonists brought on an imperial crisis that ended in the American Revolution. What inspired that commitment has seemed equally obvious to historians. Undeterred by the scarcity of documents directly relating to the ministry's decision, scholars have confidently inferred that the administration was moved by a combination of strategic, fiscal, and political considerations that virtually dictated its response. The consensus of opinion may be briefly summarized. A variety of circumstances compelled Bute and his colleagues to believe that the future security of Britain's American possessions depended on stationing a large force there. The administration also knew that the costs would be high and that the time was not propitious for Britain to shoulder new financial burdens. The nation's fiscal strength had been sapped by a long war and would be strained further in the years ahead by the necessity of servicing a huge debt. The state of Britain's finances therefore determined the ministers to require colonists to pay for the troops defending them. Their awareness that Parliament would be much more willing to agree to increasing the British force in America if Britons did not bear its cost contributed to their decision as well.[2]

The plausibility of this version of the ministry's motives has hitherto masked some shortcomings in it. These are the results of an omission in research. Because historians have largely neglected Bute's archives,[3] they have left out of their accounts the issue that George III and his ministers resolved first: a decision on basic principles to guide their planning. The king and his advisers knew, as one of the participants in their discussions later noted, that planning for the postwar military compelled them to consider "the two great ends of security and economy." They also were aware that those "great ends . . . may seem at first view to combat each other," and they accepted that "it is our duty to reconcile them."[4] Knowing what principles of policy they devised to harmonize the demands of security and economy is crucial to an understanding of how and why they decided as they did about the size, establishment, cost, and methods of supporting the peacetime army. This knowledge enables us to portray the process of decision making more accurately. In addition, it helps expose significant differences between approaches to the problems of peace by politicians experienced in the responsibilities of executive office. The administration's solutions were not the same as those of William Pitt, who had had a triumphant tenure as secretary of state during the war. The duke of Newcastle, who as first lord of the Treasury had successfully financed an unprecedentedly expensive military effort, disagreed with both Pitt and the ministers. We can thus see more clearly not only that the conventional scholarly narrative of motives and events is incomplete, but also that present conclusions about constraints on policy-making have failed to notice and take into account the existence of alternatives to the ministry's plans.

According to Bute, the administration had two essential goals. As he observed to Sir John Phillips, "in forming [the peace establishment], I had two things principally in view: security and economy." Neither consideration took priority with him: "They ought certainly to go together."[5] The earl did not go on to describe the means the ministers adopted to balance those ends, but their strategy is apparent from the process of planning itself.

The first in the government to plan seriously for the army in peace were George III and Bute. By mid-September 1762, well before peace was certain, the king had already spent "some days drawing up a state of the troops" to be stationed in Britain after the war. His plan seems not to have survived. Still, his description of its salient features in a letter to Bute reveals how the twin goals of security and economy shaped it, and how he defined those goals and worked to achieve them.[6]

When George began thinking about the postwar army, "it seemed most natural" to him to start with a knowledge of the numbers and cost of the military in 1749, the first year of peace after the War of the Austrian Succession.[7] That point of reference framed the important questions for him and for Bute and his other advisers as well. Would Britain and her enlarged empire be safe if the size of the army in 1763 was the same as in 1749? To the king, the answer was obviously no. Accordingly, his plan kept on active duty in Britain "the ten regiments [of foot] raised at the beginning of the war." George did not indicate how much this would increase the numerical strength of that force; to him, it was sufficient to tell Bute that there would now be twenty-four, rather than fourteen, infantry regiments stationed at home. But could the nation afford to pay more for its defense in 1763 than it had at the beginning of the last peace? Again, the answer seemed obvious: it could not. Thus the king was determined to find a way to ensure that the expense of this larger army would not exceed, and if possible would be less than, the cost of the much smaller force in Britain in 1749. He succeeded, happily reporting to Bute that "the expence (sic) will be some hundred pounds cheaper than the establishment . . . in 1749." How His Majesty accomplished this is clear: he sharply reduced the number of enlisted men in each regiment. All of the regiments would, however, retain close to their usual complement of officers, which meant that the army would have more officers on active duty than in earlier peacetime establishments in Britain.[8]

This part of the plan deserves elaboration. Some parliamentary critics later accused Bute of devising it solely in order to increase the patronage at the crown's disposal, a charge that the king hotly denied, and rightly so. To George III and Bute, an army with this establishment epitomized how considerations of security and economy could go together. Not only would it cost less than the army of 1749 but it would offer significant advantages when the next war began. As George put it, "the reason for keeping so many nominal corps is that an army may be formed on any new war."[9] Rather than trying to activate regiments, staff them with officers from the half-pay list, and raise soldiers for them during a national emergency, the government could simply recruit more enlisted men. Since the administrative structure would already be in place and the necessary officers present on duty, the army could expand to a wartime footing more rapidly and efficiently than ever before. Ellis publicly called attention to the merits of this plan by telling the Commons that "you could not increase your army when war came suddenly so conveniently by new corps—more speedy, more effectual this way. Without exceeding the expense of 1749, you will have an army more ready, [and] more convenient."[10] Privately, the king predicted to Bute, "If we don't take the precaution, I will venture to affirm whenever a new war breaks out we shall run great risk of losing the great advantages we are at this hour to be blessed with by this great, noble, and perfect definitive treaty [of peace]."[11]

In sum, George III, Bute, and the ministry believed that Britain's security required maintaining more, and more rapidly expandable, regiments at home than ever before in peacetime. They were also convinced that this security could not be purchased at the cost of disregarding the imperatives of economy. To be economical, to avoid straining the nation's finances further, that army would cost no more than the smaller, less easily expanded army of 1749.

353

It is obvious that the king and his ministers had the same goals and followed the same procedures to attain them when they planned for the army in Ireland and America. The government proposed increasing the number of troops in Ireland from 12,000 to 18,000, with the extra men and officers organized into 15 battalions of infantry. Units stationed there, as in Britain, would have unusually large numbers of officers for peacetime and correspondingly reduced numbers of enlisted men. The rationale was identical as well: the battalions could be expanded rapidly and efficiently if war came and would be of crucial importance in defending Britain and her possessions. Finally, the cost of the additions to the Irish army would not be passed on to Britons, because the ministers intended the Irish Parliament to bear that expense.[12]

As for America, the king originally planned to station 21 battalions there, far more than had ever been garrisoned in the New World. They would be, Ellis noted, a "small corps with a great many officers." That establishment was dictated not merely by exigencies peculiar to the colonies—the need to occupy, police, and defend vast new possessions required a great number of posts, and "no post can be without a commissioned officer, nor with one only"—but also by the consideration that dominated planning for the forces in Britain and Ireland: "you will have a bottom of an army easily to be augmented." Ellis pointed out that in 1749 "you had only four battalions in America. Now you will have the foundations of a great army there." This potentially great army would not cost more than the four battalions of 1749 because the government's intention was for America to pay the bill.[13]

It is also clear that in planning for forces outside Britain, George III, Bute, and the cabinet were resolved that security and economy would go together in those places as well, without one taking precedence over the other. The ministers decided to increase the army in Ireland because they believed that Dublin would be amenable to paying for the extra battalions. But when the king and Bute learned that opposition, not acquiescence, was the more likely Irish reaction, they immediately began preparing for that contingency by drafting a plan that did not include the additional 6,000 regulars.[14] Apparently from the beginning of planning for North America, the government intended that colonists would support the troops defending them. George noted in mid-March 1763 that the subject of a parliamentary tax on Americans to defray the cost of that army "was new to none" of his ministers, "having been thought of this whole winter."[15] Indeed, in early February, when the king drew up a comparison of the strength and cost of the troops in 1749 and 1763, he did not even include the battalions slated for America, "as [it is] proposed that being no expense to Great Britain."[16] Although lack of information and shortness of time prevented the Treasury from proposing a colonial tax for the army in 1763, Bute and his colleagues regarded this as merely a temporary setback. They were determined that in 1764 Americans would pay the full cost.[17]

There was a compelling reason for their determination, one that must be emphasized. To preserve harmony between the demands of security and economy, the total cost of the army could not exceed that of 1749. Making colonists pay was the only way Bute and his colleagues could find to accomplish this. Ellis's calculations revealed that if Americans did not pay the £214,340 estimated as needed to maintain the soldiers there, the total cost of the army would be nearly £110,000 more than in 1749, but if the government charged the American part of the bill to Americans, the cost would be about £105,000 less.[18] The success of the ministers' efforts to have a larger, more efficient army at a lower cost than in 1749 thus depended upon collecting the requisite revenue in the colonies.

When one looks from the perspective of the ministry, the origin of the decision to raise enough money in America to pay for the troops there becomes apparent. It was the result of giving equal emphasis to the ends of security and economy. Once the course was charted, the decision to raise an American revenue by parliamentary taxation followed without any debate in Whitehall. No one questioned the constitutional propriety of such a tax: as the king, Bute, and their advisers were well aware, Parliament had taxed colonists several times in the past. Nor did any of them anticipate serious political opposition, for there was no reason to do so. Collections in the colonies had been small, but Americans had at least occasionally paid the taxes.[19] Moreover, no one doubted that a substantial sum could be raised in the colonies; all believed that the Treasury, after appropriate investigation, would soon find ways to increase revenue from existing colonial duties to the point where they would cover the cost of the American army. So confident were the ministers that they expected such duties to generate over £200,000 in 1764.[20] Thus they foresaw no serious obstacles to the successful reconciliation of security and economy in the immediate future.

The fact that the king, Bute, and the ministry wished to link security and economy does not distinguish them from other monarchs and ministers before and since. It would be an optimal situation indeed for any nation at any time to be assured of being more militarily secure at a lower cost. What sets George and his ministers apart from others is their conviction that they could succeed in giving equal emphasis to "the two great ends" of policy. Their confidence was not shared by the leading politicians in opposition who had exercised executive power during the war, Pitt and Newcastle. These men insisted that considerations either of security or of economy must take precedence in planning for the peacetime army.

In Pitt's opinion, the ministers should have emphasized security over economy. Their decision to keep an unprecedentedly large force on active duty was, he thought, correct in principle. "In so early a peace," he told the House of Commons, "the nation ought to show itself on a respectable footing," particularly so in the case of a peace he stigmatized as "inadequate, precarious, and hollow" and predicted "would soon be broke." Also based on right principles was "the mode both here and in America of keeping large establishments with small corps; that had ever been the judgment of every soldier he had talked to."[21] "The best model of armies in time of peace," according to Pitt, was a "low establishment of men and high establishment of officers"[22] in order to permit rapid expansion at the beginning of war—a vital consideration since "whenever France broke with you, she would do it without giving notice."[23] Thus Pitt supported the government's plan in the Commons. He did so, though, only because it was the best option available. To his mind, the ministers committed a potentially fatal error: they did not go far enough in providing for the nation's security. Had he been in power, he would have pressed for larger armies in Britain, Gibraltar, Minorca, and especially North America, where "10,000 men [were] hardly enough to speak to one another if a communication is needed." He would have stationed 15,000 or 16,000 troops in Canada.[24]

Driving his point, and openly contemptuous of the Bute administration's emphasis on economy, Pitt seized the opportunity provided by its proposal to save £27,000 by putting 300 officers on half-pay to proclaim that "he was for economy, but in great matters, not a starving, penurious economy in little offices that amounted to nothing material and only rendered the promoters ridiculous" by costing Britain the skills of "the bravest men the world ever saw" for a paltry sum.[25] Beneath his characteristic hyperbole and equally characteristic disregard for the fact that great economies often depend on many small ones, one may discern Pitt's basic concept of the proper relationship between security and economy. Security should always have by far the preeminent role; economy, a distinctly secondary one. That his scheme would raise the cost of the army above the 1749 level did not concern Pitt in the slightest. To him, considerations of economy should never compromise, even in minor ways, the prowess of Britain's military, and hence her national security as well. It is not surprising that he did not deign to comment on the administration's intention to raise an American revenue. To Pitt, the central, overriding point was this: the safety of Britain required the maintenance of a large peacetime army, one even larger than Ellis proposed. In his eyes, the ministers' focus on how much the troops would cost and who would pay for them had caused them to lose sight of this point. Promising a colonial revenue did not make up for their failure.

The priorities of the duke of Newcastle and his allies were precisely the reverse of Pitt's. To them, the most pressing problem was the low estate of Britain's finances. They were, as H. B. Legge explained to the Commons during the debate on the army, "very much for economy, by which alone this country can be saved."[26] Newcastle's immediate reaction to the first rumors of the administration's plan was that the army would be far too large.[27] As the earl of Kinnoull, one of his intimate advisers, noted, "in the first place the general plan of economy should be observed," and on this basis the ministerial scheme should be opposed. Any increase in defense costs for 1763 over the years before the recent war, believed Kinnoull, should go to the navy, not the army.[28] Nor was expense the only part of these proposals that disturbed Newcastle and his followers. To them, the planned establishment was no effort to improve the security of Britain and her possessions at the beginning of any future war. They denied that it would have this effect; they believed the administration had concocted the scheme for entirely different purposes. "Plainly an attempt at such an extension of [executive] influence as is very dangerous" was Legge's blunt verdict on it, and he expressed the firm conviction of others in Newcastle's faction.[29] Probably no argument would have changed their minds on this point; certainly news that the administration intended to require colonists to pay for the establishment in America did not. That information also did not alter their opposition to the size of the army as a whole.

The plans for an American revenue failed as well to convince the duke and his friends that the ministers had given economy its proper primacy. Unfortunately, the specific reasons for their pessimism remain unknown. They had decided that if Pitt was not present at the debate on the plan in the Commons, Legge would "proceed, as he intended, to expose at least the American part." Because Pitt not only appeared but supported the government's proposals as far as they went, Legge did not go into the particulars of his objections to the plan for North America. He did, however, outline the basic Newcastle position on the proper uses of the time before the next war. Like Pitt, Legge expected new conflict to come quite soon. Unlike the Great Commoner, he stressed that "we shall have this dance to go over again with [a debt of] 140 millions upon our backs."[31] The way to prepare was not by enlarging the military. Rather, the government should follow France's example and reduce the army below its strength of 1749. This reduction in expenses should be accompanied by an effort to improve the collection of revenue in Britain; this could be accomplished, Legge asserted, "by lowering some of our taxes, which would both increase our trade and augment the revenue."[32] To the Newcastle faction, postwar policy should be guided by the principle that during peace considerations of fiscal economy should outweigh those of military security. Drastic retrenchment and significant reform of the nation's finances were much better preparation for wars to come than the largest peacetime army in British history. Pledging to raise an American revenue was no substitute for a genuine commitment to economy.

In sum, neither Pitt nor Newcastle believed that the government should give equal priority in 1763 to the demands of security and economy when it planned for the peacetime army. Among the men who directed and financed armies during the war, only Bute and his colleagues would make that commitment. Furthermore, neither Pitt nor the duke and his friends believed that the ministry could succeed in uniting security and economy by pledging to raise military revenues in America in 1764. They did not regard a colonial revenue as the means of easing the hard choices between the competitive considerations of military safety and fiscal soundness. That belief, too, belonged exclusively to the Bute administration.

In their accounts of the decisions of 1763, historians have generally stressed what they have seen as the absolute constraints of "the logic of the situation" that year.[33] They have argued that the need to defend new and old colonies, the condition of the nation's finances, and the prejudice in the House of Commons for reducing expenses left the Bute ministry without significant alternatives: the government had to act as it did. In making this argument, they have also implied that any administration would have been compelled by these circumstances to adopt Bute's policies.

To be sure, extensive conquests and a huge debt complicated policy making after the war. Politicians had to take these unprecedented difficulties into account as they considered the perennial problem of peace—striking the proper balance between security and economy. But there was no "logic of the situation" that imposed one inescapable solution on men at Whitehall and Westminster. The king and Bute, Pitt, and Newcastle had significantly different concepts of the right relationship between "the great ends of security and economy." They differed on the number of troops to be stationed in North America and elsewhere. They disagreed on how much of the nation's resources should be devoted to the army. Newcastle was genuinely appalled by the proposed establishment of regiments, while Pitt and the ministers saw it as essential to national security. Neither the duke nor Pitt believed the effort to collect a substantial American revenue would accomplish great things by reconciling the requirements of security and economy. The ministers believed it could; indeed, they were sure that this was the only way to effect such a reconciliation. Accordingly, they committed the power and prestige of the British government to raising that revenue in 1764, a commitment that compelled their successors to experiment with colonial stamp and trade duties, with fateful results. The argument that military, fiscal, and political circumstances at the end of the war limited politicians to only one response overlooks the historical reality of a variety of responses in 1763. It also obscures the crucial role that George III and the Bute administration played in bringing on the imperial crisis. Finally, it absolves them too much from the responsibility they should bear for the consequences of their decision to make security and economy go together, and the means they chose for doing it.

* This chapter first appeared in 1988 in the *William and Mary Quarterly* 45 pp. 499-509.

Endnotes

[1] R. C. Simmons and P.D.G. Thomas, eds., *Proceedings and Debates of the British Parliaments Respecting North America, 1754-1783* (London, 1982-), I, p. 440.

[2] See John Shy, *Toward Lexington: The Role of the British Army in the Coming of the American Revolution* (Princeton, NJ, 1965), 45-83; P.D.G. Thomas, *British Politics and the Stamp Act Crisis: The First Phase of the American Revolution, 1763-1767* (Oxford, 1975), pp. 34-39; Ian R. Christie and Benjamin W. Labaree, *Empire or Independence, 1760-1776: A British-American Dialogue on the Coming of the American Revolution* (New York, 1976), pp.30-31; John L. Bullion, *A Great and Necessary Measure: George Grenville and the Genesis of the Stamp Act, 1763-1765* (Columbia, MO, 1982), pp. 11-26, 34-36; and Robert W. Tucker and David C. Hendrickson, *The Fall of the First British Empire: Origins of the War of American Independence* (Baltimore, 1982), pp. 75-105. These accounts differ in emphasis, but the list of considerations is the same.

[3] Of the works listed in n. 2, only my book on Grenville and the stamp tax draws on unpublished Bute manuscripts, and my foray into the earl's papers was limited to the Bute letterbooks in the British Library and to the correspondence during 1762 to Bute from Nathaniel Ware, comptroller of the customs at Boston, in the Bute Papers at Mount Stuart, Isle of Bute, Scotland, and in the earl's Treasury papers in MSS North at the Bodleian Library, Oxford. See chapter XII to see how failing to consult Bute's papers has contributed to scholarly misunderstanding of his administration's reasons for stationing 20 battalions in the colonies. That neglect has had a similar consequence in the case of its decision to raise a substantial American revenue.

[4] Charles Jenkinson, draft speech endorsed "naval argument" [Jan.-Feb. 1767], Liverpool Papers, Add. MSS 38336, fol. 361, British Library. Jenkinson had been Bute's private secretary during 1762-1763.

[5] Bute to Phillips, Feb. 23, 1763, Bute Letterbook, Add. MSS 36797, fol. 4, British Library.

[6] The king to Bute [Sept. 13, 1762], in Romney Sedgwick, ed., *Letters from George III to Lord Bute, 1756-1766* (London, 1939), p. 135.

[7] For a description of the decision to begin planning by referring to information about 1749, see a War Office paper, "A representation designed to show what were the forces kept up in the year 1749, and upon what establishment: the reduction necessary to be made in the present forces to bring them to the same numbers and establishment, and what will then be the charge of the half pay at the conclusion of the war" [Oct. 1762], Charles Townshend Papers, 299/3/16, William L. Clements Library, Ann Arbor, MI.

[8] The king to Bute [Sept. 13, 1762], in Sedgwick, ed., *Letters from George III to Bute*, p. 135.

[9] The king to Bute [Feb. 17, 1763], Bute Papers, Correspondence with George III, no. 274.

[10] Ellis's speech, Mar. 4, 1763, in Sir Roger Newdigate's notes, Newdegate MSS, B. 2543/11 Warwickshire County Record Office, Warwick, England.

[11] The king to Bute [Feb. 17, 1763], Bute Papers, Correspondence with George III, no. 274. George was referring not only to the force planned for Britain but to the ones intended for Ireland and America as well.

[12] For an account of the plan for Ireland and the controversy it generated see Shy, *Toward Lexington*, pp. 73-78. Shy does not discuss either the proposed establishment of the regiments in Ireland or their military purpose; for that, see the king to Bute [Feb. 17, 1763], Bute Papers, Correspondence with George III, no. 274.

[13] For the original intent to put 21 battalions in the colonies see chapter XII; for the quotations from Ellis's speech on Mar. 4, 1763, see Simmons and Thomas, eds., *Proceedings and Debates*, I, p. 440.

[14] See Shy, *Toward Lexington*, pp. 73-76; and the king to Bute [Feb. 5, 1763], Bute Papers, Correspondence with George III, no. 195.

[15] The king to Bute [Mar. 19, 1763], in Sedgwick, ed., *Letters from George III to Bute*, pp. 201-202. See also Jenkinson to Bute, Mar. 18, 1763, in Simmons and Thomas, eds., *Proceedings and Debates*, II, pp. 562-563.

[16] The king to Bute [early Feb. 1763], Bute Papers, Correspondence with George III, no. 414.

[17] The king to Bute [Mar. 19, 1763], in Sedgwick, ed., *Letters from George III to Bute*, p.202.

[18] See Ellis's speech, Mar. 4, 1763, in Newdigate, notes, Newdegate MSS B. 2543/11, and the discussion of this and other calculations in chapter XII.

[19] For the king's and the ministers' knowledge about American taxes see: the king to the duke of Newcastle, Mar. 15, 1762, Newcastle Papers, Add. MSS 33040, fol. 309, Brit. Library; Samuel Martin to Bute, Mar. 18, 1762, Bute Papers, 4/66/1-2; the earl of Barrington to Newcastle, Mar. 19, 1762, Newcastle Papers, Add. MSS 32935, fol. 481; and "Cash in the exchequer at his majesty's disposal," May 14, 1762, *ibid.*, Add. MSS 33040, fol. 353.

[20] See the king to Bute, [Mar. 19, 1763], in Sedgwick, ed., *Letters from George III to Bute*, p. 202. For evidence that the Treasury had already discussed lowering the duty on foreign molasses imported into the colonies see Jenkinson to Bute, Mar. 18, 1763, in Simmons and Thomas, eds., *Proceedings and Debates*, II, p. 563; and, in the papers of Sir Francis Dashwood, the chancellor of the exchequer,

"Heads of the *revenue*" [Feb. 1763], Dashwood Papers, B. 7/2/5, Bodleian Library. A rationale for lowering that duty can be found in Jenkinson's files: "A state of the present branches of the customs in America, with hints for their improvement" ([Feb. 1763], Liverpool Papers, Add. MSS 38334, fols. 223-224). There are also signs that the Treasury was contemplating changing the duties on British West Indian sugars. See the letters from Claudius Amyand, a commissioner of the customs and the brother of the influential banker George Amyand, to Dashwood, Feb. 25, 26, 1763, Dashwood Papers, B. 1/1/28, 29.

[21] Pitt's speech, Mar. 4, 1763, in James West's notes, Newcastle Papers, Add. MSS 32947, fol. 285.

[22] Pitt's speech, Mar. 4, 1763, in Newdigate's notes, Newdegate MSS, B. 2543/11.

[23] Pitt's speech, Mar. 4, 1763, in West's notes, Newcastle Papers, Add. MSS 32947, fol. 285.

[24] Pitt's speech, Mar. 4, 1763, in Simmons and Thomas, eds., *Proceedings and Debates*, I, pp. 440-441.

[25] Pitt's speech, Mar. 4, 1763, in West's notes, Newcastle Papers, Add. MSS 32947, fol. 286. It must be recalled that £27,000 would not be "a paltry sum" to men who were straining to keep expenses for 1763 below the level of 1749, and who, because of the postponement of changes in colonial duties, failed to reach their goal by some £70,000. For the ministry's calculation of the comparison of the cost of the army in 1749 and 1763 see chapter XII.

[26] H. B. Legge's speech, Mar. 4, 1763, in [Jenkinson] notes [Mar. 4, 1763], MSS North, B. 5, fol. 96. Deeply interested in issues of public finance, Legge had served as Chancellor of the Exchequer from July 1757 to Mar. 1761. He was the obvious choice as principal spokesman in the House of Commons for Newcastle on fiscal affairs.

[27] Newcastle to the duke of Devonshire, Dec. 23, 1762, Newcastle Papers, Add. MSS 32945, fol. 335.

[28] Kinnoull to Newcastle, Dec. 26, 1762, *ibid.*, fol. 384. Kinnoull had read the duke's Dec. 23 letter to Devonshire and was responding to it.

[29] Legge to Newcastle, [Feb. 27, 1763], *ibid.*, Add. MSS 32947, fol. 98; see also Newcastle to the earl of Hardwicke, Mar. 3, 1763, *ibid.*, fols. 163-164.

[30] Newcastle to Hardwicke, Mar. 3, 1763, *ibid.*; see also Legge to Newcastle, Mar. 4, 1763, *ibid.*, fol. 172. Newcastle, Legge, the marquis of Rockingham, and Sir John Cavendish had decided that if Pitt appeared and spoke, as they expected, in favor of the ministers' plan, they would not risk alienating him by dividing the Commons in opposition to it. Hardwicke, who disagreed with "the principle that [Pitt's] opinion ought always to be submitted to," later recalled that Pitt had differed "with almost all of us about the plan for the troops in America . . . and

overruled [our] point by his own single opinion, to the dissatisfaction of numbers." Hardwicke to Newcastle, Mar. 3, Apr. 1, 1763, *ibid.*, Add. MSS 32947, fol. 1i68, and Add. MSS 32948, fols. 1-2.

[31] Legge's speech, Dec. 10, 1762, in Simmons and Thomas, eds., *Proceedings and Debates*, I, 426.

[32] Legge's speech, Mar. 4, 1763, in Jenkinson to Bute [Mar. 4, 1763], MSS North, B. 6, fol. 96.

[33] The quotation is from Christie and Labaree, *Empire or Independence*, p. 26. Similar arguments may be found in Shy, *Toward Lexington*, pp. 45-46; Thomas, *British Politics and the Stamp Act Crisis*, pp. 37-38; and Tucker and Hendrickson, *Fall of the First British Empire*, pp. 87-97, 105.

PART FIVE: CONSEQUENCES

Chapter XIV

"Truly Loyal Subjects": British Politicians and the Failure to Foresee American Resistance to Parliamentary Taxation, 1762-1765*

During 1762-1763, the earl of Bute's administration committed the government of Great Britain to taxing Americans to defray the expenses of the British army defending them. No one in a position of power or influence even considered the possibility of open, violent popular opposition to parliamentary taxation in the colonies. During 1763-1764, the Grenville Administration explored ways of taxing colonists. Ultimately George Grenville settled on lowering the duty on foreign molasses imported into North America and on imposing an unprecedented internal tax, the Stamp Act. No one speculated that this could conceivably bring on a serious confrontation. American taxation was discussed in Parliament on a number of occasions during 1763-1765. Only one M.P. voiced any concern at all that this policy might disrupt the profitable connection between Britain and America, and he did not specify what form a disruption might take. The followers of the Marquis of Rockingham, who were the most numerous opponents of the stamp tax in the House of Commons, did not merely fail to anticipate the reaction to it while in opposition during early 1765. Their blindness to the gathering storm continued even after they received ample information from America from August through October 1765 of a widespread, determined resistance to the Stamp Act. They were as surprised as Grenville that colonists did not relent and begin obeying it when it went into effect officially on November 1, 1765.[1] What caused this virtually universal failure to foresee any possibility of an imperial crisis over parliamentary taxation?

This question has not attracted much attention from historians of the period. That this is so is surprising. The origin and development of the changes in imperial policy during the early 1760s have been described and analyzed thoroughly and carefully by many skilled scholars. Indeed, Ian R. Christie, one of the most eminent of these, has wryly remarked that his colleagues seem to pursue their studies "into an unending spiral of more and more exact yet conflicting detail."[2] Yet examinations of why politicians could not anticipate trouble ahead have been swept into the vortex of scholarship, even though their inability to do so was crucial to the course of events. If Bute or Grenville had had sufficient reason to suspect that Americans would respond to parliamentary taxation as they did, the experiment of raising money by internal taxes would not have been tried. In the case of the other major British dependency, both administrations were determined to avoid political confrontations over fiscal affairs. Bute and his colleagues initially planned to increase the size of the army in Ireland, in the expectation that the Irish would foot the bill for it. When they discovered in early 1763 that there would be serious opposition in the Irish Parliament to paying for the additional troops, they reconsidered their plan, and then dropped it. Grenville went to considerable pains in October and November 1763 to defuse anger in Dublin over the cost of pensions charged to Ireland's establishment by reassuring Irish politicians that the king intended to stop that practice except in unusual and important instances. The two ministries would have been equally careful in dealing with the American colonies, had they been convinced of the need for caution. During the 1750s, Bute believed, and taught his young protégé, the future George III, "that the prosperity of this Nation as well as that of her Colonies, depends very much on the harmony, [and] mutual confidence [between them], and [on the] extension of their commerce with each other." As Grenville recalled in the House of Commons on March 5, 1770, if he had imagined the popular reaction to the Stamp Act, "I would not have proposed it, because I wish too well to the safety of Great Britain, to have made a proposition under such circumstances."[3] One can only add to this tale of what might have been that the history of the relationship between Britain and her American colonies would have been vastly different.

Grenville's explanation of why he failed to imagine the outcome of the stamp tax was straightforward. He denied that he was ignorant of American opinion. Indeed, he claimed he had made "all possible inquiry of the state of America." Then he observed that none of the colonial agents, who were familiar with American opinion and were "appointed by those who were best able to know," doubted that stamp duties would be collected there. Certainly they, and many important men in the colonies as well, asked for appointments for "their relations, their sons, their best friends" as stamp distributors: "Did they afterwards desire to tear them to pieces?" Thus Grenville excused his own failure to foresee the future by observing that others did too, and could not prepare themselves or warn him of the impending onslaught. What happened was the result of a change of opinion by "great bodies of people . . . in the space of a few months."[4] That development, he argued, could not have been predicted on the basis of information he had at the time.

Grenville's defense of his mistake has seemed so plausible to historians that they have accepted it without much examination as a sufficient explanation for his inability to predict the colonial reaction Why? Practically every other word he wrote or spoke has been subjected to intense scrutiny; why have these been virtually exempt from analysis? I suspect—and here I write from personal experience—that historians are reluctant to consider questions that touch on the failure of men to foresee the future. One may subscribe to the theories of the Annales School, with its emphasis on *la longue durée* and the irresistibility of underlying structural changes that govern human affairs. Conversely, one can practice a more traditional political narrative, with its stress on *l'histoire événementielle* and the role that "time and chance" play in the lives of all men. In each case, we accept as a given — to borrow again from the eloquence of *Ecclesiastes* — that "man . . . knoweth not his time: as the fishes that are taken in

368

an evil net, and as the birds that are caught in the snare; so are the sons of men snared in an evil time, when it falleth suddenly upon them." This being so, cannot anyone at any time in the past, be accused after the fact of a failure to foresee? Another pointed question comes to mind naturally: what is it we are not anticipating—as individuals and as a society—today? Wishing to be judged fairly by our successors, we are wary of applying unjust standards to others. Hindsight is, as we all know, 20/20. Armed with the knowledge of how things came out, it can be easy to condemn people for failing to think and act differently at a crucial point in their lives. Moreover, such facile judgments are not merely unfair. They give birth to historical interpretations that are superficial at best and quite wrongheaded at worst. Thus Grenville's apologia, that he could not know the future, strikes a powerful chord in those who study him in both his human and professional *personae*.

Far from denying the validity of these concerns, I share them. But they seem to me to be reasons to proceed cautiously and to try to understand without indulging in unmerited censure, rather than justifications for dismissing crucial questions after only perfunctory examination. As David M. Potter once reminded us, "history is incomplete without the dimension of human error and disaster following from error."[5] In the case of British politicians and the American question during the 1760s, it is impossible to understand the source of that error without studying why reactions in the colonies surprised them. Accepting Grenville's *ex post facto* explanation is not sufficient. Doing so overlooks the possibility that British politicians and the colonial agents failed to foresee the future for different reasons. Moreover, Grenville's remarks raise some interesting questions about the gathering and assessment of information and opinion from America by Whitehall. Were the two ministries interested in finding out what colonists thought of the principle of parliamentary taxation or of specific taxes? If so, what did they discover? What assumptions did they make about colonists? Finally, when information from the colonies was brought to their attention, how did they interpret it? After all, by late 1764 Grenville and others in power knew that two colonial assemblies had in the strongest language opposed internal taxation by Parliament in principle. Why did they fail to recognize the significance of these vehement protests? Examining their thoughts and acts before the passage of the Stamp Act fleshes out Grenville's post mortem. Answering these questions is essential to a full understanding of their inability to see what lay ahead.

I

To Bute and his colleagues, taxing Americans was the only practical way to reconcile "the two great ends of security and economy." They were convinced that the military security of the Mother Country and her colonies required maintaining the largest peacetime army in British history. They were equally certain that the fiscal strength of the nation depended upon holding the cost of that force to Britain below the expense of the army in 1749, the first year of peace after the War of the Austrian Succession. If colonists paid for the battalions stationed in America, both of these "great ends . . . [which] seem at first view to combat each other" could be achieved. Accordingly, the Bute Administration committed itself to raising the money from Americans by parliamentary taxation.[6] At first, Bute and the rest of the Cabinet were confident they could impose a tax in 1763. Lowering the duty on molasses seemed a promising course to take, and there are some indications they also considered revising the duties on British West Indian sugars. Ultimately they decided, however, that "the American tax . . . requires much information" about prices and the expenses of smuggling in the colonies "before a proper one can be stated."[7] So they contented themselves for the present with having Welbore Ellis, the Secretary at War, promise the House of Commons on March 4, 1763 that "next year America [would] pay itself" for the regulars stationed there.[8]

During these proceedings, the administration made no effort to determine colonial opinion on the general policy of parliamentary taxation to support the

American army and did not consult the agents. A number of British politicians had advance notice of Ellis's announcement to the House; the agents had none. This lack of concern about American opinion was further underlined by Ellis's remark on March 4, 1763. The Secretary at War, unlike Grenville in his later discussions of American taxation, did not try to explain the necessity and justice of this policy to the agents or a colonial audience.[9] Moreover, after the commitment was made, no one at the Treasury sought information from the agents about specific taxes. They first learned that lowering the molasses duty was being seriously considered when Charles Townshend unexpectedly introduced it in the House on March 17. Without that "insidious proposal," as George III termed it, they would have had no idea about these plans.[10]

Significantly, this unconcern about opinion on possible taxes was not typical of Bute and his colleagues. As we have seen, they tried to be certain about the Irish reaction to paying for an additional 6,000 troops to be stationed in Ireland, and tailored their plan for the postwar army there to fit what they discovered. When the Treasury considered in 1763 how to find new sources for revenue in Britain, Sir Francis Dashwood, the Chancellor of the Exchequer, privately solicited the thoughts of country gentlemen who would bear part of those burdens about the various taxes proposed to him. Then he scrupulously adopted their recommendations.[11] In the case of America, though, the ministers did not follow their usual procedures. Clearly they were certain that they could devise taxes that had the potential for raising substantial amounts of revenue in the colonies. Clearly, too, they were positive Americans would pay those taxes. What caused them to be so sure when anyone who looked, as Bute and the king had, at the tiny sums collected in America on trade in foreign molasses was well aware that colonists had not paid this duty?[12]

The roots of their optimism had nothing to do with a close examination of American conditions or opinions. Bute and his colleagues believed the molasses duty had been set so high that the profit to be gained from smuggling far outweighed both the risk of detection and the cost of legally entering the molasses. To them, the miniscule collections in America illustrated the truth of what some fiscal thinkers in Britain believed should be a general axiom of taxation: high duties on imports actually diminished the revenue because they encouraged smuggling. Lower duties, and collections would increase because merchants would have no compelling economic incentive to evade payment. Application of this principle to the North American trade in molasses would have that happy result; of this, the ministers were sure. The only question in their minds was how much to lower the duty. That did require specific information about America. The absence of such information decided them to defer action until the following year.[13]

What caused the ministers to focus on the principles and details of taxation? Why did they overlook important political questions, such as how would Americans react to a program of parliamentary taxation designed to raise significant sums each year for imperial defense? In large part, it was their interpretation of American motives for not paying the molasses duty, and their assumption that these motives were the same as those of domestic tax evaders. London did not see smuggling in the colonies as a sign of incipient or actual political disloyalty. Instead, it was the result of understandable economic considerations. Understandable and familiar. Subjects in Britain also tried to escape or reduce payment of taxes whenever legal loopholes or lax enforcement provided the chance. In the Mother Country, the successful collection of revenue depended upon finding taxes that, given the limited administrative and police capabilities of the eighteenth-century state, stood a reasonable chance of being enforceable. This awareness explained why Bute and the ministers so carefully scouted English opinion when they considered imposing new taxes in 1763. They assumed the same formula would work in America: find taxes that were reasonable enough to give little incentive for evasion; reform as much as possible a corrupt customs service; and then colonists would loyally, if perhaps reluctantly, pay them. Politics, they presumed, was essentially irrelevant to this process. Bute's successor shared these assumptions. In fact, his confidence in Americans' ultimate loyalty to Britain was so great that he had no qualms about introducing a new type of taxation.

II

After he succeeded Bute as First Lord of the Treasury; Grenville pressed ahead with plans to lower the molasses duty. Like his predecessor, he did not try to discover American opinions on the proper level for the tax, preferring instead to rely on the advice of self-designated "experts" on the colonies in London. When agents representing the New England colonies finally managed to see him, and claimed that colonists wanted the duty set at 1d. per gallon, he dismissed the wishes of Americans as a self-interested attempt to reduce it too far, and settled on 3d. instead. In the course of these deliberations he determined that this tax would not raise nearly enough money to cover the costs of the army. Additional taxes would be necessary.

At this point, Grenville made a fateful decision. He decided, as he informed the House on March 9, 1764, that "customs duties had a bound." Britain could only expect to collect so much from them. Due to the difficulty of finding good customs officers willing to go to America, it would be impossible to stop smuggling completely. To raise more money, Parliament would have to impose internal taxes directly on colonists. His choice was "a stamp duty in America; 'twas easily collected, without a large body of officers."[14] Grenville did not conclude this on the basis of any knowledge of American conditions or opinions. As Bute had done earlier that year, he gave no thought in 1763 to any possible reaction to internal taxation in principle or stamp duties in particular. But where Bute had relied on the universal applicability of an axiom of taxation, he drew upon experience with stamps in England. That tax had virtually enforced itself there, because men recognized that certain documents had to be on stamped paper to be legally binding, and their self-interest dictated payment of the tax. Grenville and his advisers took for granted that, as in England, "the people settled in the colonies must for their own security comply with the directions of the law."[15] American opinion about the justice or the wisdom of such a tax would not impede its successful execution.

However irrelevant to the collection of revenue he regarded colonial opinion as being, Grenville learned from the agents by early 1764 that it was strongly against internal taxation on constitutional grounds. This news coincided with increasing apprehension at the Treasury. Planners there feared they lacked sufficient information about documents and procedures unique to the colonies to draft a comprehensive and productive tax. Their concern led Grenville to decide to postpone the tax for one year. When he announced the decision on March 9 to the House, he took advantage of the opportunity to offer some reassurance to Americans. He wished, he told the House, "to follow to a certain degree the inclination of the people in North America, if they will agree to the end:' and he desired that "[the stamp duty] might be done with good will."[16]

These remarks were not special concessions to American opinion, any more than the postponement was. As Grenville later explained on February 15, 1765, the postponement was designed "to give time for information, not for opposition." The colonists could propose an alternate mode of parliamentary taxation, or they could make specific suggestions for a stamp tax. They could not, however, protest against Parliament's intention to raise money from them by taxation. The reason for this was obvious to Grenville. If Parliament permitted any group of subjects to object against proposed taxation that promised to fall on them, "petitions would be infinite, for *some* must be affected, propose what tax you please."[17] In sum, Americans were being offered the same limited options subjects in Britain had. After inviting the colonists to take advantage of their privilege as subjects, Grenville did not pursue the matter. He had to be prodded to countenance any departmental inquiry into American documents. When he did, he was careful not to ask the assemblies for information. By doing this, he avoided the risk of creating a precedent for officially consulting colonists before taxing them. This maneuver reveals how determined he was to preserve future ministries' freedom of action. It also shows that preserving that freedom seemed more important and useful to him than assessing opinions colonists might have on the principle or the specifics of imperial taxation. Finally, it starkly illuminates his estimate of the potential of colonial opposition for disrupting the collection of a stamp tax and creating an imperial crisis. Grenville clearly did not think these expressions of discontent were serious enough to warrant any effort either to mollify political leaders in America by contacting them, or to gather information about their intentions. To be sure, he would have been pleased had they responded by changing their opinions. That would mean that the stamp tax would be done with good will. But he did not care enough about that outcome to make any attempt to gain it. That, he believed, would not be necessary.

In fact, postponing the stamp tax intensified rather than moderated expressions of opposition from America. Toward the end of 1764, Grenville learned that the assemblies of New York and Massachusetts Bay had lent their official imprimaturs to the chorus of protest. These proceedings, according to the Privy Council, were "calculated to raise groundless suspicion and distrust in the minds of [His] Majesty's good subjects in the colonies, and have the strongest tendency to subvert those principles of constitutional relation and dependence upon which the colonies were originally established."[18]

Grenville presumably agreed with his fellow Privy Councilors that the remonstrances were shocking attempts to disturb loyal subjects in America. He did not, however, regard them as reasons to question, much less to change, his plans. To be sure, the Bute Administration had been compelled in 1763 to pay attention to expressions of opposition from members of the Irish parliament against the expense of a larger military establishment in Ireland. Since the late seventeenth century, the parliament in Dublin had chosen and levied the taxes necessary to support the troops the British government stationed in Ireland. This procedure had worked to Whitehall's satisfaction, and Bute and his colleagues never considered altering it. So the opinions of Irish politicians had to be reckoned with in London. Ultimately, Bute decided it would be politically imprudent to try to overcome that opposition, and he discarded his plan. In contrast, the American assemblies had not been—at least in the view of British politicians—helpful in the past. Moreover, Parliament had levied duties on colonists before. Grenville felt justified regarding protests from the assemblies of New York and Massachusetts Bay as merely statements from interested groups of subjects, who had no institutional claim or political power to reject imperial taxes and were resorting to a familiar ploy to evade supporting the army defending them. He knew that colonists had frequently raised constitutional points in the past; he also was aware the colonies "have in many instances encroached and claimed powers and privileges inconsistent with their situation."[19] To his mind, this was merely a political tactic, not a deep-seated ideological concern. In the case of the stamp tax, constitutional objections really amounted to a typical expression of loyal subjects' opposition to new taxes that promised to be effective. According to Jared Ingersoll, an agent for Connecticut, Grenville even told M.P.s not to "suffer themselves to be influenced by any resentments which might have been kindled from anything they might have heard out-of-doors, alluding I suppose to the New York and Boston Assemblys' (*sic*) speeches and votes—that this was a matter of revenue which was of all things the most interesting to the subject etc."[20] Americans did not like the prospect of a stamp tax; "no more does the west like the cyder (*sic*) tax; Scotland the beer tax; the middle of England, the land-tax."[21] Thus did Grenville demonstrate to his own and others' satisfaction that American protests were predictable, understandable, limited, rather than barely veiled threats to the peace of the empire.

The First Lord may even have attributed the intensity of the remonstrations to the particular nature of this tax itself. As one of his advisers observed, "a Stamp Duty has ever been born with Complaint."[22] It executed itself, and therefore gave British subjects on either side of the water no sporting chance at evasion of its charges. Certainly Grenville's knowledge that "the tax in great degree executes itself" encouraged him to dismiss any concern that American opposition might prevent or even hamper collection of those duties. Just as in Britain, no one there would trust unstamped documents. "Forgery is the only fright to be apprehended," Grenville believed, "[and] severe penalties may prevent it."[23] His equating of subjects in America with those in Britain naturally led him to predict the future payment of the tax in the colonies on the basis of past experience in the Mother Country. He could not, as he later confessed, even imagine that the reality of the colonial response would be extraordinary and revolutionary.

Given Grenville's perspective, it was inevitable that he should believe that the colonial remonstrances would have harmful consequences *only* if the government decided against going forward with the stamp tax. Their relentless seeking of every advantage they could gain would guarantee colonists would claim they had made their constitutional point. By yielding, "we shall declare that we ought not to tax the colonies. And we need not declare after a year's time that we ought not, for then we cannot."[24] In his mind, the alternatives were obvious: Britain could either establish a disastrous precedent, or she could collect a potentially lucrative revenue in America. With the choice framed this way, the decision was easy for him and the vast majority in Parliament.

The only moment of excitement during debates on the bill came on February 6, 1765 when Colonel Isaac Barré, who claimed with some justice "to know more of [North] America than most of you, having seen and been conversant in that country," objected to the stamp tax because "it creates disgust, I had almost said hatred" in the colonies. "The people [there] are as truly loyal as any subjects the King has," but they were "a people jealous of their liberties . . . who will vindicate them, if ever they should be violated." He stopped short of explicitly predicting a crisis, and abruptly concluded by saying "the subject is delicate and I will say no more." After he finished, "the whole House sat awhile as [if] amazed, intently looking and without answering a word."[25] This silence was merely a tribute to Barré's skill as an orator. It was not the result of a sudden collective vision of possible dangers ahead. Grenville had already heard comments from Ingersoll and other agents that "this tax will produce disturbance and discontent and prevent improvement among the colonies," and before Barré rose he had taken the precaution of drawing the sting from such arguments by trivializing them. Colonists, he asserted, simply did not want to pay more taxes. They would object to any type of tax at any time, and would seize upon any convenient reason for opposition. In this case, their reason was unjustifiable. Paying taxes when necessary was part of the price subjects paid for their liberties. "If [colonists] are not subject to this burden of tax, they are not entitled to the privilege of Englishmen." These commonsensical points, plus the certainty that a stamp tax "in a great degree executes itself," were far more persuasive to the House than Barré's warning.[26] The bill passed without a division. When he wrote home soon afterwards, Ingersoll sadly reported "there are scarce any people here, within doors or without, but what approve the measures now taking which regard America."[27]

III

Grenville recalled this virtual unanimity years later and cited "the repeated wish of almost all sorts and conditions of men" to impose taxes on the colonies as a justification for the Stamp Act. He also remembered that "His Majesty, ever desirous to divide the burdens amongst the people equally, wished to see them divided equally in this instance."[28] The record of the thoughts and actions of the king and his ministers during 1762-1765 reveal the significance of their understanding of Americans as essentially indistinguishable from the rest of "the people" insofar as taxation was concerned. Historians have generally understood this to mean British politicians considered colonists to be as bound as any other subjects to pay taxes imposed by Parliament. But the identification of Americans with Britons went beyond the concept of identical constitutional duties, as important as that was. Men in London believed the Americans' attitudes toward parliamentary taxes, their motives for opposition, and the significance of their opposition were indistinguishable from Britons' reactions to prospective increases in taxation. Like their fellow subjects, Americans would be opposed to bearing new burdens themselves and eager to shift them to others. Seeking their opinion on either the principle of parliamentary taxation or specific taxes would therefore yield no useful information. As was the case in Britain, their motives for opposing taxes were really economic rather than political. Neither group of subjects was much concerned about the political portents of new taxes; both fervently wished to avoid paying them. "I own I do not give entire credit to all the objections that are raised on your side of the water," an influential official at the Treasury told Ingersoll. "They are inclined to object to all taxes, and yet some are necessary."[29] Objections on constitutional grounds did not raise doubts in British politicians' minds about the future loyalty of the protesters. Such arguments were frequently raised in Britain itself, and as recently as 1763 over the extension of excise taxes on cider. The same type of argument had been used by Americans in the past on the slightest pretext. British politicians looked at protests emphasizing the constitutional dangers of certain taxes as familiar examples of a well-worn political tactic to gain self-interested ends. Thus their potential significance for American subjects' allegiance in the years ahead was hidden from them.[30] Because the ministers did not think that American loyalty could be seriously weakened by those taxes, they assumed that strategies of taxation that worked elsewhere would work in the colonies as well. Lowering molasses duties would certainly increase collections. The stamp tax would virtually execute itself in America for the same reason it did in England. Colonists would not give up all security for their legal and commercial activities, for their persons and their property, any more than Englishmen did. They might begrudge payment, but pay they would.

In retrospect, it is clear that these mistaken assumptions stemmed from a basic and unexamined premise that colonists were not essentially different from other British subjects. As a result, British politicians were sure that Americans were—to borrow Barré's words—as truly loyal as any of George III's people. But where the Colonel qualified this assessment, the politicians did not.

Unlike his contemporaries, Barré believed there were important differences in political outlook between Americans and other subjects. To him, the key to understanding them was knowledge of the history of the colonies. "[British] oppressions planted them in America; they fled from your tyranny to a then uncultivated and inhospitable country." Unaided by Britain, they created prosperity in that wilderness by "constant and laborious industry," and defended it against native and foreign foes. They still retained their determination to be free from oppression. "Remember I this day told you so," Barré warned the House, "that the same spirit of freedom which actuated that people at first, will accompany them still." Although he did not phrase his insight this way, he sensed that the allegiance of colonists to their Mother Country was conditional, and very dependent on their perception that she was not oppressing them again. He also fully appreciated how suspicious colonists could be of Britain's motives. For these reasons, Barré took their constitutional protests against the stamp tax at face value, and recognized that these had the potential of creating serious political difficulties. "Prudence" and "delicacy" made him decline to elaborate on the forms those difficulties might take. He had to satisfy himself by warning in general terms of trouble ahead, and asking his audience to "remember I this day told you so."[31]

Other politicians, however, lacked Barré's experience in America, and his connections there. Even more important, they did not share his admiration for colonists, and his sympathy for their attitudes about relations with the Mother Country. In the context of the 1760s, only a sympathetic observer of the American colonies could keep from seeing them from the perspective of the Bute and

Grenville ministries. Barré "expressed great tenderness for the Americans," noted James Harris, an adviser of Grenville.[32] Those who were harder-hearted viewed his premonition as a mark of his affection, not as a result of an informed, accurate perception of realities across the Atlantic. That his might be a prescient analysis of events to come totally escaped them. Men at Westminster and Whitehall had not yet developed the habit of coolly assessing the loyalty of British subjects and how that loyalty might be affected by new policies before they acted.

In time, of course, they learned this lesson. When William Wyndham Grenville, George's third son, drafted the Canada Act of 1791, his thoughts on the governance of colonies were clearly influenced by the different age he lived in. Men who governed now took the possibility of revolution very seriously indeed, and were keenly alert for signs of potential disloyalty in even the most seemingly placid subjects. William Grenville's primary goal was not to raise money, but to prevent, or at least delay indefinitely, political revolution. To attain that end, he tried to transplant distinctively British institutions and social classes into Canada. The intent of his bill was to encourage the development in Upper Canada of a landed aristocracy with a hereditary role in government, and the creation of a strong Anglican establishment with an independent voice in local and provincial affairs. A society and government ruled by squire and parson, peer and bishop: to his mind, this was crucial to the maintenance of loyalty and stability in Britain. Such a society and government had been significantly absent in the original 13 colonies, and that absence had prepared the way for revolution. Thus the government had to try to implant such institutions in Canada.[33]

William Grenville was not conscious of any irony in his role as colonial planner in 1791, and he certainly did not see his work as critique or correction of any failure of his father's. In many ways, this seems just. Creating an American aristocracy and strengthening the Anglican Church in the colonies had been proposed in the 1760s, but men in power did not consider either seriously and took no steps toward implementing them.[34] They could not see the necessity of "establish[ing] in the Provinces a Body of Men having that motive of attachment to the existing form of Government, which arises from the possession of personal or hereditary distinction," then relying on these men and the institutions they dominated to secure the loyalties of the common folk.[35] Nothing in their experience caused them to think to consider how Americans might differ from Britons and what effects this could have on their loyalty to the Mother Country; To Bute, Grenville, and their advisers, a dispute with the colonies over taxation was merely over the details of the tax or the fact of payment. Their assumption that colonists were essentially the same as other British subjects blinded them to the reality that in the different world of America internal taxation raised the most profound issues of political allegiance.

*This chapter first appeared in: *Connecticut Review* 11 (1989), pp. 28-42.

Endnotes

[1] In his notes for an undelivered speech, Edmund Burke hinted that the Rockingham Administration expected that Americans would obey the Act after it went into effect on Nov. 1, 1765. See Edmund Burke, "Speech on Stamp Act Disturbances," [Jan.-Feb. 1766], *The Writings and Speeches of Edmund Burke*, ed. Paul Langford, 2 vols., in progress (Oxford: Clarendon Press, 1981-), 2:43-5. Certainly Henry Seymour Conway, the Secretary of State, was "astonished" at the news of violent resistance to the tax in New York, and would have taken the bearer of those ill tidings "to the King that very day had I been fit to have been seen." Major Thomas James, letter to Cadwallader Colden [after Jan. 31, 1766], in New York-Historical Society, *Collections*, 56 (NY, 1923), *The Letters and Papers of Cadwallader Colden*, 7:98.

[2] I.R. Christie, Review of J.L. Bullion, *A Great and Necessary Measure: George Grenville and the Genesis of the Stamp Act, 1763-1765*, in: *The Historian*, 47 (1984-85), p. 226.

[3] R.C. Simmons and P.D.G. Thomas, eds., *Proceedings and Debates of the British Parliament Respecting North America, 1754-1763* (NY, 1982) III, p. 222.

[4] *Ibid.*, III, pp. 221-2.

[5] D.M. Potter, *History and American Society: Essays of David M. Potter*, 9 ed., by Don. E. Fehrenbacher (NY, 1973) p. 150.

[6] The quotation is from Charles Jenkinson, "Naval Argument," [Jan.-Feb. 1767], Liverpool Papers, Add. MSS 38336, f. 361, British Library, London. I have

discussed the significance of these concepts for the Bute Administration's plans for peace in chs. XI and XIII.

[7] R. Sedgwick, ed., *Letters from George III to Lord Bute 1756-1766* (London, 1939), pp. 202-203.

[8] Simmons and Thomas, *op. cit.*, I, p. 440.

[9] Compare Welbore Ellis's speech on Mar. 4, 1763, in: *Proceedings and Debates of the British Parliaments Respecting North America, 1754-1783*, ed. R.C. Simmons and P.D.G. Thomas, 6 vols., (Millwood, NY, Kraus International Publications, 1982), 1:440 with accounts of George Grenville's speeches on Mar. 9, 1764 and Feb. 9, 1765 in *ibid.*, 1:488-92 and 2:9-11, 14-6. A full account of Grenville's dealings with the agents may be found in John L. Bullion, *A Great and Necessary Measure: George Grenville and the Genesis of the Stamp Act, 1763-1765* (Columbia, Mo.:University of Missouri Press, 1982), pp.125-32, 168-77.

[10] George III to the earl of Bute, [Mar. 18, 1763], *Letters from George III to Lord Bute 1756-1766*, ed. Romney Sedgwick (London: Macmillan, 1939), p. 102. A letter of Jasper Mauduit, the agent for Massachusetts Bay, to Thomas Cushing, the Speaker of the House of Representatives there, on Dec. 10, 1763 reveals that the agents had no advance warning about the plans to tax Americans and to lower the molasses duty. Massachusetts Historical Society, *Collections*, 1st. Ser., 6 (Boston, 1800) "Mauduit Letters," pp. 193-4.

[11] For Sir Francis Dashwood's consultations on a proposed excise on cider, see Betty Kemp, *Sir Francis Dashwood: An Eighteenth-Century Independent* (London: Macmillan, 1967, pp. 82-8. For his consultations on a scheme to extend stamp duties in England, see Henry Reade, letter to Dashwood, December 10, 1762; "Proposal for stamp duties," [Jan. 1763]; and J. Howe to Dashwood, February 19, 1763; in Dashwood Papers, MSS. Dashwood, B. 1/1/19, 38, 33, Bodleian Library, Oxford.

[12] For their knowledge about American taxes, see George III to the duke of Newcastle, Mar. 15, 1762, Newcastle Papers, Add. MSS. 33040, f. 309, British Library; Samuel Martin to Bute, Mar. 18, 1762, Bute Papers, 4/66/1-2, Mount Stuart, Isle of Bute, Scotland; the earl of Barrington to Newcastle, Mar. 19, 1762, Newcastle Papers, Add. MSS. 32935, f. 481, British Library; and "Cash in the exchequer at his majesty's disposal," May 14, 1762, Newcastle Papers, Add. MSS. 33040, f. 353, British Library.

[13] For a cogent argument in favor of lowering customs duties articulated by Bute's most influential fiscal adviser, see [James Oswald], "notes on the excise on tea," [early 1763], Oswald Papers in the possession of Mrs. Daphne Bruton, Hockworthy House, Wellington, Somerset, England. For the application of this principle to the molasses duty, see [Oswald?], "A state of the present branches of

the customs in America, with hints for their improvement," [Feb. 1763], Liverpool Papers, Add. MSS. 38334, if. 223-4, British Library; and a paper in Dashwood's files which assumed that lowering the molasses duty from 6d. to 2d. per gallon would by itself increase revenues, "Heads of the *revenue*," [Feb. 1763], Dashwood Papers, MSS. Dashwood, B. 7/2/5, Bodleian Library.

[14] Simmons and Thomas, *op.cit.*, I, pp. 491-2.

[15] Bullion, *Necessary Measure*, p. 104.

[16] Simmons and Thomas, *op.cit.*, I, p. 489, 492.

[17] *Ibid.*, II, p. 26.

[18] Bullion, *Necessary Measure*, pp. 136-7.

[19] Simmons and Thomas, *op.cit.*, II, p. 11.

[20] *Ibid,.* II, pp. 15-16.

[21] *Ibid.*, II, pp. 14-15.

[22] Bullion, *Necessary Measure*, p. 229.

[23] Simmons and Thomas, *op.cit.*, II, p. 11.

[24] *Ibid.*, II, p. 11.

[25] Colonel Isaac Barré's speech on Feb. 6, 1765, in *Proceedings and Debates of the British Parliaments*, 2:14, 16-7. Barré went to America in 1758 with James Wolfe, served in the campaign against Quebec, and returned to England in Oct. 1760. During his time in America, he became friends with James Watts, a prominent merchant in New York City, and a member of the colony's council. Fragments of what must have been an interesting correspondence survive in Watts's papers, some of which have been printed in The New York Historical Society, *Collections*, vol. 61 (NY, 1928), *Letterbook of James Watts, Merchant and Councellor of New York, January 1, 1762-December 22, 1765.*

[26] The quotations are from Grenville's speech on Feb. 6, 1765, *Proceedings and Debates of the British Parliaments*, 2: 11. Of the three men who took notes on Barré's speech, only Jared Ingersoll, a native of Connecticut who had just arrived in England and was serving as an agent of that colony while he conducted personal business in London, recorded his veiled warning of the possibility of future trouble. Neither James Harris nor Nathaniel Ryder, two M.P.s who favored the stamp tax, included it in their accounts. This may indicate that they, and other Members, were not much impressed by this part of his speech. Cf. *Ibid.*, 2: 13-7.

[27] Ingersoll to Governor Thomas Fitch, Mar. 6, 1765, in "A Selection from the Correspondence and Miscellaneous Papers of Jared Ingersoll," ed. EB. Dexter, *Papers of the New Haven Colony Historical Society*, 9 (1918): 317. Ingersoll added that the only exceptions were a few men with interests in the West Indies or connections in America, and "a few of the heads of the minority who are sure to athwart and oppose the ministry in every measure of what nature or kind soever."

[28] Simmons and Thomas, *op.cit.*, III, p. 222.

[29] *Massachusetts Historical Society, Collections*, 6th ser. (Boston, 1897), vol. 9, p. 37.

[30] Soame Jenyns, an M.P. and a Lord of Trade, illustrated perfectly how familiarity with constitutional arguments could breed contempt when he wrote, "The liberty of an Englishman is a phrase of so various a signification, having within these few years been used as a synonymous term for blasphemy, bawdy, treason, libels, strong beer and cyder, that I shall not here presume to define its meaning; but I shall venture to assert what it cannot be; that is, an exemption from taxes imposed by the authority of the Parliament of Great Britain." Soame Jenyns, *The objections to the taxation of our American colonies, by the legislature of Great Britain, briefly consider'd* (London: J. Wilkie, Jan.1765), p. 10.

[31] Barré's speech on Feb. 6, 1765, *Proceedings and Debates of the British Parliaments*, 2:17. Barré never revealed what he believed the colonial response might be, and he never claimed later to have foreseen violent resistance. His friend Watts predicted that the Mother Country, by taxing Americans, "will not only make her Children poor and surly, but useless and disaffectionate to herself. Love is more to be depended on then Fear by half." Watts' letter to General Robert Monckton, April 16, 1765, *Watts Letterbook, 1762-1765*, p. 346. Perhaps Barré had a similar vision of things to come. There is another possibility as well. Soon after the passage of the Stamp Act, Maurice Morgann, the earl of Shelburne's private secretary, wrote a remarkable memorandum for the earl titled "On the Right and Expediency of Taxing America." Like Barré, Morgann had lived in America, albeit in the less glorious position of an apothecary in Philadelphia. Also like the Colonel, he denied the validity of the popular assumption that Americans were the same as other Britons, in this case at some length. Then he noted that although "it has been hitherto supposed that America will be intirely passive under the Imposition, . . . the Continent is not of a Temper to acquiesce under such Injuries." Morgann went on to warn that America "has even now the Spirit & the means to resist," and predicted that "Divisions & Clamours" and the seeking of aid from the French would result. Shelburne had brought Barré into Parliament for his pocket borough Chipping Wycombe, so he and Morgann certainly knew each other. Whether they shared their forebodings about the future before Barré spoke on February 6, 1765, however, is unknown. [Maurice Morgann], "On the Right and Expediency of Taxing America:' [March-

Jul. 1765], Shelburne Papers, 85: pp. 76-7, William L. Clements Library, Ann Arbor, MI.

[32] Simmons and Thomas, *op.cit.*, II, p. 15.

[33] For a discussion of the Canada Act of 1791, and William Grenville's role in it, see John Ehrman, *The Younger Pitt: The Years of Acclaim* (NY, E.P. Dutton & Co., 1969). Pp. 366-71; and Peter Jupp, *Lord Grenville, 1759-1834* (Oxford: Clarendon Press, 1985), pp. 93-7. For some suggestive remarks about its significance, see J.C.D. Clark, *English Society, 1688-1832: Ideology, social structure and political practice during the ancien regime* (Cambridge: Cambridge University Press, 1985), p. 216. The Act itself may be most conveniently consulted in *Documents relating to the Constitutional History of Canada, 1759-1791*, eds. Adam Shortt and Arthur G. Doughty, 2nd and revised edition, 2 vols. (Ottawa: J. deL. Taché, 1918), 2: 1031-51.

[34] For a thorough account of discussions about an American episcopate during the early 1760s, see Carl Bridenbaugh, *Mitre and Sceptre: Transatlantic Faiths, Ideas, Personalities and Politics, 1689-1775* (NY, Oxford University Press, 1962). 2 14-59. During 1764, Francis Bernard, the governor of Massachusetts Bay, proposed the creation of hereditary baronetcies in America. The earl of Halifax said he was enthusiastic about this and other suggestions, but did nothing about them. See the discussion of Bernard's ideas in Edmund S. Morgan and Helen M. Morgan, *The Stamp Act Crisis: Prologue to Revolution*, revised edition (NY, Collier Books, 1962). 26-8, 31-5.

[35] Shott and Doughty, eds., *Constitutional History of Canada, 1759-1971* (Ottawa, 1918), II, p. 989.

Chapter XV

British Ministers and American Resistance to the Stamp Act, October-December 1765*

Was the British government prepared during the fall of 1765 to use troops if necessary to compel Americans to pay the stamp tax? There has been a sharp division of scholarly opinion on this question. Debate has centered on rival readings of the circular letter from Henry Seymour Conway, secretary of state for the Southern Department, to the North American governors on October 24, 1765.

To Paul Langford, Conway's letter is clear proof that the ministers "really did intend the use of force in America." Noting that the secretary of state ordered governors to call for military assistance to restore public order if all else failed, Langford argues that this policy was surely inspired by the dominant figure in the king's government, the Duke of Cumberland. While conceding that direct evidence on the duke's role is lacking, Langford asserts that the use of force was compatible with Cumberland's "conservative and military cast of mind." He supports this conclusion by referring to contemporary speculation that had Cumberland not suddenly died on October 31, the ministry would have responded to the worsening crisis by sending regiments to North America. With the duke's death, the first lord of the Treasury, the marquis of Rockingham, became the actual as well as the titular head of the ministry. Far more sensitive to commercial interests, Rockingham inclined toward conciliation with the colonies.[1]

P. D. G. Thomas interprets Conway's circular differently. The letter enjoined the governors to be prudent and cautious in dealing with the disturbances. Thomas believes that this admonition diluted the letter's passages on the military. He also notes that the secretary of state nowhere specifically ordered the governors to enforce the Stamp Act. Finally, he argues that officials in Britain and America knew that the battalions in the colonies were too distant from the centers of trouble and from each other to play an effective role in suppressing resistance. These considerations lead Thomas to conclude that Conway's orders were "not intended to be put into force" and that the governors who did not follow them understood that the administration's "instructions were a piece of face-saving, promulgated to avoid any subsequent charge of negligence." Thus, even while Cumberland lived, the ministers had no plan to use the military to enforce the tax. A cabinet meeting was scheduled for the day of Cumberland's death, and the Lord Chancellor, the earl of Northington, planned to advocate sending reinforcements to America and using troops to support the civil authorities there. The duke, Thomas speculates, might have thrown his influence behind this proposal. In any event, his death ended all possibility that the British government would do anything but temporize. Rockingham and the other ministers wanted, according to Thomas, to hear what happened in America after November 1, the day the act would go into effect, before making further decisions.[2]

Resolving the controversy between Langford and Thomas depends on a fuller explanation than either gave of the ministers' reactions, expectations, and intentions between October 5, when the first news of resistance reached Whitehall, and December 10, when London learned that stamps had not been distributed in New York City on November 1. Accomplishing this enables us to reconstruct their perspective on events in America and provides the historical context for interpreting the official records of those two critical months. Fortunately, some evidence overlooked by historians illuminates the motives of the Cumberland and Rockingham administrations during that time. That evidence shows how much the special nature of a stamp tax molded ministerial policies and shaped responses to news from the colonies. It also reveals how three factors—the regulations governing the use of soldiers to support civil authority, the political implications of calling on the military to restore order, and the logistical difficulties of moving troops from Britain to North America— strongly influenced cabinet deliberations on what roles the military might play in the situation. All these considerations must be taken into account if we are to understand what the ministers did, and did not do, as they sought to comprehend and resolve the crisis in America.

This is so because Conway's circular letter and other documents touching on ministerial policy during that fall are typical examples of the official prose of the time. Their style is allusive, even elliptical; they fall short of exposing assumptions that guided decisions, alternatives rejected, or intentions for dealing with contingencies. J.C.D. Clark aptly refers to "the opacity of motive, the reticence about intention which is so marked a feature of mid-eighteenth-century politicians' relations with each other, and of their correspondence."[3] The evidence relating to imperial policy during October-December 1765 falls into this category. One cannot comprehend it without understanding the specific contexts of policy making; it must be read with a knowing eye. George Bubb Dodington, a veteran of Westminster and Whitehall, summed up this necessity in a comment on the skillful vagueness and studied omissions that Henry Pelham, first lord of the Treasury, displayed during negotiations with supporters of the prince of Wales in 1752: Pelham "spoke a little Pelham, but intelligible enough to those who know the language."[4] For the papers of the Cumberland and Rockingham administrations to be intelligible, one must try to discover what was in the ministers' minds as they deliberated on policy. To do that, one must begin with the October arrival in London of news of colonial resistance to the Stamp Act, which was contained in a lengthy letter written August 31 by Francis Bernard, the governor of Massachusetts, to the earl of Halifax, Conway's predecessor as secretary of state.

Bernard's letter gave his superiors a detailed account of violent, sustained resistance in Boston, a grim description of how narrowly "a War of plunder, of general leveling (*sic*) and taking away the distinction of rich and poor," had been averted, and a warning that this escape from anarchy might be short-lived. Even "the Horror" of a ferocious attack on the house of Lieutenant-Governor Thomas

Hutchinson had "not abated the Spirit of the People against the Stamp Act." The subsequent return to order resulted from the willingness of the town's gentlemen to stand guard, not from any action of the governor, and those same gentlemen had told Bernard they would withdraw if he tried to enforce the tax. Should they do so, he would be helpless. No British regulars were stationed in Boston. When Bernard broached to the Massachusetts Council the possibility of asking General Thomas Gage, commander in chief of the army in America, to send troops from New York, the councilors expressed their hope he would not inform Gage or his naval counterpart, Lord Colville, about the riots and refused military aid. He was certain that any future attempt by him would meet the same fate. Many councilors owned property in Boston. All of them were elected by the House of Representatives. Their "own situation and dependency would make them afraid of being answer able to the people for so disagreeable a step." This left the governor isolated and impotent. He could only hope that popular passions would somehow subside.

Bernard could see "only two things which are like to produce [such] a change." The House of Representatives would meet on September 26. The representatives might possibly fear that supporting the popular cause would risk forfeiture of the colony's charter. They might even advocate submission to the Stamp Act. Bernard placed more hope, however, on another consideration. "A nearer and fuller prospect of the Anarchy and Confusion which must take place when the Courts of Justice and public offices are shut up, as they must be on the first of November unless Stamps are allowed to be used," would compel Bostonians to pay the tax.[6] Because this expectation is central to understanding London's reaction to his letter, grasping why he believed this is essential.

The governor based his analysis on his knowledge of how duties like the stamp tax had operated in England. George Grenville had explained this succinctly on February 6, 1765, when he introduced the Stamp Act in the House of Commons. A stamp tax, he observed, was "an easy one to execute," since "bonds, conveyances, law proceedings, etc.," that were not on stamped paper were not legally binding on the parties involved. Because "instruments not stamped are null and void," self-interest would dictate buying stamps, and thus "the tax in a great degree executes itself." To reinforce self-interest, the Court of Admiralty in North America exercised initial jurisdiction over violations of the Stamp Act. Judges appointed in England and sitting in Halifax, Nova Scotia, not colonial magistrates and local juries, would interpret the law. Their decisions could only be appealed to English courts. All this would mean that no Americans would trust or use unstamped documents. That left forgery as "the only fright to be apprehended, but severe penalties may prevent it."[7] For these reasons, Grenville was sure that colonists would pay the duties, no matter how much they complained. His certainty played a major role in his decision to impose the tax.[8] Bernard shared Grenville's opinion, and the readiness of Boston's gentlemen to restore order after the destruction of Hutchinson's house buttressed his optimism.

The governor's account of popular violence was soon corroborated. On October 7, letters from Andrew Oliver, the erstwhile distributor of stamps in Massachusetts, reached the Treasury. His recital of "the great outrages committed by the people of Boston" accompanied his resignation. This news prompted the first British response to the crisis. On October 8 Rockingham and the Treasury board ordered Bernard "to take care that His Majesty's Revenue suffers no Detriment, or Diminution." To accomplish this, the governor should appoint a temporary distributor and "enforce a due Obedience to the Laws."[9]

These directives reveal more than a determination to gain revenue. Rockingham had two concerns. The first was to collect the stamp taxes. The major obstacle to that, he thought, was not mob violence but the absence of efficient distribution of the stamps: hence the orders to Bernard. The second was to restore civil authority. Bernard was to do this by encouraging local magistrates to act with "spirit and firmness" in enforcing obedience. No mention was made of calling for military assistance. This omission may be explained by the Treasury's certainty that once the stamps were distributed, the tax would enforce itself.

Further evidence of the assumptions behind the Treasury's orders to Bernard appears in Edmund Burke's January 1766 draft of a "Speech on Stamp Act Disturbances," intended as his maiden address in the Commons. As he prepared, Burke drew upon knowledge he had gained during the fall of 1765 as Rockingham's private secretary, a post he held until elected to the house in December. In this position, he was privy to the ruminations of the marquis and other ministers on America. Although he seems to have played no role in the formulation of policy during 1765-1766, he was fully informed about considerations that guided the government. Accordingly, his draft is an important source for ministerial attitudes. Presumably because it revealed both the ministers' hopes that the Stamp Act would enforce itself and their discussion of the pros and cons of sending regiments to America, and thus would embarrass them as they tried to repeal the tax, Burke never delivered this speech. His suppression of it underlines its significance.[10]

In Burke's account, the Treasury's orders of October 8 signified a decision "to try the operation of the principle of the act itself"—that is, to see what effect the prospect of "a Total vacation of Justice—a total Suspension of Dealing—a total Embargo upon Trade" would have on the American opposition to the stamp tax. The ministers were confident about the outcome, and with good reason. "No act," Burke observed, "was better calculated to execute itself"—an opinion, he noted, that was shared by Bernard even "in the very height of the Tumults." When colonists realized what was best for their own interests, "the road to their obedience was fair and open." No stamps had been destroyed, and the Treasury had given "orders very clear and precise . . . for their Effectual distribution." Burke's draft makes plain the Treasury's assumptions as it reacted to Oliver's resignation. It also reveals that the confident expectation that Americans would begin paying the tax on or soon after November 1 guided the cabinet when it informally discussed America on October 13.[11]

None of the participants in the October 13 meeting recorded any details of their discussion, nor did the meeting produce any minute of advice to the crown, as was customary. Instead, the ministers referred the matter to the Privy Council. It is evident, however, that the main topic was not how to insure collection of stamp duties in the colonies; Burke's draft emphasizes that the ministers were relying on the tax's enforcing itself, and the Treasury had taken appropriate steps to enable the "energic principle of the act" to operate. Their referral of the American crisis to the Privy Council indicates that the ministers felt that a fundamental issue was at stake. In their opinion, riots openly designed to defeat British authority and overturn Parliament's power to tax colonists demanded the formal solemnity of resolutions from one of the great institutions of British government, where the king's councilors signed their recommendations and made themselves personally accountable. Measures taken after the October 13 meeting show that the cabinet intended to formulate the Privy Council's response, with an eye mainly to demonstrating the mother country's authority and its power by restoring law and order to the colonies. This, in turn, required consideration of the role the military might play.

On October 15, clerks in Conway's office drafted an order to Lord Colville to provide assistance to any governor requesting it. This draft proves Conway's prior knowledge of the Privy Council's recommendation and shows that its substance had been agreed upon during the cabinet's session. The Privy Council announced that recommendation on October 23. It advised the king to order the secretary of state to write immediately to all governors and to the commanders of British forces in North America. The governors should be ordered to "provide by all prudent and popular methods for the support of the honour and safety of government, and [to] use all legal means to preserve peace and good order by a full exertion of the civil power," including, if necessary, an appeal to his majesty's land and sea forces. Military commanders should be ordered to provide assistance on request. George III approved this advice, and the letters to the governors and commanders went on their way to America on October 24.[12]

The Privy Council's recommendations dealt only with the king's forces already overseas. The idea of reinforcing those troops with regiments from Ireland or England may have been brought up on October 13, and Northington wanted to discuss it at a meeting scheduled for October 31. After Cumberland's death, rumors flew that the duke was ready to do this, rumors that are given credence by Langford and, to a lesser extent, by Thomas as well. In fact, for two compelling reasons the ministers never seriously considered sending regulars across the Atlantic in 1765.

One was an understandable determination to avoid expense. No one besides Northington was willing to ship men and matériel across the sea when packets from America would in all probability soon bring news that the Stamp Act had begun, on November 1, to enforce itself and that the political situation had improved. The second reason involved logistics. Cumberland was a veteran soldier who had commanded armies in Europe and experienced the rigors and dangers of a winter campaign in Scotland in 1745-1746. Rockingham had been a young volunteer on the duke's staff during that bitter struggle against the Stuart Pretender. Conway had participated in large-scale raids on the coast of France during the Seven Years' War. During the same conflict, other members of the cabinet learned about the military and political risks attendant on combined operations. All these men were familiar with the problems of moving troops and the risks of landing them on hostile shores in the eighteenth century. Langford overlooks these experiences when he asserts that Cumberland's "conservative" military background and fierce suppression of rebellion in Scotland would lead him to favor the use of force in America under any circumstances.[13]

Burke's draft makes plain what the influence of the ministers' background on their decisions really was. Experience had taught the duke and his colleagues that October was not the month to launch an expedition across the North Atlantic. As Burke explained, military operations should begin in "a Military season." Anyone favoring force, he noted, should "open your inglorious campaign against your fellow Citizens, when you open it against your Enemies, in the spring of the year. . . . Westerly winds, and that uphill Sea against you," would endanger the navy in the fall and winter. Moreover, even if these hazards were overcome, "all the accumulated Horrors of an American Winter" would prevent troops in America from coordinating operations with the regiments from Britain, and this might exacerbate the crisis. Separated detachments would "expose the force of Great Britain to the derision of her rebellious children," a situation that might enable them "to break our strength" and would "encrease their obstinancy and presumption." Accordingly, reinforcements should not leave English waters until spring. Well before then, the ministers would know whether the stamp tax was enforcing itself. If events proved a need for more troops, there would still be time to plan and execute the operation carefully. For the present, fiscal and logistical restraints, as well as the special nature of a stamp tax, determined the administration to reject sending more regulars to America.[14]

Conway's letter to the governors had two goals. First, it informed them that the king would hold them responsible for restoring and maintaining order in their colonies. Then, it pointed out the proper way to proceed. Governors should "temper [their] conduct between that caution and coolness, which the delicacy of such a situation may demand, on one hand; and the vigor necessary to suppress outrage and violence on the other." Vigorous suppression of violence, Conway stressed, included calling on the military if necessary. This would be justified because, "however unwillingly his majesty may consent to the exertion of such powers as may endanger the safety of a single subject, yet he cannot permit his own dignity, and the authority of the British legislature, to be trampled on by force and violence, and in avowed contempt of all order, duty, and decorum."[15] What made the riots in America serious was their success in overturning British authority. The governors must restore colonial obedience, by persuasion and politics if possible, but if not, by force.

The cabinet expected that some governors would have to ask for troops. Writing to Gage, Conway observed that "these Events will probably create Applications to You." When this happened, he would not have the benefit of "any particular or positive Instruction" from London. Distance would oblige the general "to take your Resolution, as particular Circumstances, & Emergencies may require." There were, however, general procedures he should follow. The king wanted his officials to seek a political solution to the crisis first. If Gage could restore order "by lenient & persuasive Methods," he would do "a most acceptable and essential service to [his] Country." But if "every Step, which the utmost Prudence & Lenity can dictate," failed, his duty was unmistakable. "You will not, . . . where your Assistance may be wanted to strengthen the hand of Government, fail to concur, in every proper Measure, for it's Support, by such a timely Exertion of Force, as may be necessary to repell Acts of Violence & Outrage, & to provide for the Maintenance of Peace, & good Order in The Provinces."[16]

Thomas's argument that these orders were "a piece of face-saving" and were understood by their recipients as "not intended to be put into force" is not persuasive.[17] The absence of specific reference to the Stamp Act in the letters that he claims supports his interpretation was the result of the ministers' confidence that it would have begun to enforce itself one week after Conway's instructions were sent to America. The careful enjoining of prudence and lenity that he believes exposed the ministers' motives was in fact typical of orders to quell popular disturbances. To be sure, as Thomas points out, some opposition members condemned the language of the circular letter as too weak, but their charges were politically motivated and utterly groundless. Eighteenth-century ministries took the preservation of public order quite seriously and recognized that it was often necessary to use troops. They insisted, however, on the proper and constitutional use of regulars by the civil authority. Magistrates should first try to disperse rioters, defuse tensions, and restore their authority by peaceful measures. Only if these failed were they to call upon the military. For their part, soldiers could not take any action against British subjects unless civil authorities requested their assistance. Failure to wait for that request meant ruined careers and criminal charges. For this reason, ministers always carefully reminded officers of their obligations whenever it appeared they might become involved in restoring order.[18] To insure that Gage did not interpret Conway's commands as anything out of the ordinary, the War Office enclosed its standard instructions governing the employment of regulars against rioters.[19]

The general could not have misunderstood another import of that enclosure. He had to comply with all proper requests for the army's help or suffer the consequences of disobedience. London's message to the governors had been much the same: the explicit commands in Conway's circular implied criticism of Bernard's failure to call for troops. Also implicit was a message meant to hearten the general. Conway's comment to Gage that "these Events will probably create Applications to You" before he could receive guidance from London shows that the ministers expected that some governors would appeal to the general before the letters of October 24 reached America.[20] This letter would reassure them that, if they had called for and used troops properly, the ministers would approve their action and support them against any complaint.

Four days after the Cumberland administration sent its guidelines for restoring order, some worrisome news from New York reached London. Gage had written Conway on September 23 that there was a "general Scheme, concerted throughout" America, to defeat the stamp tax. First, mobs would "by Menace or Force" compel stamp distributors to resign. In this, he pointed out, "they have generally succeeded." Then the stamps would be destroyed on arrival. This would provide the pretext for conducting business as usual without paying the tax. Finally, before the stamps could be replaced, the movement's leaders hoped that "the Clamor and outcry of the People, with Addresses and Remonstrances from the Assemblys might procure a Repeal of the Act." Thus far, Gage went on, no governor had asked for troops to protect distributors or stamps. He had, he assured Conway, prepared to move small units to Boston, New York, and Annapolis. In Boston and New York, however, civil authorities were inclined to "fall . . . upon other means"—as Gage tactfully put it—of preserving peace, and if troops went to Annapolis, Fort Pitt "will be extreamly (*sic*) weak." Gage underscored how thin his forces were everywhere: "they are scattered and divided, over this vast Continent, and that very few could be collected in Case of sudden Emergencys, in any part, except in Canada." Even so, he was hopeful, for everything was quiet at present. Now "people talk and Reason more cooly." Also encouraging were signs they "begin to perceive that Trade and all Business whatsoever will be thrown into great Difficultys without the Stamps." Americans were realizing that "the Certificates which they must get in Lieu of Stamps, if none are to be had, will cost much more than the Stamps themselves." Gage ended his letter almost philosophically. The stamped paper was due any day, and November 1 was only five weeks away, so "the final Issue of this Affair will be soon determined."[21]

Despite the general's optimism, his news of colonial resistance disturbed the administration. So far, no civil authorities had asked the military to suppress disorders, and this failure of will might allow the destruction of the stamps. Should this occur, the ministers would face an ominous situation after November 1. The tax could not operate as they had expected, so Britain would have no new colonial revenue. They would also have to deal with a determined defiance of British authority. Even if this did not come to pass, Gage's letter dramatically revealed how far the Stamp Act's opponents were apparently willing to go, how much support they had, and how impotent royal officials had been against them. The American crisis clearly demanded the cabinet's immediate attention. A meeting was therefore scheduled for October 31 at Cumberland's palace.

Northington's estimate of the situation's gravity impelled him to sketch a plan for remedying it. The Lord Chancellor intended to urge his colleagues to adopt four resolutions.

> 1st. . . . that the Stamp Act ought to be carried into Execution in support of the Sovereignty of the British Parl[iamen]t over the Colonies.

> 2nd. That for this Purpose immediate Orders should be given to the Respective gov[erno]rs to execute this Order & that they sh[oul]d be furnished with the Assistance of a Military Force for this Purpose.

> 3ly. That Orders should be sent to the Respective Gov to make the most diligent Inquiry to detect the Persons concerned in this Rebellion, & for which purpose they should issue proper Rewards, & the Delinquents be prosecuted & duly punished according to Law.

> 4th. That if the Contagion should prove epidemical, & elusive of Justice, that proper Laws should be proposed to the British P[arliamen]t as a Remedy.[22]

Each was a solution to the principal problems Gage described. Governors had been too timid. An explicit command to execute the Stamp Act and the arrival of military reinforcements would stiffen their resolve. The relatively few and widely dispersed troops in America weakened the hand of government. Regiments sent from Britain would provide the concentrated forces necessary to support civil authority. Opposition to the Stamp Act posed a serious threat to Britain's control over the colonies and required measures to deter demagogues and their riotous followers from renewing their resistance on future occasions. Governors should identify, prosecute, and punish resisters. Should the conspiracy be too widespread for this to be feasible, or the laws inadequate to gain convictions, the ministry would propose legislation designed to correct political and legal weaknesses.

Cumberland's fatal heart attack minutes before the cabinet met on October 31 prevented discussion of Gage's letter and Northington's proposals. What would have happened had the duke lived is unknowable, with one exception: for the reasons Burke described, the cabinet would not have agreed to send more regulars immediately to the colonies. Stunned by Cumberland's death, the ministers returned to their homes, minds focused not on America but on whether an administration bereft of its leader would survive. They did not meet to discuss the imperial crisis again until December 11. By that time, they had learned that the situation had grown much worse.[23]

Langford and Thomas emphasize differences between the Cumberland and Rockingham administrations. Langford argues that the two men did not have similar attitudes toward American affairs; Thomas, that the marquis was willing to wait on events in the colonies before he decided on policy. One difficulty with these views is that no one has uncovered any statement Cumberland made during 1765 about the colonies: assertions about distinctions between his opinions and Rockingham's are therefore speculative. In addition, important continuities from one ministry to the other are well documented. The same factors that militated against reinforcing Gage in October had even greater force in November. Neither Cumberland nor Rockingham had that option. The marquis made no effort to revise Conway's instructions to the governors and military commanders. He remained committed to supporting a constitutional and judicious use of the military in America. He continued to believe that stamp duties would be self-collecting. Finally, he was as concerned in November about the implications of colonial protests for British rule in America as he had been a month earlier. All these assumptions and concerns influenced his reactions to intelligence from America after October 31. They also informed his responses to an important letter he received from Barlow Trecothick, the current chairman of an organization established by London merchants trading with North America to lobby at Whitehall and Westminster.

Trecothick wrote to Rockingham on November 7. The stamp tax, he predicted, would have disastrous consequences not only for America but for Britain as well. He was certain that colonists would refuse after November 1 to participate in any commerce requiring stamps. When that happened, "our sugar islands will be deprived of their usual supplies of provisions lumber etc." As a result, planters in the West Indies might be "disabled from sending home their produce or even subsisting their slaves." The impact this would have on merchants trading with the islands and on the mother country's economy as a whole was so obvious that Trecothick did not pause to describe it. He did not exercise such restraint, however, when he portrayed the, significance of a stoppage of the American trade for him and his colleagues. Merchants would have "little or no chance" of collecting their debts, a circumstance that might "prove fatal" to many of them. Those who survived would have to put "a total stop . . . to all purchase of manufactures for a country whence no returns can be expected." "From this state," Trecothick asserted, "it naturally and unavoidably follows that an exceedingly great number of manufacturers are soon to be without employ and of course without bread." He refused "to pursue any further the dreadful chain of consequences." Instead, he emphasized that the administration should call Parliament into session as soon as possible to suspend or repeal the Stamp Act.[24]

Trecothick's specialized knowledge and political loyalty commanded attention and respect. He had begun his career in commerce in the 1730s in Boston as an apprentice to Charles Apthorp and had spent most of the 1740s in Jamaica as Apthorp's agent. In the late 1740s, after marrying his mentor's daughter, he moved to London. By 1765 he had achieved considerable success in the North American trade. His experiences gave him a detailed understanding of American, West Indian, and British commerce and a wide acquaintance with the men involved in each one. Trecothick put his unusually broad expertise and his numerous contacts not only to the service of his economic pursuits, but to his growing political ambitions as well. In 1764 he was elected an alderman of the City of London. Then, in February 1765, his fellow merchants chose him to lead their opposition to Grenville's stamp bill. Though unsuccessful, his performance was impressive. Rockingham's colleague, the duke of Newcastle, recognizing how useful Trecothick's knowledge and skill could be for the ministry in the

House of Commons, had asked him in September 1765 to stand for Parliament from New Shoreham—an invitation tantamount to election, since the Treasury controlled that borough. Trecothick declined, however, because he feared it would harm his prospects for entering the House as one of London's members. Refusal on these grounds did not call into question his loyalty to the ministry—a loyalty of which he reminded Rockingham by referring to a "virtuous Administration" and "the Error of their Predecessors" in his letter of November 7.[25]

Because of Trecothick's familiarity with imperial commerce and his history of political support, the marquis pondered his letter carefully. His reply on November 10 gives an illuminating glimpse of his thoughts.

He began by explaining that the difficulties confronting the administration "are great." American obedience to Parliament "is no slight matter." On the other hand, "perhaps it may be beyond doubt that the occasion which gave rise to all this confusion was ill-judged here." Political confusion and economic distress would indeed be the results of a widespread refusal in America to use stamps. Yet, he reminded Trecothick, "the particular and great inconveniences which you mention were perhaps intentionally to be so, in order to force . . . compliance" with the tax. Far from resolving these problems, calling Parliament into session early would complicate them. The ministers who sat in the House of Commons were required by law to stand for reelection, and the time necessary for that "must still be given before you could expect any moderating measures." Moreover, within a few days or weeks the government would have more knowledge of the situation in the colonies. "Upon so nice a point," Rockingham concluded, "it is both necessary and wise to wait for good grounds to proceed upon." He was willing, however, to discuss these matters more fully with Trecothick in person and invited him to come to dinner on November 12.[26]

Rockingham's signals were unmistakable. In diplomatic language suitable for a friend of the ministry he called attention to two reasons why repealing the Stamp Act was not presently an option: colonial resistance to British authority should not be rewarded, and the nature of the tax itself would in all probability defeat that resistance. At the same time, his assurances that he would listen to the grievances of British merchants and manufacturers and his reference to "moderating measures" offered guarded but real encouragement to Trecothick. Repeal might be out of the question, but softening the tax's impact on commerce was not. If merchants could convince him that specific stamp duties reduced trade, he would be willing to propose amendments to the act. The invitation to dinner meant that Trecothick could start the process of persuasion immediately. It also gave him reason to be confident of success.

On November 15, another letter from Gage reached Whitehall. Written on October 12, it seemed to clarify colonial attitudes and the Stamp Act's fate. The general informed Conway that three more assemblies had protested that the tax was unconstitutional and that "the Spirit of Democracy is strong amongst" the delegates to the Stamp Act Congress, currently meeting in New York. This, he observed, would cause them to claim the tax was "contrary to their Rights." To Gage, this amounted to "Supporting the Independency of the Provinces" by denying they were "Subject to the Legislative Power of Great Britain." Despite this development, he once more concluded with an optimistic forecast. There might not be any further opposition to the tax. Moreover, whether there was or not, "from present Appearances there is Reason to Judge, that it may be introduced without much Difficulty, in several of the Colonys, and if it is began in some, that it will soon spread over the rest."[27]

Rockingham drew two conclusions from Gage's news. First, just as he had believed, in all probability the stamp tax would execute itself. Second, assembly protests denying Parliament's authority convinced him that a response from Parliament was needed. These considerations in mind, he worked on ways to deal with the aftermath of the crisis. As he did, Trecothick's ideas strongly influenced him. In late November, he drafted a memorandum outlining his strategy.

The ministry would lay papers on disturbances in America before both houses of Parliament, then move four resolutions: first, "that the fact of riots and tumults in obstruction of [an] act of Parliament is fully proved;" second, that resolutions of assemblies had tended to inflame the situation; third, "in general words" that Parliament had authority over the colonies; and finally, that Parliament therefore formally censured the assemblies' conduct. Rockingham was uncertain whether this would suffice to repair the damage done to the mother country's authority by colonial resistance, or whether Parliament should add teeth to the resolutions by making it "high treason in the colonies to write, print, etc. doubting the right of [the] British legislature" to tax. He also wondered if it might not be better to have a declaratory act explicitly proclaiming parliamentary authority rather than relying on a generally worded resolution to settle the constitutional controversy. The remainder of his notes suggest that Rockingham may have been thinking about more than just determining the best way for Parliament to react to the challenge to its authority. He might also have been wondering which options would most fully satisfy the predictable determination of the House of Commons to respond effectively to American resistance and thereby make it easier to amend the Stamp and Sugar acts to remove some of the grievances of British merchants and their colonial correspondents.

The second part of Rockingham's memorandum reveals that he wanted to accompany the firm establishment of British authority with revisions of the stamp tax. Trecothick had convinced him that three changes were necessary. Judicial cases arising from the collection of stamp duties should be tried in local courts, not at the admiralty court in Halifax. The requirement that these duties be paid in specie should be expunged from the act, and colonial currency made acceptable. All documents required in intracolonial trade and in the commerce between Britain and America should be exempted from the stamp tax. The first two changes responded to specific colonial grievances; the second resulted as well from merchants' fears that removing scarce specie from circulation would adversely affect Americans' ability to remit payments for their debts. Trecothick's arguments about the burdens stamp duties would impose on trade between North America and the West Indies and between British colonies and the mother country inspired the third. Concern about trade between the continent and the Caribbean had another effect as well. It persuaded Rockingham that the ministry should advocate lowering the duty on foreign molasses imported into North America below the three pence per gallon required by the Sugar Act. This reduction, plus the "moderating" of the Stamp Act, would mollify colonial opinion and protect British merchants and manufacturers.[28]

Successfully executing this strategy depended on convincing the House of Commons that these revisions in the stamp tax were so essential that they must be made before there was actual evidence of how the tax affected trade and even though the changes might reduce revenue collections. Rockingham and Trecothick knew that members who had voted overwhelmingly for the stamp tax nine months earlier might be reluctant to amend it. But if they could be persuaded, vital changes could be made immediately, and the economic consequences of its flaws would be minimized. So the two men secretly plotted out a national campaign of manufacturers and merchants against the operation of Grenville's imperial legislation. The outlines of their plan are in a memorandum drafted by Burke sometime in November.

The campaign would begin with meetings of "our friends" among the London merchants, "with as little show as possible, twice a week at least, to digest business." During that time, they would learn which goods were exported to North America, who the principal merchants and manufacturers involved in that trade were, and where they lived. Then Trecothick and his associates would "get proper persons to write [to] each Town to those most interested in and best acquainted with the business—men of our principles if possible—to get information of the State of Trade." In addition to gaining knowledge, this would serve to open "proper channels of correspondence." Within London, the

ministry's friends would" talk. . . . this matter over with all they can influence."
When they were prepared, they would quietly call "a meeting in which a
Committee of *Merchants* not exceeding ten shall be chosen for conduct and
correspondence." That committee would direct and coordinate petitions from all
over Britain complaining to Parliament about the impact of recent revenue
legislation on Britain's trade and manufacturing. It would "draw drafts of
petitions, call general meetings, choose and instruct agents, and take whatever
measures shall be judged necessary."[29]

Once the petitions began arriving at Westminster, the administration
would have to realize the maximum benefit from them. According to a "Plan of
Business" Rockingham drafted on November 28, the ministers should "avoid. . .
discussion on the Stamp Act" until Parliament was "well informed of the high
Importance of the Commerce to N[orth] A[merica] to the Mother Country." The
evidence from British merchants and manufacturers would accomplish this.
Consideration of the stamp tax should also be delayed "til Good Principles are
laid down for Easing and Assisting" the colonies.[30] When this was done, he
expected the task of persuading members to adopt the administration's proposals
for asserting British authority and, especially, removing harmful provisions from
the Stamp Act would be much easier.

The early stages of this plan were entirely successful. None of the
ministry's opponents ferreted out what Trecothick was doing until his
preparations were complete and he had called a meeting of London merchants
trading to North America for December 4.[31] Nor did anyone guess Rockingham's
part in it, which meant that he did not suffer the embarrassment of explaining why
the first lord of the Treasury was soliciting petitions against a tax. Rumors had
begun to spread, though, that he and his colleagues favored repealing the Stamp
Act.[32] He did not react publicly or privately to these inaccurate reports. Perhaps
he reasoned that when the truth became known, he would have the politically
useful advantage of appearing more committed to maintaining Britain's

supremacy and revenues and more judicious and discriminating in his critique of the stamp tax than he had been painted.

Trecothick's public launching of the petition campaign marked the completion of Rockingham's preparations for the opening of Parliament and the resolution of the American crisis. The marquis had not waited for events there to determine his policy on the stamp tax, as Thomas claims. Proceeding with a decisiveness Thomas gives him no credit for, he knew what he would do when the expected news arrived that Americans were paying the stamp tax.

In fact, the news from America dashed Rockingham's expectations. A letter Gage wrote on November 4 describing continued resistance to the Stamp Act arrived on December 10. Major Thomas James, who had been present during the riots in New York, delivered it to Conway. After reading it and talking with the major, the secretary of state was "astonish'd." James later recalled that this unanticipated bad news seemed so important to Conway that he "would have taken me to the King that very day had I been fit to have been seen."[33] He did immediately inform his colleagues about the dispatch, and the next night the cabinet discussed it.

Gage's report revealed that the tax had not enforced itself in New York and probably would not do so in the foreseeable future. Moreover, the "contagion" had spread everywhere. Gage believed New York was near rebellion. He also advised that "unless the Act will from its own nature at length enforce itself, nothing but a very considerable Military force can do it."[34] The general did not need to state that this force had to come from Britain. His narrative made it obvious that small detachments of regulars could not cow the protesting crowds. To the contrary: enraged New Yorkers would have attacked and overwhelmed James and his soldiers had the government's promise to withhold distribution of the stamps not placated them. Larger concentrations of troops than were possible in North America would be necessary to restore order. "Considerable" bodies of troops would have to be sent to the colonies if the ministers chose to compel obedience to the act. Faced with this, the cabinet, according to Northington, inclined "to yield to the Insurrections & Clamors & not to support the Stamp-Act."[35]

The beginning of that consensus may be found in Rockingham's thoughts and acts during November. After December 10, he responded to the deteriorating situation by fitting conclusions he had already devised to new circumstances. In the weeks before, he had concluded that stamps on commercial documents would adversely affect Britain's trade and should be removed. The remaining duties would raise less money. Moreover, the principal attraction of those duties was the cheapness and ease—in theory, at least—of collecting them. If the stamp tax did not essentially enforce itself, that virtue would be lost. Thanks to the ministers' earlier considerations of the American crisis, Rockingham also knew that sending substantial reinforcements from Britain would plunge the ministers into the expenses, difficulties, and delays of moving a sizable force across the Atlantic. Making those sacrifices in an effort to preserve a reduced Stamp Act understandably seemed ill advised; among other things, forcing colonists to obey might cost more than the duties would raise. As for asserting British authority over America, he had already scouted out ways of affirming Parliament's supremacy, including the passage of a Declaratory Act. Finally, what he hoped would become a powerful and persuasive campaign by merchants and manufacturers against Grenville's colonial legislation had been initiated. All of this prepared him to proceed without hesitation toward persuading cabinet, king, and Parliament to repeal the Stamp Act.

Rockingham's success in persuading his fellow ministers is prefigured in their reactions during October and November to American resistance. Had they been in reality as Langford describes them, ready to reinforce and then use the army in America to coerce obedience to the Stamp Act, Rockingham would have had to overcome their initial commitment to force. No such difficulty challenged him. Cumberland and his colleagues had found compelling fiscal and logistical reasons to reject any thought of sending troops from Britain. Instead, they decided to stiffen the wills of local officials and to provide them eventually with the additional support of parliamentary resolutions. That seemed enough, because all the ministers believed that with even the most modest exertion of authority in America, the colonists would have to pay the tax. They grounded this optimism on their certainty that stamp duties virtually collected themselves. To an extent unappreciated by Langford or Thomas, this conviction dominated their estimate of the potential seriousness of colonial protests. That Conway was "astonish'd" to learn that the tax was not enforcing itself is no wonder; that news changed completely his and others' perception of the situation in the colonies. It also removed what had been, in their minds, the most appealing feature of the act: its self-executing nature. Many of them had originally opposed its passage. They, like Rockingham, were predisposed to believe it was in need of significant amendment to prevent harm to British trade. As Conway, who had spoken against the tax in the House in February 1765, put it on November 14, rioting Americans were not simply "a serious business" for government to resolve. The problem had been made "doubly difficult" for him because of his previous opposition. Conway knew that "unless we find lenity [to be] the plan" he would face the awkward necessity of defending the use of force to compel colonists to pay duties whose justice and wisdom he had publicly questioned.[36] When he and other ministers could no longer rely on the act's special nature giving them the opportunity to be lenient, modify the tax, and still collect revenue, they had to choose between confrontation and conciliation. When their expectations of American acquiescence proved incorrect, the majority of the cabinet were too familiar with the difficulties of a military response and too unimpressed with the Stamp Act to favor confrontation.

*This chapter first appeared in: *William and Mary Quarterly* 49 (1992), pp. 89-107.

Endnotes

[1] Langford, *The First Rockingham Administration, 1765-1766* (Oxford, 1973), pp. 80-83, 109-110, "The Rockingham Whigs and America, 1767-1773," in Anne Whiteman, J. S. Bromley, and P.G.M. Dickson, eds., *Statesmen, Scholars and Merchants: Essays in Eighteenth-Century History presented to Dame Lucy Sutherland* (Oxford, 1973), p. 135, and *A Polite and Commercial People: England, 1727-1783* (Oxford, 1989), p. 366. For an account that essentially agrees with Langford see Ian R. Christie and Benjamin W. Labaree, *Empire or Independence, 1760-1776: A British-American Dialogue on the Coming of the American Revolution* (New York, 1976), p. 64.

[2] Thomas, *British Politics and the Stamp Act Crisis: The First Phase of the American Revolution, 1763-1767* (Oxford, 1975), pp. 138-142. Robert W. Tucker and David C. Hendrickson, in: *The Fall of the First British Empire: Origins of the War of American Independence* (Baltimore, MD, 1982), pp. 221-222, agree with Thomas's critique of Langford but differ from all other scholars in questioning the significance of Cumberland's death. According to them, in Britain during the 1760s, there was "a consensus that militated against a resolution of the colonial conflict by armed force," and they doubt the duke could have overcome it.

[3] Clark, *The Dynamics of Change: The Crisis of the 1750s and English Party Systems* (Cambridge, 1982), p.19.

[4] Dodington, entry for Jul. 15, 1752, in *The Political Journal of George Bubb Dodington*, ed. John Carswell and Lewis Arnold Dralle (Oxford, 1965), p. 164.

[5] Bernard to Halifax, Aug. 31, 1765, C.O. 5/755, fols. 292-293, Public Record Office. For the date of its arrival in London see Langford, *Rockingham Administration*, p. 80.

[6] Grenville, Feb. 6, 1765, in R. C. Simmons and P.D.G. Thomas, eds., *Proceedings and Debates of the British Parliaments Respecting North America, 1754-1783*, I (White Plains, NY, 1982), p. 15.

[7] *Ibid.*, p. 11.

[8] See John L. Bullion, *A Great and Necessary Measure: George Grenville and the Genesis of the Stamp Act, 1763-1765* (Columbia, MO, 1982), pp. 104-107.

[9] Treasury minute, Oct. 7, 1765. I have consulted the copy in "Treasury minutes and letters relative to stamp duties in America," Rockingham Papers, R.28, Wentworth Woodhouse Muniments, Sheffield Central Library, Sheffield, England. This document was compiled early in Jan. 1766 to assist ministers in parliamentary debates by providing evidence to prove that the ministry had not been lax in administering the Stamp Act.

[10] Burke, "Speech on Stamp Act Disturbances," Jan.-Feb. 1766, in: *The Writings and Speeches of Edmund Burke, II, Party, Parliament, and the American Crisis, 1766-1774*, ed. Paul Langford (Oxford, 1981), pp. 43-44.

[11] *Ibid.*

[12] Privy Council's recommendations are quoted in: Thomas, *British Politics*, p. 137.

[13] Langford, *Rockingham Administration*, p. 83.

[14] Burke, "Speech on Stamp Act Disturbances," Jan.-Feb. 1766, in: *Writings and Speeches of Burke*, II, 44.

[15] Conway to the governors of North American colonies, Oct. 24, 1765. There are several copies of this letter; see, e.g., William Cobbett, *Parliamentary History of England*, ed. John Wright, XVI (London, 1813), pp. 116-118.

[16] Conway to Gage, Oct. 24, 1765, in: *The Correspondence of General Thomas Gage with the Secretaries of State, 1763-1775*, 2 vols., ed. Clarence Edwin Carter (New Haven, CT, 1931-1933), II, pp. 28-29.

[17] Thomas, *British Politics*, p.138.

[18] For an illuminating discussion of the use of troops in 18th century Britain to preserve public order, see: J. A. Houlding, *Fit for Service: The Training of the British Army, 1715-1795* (Oxford, 1981), pp. 57-74.

[19] See Gage to the earl of Barrington, Jan. 16, 1766, in *Gage Correspondence*, ed. Carter, II, p. 334.

[20] Conway to Gage, Oct. 24, 1765, *ibid.*, p. 28.

[21] Gage to Conway, Sept. 23, 1765, *ibid.*, I, pp. 67-69.

[22] Northington, "My Opinion intended to be d[elivere]d at the Meeting summond on Am[erican] B[usine]ss at Cumberland House, the Ev[enin]g the D[uke] of Cumb[erland] died" (Oct. 31, 1765), Northington Papers, Northamptonshire Record Office, Northampton, England.

[23] For the political repercussions of Cumberland's death see: Langford, *Rockingham Administration*, pp. 98-108. The cabinet met five times during Nov. 1765 but did not discuss American business. An informal meeting on Dec. 11, 1765, was the first since Oct. 13 to be devoted to America.

[24] Trecothick to Rockingham, Nov. 7, 1765, Rockingham Papers, R. 24-43(a).

[25] The most complete account of Trecothick is D. H. Watson, "Barlow Trecothick and other Associates of Lord Rockingham during the Stamp Act Crisis, 1765-1766" (M.A. thesis, Sheffield University, 1958). More convenient sources include Sir Lewis Namier and John Brooke, eds., *The History of Parliament: The House of Commons, 1754-1790*, III (London, 1964), pp. 557-560, Langford, Rockingham Administration, pp. 110-111, and Thomas, *British Politics*, pp. 144-147.

[26] Rockingham to Trecothick, [Nov. 10, 1765], *Rockingham Papers*, R. pp. 81-181.

[27] Gage to Conway, Oct. 12, 1765, *Gage Correspondence*, ed. Carter, I, pp.69-70.

[28] Rockingham memorandum (Nov. 1765), Rockingham Papers, R. 49-2. Neither Langford nor Thomas notices the significance of this paper for an understanding of Rockingham's position on the Stamp Act. For further evidence of his concern about the impact of requiring stamps on plantation bonds and other documents in colonial trade see two more untitled memoranda he wrote in Nov. 1765. These reveal that Trecothick's point about the harm stamp duties could do to the provisions trade between North America and the West Indies particularly worried Rockingham, even though he discovered to his relief that they would not harm that commerce in 1765. *Ibid.*, R. 49-14, 17. Possibly the persuasiveness of Trecothick's arguments against the admiralty court and in favor of permitting payment of the duties in colonial currency was enhanced for Rockingham by a paper sent him by Henry McCulloh, the progenitor of the stamp tax. McCulloh urged the marquis to make both changes, and particularly stressed that since the tax would collect itself there was no reason to fear that local juries could defeat its operation. Removing jurisdiction from the admiralty court would thus have the happy result of placating American opinion without affecting revenue collections. Rockingham endorsed the essay "Mr. McCulloh's general thoughts on the right the legislature has to tax the British colonies, in all cases of public and general concern," [1765], *ibid.*, R. 65-6. A copy of this memorandum in the papers of Thomas Townshend, a lord of the Treasury under Rockingham, has been published in Jack P. Greene, "'A Dress of Horror': Henry McCulloh's Objections to the Stamp Act," *Huntington Library Quarterly*, XXVI (1963), pp.257-262.

[29] Burke, paper endorsed "America" (Nov. 1765), Burke Papers, A. xxvii-81, Northamptonshire Record Office.

[30] Rockingham, notes, Nov. [28], 1765, Rockingham Papers, R. 49-6. Rockingham misdated the paper Nov. 27.

[31] For Trecothick's activities in December see Langford, *Rockingham Administration*, pp. 110-111, 119-124, and Thomas, *British Politics*, pp.144-150.

[32] Langford, *Rockingham Administration*, pp.110, 125-126.

[33] James to Cadwallader Colden (after Jan. 31, 1766), The *Letters and Papers of Cadwallader Colden*, VII, in New York Historical Society, *Collections*, LVI (1923), p. 98. That James brought Gage's Nov. 4 letter to his interview with Conway is confirmed by the endorsement on it in *Gage Correspondence*, ed. Carter, I, p. 72.

[34] Gage to Conway, Nov. 4, 1765, *Gage Correspondence*, ed. Carter, I, p. 71. A second letter from Gage, dated Nov. 8, reported that the resistance had succeeded

everywhere in preventing distribution of the stamps and intimidating anyone wishing to pay the tax. This letter arrived on Dec. 11 and may have been considered at that evening's cabinet meeting. *Ibid.*, p.73.

[35] Northington to the king, Dec. 12, 1765, in *The Correspondence of King George the Third from 1760 to December 1783*, ed. Sir John Fortescue, I (London, 1927), p. 429. See also L. B. Namier, *Additions and Corrections to Sir John Fortescne's Edition of the Correspondence of King George the Third* (Vol. 1) (Manchester, Eng., 1937), p. 68.

[36] Langford, *Rockingham Administration*, pp. 126-127.

PART SIX: RETREATING FROM REFORM

Chapter XVI

Roads not Taken: Lord North's Plan for Imperial Reform, 1775-76

That the many and various parts Lord North played during Britain's imperial crisis have been frequently studied is hardly surprising: whether one accepts the traditional view of him as "the prime minister who lost America" or not, he clearly was a significant figure in politics from the late 1760s to the end of the war in 1783.[1] What does surprise is this: North's commitment to imperial reform from early in his career and his efforts to convert ideas into real changes of the Empire's politics and finances during 1775-1776 have rarely been recognized.

In part, this is because of the gaps in his papers; his carelessness in handling his personal finances extended to a haphazard maintenance of correspondence files. In part, too, it is the result of his work habits; North tended to bury himself in the daily details of business at the House of Commons and the Treasury, in the process denying himself the time to craft plans for future policies. It was easy and many times comforting for such a practical politician to turn a blind eye to the contours of the forest and focus on the trees. Most of all, though, the paucity of evidence was the result of North's distinctive *modus operandi* as the King's Minister. Unlike some of his famous contemporaries on both sides of the Atlantic, he saw little to be gained by a comprehensive theoretical exploration of necessary reforms. Still less did he feel any urge to discuss his ideas in detail with others. He preferred to introduce his thoughts when circumstances demanded decisions, then tailor them to fit specific, immediate issues. This reticence preserved his options and suited his personality. Of course, it also camouflages the genesis of his plans and the principles shaping them from historians. To expose them and thereby discern the serious imperial reformer who devised them one must take his early years in politics into account, and to examine his 1775-1776 proposals to reconcile Britain and her colonies in the political context of his times. Some of his ideas he had held for years; others were the product of the crisis between the Boston Tea Party and the Declaration of Independence. Together they molded North's thoughts on how to save an empire and position it for prosperity and harmony in the years ahead.

North served on the Treasury Board during the Bute and Grenville Administrations. He participated in discussions about what to do about the huge national debt created by the struggle against France and Spain in the Seven Years War. He was part of the consensus that concluded it was essential to maintain taxes at wartime levels and to find new sources of revenue. He agreed it was also essential to reduce peacetime expenses on the military, and to find ways of doing this without weakening Britain's defenses too much. He believed much of this debt had been contracted to defend Britain's North American colonies. He knew many of the unavoidable expenses for the military in peace arose from the need to establish British authority in the new colony of Quebec, which was kept in large part to maintain the security of British North America. To him and to his colleagues, that Americans should help bear the expense of these troops and thus reduce London's costs for security was absolutely just. To raise these contributions in the most certain way possible, it was necessary for Parliament to tax Americans. Like the others, North was positive the House of Commons had the right to do this. He was sure it had to do this. And he was convinced George Grenville had found the ideal taxes to accomplish this end. Grenville had persuaded him that lowering the duty on foreign molasses imported into North America and levying a stamp tax on colonists were perfect revenue measures for people unaccustomed to paying British duties and disposed to find ways to evade them. In particular the Stamp Act would enforce itself, because it was clearly in the self-interest of the taxpayers to purchase the stamps.[2]

In the years that followed, North's commitment to three principles he adopted during the early 1760s never wavered. He was sure Americans were legally obligated to pay parliamentary taxes. He was positive they were morally obligated to help with the burdens of defense as well. Finally, he remained convinced that the Mother Country needed financial assistance from her colonies. He persisted in these convictions in the teeth of a fierce American resistance to parliamentary taxation and a persistent colonial refusal to acknowledge any moral obligation for British sacrifices during the last war. He stayed the course despite the fact the nation's finances did not collapse in the 1760s when it received no significant help from North America and successive ministries overspent the original peacetime budget for the army. Even the unexpected and unwelcome reduction of a major source of domestic revenue—the Earl of Chatham's Administration was shocked by the House of Commons' vote on February 27, 1767 to lower the land tax from 4 to 3 shillings in the pound, which subtracted from the Exchequer an estimated £500,000 in revenue—did not bring about a fiscal crisis.[3] Despite this opposition from across the Atlantic and the absence of any signs of impending financial or military disaster, North continued to believe an American tax was constitutionally and morally justified and financially necessary. He also continued to look for ways to achieve an American revenue. In that search he was inspired by more than simply concerns about raising money from the colonies. Considerations of imperial politics also compelled North's persistence. Successfully creating a source of funds from America would measurably strengthen Britain's authority over her colonies.

North did not, however, cling to a belief that British ministers could find a parliamentary tax that fell directly on individual colonists. George Grenville had been spectacularly wrong. The stamp tax did not collect itself; instead, it inspired a well-orchestrated campaign that combined violence by crowds, boycotts of British goods by merchants, and protests by assemblies and an extra-legal congress into an irresistible resistance to the tax and British authority. North shared the universal surprise in London at the powerful and widespread movement. Since he had lost his office when the king replaced Grenville with the Marquis of Rockingham, he did not have any responsibility for devising a response to the crisis. He opposed repeal, a step made easier by the fact he did not have to come up with some way of enforcing obedience. When he returned to office, it soon became clear that he had recognized and accepted a new imperial reality: if Britain repeated the experiment with direct taxation, the nation would be again confronted by massive popular disobedience. That disobedience had the potential to damage British commerce, further weaken British authority, and encourage more colonial unity against the Mother Country. Dealing with such a situation with military force was problematic. North never commented on Edmund Burke's description in 1765 on the difficulties the military would face in compelling collection of the stamp tax, but he clearly was familiar with those arguments.[4] (As we will see, during 1774-76 he listened carefully to similar misgivings about using troops against colonial protesters.) His conclusion was reasonable and realistic: Parliament unquestionably had the right to tax Americans directly, but attempts to exercise that right were unquestionably ill-advised and inexpedient. As he later confessed in the House of Commons on February 20, 1775, taxing Americans was uniquely difficult, "partly because we may not be as knowing in the detail as the American Assemblies; and we may oppress when we meant only to tax; and partly because it has been found nearly impossible for Parliament to lay taxes there, which would produce any thing in any degree adequate to their purposes."[5]

America's successful resistance to the Stamp Act helped focus North's attention on what he perceived as another reality of empire. Riots against stamp distributors, the prevention of the execution of the law, and other forms of popular resistance to British officials revealed that the executive authority in America was helpless against popular politicians and the crowds they could easily summon up. To Charles Townshend, the cause of this was obvious. The executive in all of the colonies was dependant upon annual appropriations from the popular assemblies. Governors and other officials had to cater to the public will; otherwise, their salaries and other necessary funds were in jeopardy of being cut or outright denied. This fact of life forced royal appointees to pay more attention to colonial wishes than instructions from London. It habituated them to looking first for support in America rather than toward home; it had the effect—to borrow a term from 20th century British civil servants—of making them "go native." To cure this, Townshend proposed in 1767 that the customs duties Parliament was imposing on Americans be designated to pay the salaries of royal officials and judges. Making them independent fiscally from the assemblies was a necessary reform. Without it, executive power and British authority would always be at serious disadvantage in contests with the people's representatives. North found this reasoning completely convincing. From 1767 forward, he believed royal officials had to be made as financially independent as possible of the assemblies.[6]

So committed was he on this point that in 1769 he made a fateful mistake. When the Cabinet debated whether to repeal all of the Townshend duties, North's was the deciding vote against including the tax on tea. In March 1770 he explained his decision in a major speech to the House of Commons. The duties on paint, glass, and lead fell on goods manufactured in Britain, and thus could be described as harmful to domestic manufacturers. Tea was foreign in origin. Moreover, tea was a luxury. It was not a necessity of life, so Americans could choose whether to consume it or not. They certainly could not claim they had to drink it! Finally, though the revenue it produced was small, it was more than the other duties produced. North predicted it would continue to increase as Americans became wealthier and more able to buy this luxury. Finally—and this was the most compelling reason for North—it would continue to help pay the expenses of royal government. That, he added, was "the purpose for which it was laid." And he was sure the need for that independent revenue had not disappeared.[7]

Was it possible repealing the tea duty would bring Britain and North America closer together? If so, North implied, the concession might be worth the lost funds. Such was not the case. "I am not clear that repealing the whole will appease them." In May 1769 the Earl of Hillsborough, the Secretary of State for America, had informed governors that "the opinion of the king's servants that it is by no means the intention of Administration nor do they think it expedient or for the interest of Great Britain or America to propose or consent to the laying any further taxes upon America for the purpose of raising a revenue." This concession had not moderated American protests nor convinced them to end non-importation agreements against importing British goods. Repealing the tea tax would no doubt encourage them to demand the repeal of the duty on foreign molasses. Accepting their distinction between taxes for revenue and taxes to regulate the trade would settle nothing. They would call all duties taxes for revenue; London would label them regulations of trade. "It is drawing a line which does not settle one dispute." The colonists had not earned further indulgence. Far from settling anything, this would encourage more confrontations that weakened, dependent royal executives and judiciaries were once more incapable of resisting. Given these attitudes, North's conviction that governors and judges had to be supported with permanent revenues was further fortified.[8]

So North brought with him two goals for colonial reform as he settled into being the First Lord of the Treasury and the Leader of the House of Commons in 1770. The first had its genesis during his tenure at the Treasury under Bute and Grenville: finding a way to generate mandatory, regular, sufficient, and permanent American contributions to the cost of imperial defense. The second originated in his experiences from 1767 to 1770: finding ways to grow the tea duty so it could raise a sufficient permanent revenue to make royal executives and judges in the colonies more independent of the assemblies. By the time news of the Boston Tea Party reached England, these goals had become the basis of his conception of what the empire ought to have in the future. When the crisis begun by "Mohawks" in Boston metastasized in 1774-1775, this conception became the backbone of his proposal to settle the immediate crisis and provide the basis for a peaceful and profitable empire in the future. To make them more attractive to

Americans, he was prepared to make what he felt were significant concessions on certain issues. The whole scheme he described as conciliatory; more accurately, what he was suggesting was a settlement that would reconcile Britain and America by restoring the close relationship the two had before 1763 and strengthening it significantly.

North's intimate adviser Charles Jenkinson recalled on February 20, 1775 that in 1764 Grenville had told colonial agents he was willing to consider suggestions for specific taxes from the colonies. As he remembered the episode, the colonies themselves had asked for this opportunity. Some agents had actually presented proposals to the Treasury, where they were rejected by Grenville, who, according to Benjamin Franklin's tart recollection, was too "besotted with his stamp scheme" to listen to reason. In contrast, no tax besotted North. He did not care how the assemblies raised the money. That was up to them. He expressed in straightforward terms what they would be required to do and what they would gain on February 20, 1775.[9]

When any colony by an official act "shall propose to make Provision, according to the Conditions, Circumstances, and Situation of such Province or Colony for contributing their Proportion to the common Defense (such Proportion to be raised under the Authority of the General Court or General Assembly of such Province or Colony, and disposable by Parliament) and shall engage to make Provision also, for the Support of the Civil Government, and the Administration of Justice in such Province or Colony; it will be proper, if such Proposal shall be approved by his Majesty, and the two Houses of Parliament, and for so long as such Provision shall be made accordingly, to forbear in respect of such Province or Colony, to levy any Duty, Tax, or Assessment, or to impose any further Duty, Tax, or Assessment; except only such Duties, as it may be expedient to impose for the Regulation of Commerce. The Net Produce of the Duties last mentioned to be carried to the Account of such Province or Colony respectively." What he was offering was suspension of Parliament's exercise of its right of taxation, freedom from present and future parliamentary taxes for revenue, and the allocation of net receipts from any regulations of commerce to the colonial treasuries in return for permanent revenue contributing to imperial defense and guaranteeing the basic expenses of internal government in the colonies. To North, this would mean "the quarrel on the subject of taxation was at an end." Great Britain would get what it needed; America, what it wanted.[10]

But how would the system actually work? How much would, say, Massachusetts Bay owe? How much would, for instance, Georgia have to pay? How would their respective contributions to imperial defense be determined? In February 1775 North was clear on one point: "this proposition ought not to be settled by a Congress." He explained why. "Such a mode could only tend to promote factious combinations in the colonies; who, as colonies, have no sort of relation among themselves. They are all colonies of Great Britain; and it is through her alone that they have any relation to each other." Britain would not accept propositions from any successor to the Continental Congress that had met in Philadelphia during the fall of 1774. Individual colonies would have to agree to the proposal and approach London separately. The British government would then make the decisions about what each should pay. As a result, "at present the quota which each colony ought to pay, cannot be settled." Once some or all indicated their acceptance of the deal, "the proportions (when the Americans come to make their offers) must be adjusted on the following standard—the wealth and population of each colony—its advantages relative to the other colonies—and its proportion to the wealth and other advantages, taken together with her burdens and necessities, of Great Britain." This settled, the colonies could proceed to choose and lay taxes sufficient to create a permanent establishment in each colony and to pay its share to the common defense.[11]

North did not anticipate this plan would win immediate approval in America. Instead, he expected most colonies would reject it. They would continue to press for complete freedom from annual appropriations for imperial defense and they would defend keeping royal officials in dependence on the assemblies. What North hoped was that some colonies (particularly New York) would be willing to bargain. He freely conceded that one of the attractions of his proposal was dividing the colonies against each other. Rather optimistically, he predicted to the House of Commons "if but ONE of them submitted, that ONE link of the chain would be broken; and if so, the whole [would] inevitably fall to pieces." *Divide et impera* "was a maxim never held unfair or unwise in government," and this use of that hoary tactic would restore the empire. But aside from that consideration, North felt this was the best way of resolving future disputes over imperial finance. It was not just an expedient chosen to suit the present crisis; it was meant to prevent future controversies.[12]

In the meantime, he was facing an immediate controversy right before his eyes. This proposal sparked a bitter and confused debate in the House of Commons. North had assumed he could rely on votes from the ranks of the opposition, who had been arguing for compromise with America for months. For that reason, he had taken the extraordinary step of asking them to attend and consider "a motion of importance" he intended to make. But their response disappointed him. They were skeptical. They predicted Americans would reject it, because it amounted to a tax imposed by Britain. After all, it would be Britain who determined what reasonable contributions would be from each colony, rewarding those who met the targets London set, punishing those who did not. Whether to tax or not was not an option for the colonial assemblies. How much revenue had to be raised was not up to them. What that revenue would be appropriated for was outside their control. They had to tax. They had to raise the assigned amount. They had to grant it to the British military and the royal executive. All of these choices were out of their hands. They could only choose the mode of taxation and who within the colony would pay it. This indulgence was minor beside the compulsion to raise the funds for those purposes. "To leave them the mode," argued opposition speakers like Edmund Burke and Isaac Barrè, "may be some ease as to the *Collection*; but it is nothing to the Freedom of granting; in which the colonies are so far from being relieved by this resolution, that their condition is to be ten times worse than ever . . . a far more oppressive mode of taxing than that hitherto used." Why? Because "here no determinate demand is made.... They are to be held prisoners of war, unless they consent to a ransom, by bidding at an auction against each other and against themselves, until the King and Parliament shall strike down the hammer, and say 'enough.'" And the prisoners would not be the only sufferers. The auctioneers would come in for their share of grief. Suppose an assembly made an offer Parliament felt was too low—"was not the business to walk back again to America? And so on backwards and forwards as often as the offer displeased Parliament? And thus instead obtaining peace by this proposition, all our distractions and confusions will be increased tenfold, and continued forever."[13]

Objections from his eloquent opponents must have disappointed North. He had hoped they would agree with him that this proposition promised peace in the future for Britain and her colonies. He may even have hoped that the opposition's approval would cause Americans to look on his conciliatory proposal less suspiciously and, ultimately, more favorably.

But this disappointment disturbed North less than the hostility shown by many of the supporters of government. To them, this amounted to a surrender of Parliament's right to tax. What was the purpose of this confrontation with America if not to compel colonists to accept the supremacy of Parliament and pay taxes passed by the House of Commons? North's proposal seemed to them a prelude to another series of concessions by the British government. What they fastened on was the absence of any preconditions for starting negotiations over this mode of raising funds. Welbore Ellis, a veteran friend of government, made their point most succinctly. "In any measure that I can agree to, I must expect to meet with, as the first step in the business, an express and definite acknowledgement from the Americans, of our supremacy. Without that point first settled, I can neither receive nor consent to any other propositions." Concessions had not restored stability in the empire; rather, they had encouraged more claims of immunity from parliamentary laws and more outrages by American mobs. Ellis was too loyal to his leader to observe that North himself had made that point when he rejected the repeal of the tea tax in 1770; he did not need to, for this often repeated argument was fresh in everyone's mind. In any event, Ellis's bottom line was clear: now was the time to draw the line and stick to it. It was not the time for more ambiguity and timidity on American taxation.[14]

North had answers to these objections from both sides of the American issue. Though he may have yearned for unanimity on his proposal, he was too experienced to be unprepared for debate. Over the last 15 years he had become familiar with the arguments advanced by both extremes on the spectrum of imperial debates. He had learned how to thread his way between them. This debate was no exception. North prevailed, 274 to 88.[15] What is more important than tracing this demonstration of his practiced parliamentary skills is recognizing that nothing said by anyone caused him to doubt the rightness of his conciliatory proposition. North was not trying to find by himself a resolution that suddenly and completely satisfied both parties. The participants would have to negotiate solutions between themselves. What North aimed at creating was a context that encouraged negotiation and an institutional framework that would facilitate agreement.

It is important to note that this was a familiar tactic for him and other politicians. Controversies both great and small in the eighteenth century customarily ended in negotiated settlements, with all those involved getting something and losing something. Wars did not end in conquests and dictated settlements.[16] They were ended by painstaking and protracted talks which eventuated in treaties each side could live with for the next few years. Witness the Treaty of Paris ending the Seven Years War, when Britain returned Guadeloupe and Martinique to France in order to retain Quebec. In the same way, dropping any claims to Havana enabled the nation to gain the Floridas and peace from Spain.[17] On the domestic scene, factions endlessly bargained with each other over offices and patronage. Determined to keep his step-brother the Earl of Dartmouth in the cabinet for support, North juggled appointments in 1776 until this could be achieved. The strengthening of the military effort against America by the addition to Lord George Germain depended upon finding Dartmouth a place he would accept.[18] What North was attempting to accomplish in 1775 was the extension of this process of vigorous bargaining and ultimate compromise to the American question.

The first step toward this was the submerging of assertions of Parliament's right to tax colonists. As we have seen, North believed the House of Commons could tax America in theory, but saw nothing to be gained by a noisy insistence on this principle in the face of the reality that exercising that right would be extremely difficult, endlessly destabilizing, and quite possibly counter-productive. Far better it would be to let colonists agree to reasonable taxes imposed and collected by them for defense and government. That would achieve the purposes of Parliamentary taxation without creating arguments over representation and English liberties. So eager was North to get off the subject of constitutional issues that he did not want Americans to concede Parliament's right to tax as a precondition to negotiations.[19] In his opinion, talks that started with a rehearsal of old grievances were likely to stall, if not abort. Negotiations should end with acceptance of Parliament's supremacy in theory. That should be the capstone of imperial agreement. Inserting it should follow naturally (and quietly) after every other building block had been laid.

Once talks began, the process of horse trading would, North hoped, achieve its own momentum. Bargaining over amounts and length of appropriations would proceed in a spirit of give and take. He was willing to give the House of some of his preferences on the outcome of negotiations. On February 27, 1775, he noted that his plan aimed for "preserving the right of

Parliament to tax the colonies; but for transferring the exercise of that right to the colony assemblies." Then he went on, "he did not nor could not at present to pretend to specify the exact sum they ought to raise, as it would probably fluctuate by bearing a certain proportion to the sums raised in Great Britain." North did not explain the advantage of a set percentage, but he hardly needed to: agreement on that proportion would prevent constant debate on what was a just contribution. Instead, he described the next step in the process. "Whatever propositions they might make would be received in a legal way from an assembly lawfully and properly constituted, in order to be laid before Parliament for their final approbation." One question remained: would this be an annual appropriation? Unsurprisingly, North was wary of the sort of annual battles American assemblies had been accustomed to making. He preferred an allocation that would be permanent during ordinary times. "Whether the grants [from the colonies] were to be an annual one, or for a term of years . . . he could not tell." He did tell the House his opinion, which he must have intended as a broad hint of what Britain's position would be in the negotiations. "For his part he should wish it to be the latter, otherwise it would return to interrupt the public business every session, and consequently, be a perpetual subject of discussion and disagreement."[20] This should be a perpetual settlement except in times of acute imperial emergency.

Left unstated but clearly implied was North's feeling that peace and calm on issues of finance would be conducive to not only a stable empire, but also it would allow the formation of alliances and communities of political and economic interests bridging the Atlantic. These usual eighteenth century practices of sweetening deals with understandings on patronage appointments and bounties favoring some interests would occur. The *douceurs* would lubricate negotiations and speed agreement. They would also help establish communities of interest that would operate to make future conversations easier to manage efficiently and conclude profitably. Relationships would form and political understandings would consummate. The result would be an imperial system stretching across the Atlantic that would be very similar to the one dominating decisions at Whitehall and Westminster.

In early 1775, North assumed these negotiations would be carried out between individual assemblies and London. Though he certainly was made aware by critics in the House of Commons about the complexities of this system, evidently he felt willing minds could work them out once individual colonies accepted his terms and initiated bargaining on the details. After fighting began, he expressed a willingness to add another institution to his system. The colonies had been meeting in congress since September 1774, and that congress had been deeply engaged in the organization of resistance in North America and the expression of American grievances to the king and Parliament. Americans had become accustomed to meeting together in a loosely structured central alliance, and they had dealt with the problems of making congress capable of making decisions that colonists remote from Philadelphia would accept. A loyal gathering of delegates from several colonies, one subordinate to Parliament, would facilitate agreement on quotas for imperial taxes and simplify negotiations with Whitehall and Westminster. North was prepared to negotiate with such a group. He and his colleagues carefully avoided using the word "congress" to describe it, and he vigorously denied on February 20, 1776 that he had ever communicated or negotiated with the Congress presently meeting in Philadelphia.[21] Yet clearly he was willing to discuss matters with a collective gathering of colonies, and he must have recognized that such an ad hoc arrangement could easily extend indefinitely into the future. Evidently he did not see this creation of a body that might establish quotas for each colony as a threat to the British Empire's existence. Others in London did; North did not. Why?

The answer is his confidence the same sort of connections would develop between this group and politicians in Britain that he had been sure would develop between loyal assemblymen and Britons. Deals would be sealed; friendships established; the imperial connection cemented by the stabilizing system that already ruled Britain. He himself provided examples of such deals. He told the House in November 1775 "he should also be ready to repeal the tea duty on the same grounds that he would suspend every exercise of the right of taxation, if the colonies themselves would point out any mode by which they would bear their share of the burden and give their aid to the common defense."[22] Later, in February 1776, he pointed to another concession. "The application of the port-duties to the services of the colony where such duties should happen to arise, which plainly removed the only objection that had been made to them, that of drawing the produce of such duties into the British exchequer."[23] Expanding these sorts of arrangements further and continuing them during the years ahead would be the culmination of the perfect imperial reform.

Before any of this could transpire, Americans had to be willing to start negotiations. Events between 1774-1776 left North with no illusions about the difficulty of accomplishing this. The provincial congresses in New England and the Continental Congress in Philadelphia had no interest in setting aside the issue of Parliament's right to tax and talking about other issues. To the contrary: these bodies wanted an effective renunciation of that right from London. This intransigence confirmed a corresponding stubbornness among British hard-liners. Germain, for example, suspected that North's argument that confirming Parliamentary supremacy be the last act of an imperial pact signaled a readiness to yield on this vital point; accordingly, he wanted American acceptance of Parliament's supremacy to be a *sine qua non* for any negotiations. In the end, the point was left up to the two commissioners sent to America to determine, though their instructions required an undefined "submission" by a colony to British authority before any conversation over restoration to the empire could happen. This flexibility was the best North and Lord Howe and his brother Sir William could get.[24]

And that leeway did not affect the basic stumbling block to any negotiations: Americans were not interested in North's proposition. It made its way to Congress, where it lay on the table with no formal discussion. Equally telling, the Americans were not only silent on it; but also they made no counter-proposal. Peter Thomas's observation about their position and its significance deserves underlining. North's "very real efforts to resolve the American problem . . . met only with rejection from the colonists." Thomas concluded, "There was in truth nothing that North could offer that would meet American demands."[25]

That Britain would have to compel Americans to negotiate was obvious. Equally clear was the fact military coercion must play the major role. The colonists would have to be convinced the price of armed resistance was too high and the outcome too uncertain. Then they would turn to the various political deals—North's conciliatory proposal, restoration of trade with Britain and the West Indies, pardons for rebellion—offered them.

What was the best way to apply military pressure? North's choice is by no means clear. His keen sense of his own deficiencies as a wartime leader, plus his genuine wish to avoid bloodshed, made him a wary and reluctant participant in the formulation of policy. One would think his undoubted skills as a financier and his extensive knowledge of the budget would have inspired his colleagues to ask him to estimate the comparative expense of various strategies, but there is no sign that anyone quizzed him on this. Nor is there any record of his volunteering such information. The king and his ministers accepted that this necessary enterprise would be a costly undertaking, and trusted North to find the money by a combination of increased taxes and careful agreements with public creditors. Their faith was justified. He was a very capable wartime finance minister, carefully keeping increases on the property of the well-to-do (the land tax was raised to 4s. in the pound) rather than on the necessities of the poor; finding new sources of funds (particularly ingenious was his realizing a profit from public lotteries); and keeping the principal and interest on loans manageable.[26] Still, he did not extend his fiscal ingenuity to determining the most cost-productive way of using the army and the navy.

North did, however, have a preference for which service should bear the chief responsibility for restoring the empire to peace and prosperity. Clues scattered in his public remarks and Dartmouth's private papers indicate he inclined toward the use of a naval blockade to reduce American commerce as the most promising way of bringing the colonists to their senses and to the bargaining table.

Although North did not doubt the ability of British soldiers to have their way with American troops, he had frequently heard about the difficulties of a land campaign, especially in New England. In particular, Lord Barrington urged reliance on the Royal Navy. In a private letter to Dartmouth in late 1774, the Secretary at War doubted that the troops in America could ever subdue it. The country is "of great extent and full of men accustomed to firearms." It was true, he conceded, "they have not hitherto been thought brave; but enthusiasm gives vigor of mind and body unknown before." Besides, even if New England were conquered, it would have to be garrisoned with large armies at a "ruinous and endless expense." That prospect called another objection to his mind: "the most successful campaign imaginable would produce the horrors and bloodshed of civil war." Most telling, however, of all to Barrington was the fact that conquest by land was unnecessary. The country "could be reduced, first to distress and then to obedience, by the navy in interrupting commerce and fishery and even seizing all ships in the ports, with little expense and less bloodshed."[27]

When Dartmouth shared this last thought with his step-brother, North surely was impressed, and not just because he respected the power of the Royal Navy. He had never questioned the power of economic self-interest on men's opinions. It was the dominant force in his political world. As First Lord of the Treasury, he regularly appealed to that interest as a means of furthering the public business. Where bloodshed might embitter, a return to consuming imported goods and profiting from the market in them would seem attractive. Once that happened, bargaining to renew commercial transactions would appear reasonable. That would be the ideal end of the imperial controversy for North.

Finally, relying chiefly on a blockade appealed to him personally as well. His was not a bellicose, aggressive, war-like personality. Rather than imposing his will on others, he was more comfortable reasoning and persuading, all the while maintaining polite, low key conversations about issues. His understated sense of humor and the amiable relations he preserved even with the parliamentary opposition reveal the political tactics he was most comfortable with. The Royal Navy was a gloved hand tempering the power of a mailed fist. It was—to use a 21st century term—soft power. Thus it was North's choice.

His personality foreclosed any possibility this would be the government's strategy. North was not capable of saying, as Pitt the Elder allegedly did, that he could save the country and no one else could. He did not have the drive or the energy to do this; most of all, he lacked The Great Commoner's absolute confidence during the 1750s in his own abilities. And North was incapable of bullying and compelling his colleagues to follow his lead. Despite the fact George III regarded him as indispensable, he was temperamentally prevented from taking full advantage of the support from the Royal Closet. That he would lean in the Cabinet on the slender reed of Dartmouth, a man who could not summon up enough will to defend his convictions that Britain must reconcile itself with its colonies, exposes his doubts about his own power. Neither of the brothers had the nerve or the will to resist George III and their cabinet colleagues when they insisted on reinforcing General Thomas Gage with more troops in 1775. What happened next demonstrates the aptness of a complaint Georges Clemenceau made years later at the end of the Great War: "it is much easier to make war than peace." When those regiments landed in New England after considerable trouble and expense, deciding to use them in offensive operations was politically irresistible. Not using them would have suggested to the rebellious colonists that Britain had neither the will nor the means to compel obedience. Back home, a majority in the House of Commons would be in an uproar over ministerial timidity and wastefulness. When the reinforcements proved ineffective, the decision to add even greater numbers to demonstrate superiority over armed but untrained rebels was again irresistible. No minister dared demur by suggesting this might be once more reinforcing failure with similarly unsatisfactory results.[28]

Rather than doing this, North burrowed into the fiscal details at the Treasury, focusing with equal intensity on both great issues of finance and the minutiae of daily operations. Lord George Germain, who was brought into the government to inject vigor into the war effort, beat the drums for victory on land against the Americans. Germain was also convinced he had to produce a crushing triumph; anything less might give the rebels enough wiggle room to start negotiations, which he feared would encourage North and others to make peace without requiring an explicit colonial acknowledgement of parliamentary supremacy. William Knox, the undersecretary in the American department, summed up his thinking: "Lord George having now collected a vast force, and having a fair prospect of subduing the Colonies, he wished to reduce them before he treated at all." If talks began before Americans were reduced to military impotence, "neither ministers nor Parliament would renew the war for the sake of the declaration" of the supremacy of Parliament.[29] His approach to the crisis, not North's, dominated planning of the American war during the crucial years 1776-77.

The ascendancy of Germain put an end to any chance North's ideas for imperial reform and reconciliation would shape British strategy during the pre-Saratoga years of the American War for Independence. The prospects for a breakthrough were slender in any event; the men who directed the war effort of the United States were committed to independence. Moreover, they were opposed to the idea of an American Parliament operating within the confines of the empire well before the Declaration of Independence. When Joseph Galloway proposed a colonial parliament elected by the assemblies and presided over by a president chosen by the king with the power to handle matters involving more than one colony and the right to have an equal voice with the British Parliament in passing laws and taxes affecting the Britain and America, Patrick Henry immediately argued such an American legislature would be corrupted by "that nation which avows in the face of the world that bribery is a part of her system of government."[30] North's collection of colonies willing to enter into talks with London would be even more vulnerable to British-style corruption, because it would not have had equal status with the one in London. In effect, when Congress rejected Galloway's Plan of Union by one vote in September 1774, it doomed North's reforms months before he presented them to the House of Commons.

Had that plan passed, North would have had the opening he desired to start negotiating a reformation in the political structure and the fiscal ways and means of the empire. But that chance went by the boards, just as the possibility a naval blockade could weaken the colonists' will without undue bloodshed did. George III's prediction on November 18, 1774 that "blows must decide whether they are to be subject to this country or independent" came true.[31] Negotiation and reform would have to await the uncertain outcome of an armed struggle on the North American continent.

That outcome did not favor Great Britain. As a result, North's design for imperial reform suffered the same fate as all the others advanced by public officials and private, self-appointed "experts" during the years 1763-1776. The realities of British and American politics and the swing of events made it the last of a series of failures.

Notes

[1] For biographies of Lord North, see Peter Whiteley, *Lord North: The Prime Minister Who Lost America* (London: The Hambledon Press, 1996); and Peter D. G. Thomas, *Lord North* (NY, NY, St. Martin's, 1976). The best studies of North in action are two other books by Professor Thomas: *The Townshend Duties*

Crisis: The Second Phase of the American Revolution, 1767-1773 (Oxford, The Clarendon Press, 1987); and *Tea Party to Independence: The Third Phase of the American Revolution, 1773-1776* (Oxford, The Clarendon Press, 1991).

[2] I have discussed the Grenville program at length in *A Great and Necessary Measure: George Grenville and the Genesis of the Stamp Act, 1763-1765* (Columbia MO, University of Missouri Press, 1982). Several of the chapters in this book also touch on Grenville's program. See especially ch. XIV.

[3] For concise accounts of the reduction of the land tax, see Thomas, *Townshend Duties*, p. 7; and Thomas, *North*, pp. 18-19.

[4] For Burke's remarks and a discussion of their significance, see ch. XV.

[5] See North's speech, Feb. 20, 1775, in R. C. Simmons and P. D. G. Thomas, eds., *Proceedings and Debates of the British Parliaments Respecting North America, 1754-1783*, V (Jun. 1774-Mar. 1775), (White Plains NY, Kraus International Publications, 1986), p. 436.

[6] See Thomas, *Townshend Duties*, pp. 30-35.

[7] *Ibid.*, pp. 172-174.

[8] North's speech, Mar. 5, 1770, in Simmons and Thomas, *Proceedings and Debates*, III, pp. 211-213.

[9] Charles Jenkinson's speech, Feb. 20, 1775, in *ibid.* V, pp. 445-446. Perhaps deliberately, Jenkinson's memory was in error on several important points. See Bullion, *Necessary Measure*, pp. 114-135. For Franklin's remark, see *ibid.*, p. 2.

[10] North's speech, Feb. 20, 1775, Simmons and Thomas, *Proceedings and Debates*, V, pp. 435, 440.

[11] *Ibid.*, p. 435.

[12] *Ibid.*, p. 436.

[13] See the synopsis of speeches by prominent members of the opposition in *ibid.*, pp. 437-438.

[14] Welbore Ellis's speech, Feb. 20, 1775, in *ibid.*, pp. 437, 446, 450-451. See also Thomas, *Tea Party*, pp. 202-204.

[15] A full account of both the background to this debate and the debate itself is in *ibid.*, pp. 193-204.

[16] I owe this insight to Jeremy Black, *War for America: The Fight for Independence, 1775-1783* (NY, St. Martin's, 1991), p. 24.

[17] For North's awareness of similar negotiations and "other instances in which Great powers had abandoned their pretensions, and disappointed the hopes they had held out to their allies," see his speech, Feb. 20, 1775, Simmons and Thomas, *Proceedings and Debates*, V, pp. 436-437.

[18] See Thomas, *Tea Party*, pp. 282-285; and William Knox, "Secretaries of State," in *The Manuscripts of Captain H. V. Knox*, Historical Manuscripts Commission, *Various Manuscripts*, V (London, His Majesty's Stationery Office, 1909), pp. 256-257.

[19] See Knox, "Proceedings in relation to the American Colonies," [1774-1775]; and "The First Commissioners to the American Colonies," [March 1776] in *ibid.*, pp. 257-260. See also North's speech, Dec. 1, 1775, Simmons and Thomas, *Proceedings and Debates*, VI, p. 314.

[20] North's speech, Feb. 27, 1775, *ibid.*, V, p. 475.

[21] See Thomas, *Tea Party*, pp. 318-319. For North's denial of any negotiations with Congress, see his speech, Feb. 20, 1776, Simmons and Thomas, *Proceedings and Debates*, VI, p. 397.

[22] North's speech, Nov. 20, 1775, *ibid.*, VI, p. 280.

[23] North's speech, Feb. 29, 1776, *ibid*, VI, p. 412.

[24] Thomas, *Tea Party*, pp. 313-319.

[25] *Ibid.*, p. 333

[26] The best account of North's prowess as a financier during wartime is Thomas, *Lord North*, pp. 96-106.

[27] Lord Barrington to the earl of Dartmouth, Dec. 24, 1774, Dartmouth Papers, Staffordshire Record Office, D1778II: 1035.

[28] Thomas, *Tea Party*, pp. 254-270; and Whiteley, *North*, pp. 152-153. Whiteley includes in his description Benjamin Franklin's scathing comment that since

Dartmouth "has in reality no will or judgment of his own, being with disposition for the best measures, is easily prevailed [on] to join in the worst." For the Clemenceau quotation, see Margaret MacMillan, *Paris 1919: Six Months that Changed the World* (NY,. Random House, 2001), p. xxx.

[29] Knox, "The First Commissioners to the American Colonies," [March 1776], *Manuscripts of Knox*, p. 259.

[30] Quoted in Merrill Jensen, *The Founding of a Nation: A History of the American Revolution, 1763-1776* (Oxford, Oxford University Press, 1968), p. 499. See *ibid.*, pp. 498-500 for the Galloway Plan and Congress's rejection of it.

[31] George III to North, Nov. 18, 1774, quoted in Thomas, *Tea Party*, p. 160.

Chapter XVII

The *Ancien Régime* and the Modernizing State: George III and the American Revolution*

In a variety of essays and books published over the last 15 years, J.C.D. Clark has insisted that eighteenth-century England should not be understood as a rapidly modernizing state and a precursor of the liberal politics and class society of Victorian Britain. According to him, it was a classic *ancien régime*, similar to other European governments, and like them, dominated politically by kings, courts, the aristocracy, and an established church. Like them, too, it was marked socially and culturally by an emphasis on *noblesse oblige*, deference, and tradition. Politics and governance did not separate the secular and the religious. Indeed, the worldly and the godly were closely entwined, so much so that the monarchy could still plausibly claim divine sanction for its existence and reasonably expect obedience from the realm's subjects on that basis. Society's ordered hierarchy was also divinely sanctioned. Resistance to the political state and the country's social arrangements could be condemned as both rebellion and apostasy, for God had ordained the way things were. This world-view was not unopposed in eighteenth-century England. Radical Whigs denied it, and Dissenters questioned the privileges and power of the Church of England. Because of this opposition, the government and Anglicanism had to remain united in the *ancien régime*'s defense. To underline the political and social significance of the church, which was expressed most fully in the twin beliefs that the nation had "a genuinely Christian government, guided by a Christian sovereign, on Christian principles" and that for these reasons there could not be "any notion of the justice of resistance to that government," Clark called eighteenth-century England a "confessional state."[1]

This interpretation of eighteenth-century English history is often convincing and always stimulating, though perhaps its attractiveness owes as much to Clark's considerable skill at polemics as to his wide ranging research in hitherto neglected Anglican tracts. To a historian of the American Revolution, however, there is a striking gap in his narrative. The revolution surfaces only briefly in his work. On one occasion, he did note that it raised the significant question of monarchical allegiance, but this observation did not inspire further investigation.[2] Nor did his realization that "colonial policy could sometimes make the underlying aim of a government more explicit than could domestic policy" encourage him to analyze Britain's plans for North America before and during the War for Independence.[3] But his failure to pursue these insights is less surprising than the absence of any discussion of the church's role in shaping and supporting a coercive policy toward Americans. Paul Langford has discovered that Anglican archbishops and bishops played parts thoroughly consonant with Clark's depiction of the church's function in British politics.[4] And meticulous research by James E. Bradley strongly suggests that while Dissenters tended to favor conciliation with the colonies, the Anglican clergy overwhelmingly supported waging war against rebellious subjects.[5] "Can the clergy remain silent spectators," asked an anonymous correspondent to *The Bristol Journal* on November 18, 1775, "when the church is equally in danger with the State?"[6] It is clear that the vast majority of those in holy orders, from the Archbishop of Canterbury down to the level of parish priest, answered that question "no." Certainly, Clark cannot be held accountable for overlooking research published after his major works. Even so, that he did not bother to discuss the church's responses to the imperial crisis is a significant omission.

In this chapter, I will ask what the concept of the confessional state contributes to our understanding of British reactions to events in North America during the War for Independence. In the interest of brevity, I will focus on those at the top of the political and ecclesiastical hierarchy: King George III and the bishops of the church.[7] The king is an appropriate choice to test the usefulness of Clark's arguments. He was not only the monarch but he was also a devout

Anglican who believed God intervened in the affairs of the world, and he distrusted and disliked eighteenth-century radicals at least as much as Clark does.[8] The princes of the church were the men responsible for instructing clergy and laity about the significance of the American war. They approved the *Forms of Prayer* which encapsulated the official position of the church, and promulgated it on fast days.[9] Narrowing my focus to the years of fighting is a fair test as well. What Clark defined as the fundamental issue in seventeenth- and eighteenth-century England, the question of allegiance, was obviously and inescapably at stake during 1775-1783.

I

As Paul Langford observed, the Church of England's reaction to the war against the crown's rebellious subjects "is one of the clearer aspects of the British response to the American Revolution."[10] With few exceptions, the clergy loyally supported a military solution to the crisis. Not many were as bloodthirsty as John Butler, who was serving in 1776 as a royal chaplain and was elevated in 1777 to the bishopric of Oxford. He greeted the news of the slaughter of Americans by British regulars on Long Island by observing "mankind cannot suffer by the extirpation of them," and applauded the use of Hessians because "it tends to Subjugation, which is the thing devoutly to be wished in the present case." Still, they shared that tireless seeker after preferment's enthusiasm for the cause.[11] Langford captured the institutional commitment of the church by quoting from the *Form of Prayer* published before fast days during the war. On a fast day in December 1776, clergy and laity prayed for the defeat of "the unjust attempt of their rebellious fellow-subjects against the right of our Sovereign, and the lawful authority of the legislature of these kingdoms." A second prayer asked God to "bless the arms of our gracious Sovereign, in the maintenance of His government and lawful rights, and [to] prosper His endeavours to restore tranquility among His unhappy deluded Subjects in *America*, now in open rebellion against His Crown, in defiance of all subordination and legal government." The same petitions for divine assistance were recited on fast days in 1777 and 1778. In February 1779, however, the first prayer was revised. Now the church referred only to opposing the Americans. The word "defeating" was conspicuous by its absence. A new version of the second prayer cut all references to the king's rights, open rebellion, and the defiance of subordination and lawful government. The next year the second prayer disappeared from the fast day liturgy. Then in 1782, bellicose language, complete with statements about open rebellion, due subordination, and lawful e government, abruptly reappeared in the fast service.[12]

Congregations may have wondered why the archbishops and bishops decided to return to these sentiments after the news of Yorktown reached Britain, but they had no reason to doubt the sincerity of these and earlier expressions of the church's commitment. In a political world dominated by calculations of personal and institutional self-interest, the support of the Anglican hierarchy for the attempt to prevent American independence was remarkably disinterested. They asked for no recognition or reward for their service to the cause. Even though this would seem to have been an opportune time to press for the creation of an Anglican establishment in America with a bishop at its head, the leaders of the church were less vocal in support of this proposal during the war than before it. Nor did they attempt to persuade the government to reject the Dissenters Toleration Act of 1779 by calling attention to their loyal opposition to American rebellion.[13] Evidently supporting the government in the imperial crisis was a matter of principle, a cross the church gladly bore without expectation of worldly advantage.

But what principle was at stake here? From late 1776 until early 1779, Anglicans prayed and worked for the defeat of men who were rebelling against the king and Parliament and in the process were opposing that proper subordination and lawful government the church participated in creating and sanctioned by its words and deeds. From early 1779 through 1781, however, the church merely "opposed" the Americans, just as it "opposed" two foreign enemies, the French and the Spanish. The idea of a struggle to maintain the colonies' allegiance to Britain and to defend the principles of political authority and social hierarchy as expressed in British society had been set aside. To be sure, ultimate victory was more doubtful now that Britain was fighting European enemies as well as the Americans. But if adversity affected the church's commitment to ideals it was certain were of great importance, then there must have been considerations it regarded as having equal or even greater significance. What those might have been were not revealed by its last position on the struggle in America. In a moment of catastrophic defeat, the Anglican hierarchy returned to its emphasis on the evils of rebellion. Whatever the explanation for these changes between 1776 and the end of the conflict, it is clear the attitudes of the Church of England were by no means as consistent on the nature and consequences of the American war as one might expect from reading Clark's argument that it played a crucial role in maintaining an ordered, hierarchical, confessional society and state.

II

George III's attitudes toward the imperial crisis were as strongly held and genuinely felt as those of the Anglican hierarchy. They are best studied in his private correspondence with his ministers and in the occasional memoranda he wrote to himself, where his opinions were not qualified by any need to be politic.

Soon after the Boston Tea Party, the king became an ardent convert to firmness in dealing with colonial resistance. "The fatal compliance [of] 1766," the repeal of the Stamp Act, "has encouraged the Americans annually to increase in their pretensions," claiming rights that independent nations have against each other, "but which [are] quite subversive of the obedience which a Colony owes to its Mother Country. They will be Lyons, whilst we are Lambs," he predicted, "but if we take the resolute part they will undoubtedly prove very meek."[14] When the colonial to response to the Coercive Acts was more leonine than he anticipated, he was not discouraged. "The dye is now cast, the Colonies must either submit or triumph." He did not want, he continued, "to come to severer measures but we must not retreat."[15] By November 1774, the king was ready to take "severer measures." To him, New England was clearly "in a State of Rebellion." Now "blows must decide whether they are to be subject to this Country or independent."[16] "We must either master them," the king pronounced, "or totally leave them to themselves and treat them as Aliens."[17]

This personal readiness to use force did not keep George III from grudgingly permitting Lord North to present conciliatory proposals to Parliament in early 1775, but his true preference was barely concealed. Realizing this, the minister sold him on the proposals by emphasizing that it would unify opinion in Britain even more in favor of coercing Americans. North did not hold out hope that it would be the basis for peace. At best, he told the king, it would influence only some in the colonies. The rest would have to be subdued by force. Then and only then, could the proposals be the foundation for a permanent settlement. Thereby assured that North recognized the necessity of military action, George III approved the plan.[18] Once fighting began, he pressed his minister for a quick declaration that North America was in rebellion. This, he believed, would show his subjects there and in Britain the government's determination to prosecute "with vigour every measure that may tend to force those deluded People to Submission."[19] George did not evade knowledge of what "vigour" meant: he knew the result would be suffering and death in America. In his opinion, that would be necessary. "The [too] great lenity of this Country increased their pride and encouraged them to rebel."[20] Until they had been hurt, they would not submit. Although he was not nearly as sanguinary as John Butler, he still emphasized in October 1777 that the commanders-in-chief of British naval and land forces in America, Lord Howe and his brother Sir William Howe, had to turn their "thoughts to the mode of War best calculated to end this contest;" that is, the "most distressing to the Americans," which they seem "as yet carefully to have avoided."

"To me," the king observed, "it has always appeared that there was more cruelty in protracting the War than in taking Acts of vigour which must bring the crisis to the Shortest decision."[21] When the king penned these words, Burgoyne's surrender at Saratoga was imminent, and France's open alliance with the Americans only months away.

Thus far in the war, George III's thoughts paralleled the position of the Anglican church. He regarded the conflict as a domestic controversy, and agreed with North that it was better to refer to *My Subjects in America* rather than *My American Subjects* in public pronouncements because the latter could be taken to imply colonists were somehow different than British subjects.[22] Those subjects in America had no reason whatsoever for rebelling. The king indignantly rejected the notion that "the Americans [were] poor mild persons who after unheard of and repeated grievances had no choice but Slavery or the Sword;" the opposite was the truth. Therefore restoring them to their proper subordination in the hierarchy of the empire justified making war against them. Indeed, this was the *only* justification for fighting George III cited during 1774-1777, with one exception. In late May 1777, he noted that accepting the American version of the war's origins would mean "the [West Indian] Islands would soon also cast off all obedience."[23] But this appeal to *realpolitik* was an afterthought; to the king, the fact that unjustified rebellion by subjects against the lawful exercise of legitimate authority had to be suppressed was sufficient unto itself. And, like his archbishops and bishops, he was confident that the government would succeed, even while expressing impatience for victory over the rebels.

Saratoga and the prospect of France's entry into the war dramatically changed George III's attitudes. He feared that henceforth the army in America would have to end any offensive campaigns.[24] No longer foreseeing triumph; he now could see that "perhaps the time may come when it will be wise to abandon all North America but Canada, Nova Scotia, and the Floridas." Before that could occur, he cautioned North, public opinion in Britain would have to change, too;

any such negotiation now would be repudiated.[25] Why it would be necessary soon "to end the War with that Country"—that is, America—was obvious: "to be enabled with redoubled vigour to avenge the faithless and insolent conduct of France." Why it was necessary to keep Canada, Nova Scotia, and Florida was equally clear: they "are Colonies belonging to this Country, and the more they are kept unlike the other Colonies the better, for it is by them we are to keep a certain awe over the abandoned Colonies."[26] When a French invasion threatened Britain, America became another "Country." George wanted "to secure the Dependence of America," but now he was referring to a strategic and military dependence, not a political one.[27] *Raison d'état* took precedence in a national emergency over the imperatives of defeating rebels and restoring subordination and obedience within the empire.

The king did not hold this bleak view of the future for very long. Soon a firm optimism came to dominate his thoughts about the war. He disclaimed any thoughts of giving up the coercion of America, and became instead, with Lord George Germain, the most determined opponent of American independence. But his reasons for fighting on had changed. By late 1778, he was not only grounding his decision on "the beauty, excellence and perfection of the British Constitution by law Established;" he also demanded North and others "consider that if any one branch of the Empire is allowed to cast off its dependency, that the others will infallibly follow the Example." It was therefore worth "going through any difficulty to preserve to latest Posterity what the Wisdom of our Ancestors have carefully transmitted to us."[28] When North later responded that "the advantages to be gained by this contest would never repay the expense," George stoutly replied, "this is only weighing such events in the Scale of a Tradesman behind his Counter." He elaborated, "should America succeed . . . the West Indies must follow them . . . [because] for its own interest [it must] be dependent on North America; Ireland would soon follow the same plan and be a separate State." Once Britain was reduced to itself, it "would be a poor Island indeed, for reduced in Her

Trade Merchants would retire with their Wealth to Climates more to their Advantage, and Shoals of Manufacturers would leave this country for the New Empire." Since "these self-evident consequences are not worse than what can arise should the Almighty permit every event to turn out to our disadvantage," the only sensible course was to persevere, fight, and hope for the best.[29]

As the war dragged on, George added one other consideration to his litany of disasters. Granting American independence would make him "despair of this Country being ever preserved from a state of inferiority and consequently falling into a very low class among the European states." Other nations would treat Britain accordingly, regarding her as she regarded herself.[30] That would be total ruin. "A small state," George argued, "may certainly Subsist, but a great one mouldering cannot get into an inferior Situation but must be anihilated." Britain could not think of "giving up the Game."[31]

The king's emphasis from late 1777 through the end of the war on the significance of winning the war with America for preserving the nation's prosperity, prestige, and power reflected the same concerns the church had when it amended its fast day prayers to "opposing" America. Although neither king nor church conceded independence, in effect both regarded the revolted colonies as another country, and one which, in league with the Bourbon powers, posed a major threat to the British state. The king's reasons for being optimistic about the outcome underscore this point. According to George, Britain would triumph over America because the "demagogues" and the people they deluded had not formed an efficient and powerful enough government to compete with European powers. America could not finance its war effort; its debt was already mountainous and rapidly increasing.[32] The people would soon realize they could not go on without aid from some other nation, and France would exact subservience as the price of her support. That realization, plus the other distresses their government could not prevent, and the prospect of ruin, would lead to a popular rejection of the struggle for independence and a return to the mild rule of Britain. All the nation had to do was remain firm, and offer no encouragement to its foes that it would ever give up.[33] The power of the British state would then prevail.

So insistent was the king on the necessity of this effort and the likelihood of its success that he was ready to defy the House of Commons' demand for the removal of North after the earl of Cornwallis's surrender at Yorktown. He gracelessly acceded to the prime minister's earnest advice that it would be "for Your Majesty's welfare, and even glory, to sacrifice at this moment former opinions, displeasures and apprehensions (though never so well- founded) to that great object . . . The Public Safety."[34] When he did, he had to swallow the further indignity of effectively yielding to the marquis of Rockingham's precondition for replacing North. George III had to tacitly promise that he would not veto any treaty establishing American independence.[35] Until reality compelled him to accept this, his opposition to American independence on the grounds that it would have disastrous consequences both for the nation's power and prosperity and its internal government had been furious and well-known.[36] It may well be the case that the curious *volte-face* in the fast day prayers in 1782 was the bishops' loyal effort to give moral support to their beleaguered sovereign.[37] If so, he never acknowledged the gesture. He solaced himself instead with three thoughts. Whatever evils came from independence, he was sure they could never be laid at his door. Since "knavery seems to be so much the striking feature of [America's] inhabitants," he suspected "it may not in the end be an evil that they become Aliens to this Kingdom."[38] Finally, he was confident that this "Revolted State . . . certainly for many Years cannot have any stable Government."[39]

III

What do these attitudes of miter and scepter tell us about the usefulness of Clark's interpretation for understanding British reactions to the American Revolution? The answer must be that its helpfulness is limited. So long as the crisis was defined as a domestic one, the confessional state's emphasis on deferential subordination to a hierarchy and peaceful obedience to lawful government illuminates the emotions and reasons behind the commitment to coercion during the war's early years. It also explains much of that policy's popularity among the governors of Britain. But when the crisis widened to include Europe, their dominant concerns became the future position of Britain in international economics, politics, and diplomacy. To my mind, this shifting emphasis confirms and perhaps extends a point made by J.G.A. Pocock when he reviewed John Brewer's book, *The Sinews of Power*. Pocock called attention to an arresting difference between Brewer's interpretation of eighteenth-century England and Clark's portrayal of the confessional state. As he observed, the central thrust of *The Sinews of Power* is an argument that English history during this period was distinguished by "the growth of dynamic new institutions whose function was to mobilize wealth and connect it to the making of war, and which in the process created new bureaucracies and new political interests, new practices of authority and obedience, new perceptions of political society and its values, and of the structure of human history itself." Pocock did not feel these insights refuted Clark's arguments. In his opinion, the two world-views coexisted, each depicting a part of the reality of eighteenth-century Britain. "Clark," concluded Pocock, "is describing the regime and its politics; Brewer, the state and its administration." The church "affirms the *Primat der Innenpolitik*"; eighteenth-century Whitehall, "the equally valid *Primat der Aussenpolitik*."[40]

The words of George III and the Anglican hierarchy during the War of American Independence support Pocock's point about the existence and equal importance of these two perspectives. The church revised its views in 1779, then returned to its original position in 1782. The king began by emphasizing the need to defeat rebellion. When circumstances changed after France entered the war, he stressed the necessities of the state. As the end approached, he gave the same weight to both concerns. On January 21, 1782, he swore to North that "no consideration shall ever make me in the smallest degree an Instrument in a measure [American independence] that I am confident would anihilate the rank in which this British Empire stands among the European states, and would render My situation in this Country below continuing an Object to me."[41] His keen sense of his honor, dignity, and duties as king led him briefly to contemplate abdication when that measure appeared inevitable.[42] Later, he became convinced that he had done his duty, while others failed to do theirs.[43] He even became persuaded the nation would be politically and economically better off without the American colonies.[44] Reassured, George once more dedicated himself to fulfilling his responsibilities as monarch.

Thus the thoughts and hopes of King George III and the Church of England's prelates from 1774 to 1783 provide an opportunity to see both the *ancien régime* and the modernizing state grappling with the challenges of assessing the possible consequences of rebellion in the colonies, defining war aims appropriate for the situation, and then defeating the American Revolution. With, we might add, equal lack of success.

* This chapter first appeared in *Anglican and Episcopal History* 68 (1999) pp. 67-83.

Endnotes

[1] See especially J.C.D. Clark, *English Society, 1688-1832: Ideology, Social Structure and Political Practice during the Ancien Régime* (Cambridge, 1985); and *ibid., Revolution and Rebellion: State and Society in England in the Seventeenth and Eighteenth Centuries* (Cambridge, 1986). For some trenchant comments about court society in the eighteenth century, see his introduction to his excellent edition of *The Memoirs and Speeches of James, 2nd Earl Waldegrave, 1742-1763* (Cambridge, 1988), esp. pp. 1-48. For lengthy discussions of Clark's work, and his rebuttal of his critics, see James E. Bradley, "The Anglican Pulpit, the Social Order, and the Resurgence of Toryism during the American Revolution," *Albion* 21 (1989), pp. 361-88; John Money, "Provincialism and the English *Ancien Régime*: Samuel Pipe-Wolferstan and 'The Confessional State,' 1776-1820," *ibid.*, pp. 389-425; John A. Phillips, "The Social Calculus: Deference and Defiance in Later Georgian England," *ibid.*, pp. 426-49; and J.C.D. Clark, "England's *Ancien Régime* as a Confessional State," *ibid.*, pp. 450-74. The quotations in this paragraph are from Bradley's lucid description of the ideals of the confessional state in "The Anglican Pulpit," *ibid.*, p. 376.

[2] Clark, *English Society, 1688-1832*, p. 234.

[3] *Ibid.*, p. 216.

[4] Paul Langford, "The English Clergy and the American Revolution," in Eckhart Heilmuth, ed., *The Transformation of Political Culture: England and Germany in the Late Eighteenth-Century* (Oxford, 1990), pp. 275-307. See also Langford, "Old Whigs, Old Tories, and the American Revolution," *Journal of Imperial and Commonwealth History* 8 (1980), pp. 106-30.

[5] James E. Bradley, *Popular Politics and the American Revolution in England: Petitions, the Crown, and Public Opinion* (Mercer; GA, 1986), pp.175-206.

[6] Quoted in *ibid.*, p.180.

[7] I will not examine what the implications are for Clark's theories of James Bradley's discovery that the majority of those who signed petitions to the Crown praying for conciliation with the colonies in five boroughs were Anglican laity. At the very least, this raises questions about the impact of the hierarchy's position on America on these parishioners. See Bradley, *Popular Politics*, p.192. For a general discussion of the relationship between Bradley's and Clark's works, see John Money's review of *Popular Politics* and *Revolution and Rebellion*, *Albion* 19 (1987), pp. 615-20.

[8] For a discussion of the origins of George's piety, see Chapter III; for his religious views as an adult, see John Brooke, *King George III* (London, 1972), pp. 260-62. George's views on eighteenth-century radicals—in this case, John Wilkes—are vividly portrayed in *ibid.*, pp.144-52.

[9] See Langford, "English Clergy and the American Revolution," 280n, for the authorship of the *Form of Prayer*.

[10] *Ibid.*, p. 275. Langford went on to note that the church was more unanimously opposed to the American Revolution than to the Jacobite rising of 1745. This does not seem surprising. Jacobitism tempted many in the church, particularly at Oxford University. The colonial cause did not appeal as Jacobitism did to political and ecclesiastical divisions within the clergy.

[11] *Ibid.*, p. 290 Butler approached the position of that prominent member of the Anglican laity, Dr. Samuel Johnson, who announced in 1776 he could forgive all men except Americans. For an excellent summary of the views of the Anglican clergy toward the American Revolution see Bradley, "The Anglican Pulpit," pp.66-68. As Bradley noted, the vast majority of priests enthusiastically supported war against the rebellious colonists and "were quick to point out the connection between the rebellious nature of sin against God and the sinful nature of political revolt." *Ibid.*, p. 366 In their opinions and their enthusiasm they minored the reactions of almost all of the church's hierarchy to the American war.

[12] Langford, "English Clergy and the American Revolution," p. 280. For some comments by archbishops and bishops in their sermons on the American

Revolution see Bradley, "The Anglican Pulpit," pp.366-68, especially the opinion of the archbishop of York that the rebellion "rested upon Wickedness only," and the words of the bishop of Rochester on the "political and enthusiastic furor" in America.

[13] Langford, "English Clergy and the American Revolution," pp.300-01.

[14] The king to Lord North, Feb. 4 1774 in Sir John Fortescue, ed., *The Correspondence of King George the Third from 1760 to December 1783*, 6 vols. (London, 1927-28), vol. 4, p. 59 (Hereafter cited as *Correspondence of George III*).

[15] The king to North, Sept. 11, 1774, *ibid.*, vol. 3, p. 131.

[16] The king to North, Nov. 18, 1774, *ibid.*, vol. 3, p.153.

[17] The king to North, Nov. 18, 1774, *ibid.*, vol. 3, p. 154.

[18] See *ibid.*, the king to North, Feb. 3, 1775 and Feb. 8, 1775, vol. 3, pp. 170-71; P.D.G. Thomas, "George III and the American Revolution," *History* 70 (1985), vol. 30; and ibid., *Tea Party to Independence: The Third Phase of the American Revolution, 1773-1776* (Oxford, 1991), pp. 199, 200, 218.

[19] The king to North, Aug. 18, 1775, *Correspondence of George III*, vol. 3, p. 248.

[20] The king to North, May 31, 1777, *ibid.*, vol. 3, p. 449.

[21] The king to North, Oct. 28, 1777, *ibid.*, vol. 3, p. 485.

[22] North to the king [Feb. 8, 1775], and the king to North, Feb. 8, 1775, *ibid.*, vol. 3, p. 172.

[23] The king to North, May 31, 1777, *ibid.*, vol. 3, p. 449.

[24] The king to North, Dec. 4, 1777, *ibid.*, vol. 3, p. 503.

[25] The king to North, Jan. 13, 1778, *ibid.*, vol. 4, pp.14-15.

[26] The king to North, Mar. 26, 1778, *ibid.*, vol. 4, pp.80-81.

[27] The king to North, Mar. 27, 1778, *ibid.*, vol. 4, p. 83.

[28] The king to North, Nov. 14, 1778, *ibid.*, vol. 4, pp.220-21.

[29] The king to North, Jun. 11, 1779, *ibid.*, vol. 4, pp. 350-51.

[30] The king to North, Mar. 7, 1780, *ibid.*, vol. 5, p.30.

[31] The king to North, Sept. 26, 1780, *ibid.*, vol. 5, p. 36; see also George's letters to North on Nov. 3, 1781, and Jan. 21, 1782, *ibid.*, vol. 5, pp.297, 334-35.

[32] See the king's calculation of the American debt on Jan. 1, 1779, [n.d.], *ibid.*, vol. 4, p. 244; and the king to North, Sept. 26, 1780, vol. 5, pp.135-36.

[33] The king to North, May 6, 1780, Feb. 8, 1781, Apr. 30, 1781, Jul. 19, 1781, and Aug. 7, 1781, *ibid.*, vol. 5, pp.57, 193, 224, 256, 262.

[34] North to the king, [Mar. 18, 1782], and the king to North, Mar. 19, 1782, *ibid.*, vol. 5, pp.394-97.

[35] The king to Lord Chancellor Thurlow, [Mar. 18, 1782], and the king to the earl of Shelburne, Apr. 5, 1782, *ibid.*, vol. 5, pp. 392, 445.

[36] For example, see the king to North, Nov. 3, 1781, Dec. 15, 1781, Jan. 21, 1782, Feb. 26, 1782, and Feb. 28, 1782, *ibid.*, vol. 5, pp. 297, 313-14, 334-35, 374, and 374-75.

[37] This seems more plausible to me than Langford's surmise that the prayer perhaps "was drafted in mid-1781, when military developments in the colonies were giving renewed cause for optimism." Langford, "English Clergy and the American Revolution," p. 280.

[38] The king to Shelburne, Nov. 10, 1782, *Correspondence of George III*, vol. 6, p.154.

[39] The king to Charles James Fox, Aug. 7, 1783, *ibid.*, vol. 6, p. 430.

[40] J.G.A. Pocock, review of John Brewer, *The Sinews of Power: War Money, and the English State, 1688-1783* (NY, 1989), *Eighteenth-Century Studies* 24 (1990-1991), pp. 270-71.

[41] The king to North, Jan. 21, 1782, *Correspondence of George III*, V, pp. 334-35.

[42] The king's draft message [Mar. 1782], *ibid.*, vol. 5, p. 425.

[43] For the improvement in the king's spirits, and for his growing conviction that he had acted correctly and honorably, see the king to Shelburne, Sept. 16, 1782, Shelburne to the king, Nov. 10, 1782, and reply, Nov. 10, 1782, *ibid.*, vol. 6, pp. 129, 153, 154.

[44] The king, untitled paper on the consequences of American Independence, [Jan.-Feb. 1783], Royal Archives, Additional Georgian Papers, Add. MSS. 32/2010/11. See also ch. XVIII in this work.

Chapter XVIII
George III on Empire, 1783*

No politician was more convinced of the need to prevent the breakup of the first British Empire than King George III. Loss of the American colonies, he was sure, would be a political and economic disaster that would consign Britain to "a very low class among the European states."[1] Nor did anyone in 1782 concede the inevitability of American Independence with more reluctance or greater bitterness. The king could barely bring himself to accept Lord North's resignation, and his aversion to what he characterized as a baseless rebellion continued unabated. How strongly and stubbornly he clung to these attitudes was so well known that in March 1782 he suffered the indignity of being compelled to promise the marquis of Rockingham that he would not veto a treaty recognizing the United States of America.[2] For these reasons, his contemporaries would have been astonished to read a brief *aide mémoire* he composed in January or February 1783 on British alternatives after the loss of the thirteen colonies. This untitled paper, which is in the king's distinctive handwriting, is in the Royal Archives at Windsor, filed among a miscellaneous collection of essays, notes, and exercises done by George from the mid-1750s to the mid-1780s. The document is reproduced below, with the king's spelling, punctuation, capitalization, and paragraph divisions as they are in the original.

> America is lost! Must we fall beneath the blow? Or have we resources that may repair the mischief? What are those resources? Should they be sought in distant Regions held by precarious Tenure, or shall we seek them at home in the exertions of a new policy? The situation of the Kingdom is novel, the policy that is to govern it must be novel likewise, or neither adapted to the real evils of the present moment, or the dreaded ones of the future.
>
> For a Century past the Colonial Scheme has been the system that has guided the Administration of the British Government. It was thoroughly known that from every Country there always exists an active emigration of unsettled, discontented,

or unfortunate People, who failing in their endeavours to live at home, hope to succeed better where there is more employment suitable to their poverty. The establishment of Colonies in America might probably increase the number of this class but did not create it; in times anterior to that great speculation, Poland contained near 10,000 Scotch Pedlars; within the last 30 years not above 100, occasioned by America offering a more advantageous asylum for them.

A people spread over an immense tract of fertile land, industrious because free, and rich because industrious, presently became a market for the Manufactures and Commerce of the Mother Country. An importance was soon generated, which from its origin to the late conflict was mischievous to Britain, because it created an expence of blood and treasure worth more at this instant, if it could be at our command, than all we ever received from America. The wars of 1744, of 1756, and 1775, were all entered into from the encouragements given to the speculation of settling the wilds of North America. It is to be hoped that by degrees it will be admitted that the Northern Colonies, that is those North of Tobacco were in reality our very successful rivals in two Articles the carrying freight trade, and the Newfoundland fishery. While the Sugar Colonies added above three millions a year to the wealth of Britain, the Rice Colonies near a million, and the Tobacco ones almost as much; those more to the north, so far from adding anything to our wealth as Colonies, were trading, fishing, farming Countries, that rivalled us in many branches of our industry, and had actually deprived us of no inconsiderable share of the wealth we reaped by means of the others.

This comparative view of our former territories in America is not stated with any idea of lessening the consequence of a future friendship and connection with them; on the contrary it is to be hoped we shall reap more advantages from their trade as friends than ever we could derive from them as Colonies; for there is reason to suppose we actually gained more by them while in actual rebellion, and the common open connection cut off, than when they were in obedience to the Crown; the Newfoundland fishery taken into the Account, there is little doubt of it.

The East and West Indies are conceived to be the great commercial supports of the Empire; as to the Newfoundland fishery time must tell us what share we shall reserve of it. But there is one observation which is applicable to all three; they depend on very distant territorial possessions, which we have little or no hopes of retaining from their internal strength, we can keep them

457

only by means of a superior Navy. If our marine force sinks, or if in consequence of wars, debts, and taxes, we should in future find ourselves so debilitated as to be involved in a new War, without the means of carrying it on with vigour, in these cases, all distant possessions must fall let them be as valuable as their warmest panegyrists contend.

It evidently appears from this slight review of our most important dependencies, that on them we are not to exert that new policy which alone can be the preservation of the British power and consequence. The more important they are already, the less are they fit instruments in that work. No man can be hardy enough to deny that they are insecure, to add therefore to their value by exertions of policy which shall have the effect of directing any stream of capital, industry, or population into those channels, would be to add to a disproportion already an evil. The more we are convinced of the vast importance of those territories, the more we must feel the insecurity of our power; our view therefore ought not to be to increase but preserve them. [3]

Those who are familiar with Adam Smith's arguments against empire will immediately see similar concepts expressed in this paper. One should not assume, however, that the king had suddenly become enamored of free trade or even that he knew Smith's work. Indeed, there is no evidence that he ever read *The Wealth of Nations*, and the language in this paper suggests that the source for his arguments was something else. Throughout his life, George III copied long passages from books he found persuasive and inserted them, usually without attribution, in his own essays. There is nothing here so elegantly phrased as Smith's comments on the folly of empire.[4] Who, then, inspired the king? The most likely candidate is the earl of Shelburne, the first lord of the Treasury. As Shelburne struggled to negotiate peace during 1782, he realized that it was crucial to win George's genuine acceptance of the eventual Independence of the United States. Isolated in his own cabinet, widely mistrusted by politicians of all factions, lacking the reliable support of a majority in the House of Commons, the earl had to have the unswerving support of the king in order to remain in power and in control of peace negotiations. To win that support, he was willing to employ any arguments that would be plausible and persuasive to the monarch. Those he found in a memorandum by Benjamin Vaughan, his private agent at the peace negotiations at Paris. Vaughan's "Brief for the Treaty of Peace" argued for the necessity of "Present *reconciliation, Future* peace." The points he made in support of his thesis were these:

> The Expence of Keeping up what was given away, Hope of profiting by it even in American hands, Desire of assuming merit from what was prudence, Conviction that the surer stake lay at home; & that we had been too long fighting for *colonies*; which have so truly occasioned all our late wars, that not a single trigger has been drawn by either of the four European powers in each others *principal* dominions in Europe. A few insular possessions such as Jersey, Minorca, & Gibraltar, wrested from the neighboring power, & which were the principal inciters to this war [with Spain], are all that have been attacked in Europe. The war was otherwise for the colonies, scarcely *worth* the wars at different times waged for them. Much more mad would it be to wage war for *future* unborn colonies, which cannot now advantage us, & may not hereafter belong to us. Some of these provinces & tracts which make great figuring in maps were as unprofitable to us, as many districts of Siberia to Russia, or America to Spain. Neither Florida nor Canada are possessions that have a long lease (or a profitable lease) for any but America.[5]

Although Shelburne had no high opinion of the brief's author, he recognized the potential of this paper insofar as winning the king's support was concerned. As Vaughan suggested, these arguments allowed "assuming merit from what was prudence;" they made a virtue of the necessity of accepting American Independence. Shelburne assumed that this would make the loss of the colonies more tolerable to George III. His judgment was correct. The king was sufficiently impressed to summarize the arguments in writing, a step he never took in thirty years of writing essays, papers, notes, and *aides mémoires* unless he agreed with the ideas he expressed.

What is the significance of this document? Certainly, it does not mark a permanent change of heart on George III's part. After Shelburne was forced from office in February 1783, the king became noticeably lukewarm toward efforts to improve commercial relations with the United States.[6] He also freely indulged his bitterness toward Americans with a series of petty and potentially significant insults during the late summer and fall of 1783.[7] Still, dismissing the essay as a curiosity and no more would be mistaken.

George III's paper succinctly and clearly reveals why a freer trade and a retreat from empire were the roads not taken by British policy makers during the 1780s. Well before 1783, the king had realized that if Britain lost its North American possessions, it would be in a very different relationship with other European powers. Now that had happened, and, prompted by Shelburne, he asked the appropriate questions: did the nation have resources that could sustain it, and what were they? His initial response was that these resources could not and should not be sought "in distant Regions held by precarious Tenure." Rather, they must be found "at home in the exertions of a new policy." But what that new policy would be remained unexplored by the king in his essay and presumably by Shelburne as well. How could the government direct Britain's capital, industry, and population in such ways as to improve the nation's prosperity and power? Beyond saying that none of these resources should be used either to improve existing colonies or to create new ones, George remained silent. Although he professed optimism about future profits from America and urged preservation of the fishery and the trade from India and the British West Indies, he did not identify these as cornerstones of the new policy. By process of elimination, Britain's future wealth and security would depend on improvement of its economy "at home." To judge from this essay, neither the king nor his minister had thought at all about what the new domestic policy should be. They had no answers to the questions they posed themselves.[8]

Given this failure to consider either the nature or the details of this new policy, it is not surprising that the earl of Sheffield's confident prediction in 1783 that Britain would again dominate the American trade even while denying the United States access to the British West Indies market was attractive to George III and other politicians. Sheffield did not deny what the king had stated as a truism:

"the situation of the Kingdom is novel." Unlike Shelburne, however, he offered the comforting assurance that Britain would flourish in this new world by continuing to practice the time-honored policies of mercantilism.[9] So presented, the choice between taking a familiar course of action and defining and devising new internal and external policies was easy for the king and his new ministers to make. Moreover, for George III, sticking with the old had the additional benefit of permitting him to vent his spleen on the rebels he detested. The king never bothered to refute the views he held briefly in 1783. Instead, he consigned them to the oblivion of his personal files without further comment.

*This chapter first appeared in *William and Mary Quarterly* 51 (1994) pp. 305-310.

Endnotes

[1] King George to Lord North, Mar. 7, 1780, in Sir John Fortescue, ed., *The Correspondence of King George the Third from 1760 to December 1783*, 6 vols. (London, 1927-1928), V, 30.

[2] See Lord North to King George, [Mar. 18, 1782], and the king's reply, Mar. 19, 1782, *ibid.*, V, pp. 394-397. Rockingham's requirements may be found in the marquis of Rockingham, "Chronology of conversations with Lord Chancellor Thurlow," Mar. 11-14, 1782, Thurlow to Rockingham, [Mar. 14, 1782], Rockingham to Thurlow, Mar. 15, 1782, Thurlow to Rockingham, Mar. 15, 1782, Rockingham to Thurlow, Mar. 16, 1782, Thurlow to Rockingham, [Mar. 16, 1782], and Rockingham to Thurlow, [Mar. 18, 1782], all in Rockingham Papers, R. 1/1992-1998, Wentworth Wodehouse Muniments, Sheffield Central Library, Sheffield, England. Cautiously but unmistakably, Rockingham was pressing for the king's concession on American Independence in writing. George III managed to evade a written pledge but not tacit agreement. See King George to Thurlow, [Mar. 18, 1782], and the king to the earl of Shelburne, Apr. 5, 1782, Fortescue, ed., *Correspondence of George III*, V, pp. 392-393, 445.

[3] The king, untitled paper on the consequences of American Independence, [Jan.-Feb. 1783], Royal Archives, Additional Georgian Papers, Add. MSS 32/2010/11. The paper was almost certainly written during these months because it contradicts the king's views in Dec. 1782 on the importance of India and the West Indies. King George to Shelburne, Dec. 11, 1782, and King George to the earl of Grantham, Dec. 19, 1782, in Fortescue, ed., *Correspondence of George III*, VI, 183, 192. Moreover, George remarked in it that "time must tell what share we shall reserve" of the Newfoundland fishery. In early 1783, this was still a subject of negotiation.

[4] Adam Smith on empire see: *An Inquiry into the Nature and Causes of the Wealth of Nations*, 2 vols., ed. Edwin Cannan (New Rochelle, NY, 1966), pp. 535-626, 895-900, esp. 581-582, 626, 899-900. For a description of the king's habit of copying without attribution see the account of the Prince of Wales's borrowing of ideas from Josiah Tucker's essays on naturalization during the 1750s in John L. Bullion, "From 'the French and Dutch are more sober, frugal and industrious' to the 'nobler' position: Attitudes of the Prince of Wales toward a General Naturalization and a Popular Monarchy, 1757-1760," *Studies in Eighteenth-Century Culture*, XVII (1987), pp.163-166. It is also instructive to compare George's arguments against slavery and the slave trade in his essay "Laws Relative to Government in General" (1755-1758), Royal Archives, Additional Georgian Manuscripts, Add. MSS 32/873-75, with very similar passages in Montesquieu's *De L 'Esprit des Lois* (Paris, 1748).

[5] Benjamin Vaughan, "Brief for Treaty of Peace," [Jan.-Feb. 1783], Shelburne Papers, vol. 87, fol. 212, William L. Clements Library, Ann Arbor, MI. For Shelburne's awareness of Vaughan's "foibles" see Shelburne to the king, Dec. 22, 1782, in Fortescue, ed., *Correspondence of George III*, VI, p. 193. After succinctly summarizing Shelburne's precarious political position in 1782-1783, C. R. Ritcheson cogently argued that the earl had only a superficial grasp of free trade as a system and no concept of how to implement it after the war, but still effectively used those ideas and the prospect of full reconciliation to tempt the Americans and the French into making a better peace for Britain than the circumstances of 1782-1783 warranted. Ritcheson, "The Earl of Shelburne and Peace with America, 1782-1783: Vision and Reality," *International History Review*, V (1983), pp. 338-345. In much the same way, the earl used a critique of empire and the expectation of a burgeoning trade with the former colonies to persuade George III to accept Independence. See also H. M. Scott's persuasive reflections on Shelburne's statesmanship and influence on George III in: H. T. Dickinson, ed., *Britain and the American Revolution*, (London, 1998), ch. VII esp. pp. 202-205. Essentially he wanted to depict military necessity as "magnanimous statesmanship" and incorporate America into a new Anglo-American commercial community. This is reflected in the king's essay. See also relevant sections in: L. Stone, ed., *An Imperial State at War: Britain from 1689 to 1815* (London, 1994).

[6] For correspondence that vividly conveys George III's declining interest in American trade see Charles James Fox to the king, Apr. 10, 1783, the king to Fox, Apr. 10, 1783, the duke of Portland to the king, May 10, 1783, and the king to the duke of Portland, May 11, 1783, in Fortescue, ed., *Correspondence of George III*, VI, pp. 349-350, 379-381.

[7] For instance, the king balked at receiving a minister from, and appointing a British minister to, the United States. Fox to the earl of Manchester, June 14, 1783 (private), in the Manchester Papers, vol. 3, Clements Library, and the king to Fox, Aug. 7, 1783, in Fortescue, ed., *Correspondence of George III*, VI, p. 430. George

III also flatly refused to extend the usual courtesy of giving jewelry and portraits to peace negotiators to the American commissioners in Paris. Portland to the king, [Oct.] 12, 1783, and the king's reply, Oct. 12, 1783, *ibid.*, VI, pp.451-452. The king's attitudes toward Americans in general were bewailed by Fox, who believed they would hamper the development of friendly political and commercial relations between the two countries, in a letter to Manchester, Aug. 21, 1783, Manchester Papers, vol. 3.

[8] For a telling critique of Shelburne's grasp of a policy of free trade and its implications and a judgment that the earl was "mute about speculative and theoretical systems (including free trade) because he did not really think much about them, and hence had little or nothing to say," see Ritcheson, "Shelburne and Peace with America," pp. 341-344.

[9] The earl of Sheffield's pamphlet, *Observations on the Commerce of the American States With Europe and the West Indies; Including the several Articles of Import and Export; And On the Tendency of a Bill now depending in Parliament* (London, 1783), went through six editions between May 1783, when it was first published, and July 1784. Contemporaries and historians agree that the pamphlet was very influential in defeating attempts to permit Americans to participate in the carrying trade to the British West Indies.

Chapter XIX

From an Inhuman Custom to False Philanthropy: Attitudes of George III toward Slavery and the Slave Trade, 1756-1807

By early 1805, conquests in the Caribbean had confronted the British government with a familiar problem: how should the cultivation of crops in islands taken from France be managed? Obviously sugar fields there could not be left fallow. War did not suppress the taste of Englishmen and Europeans for sweets, and the resultant trade generated welcome customs duties for the Treasury. But this did not mean that official policy should allow the number of acres in production to be increased. Wars were not perpetual, and these islands might be returned to France during peace negotiations. If they had been improved, the nation's enemy would benefit from their conquest during the conflict. After some discussion, the cabinet reached a unanimous conclusion about future policy on April 30. Earl Camden then duly communicated it to the ministers' royal master, King George III.

Camden began by pointing out the goal of that policy, "prevent[ing] the enrichment by British capital of those colonies & settlements which have been conquered by your Majesty's arms during the present war & which may possibly be restored at a general Peace." This could be accomplished, he and his colleagues believed, by controlling the supply of slave labor to those islands. "It would be expedient to prohibit the importation of slaves for the cultivation of fresh land into such colonies or settlements, & only to permit the importation of those slaves which are necessary to keep up the present stock by license from the Governors of such colonies." If the king agreed, an order-in-council limiting the slave trade to the conquered islands to numbers approved by the governors could be issued the next day. On behalf of the cabinet, Camden humbly asked for the royal approval.[1]

But the earl did not feel he could end his letter on this point. He believed it was necessary to assure George that the principles on which this policy rested "do not in any degree involve any decision upon the opinions which are entertained on the general question of the slave trade." Within the cabinet, both "those persons who are most favorable & those who are the most adverse to the abolition of that trade" agreed on the wisdom of such an order-in-council. The reason why Camden added these statements is obvious. During the nearly 20 years British politicians had debated in and out of Parliament the morality and necessity of the commerce in Africans, the king had remained firmly opposed to abolition. Arguments that had convinced men as diverse as William Wilberforce, William Grenville, Charles James Fox, and William Pitt that the slave trade must be abolished made no impression on George III. He consistently encouraged members of the royal family in the House of Lords to speak and vote against any proposed legislation on the slave trade. Pitt's conversion to the cause he shrugged off as a mere political concession to keep happy some in his coalition. "I am certain," he once confided to Henry Dundas, "the Prime Minister has all along at bottom sided with us in opinion, for his arguments have not been of his own sterling growth but . . . a display of those hatched by others."[2] Because of the king's well-known opinions on abolition, Camden had to reassure him that the order-in-council was not a Trojan horse designed to accomplish that goal by trickery.

The earl was successful. George immediately replied he could "by no means object to any measure which may prevent the West India Islands taken from the enemy during this war from being improved." But he also made clear that his assent was based on the same condition demanded by those in the cabinet who shared his view on abolition. The order-in-council had to be "clearly understood not to encourage a system that if ever adopted in the ancient colonial possessions of the kingdom in that part of the globe [I] must clearly look up[on] as in the teeth of public faith." Warming to his subject, the King excoriated ending the slave trade as "a line of conduct that would disgrace the honour and justice of the British Legislature which has ever fostered the British Islands." Parliament, he trumpeted in conclusion, "has no more right from ideas of false phylanthrophy (*sic*) to affect the property of British settlers than it would have to prevent the cultivation of land in Great Britain."[3]

The insistent emphasis on the rights of property, the unquestioning certainty that Britons' agriculture and commerce in the Caribbean could only be made profitable by slave labor, the curt dismissal of appeals against the immorality and cruelty of the trade as "false phylanthrophy"—surely none of these royal opinions either surprised or much dismayed Camden. He had heard them before, and, in any event, he had accomplished his mission by gaining approval of the order-in-council.[4] What would have surprised the earl—and perhaps George III as well—was the fact that the king had not always been so oblivious to the horrors of slavery and so accepting of the various rationales for the existence of a commerce in human beings. Fifty years earlier, as a young man preparing for the throne during the late 1750s under the tutelage of his mentor, the earl of Bute, and the influence of Montesquieu's *L'Esprit des Lois*, the prince of Wales had expressed opinions in an essay titled "Laws Relative to Government in General" that the king would have scorned. What these were help illuminate what the differences were between the youth who would be king and the ageing monarch, and what life did to him on the way.

The prince introduced the discussion of slavery in his essay by observing that it "is equally repugnant to the Civil Law as to the Law of Nature. A Slave is no member of Society, he cannot therefore be restrain'd by Laws in which [he] has no interest from attempting to procure Liberty by flight." This meant that "the legal authority of the Master only can prevent him" from seeking freedom. Although George did not elaborate further at this point, it seems clear he grasped that the absence of civil liberty for the slave required governments of societies that permitted the ownership of humans to confer by law tyrannical powers on their masters. Such was not, as he later noted, a just government or society.

What justified slavery? "The pretexts us'd by the Spaniards for enslaving the New World were," according to the prince, "extrem'ly curious." He listed two. "The propagation of the Christian Religion was the first reason; the next was the Americans differing from them in colour, manners & Customs." Merely enumerating these was sufficient for George to reach this conclusion: they "are too absurd to take the trouble of refuting." The enslavement of Indians could not be justified.

"But what shall we say, "asked the prince, "to the European traffic of Black Slaves?" Here as well he thought "the very reasons urg'd for it will be perhaps sufficient to make us hold this practice in execration." One was "the impossibility of cultivating the American Colonys without them." A second argued that even though free labor could raise crops in the New World, without slaves "the produce of these Colonys [such] as Sugar, Indigo, Tobacco, etc. would be too dear." Added to these arguments of economic necessity was this: "besides the Africans are black, wooly-headed with monstrous features, nor have they common sense as they prefer a piece of glass to gold. Such are the arguments," concluded George, "for an inhuman Custom wantonly practic'd by the most enlighten'd Polite Nations in the World." He responded to them with the contempt he felt they deserved. "There is no occasion to answer them, for they stand self condemn'd."

By process of elimination, "the true origin of the right of slavery . . . must be founded in the nature of things." One occurred "from the free choice a person makes of a Master for his own benefit, which forms a mutual convention between the two partys." This happened in despotic countries, where "people make no difficulty of selling themselves; political Slavery making the loss of civil Liberty extrem'ly easy." George cited the examples of Muscovites selling themselves into slavery, and merchants at Achim exchanging their freedom for the protection of a great lord. "Indeed in all these reched Governments, freemen have no better resource than that of becoming Slaves to tyrants in Office."

The other origin of slavery "reconcilable to reason" in George's mind was enslavement caused by climate. There were countries "where excessive heat enervates the body, & creates such indolence that nothing but the fear of chatisement can oblige Men to any laborious duty." The prince believed this came closest "to what some call natural slavery." But even if one conceded this point to the fullest extent, "it is still limitted to particular parts of the Globe for in all others no labour is so severe but free people may be found to undergo it." Then, having pointed this out, the prince went further. He argued that "in real truth there is no climate on the Earth where with proper encouragement the most painful drudgery may not be exercis'd without Slaves." Another "real truth" was this: "in some unhappy Countrys the Laws produce indolence & inaction, which very situation of mind & body never fails to give birth to or encourage Slavery."[5]

The prince ended his comments on slavery with that statement. To be sure, he did not advocate that either the slave trade or slavery itself be abolished. (Nor did Montesquieu, the inspiration for his and Bute's arguments.) Still, one should note that George wrote his analysis more than a decade before Granville Sharp began his protests, 20 years before Adam Smith denied slavery's economic importance and John Wesley attacked its morality, almost 30 years before Wilberforce underwent a religious conversion, and 35 years before William Cowper's "The Negro's Complaint" and Josiah Wedgewood's cameo of the suffering slave became popular. The prince and Bute were well ahead of their time. One would think these early beliefs would predispose George III to listen attentively to his eloquent subjects between the late 1780s and the early 1790s and lend his support and influence to reform's cause. He had determined to his own satisfaction that neither nature nor economic need created and maintained slavery and the slave trade. Rather, the cupidity and malignity of some men and the laws they devised to serve their interests produced the institution and the commerce that sustained it. Presumably the evils of the slave trade could be remedied in the same way. Moral men could devise the appropriate legislation and overturn bad laws and men. But what the king believed as a young man did not influence his ideas and acts as an older one. Why?

Two possible answers may be eliminated at the beginning of the inquiry. George III quietly opposed regulation of the slave trade before the French Revolution. His decision against exerting pressure on recalcitrants in the cabinet and the House of Lords forced Pitt to threaten resignation to secure passage of Sir William Dolben's bill to limit the number of slaves on British ships and pay bounties to masters for delivering live Africans in 1788.[6] Events in France may have hardened the king's heart further against abolition, but they did not cause him to discard earlier opinions nor did considerations of the economic importance of the West Indies to Britain's prosperity. The leading authority on the abolition of the slave trade has asserted that the king was opposed "doubtless because he saw it as a threat to the well-being of that kingdom which it was his duty to preserve."[7] This, however, overstates George III's valuation of the West Indies. During the 1750s, though he acknowledged the importance of the colonial trade from North America and the islands, he believed the commerce in British manufacturers and crops to Europe was much more crucial to the nation.[8] After the American Revolution, he placed even less emphasis on the importance of the Caribbean trade.[9] The war had convinced him defending the islands would always cost more than they could produce; therefore Britain should maintain rather than improve those possessions. Neither reaction to political revolution nor calculations of economic interest influenced his attitudes toward slavery and the slave trade. More personal considerations explain the king's shift from regarding slavery as "an inhuman Custom" to dismissing protests as "false phylanthropy."

In part, George III's change in attitudes reflects the intensity with which he held opinions about slavery and the slave trade. The strength of his language is not necessarily an accurate indication of how he felt. Throughout his life, the king had a fondness for hyperbole and vigorous expressions, especially when he was being critical. The sentences quoted above are his only comments during the 1750s on African slavery in the New World, and they were made in the context of extensive remarks on the general principles of civil government.[10] In contrast, the prince returned again and again, in public and private, to his favorite themes: the needs to end corruption in political life, to reform the nation's finances, to cease allowing Hanover to dictate the nation's European policies, and to improve morality in British life.[11] These were the subjects dearest to him. The unjust existence of slavery ranked well below these in importance. Moreover, it continued to be so even after he became critical of "false phylanthropy." George III fulminated against regulating the slave trade for 20 years, and he always forbade his ministers to make it a matter of ministerial policy—and hence a test of support for the government when parliamentary votes came up—whatever their personal position might be. But that was the extent of his opposition. Ministers allowed private members to introduce legislation throughout those two decades. If those ministers supported abolition, they spoke and voted in favor of these bills, without incurring the king's disapproval. When some of these bills passed through both Houses, the king routinely approved them without comment. He did not even protest at signing legislation ending the slave trade in 1807, even though the Ministry of All the Talents went back on its predecessors' word and used the order-in-council of 1805 as an argument in favor of abolition. One need only compare this with George III's decisive reaction against his ministers' efforts to achieve Catholic emancipation by similar tactics to see how much less crucial the slave trade was to him.[12] This record as prince and monarch indicates that he never defined the issues slavery raised as crucially important. When he changed his mind, he did not have to overcome any strongly held opinions.

This absence of intense convictions meant that the identity of the advocate was all the more important in determining George III's stance. As a young man, he wholeheartedly embraced all of the opinions of "my dearest friend," the earl of

Bute. Bute's rejection of the rationales for slavery, and his revulsion at the slave trade, were enough to convince the prince on these subjects, just as the earl's ideas about other matters were adopted by his protégé as well.[13] When his mentor's influence waned, George's commitment to his thoughts and ideals weakened apace. Those who pressed most vigorously for the end of the slave trade were, to say the least, not the sort of men who could command the respect and affection he had for Bute. Indeed, they were members of groups the mature king particularly disliked, dissenters and Evangelical Anglicans. A devout communicant and a scrupulously moral man in the domestic sphere, George III took his responsibilities as the head of the Church of England very seriously. There was no part of his coronation oath that he observed more closely than his role as defender of the faith. To his mind, Quakers, Methodists, Evangelicals, and all those he branded as enthusiasts were threats to Anglicanism. Their common insistence on the primacy of their individual visions over the ordered, hierarchical, collective wisdom of society, church, and government was disturbing to him. Wilberforce might be sure that "God Almighty has set before me two great objects, the suppression of the slave trade and the reformation of manners." But George III, who firmly believed God played an active role in human affairs, did not believe the Almighty gave such specific commands.[14] The conviction of Wilberforce and others that the abolition of the slave trade was divinely ordained was enough to make the king very suspicious of it.

Finally, and perhaps most telling of all, as he grew older the man who aspired to be a "patriot king" who would reform politics and society became convinced meaningful change was impossible. His and Bute's inability to execute their plans for national regeneration, the loss of America despite his energetic efforts, and the sinking of the prince of Wales into debauchery and political opposition after he had tried his best as father, combined to make him a monarch determined to preserve what little good he could rather than seeking reform. In 1788, he told Bute, "Every day makes me more a philosopher." This meant "[I] attempt to keep my desires within a narrow compass, that my disappointments may be fewer. When one is within a few months of 50," he continued, "one has acquired little advantage from a toilsome life if one has not learned to be moderate in expectations and thankful to divine Providence for the good one possesses, and full of diffidence of one's attempts and therefore not surprised when they prove abortive."[15] This disillusion fathered skepticism about the possibility of reform. That skepticism in turn came to include the efficacy of reform as well. That this was so is not surprising. George III, who ascended to the throne determined to change his world, had endured decades when he was the target of reformers, be they John Wilkes and his followers, Christopher Wyvill and his, Samuel Adams and his, or the various advocates of economical and parliamentary reform. His allies against them had been the defenders of the *status quo* in religion, in politics, in law, and in empire. In the case of slavery and the slave trade, George III refused to set aside the experiences of being king and return to the youthful prince who read Montesquieu with approval, hung on Bute's every word, and eagerly looked forward to the reign of the patriot king.

Endnotes

[1] Earl Camden to the king, Apr. 30, 1805, in A. Aspinall, ed., *The Later Correspondence of George III* , 5 vols. (Cambridge, 1962-1970), IV, p. 322.

[2] The king to Henry Dundas, [Feb. 16, 1796], in *ibid.*, II, 459n. For an account of George III's hostility to abolition of the slave trade, see Roger Instey, *The Atlantic Slave Trade and British Abolition. 1760-1810* (Atlantic Highlands, NJ, 1975), pp. 304-306, 322, 341, and 364; for a good introduction to the campaign against it, see John Ehrman, *The Younger Pitt: The Years of Acclaim* (NY, 1969), pp. 386-404. For parliamentary agitation against slave trade see: J.R. Oldfield, "London Opinion and the Mobilization of Public Opinion against the Slave Trade," *Historical Journal* 35 (1995), pp. 331-44; *idem.*; *Popular Politics and British Anti-Slavery* (Manchester, 1995); J. Walvin, *England, Slaves and Freedom* (London, 1982); J. Valvin and C. Elmsley, eds., *Artisans, Peasants and Proletarians 1760-1860* (London, 1985); on George III, Pitt: J. Mori, *William Pitt and the French Revolution 1785-1795* (Edinburgh, 1997).

[3] The King to Camden, [May 1, 1805], in Aspinall, ed., *Later Correspondence* IV, p. 322.

[4] Camden may have felt he had accomplished more. The earl personally favored abolition, and Wilberforce himself had prompted Pitt to propose the order-in-council as a promising start toward a new campaign for abolition. Anstey, *Slave Trade*, pp. 343-370.

[5] The prince of Wales, "Laws Relative to Government in General," [1755-1758], Royal Archives, Additional Georgian Manuscripts 32/873-75. I believe this was inspired by reading Montesquieu because of similarities between the prince's account of rationalizations of slavery and those in *L'Ésprit des Lois*. Cf. especially Montesquieu's ironical remark, "The Negroes prefer a glass necklace to the gold which white nations so highly value. Can this be a greater proof of their wanting common sense?" with the passage quoted above. Quoted in Anstey, *Slave Trade*, p. 104. For proof the prince read Montesquieu closely, see his notes from other sections of *L'Esprit des Lois* in Additional Georgian Manuscripts, 32/1044-46.

[6] See Ehrman, *Pitt*, pp. 394-95; and Anstey, *Slave Trade*, pp. 268-69. Though neither historian makes this point explicitly, I find it difficult to believe that Pitt would have had his showdown with the cabinet had George III supported him. A shrewd contemporary, Nathaniel Wraxall, shared my doubts. As Ehrman points out, Wraxall believed Pitt prevented the king from proroguing Parliament and killing the bill.

[7] Anstey, *Slave Trade*, p. 304.

[8] The prince of Wales, "On Industry in Great Britain," Additional Georgian Manuscripts, 32/260.

[9] The king, memorandum on the loss of America, [after 1783], Additional Georgian Manuscripts, 32/2010-11. Reproduced in ch. XVIII in this work.

[10] The prince did observe that "servile fetters" existed in Africa and Asia, but made no further comment other than noting both continents "breed up slavery." See "Laws Relative to Government in General," *ibid.*, 32/878.

[11] For the prince's determination to reform these areas, see chs. IV and VI.

[12] For the king's reaction to legislation affecting the slave trade, see Ehrinan, *Pitt*, pp. 394-95, 638; Anstey, *Slave Trade* pp. 268-69, 390-402; and Peter Jupp, *Lord Grenville. 1759-1834* (Oxford, 1985), pp. 388-391. In contrast to his assent to abolishing the slave trade in 1807, George III compelled his ministers to resign over the issue of Catholic emancipation in Ireland. Indeed, he gave his assent the same day Lord Grenville, the Prince Minister, resigned. *Ibid.*, pp. 399-410.

[13] See chs. IV, V, and VI in this work.

[14] Wilberforce's statement is quoted in Ehrman, *Pitt*, p. 391. For examples of the king's suspicion of "enthusiasm" and a typical reference to the role of divine

providence in men's lives, see B.D. Bargar, *Lord Dartmouth and the American Revolution* (Columbia, SC, 1965), pp.11, 191.

[15] The king to Bute, [1788], Bute Papers, Mount Stuart, Box VIII.

"The Particular Habits of His Life": Some Implications of the Legal Career of George Grenville

In the course of his famous speech on American taxation, Edmund Burke gave an intriguing explanation of George Grenville's ill-fated decision to break with tradition and past practice in colonial taxation and go ahead with an unprecedented internal tax on colonists, the Stamp Act of 1765. Grenville's error, Burke argued, was not due to any defect in character, nor to any shortcoming in mental ability, nor to any inattention to detail, nor to any failure in his dedication to duty. In all these respects, Grenville deserved his reputation as "a first-rate figure in this country." Burke therefore concluded that "if such a man fell into errors, it must be from defects not intrinsical." The source of Grenville's mistake "must rather be sought in the particular habits of his life," habits which, "though they do not alter the groundwork of [a man's] character yet tinge it with their own hue."[1]

According to Burke, two experiences molded Grenville's mental habits. One was his service for most of his adult life in one government office or another. Men who spent their time in such pursuits were "apt to think the substance of business not to be much more important than the forms in which it is conducted." As a result, they ascribed too much importance to standard procedures and past precedents, and too little to a broad "knowledge of mankind, and . . . extensive contemplation of things." Burke summed them up thusly: "men in office go on in a beaten track."[2] They were unable to respond flexibly "when a new and troubled scene is opened, and the file affords no precedent."

The other crucial experience in Grenville's life was his training as a young man in the law. Burke conceded that the law was "one of the first and noblest of sciences." Indeed, he opined that it was the science "which does more to quicken and invigorate the understanding than all the other kinds of learning put together." But studying it was "not apt, except in persons very happily born, to open and liberalize the mind in exactly the same proportion." In Burke's judgment, Grenville was not one of those happy exceptions. "His errors were owing to his having been bred to the law."[3] "He conceived," Burke believed, "and many conceived with him, that the flourishing trade of this country was owing to law and institution, and not quite so much to liberty." He was also convinced that "regulation [was] commerce, and taxes [were] revenue," without considering that on many occasions trade could generate money for the state and its subjects without legislative coercion. With his mind thus shaped by his training and his career, Grenville "attended more to the law and right, than to the expediency and propriety, of taxing America."[4]

Alexander Wedderburne, who was both a former ally of Grenville and the current Solicitor General, responded immediately to Burke's analysis. Wedderburne recalled that Grenville had studied practically the several duties and services of most offices. "Is theory," he asked rhetorically, "a better assistant than practice?" He also sarcastically observed, "I have never till now heard that the study of the law was a prejudice to a person who was to act in a public station."[5] The drift of Wedderburne's remarks was clear to his audience: despite his disclaimer of any attack on Burke's motives, he was obviously accusing his opponent of trying to blacken Grenville's reputation to serve his own immediate purposes. Burke briefly responded that no one respected Grenville more than he did, "but [Grenville] was human and therefore liable like others to error."[6] However much one respected him, one was not obliged to perpetuate his errors by venerating and repeating them. Burke closed by noting that he could see no reason to "raise the bodies of the dead, to make them vampires to suck out the virtues of the living." Wedderburne did not pursue the point, and discussion of the particular habits of Grenville's life and the origins of the Stamp Act ceased.

More amused than instructed by arguments and his exchange with Wedderburne, the House of Commons voted against repealing the tea duty, 182 to 49.[7] Despite this fact, though, and despite Wedderburne's trenchant comments on his prejudices and his motives, Burke's remarks on Grenville's mental habits are still suggestive.[8] In the eighteenth century, as today, students and practitioners of the law developed ways of analyzing situations and solving problems that were distinctive to their profession, and Grenville was not merely a student of law; he was a practicing solicitor. Moreover, Burke was not the only contemporary of Grenville's to comment on the effect of the law on his cast of mind. Both political colleagues and opponents testified at various times to the impact of his profession on his outlook toward problems of state and politics. For instance, in his reply to Burke, Wedderburne rejoiced that Grenville "had not . . . emancipated his mind" from the habits he had learned studying law when he embarked on his career in office. Other colleagues rejoiced less as they noted his ability to make "lawyerly--like distinctions." Usually, such references were critical, and, when they were made by opponents, highly so. Indeed, on one occasion an outraged Grenville found himself protesting that a man of his "rank and family be called a solicitor at the Old Bailey because he was bred to the profession of the law." To, be sure, this charge, which corresponds roughly to the present day slur of "ambulance-chaser," was partisan and unwarranted; still, even after one takes personal and political ill-feeling into account, it is clear why friends and enemies periodically identified him with the law. Grenville never hesitated to draw upon his legal expertise and training when he believed the situation called for them. The Stamp Act was such a situation. When he first introduced in 1765, and again when he reintroduced it in 1765, Grenville stressed in his arguments the legality of Parliament's directly taxing the colonies, and insisted that the House endorse his opinion.[9] So an examination of the lessons he learned as an attorney might indeed reveal interesting patterns of thought and action, and offer new insights into the background of his decision to impose a stamp tax on colonists.

I

It is impossible to analyze, or even to describe, Grenville's legal career in great detail. Many of his business papers have been lost, probably at the time of his descendant's bankruptcy during the 1840s. For the same reason, one cannot fill in some gaps of his career by studying his clients' papers. Grenville became an attorney at the insistence of his wealthy uncle, Viscount Cobham, who probably anticipated that his family would save money if his second oldest nephew could serve as their principal legal adviser. Whether or not this was Cobham's intention, it is clear that most, if not all, of Grenville's practice concerned his relatives.[10] Many of their papers have not survived, either; what is still extant provides only occasional glimpses into their legal affairs.[11]

It is possible, however, to tell from these papers that Grenville dealt most frequently with problems in what would be called today real estate law: the acquisition or alienation of real property by sale or other transfer, and the management of the various relationships between landlords, tenants, employees, neighbors, and government officials. One can also infer confidently that he was fully conversant with the statute and common law, and the local traditions, relating to these areas of the law. Had he not had a competent knowledge of these matters, his elder brother Richard, the head of the Grenville family, and his principal client, would not have kept him as a legal adviser for over 40 years. In business affairs, "nine shillings an acre, ten shillings an acre, three loads of bushels, will do twenty poles of dead-hedging" was Richard's "morning and evening song."[12] He never ceased to suspect that unscrupulous men of all social ranks were trying to relieve him of varying sums of money, and he did not fail to keep a close eye on his brother as well.[13] As he revealingly noted, "The only comfort amidst all my plagues is to think that I am by this means fortifying my own integrity by advancing my riches in an honest way, if so it be that my integrity, like that of so many of [my] acquaintance, should ever stand in need of preservatives and cordials, *alias* plain money."[14] That such a man remained

479

basically satisfied with his legal advice for so long is a tribute to Grenville's knowledge of the law.

Richard's satisfaction is a testimony to other skills of Grenville's as well. Knowledge of real estate law does not guarantee success at protecting or expanding one's property. In fact, such knowledge does little more than protect against acts so flagrantly criminal or legally unbinding that they would void an agreement or endanger possession. Ideally, an attorney should be able to use his knowledge to enhance his skills as a negotiator. Both Grenville brothers had the ability to persuade the unwary that a course of action was advantageous to them, when in reality it ultimately was not. Each of them also had in abundance the patience necessary to continue negotiations until they either got what they wanted or satisfied themselves that they could not reach agreement, and the determination to resist temptations to sign contracts quickly when they were uncertain that their interests would ultimately benefit.[15] Most important of all, both brothers understood that they could use George's legal knowledge and Richard's political connections to improve their bargaining position. Fortunately, a relatively complete record of how they used this combination of knowledge, skill, and power to attain their ends has survived in the family's papers, and it offers some interesting insights into the ways they used the law to improve their property. During the 1730s and 1740s Richard was very interested in enclosing some properties he owned in Buckinghamshire. This interest made him, to his brother, "a special client." All of the questions he asked, and all lawsuits "that you propose to enter into, some of which may not be decided immediately," led George to "fancy . . . [that] you have a design to breed your second son to the law, and do this to encourage him that twenty years hence he may not be in the condition of us young counselors (sic) without business." Still, since no one could be certain that Richard's offspring would like the profession, George planned "if possible to put a stop to the commencement of some of them."[16] The letters he wrote in November-December 1738 containing his advice, together with other materials, permit historians to reconstruct some of the Grenville brothers' thoughts and actions, during the enclosures of Ashendon and Wotton. Equally important, these documents reveal their perceptions of the law, its purposes, and its uses.

II

The Grenville family had owned land in the manor of Ashendon in Bucks since the mid-seventeenth century, and at the manor of Wotton Underwood in the same county since the twelfth century.[17] But although the Grenvilles owned most of the land in both manors, they did not own one clearly defined, contiguous block of land in either place. They had rights of commons on the meadows; that is, they and their tenants had a legal right to pasture a certain number of cattle and sheep there. Other owners had the same rights, though for fewer animals. The land under cultivation at both manors was divided in the same communal way. The Grenvilles' land lay "intermixed and dispersed in small parcels over the . . . common fields and unenclosed grounds."[18] The farmers who rented land from them planted and harvested a few strips of land in one field and other strips in another. No Grenville had ever changed these arrangements, with the single exception of Edward Grenville, who during the 1570s persuaded other holders of commons rights to a small part of the common at Wotton to give up those rights, exchange strips of land with each other until, each had a distinct, contiguous area, enclosed those areas with hedges, ditches, or fences, and acquire absolute and sole ownership to those enclosed plots. Probably Richard had no sooner assumed control of the family's estates in 1733 than he began to think about ways of persuading his neighbors to go through the process of enclosure themselves. Richard believed enclosure would benefit him in several ways. He was certain that so long as "few [of the strips of land] are commodiously situated" and "the . . . common fields, wastes, and other grounds lie open and unenclosed, many difficulties and inconveniences will attend the cultivating thereof, and the said lands will not be capable of improvement."[20] He knew he could not reasonably expect to increase the acreage being plowed at Ashendon and Wotton as long as he had to first convince several farmers working in the same field for different landlords of the necessity of expansion, and then coordinate their efforts. Nor could "a poor country haymaker," as Richard once styled himself, anticipate that his hay harvests from the large meadows at both manors would increase until his tenants could completely close off pastures from livestock.[21] Nor could he be sure of collecting full value from the timber in a forest while other men retained the traditional right of gathering wood in it.[22] In sum, improving the land's productivity depended on enclosure. And, of course, once the land was more productive, Richard could legitimately claim in his negotiations with his tenants that these improvements warranted an increase in their rents.[23]

Richard had other reasons as well for wanting to enclose the lands at Ashendon and Wotton. In both places, ecclesiastical institutions owned glebe lands and had the right to collect tithes on other lands. Used to support parish priests and religious establishments, tithes in this area of England were usually assessed each year in proportion to the amount of rent produced by estates and by the number of acres plowed, and were frequently received in the form of produce from the land and in rights to use the commons to pasture livestock. The ecclesiastics assessed the tithes themselves.[24] In the past, the Grenville family had evidently felt certain that these men of God were quick to find pretexts to raise their rates, and attempted to persuade them to accept a fixed payment in lieu of these rights.[25] During the exchange of properties before the enclosures at Ashendon and Wotton, the Grenvilles would have another opportunity to tempt the church's representatives into giving up their rights of collecting tithes, and another chance to offer men tired of annual responsibilities of assessment and collection, and the attendant disputes, into accepting land or a fixed annual payment in exchange for a renunciation of their rights. To Richard, though he was willing to give up some land, a fixed annuity was the preferable alternative. As a steward of his later remarked, a "certain payment is, and will for the future (as lands rise in value) be more advantageous for [you] and your family, than an uncertain annual sum, which may be altered at the will of the incumbent."[26]

With these goals in mind, the Grenville brothers began negotiations in 1737 with other proprietors of land at Ashendon and Wotton. Indeed, Richard was evidently so intent on realizing these goals that he was not deterred by a depression in agricultural prices, a depression so acute that pamphlet writers observed, "How shocking . . . must be the daily instances we have of the unfortunate farmers! and how great must the loss be sustained thereby, to their landlords," and bewailed the facts, that arrears in rent were sharply increasing, and that many landlords could find no tenants for their farms.[27] Nor was Richard impressed by the fact that no other landlord in Bucks had executed a parliamentary enclosure in the eighteenth century.[28] Instead, he pressed on with his plans, conducting discussions himself at the family seat at Wotton, and lubricating the proceedings with wine and other hospitalities.[29] Occasionally George was present, and he certainly was always available for consultation via the mail at his chambers in London.[30] By August 11, 1737, Richard had reached agreement with all of the proprietors at Ashendon who were not ecclesiastics on the general necessity of enclosure and the specific terms of the exchanges. Six months later, he agreed on terms with the Dean and Chapter of Christ Church, Oxford, and the Warden and Scholars of Lincoln College, Oxford.[31] The Dean and Chapter, who owned the rights of the rectory at Ashendon and all the tithes of the parish, took from Richard "a tract of land, lying together, in lieu of the said tithes and part of the glebe, being a full equivalent of the same."[32] The College estimated that its tithes were worth L 70 5s. 4d. annually, and required Richard to pay L 75 each year in lieu of these rights. "There can be no further profit upon [these rights]," Richard observed much later. "Nor," he added happily, "was it ever intended or expected that there should." The College also would annually receive L 2 15s. 9d. in place of its glebe rights.[33] As soon as Christ Church and Lincoln College were satisfied, Richard began making arrangements to obtain an

Act of Parliament ratifying all these agreements and enclosing 1,700 acres at Ashendon.[34]

An act of enclosure was necessary for three reasons. The Dean and Chapter and the Warden and Scholars were "restrained by law from alienating the rights of their Church and College." This restraint, which the men who drafted their charters had intended to protect ecclesiastical property from any unscrupulous or unwise men who temporarily occupied positions of power in these institutions, could only be circumvented by a new law, permitting alienation in a specific case. Also, some of the lay proprietors were "under family settlements, or other legal disabilities" which were designed to prevent alienation in order to guarantee that heirs and assigns would inherit the property. These men, too, needed the specific permission an Act of Parliament could provide. Finally, three other landowners had refused to sign the agreement they had verbally reached with Richard on August 11, 1737. Fortunately for Richard, these people had claims to no more than twenty acres of land and the commons rights attached to those holdings. The Grenvilles and the other proprietors had no intention of permitting these small landholders to block the consummation of the enclosure. So they planned to use the authority of a new law to compel them to submit.[35]

The Grenvilles had their petition for an act of enclosure ready by early March 1738. On March 7 Samuel Sandys, a prominent figure in the Whig opposition to Sir Robert Walpole, and a political ally of Cobham and Richard Grenville, introduced it.[36] As was the custom in the House on private legislation, Sandys also served as chairman of the select committee that examined witnesses on the truth of the petition. In theory, this committee also was responsible for drafting the legislation; in fact, the Grenville brothers drew it up, and the committee made amendments to it, probably in consultation with the parties involved.[37] The proprietors who had refused to sign the August 11, 1737 agreement were given notice to appear before the committee to state their objections to the enclosure, but none of them took advantage of this opportunity.

It is likely they had neither the time, the money, nor the inclination to travel to Westminster and dispute the wishes of Viscount Cobham, who approved of the enclosure, and the rest of the Grenvilles' economic peers. Such an errand would surely have been fruitless. On April 10, the bill passed the House. Soon afterwards, it became law.[38]

This accomplished, Richard turned to the business of dividing and enclosing the land. Commissioners to divide the land and make awards of those divisions to individual proprietors were appointed, doubtlessly by Richard, who was paying their salaries. They set to work, and apparently completed their job expeditiously.[39] Richard did not tarry, either. Before Christmas 1738, he had begun hedging his property.[40]

Indeed, Richard was so eager to start on the project that he began prematurely.[41] The commissioners had decided to allot to him the five acres that had previously belonged to James and Mary Hynd, two proprietors who had neither executed the agreement of August 11, 1737 nor consented to the Act. Taking possession of it soon after the decision, he had begun building a hedge in such a way that would cut off the Hynds' access to their former property. On at least two grounds, this was illegal, as Richard soon discovered. The five acres were not his yet, for he had neglected to obtain a formal award for it before he started the hedge. As a result, he was, so far as the law was concerned, trespassing. Moreover, even had he obtained the award, the Act required proprietors to leave gaps in new hedges for six months.

Probably this provision had been included in order to insure that persons holding the old commons rights could pasture their cattle for one more fall and winter on the fields. Richard, however, did not want to provide feed for the Hynds' livestock. Few sights irritated him more than his neighbors' taking advantage of traditional rights to graze their cattle on his lands. At the same time that he was hedging off the Hynds' beasts, he was asking his brother to find some way he could legally justify impounding other men's stock on his fields at

Westcott, near Wotton.[42] It is possible, too, that Richard felt he had a score to settle with the Hynds and an example to make to any of his other neighbors who might resist, however unsuccessfully, his plans. Clearly, he expected that the Hynds would abjectly yield their rights and transfer their herd to the acres the Commissioners had granted them. He was disappointed in this expectation. The Hynds announced that they would prevent him from completing the hedge, without specifying whether they planned to sue him or to cut gaps in the hedge themselves. Before responding to this threat, Richard asked his brother for legal advice.

George quickly soothed whatever apprehensions Richard might have felt about a possible suit for trespassing. He pointed out that while in theory the Hynds had an indisputable case against Richard for trespassing, in fact they had no case at all. They could not file a suit until the next court term. By that time, the award of the five acres might be executed, and their case would be moot. Moreover, even if the formal award had not been made by the time the courts next met, Parliament would be sitting again. Richard, who had served as the Member from the borough of Buckingham since 1734, could then take advantage of the privilege of Members, and claim freedom from suits against his person, property, or servants. The award surely would be made before Parliament adjourned again, and the Hynds would have no legal claim against him, since they would no longer have any legal interest in those five acres.

As for any fears Richard might have that James Hynd might be "insolent enough to pull up your [already completed] enclosures," George thought "there is no danger of that." But if the Hynds did cut the part of the hedge now completed, George believed that Richard could again rely on parliamentary privilege for redress. He was not entirely certain, for as he once humorously remarked, "We [lawyers] always say that the Parliament make their own privileges what they will, but the law knows of none but the safety of their persons." Still, he though that "any violence done to a [M.P.] . . . either in his person, servants, or estate, unless it is in consequence of a legal process or proceeding, is esteemed a breach of privilege though it be committed during the recess."[43] The House of Commons would probably punish the Hynds for any destruction of the existing hedge. Whether Richard should go ahead with the completion of the hedge was, however, a trickier matter. The present hedge, by virtue of its incomplete state, in effect had the required gaps in it. A completed hedge would not, and the Hynds could plausibly claim a legal right to cut them if Richard did not. If Richard wanted to go ahead with the enclosure, George suggested that he get "the Commissioners [to] send [James Hynd] a notice in writing, signed by three of them at least, that in pursuance of the power given them by Act of Parliament they have allotted to you his lands in the common fields and set out for him and his sisters . . . other lands." Such a notice would not legally absolve Richard of violating the Act, but it might impress the Hynds. Indeed, George predicted, "He will not, I believe, commit an act of violence against it." He did caution his brother, however, that if this tactic did not impress the Hynds, and if it appeared likely that they would cut the hedge, Richards should resign himself to leaving gaps in it for six months as the law prescribed.

The outcome of this situation is unknown. It is clear, though, that Richard never discussed anywhere in his correspondence during the remaining 40 years of his life any further difficulties with the Hynds. It is equally clear that he regarded the enclosures at Ashendon as a considerable success.[44]

Richard was just as proud of his successful efforts to enclose land at Wotton, though he had to wait until 1742 to complete the exchanges and obtain the Act. What caused the delay is not precisely known, but it seems most likely that the Company of the Mercers of the City of London were to blame. The Company held lands at Wotton in trust for the charity of St. Paul's School, and, because it had no interest in the land except as trustee, could not "do any act to affect the trust's estate."[45] As George Grenville explained to his brother, the only way for the enclosure to go forward would be for the Company to obtain permission to make the exchanges in Chancery Court, or for Parliament to pass an act of enclosure. The Mercers were reluctant to do either, because their Wardens feared that an application to the court or to Parliament would lead to a full-scale inquiry into their administration of the trust. George predicted that neither institution would require a comprehensive review of their administration before granting the petition. Insofar as the court was concerned, he did not think that "the novelty of [the petition] will be a sufficient objection against it, especially as it tends only to increase the jurisdiction of the court, for no maxim is more religiously adhered to in all courts than *boni judicus est ampliare jurisdictionem*." But he did believe that the court was more likely to inquire into the full administration of the trust than Parliament was. Indeed, George believed that "tis next to impossible that the Parliament should go out of their way and spend their time in an inquiry about such a probate trust as this is, when it comes before them in the usual form of bills to establish exchanges and nothing else appears."[46] Apparently the Mercers thought about these alternatives until early 1741-2, before taking the risk that George had suggested. It was, as he had predicted, in reality no risk at all. George now sat in the House himself. He introduced the petition for enclosing Wotton on March 12, drafted the bill, chaired the Committee examining the petition and bill, managed it through the stages of legislation, and personally carried it to the House of Lords on May 4.[47] Thus Richard had the pleasure later that year of inviting the Earl and Countess of Denbigh to visit his "paternal seat, the Wotton *enclosure*."[48]

III

The Grenville brothers continued to be periodically involved in enclosures for the remainder of their lives. Thus George Grenville remained familiar with this area of the law until his death in 1770. What sort of "habits of life" did such a practice create? To answer this, it is necessary to go beyond narration of the Ashendon and Wotton enclosures, and look at the principles and attitudes that guided his actions in those cases.

Clearly, Grenville's behavior reveals that he did not worship the principle of precedent to the point of being always bound by it. After all, he and his brother had made agreements that overturned traditional rights of commons, and changed radically the system of landownership and agricultural production at Ashendon and Wotton. Moreover, they had made extra-legal arrangements with other property owners that circumvented or annulled contracts and charters that past generations had established to protect the interests of unborn heirs, of charity schools, and of religious institutions. When traditional practices and arrangements prevented the Grenvilles from reaping the full benefits of their property, they did not resignedly accept the situation. Instead, they sought to change it.

They were confident that they could change it. As George observed in his letters to Richard during 1738, the institution that created law, Parliament, and the institution that interpreted and enforced it, the courts, would not prevent private efforts to overthrow old legal and customary arrangements. On the contrary: Parliament was so certain of the right of petitioners to make new arrangements among themselves, and so confident of its right to authorize and make binding enclosures, that it passed such legislation almost perfunctorily. George could be sure, for example, that it was "next to impossible" that the House of Commons would go out of its way to determine that the interests of St. Paul's School were really being served by the Mercers' agreement. As for the courts, the judges who controlled them were so committed to the principle of expanding their jurisdiction that they would not block the amendment or abrogation of centuries old contracts and rights. When property owners of sufficient power wanted them to do so, these institutions were more than willing to create and maintain new laws that destroyed the old.

Furthermore, in addition to permitting change, these institutions also legitimized it, investing it with the authority of the law, and thus helping elicit acceptance of the new way of doing things.[49] George's advice to Richard that he had the Commissioners write to the Hynds and tell them "that in pursuance of the power given them by Act of Parliament they have allotted to you his lands in the common fields and set our for [them] . . . other lands" reveals his awareness of these uses of the law. In effect, the Hynds were to be told, in an apparently official document, that the Commissioners had acted according to law, and by its authority, rather than responding to the whim of one man. Moreover, the document would inform the Hynds that the same authority had protected their rights to own property at Ashendon, and conferred upon them equivalent lands there. To be sure, George intended that this letter, which had no legal bearing on the present situation and therefore could confer no legality on Richard's actions, would deceive the Hynds into submission. Still, that he would confidently predict that James Hynds "will not . . . commit an act of violence against it" reveals his faith in the power of the law to symbolize authority, legitimacy, and fairness, and, by so doing, inspire obedience and acquiescence to change.[50]

This readiness of powerful private individuals and powerful public institutions to overthrow the past and legitimize the new when it suited private interests made the law an instrument of radical, even revolutionary change. This fact disturbed neither the Grenvilles, nor the Parliament, nor the courts. They understood that those men in their society who possessed great political and economic power would dominate the processes of writing, legislating, interpreting, and enforcing the law. So long as these men were careful, the power of the law to change would be controlled by their domination of these processes. A good example of their power and their care in the use of the law may be found in the experiences of the Hynds during 1737-1738. It was true that the Hynds' property at Ashendon did not protect them against enclosure or against an award of different acres than the ones they had had rights to use. But they owned the rights to five acres out of 1,700 at Ashendon, and there was no chance that a House of Commons composed of men of the highest economic and political statuses would permit people who owned five acres and had no powerful connections to carry their point and thwart the will of men and institutions like the

Grenvilles, Cobham, Christ Church, and Lincoln College.[51] Still, the House did take care to "apprize [the Hynds] of the intended enclosure, . . . [deliver] printed copies of the bill . . . to them," and give them the opportunity to appear against the bill.[52] This was not a charade, intended to mollify the Hynds. Carefully following this procedure preserved the right of property owners great and small to testify before a House Committee and to exert their influence against any proposed changes in their property. The testimony of people like the Grenvilles would, of course, have a greater impact on the House than people like the Hynds. Thus the weapon for change was unlikely to fall into the wrong hands, while at the same time the powerful would not be stymied by arguments supporting tradition or precedent from the powerless.

George Grenville understood this intimate relationship between his family's power and the law perfectly. When it suited his interests, he stood ready to plead the power of Parliament to sever dead hands from past and free the living to develop their estates as fully as they could. He was also ready, as the enclosures at Ashendon and Wotton prove, to take full advantage of the fact of his and his brother's membership in the House to obtain those acts, and even, if it came to be necessary, to use the privileges of a Member of Parliament to protect Richard from the consequences of trespassing on the Hynds' property. He was equally prepared to postpone or give up his plans, whenever he encountered powerful enough opposition to them.[53] And when his interests were best served by the *status quo*, he could persuasively cite past agreements and rely on the shield of both the law and customary practice to protect his property.[54] In short, he was familiar and comfortable with the manipulation of legal arguments to suit his family's interests. Burke's insinuation that the law almost inevitably made a man narrow-minded and precedent-bound would have struck him as a naive comment, made by a man who was either no attorney, or a rather poor one.

IV

Did these habits of thinking generated by his legal career influence decisions Grenville made during his political career? Can one posit a relationship between the enclosure at Ashendon and the Stamp Act similar to the legendary one between the playing fields at Eton and Waterloo?[55] Clearly there is no direct relationship between decisions reached during 1764-1765 and. those made earlier during 1737-1738. Indeed, there is no reason to believe that Grenville still recalled the details of these enclosures, which were but two of many that he had handled and was handling. The papers of his family make it clear, though, that Grenville's legal practice from 1738 to 1765 constantly required him to repeat his experiences with Ashendon and Wotton. Again and again he had to examine traditional practices and longstanding agreements, assess whether change would benefit himself and his family, and if it did, seek the best ways of effecting that change. The type of law he practiced did not narrow his mind and limit his responses to situations; rather, it frequently demanded that he think broadly and act creatively. It did not teach him to follow precedents exactly; instead, it inclined him toward using the law and legal institutions to accomplish change when he believed change was necessary and possible.

Grenville consistently applied the habits he developed during his legal career to the problems he confronted in office throughout his administrative career prior to becoming First Lord of the Treasury. Perhaps Burke's criticism of most of officialdom in eighteenth century Whitehall was accurate; it was not, however, a just charge against Grenville. Grenville had not merely "studied practically the several duties and services of most offices"; he had studied them with an eye toward improving their services when it seemed necessary.[56] In his first office, as a junior Lord of the Admiralty during 1744-1747, he soon felt confident enough to question the deployment of ships made by veteran admirals. He also interested himself in particular in the regular and efficient cleaning of ships' bottoms. In 1745, he persuaded the other Lords of the Admiralty to order the Navy Board "to take all possible care to put everything at that yard [at Kinsale] into order immediately for the cleaning of ships."[57] Soon afterwards, he fretted that "we [might] spoil all our line-of-battle ships, by keeping what formed the Western Squadron in the Downs all winter, instead of cleaning them, and putting them in order for the spring," and thus be vulnerable to a French invasion.[58] In 1746, during the planning of a Canadian expedition, Grenville insistently reminded the First Lord of the Admiralty, the Duke of Bedford, of the absolute necessity of making preparations early and sending news of the plans to America as quickly as possible.[59] This burst of energy came to naught, as the mission was scrubbed, and Grenville's efforts to create greater efficiency in the planning and execution of a major expedition in America bore no fruit. This must have seemed a typical development for Grenville, as he was less and less enchanted with his colleagues at the Admiralty with the passing of time (and they with him), and more and more eager to become a Lord of the Treasury. Finally, after a frustrating wait, he achieved that post in June 1747.[60]

Grenville's service at the Treasury was, however, equally frustrating. Henry Pelham, the First Lord, did not trust him, and he, in turn, disliked Pelham. On at least two occasions, Pelham broke promises he had made to Grenville, and the embittered Grenville later referred to his activities at the Treasury during 1747-1754 as "giving what support I was able to those who never gave any to me."[61] Despite these personal frictions, however, Grenville had a financier's appreciation for the boldness and calculation with which Pelham accomplished the reduction of the national debt. However much it may have galled him to do so, in his first speech as First Lord on the budget to the House of Commons, Grenville praised Pelham's reform, and at the same time hoped that his parliamentary opponents would be as public-spirited in assisting him with necessary reforms as Peiham's had been.[62]

For most of the time between 1754 and 1762, Grenville served as Treasurer of the Navy. He devoted much of his energy during that period to devising and attempting to enact legislation that would enable the Navy to be mobilized much more quickly in times of emergency. In his view, the principal reason why the Navy could only reach full strength over a period of years rather than months was the shortage of trained seamen in the service at the beginning of war and the difficulties of recruiting them. To solve this problem, he proposed to make the Navy more attractive to skilled volunteers, and to make it more attractive, he planned to establish "a regular method for the punctual, frequent, and certain payment of [seamen's] wages; and for enabling them more easily and readily to remit the same for the support of their wives and families; and for preventing frauds and abuses attending such payments." These, he had discovered, were among the principal grievances of the seamen. Remedy them, he assumed, and the Navy could be manned more easily. He drafted a bill that established budgetary and administrative restraints and procedures which he believed would accomplish these reforms. Ultimately, he not only succeeded in obtaining the Navy Act of 1758, which one authority has called "arguably the most single important piece of legislation attempting to grapple with [these problems] between 1696 and 1835," but he also obtained it in the teeth of opposition from the Navy Board itself.[63] The next year, Grenville again attempted a major reform. Allies of his and Pitt's introduced legislation that would have required all skilled British seamen to register with naval authorities. In time of war, the Navy would determine how many seamen it needed, and names would be chosen by lot from this list. The bill also limited their service to three years at the usual wages, and required the Navy to pay them $3d.$ per day extra if it chose to keep men a fourth year, and $6d.$ per day extra thereafter. If the bill had passed, the major reasons why few men volunteered—low pay and indefinite service—probably would have been removed to a considerable degree. But the merchant community rallied against the bill, and finally defeated it in March 1759.[64] Thus the program for naval reform remained incomplete.

Also during his tenure as Treasurer of the Navy, Grenville maintained his earlier interest in the operation of the Navy's yards. When he heard about an investigation into a fraud at the Deptford yard, he intruded himself into it, even though such an investigation lay outside his official duties.[65] This particular matter continued to concern him during his brief service as First Lord of the Admiralty from October 1762 to April 1763. When he discussed the expense of maintaining the fleet in good condition with his successor at the Admiralty, he noted, "The most reasonable and knowing part of the world have long been persuaded that all the naval money is by no means applied in the most frugal manner. I have thought so myself," he continued, "[and] I did resolve when I had the honor to be in that office, to make the strictest and most careful examination into a matter of this great moment, and had taken some steps toward it, but my short continuance in that station prevented me from carrying it into execution."[66]

In sum, Grenville spent most of his administrative career before he became First Lord of the Treasury personally examining the usual practices and procedures of important offices, testing their efficiency and usefulness, and changing them when he felt change was necessary for the service of the country. Arguments from officials and from interested parties did not deter him from these investigations, any more than their opposition to his proposals frightened him from attempting reform. Had he lived long enough to hear Burke's description of him as a follower of the "beaten track" of office, no doubt he would have laughed. On a variety of occasions in his official career, he had attempted to beat his own track. When he failed at doing this, he was not discouraged. When he succeeded, his inclination toward reform whenever he was convinced of its necessity was further strengthened.

Thus when Grenville began his ill-fated tenure at the Treasury, he had had considerable experience at applying the habits of outlook and action engendered and encouraged by his legal career to the problems of office. In both of his careers, he was accustomed to investigating customary ways of doing things, determining whether the continuance of those ways would benefit his own or the nation's interests in the future, attempting to change them when he believed change was possible and advisable, dismissing interested arguments in favor of the *status quo*, using legal arguments when appropriate in his efforts to accomplish reform, and taking advantage of the law's power and majesty to enact, enforce, and legitimize change. Often his appreciation of the benefits and virtues of carefully calculated reforms had served him well. In the case of the Stamp Act, though, these "particular habits of his life" encouraged him along the path toward imperial disaster.

Endnotes

[1] Edmund Burke's speech on the motion to repeal the tea duty, Apr. 19, 1774, *The Parliamentary History of England from the Earliest Period to the Year 1803*, William Cobbett, ed., 36 vols. (London: T. C. Hansard, 1806-1820), XVII, pp.1239-40. Hereafter this source will be cited as *Parliamentary History*. Cobbett copied this speech from the version in *The History, Debates, and Proceedings of both Houses of Parliament . . .1743 to 1774*, 7 vols. (London, J. Debrett, 1792), John Debrett, ed., VII. Debrett's source for the speech was the version first published by James Dodsley on Jan. 10, 1775. Dodsley was Burke's usual publisher, and the surviving correspondence indicates that Burke not only approved of this version, but also actively (though secretly) participated in its publication and distribution. See Richard Burke, Sr., to Richard Champion, Jan. 9, 1775, in: *The Correspondence of Edmund Burke, Volume III, July 1774-June 1778*, George H. Guttridge, ed. (Cambridge, Cambridge University Press, 1961), pp. 93-94. Indeed, this version may be very close to the remarks Burke actually made on Apr. 19. Sir Henry Cavendish, who usually tried to transcribe every speech made in the House, evidently took no notes on this speech, and explained his omission in his diary thusly: "Mr. Edmund Burke's speech copied, and printed." This comment may indicate that Cavendish knew that a confederate of Burke's was taking careful notes as he made the speech. Diary of Henry Cavendish, Egerton MSS. 255, 190, British Library, London, shorthand translation in The History of Parliament Trust, London. All of the quotations from Burke's speech in the text above, with the exception of those specifically cited, are from this version, as reprinted in *Parliamentary History*. On occasion, I have quoted from the notes taken by Matthew Brickdale, M.P., on Apr. 19, 1774, because Brickdale, a practiced abstracter of speeches in the House, expressed some of Burke's thoughts more clearly and succinctly than the speaker himself. This version may be found in Parliamentary Diaries of Matthew Brickdale, Box

IX, Apr. 19, 1774, Bristol University Library, Bristol, England, microfilm in the Library of Congress, Washington, D.C.

[2] Brickdale Diaries, Book IX, Apr. 19, 1774.

[3] *Ibid.*

[4] *Ibid.* See also Phil Lawson's article on Grenville in: R. Eccleshall and Graham Walker, *Biographical Dictionary of British Prime Ministers* (London, 1998).

[5] *Ibid.* A shorthand transcription of Wedderburne's speech may be found in Cavendish's diary. Although the characters are evidently obscure, and thus the gaps in the notes are frequent, clearly Cavendish's version agrees with Brickdale's. Cavendish Diary, Egerton MSS. 255, pp.190-91, British Library, translation, in :The History of Parliament Trust. The version of Wedderburne's speech in *Parliamentary History*, XVII, pp. 1269-70 omits these comments, merely noting that the Solicitor General said, "I differ much from [Burke] in the character of that great man, the late Mr. Grenville."

[6] Brickdale Diaries, Book IX, Apr. 19, 1774.

[7] For the vote, see *Parliamentary History*, XVII, p.1273. For an indication that Burke's effort entertained the House, see the notation in the text that Members cried, "Go on, go on," when he said, "I hope I am not going into a narrative troublesome to the House." *Ibid.*, p. 1246. This sort of attention and indulgence was not often accorded to Burke, another indication of how interested the House was. See P. D. G. Thomas, *The House of Commons in the Eighteenth Century* (Oxford: Clarendon Press, 1971), pp. 225-26.

[8] Indeed, Ian R. Christie has noted that "Grenville's character displayed both strengths and weaknesses which may have contributed to the growing friction within the Empire," and praised Burke's comments on Apr. 19, 1774 on his character as "both shrewd and fair." Ian R. Christie and Benjamin W. Labaree, *Empire or Independence, 1760-1776: A British-American Dialogue on the Coming of the American Revolution* (NY, W. W. Norton & Co., 1976), p. 26.

[9] For Wedderburne's comment, see Cavendish Diary, Egerton MSS. 255, 191, British Library, translation in The House of Parliament Trust. For the comment on Grenville's "lawyerly-like distinctions," which was the Earl of Bute's, see Richard Rigby to the Duke of Bedford, Sept. 29, 1762, *Correspondence of John, fourth Duke of Bedford, selected from the originals at Woburn Abbey*, ed. by Lord John Russell, 3 vols. (London, John Murray, 1842-46), III, p. 127. For the comparison of Grenville to a solicitor at the Old Bailey, see [John Almon, writing as An Independent Whig], *A letter to the right honourable George Grenville* (London, 1763), p. 34; for Grenville's reply, see [George Grenville], *A reply to a letter addressed to the right honourable George Grenville, etc. In which the truth of the facts is examined, and the propriety of the motto fully considered* (London,

1763), p.17. For Grenville's reference to legal principles when he introduced the stamp tax, see his speeches, Mar. 9, 1764 and Feb. 6, 1765, "Parliamentary Diaries of Nathaniel Ryder," ed. by P. D. G Thomas, *Camden Miscellany vol. XXIII,* Camden Fourth Series, Volume 7 (London, The Royal Historical Society, [1969]), pp. 235, 254-55.

[10] For Cobham's role in Grenville's choice of a career, see George Grenville, "narrative," Apr. 12, 1762, in: *The Grenville Papers: Being the Correspondence of Richard Grenville Earl Temple K.G. and The Right Hon: George Grenville, Their Friends and Contemporaries,* ed. by William James Smith, 1 (London, John Murray, 1852-53), I, p. 423, hereafter cited as: *Grenville Papers*; and Lewis M. Wiggin, *The Faction of Cousins: A Political Account of the Grenvilles, 1733-1763* (New Haven: Yale University Press, 1958), pp.5-6. Grenville apparently paid little attention to legal affairs that did not touch on his family; he even confessed that he was "so very little of the counsellor and so entirely George Grenville" that he preferred the country to the city. Grenville to Lady Suffolk, n.d., in *ibid.,* p. 65. His lack of enthusiasm may be traceable to a lack of business, for in 1738 he facetiously called his brother "a special client" because he proposed to bring on enough lawsuits to employ not only Grenville but also any son Richard might choose to breed to the law, and thus keep that son from being in "the condition of us young counsellors, without business." Grenville to R. Grenville, Dec. 14, 1738, Grenville Papers, STG 192-(7), Henry E. Huntington Library, San Marino, CA. Later in his life, Grenville may have fallen in the habit of referring some of the family's legal affairs to attorneys of his choosing. For example, see Thomas Ryder to [Richard Grenville], July 28, 1753, Grenville Papers, STG 423-(58).

[11] For a good brief description of the Grenvilles' business papers, see Wiggin, *Faction of Cousins,* pp. 75-76n. Since Wiggin wrote this, archivists at the Huntington Library have imposed some order on these papers and made them easier to use, but his observations about the *lacunae* in them and the whimsical and incomplete nature of the surviving account books are unfortunately still appropriate ones.

[12] [Richard Grenville] to the Countess of Denbigh, Sept. 26, 1742, Historic Manuscripts Commission, *Report on the Manuscripts of the Earl of Denbigh Preserved at Newnham Paddox, Warwickshire, (Part V.),* (London, His Majesty's Stationery Office, 1911), p. 237, hereafter cited as HMC, *Denbigh.*

[13] For indications of Richard's care in the handling of even small sums of money, see his anger at spending two guineas for "pretended services" by poor men at Wendover in Richard Grenville's Account Book, 1732-1779, entries for Michelmas 1740 to May 9, 1741, Grenville Papers, ST 164; his noting a steward's entering L 11-7*s.-d.* in an account instead of the correct L 11-17*s.-6d.,* Richard Grenville to R. Codrington, Sept. 28, 1772, Grenville Papers, STG 1419-(12); and his fury at arrears in another steward's accounts amounting to 30 guineas, John

King to Earl Temple [Richard Grenville], Feb. 21, 1762, Grenville Papers, STG 1421-(62). For Richard's periodic suspicions that his brother wished "to divide the family, and put [him]self at the head of a party in it," see "narrative," Apr. 12, 1762, *Grenville Papers*, I, pp. 427-28. Perhaps it was during one of these periods that Richard approached another attorney for advice on an unknown subject, and made him promise not to mention "a syllable of your intentions to Mr. G. Grenville or anyone else." James Booth to [Richard Grenville], July 11 1752, quoted in Wiggin, *Faction of Cousins*, p. 163.

[14] [Richard Grenville] to the Countess of Denbigh, Sept. 26, 1742, HMC, *Denbigh*, p. 237.

[15] Examples of the Grenvilles' skill and patience as negotiators abound in their surviving business records. Perhaps the most incredible may be found in Grenville Papers, L9D10, Huntington Library, where documents reveal that the family annually denied any obligation to repair a road called Long Lane in Bucks from 1752 to 1778, at which time the Grenvilles' opponents finally conceded the point. For an example of George Grenville's carefulness, see Edward Gibbon to Grenville, Apr. 22 and May 17, 1765, Grenville Papers, STG 365-(41), (43); and Grenville to Gibbon, Apr. 25 and May 11, 1765, George Grenville Letterbooks, ST 7, II, Huntington Library.

[16] Grenville to Richard Grenville, Dec. 14, 1738, Grenville Papers, STG 192-(7).

[17] *The Victoria History of the County of Buckinghamshire*, William Page, ed., 14 vols. and a separately published index (London: Archibald Constable and Company Ltd, vols. I, II, 1905-08; and The St. Catherine Press, vols. III, IV, and the index, 1925-28), IV, 4, 131. Hereafter this source will be cited as VCH, *Bucks*.

[18] The quotation is from Richard Grenville's petition for an act enclosing certain lands at Ashendon, Mar. 7, 1737/8, *Journals of the House of Commons*, XXIII, p.64. The Grenvilles used precisely the same language in Richard's petition for an act enclosing land at Wotton on Mar. 12, 1741-2, *ibid.*, XXIV, p. 120. Hereafter this source will be cited as *Commons Journals*. There is no reason to assume that this description was inaccurate. Indeed, given the strict regulations governing the introduction of private legislation, it is likely that the Grenvilles chose the language for their petitions carefully. See Thomas, *House of Commons*, pp. 57-58.

[19] VCH, *Bucks*, IV, p.130.

[20] Petition for enclosing Ashendon, Mar. 7, 1737-8, *Commons Journals*, XXIII, p.64.

[21] For Richard's characterization of himself as "a poor country haymaker," see Richard Grenville to the Countess of Denbigh, June 19, 1743, HMC, *Denbigh*, p. 241. For his concern about the damage his neighbors' cattle were doing to his

fields at a partially hedged area at Wotton, see Grenville to Richard Grenville, Dec. 14, 1738, Grenville Papers, STG 192-(7).

[22] As its name suggests, Wotton Underwood was heavily wooded. VCH, *Bucks*, IV, p.130. For examples of the Grenvilles' constant concern over the profits they gained by harvesting timber on other property they owned in Bucks, see J. Oxlade to Richard Grenville, Aug. 17, 1742, Edward Bacon to Grenville, Aug. 7, 1753, [Richard Grenville] to Edward Bacon, Mar. 10, 1755, and John Fessey to Grenville, Dec. 10 and Dec. 27, 1765, and Feb. 26, 1766, Grenville Papers, STG 423-(9), 365-(15), 1425-(3) and (39) and 365-(36-38). By 1749, Richard's reputation as "a gentleman of honor and knowledge in the rural . . . sciences" was such that a neighbor asked him to arbitrate a dispute he was having over the value of some trees. William Ince to [Richard Grenville], Aug. 2, 1749, Grenville Papers, STG 421-(48).

[23] Information on rents at Ashendon and Wotton immediately before and after enclosure is no longer extant. However, a notation on Richard Grenville's "Account of expenses concerning the Ashendon enclosure" [1737-1739] reveals that he expected that these expenses would be "charged in rentals" to his tenants. Richard Grenville's Account Book, 1732-1779, ST 164, p. 310.

[24] For a list of these institutions, see Mar. 7, 1737-8, and Mar. 12, 1741-2 in *Commons Journals*, XXXIII, p. 64 and XXIV, p.120. For a description of the customs regulating the assessment of tithes on the Grenvilles' lands in Bucks, see copies of the agreement between Lord Cobham and Thomas Price, May 28, 1722, the indenture between Cobham and Thomas Price and Campbell Price, July 7, 1729, and Richard Codrington to [Richard Grenville], Mar. 23, 1769, Grenville Papers, L9D10 (for both the agreement and the indenture), and STG 419-(4).

[25] For examples of these efforts in the past, see the agreement between Cobham and Thomas Price, and the indenture between Cobham and the Prices, cited in note 24 above. See also the description of codicils to the wills of Cobham and his sister regarding the annuity to the vicar at Stowe in Grenville Papers, STG 192-(50). For other correspondence regarding this annuity, see STG 225-(25-32) and STG 423-(58).

[26] Richard Codrington to [Richard Grenville], Mar. 23, 1769, Grenville Papers, STG 419-(4).

[27] For these quotations, see G.E. Mingay, "The Agricultural Depression 1730-1750, *Economic History Review*, 2nd Ser., VIII (1956), pp. 323-24. In this article, Mingay reached the conclusion that these writers were accurately describing the situation in some areas of England. It is highly unlikely that a man as interested in business as Richard Grenville would have been unaware of this depression and of the pamphlet literature that touted cures for it.

[28] See VCH, *Bucks*, II, p. 82. Again, it is highly unlikely that Richard Grenville, who was active in county affairs and in other sorts of economic improvements,

especially turnpikes, would be unaware of this fact. Indeed, enclosure by Act of Parliament was rare in all areas of England during this period. During the years 1735 through 1745, an average of only four enclosures per year were enacted by Parliament. By way of comparison, during 1755-1765, the average was 31 acts a year, and during 1765-1775, 47 acts. "Report from the committee on the means of permitting the cultivation and improvement of the wastes, unenclosed, and unproductive lands, etc. of this Kingdom," Apr. 27, 1797, *Reports from Committees of the House of Commons Vol. IX Provisions: Poor: 1774-1802,* (London: by order of the House of Commons, 1803), pp.219-20.

[29] Richard's account book for the years 1732-1779 reveals that he made special trips to Wotton for this purpose that he otherwise would not have made, and that he incurred expenses for "additional housekeeping, wine, etc." The account book does not, however, give any hint as to the amount of these expenses. Grenville Papers, ST 164, p. 310.

[30] See Grenville to Richard Grenville, Nov. 23, Dec. 14, Dec. 24, 1738, Grenville Papers, STG 192-(6-8).

[31] Report of the committee on Richard Grenville's petition to enclose Ashendon, Mar. 17, 1737-8, *Commons Journals,* XXIII, p. 100.

[32] Richard Grenville's petition to enclose Ashendon, Mar. 7, 1737-8, *ibid.,* p. 64.

[33] For these details of the agreement, and for the quotation from Richard, see his draft of a letter to the Dean and Chapter of Christ Church, Oxford, [1758], Grenville Papers, STG 225-(41). In 1758, Christ Church attempted to use this agreement to justify raising the fine that Richard owed them higher than they usually did. They reasoned, "Have we not some reason to complain that we only have lands allotted to us that are unimprovable?" and then pointed out, "Whatever advantage is made in the value of the tithes and of the lands which were originally ours (which by this time must be considerable), [Richard Grenville] enjoys." Richard Hanwell to John King, Mar. 14, 1758, STG 225-(47). Christ Church, however, had already ceased their efforts to raise the fine that year. Hanwell to King, Mar. 8, 1758, STG 225-(46). In 1771, the controversy was renewed. Richard observed to his steward then, "It appears that the Commissioners have dealt very hardly with the college in their allotment for the unenclosed glebe, as the advance should have been greater. But the chapter had [the opportunity to object] and they were unanimous [in favor of accepting it]." [Richard Grenville] to John Jeffrey, June 11, 1771, STG 425-(24).

[34] Christ Church and Lincoln College reached an agreement with Richard Grenville on Feb. 24, 1737-8. On Mar. 7, 1737-8, he petitioned the House of Commons for an act enclosing Ashendon. *Commons Journals,* XXIII, 100, 64. For the size of the enclosed area, see VCH, *Bucks,* IV, p. 3.

[35] *Commons Journals*, XXIII, pp. 64, 100. One of those who refused to sign the articles when they were presented to him on Mar. 9, 1737-8 gave this excuse: "he could not advise with his attorney, he being absent; and that, as he was ignorant of the law, he did not care to execute, without first advising with him; but was very willing, that Mr. Grenville should go on with the same." *Ibid.*, p.100.

[36] Sandys was appointed chairman of the committee that considered Richard Grenville's petition, and during the eighteenth century this usually meant that he had presented the petition. See *Commons Journals*, XXIII, p. 64; and Thomas, *House of Commons*, pp. 57-58. For biographical information about Sandys, see Romney Sedgwick, ed., *The History of Parliament: The House of Commons, 1715-1754*, 2 vols. (Oxford: Oxford University Press, 1970), II, pp. 406-408.

[37] Richard Grenville's account book, 1732-1779, reveals that the Grenvilles were responsible for drawing up the act. Grenville Papers, ST 164, p. 310. For a reference to amendments made by the committee, see Apr. 7, 1738, *Commons Journals*, XXIII, p. 136. For some stylistic amendments, see Apr. 10, 1738, *ibid.*, p. 141.

[38] See *ibid.*, pp. 136, 141.

[39] Richard Grenville bore the entire expense of enclosing Ashendon. See King to [Hanwell]?, Nov. 20, 1757, Grenville Papers, STG 225-(35). He paid seven commissioners five guineas each, a total expense of L 36-15s. Richard Grenville's account book, 1732-1779, ST 164, p. 310. Perhaps one can judge how quickly these men worked by noting that at the end of the eighteenth century the usual salary for commissioners was two guineas a day. "Report from the select committee appointed to consider of the most effectual means of facilitating bills of enclosure," Apr. 17, 1800, in *Reports from Committees of the House of Commons, Vol. IX Provisions: Poor: 1774-1802*, pp. 230, 232. J.M. Martin has pointed out that in Warwickshire commissioners' fees apparently increased as time passed during the century. In 1767, the commissioners making the award at Wixford, Warwick received a guinea a day. Probably Richard was charged a similar rate, which would mean each commissioner worked five days. J.M. Martin, "The Cost of Parliamentary Enclosure in Warwickshire," in E. L. Jones, ed., *Agriculture and Economic Growth in England 1650-1815*, (London, Methuen & Co., Ltd., 1967), p. 134.

[40] See Grenville to Richard Grenville, Dec. 14, 1738. Grenville Papers, STG 192-(7). Richard's eagerness to enclose Ashendon may perhaps be gauged by Martin's observation that in Warwick during the early part of the eighteenth century "the application for the act was usually followed *in the next year* by the commissioners' award (italics mine)." Martin, "Cost of Parliamentary Enclosure," in Jones, ed., *Agriculture and Economic Growth*, p. 135.

[41] The next four paragraphs in the text are based upon the information in Grenville to Richard Grenville, Dec. 24, 1738, Grenville Papers, STG 192-(8). All

quotations are from this source as well. Where I have drawn information from another source in these four paragraphs, I specifically noted it in note 42 below.

[42] Grenville to Richard Grenville, Dec. 14, 1738, Grenville Papers, STG, 192-(7).

[43] *Ibid.* For a discussion of the various privileges of the House of Commons and its Members, see Thomas, *House of Commons*, pp. 334-38.

[44] Richard Grenville's pleasure at the fact that enclosing Ashendon relieved him from the weight of tithes that would have been regularly raised is obvious in his and his agent's correspondence with Christ Church during 1757-1758 in Grenville Papers, STG 225 - (19-47). One may take his comment to the college that "the expense of Ashendon enclosure was very great, and the profit upon the whole but small, on account of the high rate the land was let at unenclosed" with several grains of salt. Certainly Christ Church did. See draft of a letter to Christ Church, [1758], STG 225 - (41), and Hanwell to King, Mar. 14, 1758, STG-(47).

[45] Grenville to Richard Grenville, Dec. 14, 1738, Grenville Papers, STG 192-(7).

[46] Grenville to Richard Grenville, Nov. 23, 1738, Grenville Papaers, STG 192-(6).

[47] See Mar. 12, 1741-2; Apr. 9, 14, 29, 1742; and May 4, 1742, *Commons Journals*, XXIV, pp. 120, 171, 181, 188, 195.

[48] [Richard Grenville] to the Countess of Denbigh, Sept. 26, 1742, HMC, *Denbigh*, p. 237.

[49] For an excellent discussion of how judges manipulated the criminal laws of the eighteenth century to achieve this purpose, see: Douglas Hay, "Property, Authority, and the Criminal Law," in Douglas Hay, et.al. eds., *Albion's Fatal Tree: Crime and Society in Eighteenth Century England* (New York, Pantheon Books, 1975), pp. 17-63.

[50] Grenville to Richard Grenville, Dec. 24, 1738, Grenville Papers, STG 192(8).

[51] The report of the committee investigating the petition to enclose Ashendon emphasized carefully on Mar. 17, 1737-8 that "James Hynd and Mary his wife . . . are entitled to an undivided fourth part of 20 acres *only*" (my emphasis). The committee again noted on Apr. 7, 1738 that the Hynds "have an undivided fourth part of one half yard land, and the right of commons belonging to the same; which half yard of land does not contain above 20 acres." *Commons Journals*, XXIII, pp. 100, 136. It is interesting to note that in 1738 Richard Grenville was considering the wisdom of parliamentary enclosures at Wescott and at Ludgershall, Bucks. When these areas were finally enclosed, in both cases some proprietors did not agree to the bill of enclosure. At Westcott, one proprietor "possessed of three quarters of a yard land in the said fields, who lived at a great distance, . . . could not be applied to." The committee carefully noted that the entire enclosure contained about 34 yard lands. At Ludgershall, where the

commons caused "frequent trespasses and disputes among the proprietors and their tenants," owners of "eight yard lands . . . refused to sign the bill." The committee added, "the whole of the lands intended to be enclosed consisted of fifty-one yard lands and one quarter, and . . . no person appeared before the committee to oppose the bill." For Richard's interest in these lands, see Grenville to Richard Grenville, Dec. 14, 1738, Grenville Papers STG 192-(7). For the information on Westcott and Ludgershall, see Feb. 13, 1765, *Commons Journals*, XXX, p. 128; and Feb. 3, Mar. 11, 1777, *ibid.*, XXXVI, pp. 106, 259.

[52] *Ibid.*, XXIII, p.136.

[53] As mentioned in note 51, in 1738 Richard was also interested in enclosures at Westcott and Ludgershall, Bucks. For some reason, his plans did not immediately bear fruit. Westcott was finally enclosed by Act of Parliament in 1765, and Lugershall in 1777. Grenville to Richard Grenville, Dec. 14, 1738. Grenville Papers, STG 192 - (7); VCH, *Bucks*, IV, pp. 69, 108. George Grenville apparently was not directly involved in moving the Westcott enclosure through the stages of legislation, but this is unsurprising, considering that it was before the House debates on the budget in 1765. See Jan. 24, 29, Feb. 2, 13, 14, 1765, *Commons Journals* XXX, pp. 56, 66, 77, 128, 137. Grenville's son did play an active role in the passage of the Ludgershall enclosure. See Feb. 3, 12, 20, Mar. 11, 18, 1777, *ibid.*, XXXVI, pp. 106, 158, 198-99, 259, 285.

[54] For an example, see the negotiations over the proposal of the Warden of New College, Oxford, that Grenville assist in the enclosure of land leased to him at Tetchwick, Bucks. Grenville to Rev. Mr. Price, Oct. 6, 1764, and to Rev. Mr. Hayward, Oct. 23, 1764, in Grenville Letterbook, ST 7, II, and [to Grenville, [Hayward] to Grenville, [Nov. 1766], Grenville Papers, STG 366 - (2). By 1777 Grenville or his son had evidently purchased the land from New College. In that year, Grenville's son refused to include his property at Tetchwick in the enclosure at neighboring Ludgershall. See VCH, *Bucks*, IV, pp. 69, 71.

[55] As Elizabeth Longford has observed, it is highly unlikely that the Duke of Wellington ever remarked on any relationship between Eton's fields and Waterloo. Elizabeth Longford, *Wellington: The Years of the Sword* (London, Weidenfield and Nicolson, 1969), pp. 16-17.

[56] The quotation is from Wedderburne's speech, Apr. 19, 1774, Brickdale Diaries, Book IV. One should remember that no matter how trenchant Burke's remarks may seem to an age complicated by bureaucracies and their regulations that he spoke in 1774 from no practical knowledge of eighteenth century administration.

[57] Grenville to Thomas Grenville, May 13, 1745, *Grenville Papers*, I, p. 35. For his comments on naval strategy, see another letter to his brother Thomas, Oct. 10, 1745, *ibid.*, p. 44. During his stay at the Admiralty, Grenville worked ceaselessly to further his brother's career in the Navy. In the case of the yard at Kinsale, reform served not only the nation's interest but his family's as well.

[58] Grenville to Thomas Grenville, Dec. 28, 1745, *ibid.*, pp. 48-49.

[59] See Grenville to the Duke of Bedford, Oct. 2 Nov, 19, 1746, *Bedford Correspondence*, I, pp. 182, 196; and Bedford to Grenville, Nov. 11, 24, 1746, *Grenville Papers*, I, pp. 54-55.

[60] Much of Grenville's frustration with his colleagues stemmed from their constant refusal to fulfill a promise they had made to him that Thomas Grenville would have a separate command. His ill-tempered persistence may have actually hindered his brother's career. See N.A.M. Rodger, *The Wooden World: The Anatomy of the Georgian Navy* (London, 1986), pp. 278, 315-316. See Grenville to Thomas Grenville, Apr. 2, 1747, *ibid.*, pp. 58-60. For his efforts to get an appointment to the Treasury, see Grenville, "narrative," Apr. 12, 1762, *ibid.*, pp. 425-26.

[61] *Ibid.*, p. 426.

[62] Grenville's speech, Mar. 9, 1764, "Diaries of Ryder," Thomas, ed., Camden Miscellany Vol. XXIII, Camden Fourth Series, Vol. 7, p. 234. The best description of Pelham's accomplishment may be found in P.G.M. Dickson, *The Financial Revolution in England: A Study in the Development of Public Credit* (NY, St. Martin's Press, 1967), pp. 228-43. On Pelham's accomplishments see, more recently: R.T. Connors, "Pelham, Parliament and Public Policy, 1746-1754," (Cambridge, Ph.D [1993]) and the excellent article by Andrew Hanham in: R. Eccleshall and Graham Walker, *Biographical Dictionary of British Prime Ministers*, (London, 1998), pp. 17-28. There is also the arguable question of deficient foresight on his part when it came to foreign affairs, a point made recently by G. Holmes and D. Szechi, though admittedly, they probably overlooked the serious political/financial constraints within which Pelham had to work.

[63] The information in this paragraph is from Stephen F. Gradish, "Wages and manning: The Navy Act of 1758," *English Historical Review*, xciii, 1978, pp. 46-67. The quotations are from pp. 61-62. For an incisive analysis of the strengths and shortcomings of Grenville's Act, see Rodger, *Wooden World*, pp. 132-135.

[64] *Ibid.*, pp. 63-64; and Philip Lawson, *George Grenville: A Political Life,* (Clarendon Press, Oxford, 1984), pp.105-108. Ultimately Grenville succeeded in shepherding a bill through the Commons and into law. It did not function as well as its author hoped, thanks to persistent merchant opposition.

[65] *Ibid.*, p. 105.

[66] Grenville's comments to the Earl of Sandwich are quoted in: *ibid.*, p.111.

Escaping Boston: Nathaniel Ware and the Beginnings of Colonial
Taxation, 1762-1763*

Years after Britain's American colonies won their independence, a former
colleague of George Grenville sardonically observed that "Mr. Grenville lost
America because he read the American dispatches, which his predecessors had
never done."[1] The kernel of truth in this witticism enabled it to survive in men's
memories: Grenville and his colleagues had in fact studied reports from America
more closely, and with a keener eye for ways to maintain British domination over
the colonies, than most of the men who came before them in office. But historians
have long known that what Grenville heard from men in London about America
often had at least as great an influence on his decisions as what he read from men
in America. In particular, students of the first British Empire have fully described
the part Henry McCulloh, a Scots merchant and resident of London who had
served as inspector and comptroller of the royal quitrents in the Carolinas, played
in the origins of the Stamp Act. For years, he was as persistent an advocate of
various colonial reforms as he was a defender of his title to the vast acres he
speculated on in North Carolina. In 1751, he had suggested to the Earl of Halifax
that a stamp tax on colonists would be an ideal way of raising a colonial revenue.
During the summer of 1763, he made the same proposal to Grenville. Impressed
by this suggestion, Grenville set McCulloh to work in early September drafting a
bill for the House of Commons' consideration.[2]

Still, despite the attention scholars have paid to McCulloh's moments of
influence on Grenville, historians have not investigated the possibility that other
self-appointed colonial "experts" might have gained the First Lord's attention.
This is a curious omission, because a report from an American customs officer on
leave in England may be found in Grenville's files. Moreover, the report reveals
that during the summer of 1763 Grenville asked this officer to examine the state

of an important colonial trade, and then assess the possibility of extracting a sizeable revenue from it. The following is an effort to reconstruct this officer's motives and actions, and to assess his influence during the beginning stages of the planning of Grenville's ill-fated taxes on the American colonists.[3]

I

In 1755, Nathaniel Ware, the comptroller of the Customs at Boston, asked the Commissioners of the Customs for a temporary leave of absence. Massachusetts' severe climate, Ware told his superiors, had greatly weakened his health. To recover his strength, he would have to return to England for a few months. On November 28, 1755, the Commissioners granted his request. After arranging for a substitute to execute his duties, Ware left for London.[4]

Soon after his arrival, Ware informed his superiors that his concern for his health had been only one of the reasons he desired a leave. Ever since his appointment in 1750, he had tried to be a conscientious officer, endeavoring, "though under various discouragements . . . faithfully to discharge a trust which could not but appear to me of great national concern," the halting of New England's clandestine trade.[5] His colleagues, however, left him "unassisted, unsupported, and even denied [me] the customary instructions for my conduct." Fearful that he would reveal their shortcomings in London and endanger their places, they had vigorously opposed his request for leave. These apprehensions were justified. Though Ware later insisted that "it was not men, . . . but abuses that I aimed to expose," upon his arrival "I laid before Mr. Legge, then Chancellor of the Exchequer, both in words and writing, several practices in the American trade apparently hurtful to the manufactures and commerce, and consequently to the revenue of Great Britain, if not disgraceful to the government of the Mother Country and to His Majesty's Administration where the subjects, by their extreme remoteness, are prevented judging of either except from the specimen before their eyes."[6]

Ware's report evidently impressed Legge. After listening to it, he agreed that "the necessity of [Ware's] being protected was apparent." He also thought the Comptroller's petition that "rather than return among a people who must of course disapprove any attempts to throw light upon their transactions, I . . . be removed elsewhere" was "but reasonable." And, most significant from Ware's standpoint, Legge "permitted me to make use of his name in my application" to the First Lord of the Treasury, the Duke of Newcastle, for an equivalent place in England.[7]

Ware took full advantage of Legge's offer when he laid "the nature of my case before the Duke." To his delight, it had the desired effect. Newcastle "instantly" granted his every wish. "Not only [was] the remove [from Boston] promised, but I was myself to mention the department or office I chose to be in."[8] And, to protect Ware's present salary while he made his choice, the Treasury granted him an extension of his leave in February 1757.[9]

Painful delay and disappointment followed this auspicious beginning, however. Offices came open and Ware made his choices, but he received none. His contacts at the Treasury explained that "prior engagements," claimed some of these places; other jobs fell prey to "more pressing engagements from other quarters." This last excuse must have been deeply discouraging, for it reminded Ware that men who did not enjoy constant support from powerful friends had to be fortunate indeed to get office in England. Still, he persisted, despite the financial difficulties of living in London on a salary reduced by payments to his substitute in Boston and the emotional frustrations of unsuccessful applications to the Treasury. No doubt he was sustained in part by frequent assurances of Newcastle's favor, even though these assurances bore no more immediate fruit than two more extensions of his leave. Also, his memories of New England's winters, and of "my perpetual want of health in America through the extreme savagery of that climate," were vivid enough to enable him to continue the struggle. As he confessed to Newcastle, "the apprehension of being obliged to return for life to the same painful and comfortless state which for so many years I have already experienced . . . [causes me] extreme alarm." Without question, too, his apprehensions about his probable reception in Boston from his fellow officers and illicit traders strengthened his resolve as well.[10] So he persisted. Years passed, Québec fell, official concern over American smuggling increased, a pamphlet debate over the terms of peace and over the merits of keeping Canada or Guadeloupe began, and Ware remained in London, working for an English appointment as reward for his "having faithfully discharged, even to the neglect of my fortune as well as health, the several duties I have hitherto been employed in."[11]

Sometime after the spring of 1760, Ware adopted a new approach toward the problem of getting a place; one he hoped would impress a new patron. He drafted a long paper, which he titled "Observations on the British Colonies on the Continent of America." In it, he placed colonial attitudes toward Britain in historical perspective, assessed the colonies' future importance to the mother country, described problems Britain had had in enforcing her control over them in the past, and offered some suggestions for solving those problems in the future.[12] The length and style, and the depth and breadth, of this *tour d' horizon* seem at first glance to hint that Ware intended to publish it as a pamphlet. If he ever entertained such plans, doubtless he hoped that it would capture the political world's interest as Israel Mauduit's *Considerations on the present German War* and Benjamin Franklin's *The Interest of Great Britain Considered, With Regard to her Colonies, And the Acquisitions of Canada and Guadeloupe* had.[13] Such a triumph might dramatically improve his chances of being awarded an English place. But if Ware did consider such a course, he ultimately rejected it. He sent a copy of "Observations" not to a printer, but to the president of the Board of Trade, the Earl of Halifax, a man well known in London for his "distinguished attention to whatever relates to the British colonies."[14]

This step was not a desperate gamble on a long shot. Halifax's interest in colonial reform was no secret to men familiar with Whitehall; indeed, in late 1758 he had presented the Treasury and the Customs Commissioners with evidence testifying to the extent and seriousness of illicit trade in America. Thus Ware could be certain that Halifax would read his paper carefully and receptively.[15] Moreover, he could be confident that Halifax would take his "Observations" seriously for other reasons as well. Ware had studied the arguments in favor of retaining Canada rather than Guadeloupe in Franklin's pamphlet carefully.[16] Certainly he had considered the arguments in favor of keeping Guadeloupe with equal care, for they had been convincing to him. It was clear to him that both sides agreed on one central point: Britain's future power and prosperity would depend to a large extent on the growth of her commerce with her dependencies in the New World. This consensus hinted at a much greater interest in this trade at Whitehall and Westminster than before the war. Ware did not lack confirmation for this impression, either. He had learned that men were beginning to suggest changes in the policing of trade regulations in America. Some were advising the establishment of more ports of entry; others were arguing for "employ cruising ships along the sea coast." This new interest in colonial commerce and the resulting debate over law enforcement gave Ware an opportunity. To his experienced eye, and surely to Halifax's as well, it was apparent that much of the discussions were based on "the vague conversations of this town, . . . the authority of pamphleteers or news writers, the groundless reports of cursory travelers, *or more criminal misinformations of interested men.*" In contrast, he could supply "that exact and minute detail which the importance of the subject merits."[17]

No one could know for sure, Ware pointed out to Halifax, the exact amount of goods smuggled into the colonies. Nor could one assess precisely the seriousness of the damage done to the mother country by the various types of goods smuggled. Still, it was possible to make an informed estimate on both points. During his own time there, he had noticed that New Englanders frequently smuggled in foreign molasses. This trade did not disturb him much: it insured the dependence of the French islands on the British mainland, benefited the British carrying trade, and allowed Americans to buy more manufactured goods from the mother country. Indeed, Ware felt Parliament might be well-advised to repeal the duty. "The great point" to him, the one in which Americans "are really culpable, is their clandestine trade" with the European nations. There was a simple procedure that could be used to map the dimensions of this illicit commerce. If one took the population of the colonies in 1754, then divided that figure into the value of goods exported there from Britain in that year, one discovered that Americans paid about twenty shillings each for British goods. This sum was low, and remarkably so when one realized it did not include the slaves and remembered that "the lowest orders of people there are really better fed, clothed, and in every way accommodated than the most industrious and discreet of our journeymen artificers in London." "The smallness of the export," observed Ware, could only be accounted for by "supposing the people to be [further] supplied by a clandestine trade or their own manufactures." And, in fact, the manufactories in America were quite small, so the bulk of this illegal supply must be foreign in origin. To corroborate this point further, Ware noted that "tea throughout America is of so general a consumption that at the [East India] Company's price, [it] . . . probably amounts to one-fifth of what is said to be the value of the whole British export." The Company's books would surely reveal that it was not shipping tea in these quantities to America. In sum, British merchants and manufacturers were presently losing a sizeable share of the American market to illicit traders. Even worse, this already bad situation could deteriorate in the future. "What calls for the speediest attention of government," Ware concluded, "is their *clandestine trade*. . . [for] the profits are excessive, [and] should the people generally rush into it, what adequate remedy to apply except fleets and armies, might be difficult to conceive."[18]

Stopping this smuggling depended on knowing why it was so easy to run goods into America. Some men had explained this by noting that the colonial coast's geography favored smugglers; others by observing that illicit traders enjoyed the colonists' wholehearted support. These were advantages, Ware agreed, but they were not, he believed, the smugglers' principal advantage. Illicit traders could not make a profit unless they brought their cargoes directly into the major ports. If the customs officers were doing their duty, in Ware's judgment "it would be impossible for a smuggler to dispose of a whole contraband cargo." But the smugglers had no trouble bribing some officers to look the other way. Corruption in the American customs service, the Comptroller at Boston emphasized, made the clandestine trade safe and profitable.[19]

To prevent this corruption in the future, Ware advised that officials in Britain and America keep up "a steady and constant inspection into [the officers'] conduct." The Treasury should begin by requiring them to maintain detailed records of their collections and keep "general accounts of all exports whither, and all imports whence" at their ports, whether those goods were taxed or not. Each quarter, the officers would have to send copies of their records to the Customs Commissioners in London. The Commissioners would then compare them with reports from other British and colonial ports. This comparison would enable them to tell at "a single glance . . . any fraud that shall arise, and in what ports." The Surveyors-General of the Customs in America could supplement this procedure by personally inspecting every year the books and behavior of all officers in their districts and suspending officers when necessary. Ware was sure corruption could not flourish under these circumstances. Smuggling would decline correspondingly, and "the exports from Great Britain [would] clearly . . . increase."[20]

Halifax was impressed by "Observations." As Ware later recalled, he, like Legge and Newcastle, "was likewise pleased to honor me with his countenance," and added his good opinion and best wishes to theirs.[21] Unfortunately for Ware, the President of the Board of Trade's good wishes had the same result as those of the First Lord of the Treasury. Ware still was unable to exchange his office for an English one. Then, in May 1762, an ominous development occurred. Newcastle resigned as First Lord of the Treasury, and the King's favorite, the Earl of Bute, took his place. Ware had not had the long-term relationship with Bute that he had had with Newcastle, a fact which diminished his chances of at long last completing an exchange of offices satisfactorily. But this prospect probably troubled Ware much less than the possibility that the new First Lord might compel him to choose between returning to America or giving up his job. At the moment Bute took office, Ware was technically in England without official permission. The last extension of his leave had expired in January 1762, and no renewal had as yet been granted. Since he was a stranger to Bute, he must have felt peculiarly vulnerable. To forestall an order to return or resign, as well as to affect the exchange, he moved quickly to describe his sad history to Bute, establish his qualifications for advising on the reform of the customs service in America, and make his plea for an English place. Probably the truest measure of his desperation was the fact that he was now willing to accept any job, even one that paid less than the one he currently held. He did, however, retain enough dignity to make this eloquent appeal in a letter to Bute.

> If national industry be the true principle of this empire, and commerce rather than conquest its most interesting object; if Great Britain in return for so much blood and treasure can never derive any advantage from these American colonies, whatever vague ideas may be conceived of their value, except by their trade; if in the amazing growth of the British settlements upon that continent the seeds of a future independency be already discoverable; if the time approaches when any force the Mother Country shall be able to apply at such a distance may prove very ineffectual, should the authority or reputation of her government be unhappily lost; and if that opinion or reputation of that must really after all depend, among the inhabitants as it were of another world, upon the conduct of such as are appointed over them from hence, your lordship will best judge whether His Majesty's future service . . . may not in those distant parts probably be affected by the apparent discouragement of an officer who endeavored to act upon the above principles, and was notoriously known to reject the usual methods of accumulating.[23]

Bute's response to these pleas has evidently not survived. He did not offer Ware an English place. Moreover, the Customs Commissioners never renewed Ware's leave. Still, they did not force him to return to America. He continued in London, doubtless ready to discuss the ideas he had expressed to Halifax with Bute, since he had informed the new First Lord about the existence of his "imperfect observations on the present state of the Northern colonies."[24] Did Bute or someone else from the Treasury ever contact Ware about these ideas? It is intriguing to note that years later John Almon recalled the political gossip of the time that Bute had studied closely "a plan . . . by a naval officer from Boston, of new modeling the governments of that country" and had begun "this scheme . . . in idea, before the conclusion of the peace in 1763."[25] Lacking more specific and conclusive evidence, one cannot do more than wonder if Ware was consulted by Bute's Treasury. It is certain, though, that two men who served at the Treasury with Bute's successor, George Grenville, did become familiar with him and his particular claim for a place. Lord North clearly knew about Ware, because one of his petitions to Bute for a job in England is in North's files. Charles Jenkinson also knew about the Comptroller of Boston, for Jenkinson, in his capacity as Bute's secretary, read, endorsed, and apparently filed the letter Ware wrote to Bute on July 6, 1762.[26] The hints that Ware threw out in that letter about his intimate knowledge of smuggling and corruption in the colonies, and his transparent desire to gain a place by suggesting ways of hindering the one and ending the other, cannot have escaped the vigilant and dedicated Jenkinson's attention. When those matters became items of important business at Grenville's Treasury, Ware was an obvious man to ask for information about the clandestine trade and ideas about how to reduce it.

II

That he had managed to become an advisor of Grenville must have heartened Ware. At the same time though, he must have been apprehensive about the future. In February 1763, Bute's Treasury had asked the Customs

Commissioners to provide a list of all officers who were absent, with or without leave, from their posts in America.[27] Then, in March, Members of the House of Commons made "heavy complaints . . . about the state of our revenues in North America," and blamed the pitiful sum collected there on "making all [the customs] offices sinecures in England."[28] It seems reasonable that Ware, through his contacts at the Customs House, was aware of the signs of coming official displeasure with men like him. As he contemplated advising Grenville, Ware may have felt optimism, but he surely also must have realized that this could be his last opportunity to escape Boston.

In Grenville Ware found, as others did, a man who prided himself on his accessibility to those with useful information on the colonies and who was more than willing to adopt others' suggestions when he thought they would be likely to increase the benefits Britain derived from America.[29] During their first contact, the two men evidently concentrated upon "the great point," the clandestine trade, for Ware referred in his August 22, 1763 letter to an estimate of the yearly volume of smuggled molasses he made "upon another occasion, when, *without the least view to a tax*, any random guess, which I took care should be within the truth, was sufficient for any purpose."[30] Grenville obviously received Ware's information with respectful and concerned attention. When he had served as First Lord of the Admiralty during Bute's ministry, he had been concerned about the possibilities of smuggling French goods into America. What he learned from Ware removed this illicit trade from the realm of possibility and helped convince him that, as he later told the House of Commons, "many colonies have such a trade; such a trade has been opened by three or four colonies with France to the amount of £4 or 500,000 a year."[31] There is also reason to believe that the men at the Treasury were impressed by the procedure Ware had used to calculate the dimensions of the illicit trade. In late 1764, when Thomas Whately wrote a pamphlet defending the Administration's colonial policies, he used an identical method, mode of argument, and examples to reach the conclusion that smugglers brought into the colonies £700,000 worth of contraband each year.[32] Finally, Grenville and his colleagues apparently borrowed Ware's suggestion for impeding that trade by a rigorous inspection of American customs officers' behavior and books. On July 25, 1763, the Treasury directed the Customs Commissioners to order their officers in America to "transmit . . . exact accounts of the imports and exports of the several ports, and what may from time to time be the state of the revenue" to England on a regular basis. The purpose of this regulation, as the Plantation Clerk at the Customs Board explained it, was strikingly similar to Ware's prediction of the effect of his proposed reform. These accounts "should be a check on the account of exports of another [port] to detect any irregular importation [of dutied goods] . . . and to be enabled by the returns made from the second ports, to form a general state of the trade and produce of the colonies and amount of the revenue received therein."[33]

The Treasury's adoption of Ware's proposal was a considerable testimony to the value of his information and ideas. Moreover, Grenville paid him the further compliment of asking him to assist the Treasury in the formulation of its future policy toward the colonial trade in foreign molasses. That Grenville asked Ware to help him was not surprising. Ware was the comptroller at a port where, as the First Lord knew, ships reputedly brought in large amounts of French molasses without paying the 6d. per gallon duty on it that Parliament had set in 1733. He might, therefore, have a pretty good idea about how that trade operated. Even if he did not know everything, he would know what sorts of inquiries to make to find out additional information. As he made those inquiries, he would have the knowledge and experience necessary to recognize improbable rumors and estimates, no matter how plausible they might seem to the uninitiated. Finally, Grenville could be sure Ware's eagerness for an English place would impel him to deliver accurate information to the Treasury as quickly as he could, and speed in this case was almost as important to the First Lord as accuracy.[34] He needed the information before Parliament next met. During the previous session, Charles

Townshend had discomfited the ministry by suddenly moving that the House reduce the duty on foreign molasses imported into the colonies from 6*d*. to 2*d*. per gallon. He had supported his motion by arguing that "the high duties produce nothing by driving all people to smuggle from the enormity of the gain." In reply, Grenville had spoken "against lowering them," and had persuaded the House to kill the motion procedurally. He could be certain, though, that Townshend would raise the question again during the next session. Moreover, Grenville knew that the Treasury had to make a decision on this tax by that time for administrative as well as political reasons: the duty would automatically expire in 1764 unless Parliament renewed it.[36] So the First Lord was eager for Ware to investigate the trade, then answer two questions in a report. First, what was the annual volume of molasses smuggled into America? Second, could the Treasury reasonably expect to collect the 6*d*. duty?[37]

Given his personal opinions that this tax "apparently is in itself prejudicial to British navigation" and that "nothing could more effectually palliate any necessary severity in putting an effectual stop to future clandestine importations from Europe than repealing it," Ware may not have been enthusiastic about his assignment.[38] But if he was unenthusiastic, he was also sensible enough to realize that he had no choice. He had to do a good job to retain any hope of an English place. Moreover, as he was going about the investigation, his situation abruptly worsened. The Customs Commissioners, at the Treasury's orders, commanded all officers absent from America to set out for their posts by August 31, 1763 or be dismissed.[39] Successful completion of his assignment was now his last chance to avoid the unpleasant dilemma of resignation or return.

In the course of his investigation, Ware discovered that men in London firmly believed that "the importation of foreign molasses has increased greatly during the war to the amount of, it is said, of 60,000 hogsheads annually." He himself did not accept this figure, which was much higher than his conservative estimate of 12,000 hogsheads, at face value. And, after investigation, he discovered that the higher figure was based on conjecture, and thus was "too vague to be depended upon." He decided that a more accurate estimate could be obtained by determining first how many distilleries were in America, then by finding out how many hogsheads of molasses the average distillery would use every year. To this total, he planned to add an estimate of the amount of molasses Americans consumed in their beer and food. Moreover, he decided to collect his data only from those Americans in London who seemed familiar enough with that country's commerce to give reliable answers. Unsurprisingly, he found these colonists "extremely cautious of giving any light into their own affairs," but through his patient use of "various shifts and pretences" he ultimately succeeded, On August 22, 1763, he reported to Grenville that American distilleries probably consumed at least 38,625 hogsheads per year. In addition to this total, colonists added to their food and beer "5,000 hogsheads more than is said to be imported from all the British islands, so that, if our calculations be just, the foreign only must exceed 43,625 hogheads."[40]

Could 6*d*. per gallon be collected on these molasses? Ware's researches indicated that the trade was thriving despite costs of bribes and provincial taxes that approximated that figure. He cautioned Grenville, though, that the trade would not survive adding the British duty to the weight of the provincial taxes. The margin of profit, already fairly slender, would absolutely vanish, and "that trade must totally fail." Ware did not think that this was desirable. Not only would the provinces most deeply involved in it be ruined, but also other colonies would quickly feel the contraction of their market for lumber. Moreover, in the present circumstances, the French were dependent on America for supplies and "in case of a rupture, what use may not be made of such advantage?" This advantage would be lost if the commerce ceased. The only solution, therefore, was to collect the 6*d*. duty if "all provincial duties are taken off."

This was not the only change the Treasury should make, either. Ware also warned Grenville that taxing foreign molasses heavily without placing some duty on British molasses, would encourage illicit traders to try to bribe customs officers in the British West Indies to officially represent foreign as domestic molasses. Such efforts, he predicted, would be successful to the point that "the quantity [of British molasses imported] will probably be doubled by collusion of the people in our islands." "This it seems," he added, "is no more than has formerly been practiced."[61] And even if the Treasury did put some duty on domestic molasses, it would be necessary to tax rum produced in the Caribbean as well. "Was the duty to extend to molasses only, the foreign islands would manufacture theirs into rum for the use of the continent, as in part they do already; or, which would be much the same in the end, our own islands would do it for them."[62] Ware did not insult the First Lord's intelligence by drawing the obvious conclusion. If the Treasury wanted to avoid disrupting the American colonies' commerce in molasses, and to collect much money at all from this duty, it would have to take these steps.

Ware closed with one final recommendation. He anticipated that collections of the molasses duty would "fall short of expectation." "There must, I fear, after all be a large deduction for frauds, under the term 'leakage.'" So he suggested that the Treasury tax some other goods and services that the assemblies had already successfully taxed. These included a duty on all sugar imported into America, excises on wine and Mediterranean fruits, and a tonnage duty on ships entering American ports. Since Britain now paid for the defense of the American frontier, the assemblies could not reasonably protest to the mother country's tapping these sources of income. On this note, Ware ended his report.

III

No document describing Grenville's response to Ware's letter has survived. Probably none ever existed, for the First Lord's usual way of dealing with reports was to read them, digest their contents, and file them away without notation or comment. Still, one can safely infer that Grenville did not dismiss Ware's opinions or his information as insignificant. In the months after August

1763, he received at least two estimates that put the quantity of molasses annually smuggled into America at amounts higher than Ware's. These two estimates were produced by informants who reported directly to two men whom Grenville trusted, Thomas Whately and Charles Jenkinson, the Secretaries to the Treasury.[43] Yet Grenville was made sufficiently wary by Ware's calculations and his skepticism about estimates based on conjectures "too vague to depend upon" that he admitted in the House of Commons that "the quantity [of molasses annually smuggled into the colonies is] so doubtful, that [I] cannot form any certain estimate [of the yearly produce of a 3d. duty]; perhaps £40, 50, or 60,000."[44] Grenville also learned about the political and economic complexities of taxing molasses from Ware, and this lesson must have helped convince him that it would be necessary to lower the duty from 6d. Moreover, Ware's report of August 22 repeated and reinforced an observation the First Lord's informants, both official and unofficial, had already called to his attention. Flat predictions by Ware that enforcing the 6d. duty would inspire "collusion by the people in our islands" in declaring foreign molasses to be domestic, and encourage merchants to evade the tax by making fraudulent claims of leakage must have reminded him that he should never underestimate the ingenuity and determination of American smugglers. Finally, Ware's comment that American officers were accustomed to receiving a 1d. per gallon bribe, surely recalled to his mind that he could never overestimate the dedication of the men who would be dealing with those smugglers. These facts of law enforcement in the colonies were other reasons why lowering the molasses duty would be wise.[45]

Grenville's acceptance of these realities had another, and more significant impact on his colonial policies. As he later told the House, the molasses duty and other regulations would be difficult to execute, because it was "difficult to find good officers who will go to North America." He went on, "Smuggling will continue, and therefore, as this will diminish the revenue, some further tax will be necessary to defray the expense of North America."[46] In Grenville's opinion, that tax should be a stamp tax. Such a tax was enforced not by officers, but by the fact that papers used for certain purposes that were unstamped had no legal force to bind parties using them. Thus, as Henry McCulloh said, the tax "in great measure would execute itself, except in a few particulars; for in all suits depending, the people settled in the colonies must for their own security comply with the directors of the law." "In all cases," he added, "of warrants of attorney, procurations, protests, and other matters in the intercourse of business, the safety of the parties concerned would likewise enforce an obedience."[47] Grenville could see the point of these observations. Americans would have to buy the stamps or place their property and persons in jeopardy. Self interest would, therefore, force them to obey the tax. "Stamp duties [are] the least exceptionable [new tax]," he told the House, "because [they] require few officers and even collect [themselves]. The only danger is forgery."[48] It was the perfect tax to impose on people who were used to evading British taxes by bribery and fraud.

Grenville's enthusiasm for a stamp tax was not, however, so great that he would have recommended Parliament impose it even if collections from other duties were high. A stamp tax, the First Lord was keenly aware, had nearly as many unattractive features as attractive ones. To begin with, it would be not merely a new tax, but a new type of tax, insofar as the colonies were concerned. This might cause political difficulties in Parliament as well as in America.[49] Moreover, officials at Whitehall were largely ignorant of legal forms and business practices in the colonies. As Grenville freely confessed to the House, in many of these matters "the officers of the revenue must strike in the dark." While they did so, the possibility that they might tax some documents too heavily, and thereby harm the colonial market for British goods, certainly existed. But, as Grenville also told the House, he did not believe that Britain could afford not to impose some new tax. Additional revenue from the colonies had to be found. A stamp tax, he thought, was "the best plan" for raising it.[50]

Unquestionably, Ware's report helped Grenville reach this fateful conclusion. The First Lord could not brush aside as unimportant the prediction of an experienced American customs officer that collection of the molasses duty would never reach the optimistic expectations of some men. The fact that Ware made his prediction after a careful investigation gave it additional weight. As a result, the hint he diffidently dropped in his conclusion—that Britain would have to find other sources of revenue in America to supplement the molasses duty— was not lost on the First Lord. To Grenville, as to Ware, the results of this investigation made such a search necessary. Ware's report surely was not the sole inspiration for Grenville's decision to have a colonial stamp tax prepared. Still, it may well have been the piece of information that determined him to pursue the policy he did. On September 8, two weeks after Ware wrote his letter, the Treasury ordered Thomas Cruwys, the Solicitor for the English Stamp Commissioners, to assist McCulloh in drafting a stamp tax for America.[51]

IV

There is no sign that Grenville gave Ware another assignment after he completed his inquiries into the molasses trade. That is not surprising: there was no other colonial business pending that Ware's particular expertise could deal with, and thus his usefulness to Grenville as adviser and investigator was at an end. Moreover, Grenville did not exempt Ware from the Treasury order of July 25, 1763. He would have to return to Boston, or lose his place. Again, this is not surprising. Grenville was being besieged by petitions for exemptions from men with strong political connections, and any breach of his orders might ultimately destroy this policy.[52] So, as the end of 1763 approached, Ware was finally confronted with the decision he had evaded for years. He could not bring himself to return to Boston. On January 3, 1764, the Customs Commissioners informed the Treasury that he had been disciplined, presumably for his failure to go to America. Eight weeks later, on February 27, the Treasury Lords signed the official warrant of Benjamin Hallowell as Comptroller at Boston, "in the room of Nathaniel Ware, resigned."[53]

Ware's services did not go unrewarded, however. Although the mechanics of the exchange are obscure, probably through Grenville's intervention, and with the concurrence of Halifax, who controlled the office in question, he was appointed British Consul at Málaga. It was a place ideally suited for a man with a knowledge of trade and commercial regulation, and a location perfectly chosen for a man who suffered in cold weather. Ware did not enjoy his good fortune for long; he died at Málaga in 1767.[54] Still, he did have the pleasure of living his last years in a post both profitable and important and in a place with a warm climate, far from the New England winters and the vengeful colleagues and colonists he had tried so hard and for so long to escape.

*This chapter first appeared in the *Huntington Library Quarterly*, vol. 45 (1982), pp. 36-58.

Endnotes

[1] The Earl of Albemarle, *Memoirs of the Marquis of Rockingham and his Contemporaries, with Original Letters and Documents now first published* (London, 1852), 1, p. 249. The person who made this remark was identified only as a "former undersecretary."

[2] For information on McCulloh's background and on his role in the formulation of the stamp tax, see Charles G. Sellers, Jr., "Private Profits and British Colonial Policy: The Speculations of Henry McCulloh," *William and Mary Quarterly*, 3rd ser., 8 (1951), pp. 535-51; Charles R. Richeson, "The Preparation of the Stamp Act," *ibid.*, 10 (1953), pp. 543-59; John Cannon, "Henry McCulloch and Henry McCulloh," *ibid.*, 15 (1958), pp.71-3; Jack P. Greene, "'A Dress of Horror: Henry McCulloh's Objections to the Stamp Act," *The Huntington Library Quarterly* 26 (1963), pp. 253-62; and P. D. G. Thomas, *British Politics and the Stamp Act Crisis: The first phase of the American Revolution, 1763-1767* (Oxford, 1975), pp. 69-72, 83.

[3] I have appended this report, made by Nathaniel Ware to [George Grenville], Aug. 22, 1763, to this chapter. I acknowledge with thanks the permission of the Trustees of the Huntington Library to publish this chapter, and to quote from other documents in their possession. Scholars wishing to consult the original will find it in the George Grenville Papers, Huntington Library, STG 12-(14).

[4] For a description of his application for leave, see Ware to the Duke of Newcastle, Jun. 26, 1755, Newcastle Papers, British Library, Add. MSS 32881, f. 62. For the Commissioners' action, see "Copy of the list of officers in the plantations who were absent from their duty," Mar. 8, 1763, Liverpool Papers, British Library, Add. MSS 38335, f. 37. One reason why historians have overlooked Ware's role in the formulation of imperial policy is their assumption that he was in Boston between 1756 and 1764. See, for example, Thomas C. Barrow, *Trade and Empire: The British Customs Service in Colonial America, 1660-1775* (Cambridge, MA, 1967), p. 176. For evidence to the contrary, see the "Copy of the list of officers" cited above; the appendix to this article for Ware's reference to his having gone to the offices of the Board of Trade during the summer of 1763; and John Fremantle, acting Secretary to the Customs Commissioners, to Charles Jenkinson, Secretary to the Treasury, Jan. 3, 1764, Treasury Papers, National Archives, T. 1/429, no. 57. I acknowledge with thanks the permission of the Trustees of the British Library, and the Keeper of the Records at the National Archives (formerly Public Record Office) for permission to quote documents in their possession.

[5] Ware described his adventures in Boston and London in a letter to the Earl of Bute, Jul. 6, 1762, Bute Papers in the possession of the Marquess of Bute, Isle of Bute, Scotland. I am indebted to the Marquess of Bute for permission to quote from this document. Apparently Ware was not exaggerating his conscientiousness. Soon after he began his service in Boston, he personally seized on Dec. 29, 1750 six hogsheads of molasses and two hogsheads of rum. Not only were seizures rare in Boston during his tenure there, but also it was unusual for a comptroller to make seizures at any time or place. See *Boston Post Boy*, Jan. 26, 1750/1. I have found few clues to Ware's background before he became comptroller at Boston. In his letter to Bute on Jul. 6, 1762, he commented that he received the post in 1750 "through the recommendation of the Secretary at War [Henry Fox], to whom I was known only by some faint expressions of my duty in the preceding war." And in a long letter he wrote in the early 1760s, Ware mentioned he had been in Albany during the war, so he may have had a part in the abortive Canadian expedition of 1745-6. See Mr. Comptroller Weare to the Earl of,_____, [n.d.], Massachusetts Historical Society, *Collections*, 1st ser. (Boston, 1795), 1:75. Hereafter I shall cite this letter as Ware to the Earl _____. John Shy has asserted that this paper was one of those sent by Paine Wingate to Jeremy Belknap on Oct. 23, 1775, and therefore concluded that Ware was the grandfather of Colonel Mesech Weare, a revolutionary leader in New Hampshire during the 1770s and 1780s. John Shy, *Toward Lexington: The Role of the British Army in the Coming of the American Revolution* (Princeton, 1965), 63n. But Wingate's later account of Mesech Weare's career makes it clear that the Nathaniel Weare referred to in this letter served as New Hampshire's agent in London in 1663, and thus could hardly be Ware. New Hampshire Historical Society, *Collections*, (Concord, NH, 1837), 5:244. Moreover, the records of the Massachusetts

Historical Society reveal that Edward Davis, not Paine Wingate, gave Ware's letter to the Society. Minutes of the Society, Dec. 21, 1791, Massachusetts Historical Society, *Proceedings* (Boston, 1839), 1:26.

[6] Ware to Bute, July 6, 1762, Bute Papers, Scotland. The written portion of Ware's presentation to Legge has not survived. Undoubtedly its information about the American customs service and colonial commerce and its suggestions for reforming the one and controlling the other were very similar, if not identical, to those in Ware to the Earl of _____, pp. 78-83.

[7] Ware to Bute, Jul. 6, 1762, Bute Papers, Scotland. In this letter, Ware claimed he told Legge he would accept a post with a smaller salary. This is probably a reflection of his desperation in 1762 and not an accurate account of his past petitions. The letters of his that have survived from the 1750s reveal he was asking for a place with an equivalent salary. See Ware to [Legge?], Jan. 28, 1758, Treasury Papers, National Archives, T. 1/384, no. 144; and Ware to Newcastle, Jun. 26, 1758, Newcastle Papers, British Library, Add. MSS 32881, f. 82. Ware's salary at Boston was £70 a year. Barrow, *Trade and Empire*, p. 264.

[8] Ware to Bute, Jul. 6, 1762, Bute Papers, Scotland.

[9] For the dates the Treasury granted Ware's leaves, see "Copy of the list of officers," Mar. 8, 1763, Liverpool Papers, British Library, Add. MSS 38335, f. 37.

[10] For the information in this paragraph, see Ware to [Legge?], Jan. 28, 1759, Treasury Papers, National Archives, T. 1/384, no. 144; Ware to Newcastle, Jun. 26, 1758, Newcastle Papers, British Library, Add: Mss. 32881, f. 82; "Copy of the list of officers," Mar. 8, 1763, Liverpool Papers, *ibid.*, 38335, f. 37; and Ware to Bute, Jul. 6, 1762, Bute Papers, Scotland.

[11] Ware to Newcastle, Jun. 26, 1758, Newcastle Papers, British Library, Add. MSS. 32881, f. 82.

[12] Ware to the Earl of _____, pp. 66-84. Ware's paper comprises the body of this letter, from pp. 67-84. It is clear he wrote it after the spring of 1760, for the paper includes a reference to Benjamin Franklin's *The Interest of Great Britain Considered, with Regard to her Colonies, And the Acquisitions of Canada and Guadeloupe*, which was published on Apr. 17, 1760. See Ware to the Earl of _____, p.78; and Leonard W. Labaree, ed., *The Papers of Benjamin Franklin* (New Haven, 1966), 9, p. 52. It also is apparent that he wrote it before Jul. 6, 1762, for he refers to such a paper in his letter to Bute of that date. Even if one questions whether this is the same paper, Barrow certainly erred in *Trade and Empire*, p. 176, when he argued that Ware wrote it in 1763. A man so desperate for a place as Ware would not likely argue for keeping Guadeloupe and returning Canada after the publication of the preliminary treaty in Nov./Dec. 1762.

Moreover, had he been so foolhardy, he would have referred to the ministry's decision to keep Canada as a mistake.

[13] Horace Walpole believed that Mauduit's *Considerations on the present German War* (London, 1760) "had more operation in working a change on the minds of men, than perhaps ever fell to the lot of a pamphlet." For its full publishing history and political impact see: K.W. Schweizer, "Pamphleteering and Foreign Policy in the Age of the Elder Pitt," *Hanoverian Britain and Empire*, S. Taylor and C. Jones, eds., (London, 1998), pp. 94-108. Walpole, *Memoirs of the Reign of King George III*, G. F. Russell Barker, ed. (London, 1894), 1, p. 25. For an able introduction to Franklin's pamphlet, and the text itself, see Labaree, ed., *Franklin Papers*, 9. pp. 47-100.

[14] The quotation is from Ware to the Earl of _____, p. 67. Shy guessed that Ware might have been addressing this paper to Bute, *Toward Lexington*, 63n. But Bute did not have a reputation for paying close attention to colonial affairs. Moreover, Ware told Bute that he "had presumed to offer some imperfect observations on the present state of the Northern Colonies" to Halifax. Ware to Bute, Jul. 6, 1762, Bute Papers, Scotland.

[15] For a good summary of Halifax's interests and activities, see Barrow, *Trade and Empire*, pp.163-5. Almost certainly Ware was aware of this, for his letter to Bute of Jul. 6, 1762 reveals that someone in the Customs office was permitting him to read correspondence from officers in New England relating to inquiries about the illicit trade.

[16] Ware gave a summary of arguments for "the entire removal . . . of the French off that continent . . . by one of our colonists" that is clearly drawn from Franklin's *The Interest of Great Britain Considered*. See Ware to the Earl of _____, p. 78.

[17] *Ibid.*, p. 67.

[18] *Ibid.*, pp.79-80. Ware's knowledge of this trade was based upon his experiences at Boston. Apparently it was so notorious that "great quantities of European and Asiatic [goods] were being brought from [Holland and other parts of Europe to the neighboring colonies, and from] thence into this port," that Sir Henry Frankland, the Collector at Boston, felt compelled to make a public proclamation against "a trade so prejudicial to our Mother Country and detrimental to the fair trader," and promise handsome rewards and anonymity to in formers. *Boston Post Boy*, Feb. 19, 1753. And four times during Ware's stay in Boston officers seized small quantities of these goods. See *Boston Post Boy*, Sept. 3, 1750, Sept. 24, 1750, Oct. 14, 1751, and Nov. 4, 1754.

[19] Ware to the Earl of _____, pp. 81-2.

[20] *Ibid.*, p. 82.

[21] Ware to Bute, Jul. 6, 1762, Bute Papers, Scotland.

[22] In and of itself, this was not cause for much alarm. The "Copy of the list of officers" reveals that during the 1750s Ware had been in England for periods as long as a year between the expiration of one leave and the approval of another. The replacement of Newcastle, however, made this interregnum a period of much greater uncertainty. Moreover, the Treasury had granted Ware only a six month's extension of his leave in Jul. 1761, which was a departure from the grant of a year in May 1759. Perhaps Ware saw this as a sign that even Newcastle was tiring of his presence in London. "Copy of the list of officers," Mar. 8, 1763, Liverpool Papers, British Library, Add. MSS 38335, f. 37.

[23] Ware to Bute, Jul. 6, 1762, Bute Papers, Scotland.

[24] *Ibid.*

[25] It is unclear whether Almon was referring to Ware's ideas or not. Still, a "naval officer" was a provincial customs officer in many colonies, and Ware did recommend in his "observations" that the Crown pay the salaries of colonial governors and other executive officers, a part of the scheme by the gentleman from Boston that Almon found particularly sinister. Almon attributed tremendous significance to this plan, crediting it as the inspiration of British policy until 1777. Needless to add, that analysis is incorrect. Still, Almon's recollection may indicate Ware's ideas were taken seriously before Grenville was in office. See [John Almon], *Biographical Literary, and Political Anecdotes of Several of the Most Eminent Persons of the Present Age, Never Before Printed* (London, 1797), 2, p. 81.

[26] Ware to the Earl of Bute, [1762], North Papers, Bodleian Library, Oxford, a. 6, f. 238. I am indebted to the Bodleian Library for permission to cite this document. The archivist for the Bute Papers, the late Catherine Armet, in a private communication of Feb. 5, 1981, pointed out that the endorsement on Ware to Bute, Jul. 6, 1762, is in the handwriting of Charles Jenkinson. I am indebted to Miss Armet for her kind assistance and for her observations on this point.

[27] For the Treasury's request, see Jeremiah Dyson, Secretary to the Treasury, Feb. 16, 1763, Treasury Papers, the National Archives, 1. 11/27, f. 128.

[28] For an account of the debates in the House of Commons in Mar. 1763, see Grenville to Horace Walpole, Sept. 8, 1763, W. J. Smith, ed., *The Grenville Papers: Being the Correspondence of Richard Grenville, Earl Temple, K. G., and the Right Honourable George Grenville, their friends and contemporaries* (London, 1852), 2, p.114.

[29] William Knox, whose career as colonial "expert" and Secretary to the American Department spanned the period 1763-83, recalled that Grenville

received information "with as much candor and openness to conviction as any man I ever knew." Knox, *Extra Official State Papers* . . . (London, 1789), 2. p. 32.

[30] See the Postscript. The words I have italicized indicate that during his earlier contact with the Treasury, Ware had discussed the colonists' various clandestine commerces without any discussion of the revenue-producing potential of any of them.

[31] For Grenville's earlier concern, see his copies (in his own handwriting) of reports of the Board of Trade to the King on the clandestine commerce between Newfoundland and the St. Lawrence on Mar. 15 and 21, 1763, Grenville Papers, Huntington Library STG-17, (28-9). For his instructions to naval commanders in those areas, see Admiralty to the Earl of Egremont, Mar. 21, 1763, State Papers Domestic, Public Record Office, S. P. Dom. 42/64, 150/18, and Instructions to Commanders, Mar. 29, 1763, Grenville Papers, Huntington Library, STG-17, (30). For his remarks to the House on Mar. 9, see P.D.G. Thomas, ed., "The Parliamentary Diaries of Nathaniel Ryder, 1764-1767," *Camden Miscellany Vol. XXIII*, Camden 4th ser. (London, 1969), 7, p. 234. Hereafter I shall cite this as "Ryder Diaries."

[32] Cf. [Thomas Whately], *The regulations lately made concerning the colonies, and the taxes imposed on them, considered* (London, Jan. 1765), pp. 92-3, with Ware to the Earl of _____, [1762], pp. 79-80. Whately was a Secretary to the Treasury.

[33] Jenkinson to the Customs Commissioners, Jul. 25, 1763, Treasury Papers, National Archives, T. 11/27, F. 147; and Henry Hulton to the Treasury. May 16, 1765, *ibid.*, T. 1/442, f. 333. Historians have generally assumed that this order was inspired by the Customs Commissioners' Jul. 21, 1763 report to the Treasury. But the only part of the text that might conceivably relate to that order deals solely with the collection of plantation duties on West Indian goods. This section advised that frauds in this trade "may possibly be remedied in some degree by farther checks and restraints to be imposed by Parliament, where by the identity and quantity of goods shipped in the West Indies, and the duties paid there, may be better ascertained and determined upon their arrival at the port for which they cleared out." Customs Commissioners to the Treasury, Jul. 21, 1763, *ibid.*, T. 1/426, f. 269. The order of Jul. 25 was imposed by the Treasury, not by Parliament, and covered all goods, whether taxed or not, from everywhere rather than only on Caribbean goods on which plantation duties were paid. That the Treasury appreciated the differences between the Jul. 25 order and the Commissioners' suggestion may be seen by their order on Aug. 1 for the Commissioners to elaborate on the suggestion they made on Jul. 21. Jenkinson to Customs Commissioners, Aug. 1, 1763, *ibid.*, T. 11/27, f. 137. Moreover, it is improbable that the Treasury Lords thought of the Jul. 25 order themselves, then implemented it, without the authority of a source they respected. As Elizabeth F. Hoon observed in her study, *The Organization of the English Customs System,*

1696-1768 (NY, 1938), pp. 45-61, eighteenth-century Treasuries rarely formulated specific reforms of commercial regulations, preferring instead to rely on the expertise of outside authorities. In the specific case of Grenville and his colleagues, they knew very little about the procedures and forms of customs officers in 1763. By 1764, their ignorance so disturbed Grenville that he tried to educate himself in these officers' procedures. See C. Amyrand to Jenkinson, Jul. 27, 1764, Liverpool Papers, British Library, Add. MSS 38203, f. 49. If neither the Commissioners nor the Treasury thought of the order of Jul. 25, who did? The most probable explanation is that Ware, who had earlier formulated such a reform and been in contact with Grenville in 1763, discussed his idea with the First Lord, who adopted it.

[34] Note in the P.S. to the Postscript that Ware was careful to justify his delay in making the report. Had he not been aware that the First Lord wanted the report as soon as possible, he would not have added these remarks.

[35] See Mar. 30, 1763, James Harris Diary, quoted *in extenso* in Sir Lewis Namier and John Brooke, *Charles Townshend* (London, 1964), p. 92. For an account of the procedural death of Townshend's motion, see Thomas, *British Politics*, pp. 39-40.

[36] For the expiration date of the molasses duty, see Mar. 9, 1763, *Journal of the House of Commons*, 29, p. 537.

[37] Since Ware was skeptical of the wisdom of taxing foreign molasses, it is reasonable to assume that he did not suggest this investigation to the First Lord. Grenville's desire for a reliable estimate of the quantity of smuggled molasses is apparent in the first paragraph of the report. Note how Ware begins without any description of the question under examination because he knows his reader is already familiar with the subject of the inquiry. And, because Ware does not even mention the possibility of lowering the duty when such a step would have solved some of the Treasury's difficulties fully as effectively and with fewer political repercussions than having the Privy Council annul provincial taxes, it is equally reasonable to believe that Grenville had commanded him to consider only the feasibility of collecting the 6*d.* duty. Since Grenville had declared in the House on Mar. 30 that this duty was not too high, and since he certainly wanted to raise the maximum revenue possible from the molasses trade, he naturally began his inquiry into that tax by seeing if he could possibly collect 6*d.*

[38] Ware to the Earl of _____, p. 83.

[39] For the Treasury's orders, see Jenkinson to Customs Commissioners, Jul. 25, 1763, Treasury Papers, National Archives, T. 11/2 7, f. 147. Fremantle reported to Jenkinson on Aug. 11 that he had notified all absent customs officers to set out for America by Aug. 31 or face the consequences. Fremantle to Jenkinson, Aug. 11, 1763, *ibid.*, T. 1/426, f. 274.

[40] Ware's report of Aug. 22 is confusingly phrased—the work of a hurrying desperate man, perhaps?—and his calculations are difficult to understand. Since he was inquiring into the amount of foreign molasses annually consumed in America, it seems reasonable to read his reference to "38,625 hogsheads molasses" in the second paragraph as a reference to the foreign product. There is no sure way of gauging the accuracy of his work. But after 1766, when Parliament imposed a 1d. per gallon tax on all molasses imported into the colonies, a tax that most observers believed would be paid because smugglers were already used to paying 1d. as a bribe, customs receipts for the years 1768 and 1769 indicate that in those years 30,977 and 32,433 hogsheads entered America. Accounts, 1768-1770, *ibid.*, T. 1/465, f. 122, and T. 1/471, f. 90.

[41] Grenville took this warning seriously. A 3d. duty on molasses went into effect on Sept. 29, 1764. On Oct. 20, the Treasury studied accounts of molasses entered at Boston as shipped from Dominica, Granada, and Antigua from Dec. 1, 1763 to Aug. 17, 1764, and discovered that "it appears thereby that a much greater quantity has been exported from [there] . . . than can be supposed to be the product of those islands." Grenville then ordered the Commissioners to investigate the situation in the islands. Jenkinson to Customs Commissioners, Oct. 20, 1764, *ibid.*, T. 11/27. f. 236. See also the order for officers from those islands to send their records to the Treasury "in order to see how far it is probable that the same are the product of these islands." Whately to Customs Commissioners, Oct. 25, 1764, *ibid.*

[42] Ware's concern that the French islands might begin the production of rum was based on his experience in Boston. Massachusetts merchants were fearful that the French would establish distilleries, and promised to inform on all men who might encourage that development by smuggling equipment into the colony. See their advertisement in *Boston Post Boy*, Oct. 29, 1750. Grenville was sufficiently impressed with this argument, which was repeated in a petition presented to the Treasury by merchants trading to America in Feb. 1764, to include in the Sugar Act a clause forbidding the importation of foreign rum into America, and imposing a harsh penalty, the loss of the spirits and the ship carrying them, on those caught smuggling. See 4 Geo. 3, c. 5, sec. 18, in *Statutes at Large*, 26, pp. 39-40.

[43] See [Thomas Whately], "Calculation concerning the molasses duty," [1763-64], National Archives, T. 1/434, f. 52. The credit for identifying this as Whately's work belongs to Allen S. Johnson, "The Passage of the Sugar Act," *William and Mary Quarterly*, 3rd ser., 16 (1959), p. 511. See also [Charles Jenkinson], "An estimate of tea, sugar, and molasses, illegally imported into the continent of North America in one year," [1763-64], Liverpool Papers, British Library, Add. MSS 38335, f. 12. Whately estimated the annual volume at 80,000 hogsheads, which he believed would be reduced to 62,222 hogsheads by a 3d. duty. Jenkinson guessed that colonists illegally imported 90,000 hogsheads annually.

[44] Grenville's speech, Mar. 9, 1764, "Ryder Diaries," p. 234.

[45] Eighteenth-century Commissioners of the Customs were usually, as Sir Lewis Namier observed, "men broken in health or disappointed in their bolder hopes and ambitions" who were traditionally reluctant to lead where First Lords of the Treasury were unwilling or unable to follow. With this in mind, it is possible to tell roughly about what time Grenville decided to lower the molasses duty by comparing the statements they made on that tax in their reports of Jul. 21 and Sept. 16, 1763. In the earlier report, when the Commissioners were uncertain of Grenville's opinion, they merely admitted that huge amounts of molasses were smuggled, pointed out that some of the officers in America believed that it would be impossible to stop this trade unless the duty were lowered, and referred to a report of May 10, 1759, in which the Commissioners in office at that time had concluded that "so long as the high duties imposed on [molasses] continue, the running the same [into] His Majesty's colonies will be unavoidable." But they stopped short of directly recommending such a change themselves, despite the fact that the Treasury had asked them for suggestions for improving the collection of the revenue. By Sept. 16, though, the Commissioners felt confident enough to state flatly that "the establishing . . . proper duties [on molasses] at a lower rate than at present . . . seems to be an object at this juncture of importance to the revenue." At some point between late Jul. and mid-Sept., therefore, the Commissioners probably had what they regarded as reliable information that Grenville planned to lower the duty. Coming as it did in the middle of this period, Ware's report must have either confirmed the First Lord's decision, or helped to change his mind. On the political attributes of Customs Commissioners, see Sir Lewis Namier, *The Structure of Politics at the Accession of George III*, 2nd ed. (London, 1957), p. 21; and W. R. Ward, "Some Eighteenth Century Civil Servants: The English Revenue Commissioners, 1754-98," *English Historical Review 70* (1955), pp. 27-35. For the Commissioners' reports of Jul. 21 and Sept. 16, 1763, see Treasury Papers, National Archices, T. 1/426, fols. 269, 289.

[46] Grenville's speech, Mar. 9, 1764, "Ryder Diaries," p. 235.

[47] Henry McCulloh, "General thoughts . . . with respect to the late American stamp duty bill" [1765] Rockingham Papers, Sheffield Central Library, Wentworth Wodehouse Muniments, R pp. 65-6. I acknowledge with thanks the permission of the Trustees of the Fitzwilliam (Wentworth) Estates and the Director of Sheffield City Libraries to quote this document. McCulloh made a similar statement in the paper he sent Halifax in 1755, so surely he made the same general remarks to Grenville in 1763. Unfortunately, the copy of the 1763 paper has been lost. For the earlier one, see McCulloh to Halifax [1755], Newcastle Papers, British Library, Add. MSS 33030, fols. 334-5.

[48] Grenville's speech, Mar. 9, 1764, "Ryder Diaries," p. 235.

[49] Grenville made an effort to settle all constitutional objections M.P.s might possibly have to taxing the colonies in this manner as soon as he introduced the subject of the stamp tax. See *ibid.*

[50] *Ibid.*

[51] [Thomas Cruwys], "Law Bill," Sept. 8, 1763, Hardwicke Papers, British Library, Add. MSS 35911, f. 15. McCulloh later stated that he "was desired to assist Mr. Cruwys in drawing the stamp duty bill." His comment reveals that Grenville wanted the two men to act as a team and started them on the job about the same date. The First Lord therefore did not call in the expert Cruwys to help on a project that the amateur McCulloh had been working on for some time. This permits historians to place his decision to go ahead with a colonial stamp tax in early Sept. See McCulloh, "General thoughts . . . with respect to the late American stamp duty bill" [1765], Rockingham Papers, Sheffield Central Library, Wentworth Wodehouse Muniments, R 65-6.

[52] Grenville probably excused himself from making an exception in Ware's case in much the same way that he did in the case of Grosvenor Bedford, Collector at Philadelphia. "It will be," he explained to a friend of Bedford's, "attended with difficulty to make an exception, as [the absent officers] are everyone of them applying to be [excepted] out of the order. If Mr. Bedford can suggest to me any proper means of obviating it without overturning the whole regulation, he will do me a sensible pleasure." Grenville to Walpole, Sept. 8, 1763, Smith, ed., *Grenville Papers*, 2, p.114. Because Bedford's warrant explicitly permitted him to hire a deputy, he kept his place, and stayed in London. Ware had no such loophole to escape through.

[53] Fremantle to Jenkinson, Jan. 3, 1764, Treasury Papers, National Archives, T. 1/429, no. 87; and Treasury Warrants, 1764, *ibid.*, T. 11/27, f. 224.

[54] The only evidence I have uncovered so far of Ware's appointment is the notice of his death at Málaga in the *London Magazine 36* (1767), p. 596. The introduction to Ware to the Earl of _____, 66, mistakenly described him as the consul at Madeira, and incorrectly gave the date of his death as "about the year 1769."

Postscript*

Nathaniel Ware to George Grenville

Sir

I find upon Enquiry that ye Importation of foreign Molasses into America has increased greatly during the War to the Amount, it is sayd, of Sixty thousand

Hogsheads annually: five times the quantity I had mentioned upon another occassion, when, without the least view to a Tax, any random guess, which I took care should be within the Truth, was sufficient for any Purpose.

However the above conjecture as to quantity being too vague to depend upon, I have endeavoured to ascertain the Number of distilleries at present on that continent; & I find in Nova-Scotia 2—in New-Hampshire 1—in Massachusetts-Bay 64—in Rode-Island & Connecticut upwards of 40—in New-York & the Jerseys 4—in Pennsylvania 7—(those of ye Southward are many but too inconsiderable to be mentioned)—in ye whole 117 distilleries working off, at a medium between 100 and 550 Hogsheads each, 32625 Hogsheads Molasses annually.

When the great & universal consumption of Rum amongst these People in their Fisheries, Navigation, Seamen, Laborers, the Indian Supply, the Exportation to NfoLand, guinea, & sometimes even to Ireland are considered, the above quantity, besides ye usual Importation from our own Islands for use of the better Sort of People only, seems not to exceed what may be supposed necessary.

But beside what goes to the [?] there is a farther consumption of Molasses in Beer & in their Food, thro' out all that continent, to the amount of five thousd Hogsheads more than is sayd to be imported from all the British Islands, so that, if our calculations be Just, the foreign only must exceed 43625 Hds.

There has always been a considerable Charge attending the Importation; first, about one peny Sterl. to the officer for Connivance, then a provincial Impost in, I believe, all the Colonies: & in 1758 the Massachusetts-Bay, a People of all others the most concerned in this Article, ventured to raise a former Excise on the Home consumption of Rum from 4 to 8 pence currency, that is, from 3 pence to 6 pence sterl. p^r gallon. this Excise, after one years Experience, was continued for the next; & afterwards renewed for two years more.

The old duty therefore of 6 pence sterl. on foreign Molasses may very well be exacted, provided all those provincial Impositions are taken off. otherwise that Trade must totally fail.

Now should this last be the Intention, beside the difficulty of forcing a whole People to a Sudden Change of an article of so universal a consumption, it must ruin the Provinces more immediatly concerned, & greatly distress the others. for where shall they all find a market for their Lumber? at present any of them could probably supply all y^Y Wst Indies.

did the Molasses or Rum of our own Islands, or any other article of their Produce lye on Hand, even at a much higher Price than in any of the foreign Islands; or were not ours abundantly supplyd with Lumber, or whatever else ye continent affords, it were indeed something: but this is so far from being the case that Lumber does not in the West Indies pay the carryage thither; the Profit is made in ye Return & as to the Price of their Produce, that of Molasses the article under consideration is in our Islands from 8 to 9 pence sterl. per gallon; in the other Islands from three half pence to four pence half peny, which difference in the price cost establishes the certainty of ye payment of the old duty on the Importation; provided, as above, all provincial Impositions are taken off.

But we contribute by this Trade to the support of the colonies of a rival Power. true, but at the same time they become thereby dependent upon us. & in case of a Rupture what use may not be made of such an advantage?

The British Molasses imported is sayd not to exceed, at present, 15 thousand Hogsheads. should a high duty be layd on the foreign only, that quantity will probably be doubled by collusion of the People in our Islands. this it seems is no more than has formerly been practiced.

Was the duty to extend to molasses only, the foreign Islands would manufacture theirs into rum for ye use of ye continent, as in part they do already; or, which would be much ye same in the end, our own Islands would do it for them.

Should the proposed duty fall short of Expectation, (and there must, I fear, after all be a large deduction for Frauds, under the Term Leakage) there are other articles pointed out by their own assemblys which may be brought in aid. Such are—a Tonage on shipping—a duty on Sugars—an excise on Wine, Lemons, Oranges, & Limes, which may the more reasonably be adopted by Government as those Provinces are now rid of all Expense in garrisoning their Frontiers etc. I am

S^r.

with profound respect.

22th August

1763

Your most obdt

& most devoted

humble servt

Nath: Ware

P.S.

as ye foregoing Information could be collected only from ye People of that country, who are extremely cautious of giving any Light into their own affairs, the various shifts & pretenses I was obliged to make use of in my Enquiry has occasioned this delay. I likewise proposed adding an account of all Impositions on Molasses and Rum thro'out the several Provinces, but applying to the Board of Trade was disappointed: either they had not those Laws, or knew not where

534

readily to come at them, or perhaps did not think proper to give every one access to them, without a particular order.

*Original spelling and punctuation retained throughout Postscript.

Conclusion

"There's something exceedingly ridiculous in the composition of monarchy," Thomas Paine famously opined in *Common Sense.* "It first excludes a man from the means of information, yet empowers him to act in cases where the highest judgment is required." More precisely, "the state of a king shuts him from the world, yet the business of a king requires him to know it thoroughly." To Paine, "the different parts, by naturally opposing and destroying each other, prove the whole character to be absurd and useless."[1]

However true this description in *Common Sense* may have been of *ancien régime* monarchs in general, it does not apply to George III. The essays in this book demonstrate how carefully he was prepared for the business of ruling Britain and its empire. His mother taught him morality and imprinted its importance in his heart and mind; Lord Bute readied him for the throne by emphasizing how significant a patriot king would be and instructing him in the rudiments of public finance, national politics, and international relations. Both Augusta and his "dearest friend" also taught him that the fate of his reign and the happiness of his country depended on his serving as an agent of reform where change was necessary. George studied their lessons conscientiously. He absorbed the information and accepted the arguments. And what he learned affected him, sometimes subtly, sometimes obviously, for the rest of his life.

What was the result? Again, it is instructive to turn to *Common Sense.* According to Paine, "men, who look upon themselves born to reign, and others to obey, soon grow insolent; selected from the rest of mankind their minds are easily poisoned by importance." Since "the world they act in differs so materially from the world at large, . . . they have but little opportunity of knowing its true interests, and when they succeed to government are frequently the most ignorant and unfit of any throughout the dominions."[2] Once more, the description does not fit the man Paine condemned in his pamphlet. A crucial part of his business was knowing the world's business. Convinced of this early in life, he constantly worked at doing that business. It is not surprising, for instance, that when Thomas Hutchinson had a lengthy discussion with the king on July 1, 1774 on the state of affairs in Massachusetts Bay he was struck by the breadth and depth of George's knowledge about North America.[3]

Peter D. G. Thomas, who has written thoughtful, careful studies of George III and British politics during the American Revolution, leveled a different critique of the king's grasp of business. 'It is impossible," argued Thomas, "to ascertain how many of the ideas and suggestions to be found in his correspondence had been put in his head either by way of conversations or by letters that no longer survive."[4] He has a point: especially in briefer letters in his daily correspondence references can be elliptical. It is not, however, true of longer memoranda and essays. Two of the chapters in this book focus on the provenance of the king's writings. Most of the others accurately attribute sources for his information and ideas. And Professor Thomas misses a larger point. What he wanted to assess was the originality of the king's mind and the sharpness of his intelligence. No one studying George III has ever concluded that he had a powerful intellect or an original mind. In a review, I once characterized the king as "a testimony to the determination and cunning of the strong and stupid."[5] More important than the source of his thoughts and, for that matter, more important than his relative intelligence or stupidity, are three considerations: are these positions congruent with the realities of the world rather than being half-baked or fantastical; did the king believe what he wrote; did he act on these convictions. The essays in this book reveal that he adopted practical solutions for changes in policies and that he believed what he wrote when he wrote it. Very rarely does one find George III attempting to "spin" information. When he does, it is obvious what he is doing and why he is doing it.

Did he act on his ideas? Put another way, what impact did he have on his government's policies? As Thomas and others have observed, this can be difficult to gauge because of the nature of the evidence. That led Thomas to conclude that George III bore only limited responsibility for the decline and fall of the First British Empire.[6] What these historians failed to consider is what usually prevented any contemporary discussion of George's reactions and contributions. The king's role was obscured by one of the constitutional fictions of the time. The monarch could do no wrong; ministers, in contrast, could misadvise him and could be removed from office for their errors. Accordingly, George's advisers would publicly and privately claim complete responsibility for the direction of policy in order to preserve that fiction and the authority of the throne. What my essays do make clear is that George III was well informed about discussions on policy, participated in examining proposed changes, and once decisions were made supported them. Clearly, he felt secure giving that support because whether he agreed on all details or not, the ministers and he were united in the belief that those policies helped do the true essential business of the kingdom. He shared with most of the men who served him a readiness to reform. That commitment to reform dated from his experiences as a young man. He never abandoned it completely, though the older monarch became more discriminating in determining what needed change and what could not be safely changed. Others such as George Grenville brought a propensity toward change with them to office. In Grenville's case, his experience arranging enclosures of common fields and regulating the payment of seamen's wages helped prepare him for colonial reform. Only rarely did the king disagree with his ministers on principle. None of the most famous occasions when this occurred—the Regency Act of 1765, Charles Fox's proposed East India Bill in 1783, and William Pitt the Younger's support of Catholic Emancipation during 1799-1801—fall within the purview of this book. It is worth noting that all three times George III intervened decisively.

Given his constant involvement in and concern for the business of the state, it is clear that George III fully shared the responsibility for policy decisions on the Seven Years War and the War of American Independence, on public finance from 1760-1765, on the peacetime military in 1762-63, on taxation, and on the American colonies from 1760 to 1783. His impact on decisions and events is most apparent while Bute held office between 1760-1763, but his influence is discernible during the following years. He did the business of the king.

Where should scholarship go in the future? George III himself has been the subject of very good extended studies.[7] The most promising approach to extending our understanding of him is via thorough examination of his relationships with those closest to him. In particular, a full length account of Princess Augusta would illuminate not only the king but his times. So would a biography of the Earl of Bute. In fact, the absence of such a study is one of the major gaps in the historiography of Britain in the eighteenth century. Insofar as the king and the colonies are concerned, a synthesis of the many books and articles on George III, British politicians, and the American question from 1760-1783 would usefully chart where we historians are now on that subject, and in the process highlight where we should go next.

The "True Essential Business of a King" does not fill any of these gaps. My hope is it will be a good start toward closing all of them.

Endnotes

[1] Thomas Paine, *Common Sense*, 2nd printing, expanded edition (Philadelphia, Feb. 1776). I have used the version printed in Thomas P. Slaughter, ed., *Common Sense and Related Writings by Thomas Paine* (Boston, 2001). The quotation is on pp. 77-78.

[2] *Ibid*, p. 84.

[3] Thomas Hutchinson's Diary, Jul. 1, 1774, P. O. Hutchinson, ed., *The Diary and Letters of His Excellency Thomas Hutchinson, Esq.* (London, 1883), vol. I, pp. 175-179 .

[4] Peter D. G. Thomas, *George III: King and Politicians, 1760-1770* (Manchester, 2002), p. 43.

[5] See my review of *ibid.* and G. M. Ditchfield, *George III: An Essay in Monarchy* (NY, 2003) in *Albion*, vol. XXXVI (2004), pp. 529-531.

[6] P. D. G. Thomas, "George III and the American Revolution," *History*, vol. LXX (1985), pp. 16-31.

[7] See the works by Thomas and Ditchfield cited above; each of these historians has widened our knowledge of George and his times. The best recent biography is Jeremy Black, *George III: America's Last King* (New Haven, CT, 2006). For a stimulating discussion of public opinion about George, and the king's role in the creation of the British nation, see Linda Colley, *Britons: Forging the Nation, 1707-1837* (New Haven, CT, 1992), pp. 195-236.

Bibliography

Archives

Below I have listed the volumes cited in these essays. They are, of course, only parts of larger collections. Historians researching other issues and events during the years 1754-1783 would be well advised to look at the entire corpus of these collections; my experience has convinced me that there must be a considerable number of treasures buried among them.

Bedford Estates Office (London)

Papers of the second Duke of Bedford, vols. 54, 56, 58. Of particular value are the speech drafts, memoranda, and letters of Richard Rigby, Bedford's "man of business" in the House of Commons. (These papers are now located at Woburn Abbey, Bedfordshire).

Bodleian Library (Oxford)

Papers of Sir Francis Dashwood, vols. B. 1/1/19, 28, 33, 38; and vol. B. 7/2/5. Dashwood was Bute's Chancellor of the Exchequer, and his files contain many papers relating to Britain's financial condition after the Seven Years War and a valuable set of plans for future taxation. This collection also holds a large number of Treasury Office papers from 1762-1763.

Papers of Lord North, vols. MSS. North a. 4, 6; b. 1-6; c. 1-3. North was a Lord of the Treasury when Bute was First Lord. Somehow many of the Treasury's official papers and the drafts of plans and legislation found their way into this collection. It is the most complete and most valuable source for Bute's tenure at the Treasury.

Bristol University Library (Bristol)

Parliamentary diaries of Matthew Brickdale, M. P. Brickdale abstracted most of the speeches made in the House of Commons during 1768-1774. His outline of Members' remarks is generally very accurate.

British Library (London)

Birney Collection of Eighteenth Century newspapers (microfilm). This is the most complete collection of London newspapers in existence.
 I read:
The Briton
The Gazetteer

The Monitor
The North Briton
Lloyd's Evening Post
London Chronicle
London Magazine
Public Advertiser
Public Ledger
The Royal Gazette
St. James Chronicle

Bute Letterbooks, Add. MSS. 36796, 36797. These contain copies of much of Bute's political correspondence during the 1760s. When he gauges the reaction of Westminster to proposed legislation they usefully illuminate his thinking.

Parliamentary Diary of Henry Cavendish, Egerton MSS. 250-300. Transcripts of speeches made in shorthand by Cavendish. Most of those pertaining to the North American colonies have been published and annotated. On other subjects they continue to be a valuable source of information about attitudes in the House of Commons.

Grenville Papers, Add. MSS. 57834. These files contain important information about Britain's fiscal condition at the end of the Seven Years War, and illuminate George Grenville's strategy and tactics in cabinet politics about diplomacy and peace negotiations.

Hardwicke Papers, Add. MSS. 35352, 35912. These volumes contain the correspondence between the Earl of Hardwicke and the Duke of Newcastle during 1762-1763. They are full of comments about Bute and peace negotiations from the perspective of Newcastle as he steadily lost influence and power.

Holland House Papers, Add. MSS. 51379, 51380, 51420. These documents outline the positions taken by Henry Fox during 1760-1763. They include some financial material, some papers relating to the military, and comments on the politics of defending the peace in Parliament and the newspapers.

Liverpool Papers, Add. MSS. 38200, 38203, 38334, 38335. 38336. Historians have long been familiar with the political correspondence of Charles Jenkinson. These volumes are a rich collection of materials relating to finances, the power of France, and the taxation and regulation of North America that have been surprisingly under-utilized by scholars of the period.

Martin Papers, Add. MSS. 51435. Samuel Martin as Secretary of the Treasury during 1762 was a central figure in the controversy over the amount to be requested by the government as a Vote of Credit. This volume is an invaluable collection of papers and correspondence relating to the financing of the war. It too has been comparatively neglected by historians.

Newcastle Papers, Add. MSS. 32881, 32888, 32914, 32918, 32929, 32931, 32932, 32933, 32935, 32936, 32937, 32938, 32999, 33030, 33040. Most of these volumes contain the well known and often studied correspondence of Newcastle with politicians during 1760-1765. Add. MSS. 33030 and 33040 are stuffed with miscellaneous memoranda and materials relating to fiscal and diplomatic policies. Much of it is Treasury material from the Duke's days as First Lord. Studying them carefully is amply rewarded.

Bute Papers (Mount Stuart, Isle of Bute, Scotland)

Bute Correspondence, Boxes 1, 4, 6 (undated), 8, 11. A complete run of Bute's political correspondence during the 1760s, this is essential to an understanding of the politics of the period.

Correspondence with Henry Fox. Bute's contacts with Fox when he was Leader of the House of Commons during 1762-1763; they illustrate the domestic politics of making peace and planning for the war's aftermath.

Correspondence with George III. There are over 500 letters in this file. Very few have been published. They include documents outlining the ministry's strategy for the army in the colonies after the war and revealing the genesis of schemes to tax Americans. They also further illuminate the relationship between George and his "dearest friend." Formerly in the Central Library, Cardiff, Wales.

Clements Library (Ann Arbor, Michigan)

Henry Clinton Papers, Miscellaneous. Clinton's files include interesting documents written by Henry McCulloh, the progenitor of the Stamp Act.

Manchester Papers. This relatively small collection includes interesting material relating to George III's reactions to peace negotiations with the United States in 1782-1783.

Shelburne Papers, vols. 85, 87. These are Shelburne's files on North America. They include memoranda relating to peace negotiations in 1782, and are especially illuminating on Shelburne's relations with George III.

Charles Townshend Papers, vols. 8/3B/2, 299. These are Townshend's calculations of the potential for raising a revenue by parliamentary taxation in

America. They also reveal his ideas on the British Army in America after the Seven Years War.

East Suffolk Record Office (Ipswich, England).

Barrington Collection. Papers of Viscount Barrington, Secretary of War, 1755-1761 and Chancellor of the Exchequer, 1761-2, and treasurer of the Navy, 1762-1765.

Hockworthy House (in the possession of Mrs. Daphne Bruton, Wellington, Somerset)

Papers of James Oswald, Autograph Letters, Chest 4. Oswald was a close ally of Bute's at the Treasury and in Scotland. These papers are a rich source for Bute's calculations of the fiscal condition of Britain in the late summer and early fall of 1762. They include new and significant material on the background of the peace negotiations.

Henry E. Huntington Library (San Marino, California)

Grenville Letterbooks, ST 1, 2. These comprise copies of most of Grenville's political correspondence to other people from 1762-1770. They also include some papers not in the published *Grenville Papers*.

Grenville Papers, STG-12, 17, 18, 164, 192, 225, 365, 419, 421, 423, 425; L9D10. These are letters and memoranda written to Grenville, with some replies interspersed throughout the files. It is valuable for information about the Grenville family's efforts to enclose common lands as well as an important source for policies on American taxation.

ST 164, Richard Grenville's Account Books, 1750-1779. A valuable source on family financial and business dealings. It includes some material on enclosures.

National Archives (Kew, London)

I continue to prefer the old name of Public Record Office for this wonderful depository, not only out of affectionate memories of working at Chancery Lane—which a colleague once described to me as "the coal mine" of English libraries—but because it holds mostly the public records of the great departments, sprinkled with the private papers of men who ran them. Kew is clearly not a coal mine. Nor is it terribly convenient. But it still is the place to go to study official records.

Chatham Papers, PRO 30/8/76, 81. Pitt the Elder's files on finances.

Colonial Office Papers (Massachusetts Bay), C. O. 5/755. Boston during the Stamp Act Crisis.

Egremont Papers, PRO 30/47/21. The Secretary of State for the South's files for 1762-1763.

Gower Papers, PRO 30/29/14. Correspondence of a cabinet officer during the late 1760s and 1770s.

Neville Papers, PRO 30/50/48, 52. Important assessments of the strength of France immediately after the Seven Years War.

State Papers Domestic, S. P. Dom. 42/64, 150/18. Reactions to negotiations with France and Spain in 1762-1763.

Treasury Minutes, 1762-1766, T. 29/34. Official minutes of decisions of the Treasury Board.

Treasury Papers, T. 1/384, 408, 426, 429, 434, 442, 465, 471; T. 11/27; T. 27/28. Official papers collected at the Treasury during 1762-1765. They reveal the background to many policy decisions on the national debt, the budget, and taxation.

War Office papers, W. O. 4/987. Stamp Act Crisis materials.

National Library Of Scotland (Edinburgh)

Minto Papers, MS. 11036. The notes and speech drafts of Sir Gilbert Elliot, an ally of Bute and later a King's Friend, during parliamentary session of 1762-1763. His notes include valuable material on the decision to raise an American revenue to help support the British regulars stationed there.

Northamptonshire Record Office (Northampton, England)

Edmund Burke Papers, a. xxvii-81. Papers relating to cabinet decisions on the debates over the repeal of the Stamp Act. They reveal how the ministry raised petitions from merchants in favor of repeal, and thus enhance out understanding of events in 1766.

Northington Papers. This collection includes Lord Chancellor Northington's advocacy in October 1765 for using troops against colonists protesting the stamp tax and preventing its execution.

Royal Archives (Windsor Castle, Windsor, England)

Additional Georgian Manuscripts, 32/1-2483. Essays and papers written by George III, mostly under Bute's tutelage while he was Prince of Wales during the 1750s but also some memoranda as king, including an important discussion in 1783 of Britain without her North American colonies. To begin to understand George's mind and his principles and prejudices, one must read these files.

Sheffield Central Library (Sheffield, England)

Marquis of Rockingham Papers, R. 1/ 1992-1998; R 24-43(a); R. 28; R. 49-2, 14. 17; R. 65-6; R. 65-6. These are Rockingham's files relating to the execution and repeal of the Stamp Act.

Staffordshire Record Office (Stafford, England)

Earl of Dartmouth Papers, D 1778II: 1035. The Earl of Barrington's 1774 letter warning Dartmouth (and by extension Lord North) that the army was not the service that should be given the task of subduing the rebellious colonists.

Warwickshire Record Office (Warwick, England)

Sir Roger Newdigate's Parliamentary Diary for 1762-1763, Newdegate MSS, B. 2539, 2540, 2543. A prominent country gentleman with an eye to greater economy in government, Sir Roger was deeply interested in the debates over the American revenue and the regulars in America. They are very important notes on those topics.

Newdegate MSS, pamphlets on investing in government bonds. This is an illuminating collection of primers on the national debt written for young men and young women who wanted to learn how to invest. They are the clearest descriptions I have ever read. Particularly useful is *The Daily Journal*; or, *The Gentleman's and tradesman's complete annual account book for the pocket, or desk. For the year of our Lord 1761* (London, 1760). In an appendix to the account book may be found a precise description of the funding of the national debt and advice on which funds are most promising.

Printed Primary Sources

Almon, John, *A letter to the right honourable George Grenville* (London, 1763).

_____, *Biographical, literary, and political anecdotes of several of the most eminent persons of the present age, never before printed* (London, 1797).

Annual Register, 1760-1776

Bedford, Duke of, *Correspondence of John, Fourth Duke of Bedford, selected from the originals in Woburn Abbey*, 3 vols., ed. by Lord John Russell (London, 1842-1846).

Boswell, James, *James Boswell: The Earlier Years, 1740-1769*, ed. by Frederick Pottle, (NY, 1966).

Buckhamshire, *The Victorian History of the County of Buckinghamshire*, 4 vols. (London, 1905-1908, 1925-1928).

Burke, Edmund, *The Writings and Speeches of Edmund Burke: Party, Parliament, and the American Crisis, 1766-1774, II*, ed. by Paul Langford (Oxford, 1981).

_____, *The Correspondence of Edmund Burke, July 1774-June 1778, II* ed. by G. H. Guttridge (Cambridge, 1961).

Bute, Earl of, "The Cabinet Crisis of August 1761: unpublished letters from the Bute and Bedford manuscripts," ed. by Karl W. Schweizer, *Bulletin of the Institute for Historical Research*, vol.59: 225-229.

Constitution Of Canada, *A Constitutional History of Canada, 1759-1791*, ed. by Shortt, A. and Doughty, A. G., 2 vols. (Ottawa, 1918).

Commons Committees, *Reports from Committees of the House of Commons, vol. ix Provisions: Poor, 1774-1802* (London, 1803).

Denbigh, Earl of, *Report on the Manuscripts of the Earl of Denbigh Preserved at Newnham Paddox, Warwickshire (Part V)* Historical manuscript Commission (London, 1911).

Devonshire, Duke of, *The Devonshire Diary: William Cavendish, Fourth Duke of Devonshire: Memoranda on State of Affairs, 1759-1762*, ed. by P. D. Brown and K. W. Schweizer, *Camden Miscellany Vol. XXVII, Camden 4th Ser.* (London, 1982).

Dodington, George Bubb, *The Political Journal of George Bubb Dodington*, ed. by J. Carswell,and L. A. Dralle (Oxford, 1965).

Egmont, First Earl of, *Manuscripts of the Earl of Egmont: Diary of Viscount Percival Afterwards First Earl of Egmont*, 3 vols. Historical Manuscript Commission (London, 1920-1923).

Egmont, Second Earl of, "Leicester House Politics, 1750-1760, From the Papers of John, Second Earl of Egmont," *Camden Miscellany Vol.XXIII*, Camden 4th Ser., vol. 7 (London, 1967).

Fox, Henry, "Memoirs on the events Attending the Death of George II, and the Accession of George III, " in *The Life and Letters of Lady Sarah Lennox, 1745-1826*, ed. by Countess of Ilchester and Lord Stavordale (London, 1902).

Franklin, Benjamin, *The interest of Great Britain considered, with regard to her colonies, and the acquisitions of Canada and Guadeloupe* (London, 1760).

Gage, Thomas, *The Correspondence of General Thomas Gage with the Secretaries of State, 1763-1775*, 2 vols., ed. by C. E. Carter (New Haven, CT, 1931-1933).

Grenville George, *A reply to a letter addressed to the right honourable George Grenville* (London, 1763).

_____, *The Grenville Papers*, 4 vols. , ed. by W. J. Smith (London, 1852-1853).

_____, *Additional Grenville Papers, 1763-1765*, ed. by J. R. Tomlinson (Manchester, 1963).

George III, *The Correspondence of King George the Third from 1760 to December 1783*, 6 vols. ed. by Sir John Fortescue (London, 1927-1928).

_____, *Additions and Corrections to Sir John Fortescue's Edition of the Correspondence of King George the Third (Vol. I)*, ed. by Lewis B. Namier (Manchester, 1937).

_____, *The Later Correspondence of George III*, 5 vols., ed. by A. Aspinall (Cambridge, 1962-1970).

_____*Letters from George III to Lord Bute, 1756-1766*, ed. by Romney Sedgwick (London, 1939).

Hardwicke, Earl of, *The Life and Correspondence of Philip Yorke, Earl of Hardwicke, Lord High Chancellor of Britain*, 3 vols., ed. by P. C. Yorke (Cambridge, 1913).

Hervey, Lord, *Lord Hervey, Memoirs of the Reign of George the second from his Accession to the death of Queen Caroline*, 2 vols. ed. by J. W. Croker (London, 1848).

_____, *Lord Hervey's Memoirs*, ed. by Romney Sedgwick, (London, 1952).

Ingersoll, Jared, "A Selection from the Correspondence and Miscellaneous Papers of Jared Ingersoll," *Papers of the New Haven Colony Historical Society*, vol. 9, ed. by F. B. Dexter (New Haven, CT, 1918).

Hutchinson, Thomas, *The Diary and Letters of His Excellency Thomas Hutchinson, Esq*, 2 vols., ed. by P. O. Hutchinson (London, 1883).

Jenyns, Soame, *The objections to the taxation of our American colonies, by the legislature of Great Britain, briefly consider'd* (London, 1765).

Johnson, Samuel, *A Dictionary of the English Language* (London, 1755).

Journals of the House of Commons, 1760-1776

Knox, William, *Extra-Official State papers, addressed to the Right Hon. Lord Rawdon*, 2 vols. (London, 1789).

_____, *The Manuscripts of Captain H. V. Knox, Various Manuscripts*, V Historic Manuscript Commission (London, 1909).

McCulloch, Henry, "'A Dress of Horror": Henry McCulloh's Objections to the Stamp Act," ed. by Jack P. Greene, *Huntington Library Quarterly*, vol.26 (1963), pp. 257-262.

Mauduit, Israel, *Considerations on the Present German War* (London, 1760).

_____, Israel Mauduit letters, *Massachusetts Historical Society Collections*, 1st Ser., vol. 6 (Boston, 1800).

Oswald, James, "A letter to a gentleman in the City," in the *St. James Chronicle* Sept. 7-9, 1762). This essay was better known to contemporaries as "the Wandsworth letter."

Paine, Thomas, *Common Sense* (Philadelphia, 1776).

Parliamentary Debates, *The History, Debates, and Proceedings of Both Houses of Parliament*, vol. 7, ed. by John Debrett (London, 1792).

_____, *The Parliamentary History Of England*, vols. 15-17, ed. by William Cobbett (London, 1806-1820).

_____, *Proceedings and Debates of the British Parliaments Respecting North America, 1754-1783*, vols. 1-6, ed. by P. D. G. Thomas and R. C. Simmons (London, 1982-1987).

_____, "New Light on the Commons Debate of 1763 on the American Army," ed. by P. D. G. Thomas, *William and Mary Quarterly*, 3rd ser., vol. 38 (1981), pp. 110-113.

Pitt, William, *Correspondence of William Pitt, Earl of Chatham*, 4 vols., ed. by W. S. Taylor and J. H. Pringle (London, 1838).

Postlethwayt, Malachy, *The Universal Dictionary of Trade and Commerce*, 2 vols. (London, 1751, 1755).

_____, *Great Britain's True System* (London, 1757).

_____, *Britain's Commercial Interest Explained and Improved*, 2 vols. (London, 1757).

Rockingham, Marquis of, *Memoirs of the Marquis of Rockingham and his Contemporaries, with Original Letters and Documents now first published*, ed. by the Earl of Albemarle (London, 1852).

Ryder, Nathaniel, "Parliamentary Diaries of Nathaniel Ryder," ed. by P. D. G. Thomas *Camden Miscellany*, vol.XXIII, Camden 4th Ser., vol 7 (London, 1969).

Shelburne, Earl of, *Life of William, Earl of Shelburne, First Marquis of Lansdowne*, 2 vols., ed. by Earl Fitzmaurice (London, 1912).

_____, "speech in the House of Lords on America, December 1762," ed. by R. B. Morris, *The American Revolution, 1763-1783: A Bicentennial Collection* (Columbia, SC, 1970).

Smith, Adam, *An Inquiry into the Nature and Causes of the Wealth of Nations*, 2 vols., modern edition, ed. by Edwin Cannan (New Rochelle, NY, 1966).

Tucker, Josiah, *Reflections on the expediency of a law for the naturalization of foreign Protestants in two parts: part II* (London, 1751).

_____, *A letter to a friend concerning naturalization* (London, 1753).

_____, *A second letter to a friend concerning naturalization* (London, 1753).

_____, *A brief essay on the advantages and disadvantages which respectively attend France and Great Britain, with regard to trade* (London, 1753).

_____*Four tracts together with two sermons on political and commercial subjects* (Gloucester, England, 1774)

_____, *Josiah Tucker: A Selection from His Economic and Political Writings* , ed. by R. L. Schuyler (NY, 1931).

Waldegrave, Earl, *The Memoirs and Speeches of James, 2nd Earl Waldegrave*, ed. by J. C. D. Clark (Cambridge, 1988).

Walpole, Horace, *The Yale Edition of Horace Walpole's Correspondence*, vol. 9, ed. by W. S. Lewis (New Haven, CT. 1948).

_____, *The Yale Edition of Horace Walpole's Memoirs of King George II*, vol. 2 ed. by John Brooke (New Haven CT, 1985).

[Ware, Nathaniel], "Mr. Comptroller Weare to the Earl of _____," *Massachusetts Historical Society, Collections*, 1st ser., vol. 1 (Boston, 1795).

[Whately, Thomas], *The regulations lately made concerning the colonies, and the taxes imposed in them, considered* (London, 1765).

Select Secondary Works

I have listed below the books and articles that influenced my thinking on these subjects the most. In most cases, I have excluded the works cited only once in the end notes.

Anderson, Fred. *A People's Army: Massachusetts Soldiers and Society in the Seven Years War* (Chapel Hill, NC, 1984).

Appleby, Joyce Oldham. *Economic Thought and Ideology in Seventeenth-Century England* (Princeton, NJ, 1978).

Ayling, Stanley. *George the Third* (London, 1972).

Bailyn, Bernard. *The Ideological Origins of the American Revolution* (Cambridge, MA, 1967).

Bargar, B. D. *Lord Dartmouth and the American Revolution* (Columbia, SC, 1965).

Barrow, Thomas C. *Trade and Empire: The British Customs Service in Colonial America, 1660-1775* (Cambridge, MA, 1967).

Baugh, Daniel. "Great Britain's 'Blue Water' Policy, 1689-1815," *The International History Review*, vol. 10 (1988).

Beckett, J. V. "Land Tax or Excise: the levying of taxation in seventeenth- and eighteenth-century England," *English Historical Review*, vol. 100 (1985).

Black, Jeremy. *The English Press in the Eighteenth Century* (London, 1987).

_____. *War for America: The Fight for Independence, 1775-1783*, (NY, 1991).

_____. *King George III* (New Haven, CT, 2006).

Bradley, James E. *Popular Politics and the American Revolution in England: Petitions, the Crown, and Public Opinion* (Mercer, GA, 1986).

_____. "The Anglican Pulpit, the Social Order, and the Resurgence of Toryism during the American Revolution," *Albion* vol.21 (1989).

Brewer, John. *Party Ideology and Popular Politics at the Accession of George III* (Cambridge, 1976).

_____. *The Sinews of Power: War, Money, and the English State, 1688-1783* (NY, 1989).

_____ *The Pleasure of the Imagination: English Culture in the Eighteenth Century* (NY, 1997).

_____. "The Faces of Lord Bute: A Visual Contribution to Anglo-American Political Ideology," *Perspectives in American History*, vol. 6 (1972).

_____. "The Misfortunes of Lord Bute: A Case Study in Eighteenth-Century Political Argument and Public Opinion ," *Historical Journal* vol. 16 (1973).

Brooke, John. *King George III* (London, 1972).

Browning, Reed. *The Duke of Newcastle* (New Haven, CT, 1975).

_____. *Political and Constitutional Ideas of the Court Whigs* (Baton Rouge, LA, 1982).

Bullion, John L. *A Great and Necessary Measure: George Grenville and the Genesis of the Stamp Act, 1763-1765* (Columbia, MO, 1982).

Caretta, Vincent. *George III and the Satirists from Hogarth to Byron* (Athens, GA, 1990).

Christie, I. R. and Labaree, B. W. *Empire or Independence, 1860-1776: A British-American Dialogue on the Coming of the American Revolution* (NY, 1976).

Clark, J. C. D. *The Dynamics of Change: The Crisis of the 1750s and English Party Systems* (Cambridge, 1982).

_____. *English Society, 1688-1832: Ideology, Social Structure, and Political Practice during the Ancien Regime* (Cambridge, 1985).

_____. *Revolution and Rebellion: State and Society in England in the 17th and 18th Centuries* (Cambridge, 1986).

_____. "England's Ancien Regime as a Confessional State," *Albion* vol. 21 (1989).

Clark, W. E. *Josiah Tucker, Economist: A Study in the History of Economics* (NY, 1903).

Coats, A. W. "Changing attitudes to labour in the mid-eighteenth century," *Economic History Review*, 2nd Ser., vol.11 (1958-1959).

_____. "Economic thought and poor law policy in the eighteenth century," *Economic History Review*, 2nd Ser., vol. 13 (1960-1961).

Coleman, D. C. "Labour in the English economy of the 17th century," *Economic History Review*, 2nd Ser.. vol. 8, (1955-1956).

554

Colley, Linda. *In Defiance of Oligarchy: The Tory Party, 1714-1760* (Cambridge, 1982).

_____. *Britons: Forging the nation, 1707-1837* (New Haven, CT, 1992).

_____. "The Apotheosis of George III: Loyalty, Royalty, and the British nation, 1760-1820," *Past and Present*, vol.102 (1984).

Davis, Ralph. "The rise of protection in England, 1689-1786," *Economic History Review*, 2nd Ser., vol. 18 (1965-1966).

Deane, Phyllis. *The First Industrial Revolution* (Cambridge, 1965).

_____ and Coats, W. A., *British Economic Growth, 1688-1959* (Cambridge, 1969).

Dickson, P. G. M. *The Financial Revolution in England: A Study in the Development of Public Credit* (NY, 1967).

Ditchfield, G. M. *George III: An Essay in Monarchy* (NY, 2003).

Ehrman, John. *The Younger Pitt: The Years of Acclaim* (NY, 1969).

Elliot, G. F. S. *The Border Elliots and the Family of Minto* (Edinburgh, 1897).

Fliegelman, Jay. *Prodigals and Pilgrims: The American Revolution against Patriarchal Authority* (Cambridge, 1980).

Gelles, Edith B. "Gossip: An Eighteenth-Century Case," *Journal of Social History*, vol. 22 (1989).

Gipson, Lawrence Henry. *The Triumphant Empire: Thunder-Clouds gather in the West, 1763-1764* (NY, 1961).

Gradish, Stephen F. "Wages and Manning: The Navy Act of 1758," *English Historical Review*, vol. 93 (1978).

Greene, Jack P. "An Uneasy Connection: An Analysis of the Preconditions of the American Revolution," Stephen G. Kurtz and James E. Hutson, eds., *Essays on the American Revolution* (Chapel Hill, NC, 1973).

_____. "'A Posture of Hostility': A Reconsideration of Some Aspects of the Origins of the American Revolution," *Proceedings of the American Antiquarian Society* vol. 87 (1977).

_____. "The Seven Years' War and the American Revolution: The Causal Relationship reconsidered," *Journal of Imperial and Commonwealth History*, vol. 8 (1980).

Hausman, W. J., and Neufield, J. L. "Excise Anatomized: The Political Economy of Walpole's 1733 Tax Scheme," *The Journal of European Economic History*, vol. 10 (1981).

Hay, Douglas. "Property, Authority, and the Criminal Law," Douglas Hay, et. al. eds. *Albion's Fatal Tree: Crime and Society in Eighteenth-Century England* (NY, 1975).

Hoon, Elizabeth. *The Organization of the English Customs System, 1696-1768* (NY, 1938).

Houlding, J. A. *Fit for Service: The Training of the British Army, 1715-1795* (Oxford, 1981).

Hyam, R. "Imperial Interests and the Peace of Paris (1763)" R. Hyam and G. Martin, eds., *Reappraisals in British Imperial History* (London, 1975).

Instey, Roger. *The Atlantic Slave Trade and British Abolition, 1760-1810* (NJ, 1975).

Jensen, Merrill. *The Founding of a Nation: A History of the American Revolution, 1763-1776* (Oxford, 1968).

Johnson, Allen S. "The Passage of the Sugar Act," *William and Mary Quarterly*, 3rd Ser., 16 (1959).

Jupp, Peter. *Lord Grenville, 1759-1834* (Oxford, 1985).

Kemp, Betty. *Sir Francis Dashwood: An Eighteenth-Century Independent* (London, 1967).

Kennedy, William. *English Taxation, 1640-1799: An Essay on Policy and Opinion* (London, 1913).

Kramnick, Isaac. *Bolingbroke and his Circle: The Politics of Nostalgia in the Age of Walpole* (Cambridge, MA, 1968).

Langford, Paul. *The First Rockingham Administration, 1765-1766* (Oxford, 1973).

_____. *A Polite and Commercial People: England, 1727-1783* (Oxford, 1989).

_____. "The Rockingham Whigs and America, 1767-1773," Anne Whiteman, et. al., eds., *Statesmen, Scholars, and Merchants: Essays in Eighteenth-century History presented to Dame Lucy Sutherland* (Oxford, 1973).

_____. "Old Whigs, Old Tories, and the American Revolution," *Journal of Imperial and Commonwealth History*, vol. 8 (1980).

_____. "The English Clergy and the American Revolution," E. Hellmuth, ed., *The Transformation of Political Culture: England and Germany in the Late Eighteenth Century* (Oxford, 1990).

Lawson, Philip. *George Grenville: A Political Life* (Oxford, 1984).

Levinson, Daniel, et. al. *The Seasons of a Man's Life* (NY, 1978).

McKelvey, James L. *George III and Lord Bute: The Leicester House Years* (Durham, NC, 1973).

Marples, Morris. *Poor Fred and the Butcher: Sons of George II* (London, 1970).

Martin, J. M. "The Cost of Parliamentary Enclosure in Warwickshire," E. L. Jones, ed., *Agriculture and Economic Growth in England, 1650-1815* (London, 1967).

Mathais, Peter. *The Brewing Industry in England, 1700-1830* (Cambridge, 1959).

Middlekauff, Robert. *The Glorious Cause: The American Revolution, 1763-1789*, 2nd ed. (NY, 2005).

Middleton, Richard. *The Bells of Victory: The Pitt-Newcastle Ministry and the Conduct of the Seven Years War, 1757-1762* (Cambridge, 1985).

Mingay, G. E. "The Agricultural Depression, 1730-1750," *Economic History Review*, 2nd ser., vol. 8 (1956).

Money, John. "Provincialism and the English 'Ancien Regime': Samuel Pope-Wolferstam and 'The Confessional State,' 1776-1820," *Albion*, vol. 21 (1989).

Murdock, A. "Lord Bute, James Stuart Mackenzie, and the Government of Scotland," K. W. Schweizer, ed., *Lord Bute: Essays in Re-interpretation* (Leicester, 1988).

Namier, Sir Lewis. *The Structure of Politics at the Accession of George III*, 2nd. Edition (London, 1957).

_____. *England in the Age of the American Revolution*, 2nd edition (London, 1961).

_____. *Crossroads of Power: Essays on Eighteenth-Century England* (London, 1962).

_____ and Brooke, John. *Charles Townshend* (London, 1964).

_____. (eds.) *The History of Parliament: The House of Commons, 1754-1790*, 3 vols. (London, 1964).

Newman, A. N. "Communication: The Political patronage of Frederick Lewis, Prince of Wales," *Historical Journal*, vol. 1 (1958).

Nicholas, J. D. "The Ministry of Lord Bute," unpublished Ph. D thesis, University of Wales, 1989.

Pares, Richard. *King George and the Politicians* (Oxford, 1953).

_____. "American versus Continental Warfare, 1739-1763," *English Historical Review*, vol. 51 (1939).

Perkin, Harold. *The Origins of Modern English Society, 1780-1800* (London, 1969).

Perry, Thomas W. *Public Opinion, Propaganda, and Politics in Eighteenth-Century England: A Study of the Jew Bill of 1753* (Cambridge, MA, 1962).

Peters, Marie. *Pitt and Popularity* (London, 1980).

_____. "The 'Monitor' on the Constitution, 1755-1765: New Light on the Ideological Origins of English Radicalism," *English Historical Review*, vol. 86 (1971).

Phillips, John A. "The Social Calculus: Deference and Defiance in Later Georgian England," *Albion*, vol. 21 (1989).

Plumb, J. H. *New Light on the Tyrant George III* (Washington, DC, 1978).

Rashed, Z. E. *The Peace of Paris* (London, 1951).

Reitan, E. A. 'The Civil List in Eighteenth-Century British Politics: Parliamentary Supremacy versus the Independence of the Crown," *Historical Journal*, vol. 10 (1966).

_____. "The Civil List, 1761-77: Problems of Finance and Administration," *Bulletin of the Institute of Historical Research*, vol. 47 (1974).

Ritcheson, C. R. "The Earl of Shelbourne and Peace with America, 1782-1783" Vision and Reality," *International History Review*, vol. 5 (1983).

Rodger, N.A.M., *The Wooden World: An Anatomy of the Georgian Navy* (London, 1986).

Schweizer, Karl W. (ed,) *Lord Bute: Essays in Re-interpretation* 9Leicester, 1988).

_____. *Frederick the Great, William Pitt, and Lord Bute: Anglo-Prussian Relations, 1756-1763* (NY, 1991).

_____. (ed.) *Parliament and the Press, 1689-1939)* Edinburgh, 2006).

_____. *William Pitt, Earl of Chatham*, (Greenwood Press, 1993).

_____. *Statesmen, Diplomats and the Press* (Lewiston, 2002).

_____. "John Stuart, 3rd Earl of Bute, 1713-1792," *Dictionary of National Biography*, (Oxford, 2004), vol. 53, pp. 173-179, A.W. Matthews and B. Harrison, eds.

_____. "Imperial Britain at War," *European Legacy*, vol. 2, no. 6, pp. 1031-1035, (1997).

_____. "Chatham Revisited," *History of European Ideas*, vol. 18, no. 3, pp. 417-420, (1994).

559

_____. "The Parliamentary Speeches of William Pitt, Earl of Chatham," *Canadian Journal of History*, (April 1992), pp. 185-190.

_____. "Some Additions to the Devonshire Diary," *Notes and Queries*, pp. 64-67, (March 1986).

_____. "Lord Bute and William Pitt's Resignation," *Canadian Journal of History*, vol. 7 (1973).

_____. "The Draft of a Pamphlet by John Stuart, 3rd earl of Bute," *Notes and Queries* (September 1981).

_____. "The Bedford Motion and the House of Lords Debate, 5 February 1762," *Parliamentary History*, vol. 5 (1986).

_____. "Some Additions to the Dodington Diary," *Notes and Queries* (March 1992).

Sedgwick, Romney. *The History of Parliament: The House of Commons, 1715-1754*, 2 vols. (Oxford, 1970).

Sellers, Jr., Charles G. "Private Profits and British Colonial Policy: The Speculations of Henry McCulloh," *William and Mary Quarterly*, 3rd Ser., vol. 8(1951).

Shelton, W. G, *Dean Tucker and Eighteenth-Century Economic and Political Thought* (NY, 1981).

Shy, John. *Toward Lexington: The Role of the British Army in the Coming of the American Revolution* (Princeton, NJ, 1965).

_____. *A People Numerous and Armed: Reflections on the Military Struggle for American Independence* (NY, 1976).

Simmons, R. C. *The American Colonies: From Settlement to Independence* (NY, 1976).

Stone, Lawrence. *Family, Sex, and Marriage in England, 1500-1800* (London, 1977).
_____. (ed,) *The Imperial State at War: Britain from 1689-1815* (London, 1994).

Thomas, P. D. G. *The House of Commons in the Eighteenth Century* (Oxford, 1971).

_____. *British Politics and the Stamp Act Crisis: The First phase of the American Revolution, 1763-1767* (Oxford, 1975).

_____. *The Townshend Duties Crisis: The Second Phase of the American Revolution, 1767-1773* (Oxford, 1987).

_____. *Tea Party to Independence: The Third Phase of the American Revolution, 1773-1776* (Oxford, 1991).

_____. *Lord North* (NY, 1976).

_____. *George III and the Politicians, 1760-1770* (Manchester, 2002).

_____. "The beginning of Parliamentary Reporting in Newspapers, 1768-1774," *English Historical Review*, vol. 74 (1959).

_____. "George III and the American Revolution," *History* vol. 70 (1985).

Tucker, Robert W. and Hendrickson, David C. *The Fall of the First British Empire: Origins of the War of American Independence* (Baltimore, MD, 1982).

Vivian, Frances. *A Life of Frederick, Prince of Wales, 1707-1751: A Connoisseur of the Arts*, ed. by Roger White (Lewiston, NY, 2006).

Walters, J. *The Royal Griffin: Frederick Prince of Wales, 1707-1751*, (NY, 1972).

Ward, W. R. "Some Eighteenth-Century Civil servants: The English Revenue Commissioners, 1754-98," *English Historical Review*, vol. 70 (1955).

Watson, D. H. "Barlow Trecothick and Other Associates of Lord Rockingham during the Stamp Act Crisis, 1765-1766," unpublished M. A. thesis, Sheffield University, 1958.

Whiteley, Peter. Lord North: The Prime Minister Who Lost America (London, 1996).

Wiggin, Lewis M. *The Faction of Cousins: A Political Account of the Grenvilles, 1733-1763* (New Haven, CT, 1958).

561

Wiles, R. C. "The Theory of Wages in Later English Mercantilism," *Economic History Review*, 2nd Ser., vol. 21 (1968).

Young, Sir George. *Poor Fred: The People's Prince* (Oxford, 1937).

Index

John L. Bullion

Dr. John Bullion received his doctorate in history from the University of Texas-Austin. Dr. Bullion is a member of the Department of History at the University of Missouri-Columbia. His research focuses on two very different peoples, times, and places in Anglo-American history: British politicians during the era of the American Revolution, and the America of Lyndon Johnson.